Explorations in

Political Psychology

Duke Studies in Political Psychology

Shanto Iyengar and

William J. McGuire, Editors

Explorations in

Political Psychology

Duke University Press   *1993*   *Durham and London*

Second printing, 1995

© 1993 Duke University Press

All rights reserved

Printed in the United States of America on acid-free paper ∞

Designed by Cherie Holma Westmoreland

Typeset in Bembo by Keystone Typesetting, Inc.

Library of Congress Cataloging-in-Publication Data

Explorations in political psychology / Shanto Iyengar and William J. McGuire, editors.

p.   cm. — (Duke studies in political psychology)

Includes bibliographical references and index.

ISBN 0-8223-1301-4 (alk. paper) — ISBN 0-8223-1324-3 (pbk.)

1. Political psychology.   I. Iyengar, Shanto.   II. McGuire, William James, 1925–   .   III. Series.

JA74.5.E96   1993

320'.01'9—dc20   92-27503   CIP

Contents

IV *Decision Making and Choice*

Tables and Figures

Acknowledgments

The editors are indebted to a number of people whose assistance, guidance, and support made this book possible. Larry Malley, Director of Duke University Press, who has long been a proponent of interdisciplinary studies, lent his support and encouragement to the project from its inception. The fourteen individual contributors, whose sterling credentials in political psychology need no embellishment, exhibited a sense of responsibility that is uncommon in the academic world: they adhered without exception to their deadlines and responded fully to the editors' and reviewers' suggestions. Finally, we acknowledge with gratitude the masterful assistance provided by Ms. Sharmaine Vidanage who coordinated the entire process, provided editorial guidance, revised the individual chapters, and compiled the massive bibliography.

I

Interdisciplinary Cross-

Fertilization

Researchers congregate around the core topics of a discipline, a central self-positioning that is probably the most advantageous for success in the academic world; yet a disproportional number of innovations arise from work done at the frontiers where disciplines meet. Perhaps the disproportional productivity of interdisciplinary workers results from the cross-fertilization produced by contact across disciplinary borderlines, analogous to the population genetics thesis that the optimal condition for the emergence of new species is to have semi-isolated communities among which there is a small amount of interbreeding.

Even its name reveals political psychology's essentially interdisciplinary nature. While the grammar of "political psychology" gives the more substantial noun status to psychology, a more diffuse rubric such as "psychological aspects of politics" would be fairer in recognizing the field's having been more popular in political science, as illustrated by university doctoral programs on the topic that usually are located in political science rather than psychology departments (Sears & Funk, 1991). The label is even more inadequate in failing to convey the relevance and contributions of many disciplines other than political science and psychology. From the outset, workers in a wide variety of union locals have been major contributors: for example, anthropologists such as Linton, Mead, Benedict, Whiting, and Murdock; sociologists such as Lazarsfeld, Dollard, Berelson, Lipset, and Converse; psychiatrists such as Freud, Kardiner, Langer, Coles, and Lifton; and people who rode into this frontier territory from even more distant disciplines such as Erikson from art and Adorno from musicology.

Together, the two chapters in this section on interdisciplinary cross-fertilization provide a tour of the interdisciplinary collaboration, not only across disciplinary space but over time, identifying three successive eras during the past half-century of work on political psychology. The field first reached a critical mass in the 1950s–1960s era when it focused on the culture and personality aspects of political psychology; followed by the 1960s–1970s, which were preoccupied by the study of attitudes and voting behavior; and then by the 1980s and 1990s cognitive era concerned with political ideology and decision-making. This first chapter describes each era connotatively in regard to its distinctive subject-matter topics, theoretical explanations, and methods. It also describes each era denotatively by citing both humanistic and scientific work on micro and macro levels. While emphases have shifted, the preferred topics of each era have remained popular throughout the half-century. Hence, the evolution sketched in McGuire's chapter puts into context the chapters in the book's other three sections.

In sketching out a future fourth era, McGuire predicts increasing participation by historians capitalizing on both the increasing data archives that have time-series political data and on recent developments in causal modeling that can test sequential relations among multiple, naturally varying factors. In the second chapter of this interdisciplinary section, William McKinley Runyan deals in more detail with the intersections between history and political psychology—currently and during past decades. He traces the many strands of psychohistory and its psychobiography subfield, particularly as they have impinged on political psychology. Runyan illustrates the uses of psychology in historical interpretation at five different levels of the social system, starting with individuals and moving up through increasingly complex groupings to the level of international relations, an extended and more refined analysis of McGuire's dichotomous micro versus macro division. Runyan's analysis of the relationships between psychology and history as they contribute to political psychology leads to the conclusion that the enterprise involves not only those fields but a number of other social science disciplines that include anthropology, demography, economics, linguistics, and sociology. Both chapters in this section, then, show that political psychology is broadly interdisciplinary.

Shanto Iyengar

1. An Overview of the Field of Political Psychology

Political psychology is the field of inquiry at the intersection of political science and psychology. Political scientists, psychologists, historians, psychiatrists, sociologists, and legal scholars have all contributed to this body of research. The primary objective of this volume is to survey areas of current interdisciplinary interest and to illustrate the rich eclecticism of the theories, concepts, and methods that make up research in political psychology, while giving emphasis to what we regard as the most promising trends. In their present form, the various social sciences are largely autonomous and parochial enterprises. In imperialistic fashion, political scientists, economists, sociologists, or psychologists impose their distinctive disciplinary stamps on the phenomena they investigate. This tendency toward "disciplinary egocentrism" runs counter to the natural overlap in subject matter interests across disciplines. As those pioneers of interdisciplinary collaboration Muzafer Sherif and Carolyn Sherif observed: "man does not arrange his problems or divide them up neatly along lines laid down by academic disciplines . . . a single discipline which buries itself in order to concentrate on its own problems, theories, techniques, and data collection to the exclusion of others will end up being a know-nothing. The self-insulation of a social science discipline is ostrich-like. It will not and cannot protect the bird from impending danger" (1969, p. 7).

The different social sciences tend to cross paths only when some basic theoretical framework or methodology penetrates a disciplinary boundary. In the case of research on "political economy," for example, economics is typically the "source" discipline and political science the "receptor" discipline. The intellectual exchange is essentially unidirectional as political scientists use the methods of economic analysis and game theory to study phenomena of political relevance. (For further discussion of the hierarchical nature of interdisciplinary exchanges, see Schwartz, 1990.)

As William McGuire points out in his overview of the history of political psychology, the relationship between political science and psychology cannot be easily characterized in terms of disciplinary dominance. Indeed, political psychology is unusual in that each parent discipline has sparked research in the other. Political scientists, especially those working in the fields of public opinion and voting, may have been the more enthusiastic participants in this joint venture (most graduate training programs in political psychology are housed in departments of political science), but the range of phenomena and activities studied by them and the methods they use are increasingly migrating toward psychology. In this sense, political psychology is a dialogue marked by genuine intellectual exchange.

The methodological ebb and flow across the disciplines is of particular significance. Writing in 1959, the social psychologist Carl Hovland lamented the tendency of psychologists to rely exclusively on manipulational laboratory experiments while political scientists relied chiefly on the sample survey. As he pointed out, these distinct methods of research, each with its own strengths and weaknesses, yield different accounts of closely related phenomena. At the time of Hovland's analysis, the psychological literature on attitude change suggested that human beings were malleable, even capricious, creatures and that attitudes and choices were subject to any number of powerful external influences. Yet the contemporaneous literature on political persuasion indicated that voters were stubbornly resistant to the effects of communication and that political campaigns typically induced only minor shifts in support for candidates or public policies. Hovland demonstrated that these inconsistent results were largely a function of the respective strengths and weaknesses of the experimental and survey methods of research. He concluded that research into attitudes and attitude change must avoid the pitfalls of methodological orthodoxy:

> What seems to me quite apparent is that a genuine understanding of the effects of communications on attitudes requires both the survey and the experimental methodologies. At the same time, there appear to be certain inherent limitations of each method which must be understood by the researcher if he is not to be blinded by his preoccupation with one or the other type of design. . . . I should like to stress in summary the mutual importance of the two approaches to the problem of communication effectiveness. Neither is a royal road to wisdom, but each represents an important emphasis. The challenge of future work is one of fruitfully combining their virtues. . . . (p. 17)

If Hovland were alive today, he would be less troubled by the state of political psychology. While experiments and surveys still enjoy privileged status within political science and psychology, the two fields are moving closer together in methodological terms. Political scientists are increasingly turning to experimentation to test hypotheses about real-world phenomena (including mass media effects, social cooperation, voting, legislative outcomes, and international conflicts). Psychologists are increasingly moving outside the laboratory to examine behavior in naturalistic contexts (such as subways, elevators, or shopping malls). In addition to adopting "quasiexperimental" methods, psychologists are also turning to alternative sources of evidence (such as surveys and content analysis) and alternative nonexperimental techniques of hypothesis testing (for an early prediction of this trend, see McGuire, 1969). The disciplines are also converging on nonmethodological grounds. Thus, as the essays invited for this volume illustrate, political scientists are employing psychological explanations of political attitudes and foreign policy decisions, while psychologists are beginning to examine phenomena, including voting, group conflict, and elite rhetoric, that have considerable political significance.

Notwithstanding increasing interdisciplinary contact, political psychology is still far from attaining mainstream status. Researchers in political psychology are more prone to violate the norms of their "host" disciplines, and they face an uphill battle in gaining recognition for and publication of their work. The proportion of journal articles in social psychology that employ nonexperimental methods remains low (see Sears, 1986), and experimental studies rarely appear in political science journals. While the obstacles are gradually being overcome, political psychologists have seen fit to form their own organization, the International Society of Political Psychology. Founded in 1978, this organization has rapidly acquired the indicia of scholarly legitimacy—a large dues-paying membership, an annual research conference, and a refereed journal (*Political Psychology*). The emergence of political psychology as a distinct area of research also has had important pedagogical consequences. Virtually every major psychology and political science department in the United States offers specialized courses in the field, and a few (including CUNY Graduate Center, Minnesota, Ohio State, SUNY—Stony Brook, UCLA, Wisconsin, and Yale) offer political psychology as a formal component of their graduate curriculums.[1]

The extent of the interdisciplinary exchange, the rapid institutionalization of the field, and the growing number of graduate students being trained as researchers and teachers are clear testimony to the growing interest in political psychology. This collection of essays, selected to illustrate a wide range of the most promising trends in the field, will be the first volume in a series devoted exclusively to research in political psychology. It is intended as an introductory overview of the heterogeneous approaches and research topics (ranging from public opinion to foreign policy-making) that make up the field. The authors, drawn evenly from political science and psychology, are all established researchers whose varied contributions to the field have been numerous and significant.

The book is organized into four sections. The first (Interdisciplinary Cross-Fertilization) includes chapters by William McGuire and William Runyan that trace the intellectual traffic among psychology, political science, and history. While McGuire describes the various research traditions that have emerged from the cross-fertilization of psychology and political science, Runyan locates the study of "psychohistory" within a broader multidisciplinary context.

The remaining sections are devoted to the three principal traditions of research in contemporary political psychology: attitude formation, information processing, and decision-making. It must be emphasized that these thematic categories are far from mutually exclusive. Indeed, there is considerable overlap and supplementation among the guiding assumptions and concepts that appear in the various chapters. The distinction between the three subfields is subtle and most apparent at the level of the researcher's worldview of human behavior.

Research on attitude formation and change typically traces individual behavior to long-term historical and cultural factors, including society's political and economic situation, values, personality characteristics, group affiliations, and other distal antecedents. Political behavior is seen as "dispositional" in that attitudes and their antecedents are considered stable properties of the individual. (In fact, stability is generally posited as a defining characteristic of attitudes.) Attitude researchers also explain behavior in terms of motivational factors, particularly the motive to attain attitudinal states that are consistent, gratifying to the ego, socially adaptive, etc. Granberg's essay is explicit in this regard; he uses a variant of consistency theory (balance theory) to account for a variety of political beliefs and opinions. Sidanius explains intergroup conflict in terms of the drive to make evaluations of individuals consistent with perceptions of their group membership, and Sears makes the argument that individuals react to current issues or events by sorting them into long-standing cognitive and affective categories. What these arguments have in common, then, is a view of human beings as motivated to achieve consistent psychological outcomes.

Researchers who study information processing, in contrast, give short shrift to motivational factors in accounting for individual behavior. Their preference is for mechanistic or "black box" accounts rooted in components and structures of human cognition. These researchers thus use directive rather than dynamic processes—a capacity-based rather than a motive-based logic. The technological aspects of human information-processing ability (e.g., the form in which concepts are stored in long-term memory and the processes by which information can be retrieved) are thought to be more important in explaining behavior than dispositional attributes such as early childhood experiences or personality traits. Naturally, political psychologists in this subfield rely heavily on the research of cognitive psychologists.

The chapters in the final section address decision-making by both political elites and ordinary citizens. Decision-making research in political psychology relies on elements of both motivational and information-processing arguments, but its distinctive character stems from its use of well-developed normative criteria for assessing the quality of decisions. The criteria posited by the two disciplines diverge, however. The dominant theoretical framework within political science for the study of decision-making, drawn from microeconomics, assumes that individuals strive for decisions that maximize their expected gain. The dominant framework within psychology, however, suggests that decision-makers typically expend the minimal effort necessary to reach satisfactory outcomes. The chapters by Tetlock, Jervis, Popkin, and Ansolabehere and Iyengar, to varying degrees, are concerned with these alternative conceptions of rationality in political decision-making (as applied to both ordinary citizens and political elites). Proponents of economic and psychological models of rationality typically have little to say to each other, both groups accepting a cost/utility model; but political science focuses on utility maximization, and psychology focuses on cost minimalization. As Ansolabehere and Iyengar point out, one of the most exciting prospects offered by political psychology is the potential for reconciling "optimizing" with "satisficing" theories of decision-making.

The emergence of political psychology thus represents a small but nevertheless important step away from the illusion of "unidisciplinary competence" (Campbell, 1969). There can be no denying that political science and psychology remain widely separated in matters of epistemology and in their respective criteria for determining what issues are worth investigating. Truly collaborative research involving scholars from both disciplines is also still rare. The programs of research described in this book, however, are testimony to the existence of a number of areas of mutual interest. The editors hope this volume will help to further erode disciplinary boundaries and the fallacy of disciplinary autonomy.

Notes

1. For evidence of these curricular trends, see David O. Sears and Caroline L. Funk, "Graduate education in political psychology in the United States," presented at the annual meeting of the International Society of Political Psychology, July 1991.

William J. McGuire

2. The Poly-Psy Relationship:
Three Phases of a Long Affair

Interdisciplinary cross-fertilization during the past half-century, while always at a modest level, has been as active and sustained between political science and psychology as between any two social sciences, which is surprising considering that each discipline has more extensive frontiers with other fields—political science with economics and history, psychology with sociology and anthropology. This intellectual border traffic has persisted through three successive eras that have differed in preferred topics, theories, and methods. In all three eras the main enthusiasm within political science has come from students of political behavior, while within psychology the enthusiasm has shifted over the three eras from personality, to social, and now to cognitive psychology.

Each of these three collaborative eras has had its preferred topics of study, its favored theoretical explanations, and its high-table nihil obstat methods. Here we shall label each era by its popular topics of study, so that the first interdisciplinary flourishing in the 1940s and 1950s is called the "personality and culture" era; the second, in the 1960s and 1970s, the "attitudes and voting behavior" era; and the third flourishing, likely to dominate the 1980s and 1990s, the "ideology and decision" era. This nomenclature, which for simplicity and consistency emphasizes the era's preferred topic, should not obscure the fact that in some eras a shared theory or shared method has constituted a stronger bond among the interdisciplinary workers than has the shared topic used to label them.

Contributions were made during each of the three eras by both humanistic and scientific approaches, and within each approach on both

The writing of this article was substantially aided by Grant MH 32588 from the National Institute of Mental Health.

micro and macro levels. We classify as "humanistic" those researchers who use their era's theoretical insights idiographically to account for the thick texture of complex concrete cases, and we call "scientific" those researchers who use these insights nomothetically to study an abstract general principle as it manifests itself across a wide range of cases whose peculiarities will, it is hoped, cancel each other. The idiographic humanistic workers bring theory and empirical observation into confrontation better to understand the specific case; the nomothetic scientific workers bring them into confrontation better to understand the theory. Within each approach some work is at the micro level, investigating the variables of interest as they relate across individual persons as the units of study; other work is at the macro level, investigating the relations across collectives (e.g., nations, social classes, historical epochs) as the units of study.

Table 2.1 gives an overview of this half-century of interdisciplinary collaboration. Its rows list three successive twenty-year eras, the 1940s–1950s personality and culture era, the 1960s–1970s attitudes and voting behavior era, and the 1980s–1990s ideology and decision era. Of the columns in table 2.1, the three on the left constitute a connotative definition of each era in terms of its characteristic topics, theories, and methods; and the four columns on the right provide a denotative definition of each era by citing some of its important contributions, partitioned first between the idiographic humanistic and the nomothetic scientific approaches and, within those, between work at the micro and the macro levels. The three sections of this chapter describe, in turn, the three successive row eras, each in terms of these seven columns of information sketched in table 2.1.

The evolution of interdisciplinary research in political science and psychology during the past half-century is summarized in table 2.1 with stylized symmetry, as if it has passed neatly through three successive eras of different content and similar structure. In this depiction of the historical process we have superimposed sharp contours and contrasts on an amorphous body of research, which in actuality had more continuity and less direction than are highlighted in our description of it. Intellectual history (and indeed any representational knowledge) must highlight regularities and distinctions if it is to call attention to the faint signals masked by background noise, as is discussed more fully in my expositions of a "perspectivist" (or "contextualist") epistemology (McGuire, 1982, 1986b). Other historians of the topic might abstract different themes from this interdisciplinary effort that are as useful as my own for revealing directions. Alternative depictions based on concurrent European political psychology would be particularly useful because this sketch focuses primarily on the developments in North America. Each such complementary depiction would in its own distinctive way sharpen contours of the long collaboration and bring out additional underlying structures that give it coherence and suggest its directions.

This chapter is not arguing that all research was confined strictly within the borders of this sketch or that the boundaries between eras mark discontinuities at which successive enthusiasms abruptly replaced one another. Noteworthy work involving the favored topics, theories, and methods of each era has been done throughout the half-century and will probably continue to be done for decades to come. Indeed, the chapters that follow report current work on topics, theories, and techniques that were especially favored in each of the three eras, illustrating their continuing evolution and health. There have been successive waves of enthusiasm, however, that have thrown the spotlight on different parts of the interdisciplinary enterprise, each with its own organic structure characterized by distinctive topics of interest, theoretical orientations, and methods of investigation.

The 1940s–1950s Personality and Culture Era

Each era has its distinctive topics, theories, and methods but in each the main intellectual impetus has come from a different one of these three components. In the first, the personality and culture era, the main common ground among researchers was a shared theoretical enthusiasm to explain political thoughts, feelings, and actions in terms of environmental (versus hereditary) determinism, using explanatory concepts drawn from psychoanalysis, Marxism, and behaviorism, in declining order of importance.

By the 1940s some students in each of the social sciences had become fascinated by the promise of psychoanalytic theory, not so much for its hereditarian conjectures about racial unconscious, innate instincts, and rigid developmental stages, but rather for its environmentalistic theories about the vicissitudes of these genetic trends when shaped by the individual's early experiences. For political psychologists, psychoanalysis suggested how early childhood experiences provided by a society shape the leaders' and the public's mature political personalities and their consequent political behaviors. Reflecting Freudian theory's psychiatric origins, particular attention was paid to pathological aspects of personality

Table 2.1. Synopsis of the features and products of the three successive eras of political science/psychology collaboration.

	Connotative definition: Distinctive characteristics		
Eras	Preferred topics	Preferred theories	Preferred methods (and statistics)
1. 1940s and 1950s	Political personality (in leaders and in masses)	Environmental determinisms (psychoanalysis, Marxism, S-R behaviorism)	Content analysis of records and interviews (contingency and correlation co-efficients)
2. 1960s and 1970s	Political attitudes and voting behavior	Rational person (subjective-utility maximizing, cognition→affect→action)	Questionnaires in survey research; participant observation (factor analysis)
3. 1980s and 1990s	Political ideology (content and processes of belief systems)	Information processing (cognitive heuristics, decision theories, schemata theories)	Experimental manipulation; computer flowchart (structural equation models)

and political behavior. A second prevalent theoretical orientation, Marxist historical materialism, shared with psychoanalysis the view that cultural institutions determine political personality and behavior, but Marxism focused less on early childhood experiences as determinants and was concerned with mass personality as an effect, to the neglect of leader personality as a cause, of social and material conditions. The third environmentalistic-theoretical inspiration for researchers in this era was

Denotative definition: Notable contributions by each of four approaches			
Humanistic approaches (idiographic, synthetic)		Scientific approaches (nomothetic, analytical)	
Micro	Macro	Micro	Macro
Psychobiography: Fromm (1941) Langer (1972) George and George (1956) Erikson (1958)	National character: Benedict (1946) Mead (1942) Gorer (1948) Riesman (1950)	Dollard et al. (1939) Adorno et al. (1950) Smith, Bruner, and White (1956) McClosky (1958)	Sorokin (1937–41) Kluckhohn and Murray (1948) HRAF (Murdock, Ford) Whiting and Child (1953)
Lane (1959, 1962) Goffman (1959, 1961)	Ariès (1960) Annals (Block) Foucault (1961, 1984)	Election studies, e.g., Campbell et al. (1954, 1960, 1966) Roper Center	Lipset (1960) McClelland (1961) ICPSR (1962) Rokkan (1962) Almond and Verba (1963) Russett et al. (1964) Inkeles and Smith (1974)
George (1980) Larson (1985) Doise (1986)	Lebow (1981) Jervis et al. (1985, 1986) Radding (1985)	Tetlock (1981) Simonton (1984)	Archer and Gartner (1984) Tetlock (1985)

the stimulus-response behaviorism that described how the individual's political personality is conditioned by the stimuli, responses, drives, and reinforcements provided by the society's institutions. In addition to this basic bond of environmentalistic theorizing, the invisible college that constituted this first, 1940s and 1950s, interdisciplinary politics and psychology era had a secondary bond in a shared subject matter (its interest in personality) and a tertiary bond in a shared methodology (its predilection for documentary analyses). These three shared enthusiasms of the era will be discussed more fully in the next section.

Mention of a few key works contributed by each of the four approaches (humanistic micro and macro, and scientific micro and macro) will provide a preliminary denotative definition of this political personality era. Within the humanistic approach, an archetypical microstudy is the George and George (1956) depiction of how Woodrow Wilson's childhood experiences with a demanding father laid down a personality style that led to his fractious behavior in authority situations, as illustrated by his recurring problems in dealings with the Princeton University trustees, the New Jersey legislature, and the U.S. Senate. The macro branch of humanistic studies in this era is illustrated by influential studies of modal personality, such as Ruth Benedict's (1946) analysis of Japanese national character and Riesman's (1950) analysis of the evolution across epochs from tradition-directed, to inner-directed, to other-directed personalities. Within the scientific tradition, a paradigmatic microstudy is the Adorno et al. (1950) authoritarian personality analysis of how hostility to low power groups and subservience to high status leaders can develop as a mode of coping with a difficult Oedipal situation. Scientific studies at the macro level are illustrated by those using the Human Relations Area Files, such as Whiting and Child's (1953) cross-cultural investigation of how cultural differences in child rearing produce the societies' distinctive adult modal personalities. These prototypical examples of 1940s and 1950s political personality research illustrate that the interdisciplinary aspects of the work extend beyond political science and psychology, in that Benedict and Whiting were card-carrying anthropologists and Adorno a philosopher and musicologist.

Characteristics of the 1940s–1950s Personality and Culture Era

The preceding précis of the connotative and denotative definitions of the political personality movement in the 1940s and 1950s will be fleshed out here, first by detailing the movement's connotational definition in terms of the decade's characteristic theories, topics, and methods, and then by expanding its denotational definition by further citations of the era's notable contributions within each of the four approaches.

Preferred theories. The unifying assumption behind this 1940s–1950s interdisciplinary flourishing is that political personality and behavior are formed by ontogenetic socialization experiences, an assumption that encouraged the era's students of political personality to use the environmentalistic components of psychoanalytic, Marxist, and behavioristic theorizing. The era's environmentalistic metatheorizing may have been an embarrassed and indignant reaction to the excesses of the social Darwinism earlier in the century (Hofstadter, 1944) as well as a desire to understand and then ameliorate the disturbed economic and political conditions of society in the aftermath of the 1914–1918 war. This chapter focuses on the work produced in each era, ignoring the further question of what were the driving forces that motivated and shaped the successive enthusiasms in this interdisciplinary field. Elsewhere (McGuire, 1986a) I have argued that when, as here, a field of scholarship advances by a succession of enthusiasms, the dampening of the earlier enthusiasm tends to be brought about by internal factors, usually by excesses of virtues (excessive quantification, conceptual elaboration, application, etc.), whereas the shaping of the succeeding enthusiasm tends to be determined by external factors, such as developments in neighboring disciplines or in the broader society.

Psychoanalytic theory arguably has had a broader impact on social science during the first half or three-quarters of the twentieth century than has any other theory. Behind the 1930s introjection of Freudianism by many American political psychologists looms the father figure of Harold Lasswell (1930, 1935) whose influence launched the use of Freudian notions of unconscious erotic (and thanatotic) motivations, of defense mechanisms that adaptively channel the expression of these drives, and of Freud's psychosexual developmental notions of how oral, anal, and phallic frustrations of early childhood form the id, ego, and superego aspects of personality. These rich notions provoked a gold mine of hypotheses about the development and operation of politically relevant thoughts, feelings, and actions in the public and its leaders. In the 1940s and 1950s enthusiasts made vigorous use of this psychologizing, but a few critics, such as Bendix (1952), objected to the reductionism of such undertakings.

A second manifestation of environmental determinism in this 1940s–1950s political personality theorizing was a vague use of Marxist historical materialism which attributed the formation of any society's political consciousness to the social and political institutions shaped by its modes and relations of production, which in turn was determined by its physical realities. The Marxists generally accepted Engels' (1884/1972) low opinion of the bourgeois family (the *Communist Manifesto* called for abolition of the family), but unlike the Freudians they did not detail the baleful effects of the early childhood home on adult political personality.

A third theory, s-r (stimulus-response) behaviorism or "learning theory," also provided some inspiration for the political personality movement, particularly through the circle of interdisciplinary workers around Clark Hull at the Yale Institute of Human Relations. These theorists seasoned a "liberated" behaviorism with a generous sprinkling of psychoanalytic theory and a dab of Marxism, as illustrated by the Dollard et al. (1939) work on frustration and aggression and later the Miller and Dollard (Dollard & Miller, 1950; Miller & Dollard, 1941) work on social learning, personality formation, and psychopathology. Brown (1936) interwove several of these theoretical strands (plus field theory) in explaining political personality.

Another ideological orientation, supplementing environmental determinism, that at least implicitly directed and energized many of these interdisciplinary researchers was a loathing for the fascistic personality, a syndrome hard to define but (at least in those days) one knew it when one saw it. The era's underlying revulsions for social Darwinism and fascism are not unrelated (Hofstadter, 1944; Stein, 1988).

Preferred topics. A secondary unifying focus of these 1940s–1950s political science/psychology interdisciplinary researchers was a shared subject-matter interest in personality as a mediating variable—how it is determined by the individual's cultural experiences and how it determines the politically significant behavior of the masses or their leaders. "Personality" was used broadly to include motivations and values, perceptions and stereotypes, cognitive and interpersonal styles, characteristic modes of coping, etc. Popular independent variables to account for these mediating personality variables were the early childhood socialization experiences stressed by psychoanalytic theory. Other popular independent-variable determinants, reflecting the behavioristic and Marxist materialism of the era's theorists, were the institutions of society as regards the stimuli they presented, the response options they made available, the drives they fostered, and the schedules of reinforcement they provided. For example, the aggressive foreign policy of a national leader or the bellicose attitudes of the population might be attributed to (a) the culture's displacement of an Oedipal hostility or ambivalence regarding the father to outgroup targets, or (b) to frustration caused by economic deprivation (absolute or relative to others' or to one's rising expectations), or (c) to alienation and felt loss of control due to bureaucratization, the estrangement of the worker from the product of his/her labor, or (d) to social modeling and reinforcement of aggressive responses in childhood.

Preferred methods. Researchers in this first era were not as self-conscious about their methodologies as were the workers in the next two eras. Scholars in its humanistic branch used secondary analysis of the textual record, occasionally supplemented by nonparticipant observation and interviews, procedures whose popularity with humanists continued during the two later eras as well. Methodological differences among the three eras are less pronounced in the humanistic than the scientific approaches. Scientific workers in this era characteristically used data from questionnaires or from content analyses of archival data in correlational designs. Their preferred descriptive statistics were measures of simple association such as contingency and correlation coefficients, statistics that were inefficient for the study of nonmonotonic and interactional relations but have the attractions of allowing use of discontinuously- and even nominally-scaled variables and of being computationally simple, a more important desideratum in the precomputer era.

Notable Contributions in the 1940s–1950s Personality and Culture Era

The preceding section presents a connotative definition of this first, culture and personality, interdisciplinary era by describing its characteristic topics, theories, and methods. Now its denotative definition will be extended by identifying some major studies done during the era by each of the four types of research, illustrating successively humanistic work on the micro and macro levels and then scientific work on each level.

Political science, despite its name, has always included a large amount of humanistic research, using "thick" descriptive analyses (Geertz, 1973, 1983) to demonstrate how some theory or constellation of factors can account in depth for a concrete case. Such idiographic studies are typically designed to advance understanding of the specific case more than of the theory. Scientific studies, on the other hand, apply the theoretical explanations to multiple cases, paying the costs of abstractness and superficiality to gain breadth and disconfirmability. The scientist's nomothetic studies are usually designed to advance understanding of the theory more than of the cases. Each approach, the humanistic and the scientific, has its uses and each includes studies on the micro level using individuals and on the macro level that use collectives (such as nations or historical epochs) as the units of analysis.

Humanistic psychobiography studies on the micro level. The humanistic micro branch in this political personality era has come to be known as "psychobiography" or "psychohistory," the evolution and cultural status of which is reviewed by Runyan in the next chapter; and its macro branch has been labeled "national character" study. The master himself (Freud, 1910) contributed one of the earliest psychobiographies in his description of Leonardo DaVinci as having low sexual drive and trouble in completing his artistic undertakings, which Freud attributed to the ambivalences laid down in Leonardo's early childhood by his unusual experience of having biological and adoptive mothers, both of whom were warmly indulgent. Some psychobiographies continue to be done on non-political personages such as artists or religious figures like Luther (Erikson, 1958), but political leaders have become the most popular subjects (Glad, 1973; Greenstein, 1969). As was pointed out in the précis of this first era, a seminal contribution was the George and George (1956) analysis of Woodrow Wilson's personality as instigating his troubles with legislatures. Freud himself purportedly co-authored a psychobiography of this psychologically intriguing president, if one accepts the authenticity of the "Freud and Bullitt" (1967) hatchet job on Woodrow Wilson (Erikson & Hofstadter, 1967). Neo-Freudian, Marxist, and ego-psychological theorists contributed political psychobiographies of Hitler (Erikson, 1950; Fromm, 1973), Richelieu (Marvick, 1983), Atatürk (Volkan & Itzkowitz, 1984), etc. This movement gained status among policy makers by its World War II use in intelligence work, illustrated on the micro side by Langer's (1972) psychobiography of Hitler and on the macro side by Benedict's (1946) analysis of Japanese national character.

Humanistic national character studies on the macro level. Most of the 1940s national-character research in the macro humanistic line were more explicitly psychoanalytic than Benedict's, even in regard to her own topic of Japanese modal personality. Psychoanalytically-oriented theorists demonstrated that the Japanese national character was oral (Spitzer, 1947), and anal (LaBarre, 1945), and phallic (Silberpfennig, 1945), illustrating the protean quality, at once admirable and worrisome, of psychoanalytic theory. Contemporaneous analyses of American national character tended to be less Freudian (Gorer, 1948; Mead, 1942).

In identifying the 1940s and 1950s as the main flourishing of political personality research I do not mean to imply that such work ceased abruptly with the decadal dawn on New Year's Day, 1960. Notable work in the humanistic tradition has continued to the present, as reviewed by Runyan in the next chapter. The more recent work has flourished, particularly in its micro, psychobiography branch, as reviewed by Barber (1972), Mazlish (1972), Knutson (1973), Greenstein (1975), Glad (1980), Runyan (1982, 1988), and Cocks and Crosby (1987). The challenge of

Richard Nixon's personality (Brodie, 1981) could all by itself have suf-ficed to revive the enterprise. The macro branch has been less active (Patai, 1973, 1977) since its 1940s and 1950s popularity, perhaps because describing national characters as distinctive could appear racialistic, as illustrated by some hostile reactions to Lewis's (1961) well-intentioned "culture of poverty" concept. The cautious scholar builds a fence around the law to avoid being tarred by the racialism brush (Bendersky, 1988). The shocku of Japan-Incorporated has evoked a flood of books that only a yuppie could love on Japanese culture and character, subspecies homo economicus (Morita, Reingold, & Shimomura, 1986; Imai, 1986). The comparable shock of the revolting youth of the late 1960s promoted macro analyses of epoch personality of successive youth generations who were given picturesque labels such as teddy boys, skin heads, beats, flower people, punks, yuppies, dincs, yucas, etc., showing that the con-cept of adolescent political cohorts is a vigorous one (Mannheim, 1923/ 1952; Jennings & Niemi, 1981; Jennings, 1987). Perhaps at this very moment a new generation of students of national, subnational, epoch, and generational character are slouching toward Bethlehem (somewhere in California?) to be born (Peabody, 1985). We depict three twenty-year waves of enthusiasm as passing successively from political personality to political attitudes to political ideology topics, but each exercised only relative hegemony, not interdictive dominance; a respectable level of work on each of these three important topics can be found in every era.

Scientific studies on the micro level. The scientific approach involves sampling cases from a designated universe of generalizability and mea-suring each case, both on the independent variable (in this first era, often on some psychoanalytically relevant dimension of early childhood expe-rience), and on the dependent variable (usually some politically sig-nificant dimension of personality). Then the relation between indepen-dent and dependent variables' distributions of scores is calculated. The scientific approach, like the humanistic, has both micro versus macro branches, the micro using as its cases (its units to be measured on the independent and dependent variables) individual persons, whereas stud-ies on the macro level use as their cases multiperson social composites such as nations, subnational units, or epochs.

Both micro and macro scientific examples of this 1940s–1950s politi-cal personality work are reported in the Dollard et al. (1939) volume on the frustration-aggression hypothesis that individuals, as their frustra-tions rise, become increasingly likely to aggress against scapegoats (cho-sen as targets on the basis of their availability and weakness rather than their responsibility for the frustration). This frustration/aggression notion had Freudian underpinnings although it does not fully exploit the rich contradictions in Freud's three theories of aggression (Stepansky, 1977). Microstudies in the Dollard et al. (1939) volume systematically manipulated the frustration levels of individual rats and then measured these rats' aggressiveness toward targets that were in no way responsible for or associated with their frustration. A macrostudy in the Dollard book measured annual fluctuations in U.S. economic frustration (calculated from aggregated annual gross national product) and correlated these annual economic frustration scores with annual scapegoating scores (measured by yearly numbers of lynchings in the United States).

A comparably important scientific microstudy in the political personality era is the Adorno et al. (1950) authoritarian personality research derived from Freudian and Marxist orientations. Its basic postulate was that the authoritarian (fascist) personality syndrome, characterized by hostility to Jews and various out-groups along with idealization of high-power individuals and groups, could result from an Oedipal situation in a male's early childhood such that his punitive father had severely punished any manifestations of hostility, resulting in the boy's growing up rigorously repressing aggressive feelings by the reaction-formation mechanism of idealizing the father (and by generalization, other authority figures) and by releasing the pent-up hostility vicariously toward out-groups whose demographics or life styles place them outside the Establishment's authority structure.

Other scientific micro studies in the era included Almond's (1954) on appeals of communism, Srole's (1956) on anomie and prejudice, Smith, Bruner, and White's (1956) on the functional bases of political attitudes, and McClosky's (1958) on political conservatism and personality. While scientific micro research on political personality became rarer after the 1950s, occasional studies in this vein continue to attract attention, such as Rokeach's (1960) work on dogmatism, Rotter's (1966) on locus of control, and Christie and Geis's (1970) on Machiavellianism. However, interest in these politically relevant personality orientations has largely shifted from their psychoanalytical antecedents to their behavioral consequences.

Scientific studies on the macro level. A precursor of the macro scientific studies of political personality was Sorokin's (1937–1941) formidable four-volume quantitative analysis of many cultural manifestations of Western civilization during the past two and a half millennia to test his theory of sensate, ideational, and idealistic (and other mixed) types of personality orientations. More sophisticated later analyses of Sorokin's data (Simonton, 1984) raise doubt about some of his conclusions but the work is a remarkable achievement for its time. Another prototypical macro scientific study is Richardson's (1960) work on the statistics of deadly quarrels, done contemporaneously with Sorokin's although the findings were published only posthumously. These pioneers had to do Stakhanovite labor—in those days before large federal research grants, computer entry and manipulation of data, and interuniversity data consortia—to assemble personally (with a little help from their friends and students) these large-scale historical data archives. Macro empirical research on personality was given a major impetus in the 1940s by the development of social-data archives, beginning with G. P. Murdock, C. S. Ford, and others at Yale in setting up the Human Relations Area Files that allowed efficient macro research on how child rearing practices, social structure, etc., related to cross-cultural differences in modal personality (Kluckhohn & Murray, 1948).

In summary, this 1940s–1950s personality and culture era was an exciting time when a small invisible college of interdisciplinary researchers, sharing overlapping explanatory targets and theoretical orientations, reached a critical mass. Operating *à cheval* across disciplinary frontiers, using psychoanalytic and, to a lesser extent, Marxist and behaviorist theorizing, they proposed interesting conjectures regarding how individual and societal differences in politically relevant personality syndromes and behavioral styles can be accounted for in terms of the society's early child rearing practices or prevailing socioeconomic institutions and can in turn account for politically significant consequences.

Cross-disciplinary research at an interface of two fields tends to be an exciting participatory sport but it is a young person's game, drawing few spectators and fewer participants from the parent disciplines' established leaders who tend to be preoccupied by the traditional topics with which the field has become fairly comfortable. Because workers at interdisciplinary borders are relatively few, their focusing narrowly in any one era in regard to topics, theories, and methods is excusable in order that they may attain a critical mass of mutually stimulating work. This narrowness tends to be corrected by sizable shifts of focus from one era to the next.

The 1960s–1970s Attitudes and Voting Behavior Era

In the second—1960s and 1970s—interdisciplinary flourishing of political psychology the focus shifted from political personality and behavioral pathology to political attitudes and voting behavior. This second era, like the first, had its preferred topic, theory, and method, but the relative emphasis on the three reversed between the two eras. The earlier period had been characterized especially by its distinctive theoretical enthusiasms for psychoanalytic, Marxist, and behavioristic environmentalism explanations. It had only a secondary bond in shared topical interests such as how the conditions of early childhood home and other social institutions shaped politically relevant personality; and it had only a weak tertiary bond in its preferred methodology, vaguely characterized by content analyses of documentary materials and correlational analyses. In the succeeding 1960s and 1970s attitudes and voting behavior era the relative importance of these three components in providing a common ground for the participants was reversed. The primary commonality of the 1960s and 1970s political attitude workers was a shared methodological enthusiasm for survey research; their secondary bond was a shared topic preoccupation with political attitudes and voting behavior; while a subjective-expected-utility (seu), benefits/costs maximizing theory supplied only a weak tertiary bond, often used only implicitly.

A brief denotative definition of the second era might include, as prototypic works in the humanistic branch, Lane's (1962) study of political ideology as a micro example and Foucault's (1961/1965) of the cross-epoch development of attitudes toward deviancy and restraint as a macro example. In the scientific branch a precursor micro study was Lazarsfeld, Berelson, and Gaudet's (1944) research on voters' decision making. However, institutionally sustained work on the influence of political campaigns on voting behavior, focusing especially on its mass-mediated psychological determinants, begins with the 1960s Michigan studies (Campbell, Converse, Miller, & Stokes, 1960). On the macro level, notable early contributions include those of Lipset (1960) on the social bases of politics and McClelland (1961) on the attitudinal correlates of the rise and fall of national power and economic success.

These early examples of second era studies, being done in the transition from the political personality to the political attitude period, show subject matter overlap with the first era, their dependent-variable focus having shifted to attitudes, but attitudes that shade into motivational and personality characteristics. Their independent variables continued to be social conditions but with less use of the family structure and child rearing practices variables stressed by psychoanalytic theory and more use of mass media and other institutional determinants. This was an end-of-ideology period (Bell, 1960; Mills, 1959; Namier, 1955) so it is not surprising that theoretical explanations were becoming eclectic and ad hoc—although now it appears that ideology was not dead but hiding out in Paris and Frankfurt (Skinner, 1985). Mentalistic explanatory constructs were often left implicit and when economic determinism was assumed, it was likely to be based on the simplistic SEU rationalism of marketing theory rather than on complex Marxist concepts such as historical materialism, exploitation, and added value.

As we did for the first era, we shall describe this second, political attitudes, era by expanding this introductory précis: first connotatively, in terms of its preferred methods, topics, and theories; and then denotatively by citing notable contributions made in each of the four approaches, humanistic micro and macro and scientific micro and macro.

Characteristics of the 1960s–1970s Attitudes Era

Preferred theories. The interdisciplinary researchers in this political attitudes second era, working after the "end of ideology," were not doctrinaire in regard to their own theoretical orientation; neither did they impute highly organized thought systems to the public (Converse, 1964). However, underlying much of the research there was an implicit assumption of the hedonic person operating in accord with a self-interest subjective-utility maximizing model. When formalized, it depicts the favorability of a person's attitude or behavior toward a political figure or position as a positive function of the algebraic sum (or the mean) of the products of each of the political figure's perceived properties (or consequences) multiplied by that property's (consequence's) subjective desirability (Feather, 1982). For example, a voter's preference for a candidate was predicted to be an additive or averaging function of the candidate's perceived position on the party dimension, on issues and demographic dimensions, etc., each weighted by the voter's own position on the dimension and its perceived importance.

Supplementing this expected-utility conceptualization was a second rationality assumption, the "cognitive → affective → conative" concept of the person as having beliefs that lead to attitudes that lead to actions (Krech & Crutchfield, 1948). A third underlying assumption was the "reference group" consistency concept that the person maximized in-group homogeneity by adopting attitudes and behaviors normative within his/her demographic or social groups (Newcomb, 1943). These three rationality presuppositions of the 1960s and 1970s political-attitudes era went almost without saying, in contrast with the belligerent assertiveness of the psychoanalytic, Marxist, and behavioristic theorizing during the 1940s and 1950s political-personality era. An environmental determinism bridged both eras; the reawakening appreciation of the evolutionary and genetic contributions to human proclivities in other fields had little influence on these students of politics and psychology.

Preferred topics. We are discussing an interdisciplinary field that falls primarily within the jurisdictions of psychology and political science but our account would be unrealistically parochial if confined to work by members of these two union locals. In the opening scenes of this second act the main roles were played by confessed sociologists such as Lazarsfeld at Columbia, Berelson at Chicago, and Lipset at Berkeley. Their topics of common interest were voting behavior and attitudes on political issues, parties, and candidates, especially in regard to how attitudes are affected by group memberships, personal interactions, and mass media. Earlier in the century political elections had been regarded as a great American game (Farley, 1938), an uncouth sport like prizefighting and baseball. Brahmin scholars, both in the academy, such as Frederick Jackson Turner, or outside it, such as Henry Adams, were willing to leave the practice to the upwardly mobile hinterland provincials and immigrant urban proletarians. As some of these outsiders shouldered or sidled their way into academic halls, and as the Great Depression and the proselytizing of international socialism and the terrors of National Socialism riveted scholars' attention on politics, the study of political attitudes and voting behavior in the relatively democratic nations became respectable research topics, first in the humanities and then in the social sciences.

Turn-of-the-century political scientists had found the electoral process and the public exercise of power distasteful (Acton, 1907). By midcentury students of politics had become quite comfortable, even obsessed, with power (Dahl, 1961; Hunter, 1953; Lasswell, 1948; Leighton, 1945; McClelland, 1975; Winter, 1973), perhaps because of their having seen governmental power exercised both to perpetrate genocide and to defeat fascism in a war that also caged the big bad wolf of economic depression. Indeed, many of these post–1940 students of politics had played participatory Dr. Win-the-War roles. After the 1939–1945 war, in most countries where political science flourished, power was perceived as coming from elective office, office from votes, and votes from influencing public attitudes regarding participation and partisanship in the electoral process.

Preferred methods. Shared methodology united these 1960s–1970s political attitudes and voting researchers more than did their shared rational-person theoretical orientation or even their shared interest in the topic of political attitudes and voting. Administering questionnaires in public opinion surveys was the preferred method of data collection. Researchers had a "Do surveys, will travel" modus operandi. This method involved designing a questionnaire for asking a (representative) sample of some population about their demographic, media consumption, political information, or other personal characteristics (as measures of the independent variables) and about their political attitudes and voting intentions or behaviors (to measure the political participation and partisanship mediating or dependent variables). In the early years of the era when labor was cheaper, phone networks less inclusive, and streets safer, the interviews were usually administered on the doorstep by the proverbial little old lady or gent in sensible shoes. More recently the preferred channel has switched to telephone interviews, made more cost-effective by 800 numbers and random-digit dialing. Two complementary schools went for depth versus breadth, respectively, a panel school (Lazarsfeld, Berelson, & Gaudet, 1944) that used repeated interviews of a sample selected from a circumscribed community versus a cross-sectional school (Berelson, Lazarsfeld, & McPhee, 1954; Campbell, Gurin, & Miller, 1954) that used single interviews of a sample drawn from a broader (often national) population. The two variants offered alternative process versus product advantages, respectively, the analysis of time-series changes versus subgroup analyses and broad generalizability. Such formal survey-research methods characterized the scientific branch of political attitudes work, while the humanistic branch often used less formalized depth interviews that allowed open-ended responses to general probes.

A secondary method, more popular in the humanistic branch, was participant observation, earlier improvised by descriptive anthropologists to allow depiction of the cultures of nonliterate societies. Participant observation gained some early acceptability within sociology from its fertile use by Whyte (1943, 1949) in his studies of street corner and restaurant societies and by Goffman (1959, 1961) in his analyses of self-presentation in settings as varied as gambling casinos and asylums. These observational methods seem more promising for the description of public behavior than of private attitudes, but its skilled practitioners readily extrapolated from the overt actions to the mentality of the actors.

Notable Contributions in the 1960s–1970s Political Attitudes Era

To provide a denotative definition of this 1960s and 1970s research on political attitudes and voting behavior, prototypical contributions will be described in each of the four approaches: the humanistic micro and macro and the scientific micro and macro. The previous era's personality researchers derived their inspiration from intricate theories such as psychoanalysis and Marxism that were more notable for their provocativeness than for their falsifiability (Popper, 1945), making the humanistic branches particularly productive. This second, political-attitudes era, being more methodologically inspired in its avidity for survey data that could be put on punched cards (and later on computer tapes and disks), resulted in a more exuberant flowering of the scientific branches, although some fine blossoms bloomed also on humanistic branches.

Humanistic studies on the micro level. Throughout the century of progress following Henry Mayhew's (1861) interviews of the poor in early Victorian London to the sophisticated survey methods taught and utilized at the University of Michigan Institute for Social Research, students of society and mentality have made thoughtful use of the interview method, developing it from an art to a craft, if not yet quite to a science. As an intuitive art, it calls for a virtuoso such as Henry Mayhew or Studs Terkel who use intuitive techniques difficult to communicate. The procedure evolved to craft status as its experienced practitioners became able to articulate rules of thumb teachable to apprentices. It is only beginning to develop to the status of a science with an organized body of theory from which new testable relations can be generated and which can evolve by assimilating new findings.

An early contributor of microhumanistic depth studies of political attitudes (their nature, origins, and relations to behavior) was Robert E. Lane (1959, 1962) in his investigations of attitudes associated with political participation, and then of the nature and origins of the attitudes themselves. Lane's (1962) methods were prototypical of the microhumanistic research on political attitudes in his use of an informal content analysis of the responses given by a diverse sample of interviewees to semistructured or open-ended questions.

These micro humanistic researchers usually present their results in the form of general relations illustrated by summaries of the interview material made concrete by pithy quotes. Occasionally, tabular material is added in the form of frequency data in contingency tables that give some indication of the sample's distributions over the dependent and independent variables and of the strength of the obtained relations between the variables. Such tabular presentations straddle the borderline between the humanistic and scientific approaches and call for a more serious attempt to obtain a large and representative sample of interviewees than does the strictly humanistic approach. Closer to the humanistic pole are popular culture uses of this approach, including the radio and television interview shows that are the most popular form of electronic political communication, with some popularity having been achieved even in print (Terkel, 1967, 1970). Oral history archives promise to expand the collection and availability of useful bodies of interview materials for scholars in the future.

Humanistic studies on the macro level. Macrohumanistic studies of modal attitudes of collectives (nations, regions, eras, etc.) have been conducted on a modest level in the United States and more vigorously in France. Precursory was Myrdal's (1944) analysis of the American dilemma constituted by egalitarian attitudes at odds with racially discriminatory behavior. Regional studies, often centered on an archetypical community ("Jonesville," "Yankee City," "Middletown," etc.) by Dollard (1937), Cash (1941), Key (1949), Warner & Lunt (1941), Lynd & Lynd (1937), etc., depicted the political minds of the South, of New England, and of the American heartland; the Far West alone was neglected because in those pre-jet days academic researchers were loathe to travel three thousand miles from the ocean to collect their data. These precursory macrohumanistic attitude studies evolved by the 1960s and 1970s into a wide spectrum of styles that varied from the literary-anecdotal to the sociological-descriptive poles. Paradoxically, this macrohumanistic research, originally preoccupied with the minutia of overt behavior and objective physical data, metamorphosed into a depiction of subjective group mentality, a surprising development that occurred independently in the U.S. participant-observer movement and the French record-reading *Annals* group. The procedures of the U.S. participant observers such as Goffman provide data mainly on external gross behavior but their interpretative accounts depict mentality more than do accounts by the survey researchers even though this verbal interview material would seem to access more directly the subjective worlds of the respondents. A similar paradox appears in the earlier-born, livelier French *Annaliste* school stemming from Block and Febvre (Le Roy Ladurie, 1978/1981). Its initial preoccupations were with material conditions and products as the primary impetus and manifestation of cultural development (Braudel, 1949/1972), but a subsequent generation ingeniously explored the material surfaces to discover the evolution of *mentalité,* as in Ariès's (1960/1962, 1977/1981) tracings of the development of attitudes about childhood and death, Foucault's (1961/1965, 1984/1986) of attitudes toward the concept of normality in health, sexuality, etc., and Ricoeur's (1967) on attitudes regarding evil.

Scientific studies on the micro level. In the 1940s–1950s political personality era the complexity and uniqueness of its individual personality topic made good use of the depth analysis potential of the idiographic humanistic approach; but in the political attitudes era of the 1960s and 1970s the atomistic quality of voting and of political attitudes, especially as conceptualized and measured by the popular scaling methods, facilitated the counting procedures and broad sampling of cases favored by the nomothetic scientific approach.

Prototypical of the micro scientific research on political attitudes were the early voting studies by Lazarsfeld, Berelson, and their colleagues (Berelson, Lazarsfeld, & McPhee, 1954; Lazarsfeld et al., 1944) associated with Columbia University and the University of Chicago. The most sustained program of such research has been at the University of Michigan under Campbell, Converse, Miller, and their colleagues (Campbell et al., 1954; Campbell et al., 1960, 1966). The 1960s and 1970s were the great decades of this micro scientific research on political attitudes and voting as summarized by Kinder and Sears (1985) but interest in the topic has continued (as might be expected because of the intrinsic importance of its issues), both by the panel method (Himmelweit, Humphreys, & Jaeger, 1985; Patterson, 1980) and the cross-sectional method (Nie, Verba, & Petrocik, 1976).

Lines of work that furnish a bridge between the 1960s and 1970s survey research on political attitudes and the emerging 1980s and 1990s experimental research on political ideology include the reviving interest in agenda setting (Berelson, 1942; Iyengar and Kinder, 1987; McCombs, 1981; Protess and McCombs, 1991), in the development of the structure of political thought during adolescence (Jennings, 1987; Jennings and Niemi, 1981; Sears, 1975), and in the work on "symbolic racism" (Sears, Lau, Tyler & Allen, 1980) as it evolves from studying the relation between political attitudes and behaviors to investigating the structure of ideology. Further evolution of this work is discussed in Sears's chapter in the next section of this volume.

Scientific studies on the macro level. Fewer than these micro scientific studies on political attitudes are the macro scientific studies that use conglomerates such as nations or different historical epochs as the units of measurement. A macro scientific study transitional between the 1940s and 1950s political-personality era and the 1960s and 1970s political-attitudes era is McClelland's (1961) study of how societies' child rearing practices affect their citizens' achievement, power, and affiliation motivations, and how these in turn affect the rise and fall of the societies' political dominance, cultural influence, and economic affluence. McClelland's motivational mediating variables have elements both of the earlier era's personality characteristics and of this second era's attitudinal variables.

Because nations had been more frequently scored in regard to modal actions than modal attitudes, many of these macrostudies focused on behaviors such as participation in voting or political violence rather than on the attitudes presumably underlying them (although macrostudies that focus directly on attitudes are becoming more feasible now as cross-national political attitude data are made conveniently available in social data archives such as the Roper Center headquartered at the University of Connecticut). Much of this macro work concentrated on politically disruptive behavior such as war, revolution, and crime, which presumably manifest national differences in attitudes toward aggressive behavior. Investigations of national correlates of internal and external violence became popular in the 1960s (Archer & Gartner, 1984; Davies, 1962; Feierabend & Feierabend, 1966; Gurr, 1970; Naroll, Bullough, & Naroll, 1974; Singer & Small, 1972) when the cold war, the Vietnam conflict, student unrest, and crime in the streets became more salient issues in North and South America, Europe, and Asia. While disruptive behavior was the most popular dependent variable, some scientific macro studies focused on more constructive characteristics, for example, Lipset's (1960) on political stability, Rokkan's (1962) and Almond and Verba's (1963) on cross-national differences in attitudes and political participation, Inkeles and Smith's (1974) on modernization attitudes, and Cantril's (1965) and Szalai and Andrews' (1980) on cross-national differences in felt quality of life and uses of leisure.

Some of the macro work programmatically identified the dimensionality of nations (Rummel, 1972; Russett, Alker, Deutsch, & Sewell, 1964) and so facilitated subsequent cross-national studies by providing a macro social data bank to parallel archives like the Roper Center which made conveniently available micro political data on individuals. Some macro archives include data for subnational units. For example, the Interuniversity Consortium for Political and Social Research (1988) centered at the University of Michigan, includes more than a century of U.S. voting statistics and social census information on a county-by-county basis. The value of these social data archives will grow progressively as longer multivariate time series data accumulate and causal analyses such as structural equation models are improved to allow better adjustment for differential reliabilities and other technical improvements that facilitate discovery of, or at least testing among, multiple causal paths of influence.

The 1980s–1990s Political Cognition and Decision Era

The preferred interdisciplinary bordercrossing has in the past decade shifted to a third frontier, political cognition. The volume of research on this new topic may still be smaller than that on political attitudes but the future appears to belong to this growth topic—the content, structure, and operation of ideological systems (McGuire, 1986a, 1988, 1991)—that underlies political decision making by the masses and the classes.

Characteristics of the 1980s–1990s Political Ideology Era

Already discernible in this third, ideological systems era are its characteristic subject matter, method, and theory. The two previous waves also had their distinguishing features in each of these regards but the relative importance of these features has shifted among the three eras. In the first, the political personality era, researchers were united mainly by their shared theoretical orientations—psychoanalytic, Marxist, and behavioristic forms of environmental determinism. The second era, focused on political attitudes and voting, was most defined by its characteristic method, survey research. This new third era is best defined by its distinctive subject-matter focus, the content and operations of cognitive systems and choice behavior. Shared theoretical and methodological orientations provide only weaker bonds, underlying both of which the computer metaphor is discernible. Depicting the person as an information-processing machine is the dominant theoretical model with specifics drawn from cognitive science assumptions regarding how information is stored in memory and from decision theory assumptions regarding the heuristics of selective information retrieval and judgment (Axelrod, 1976; Tversky & Kahneman, 1983). Hastie (1986) provides a useful summary of this cognitive science theorizing, conveniently oriented toward political psychology. Depicting political ideological systems as types of schemata (Lau & Sears, 1986) reflects the "cold" information-processing preoccupations of cognitive science (Brady & Sniderman, 1985). Wyer and Otatti, in their two chapters in this volume, show how both cold cognition and hot affect might be taken into account.

The computer inspiration of this third era is apparent also in its characteristic methods, if only on the programmatic level that the operation of the person's ideology and decision processes are often depicted as computer flow charts (Janis, 1989). Studies reported in this volume trace the cost-reducing simplifications (and distortions) at the successive steps in information processing from the stage of perception (see the chapters by Granberg, by Masters and Sullivan, and by Sears in the next section) through central processing (see chapters by Wyer and Otatti, by Lodge and Stroh, and by Tetlock) to inferential decision-making (see chapters by Jervis, by Popkin, and by Ansolabehere et al.).

The need to depict complex cognition systems and processes in this third era is likely to require use of manipulational laboratory experimentation (Beer, Healy, Sinclair, & Bourne, 1987; Lodge and Hamill, 1986) more than did the first two eras, as illustrated in the chapter by Masters and Sullivan in the next section; but most data will continue to be drawn from the natural world, as illustrated by Tetlock's chapter in the final section. The complexity of using these natural world data to clarify the structure and operation of ideology will require increasing use of path analysis and structural equation modeling (Hurwitz & Peffley, 1987). The complexity of systems' theorizing and the availability of computers and programming skills are tempting some researchers to use computer simulation as a method in lieu of data collection (Ostrom, 1988; Rumelhart, McClelland, & the PDP Research Group, 1986).

Notable Contributions in the 1980s–1990s Political Ideology Era

Humanistic micro contributions. It would be premature this early in the third, the political ideology era, to attempt a definitive listing of its major research contributions, but it will be useful as a working denotative definition of the era if we mention illustrative contributions made in each of the four approaches. As regards the humanistic micro approach, noteworthy is Larson's (1985) use of cognitive heuristics to analyze the origins of the U.S. containment policy toward the Soviet Union during the early years of the cold war. George (1980) describes the effective use of information in presidential foreign policy decisions. Purkitt and Dyson (1986) analyze the role of cognitive heuristics in affecting recent U.S. policy toward South Africa. Jervis (1986) analyzes how laboratory-studies findings, that decision makers tend to ignore base-rate information, may show up differently in actual foreign policy decision making. The difference between laboratory and natural world information processing is further analyzed by Jervis in his chapter in the final section of this volume. A different kind of microhumanistic approach is Doise's (1986) analysis of how Mussolini's political ideology derived from his reading of Le Bon, Orano, and Sorel and affected his political policies and tactics. Depth interviewing is used to study the development of political consciousness and ideology in children by Coles (1986) and in adults by Reinarman (1987).

Humanistic macro contributions. Cognitive era studies in the macro humanistic line typically use case history analyses such as those by Lebow (1981) on brinkmanship crises, by Jervis, Lebow, and Stein (1985) on the efficacy of a deterrence policy for averting war, and by Frei (1986) on how perceptual and cognitive patterns interfere with progress on disarmament. Popkin's chapter in the last section of this volume cites numerous cases of cognitive distortions affecting arms policies at diverse times and places in the past half century. Neustadt and May (1986) provide illustrations of the use of case histories by political decision makers. A macro humanistic study that uses epochs as the units of measurement is Radding's (1985) application of Piaget's theory of cognitive development to account for a purported transformation toward abstractness in the mentality and society of Western Europe from 400 to 1200 C.E.

Scientific micro contributions. As to the scientific approach, the micro level is illustrated by Suedfeld and Rank's (1976) and Tetlock's (1981) analysis of the cognitive complexity required in revolutionary leaders if, like Fidel Castro, they are to avoid the classic Robespierrean trajectory of being consumed by their own revolution. First to guide their revolution and then to survive its success, their ideological structure must be complex enough to include both the single-minded fanaticism useful in winning a revolutionary struggle and also the flexibility to employ compromise and accommodation useful in governing a postrevolutionary regime. Tetlock, in his chapter in this volume, discusses further the role of cognitive complexity in effective political leadership. Intriguing scientific micro studies of social factors affecting the productivity and processes of eminent political and cultural leaders are included in the program carried out by Simonton (1984).

Scientific macro contributions. Illustrative of the scientific macro approach to political ideology are Archer and Gartner's (1984) analysis of cross-national differences in violence in terms of social conditions that would affect the cognitive salience of aggression as a mode of coping, Reychler's (1979) analysis of national differences in patterns of diplomatic thinking, and Tetlock's (1985) discussion of complexity in Soviet and U.S. foreign policy rhetoric. Illustrative in style, although not focused on dependent variables typical of political science, are Martindale's (1981) cross-epoch analysis of the evolution of stylistic consciousness in poetry and other arts, and Reiss's (1986) cross-cultural analyses of the role of societal-level factors affecting the conceptualization of sexuality.

Future Directions

This politics and psychology relationship has been lively and long-lasting as interdisciplinary affairs go, its longevity fostered by the protean nature of the collaboration, with frequent shiftings of its popular topics, methods, and theories. The fluidity has made participation in the enterprise both exciting and precarious. The shifting enthusiasms promise novelties that lure new recruits and promote timely discarding of tried-and-trivialized old constructs. The obverse face of this tradition of novelty is painfully rapid obsolescence, as when the depth analysts of the political personality era were edged out of the fast lane by the survey researchers of the political attitudes era with their rich grants for presidential election surveys. Now these second-era survey researchers are finding the third era's cognitive science ideologues tailgating them to move them out of the passing lane.

Participants in This Interdisciplinary Work

Recruitment of workers for the successive eras has been accomplished more by replacement than by retooling. A few like Lasswell, George, Lane, and Converse have managed to move with the changing interests of successive eras. More typically, researchers who initially created each era have continued to do good work in that old line after time has dulled the cutting edge it had when first they honed it. These actors in earlier dramas that have ceased to occupy main stage can continue to play excellently their parts in the old favorites, even if the younger members of the interdisciplinary company prefer a new repertory.

There have been asymmetries in disciplinary inputs over the three eras. The concerned subdiscipline of psychology has shifted from personality/clinical in the 1940s and 1950s political personality era, to social/communication in the 1960s and 1970s political attitudes era, to cognitive/information science in the 1980s and 1990s political ideology era. In contrast, political science participants throughout the half-century have come mainly from its political behavior subdiscipline. Thus, three different areas of psychology have been enlivened by the new questions and new approaches that interdisciplinary contacts tend to evoke; but so far the cross-fertilization benefit within political science has been confined mainly to the subareas of personality and politics and political behavior, although in recent years there has been a growing participation by students of international relations (Sears & Funk, 1991).

There has been a shift across the three eras also as regards which auxiliary disciplines, outside the two main ones of political science and psychology, have contributed most to this collaboration. In the first, the political personality era, outside help came primarily from psychiatrists and anthropologists (Stocking, 1987). In the second era, focused on political attitudes and voting behavior, the main outside collaboration was from sociologists and communication theorists; indeed, sociologists' contributions to the study of voting behavior may have exceeded that of the political scientists or the psychologists . . . but who's counting? In the third, the political ideology era of the 1980s and 1990s, the cognitive scientists are the main outside contributors. During recent years historians, particularly the cliometrics branch not always admired by more orthodox humanistic historians (Barzun, 1974; Bogue, 1983), have been substantial participants in the collaboration (McGuire, 1976).

A Possible Fourth Era

These past trends allow projecting at least through a glass, darkly, a fourth flourishing of political science/psychology collaboration that might succeed the current 1980s and 1990s political ideology era. The past three eras have focused largely on intrapersonal topics (personality, attitudes, ideology), albeit as these processes within the individual are affected by social factors and as they in turn affect society. We anticipate a quantum leap of topic in the fourth era, not just to another intrapersonal topic, but to interpersonal (and intergroup) processes. The beginnings of such a shift are adumbrated in the current work on how stereotypical perceptions and selective information encoding affect international relations (Jervis, 1976) and on jury decision-making (Hastie, Penrod, & Pennington, 1983). The work described in the chapters by Sidanius and by Jervis adumbrate this predicted wave of research on the intergroup processes.

If interest does move from intra- to interpersonal and intergroup processes, the local origins of the psychological participants is likely to shift again, this time to organizational psychology; and participants from within political science are likely to come more heavily from foreign policy and international relations relative to politics (Tetlock, 1986). Third-party collaboration from outside the two core disciplines is likely to come from historians and area specialists. It is also likely that macro research will grow relative to micro research, because a new group-processes era would investigate intergroup as well as interpersonal issues. Both humanistic and scientific branches are likely to flourish: the humanistic, because the complexity of many-player group issues invites its idiographic descriptive approach; and the scientific, because increasing technical capacity for collecting and analyzing multivariate time series data makes modeling such complexities more possible. The fourth era's characteristic theories and methods are likely to reflect systems analysis. It would be hubris to prognosticate in fuller detail than this the shape of a fourth, 2000 to 2020, flourishing that would require clairvoyance into a new millennium.

William McKinley Runyan

3. Psychohistory and Political Psychology:
A Comparative Analysis

Political psychology and psychohistory both began their twentieth-century lives with applications of psychoanalysis to biography and history, as with Freud's *Leonardo Da Vinci and a Memory of His Childhood* (1910/1957) or Erikson's *Young Man Luther* (1958), or with applications of psychoanalysis to political figures as in Lasswell's *Psychopathology and Politics* (1930). In recent years, political psychology has become increasingly cognitive, drawing on findings and methods from attitude research and cognitive psychology (Jervis, 1976, 1989a; Lau & Sears, 1986; McGuire, this volume), while psychohistory has continued to draw primarily, although not exclusively, on developments within psychodynamic theory.

This chapter attempts to provide a relatively comprehensive conceptualization of the uses of psychology in historical interpretation, one that reveals the internal structure of psychohistory and that suggests its multiple relationships with political psychology. Psychohistory can be defined as the explicit use of formal or systematic psychology in historical interpretation. Two aspects of this definition should be noted. First, the field is defined by the use of psychology, which may or may not be psychoanalytic. Second, the interpretive use of systematic psychology must be explicit or visible in order to distinguish psychohistory from all of those historical works that make implicit use of commonsense psychology. Early workers in psychobiography and psychohistory saw it as "applied psychoanalysis," but in the past two decades, many have argued that psychohistory should be defined more broadly so that it draws not only from psychoanalysis, but also from the contributions of personality, developmental, abnormal, social, and cognitive psychology. While a variety of psychodynamic approaches—ranging from drive theory to ego psychology, object relations theory, and self psychology still predominate in psychohistory (see Loewenberg, 1988), there is an increasing use of other psychological theories and methods in psychobiography and psychohistory (Craik, 1988; Gilmore, 1979; McAdams & Ochberg, 1988; Runyan, 1982, 1988a).

The question of how psychological structures and processes are related to the flow of historical events is a fundamental one, with implications cutting across all of the human sciences. Sociology, anthropology, economics, and political science all wrestle with a common set of problems in understanding relationships between individual or collective psychology and continuity or change in social institutions. A clearer conception of psychohistory can help in visualizing the uses of psychology in all of the institutional-level social sciences, with particular attention given in this chapter to political science and political psychology.

The second section will outline the uses of psychology in psychohistory at six different system levels, ranging from individuals up through groups, organizations, institutions, sociocultural systems (e.g., nations), and international relations. This conceptual framework will be illustrated with a set of interconnected examples from Nazi Germany that illustrate in substantive detail the extent of the overlap between psychohistory and political psychology. The third section will outline the disciplinary-mediated relationships between psychology and history, with political psychology as one hybrid field, along with others such as psychological anthropology, which can serve to link history and psychology. The fourth section outlines work in historical psychology and argues that such research cannot only facilitate the use of psychology by historians and political scientists, but can make basic contributions to the discipline of psychology.

The fifth section will briefly discuss several of the implications of this comprehensive conceptualization of psychohistory for the field of political psychology. The sixth and final section will compare the fields of psychohistory and political psychology on a number of intellectual and institutional dimensions. This comparative perspective will, it is hoped, be useful in bringing both fields into sharper focus and in shedding light on their interrelationships.

The history of psychohistory and psychobiography has often been told (Barnes, 1925; Hoffman, 1982; Mack, 1971; Manuel, 1972; Runyan, 1988b), but it may be useful to briefly note it here as background to discussions of the conceptual structure of the field that follow. The history of psychohistory is traditionally defined as beginning in 1910 with Freud's study of *Leonardo da Vinci and a Memory of His Childhood* (1910/1957), which was followed by his historical and anthropological studies in *Totem and Taboo* (1913/1955), *Group Psychology and the Analysis of the Ego* (1927/1955), *The Future of an Illusion* (1927/1961), *Civilization and Its Discontents* (1930/1961), and *Moses and Monotheism* (1939/1964).

Much of the work applying psychoanalysis to history and biography in the 1920s and 1930s by psychoanalysts and others was reductionistic and unsatisfactory, and was widely criticized. However, the rise of Hitler and National Socialism in World War II led to an increased willingness to consider irrational forces in history and biography and provided material for a stream of psychobiographical and psychohistorical works on Nazi Germany beginning during the war with a psychobiographical study of Hitler commissioned by the Office of Strategic Services (Langer, 1972), picking up steam in the 1960s and 1970s, and continuing through the present (see reviews in Cocks, 1979, 1986; Hoffman, 1982; Kren & Rappoport, 1980; Loewenberg, 1975, 1983; and Runyan, 1988a).

The modern period of psychohistory is frequently identified as beginning in 1958, the year of publication of Erik Erikson's *Young Man Luther* and of William Langer's presidential address to the American Historical Association on "The Next Assignment," in which he urged his colleagues to deepen their historical understanding through the use of the concepts and findings of depth psychology.

The field of psychohistory has not developed within one unified and coherent stream but has evolved within several partially autonomous subtraditions, which cluster in part within traditional disciplinary boundaries, with relevant groups including the psychoanalytic and psychiatric community and those in history, political science, academic psychology, literature, the deMause group, and an assortment of others with backgrounds in art, music, religion, and other fields. For a more detailed analysis of the intellectual history of psychohistory across these different fields and of the institutional growth of psychohistory as indicated by a rise in the number of publications, conferences, professional organizations, specialty journals, academic courses, and dissertations in the field, see Runyan (1988b).

Conceptualizing the Structure of Psychohistory

Much of the debate about the accomplishments and failings of psychohistory has centered on the problems and potentials in applying psychoanalysis and psychology to history and biography. Many commentators agree that reductionistic errors are too often made in overemphasizing psychology while neglecting the social–institutional environment, in focusing excessively on psychopathology, or in neglecting basic canons of evidence and inference (Runyan, 1988a). The literature on psychohistory is strewn with examples of inadequate psychohistorical interpretation, which are embarrassing to serious practitioners, as well as with slipshod critiques of the field, which may be equally embarrassing to responsible critics. Whatever the reasons for its embattled status, psychohistory is sometimes perceived as marginal or disreputable by both historians and psychologists. However, the legitimate problem of the relationship of psychological structures and processes to historical events is a fundamental and enduring one, even if it temporarily falls out of intellectual fashion, and no matter how many simplistic or wrong-headed solutions to it are proposed. "Legitimate questions . . . are not invalidated by misconceived answers" (Geertz, 1973, p. 61). The problems of history and psychology, or of the mutually determining nature of human agency with continuity and change in social structure, are fundamental issues within psychology, the social sciences, and historiography.

How can we best conceptualize the relationships among psychological structures, elements, and processes and the flow of historical events? Given the internal diversity of psychology and the multifarious branches of history, divided by time period, area of the world, and substantive focus, these questions are enormously complex and at times feel overwhelmingly so.

It can be frustratingly elusive to get a grasp on what counts as "history." Everything has a history, in the sense of extension over time, but what is the discipline of history the history of? Historians often state that history is primarily concerned not with the history of individual persons (i.e., biography) but with the history of aggregates of persons, with institutions, and with stability and change in society as a whole.

There is considerable controversy about the role of persons versus that of larger impersonal, institutional, demographic, and economic forces in shaping the course of history. Historians often have grave reservations about the study of individuals, believing that their importance in the overall historical process is naively overemphasized (Runyan, 1988b). If individuals are not so significant, then their internal psychological processes are not so important either, and there is no need for historians to be concerned with the details of psychological processes of perception, interpretation, unconscious motivation, belief, decision, and action. For other historians, the solution is not to deny the relevance of psychology to history, but rather to argue that a social psychology, dealing with the psychology of groups, is more relevant than the psychology of individuals (e.g., Barraclough, 1978; Marwick, 1981). According to this view, the most significant contributions of psychohistory would not be in individual psychobiography but in group psychohistory.

What, if anything, does an understanding of psychological structures and processes have to do with the whole range of traditional and contemporary historiographic questions about continuity and change in such large-scale phenomena as international relations? the history of Germany, England, China, or the United States? the French, American, or Russian revolutions? peasants in sixteenth-century France? intellectual history? the history of women? the history of blacks, Native Americans, or Chicanos? the history of social classes? the history of popular culture? or other major historiographic questions?

I shall argue that psychology is relevant to understanding such central historical questions, and not merely in peripheral ways. One way of addressing these questions about the relationships between psychological processes and historical events is outlined in figure 3.1. Figure 3.1 outlines six different system levels, from persons up through international relations, and three levels of aggregation within each system level, from one to some to all. This figure is based on the premise that history can usefully be analyzed as the history and interaction of a number of distinguishable system levels. The six system levels used here are those of persons (including their psychological processes), groups (defined as sets of persons interacting with each other, ranging from two-person relationships, through families, to social groups), organizations (such as formally organized business, church, or political organizations), institutions (such as economic, political, military, and religious institutions, which would include a number of specific organizations within them), nations (or entire sociocultural systems), and, finally, international or intersocietal relationships.[1]

The diagram in figure 3.1 is intended to provide a framework for exploring three kinds of questions, about first, the relationship of psychological structures and processes to historical events; second, the issue of studying individuals versus (or in conjunction with) aggregates of persons; and third, the role of individuals in history versus that of larger impersonal structures.

The discipline of history unquestionably includes the history of international relations, the history of nations, the history of major social

	One	Subsets	All
International relations	1	2	3
Sociocultural systems	4	5	6

Institutions
  Economic
  Political
  Military
  Religious
  Educational
  Scientific
  Social welfare
  Mass media
  Other
	7	8	9

Organizations	10	11	12
Groups	13	14	15
Persons	16	17	18

Figure 3.1. Six system levels and three levels of aggregation.

institutions (economic systems, political systems, higher education), the history of particular organizations (Standard Oil, the Democratic party, the *New York Times*), the history of particular groups or social movements (abolitionists, student activists in the 1960s), and the history of aggregates of people (women, blacks, immigrant groups).

While historians often focus on the history of a particular system, they also may analyze the history of a period, event, or process that cuts across system levels. For example, historical works are often organized in relation to a particular period (such as Victorian England, or Germany from 1933 to 1945), a single event (French Revolution, American Civil War), or process (industrialization, colonization). For these kinds of questions, it is typically useful to draw on material from a variety of relevant system levels and to analyze their interactions over time. History just *is* the history of different entities within these various system levels and relationships among them and of the periods, events, and processes that cut across them.

Psychological processes of perception, sensation, learning, memory, motivation and emotion, unconscious dynamics, decision-making, planning, and action all occur within people (in interaction with their environment) in the bottom row of figure 3.1. The relationships between psychological structures and processes within persons and aggregates of persons to the course of history are outlined by the multiple connections between the bottom row and the top five rows.

If one could demonstrate the relationships between psychological processes within cells 16–18 to each of the other system levels, then one would have laid out the relationship of psychological structures and processes to historical events and have established the relationship of psychology to problems and interests that are central to historians. Such a framework also would clarify the relationships of psychology to political phenomena and events.

Conversely, those maintaining that history has no need for psychology would need to contend that the history of groups, organizations, institutions, nations, and international relations are unaffected by the psychological functioning of individuals, groups, and populations within those systems. Formulated in this light, it is difficult to see how an antipsychological position could be seriously maintained or plausibly defended.

To illustrate the application of the framework outlined in figure 3.1, consider the range of examples of *Our Selves/Our Past: Psychological Approaches to American History* (Brugger, 1981), which suggests the range of psychological approaches that have been taken toward events in American history. The book includes chapters on the psychology of witchcraft in colonial New England; the psychology of revolutionaries versus Tories during the American Revolution; the psychology of slavery; the psychology of abolitionists; the psychology of the progressive movement; the psychology of sex roles and female hysteria in the nineteenth century; the psychology of populists of the 1890s; the psychology of anger and survival guilt among American soldiers in the My Lai massacre; and the psychology of narcissism in contemporary American society, as well as psychological studies of prominent individuals including Theodore Roosevelt, Jonathan Edwards, Abraham Lincoln, and Richard Nixon.

In each of these examples of group or collective psychohistory, analyses are made of the relationships between psychological structures and processes and an important group, social movement, institution, or event in American history. The point is that psychological structures, elements, and processes within individuals and collectivities of individuals are inextricably related to events and processes at each of the other system levels; are actively involved in producing a Revolutionary War, maintaining slavery or fighting to abolish it, living within or rebelling against women's roles in the nineteenth century, participating in or demonstrating against the Vietnam War, and so on.

To take a second and more detailed historical illustration, the relevance of psychological processes for understanding each of the six system levels in figure 3.1 may be illustrated with examples from the Nazi era. Psychological analyses may be useful, or probably even necessary, for understanding those who joined the Nazi party and the ss, those engaged directly in the killing of Jews, those Germans who actively opposed Hitler or aided Jews, the behavior of Jews in the ghettos and concentration camps, the instances of violent resistance by the Jews and other victims, the bystanders in other nations who failed to intervene, and, finally, the psychological impact of the Nazi era and the Holocaust on survivors of the concentration camps, former Nazis, emigrants, descendants of those directly involved, and on all those who study it.

To illustrate the relevance of the relationships between psychological factors and the six system levels of persons, groups, organizations, institutions, sociocultural systems, and international relations within the Nazi era, let us begin with the bottom row of figure 3.1, the level of persons.

The most obvious starting point for studies of individuals is with analyses of Adolf Hitler. In a population with widespread anti-Semitism, what contributed to the unusual intensity of his own anti-Semitic feelings? How did he manage to attain and wield so much power, and then to contribute to his own destruction? The psychobiographical literature on Hitler is enormous, from an early study by Erik Erikson (1942), to William Langer's study for the U.S. Office of Strategic Services in World War II (published in 1972 as *The Mind of Adolf Hitler*), to Rudolf Binion (1976) who argues that Hitler's anti-Semitism had its emotional origins in the trauma caused by his mother's death while being treated by a Jewish physician and in linking the traumatic German loss in World War I to Jews, to Helm Stierlin's (1976) argument that Hitler's hatred of his authoritarian father was displaced onto the Jews against whom Hitler protected his German "Motherland," to perhaps the most comprehensive psychobiographical analysis in Robert Waite's *The Psychopathic God: Adolf Hitler* (1977), which critically evaluates a number of earlier interpretations and argues for, among other factors, the importance of Hitler's abnormal sexual development.

There are, of course, also biographical, autobiographical, and psycho-biographical analyses of an immense number of other individuals within the Nazi era, including Heinrich Himmler, Joseph Goebbels, Herman Goering, Adolf Eichmann, war criminals tried at Nuremberg, concentration camp directors such as Rudolf Hoess, Commandant of Auschwitz from 1941 to 1943, Raoul Wallenberg and others who aided Jews in escaping, autobiographical accounts by concentration camp survivors, and many others (see Cargas, 1985; Mensch, 1979).

Staying at the level of persons, but moving to their aggregation into sets of persons (cell 17 in figure 3.1), a variety of additional psychological questions come to mind. For example, (1) What psychological processes were involved in supporting, voting for, and joining the Nazi party? What psychological (and other) differences were there among those who joined the party in its early years in the 1920s, those who joined in the early 1930s, and those derogatorily nicknamed "March violets" who joined in March 1933 or later after Hitler had come to power? (2) What was the psychology of those actively engaged in mass murder? (3) What was the psychology of the Jewish and non-Jewish victims of the Holocaust? What psychological considerations are necessary in order to understand their behavior and experience, such as widespread disbelief in the death camps, processes of adaptation to and survival in the concentration camps, or longer-term psychological consequences for survivors and their families? (4) What psychological and/or social attributes and processes characterized those who actively fought against Nazism? For example, what was the psychology and social organization of those Jews involved in the Warsaw ghetto revolt of 1943? or the armed revolts of the Treblinka and Sobibor death camps in 1943? or of the German "White Rose" student group who distributed anti-Hitler leaflets in 1942–43 for which they were beheaded; or of those involved in various plots to assassinate Hitler (Hoffman, 1977; Scholl, 1983; Trunk, 1979)? (5) What were the psychological and social circumstances of all the bystanders in Germany, Britain, the United States, and elsewhere who might have helped end the Holocaust, but did not? (6) What about the psychology of the refugees and emigrants from Nazi Germany? Focusing on a subgroup of scholars and intellectuals who emigrated from Nazi-controlled territory, what was the impact of their emigration-related experiences on their later lives, ideas, motivations, and subsequent intellectual careers (see Bailyn & Fleming, 1969; Coser, 1984)?

In each of these six groups, there is a substantial internal heterogeneity, and psychological elements are *only one* of several kinds of operative factors, yet psychological analyses are still a necessary component of any comprehensive understanding.

Moving to questions about psychological aspects of the population of Germans (cell 18 in figure 3.1), a great deal of earlier research focused on questions about the authoritarian personality and German "national character," characterized by features such as ethnocentrism, anti-Semitism, anti-intraception (impatience with fantasies, feelings, and inner subjective phenomena), idealization of parents, and a rigid conception of sex roles (Sanford, 1973). Paralleling the wider course of research on national character (Bock, 1988), it became clear that such global psychological characterizations of a population had to be disaggregated, as there was a wide range of personality types within a population. This more differentiated analysis, working downward from population-level data to finer and finer subgroups (and hence into cell 17), has probably progressed furthest in analyses of who voted for the Nazi party, moving from initial aggregate data about the number of people voting for the Nazis in 1928, 1930, or 1932, to ever more differentiated analyses of election-by-election voting patterns broken down by town, geographical area, religion, age, income, occupation, and other factors (see Childers, 1984; Hamilton, 1981).

To be complete, psychohistorical analyses at the level of persons cannot be restricted to individual psychobiography, but rather must move along the whole continuum of levels of aggregation, from one, to some, to all, and correspondingly, to move along the whole continuum of levels of analytic generality, discovering what can truthfully be said about the population as a whole, about various groups within it, such as perpetrators, victims, bystanders, and resisters, and, finally, about particular persons within each of these groups. Such psychohistorical analyses, moving back and forth across the whole continuum of levels of generality, hold promise for reducing both psychological and historical oversimplification.

Let us now consider the second system level, that of groups, families, and interpersonal relationships (the fifth row in figure 3.1). The distinguishing feature of this system level is people interacting directly with each other, whether in two-person relationships, families, or informal social groups. These face-to-face groups are to be distinguished from analytically defined groups of people who may never interact with each other, such as the set of males versus females in cell 17. Within the Nazi era, examples would include the structure of the German family and processes of childrearing, the interpersonal relationships of Nazis, Jews,

Gypsies, and others, and a variety of informal face-to-face groups, such as the group of Nazis confined with Hitler in Landsberg prison in 1924, or the group of death camp inmates planning the escape from Sobibor in 1943. Within this system level, it is also possible to distinguish between three levels of aggregation, namely, the analysis of a single group, a set of groups, or a whole population of groups. Using the example of interpersonal relationships, attention might be focused on psychological aspects of Hitler's relationships with a particular person, such as Joseph Goebbels, his relationships with a set of people, such as the seven women he presumably had intimate relationships with, six of whom attempted or committed suicide (Waite, 1977, p. 239), or, finally, on the entire set or population of his interpersonal relationships. Similarly, attention to German childrearing processes might focus on characteristics of the population as a whole, on childrearing patterns in different social classes or religious groups, or finally, in childrearing processes in a particular family.

At the next system level, that of formal organizations (the fourth row in figure 3.1), attention can be directed to psychological structures and processes related to a variety of formal organizations, such as the Storm Troops, the Hitler Youth, the Gestapo, the Judenrat (organization of Jewish leaders in the ghettos), or a particular business organization such as I. G. Farben, the chemical company that ran a large synthetic rubber plant near Auschwitz using Jewish slave labor.

To take an example of just one organization, consider the psychology of and the psychological changes over time in the ss (*Schutzstaffeln*, or "protective squads"), which began in 1923 as a group of eight men selected as a personal bodyguard for Hitler. The group, renamed the ss in 1925, was taken over by Heinrich Himmler in 1929, and the membership grew from 280 in that year to approximately 30,000 in 1932, to 250,000 in 1942, to more than a million in 1944, including some 24,000 concentration camp guards, the infamous "Death's Head" detachments (Höhne, 1969; Kren & Rappoport, 1980, chap. 3; Steiner, 1980).

When Germany invaded the Soviet Union on June 22, 1941, the troops were followed by four *Einsatzgruppe*, or "special action groups," whose job was to liquidate Jews, Bolsheviks, Gypsies, the deranged, and other "racial enemies." Hundreds of thousands of victims were rounded up, sometimes ordered to dig their own graves, and then shot. A psychological consequence faced by the ss was the effects of these murders on the soldiers, a number of whom committed suicide, or suffered nervous breakdowns, nightmares, and alcoholism. After the war, one of their leaders, Paul Blobel, made the not overly sensitive claim that "The nervous strain was far heavier in the case of our men who carried out the executions than in that of their victims. From the psychological point of view they had a terrible time" (Höhne, pp. 969, 364). After watching two hundred Jews being shot in Minsk, Himmler was so shaken that he said a new method of killing must be found, which led to the development of gas vans (Höhne, 1969, p. 366), which were followed by gas chambers. A number of other questions can be raised about the psychology of the ss, such as what motivated men to join at different periods, whether they were disturbed or relatively normal, and how they adapted after the war (Runyan, 1988c; Steiner, 1980; Sydnor, 1977).

Working within the organizational system level, and moving to higher levels of aggregation, the study of a specific organization such as the ss may be compared with the study of other organizations within Nazi Germany, or with paramilitary police groups in a number of other countries. Or, if one starts by focusing on a smaller organization, such as a particular concentration camp, a particular church, or a specific business organization, then analyses can be made of a specific group or population of comparable organizations within Nazi Germany. For example, one recent study of a set of death camps is Arad's *Belzec, Sobibor, Treblinka: The Operation Reinhard Death Camps* (1987).

The next system level to be concerned with is that of institutions (the third row in figure 3.1), with each institution including a number of specific organizations within it. This level would include an analysis of the psychological aspects of each of the major social institutions in Germany from 1933 to 1945. Extensive studies have already been made of the functioning of political, military, legal, business, church, educational, scientific, cultural, mass media, and other institutions during the Nazi era (Cargas, 1985; Szonyi, 1985). As just a sample of this literature, there is Turner's *German Big Business and the Rise of Hitler* (1985), arguing that big business was less responsible for Hitler's rise to power than commonly believed; Conway's *The Nazi Persecution of the Churches, 1933–1945* (1969), detailing Hitler's undermining of the churches; Beyerchen's *Scientists Under Hitler* (1977), analyzing the responses of physicists to National Socialism; Blackburn's *Education in the Third Reich* (1984), outlining the massive educational propaganda efforts to shape the minds of German youth in line with Nazi racial theories, political beliefs, and anti-Christian and anti-Marxist ideology; and studies of Nazi physicians in Lifton's *The Nazi Doctors* (1986) and psychiatrists in Cocks's *Psychotherapy in the Third Reich* (1985).

Psychohistorical study would analyze the psychological elements and processes related to the history and functioning of each of these institutions during the Third Reich. In spite of the massive amounts of literature on the Nazi era, and even massive amounts of psychohistorical literature (Gilmore, 1984; Loewenberg, 1975; Mensch, 1979), there is still much more that remains to be done with psychologically informed analysis of each of the major institutions in Nazi society.

Questions about the sociocultural system as a whole (the second row in figure 3.1) have troubled students of the Nazi era and of the Holocaust for decades. As expressed by Lucy Dawidowicz, "(1) How was it possible for a modern state to carry out the systematic murder of a whole people for no reason other than that they were Jews? (2) How was it possible for a whole people to allow itself to be destroyed?" (1975, p. xxi). How are we to understand the values and beliefs of a culture, the interpenetration of political, legal, religious, educational, scientific, and other institutions, the variety of specific organizations, and the array of individual persons from Hitler on down that made this possible?

The entire literature on the Nazi era and the Holocaust deals with different aspects of these questions. Questions about the functioning of the sociocultural system as a whole may be pursued by focusing on the specifics of Nazi Germany, or by comparisons with the histories of other societies such as Franco's Spain, Italy under Mussolini, the Soviet Union under Stalin, or Cambodia under Pol Pot.

At the level of international relations (the first row in figure 3.1), there are a good many issues that have been examined in detail, including (1) most obviously, the psychology of diplomatic and military relations between Germany and the Soviet Union, Austria, Poland, France, Great Britain, the United States, and other countries throughout the Nazi period (for an interesting psychological study of German-British diplomatic relations at the end of the nineteenth century, see Hughes, 1983); (2) the participation of international business with the Third Reich, including officials from firms such as ITT, Ford, Standard Oil of New Jersey, and the Chase Bank (Higham, 1983); and (3) the response or lack of response of other nations to the events of the Holocaust, as in Wyman's *The Abandonment of the Jews: America and the Holocaust, 1941–1945* (1984).

This discussion of the psychological aspects of six system levels does *not exhaust* the range of important psychohistorical questions. Within a given historical period and geographical area, such as Nazi Germany from 1933 to 1945, important questions can also be investigated about the psychological aspects of a chain or sequence of *events* occurring throughout the period, interwoven with the six system levels. This would include events such as Hitler's accession to power on January 30, 1933; the Night of the Long Knives on June 30, 1934, when the ss murdered the leaders of the Storm Troops and took power over their rival organization; *Kristallnacht* (Night of the Broken Glass) on November 9–10, 1938, when the Nazis attacked Jews in the streets and looted their shops; the psychology of the German invasion of Poland on September 1, 1939; the German defeat at Stalingrad in early 1943; the psychology of the Warsaw ghetto revolt in April 1943; the Allied invasion at Normandy beginning June 6, 1944; the psychology of Hitler's suicide on April 30, 1945; and the surrender of Germany on May 8, 1945. Specific events such as these may occur within a single system level, yet have ramifications across other system levels (such as Hitler's suicide), while the very constitution of other events cuts across a variety of system levels (such as the Allied invasion at Normandy). Graphically, events could be represented as circles or uneven puddles of different sizes on figure 3.1, some within single levels but others spreading across several levels.

For each event, important psychohistorical questions can be asked about (a) the antecedent psychology of hopes, plans, fears, expectations, efforts, etc., which led up to it; (b) the concurrent and constitutive psychology of beliefs, perceptions, feelings, interpretations, statements, and actions directly involved in the event; and (c) finally, the psychological consequences, subjective meanings, and later interpretations of the event.

To illustrate with a single event such as the Kristallnacht pogrom on November 9–10, 1938, psychohistorical analysis would include research about the psychological antecedents of the events, such as the anti-Jewish riots following the assassination of a German diplomat in Paris, the fanning of the flames by Hitler, Goebbels, and Heydrich; the psychology of those participating in the looting, of those refusing to participate, or of those actively opposing it; the psychological experience of the Jews associated with the two hundred synagogues that were destroyed, some 7,500 shops that were looted, and the families of the more than twenty thousand Jewish men who were sent off to concentration camps; and the subsequent psychological impact of this event as it was perceived and interpreted by Jews, Nazis, Germans, and citizens around the world (Gorden, 1984).

The discipline of history may focus on the history of a period and geographical area, the history of a particular system within a period, the history of events and processes, or, finally, the history of particular topics or themes. Psychohistorical analysis of *topics* in the Nazi era would include different classes of behavior and experience within the period, such as the psychology of mass murder, the psychology of obedience to authority, the psychology of violent resistance or passive accommodation, the psychology of denial and disbelief at what was happening in the death camps, the psychology of lying and deceit, the psychology of survivor guilt, the psychology of mourning and denial, and so on.

One additional topic with particular relevance to the Nazi era is that of "countertransference," or, more generally, the psychological relationship of the researcher to his or her subject. Studying the period is gut-wrenching for almost everyone, including myself. The strong emotional reactions that the topic engenders are intensified and complicated by the variety of interests involved, whether on the part of concentration camp survivors, former Nazis, other Germans, descendants of those involved, or even those encountering it solely through the literature.

The Nazi period is of particular interest to psychohistorians, as well as to political psychologists, as it has claimed the attention of so many significant contributors to the field, beginning with Erik Erikson's study of Hitler's imagery and German youth (1942), and including studies by Peter Loewenberg of the Nazi Youth cohort, Himmler's adolescence, and overviews of psychohistorical work on modern Germany (Loewenberg, 1971, 1975, 1983); Saul Friedlander on anti-Semitism, the Catholic Church's lack of protest, and contemporary German treatment of the Nazi period (1971, 1975, 1984); Kren and Rappoport's overview of Nazi psychohistory in *The Holocaust and the Crisis of Human Behavior* (1980), Weinstein's study of the *Dynamics of Nazism* (1980); the many psycho-biographies of Hitler, including those by Langer (1972), Binion (1976), Stierlin (1976), and Waite (1977); and most recently Geoffrey Cocks on *Psychotherapy in the Third Reich: The Göring Institute* (1985) and Robert J. Lifton on *The Nazi Doctors* (1986). Psychohistorical studies of the Nazi era are so extensive that they are on the cutting edge of helping to define both the possibilities and the limitations of psychohistorical analyses.

To summarize, the study of psychological aspects of each of the six system levels in figure 3.1 from persons up through international relations, as well as of events and topics cutting across these levels, provides a far more differentiated and fine-grained analysis of the structure of the field of psychohistory than one that makes only the gross distinction between individual psychobiography and group psychohistory.

The more one studies the Nazi period, from the cruelty of individual Nazis, to the brutality of certain organizations, to the agony of the victims, to the heroism of resistant Jews and Germans, to the complex thoughts and emotions of scholars engaged with the period, the more one sees a need for psychologically informed analyses of the issues. To emphasize again, analyses of psychological threads of these events and processes are *not* a substitute for sociological, economic, political, demographic, cultural, and other forms of analysis, but rather their necessary complement.

I have found this diagram helpful in analyzing a wide range of questions about the relationships between psychology, biography, and history, but several comments about its limitations need to be made. First, the particular system levels outlined here are for contemporary Western culture and are not immutable in time and space. For working with the medieval, classical, or prehistoric world, one would need to use a somewhat different set of social system levels, including systems such as tribes, feudal estates, or city-states. There is, in short, a history both of particular entities and of the system levels themselves. Second, the six system levels in figure 3.1 need to be seen against a background of, and in continual reciprocal interaction with, the physical, biological, and technological world. Geographical, climatic, agricultural, technological, and other aspects of the physical world are in continual interaction with the human-social systems sketched in this diagram. Figure 3.1 does not provide a comprehensive analysis of the historical process, but rather focuses on the interconnections between psychological processes within individuals and collectivities to the histories of groups, organizations, institutions, nations, and international relations.

Disciplinary-Mediated Relationships

The uses of psychology by historians need not all be direct ones, in that history can draw from fields such as sociology, anthropology, or political science, which themselves have drawn on psychology. From another perspective, each aggregate level or institutional-level social science has a historical side concerned with the history of phenomena under question (as in historical sociology or historical anthropology) and a psychological side concerned with relevant psychological processes in individuals and collectivities (as in psychological anthropology or political psychology). The relationships of these aggregate-level social sciences to history and psychology are outlined in figure 3.2.

The emphasis in figure 3.2 is on those areas of the social sciences that have explicitly developed their connections with psychology. In sociol-

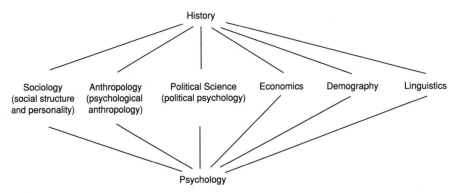

Figure 3.2. Disciplinary-mediated relationships between history and psychology.

ogy, anthropology, and political science, there are formally developed subfields focusing on relationships with psychology, including social structure and personality, psychological anthropology, and political psychology.

The essential point of figure 3.2 is that all of the connections between history and psychology need not be direct ones. Contributions of psychology to history may come not only directly from the discipline of psychology, but indirectly through other disciplines that in turn have made use of psychology. There is a substantial literature in each of these hybrid fields for historians to draw on. The literature is too vast to review in detail, but to mention only a few significant works, with an emphasis on overviews, historically relevant work is discussed in the literature in social structure and personality (e.g., Inkeles, 1983; Rosenberg & Turner, 1981; Smelser & Smelser, 1970, 1981; Yinger, 1965), in psychological anthropology (e.g., Barnouw, 1985; Bock, 1988; LeVine & Shweder, 1984; Spindler, 1978), and in political psychology (e.g., Davies, 1980; Elms, 1976; Greenstein, 1975; Janis, 1982; Jervis, 1976; Jervis, Lebow, & Stein, 1985; Long, 1981; McGuire, this volume; Sears, 1987; White, 1986). To the best of my knowledge, the literatures on relationships between psychology and economics (e.g., Katona, 1975; Maital, 1982), and between psychology and demography (e.g., Easterlin, 1980; Miller & Godwin, 1977), are not as extensively developed, although there may be more to draw on over time.

Psychological history is not some bizarre fringe movement that just ought to go away and stop bothering people, but rather it is intimately related to a number of those aggregate-level social sciences with which historians have already established relationships and are often more comfortable dealing with. As Lawrence Stone (1981) has noted, there are historical trends in the relationships between history and the social sciences, with history borrowing at first most heavily from economics, then from sociology, and most recently from anthropology. Psychology is sometimes mentioned as a possibility, but the reception of psychology by historians has often been far more ambivalent (Gay, 1985). Historians in the future will have the option of borrowing not only directly from psychology, but also from each of these interdisciplinary hybrids, including psychological anthropology, psychology and social structure, and political psychology.

Historical Psychology as a Resource for Psychohistory

One of the most common criticisms of psychohistory is that it relies on a parochial psychology that is naively presumed to hold across space and historical time. The problem was clearly formulated in 1938 by historian Lucien Febvre: "How can we as historians make use of psychology which is the product of observation carried out on twentieth-century man, in order to interpret the actions of the man of the past?" (quoted in Gilmore, 1979, p. 31). It is claimed that many psychohistorians "begin by postulating that there is a theory of human behavior which transcends history" (Stone, 1981, p. 40). Or "The psychohistorian employs theoretical models and cognitive assumptions created from the material of the present— and then imposes them on the past. In so doing, he or she must assume that in most fundamental ways all people, at all places, at all times, have viewed themselves and the world about them in substantially the same fashion" (Stannard, 1980, p. 143).

One way of addressing this concern is to develop a historical psychology that explicitly examines the extent to which psychological concepts and theories do or do not apply across historical eras. As Kluckhohn and Murray (1953, p. 53) stated, every person is in certain respects (a) like all other persons, (b) like some other persons, and (c) like no other persons. If this is true, then some psychological generalizations can be expected to hold across all historical periods, others for limited historical periods, and others perhaps only within specific historical circumstances. This is directly analogous to the more familiar conceptual problem of psychological anthropology, in which questions arise about the extent to which psychological structures and processes hold across all cultures, some cultures, or only within a particular culture. Psycho-historical interpretation is a complex three-tiered intellectual enterprise, which needs to draw on psychological theories that hold universally, other theories holding only within limited social-historical contexts, and finally idiographic relationships holding only within specific cases. A range of idiographic relationships, such as particular subjective meanings, idiosyncratic patterns and correlations, and causal relationships holding only within a single case are reviewed elsewhere (Runyan, 1983).

Psychologists often talk about the generality of a theory as an ideal, but only rarely do they explicitly assess the transhistorical generality of theories. There is considerable concern for generalizing across subjects, across situations, across cultures, and across measurement instruments, but far less research on generalizing over time. To the extent that psychologists intend to develop truly general psychological theories holding across space *and* time, there is a crying need for research on the historical stability and mutability of psychological relationships.

This need has been expressed most vividly within social psychology, with a seminal article by Kenneth Gergen on "Social Psychology as History" (1973), a rebuttal on "Social Psychology as Science" by Schlenker (1974), a symposium on the issue in the *Personality and Social Psychology Bulletin* (Manis et al., 1976), and subsequent publications by Cronbach (1975, 1986), Gergen (1982), Gergen and Gergen (1984), and others. Gergen's central arguments are, first, that since social phenomena and relationships are undergoing rapid historical change, many social-psychological generalizations have only a short half-life, and, second, that social-psychological research can produce reflexive "enlightenment effects" and change the phenomena under investigation.

Fortunately, an increasing concern with the transhistorical generality of theory seems to be emerging across several branches of contemporary psychology. For example, within historical social psychology, there is new research on historical changes in attitudes and motives, in gender relationships, in structure of the family, in aesthetic tastes, in expressive gestures, and in conceptions of the self (Gergen & Gergen, 1984).

Steps toward a historically sensitive psychology also are being taken within life-span developmental psychology, where there has been an increasing recognition of the importance of historical or cohort effects on the course of human development, with many features of the developmental trajectory, such as intellectual capacity, achievement, gender roles, and parenting, varying widely across different generations (Bronfenbrenner, 1979; Keniston, 1971; McCluskey & Reese, 1984; Nessel-roade & Baltes, 1974).

Third, there is also a long tradition of inquiry into historical changes in national character, as in the work of Riesman in *The Lonely Crowd* (1961) on changes from traditional to inner-directed to outer-directed American social character; or Barbu (1960) on the formation of personality in classical Greece and early modern England; to the extensive research on "modernization" of personality in developing countries (Inkeles, 1983; Inkeles & Smith, 1974); to Philip Greven (1977) in delineating three types of early American character, the evangelical, the moderate, and the genteel; to Christopher Lasch (1979) on the narcissistic personality of our time; and others (Bellah et al., 1985; Direnzo, 1977; Fromm, 1941; Horney, 1937; and Marcus, 1984).

Fourth, there is research on the history of cognitive structures and processes, as in Julian Jaynes's speculative and thought-provoking *Origin of Consciousness in the Breakdown of the Bicameral Mind* (1976); Radding's (1985) study of cognitive processes in the Middle Ages, arguing that most people made only very limited progression in terms of the stages of cognitive development outlined by Piaget; a study of the increase in intelligence of the American people from 1750 to 1870 (Calhoun, 1973); studies of the evolution of artistic styles and aesthetic tastes (Blatt, with Blatt, 1984; Martindale, 1984); and a line of work influenced by Vygotsky on historical changes in cognitive development (e.g., Luria, 1971, 1976; Scribner & Cole, 1981; Wertsch, 1985).

In short, just as there is a *Historical Social Psychology* (Gergen & Gergen, 1984), there are possibilities for a historical developmental psychology, historical personality psychology, historical cognitive psychology, and historical abnormal psychology. For example, in abnormal psychology there is research on historical changes in hysteria, depression, narcissism, and anorexia nervosa. In every branch of psychology, important questions can be asked about the transhistorical generality or specificity of psychological phenomena that have remained constant over long, medium, or short periods of time.

The scope of inquiry in historical psychology is suggested by the following question. Starting with any contemporary psychological theory of interest (whether in social, developmental, personality, cognitive, or abnormal psychology), what hypotheses can be formulated about its transhistorical generality or specificity, and what bodies of evidence can be brought to bear on these questions? Some questions cannot be answered because of gaps in the available evidence, but there are still intriguing possibilities for research in historical psychology, glimpses of which are provided by the body of work already done.

Implications of Psychohistory for Political Psychology

The preceding analysis of the conceptual structure of psychohistory has several implications for the study of politics and the discipline of political psychology. First, the six system levels of persons, groups, organizations, institutions, sociocultural systems, and international relations useful in psychohistory also can be fruitfully applied within political psychology. In political psychology, however, the focus will not be on all institutional domains, but rather on political processes at each system level, ranging from studies of the political beliefs, attitudes, decisions, and behaviors of individuals, to studies of the political functioning of informal groups, to analyses of political parties and organizations, to studies of major political institutions, to analyses of political processes in the whole sociocultural system, to research on the political psychology of international relations, including diplomacy, international conflict, and war. Political psychology, as a partly nomothetic discipline concerned with developing and testing theories about classes of political behavior, may have a somewhat greater emphasis on comparative and quantitative studies of large numbers of entities at each system level, while psychohistory may have a greater emphasis on the descriptive and interpretive analysis of single cases and events. This is not to say that political psychology is unconcerned with single political processes and events, but that it *also* is concerned with nomothetic theories about classes of political behavior such as voting, political participation, attitude change, and violence (see McGuire's discussion in the introduction to this volume on humanistic [idiographic] and scientific [nomothetic] approaches within political psychology).

A second implication of psychohistory for political psychology is the relevance of a "historical psychology" that systematically assesses the transhistorical generality or specificity of its findings. There are, for example, historical changes in attitudes and motives, in gender relationships, in structure of the family, and in conceptions of the self (Gergen & Gergen, 1984), all of which have relevance for political psychology. There also are historical changes in personality and national character (Inkeles, 1983; Lasch, 1979; Riesman, 1961), in life-span developmental processes (Bronfenbrenner, 1979; McCluskey & Reese, 1984); and even in cognitive processes (Luria, 1971, 1976; Radding, 1985), all of which are related to political processes and institutions.

A third implication of psychohistory for political psychology is the recent attention given to the emotional reactions of authors to their research material. This may be most evident in work in political psycho-biography, where it is essential for the biographer to be aware of his or her subjective reactions to the subject. Erik Erikson has long written about the importance of "disciplined subjectivity" (Erikson, 1975) for psychohistorians. Robert Tucker (1988) has written eloquently about the strength of his loathing for Joseph Stalin, which increases the more he finds out about the man and his deeds and about the extent to which this does or does not compromise the scholarly rigor of his psychobiographical analysis of Stalin (Tucker, 1973). Related essays by biographers grappling with this issue of their subjective relations with their subjects are contained in *Introspection in Biography: The Biographer's Quest for Self-Awareness* (Baron & Pletsch, 1985).

Implications between psychohistory and political psychology do, of course, not all flow in one direction. Although not the focus of this chapter, two implications of political psychology for psychohistory may be mentioned here. First, the extensive use by political psychologists of cognitive psychology is something that psychohistorians might learn from. Second, the methodological pluralism of political psychologists might contain useful suggestions for the field of psychohistory in making greater use of quantitative, survey, or experimental methodologies.

Contrasts Between Psychohistory and Political Psychology

As the discussion of psychohistorical literature on Nazi Germany illustrated, there can be significant substantive overlap between psychohistory and political psychology. There are, however, a number of contrasts or differences between psychohistory and political psychology which can be identified. The following comparisons are based primarily on my own informal observations. I cannot stress too strongly that these are hypothesized possible differences, requiring more systematic research to corroborate or disprove them, to revise or replace them. With that proviso, let me offer the following comments on ways in which psychohistory and political psychology seem to have developed along somewhat different paths and on dimensions on which they can be compared.

First, psychohistory seems predominantly psychoanalytic or psychodynamic, while political psychology has a stronger cognitive emphasis, particularly in recent years. Although both psychohistory and political psychology started out as primarily psychoanalytic (e.g., Freud, 1910/1957; Lasswell, 1930), psychohistory seems to have remained primarily psychodynamic, although not exclusively so (Runyan, 1988a), while political psychology has acquired a stronger cognitive component. An interesting research question would be to investigate exactly how political psychology became "cognitivized," while a similar process seems not to have happened within psychohistory.

Second, political psychology seems more methodologically pluralistic than psychohistory. While psychohistory seems to rely primarily on archival resources interpreted psychodynamically, research in political psychology seems to draw not only on archival records, but on survey research in studies of attitudes and voting; on small group experiments; on prisoner's dilemma games; on projective testing; on simulations and other methods (see Hermann, 1986; and McGuire, this volume, on the evolution of methods in political psychology).

Third, political psychology seems to have more of a hard science wing to it than does psychohistory. While psychohistory is primarily idiographic and interpretive, political psychology is also concerned with formulating and testing nomothetic theories about political behavior. This contrast may come in part from a difference in the definition and goals of the two hybrid fields. While psychohistory is concerned with using systematic psychology in studying historical phenomena, political psychology is concerned not only with psychologically analyzing particular political events, but also with developing and testing nomothetic hypotheses about classes of political behavior such as voting, political participation, or political violence.

Fourth, and perhaps as a result of this last feature, political psychology may be more widely accepted within its parent discipline of political science than is psychohistory within its parent discipline of history. It is my impression that political psychology is more adequately represented in meetings and publications of the American Political Science Association than is psychohistory in conventions and publications of the American Historical Association. As for the other parent, I shall leave as an open question the relative acceptance of political psychology and psychohistory within academic psychology and psychoanalysis. My guess, though, is that political psychology is more popular than psychohistory within academic psychology, while in psychoanalysis, psychohistory (including psychoanalytic studies of writers, artists, and musicians) may be equally or more popular than political psychology. In short, I am suggesting that political psychology, perhaps on the grounds of compatible (and partly nomothetic) theoretical objectives and methodological approaches, seems better accepted within political science than is psychohistory within history.

Fifth, political psychology seems to have more of a practical or "applied" side than does psychohistory. For example, there is an extensive literature in political psychology dealing with topics of nuclear deterrence, of cognitive processes involved in diplomacy, and of cognitive processes involved in individual and group decision-making, all of which policy-makers or advisers may draw from on occasion. However, it is not as clear to me that there is an equivalent applied wing of psychohistory, although the CIA does commission psychobiographical profiles of political leaders around the world.

Sixth, a quantitative analysis of publications in psychohistory (Runyan, 1988b) indicates an enormous and geometrically increasing growth of them from before 1920 until 1980. From before 1920 through 1979 there were at least 135 dissertations, 1,131 articles, and 457 books in psychohistory. Of all 1,723 publications from those years, 1,062 (62 percent) appeared between 1970 and 1979. In other words, more than three-fifths of all studies were published in the most recent decade covered by the survey. Of 1,562 psychohistorical publications dealing with subjects in the United States, Europe, and the Soviet Union, approximately 60 percent were group psychohistory, and 40 percent were psychobiographical studies of individuals. Up through 1979, more than four hundred additional methodological or theoretical publications in psychohistory appeared. (A more detailed analysis of the quantitative growth of articles, books, and dissertations in psychohistory from pre-1920 through 1979, broken down by five-year periods, by focus on psychobiography or group psychohistory, and by area of the world, is reported in Runyan, 1988b. I am not aware of quantitative studies of the growth of literature in political psychology that could be used for comparison.)

Seventh, and finally, political psychology seems currently to have a more firmly established institutional infrastructure. While political psychologists may sometimes consult with the powerful around long, polished mahogany tables, psychohistorians are more likely to huddle around a grubby formica table in someone's kitchen. These differences in institutional wealth and establishment seem to exist on a number of dimensions. For example, the main professional society in political psychology, the International Society of Political Psychology, organized by Jeanne Knutson in 1977, seems better-established and to attract higher-quality intellectual talent on the average than does the International Psychohistorical Association, founded by Lloyd deMause in 1973. In journal publications, the quality of articles in *Political Psychology* seems to attain a higher mean level than do those in the *Journal of Psychohistory*. (Although the *Psychohistory Review* is of higher quality than the *Journal of Psychohistory,* it still may not equal *Political Psychology.*)

From a survey of college and university catalogs, Bruce Mazlish (1977) estimated that there were more than two hundred courses offered in psychohistory around the country. In political psychology, extremely informative surveys of graduate education and undergraduate courses in political psychology (Sears & Funk, 1990; Funk & Sears, 1990) indicate that there are at least ninety-nine undergraduate course offerings in political psychology from seventy-seven different institutions in the United States and Canada, and forty-five graduate courses in political psychology. In terms of graduate training, several universities, such as UCLA and Kansas State, offer graduate specializations in psychohistory, while Sears and Funk (1990) have identified at least nine doctoral training programs in political psychology, including those at Yale, the State University of New York at Stony Brook, the University of Wisconsin at Madison, UCLA, UC Irvine, CUNY Graduate School, Ohio State, George Washington University, and the University of Michigan.

As for academic positions, there are now a few job offers explicitly designed to hire someone in political psychology, while I am not aware of similar job openings in psychohistory. I do not have any hard numbers, but my impression is that more grant money is available in political psychology from sources such as the Carnegie Foundation or the McArthur Foundation than there is in psychohistory.

To my surprise, and somewhat to my dismay, as my own past work has been primarily on methodological problems in psychobiography and psychohistory (Runyan, 1981, 1982, 1988a, 1990), these comparisons seem generally to favor political psychology. On the dimensions of theoretical range, methodological pluralism, acceptance by parent disciplines, applied utility, and institutional infrastructure, political psychology seems at present to be doing better than psychohistory. It is, again, important to remember that these are impressionistic contrasts, and more systematic research on these issues might well lead to different results.

These comparisons may also exaggerate the differences between psychohistory and political psychology. There is, in fact, substantial overlap between them in that many publications are seen as contributing to both fields, a number of people belong to both organizations, and intellectually there is substantial overlap in objectives and methods.

In favor of psychohistory, it is in some ways intellectually more comprehensive than political psychology. While psychohistory is concerned with the use of psychology in all areas of historical analysis, political psychology is concerned with the overlap of psychology with only one institutional sphere, that of politics. Psychohistory is more comprehensive in that it deals not only with political institutions and events, but with the use of psychology in analyzing other institutional spheres such as literature, art, music, mythology, religion, education, science, social welfare, mass media, and family structure and childrearing.

Is it fair to say that political psychology is just one institutional branch of psychohistory (although a particularly well-developed branch)? Or, is it that psychohistory is a significant contributor to and constituent of political psychology? There seems to be some merit in both of these claims, as the two fields might best be seen as two partially overlapping circles (with perhaps 20 percent to 30 percent common territory?). Psychohistory has greater institutional range and inclusiveness than does political psychology, so political psychology is one of its institutional branches; while political psychology has both an idiographic-interpretive wing, which overlaps with psychohistory, and a scientific-nomothetic wing which does not.

Conclusion

In summary, this chapter began by providing a relatively comprehensive conceptualization of psychohistory, defining it as the explicit use of formal or systematic psychology in historical interpretation. The array of uses of psychology in historical inquiry was illustrated at six system levels—from persons through groups up to institutions and international relations—with examples drawn from Nazi era psychohistory. The third section focused on the place of hybrid disciplines such as political psychology and psychological anthropology in mediating relationships between history and psychology.

The fourth section briefly outlined work in "historical psychology" and argued that historical psychology not only can contribute to psychohistory and political psychology, but can make basic contributions to the discipline of psychology.

The fifth section discussed several implications of the proposed conceptualization of psychohistory for the field of political psychology. Three implications of psychohistory for political psychology are (1) the relevance of the six system levels and three levels of aggregation for political psychology as well as psychohistory, (2) the importance of subjectivity and countertransference for political psychology as well as psychohistory, and (3) the use of "historical psychology" in both psychohistory and in political psychology.

The sixth and final section offered a number of impressionistic comparisons between psychohistory and political psychology. (1) Psychohistory tends to rely more heavily on psychodynamic theory, while political psychology has made greater use of cognitive psychology in recent years. (2) Political psychology seems more methodologically pluralistic, using archival, survey, quantitative, experimental, and simulation methods, while psychohistory relies more heavily on archival and psychodynamic interpretive methods. (3) Political psychology seems to have more of a nomothetic and hard science look to it in that it is concerned not only with specific political events and processes, but also with developing and testing general theories. (4) Political psychology may be more favorably regarded by its co-parent discipline of political science than is psychohistory by history. (5) Political psychology seems to have a more extensive "applied" side than does psychohistory. (6) Political psychology may currently have a more solid institutional infrastructure in terms of professional organization and publication outlets, available outside funding, and possibly in terms of academic institutionalization.

Perhaps the more important issue is not the relative status of the two fields, but what they can learn from each other, and what they can jointly achieve. Together, political psychology and psychohistory are part of a larger story, that of the interrelations of psychology with all of the human-social-historical sciences, and they share a number of common theoretical and methodological problems with other hybrid fields such as psychological anthropology and social structure and personality. There is, without doubt, a great deal that remains to be done in clarifying the uses and limitations of both academic-scientific and psychodynamic-experiential psychology for understanding social, political, and historical phenomena. This is a story that will be played out in part through the future histories of, and relationships between, psychohistory and political psychology.

Notes

Portions of this analysis are adapted, with permission, from W. M. Runyan, *Psychology and Historical Interpretation* (New York: Oxford University Press, 1988).

1. The six system levels outlined here bear some similarity to the system levels outlined by James G. Miller in *Living Systems* (1978), although he includes suborganismic system levels of cells and organs, and I include a level of institutions between organizations and social systems.

II

Attitudes and

Behavior

Each of the four chapters in this section uses attitudes as a key mediating variable, discussing them in terms of a wide range of their determining antecedents and the diverse behavioral consequences that they in turn determine. Granberg's chapter focuses on how someone's perception of parties, candidates, and other political stimuli affect and are affected by his or her attitudes. Sears discusses symbolic politics in regard to how political issues evoke one versus another symbolic predisposition and how these predispositions affect attitudes. The Masters and Sullivan chapter describes how candidates' nonverbal cues affect the public's attitudes and voting preferences. Sidanius moves from the intrapersonal to the interpersonal and intergroup levels of analysis, theorizing how societies evolve into hierarchically organized groups that lead to conflict and oppression and to the attitudes that sustain these groups. Within its domain, each chapter reviews a wide range of state-of-the-art theories, methods, and results, with each author giving sympathetic attention to a wide range of possibilities, but also proposing an integrative viewpoint on the topic.

These four chapters share a metatheoretical orientation long used in psychology: a person's thoughts, feelings, and actions are determined, not only by the world as it is, but more precisely by the world as the person perceives it. Hence, the differences among people's reactions to a given political situation reflect their differing ways of perceiving what the situation is, as well as their differing ways of responding to it. A person's idiosyncratic complex of political attitudes, beliefs, and voting choices that may seem disorganized, irrational, and even perverse from an observer's perspective may turn out to be perfectly comprehensible in terms of the person's attitudinal transformations of the information in the situation.

Donald Granberg's chapter focuses on the transformational rules that convert the objective political situation into the individual's perceptual world. He considers the interrelations among the public's liking for these political actors, the public's own stands on these issues, and the salience of the issues in the public's perceptual world. Granberg pits against one another and against his own theory the conflicting hypotheses regarding perceptual transformation derived from various theories (e.g., balance, social judgment, political cue, and distinctiveness). He derives distinctive predictions from these clashing theories and then tests the predictions by means of elegant statistical analyses of a considerable body of data from North American and European public opinion surveys and election results.

Such perceptual-mediational metatheorizing also is basic to David O. Sears's analysis of symbolic politics, but while Granberg is especially concerned with perceptual transformation, Sears focuses more on perceptual selectivity. He postulates that formative experiences in adolescence establish persisting affective responses to political symbols that determine a wide range of attitudinal responses. Sears describes earlier work on effects of these symbolic predispositions but then shifts his focus to their antecedents. He analyzes political issues such as busing, bilingual education, and national health insurance in regard to what evokes one versus another of the alternative symbolic predispositions latent in that ideological domain. Sears considers determinants like issue wording, framing, linkage by conceptual schema, and especially the similarity (latent as well as manifest) of symbolic predispositions. He contrasts various other approaches to the symbolic predisposition approach to political attitudes and behaviors. Among these contrasting alternative formulations are motivational theories postulating status needs, self-interest, and real conflict; personality theories regarding Machiavellianism, authoritarianism, etc.; rational theories such as expectancy × values and reasoned action; and cognitive heuristic, work-minimizing conceptualizations. While symbolic politics theorizing has usually dealt with survey research, Sears reviews its relevance to manipulable laboratory research on topics such as ego involvement, salience, and priming. He then illustrates symbolic politics theorizing in depth as it relates to the several symbolic meanings of bilingual education, and he makes further predictions about cognitive coding, schemas, and political socialization.

Most research on how persuasive communication forms political perceptions, changes political attitudes, and channels political behavior, including that described in Granberg's and Sears's chapters, has focused on verbal communication. Roger Masters and Dennis Sullivan's chapter provides balance by concentrating on how political leaders' nonverbal communication (particularly their facial cues) may be processed in parallel to verbal information to produce a joint effect on the public's political attitudes. They argue that before the mid-twentieth century advent of television, the public's attitudes toward candidates were affected mainly by the candidates' party affiliation and issue stands, which are easily communicated by means of verbal messages in print or speech; but ever since the diffusion of television provided wider transmission of candidates' facial expressions and other nonverbal cues, the public's attitudes are increasingly affected by their emotional reactions and trait attributions to the candidates. Masters and Sullivan review the results from laboratory experiments in the United States and France on how the public infers the emotional states of candidates from their facial cues, how the public responds affectively, and how specified facial cues change the public's attitudes regarding candidates. The magnitude of these nonverbal cue effects are shown to interact with a variety of situational dispositional variables. Masters and Sullivan's work illustrates how such complex interactions can be most efficiently advanced by a coordinated program that includes both laboratory experiments and survey research.

What Donald Granberg does for intrapersonal processes in his chapter, James Sidanius does for intergroup processes in the fourth chapter of this section, where he focuses on intergroup conflict and oppressive discrimination, along with their attitudinal underpinnings. Sidanius provides a tour of current theories about intergroup relations, providing descriptions and evaluations of five classes of theories: self-enhancement ego theories; rational actor utility-maximizing theories; belief-attitude-behavior theories (including Sears's symbolic racism, Tajfel's social identity theory, and Turner's social categorization theory); evolutionary biopolitical theories; and theories that combine several of the above. Most prominent among the latter is Sidanius's own Social Dominance Theory, which postulates that human societies evolve by adaptive selection into hierarchically organized structures of subgroups, and that social conflict and group oppression, as well as the political attitudes and institutions that support them, develop to maintain the hierarchy. From these assumptions, Sidanius derives a rich set of provocative concepts such as legitimizing myths; behavioral asymmetries in the form of deference, self-handicapping, ideological asymmetries, and systematic terror; oppressive equilibrium brought about by ideological, economic, and instability constraints; and differential sex roles in social dominance.

The authors in this section review the theorizing and empirical findings on the antecedents and consequences of political attitudes. In doing so, they focus on a wide variety of conceptualizations and approaches, to which they give careful and sympathetic consideration. However, these authors also accept the responsibility for making choices among competing formulations by providing their own integrations and extensions of the extensive bodies of current research.

That the four complementary chapters in this section are inclusive in the theoretical positions they take into consideration is indicated in the wide range of theories that are discussed, often in several chapters, to account for political attitudes and their antecedents and consequences. All of these authors are social scientists, but even so they give sympathetic attention to biological formulations such as evolutionary and biopolitical theories, neuroscience constructs, and physiological indices of attitudes and effects. The four chapters pay particularly close and inclusive attention to cognitive formulations, which the preceding chapter by McGuire identifies as central to the current (third) wave of political psychology research. The cognitive constructs that they consider include information processing, cognitive heuristics, parallel processing, attribution theories, social judgment, episodic memory, schema theories, and the theory of reasoned action. Their chapters also cover a wide range of motivational and personality conceptualizations such as situationalism versus dispositionalism, authoritarianism, trait theory, rational-man theories, subjective-utility theories, and self-enhancement and self-interest theories. Interpersonal and intergroup theories also are taken into consideration, including real-conflict and distinctiveness theories, social identity and social categorization theories, and leadership conceptualizations. While offering sympathetic consideration to these widely varied theories, the authors give a coherent structure to their subject matter by organizing their coverage around a preferred integrative position such as social dominance theory or symbolic politics.

These four chapters also show openness to methodological tactics. Besides the field methods (such as survey research) that dominated the second-wave voting behavior era, and that remain the most popular data-collection procedure, the authors give sympathetic attention to laboratory experimentation where it is more practicable or efficient than field research in controlling extraneous variables or in allowing individual measurement. Until recently, students of political psychology coming from the political science or sociology disciplines usually did survey research in the field, while those coming from the psychology discipline confined themselves mostly to manipulable research in the laboratory. The chapters in this section show that researchers from each of the disciplines are becoming more eclectic in their methods, choosing between field and laboratory research on the basis of suitability to the problem rather than adherence to disciplinary tradition. While most political psychology studies continue to have simple designs, these chapters demonstrate how traditional designs can be supplemented by varying multiple independent variables orthogonally, by getting direct measures of theorized mediators, and by using complex mathematical analyses that assess the extent to which those mediators account for the ultimate effect as theorized. The use of causal models to choose among multiple paths of influence among the variables is illustrated in state-of-the-art studies described here.

In summary, the authors of the four chapters in this attitudinal section have not winced at the obvious complexity of the political psychology issues with which they deal. Rather, they have recognized the need for an ecumenical approach to explanatory concepts, research methods, and demographic and situational contextual limitations to the relations hypothesized or found. In this openness, the authors do (and the readers should) acknowledge that to describe the pretzel-shaped universe for which students of political psychology must account it may be necessary to use pretzel-shaped theories and methods. In each of these chapters the author has attempted to show the reader a path through the maze of confusion, not by denying its complexity, but by identifying an integrating formulation by which the reader can trace a coherent route through a difficult intellectual terrain.

Donald Granberg

4. Political Perception

Political perception refers to the process by which people develop impressions of the characteristics and positions of political candidates, parties, and institutions.[1] In research in political psychology we often analyze the outcome of that process, that is, a person's answer to a survey question designed to tap some manifestation of political perception. This chapter focuses on perceptions of issue and ideological positions of individual politicians and parties (Berelson, Lazarsfeld, & McPhee, 1954).

Stimulus Versus Perceiver Determinants of Perception

A venerable but still relevant question in the study of political perception is whether the perceptual process is determined primarily by external stimulus conditions or by a perceiver's internal features (McGrath & McGrath, 1962; Nimmo & Savage, 1976; Sigel, 1964). In more concrete terms, are the qualities we ascribe to President George Bush determined by Bush's actual features (or the image of him transmitted by means of the mass media since most people do not see Bush in person)? Or are perceptions of Bush determined more by the values, attitudes, beliefs, and other properties inside the head of the individual perceiver? If ever a question deserved the answer that it depends on the context, this must be the one.

To address this matter adequately, it is advisable to simultaneously consider the perceptions of two or more political stimuli. ANOVA designs, where one looks at the main and interactive effects of certain independent variables (say, the respondent's attitude on an issue and the respondent's attitude toward the stimulus object) on a single dependent variable (say, the respondent's perception of the stimulus object's position on the issue) will not suffice. The most one could hope for in such an analysis is to demonstrate that features within the person's mind do (or do not) have some discernible influence on the perceptual process (Granberg & Brent, 1974; Sherrod, 1972). Since both of the independent variables in such analyses are internal factors, that mode of analysis provides no way of assessing the relative contribution of external and internal factors to determining systematic variance in perception.

What is needed is a more complex analysis in which two or more perceptions—that is, more than one dependent variable—are considered simultaneously in the same analysis. This can be done with MANOVA, which should enable one to apportion the variance in perceptions to internal and external sources, at least as it has occurred under that contextual condition. This seems to be the central thesis in some recent work by Victor Ottati, who has shown how internally generated tendencies toward perceptual distortion are constrained by external stimulus conditions. His analyses show that when the perceptions of more than one candidate are considered, the "real" position of the various candidates can have an effect (Ottati, 1990; Ottati, Fishbein, & Middlestadt, 1988; Ottati & Terkildsen, 1989).

Related to stimulus versus perceiver determination of perception is the "message tailoring hypothesis" (Googin, 1984), which suggests that when people differ in their perceptions of a candidate, this stems from the candidate saying different things in different places. Not only are different positions taken, but the various messages are crafted to suit particular audiences. It was convincingly shown by Miller and Sigelman (1978) that Lyndon Johnson made more hawkish speeches to more hawkish audiences. Similarly, in 1988 George Bush spoke in California as if he opposed new leases for offshore oil drilling where the public may have leaned toward opposition, but he campaigned in Texas, where the public may have been more favorable, as if he favored new leases. It is not impossible to square this circle, but it is awkward.

In modern national campaigns the close scrutiny given to campaigns by the mass media limits the extent to which candidates or parties can tailor their message to suit (or soothe) the audience being addressed. Nonetheless, candidates still have some latitude in choosing the topics and positions to be emphasized, and they can fine-tune their message for particular situations.

Sometimes even a symbolic gesture may contribute significantly to voters' perceptions of candidates. Recall 1960, a time when the black vote was far more divided and much less monolithic than in recent years. In the course of a busy campaign, the Democratic candidate, John Kennedy, took the time to telephone Coretta Scott King and express concern about her jailed husband, Martin Luther King, Jr. This was regarded as a significant symbolic act and is often viewed as one of many decisive events in that extremely close election.

If candidates or parties engage in efforts at impression management in which they deliberately try to be different things to different people in different settings, how can this variability be taken into account? Moreover, if Lyndon Johnson says substantively different things about the Vietnam War to difference audiences, does this mean that each time he has a different position on the war? Theoretically, can he have as many positions as he has audiences? A more fruitful approach may be to consider each of his public utterances, taken separately, as an imperfect guide or cue to his real or actual position on the war. It may not be unreasonable to assume that usually the real or actual position of a candidate or party is roughly constant during a campaign, although it may be difficult to precisely define or quantify. Recently, Rabinowitz and MacDonald (1989, p. 98) put forth an intriguing "directional theory of issue voting" which assumes that "all voters are reacting to the same candidate stimulus." There is, of course, the possibility that a candidate's position may evolve or crystallize during a campaign (Page, 1978). Generally, this is less likely in a strong party system in which political parties are the principal actors (Granberg & Holmberg, 1990).

Many times there is no question that a politician has changed his position. Senator Arthur Vandenberg's shift from isolationist to internationalist was a historically important instance. In 1964 when the Tonkin Gulf resolution, later viewed by some as functionally equivalent to a declaration of war, was passed by the U.S. Congress, only two senators (Ernest Gruening of Alaska and Wayne Morse of Oregon) voted against it. Not a few senators later turned against the war effort and publicly renounced this earlier vote. If political perceptions are, at least in some measure, stimulus-determined, then if politicians or parties actually change their positions, there ought to be a corresponding shift in political perceptions. A related question is the degree to which political perceptions are sensitive to changes in the content of the scale. That is, if the public's political perceptions are no more than gross impressions, one would not expect them to be much affected by minor changes in the way the question is asked or how the scale is devised (Schuman & Presser, 1981).

On these matters, the 1986 Dutch election study is an unusually rich

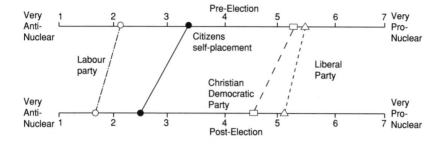

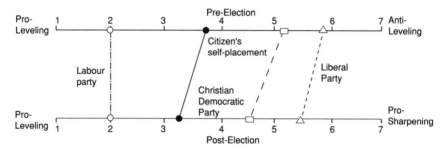

Figure 4.1. Average self-placement and perceptions of the three largest political parties on the scales for nuclear power and income differences in the Netherlands 1986 election study.

source of data. First, there is the extraordinary situation that the major political parties in the Netherlands openly and unambiguously changed their positions on the issue of nuclear power plants during the campaign. In the wake of the Chernobyl disaster, the parties all became more opposed to reliance on nuclear power. By a fortuitous coincidence, the preelection interviewing had been essentially completed at the time of the tragedy at Chernobyl, and that interview included questions on perceptions of the parties' positions on nuclear power as well as associated attitude questions. These questions were then repeated in postelection interviews with the same people. Thus, from a social-psychological point of view, with the nuclear disaster and the subsequent changes in the parties' positions as intervening events, the two interviews form a sort of "natural experiment."

Figure 4.1 shows the mean values for placement of the parties on the pre- and postelection interviews on the nuclear power questions. There is no doubt that the shift in the parties' actual positions is reflected in Dutch citizens' perceptions. This is a stimulus-determined shift. Figure 4.1

shows evidence that the respondents' own attitudes also shifted in the antinuclear direction.

The other unusual feature of the 1986 Dutch study involves a social equality or income differences scale. On this issue, there is no reason to think that the public or the parties changed their actual positions from pre- to postelection. But in this case the scale was changed. The question, closely related to the classical left-right dimension in European politics, was whether governmental policy ought to be used to reduce inequality in income. On the preelection survey, the scale essentially went from the leftist view favoring a leveling of incomes policy to the rightist view opposing a leveling policy (i.e., favoring the status quo). On the post-election survey, the scale was expanded so that it went from pro-leveling to pro-sharpening, the latter referring to a position that advocated increasing the inequality or differences in income. On the postelection scale, the status quo becomes, in effect, the midpoint. This type of change in the scale, albeit in only one direction, lends itself to an application of perspective theory (Ostrom, 1966; Upshaw, 1969; Upshaw & Ostrom, 1984). Figure 4.1 shows that people shifted their own position on the scale from 3.7 (preelection average) to 3.2 (postelection). Perceptions of the rightist parties, which formed the governing coalition both before and after that election (and whose side of the scale changed), shifted from 5.2 (preelection) to 4.5 (postelection) for the Christian Democratic party and from 5.9 to 5.5 for the smaller coalition partner, the Liberal party. At the same time, there was no shift in the average perception of the Labour party (2.0 on both the preelection and postelection scale). Thus, people shifted their perceptions to correspond with a shift in the definition of an end point on the scale, but it was not an across-the-board-shift, as happened on the nuclear power scale. Rather, the parties closer to the end of the scale that changed were subject to the largest shift in perceptions, but the party farthest from the end of the scale that changed was essentially unchanging in the perceptions it evoked. The evidence suggests that Dutch voters are alert and their political perceptions are responsive to shifts in the actual positions of the parties and also to variations in the wording of the scale being used.

There is, of course, no simple solution to the general question of the extent to which political perceptions are stimulus-determined or perceiver-determined. The answer must have something to do with the ambiguity of the parties and candidates as stimuli (Page, 1976; Shepsle, 1972). Gestalt-oriented social psychologists, such as Muzafer Sherif and Carolyn Sherif (1969), would certainly invoke some of their very general propositions, such as how structured stimulus situations limit the alternatives in psychological structuring. The more unstructured (ambiguous) the external stimulus situation, the greater will be the role played by internal factors in psychological structuring by the individual. A relatively well-structured political stimulus can lead to political perceptions with a high consensus, in which the perceptions correspond to reality and are determined primarily by features of the stimulus rather than by personal characteristics that individuals bring to the perceptual task.

Balance Theory

There is an important distinction between the assumption that people are motivated to be accurate (i.e., "to get it right") and the alternative assumption that people are motivated to maintain cognitive balance. Balance theory, developed by Fritz Heider (1946, 1958), has been the most influential theory guiding analyses of political perception. Heider's theory has as its focus the cognitive dialectic going on within the mind of the individual. In that sense, it is very much a psychological theory. The central thesis of balance theory is that, other things being equal, a balanced set of cognitions is more stable than an imbalanced set. People find an imbalanced set of cognitions unpleasant and proceed to change one or more of them to move toward a balanced state. Heider's theory deals not only with cognitions. Rather, his basic P-O-X model deals with two attitudes and a belief, or, in other words, two affective orientations and a cognition. These components are P (person, citizen), O (another person, politician, political party), and X (some issue, e.g., a mandatory deposit on all cans and bottles). The crucial factors in the configuration are P's attitude toward O (an interpersonal attitude when O is an individual candidate or officeholder), P's attitude toward X, and P's impression of O's attitude toward X. Note that it is not a question of O's actual orientation toward X, but rather P's estimation of O's attitude toward X. The latter is most directly implicated in studying the process of political perception. The first two factors are referred to as *sentiment relations*.

Heider's theory also included the concept of a *unit relation,* referring to whether or not P and O are part of the same unit (Kinder, 1978). All U.S. citizens had a unit relationship with George Bush, at least until January 20, 1993, because he was president of their country. This, of course, says nothing about the sentiment relationship a citizen had with Bush, which could range from loathing through indifference to adoration.

Not too much has been done with Heider's concept of a unit relationship, but it is closely analogous to the sociological concepts of membership group and reference group. That is, sentiment is to a unit relationship as reference group is to membership group (Granberg, 1987b; Granberg, Jefferson, Brent, & King, 1981). Heider's theory implies that psychological pressure to achieve, maintain, or restore a state of cognitive balance is greater when P and O share a unit relationship. Kinder (1978) made the unit relationship operational by focusing on which candidate that people expected to win the upcoming election. The presumption was that a person who expects Nixon to win has or anticipates having a unit relationship with him. An alternative would be in terms of party identification or membership. People who are members of the British Labour party have a unit relationship with the party's current leader, whether they like him or not.

Heider's theory has had considerable heuristic value in stimulating and guiding much research (Luttbeg, 1981). Some additions and modifications have ensued. For instance, Heider's theory provided no basis for predicting that people would find agreement with someone they liked (a liked other) more pleasant than disagreement with someone they disliked (a disliked other). On logical grounds and in Heider's theory, the categories are equally well-balanced. Yet in social-psychological experiments, people find agreement with a liked other more pleasant (e.g., Insko, Songer, & McGarvey, 1974). This line of research led people to posit, in addition to a balance effect (which deals with all three factors), an agreement effect and a positivity effect. The agreement effect, which deals only with the P-X and the O-X relations, suggests that other things being equal, people find agreement more pleasant than disagreement. This finding has important implications for the study of political perception (Crockett, 1974). The positivity effect, which deals only with the P-O relationship, occurs when a situation is experienced as more pleasant when P likes O, over and above any balance and agreement effects.

Before looking at some of the ways in which balance theory has been used in the analysis of political perception, we should ask whether Heider's balance model is a useful metaphor that bears at least a resemblance to reality. Do people really think in a way that is depicted in his theory? Heider's theory oversimplifies reality, of course, but then so does any other theory.

In fact, there are many real life examples illustrating that Heider's theory does penetrate, at least to some degree, the way in which people think. In Kristen Luker's (1984) study of abortion activists in California, one of the antiabortion activists volunteered the judgment that she could not be a friend with someone who disagreed with her about abortion. In 1989 the U.S. Supreme Court decided that it was all right for states to execute people who had been as young as sixteen when a murder was committed. One young man who was convicted of murder and whose appeal formed part of the basis of the Supreme Court's decision had vacillated. At first, he said he wanted to be executed rather than face life imprisonment, but later he changed his mind and appealed, seeking to avoid execution. The response of the victim's family was most interesting. When the young man wanted to be executed, the family of the victim wanted to have him sentenced to life in prison; however, when he changed his mind and strove to avoid execution, then the family wanted him to be executed (Rosenbaum, 1989).

Surely, there is a kind of "psychologic" in these examples. Of course, the need for cognitive balance is not the touchstone for understanding human relations. It is not that important, but then probably nothing else is either. The human tendency to move toward cognitive balance is probably rather basic and pervasive and can be thought of as part of the more general tendency for individuals to impose order and structure on the world in the psychological processing of events.

Regardless, balance theory has been found useful by a variety of investigators considering the process of political perception. Let us look at some data from the 1988 U.S. presidential election. In the national survey done by the Center for Political Studies at the University of Michigan prior to the election, people were asked to place themselves, the two largest parties, and the presidential nominees of these parties on nine (1–7) scales, including the abstract liberal-conservative scale. On each of these scales the end points were well-defined and represented distinct and relatively extreme positions. The forty-five mean placements are shown in table 4.1. On every scale except women's rights, the average self-placement was between the average perception of Dukakis and Bush. On six issues, the average self-placement was closer to the average perception of Bush's position (abstract ideology, government services, guaranteed jobs and living standard, government help to blacks, aid to minorities, and relations with the then–Soviet Union).[2] On the other three scales (defense spending, health insurance, women's rights), the average self-placement was closer to the average perception of Dukakis's position. On all but one scale, Dukakis was perceived to be slightly to the left of the Democratic party. Bush and the Republican party were perceived very similarly.

From the point of view of balance theory, it is essential to have some

Table 4.1. Average self-placement and perceptions of the two parties and the presidential nominees of those parties in the 1988 U.S. National Election Study.

Scale	Average placement				
	Michael Dukakis	Democratic party	Citizens	Republican party	George Bush
A. Liberal-conservative ideology	3.2	3.3	4.4	5.1	5.1
B. Expand or cut government services	2.9	3.1	3.9	4.4	4.4
C. Military spending	3.3	3.7	3.9	5.2	5.3
D. Government-provided health insurance	3.1	3.3	3.8	5.1	5.1
E. Government-guaranteed jobs and standard of living	3.4	3.5	4.4	5.1	5.0
F. Government aid to blacks	3.5	3.4	4.7	4.7	4.9
G. Aid to minority groups	3.2	3.3	4.3	4.7	4.8
H. Relations with the Soviet Union	3.4	3.5	3.8	3.9	4.1
I. Women's rights	2.9	3.1	2.6	3.8	3.7

Note: Each scale has been coded so that 1 represents the liberal end and 7 the conservative end of the scale.

measure of the citizen's orientation toward the candidate (P-O), a measure of the citizen's orientation toward an issue (P-X), and the citizen's perception of the candidate's position on the issue (O-X). This relationship can be represented in various ways. One way is to examine the cross-tabulations of attitude and perception while controlling for candidate preference. Here we are working with a very large number of instances, in fact, 19,421 instances when someone who preferred Bush or Dukakis placed themselves and a candidate somewhere on the same 1–7 scale. By chance, one would expect attitude and perception to be exactly the same in about 14 percent of the cases. In fact, people intending to vote for Bush placed Bush at the same position as themselves 36 percent of the time and Dukakis at the same position as themselves 13 percent of the time. Correspondingly, people intending to vote for Dukakis perceived Dukakis to be at exactly the same position on the 1–7 scales as themselves in 37 percent of the instances and Bush at the same position as themselves in 12 percent.

Another possibility is that people might seek through their political perception and self-placement to maximize the distance. When people at positions 1–3 perceive a candidate at 7, people at position 4 place the candidate at 1 or 7, and people at positions 5–7 perceive a candidate at position 1, the distance between self-placement and perception is maximized (Granberg & Brent, 1980). If people answered at random, this would occur in 16 percent of the cases. Dukakis intenders maximized the distance between themselves and Dukakis 6 percent of the time and maximized the distance between themselves and Bush 19 percent of the time. The corresponding figures for the Bush intenders were 16 percent and 8 percent for Dukakis and Bush, respectively.

These percentages imply a certain asymmetry. The tendency to maximize the similarity between oneself and a preferred candidate is considerably stronger than the tendency to maximize the distance between oneself and a nonpreferred candidate. The percentage who maximized the similarity between themselves and a preferred candidate exceeded the chance level by a considerable margin. However, the percentage who maximized the distance between themselves and a nonpreferred candidate exceeded the chance level by a very small margin if at all.

This asymmetrical tendency is exactly the pattern one would expect if both a balance effect and an agreement effect were operating. That is, a balance effect by itself would produce a tendency to maximize both the similarity between self and a preferred candidate and the dissimilarity between self and a nonpreferred candidate. However, these tendencies will be offset to a degree by an agreement effect in which, regardless of whether the candidate is liked or not, agreement is experienced as more pleasant and therefore preferred over disagreement.

The same pattern emerges when these data are summarized in correlational terms, as shown in table 4.2. For Dukakis intenders, the positive correlation between where they placed themselves and where they placed Dukakis was of a much stronger magnitude than the negative correlation between where people placed themselves and where they placed Bush

Table 4.2. Average correlations between self-placement and perception of the presidential candidates' positions in the 1988 U.S. National Election Study.

People intending to vote	Average correlation between self-placement and placement		
	Michael Dukakis	George Bush	Average N
Dukakis	+.51	−.18	510
Bush	−.14	+.45	569
People rating the candidate being placed on the feeling thermometer at:			
100	+.63	+.56	120
85	+.52	+.47	194
70	+.34	+.25	160
60	+.14	+.05	135
50	+.10	−.05	188
40	−.05	−.09	118
30	−.18	−.24	70
15	−.36	−.23	53
0	−.35	−.40	79

Note: Each correlation is actually the average of eight correlations, corresponding to the eight 1–7 point scales used in the preelection portion of the 1988 U.S. National Election Study, shown in table 4.1.

(+.51 to −.14). A similar pattern occurred among the Bush intenders. Moreover, this pattern has been observed to occur in each of the previous six U.S. elections through 1988 (Brent & Granberg, 1982; Granberg & Brent, 1974, 1980; Granberg & Jenks, 1977; Granberg, Kasmer, & Nanneman, 1988; King, 1978).

Shaffer (1981) claimed that this apparent asymmetry in political perception is a methodological artifact resulting from the use of voting intention as a measure of attitude toward the candidate. However, this is demonstrably not so. If we take the person's rating of the candidate on a 0–100 affective feeling thermometer as the measure of P's sentiment toward O, which may indeed be closer to Heider's theory, the results are essentially the same. That is, the positive correlation between self-placement and perception of a candidate is stronger for people who rated

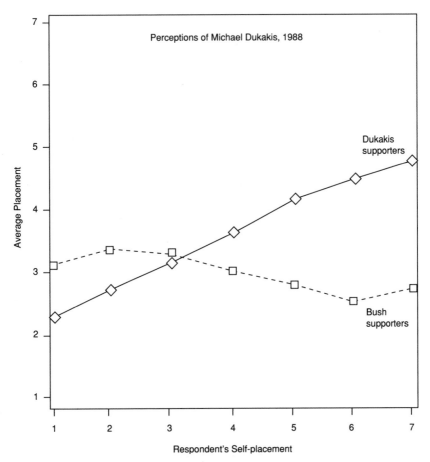

Figure 4.2 Average placement of Michael Dukakis in 1988 as a function of candidate preference and self-placement, based on a composite of all nine scales in table 1.

the candidate at 100 on the feeling thermometer than is the corresponding negative correlation for those who rated the candidate at 0. Similar conclusions are drawn for those who rate the candidates at 85 and 15, 70 and 30, and so on, as shown in the lower portion of table 4.2. It also does not matter much whether a nonlinear measure of association (eta) is used instead of a linear correlation. We can assert that there is more shared variance between self-placement and perception of a liked candidate than between self-placement and perception of a disliked candidate. A composite picture of political perceptions in the 1988 U.S. election is shown in figures 4.2 and 4.3. By combining across issues, the minor irreg-

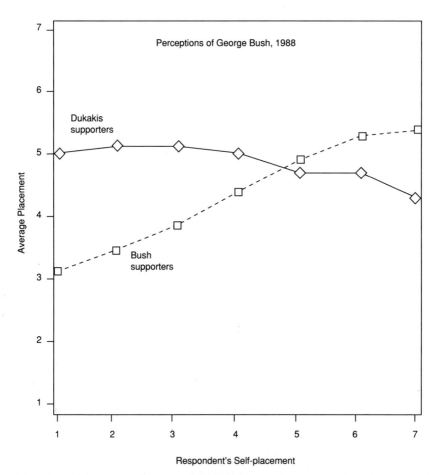

Figure 4.3. Average placement of George Bush in 1988 as a function of candidate preference and self-placement, based on a composite of all nine scales in table 1.

ularities associated with particular issues tend to disappear. These findings essentially replicate earlier analyses of U.S. elections from 1968 through 1984 (Granberg & Brent, 1980; Granberg, Kasmer, & Nanneman, 1988).

Figures 4.2 and 4.3 strongly imply that some systematic effects are occurring in these political perceptions. The eta values are .54 and .16 when Dukakis is placed by Dukakis and Bush supporters, respectively, in figure 4.2; .13 and .53 when Bush is placed by Dukakis and Bush supporters, respectively, in figure 4.3. It is not, however, a simple matter as to how such relationships are to be interpreted. Thus far, we have studiously avoided labeling or naming the apparent effects readily observable in political perceptions.

Social Judgment Theory

One interpretation of the relationships depicted in table 4.2 and figures 4.2 and 4.3 is to view them as a manifestation of underlying psychological processes called assimilation and contrast effects. These terms are derived from social judgment theory, developed by Muzafer Sherif and Carl Hovland (1961). Drawing on what they regarded as well-established principles from psychophysics, they set out to analyze how individuals place a communication. By a clever but rather tenuous extrapolation, they developed the thesis that in perceiving the position taken by a communication, the individual's own attitude would act as an anchor. Thus, the position of a communicator would be placed relative to the individual's own attitude. Communications near the individual's own position, within the latitude of acceptance, would be pulled toward the individual's attitude in the process of perception. When the similarity between self and other is overestimated by a person, that is *assimilation*. In other words, assimilation refers to a perception in which the perceived similarity exceeds the actual similarity.

On the other hand, when a communication was at some distance from the person's own position and fell within the latitude of rejection, a contrast effect was expected to occur. Contrast refers to the perceptual process in which a person psychologically pushes a communication away from the person's own attitude so that the actual distance is exaggerated. In other words, *contrast* occurs in perception when the perceived distance exceeds the actual distance. Together, the two processes compose a push-pull theory of social judgment. The theory also acknowledged that a zone or latitude of noncommitment could exist between the latitudes of acceptance and rejection, but it was not clear whether assimilation or contrast would occur when a communication took a position within the latitude of noncommitment (Sherif, Sherif, & Nebergall, 1965).

Ambiguity was a crucial concept in social judgment theory. No systematic displacement effect (i.e., neither assimilation nor contrast) was expected when a communication was very unambiguous. A pervasive assimilation effect was expected when the communication was highly ambiguous. When a communication was moderately ambiguous, the push–pull combination of assimilation and contrast effects was expected to occur. With a moderately ambiguous communication, assimilation was predicted when the actual discrepancy between self and other was relatively small, and contrast was predicted when the actual discrepancy was relatively large. In the study of political perception it is not easy to determine how ambiguity should be measured or operationalized. Certainly, the percentage of people who say they "don't know" a candidate's or party's position is one possibility (Wright & Niemi, 1983). The standard deviation of the perceptions is another (Granberg & Jenks, 1977). Unfortunately, these two indicators of ambiguity are not always highly correlated and may not yield the same ordering of issues. On perceptions on the abstract ideology dimension, the percentage of "don't knows" is relatively high, but the standard deviation among those who "do know" is relatively low.

A person's level of ego involvement was also expected to play a role in social judgment theory. Ego involvement is the extent to which the individual personally regards the issue under consideration as important. As ego involvement increases, it was anticipated that the normal tendencies toward assimilation and contrast would be enhanced.

Although the theory was alleged to be grounded in well-established principles of psychophysics, others have questioned whether this is so (Eiser & Stroebe, 1972; Petty & Cacioppo, 1981). Contrast effects are easier to document in psychophysical judgments, but it is hard to find evidence of assimilation and contrast effects occurring systematically within the same study in relation to the same stimulus array. Sherif and Hovland (1961) never really provided a good explanation as to why assimilation and contrast effects occur in either the psychophysical or psychosocial realm.

Perhaps assimilation and contrast effects are functional, but they certainly are not rational. In fact, if one disregards the degree to which assimilation and contrast occur, there is only one other alternative, and that is a veridical, which is to say accurate, perception. That is, assimilation and contrast effects are forms of perceptual distortion, underestimating and overestimating, respectively, the distance between self and other. To use a somewhat kinder and gentler label, one can refer to assimilation and contrast effects jointly as displacement effects.

The potential application of these concepts from social judgment theory to the analysis of political perception was obvious. Of course, the concepts could not be applied in a simpleminded or uncritical manner. Social judgment theory, as developed by Sherif and Hovland (1961), concentrated on how and where people place statements and messages coming from anonymous communicators. Although some political communications come to us anonymously (e.g., that unknown and unseen speaker in negative television advertisements), political candidates and parties are hardly anonymous communicators. Some U.S. candidates begin an election year with a low level of name recognition, even those who win the nomination such as George McGovern, Jimmy Carter, and Michael Dukakis; but they are reasonably well-known by the time the election campaign is fully under way and interviewers are busy asking questions (Markus, 1982). The perception process occurs differently when the identity of the communicator is known (Eiser, 1971; Manis, 1961).

Initially, when the key variables in social judgment theory, the individual's own attitude position, and the level of ego involvement in the issue were used in a study of political perceptions on the issue of the Vietnam War, only weak effects were observed (Granberg & Brent, 1974). It was only when a control was introduced for the person's attitude toward the communicator, in this case Hubert Humphrey or Richard Nixon, that strong and theoretically interesting effects began to appear. Within social judgment theory per se, there is no reason that people ought to assimilate only when estimating a preferred candidate's position and contrast only when estimating a nonpreferred candidate's position. Conceivably, people could assimilate (or contrast) when perceiving any candidate's position. It was only when the analysis combined the concepts of social judgment theory and balance theory that coherent effects began to be observed. Assimilating while estimating the position of a nonpreferred candidate or showing contrast when estimating the position of a preferred candidate would, of course, run counter to the implications of balance theory.[3]

It is plausible to interpret the effects shown in figures 4.2 and 4.3 and table 4.2 as assimilation and contrast effects in political perception. This line of research can be summarized in a set of empirically grounded propositions:

1. People tend to assimilate when attributing a position to a preferred party or candidate.
2. The degree to which assimilation of a preferred candidate occurs is a direct function of the level of positive affect felt by the person toward the preferred candidate.
3. The tendency to assimilate in perceiving the position of a preferred party or candidate is pervasive, occurring at both the level of the average citizen

and extending to people in elite positions (Carlson, 1990; Holmberg & Esaiasson, 1988).

4. The tendency toward assimilation in estimating a preferred candidate's position is enhanced among people who are high in involvement, who attribute great importance to the issue under consideration, or who are very concerned about the outcome of the election.[4]

5. Assimilation effects in the perception of a preferred party or candidate are more reliable and more robust than contrast effects in the perception of a nonpreferred party or candidate.

6. When contrast effects occur, they are more likely to occur in perceptions of an incumbent than in perceptions of a challenger. This implies that the relative novelty of most challengers may inhibit contrast; if true, it may be that a certain lack of ambiguity is necessary for contrast to occur. Assimilation, on the other hand, appears to be facilitated by ambiguity (Granberg & Jenks, 1977).

7. Assimilation of a preferred candidate and contrast of a nonpreferred candidate occur both before and after an election. The degree to which these effects occur does not appear to be affected by whether the questions are posed before or after an election.

If assimilation effects were truly pervasive, and wishful thinking were complete, there would be no limit. We know that is not the case. In the 1980 Swedish referendum on nuclear power, for example, people who decided to vote for an alternative other than that endorsed by their preferred party did not assimilate when attributing a position on nuclear power to their preferred party (Granberg & Holmberg, 1988). In Sweden the Center party led the antinuclear movement, and its position on the issue was widely publicized and well-known. On that issue, only the Center party supporters whose attitudes were on the same general side of the issue as their party showed a tendency toward assimilation. Center party supporters who were pronuclear in their attitudes attributed to the Center party a more extreme antinuclear position than it actually had (Granberg & Holmberg, 1986b). Even though this is an unusual case, those people actually showed a tendency toward contrast when placing their preferred party.

Although it is evident that ambiguity is involved, it is usually mixed with other things in a complex manner. George Wallace made his reputation on trying to maintain segregation and taking a strong "law and order" approach. His views on Vietnam and other matters of foreign policy were much less well known. By comparison, George McGovern's presidential campaign emerged largely on the basis of his opposition to the Vietnam War. His liberal position on domestic matters was not well-known. It is revealing that among their respective supporters, Wallace was assimilated more on the Vietnam War issue than on the issue of urban unrest, while McGovern was assimilated more on urban unrest than on Vietnam (Granberg & Seidel, 1976). For Wallace on urban unrest as with McGovern on Vietnam, their respective positions were so well-known and well-publicized that this constrained the voters' propensity to assimilate in their perceptions of a preferred candidate.

Perhaps it is a combination of involvement and information that produces tendencies toward displacement. Granberg and Brent (1983) reported that the tendency toward wishful thinking in expectations about the outcome of a presidential election occurred most strongly among people who were highly involved but poorly informed. It may be the highly involved but poorly informed people in a campaign who are especially likely to assimilate when perceiving the views of a preferred candidate. This may have been obscured in many analyses in that the natural tendency will be for those people who are highly involved to also be well-informed.

While contrast effects are more rare and less robust than assimilation effects in political perception, it is not the case that contrast effects never occur. In 1984, for instance, Mondale supporters showed a composite contrast of $-.41$ in their perceptions of the incumbent Reagan, which is suggestive of a substantial tendency toward contrast and only slightly weaker than the assimilation tendency these same people showed in their perceptions of Mondale ($+.51$). Granberg and Robertson (1982) reported significant contrast on each of three issues when U.S. citizens gave their estimates of current governmental policy. The more conservative the person's own position, the more liberal the perception of governmental policy.

As an additional demonstration that contrast effects can occur in political perception, consider the placements of the small Centrum Parti in the Netherlands. It was in the unusual situation of being a much disliked party (average rating = 5.2 on a 0–100 feeling thermometer), being outside the mainstream of Dutch politics, but, nonetheless, calling itself the Center party (Van der Eijk, Irwin, & Niemöller, 1986). On the 1–10 left-right scale, people were most likely to place it at the extreme right (57 percent) and next most likely to place it at the extreme left (25 percent). To examine for a contrast effect, we also need to take into account the person's self-placement. Overall in placing the Center party on the left-right scale, 3 percent maximized the similarity (placed themselves and the party at the same point), and 51 percent maximized the

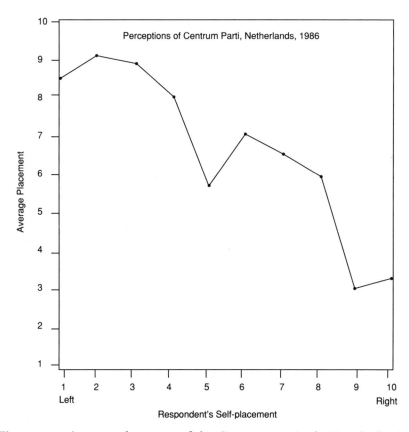

Figure 4.4. Average placement of the Center party in the Dutch election study of 1986 as a function of the respondent's self-placement.

distance. The mean perceptions of the Center party, as a function of self-placement, are shown in figure 4.4. Although the curve is somewhat irregular, the eta value of .40 and the correlation of $-.35$ certainly can be taken as indicating that a contrast effect was occurring.

Rational Selection, Persuasion, and Perceptual Distortion

Heider's theory clearly implied that an imbalanced set of cognitions would be more unstable than a balanced set. The theory was not so clear, however, on the matter of which of the three elements in an imbalanced set would be most likely to change. One might suppose that the attitudinal or sentiment relations would be more firmly established, and that it would be the perception, belief, or cognition that would be most susceptible to change. That generally may be the case, although it is not difficult to conjure up a counterexample.

Consider for instance an American Catholic who is pro-choice on abortion. Insofar as the person has a positive sentiment relation to the Roman Catholic Church as well as a unit relation with it, the person is almost by definition in a state of cognitive imbalance on the question of abortion. Just how plausible is it that a pro-choice Catholic could deny that the church is really against abortion?

Of course, the three alternatives for changing should not be regarded as mutually exclusive. That is, a person in a state of cognitive imbalance may adopt a complex combination of alternative ways to move toward cognitive balance. Granberg and Campbell (1977) showed that on a relatively uninvolving judgment task, when the discrepancy was large, assimilation and opinion shift were actually complementary. That is, people who did one also were more likely to do the other. The pro-choice Catholic might maintain membership but hold a slightly less favorable view toward the Catholic Church, contribute a little less money, be a little less insistent that his or her children are educated in Catholic schools, but also slightly change the attitude away from an extreme pro-choice position and find exceptions so that Catholics are not perceived as monolithic or absolute in their opposition to abortion.

We also should not fail to recognize that people can live with a certain amount of dissonance or cognitive imbalance (Aronson, Turner, & Carlsmith, 1963). This is especially true if the issue under consideration is not highly salient or does not highly involve the individual's ego. At the same time, if the issue is at the top on the public agenda, as with the Vietnam War in 1968, and the person regards it personally as the most important issue at the time, then it seems unlikely that the individual could comfortably abide a state of cognitive imbalance.

For better or worse, the positions of politicians on current issues are rarely as unambiguous as the position of the Catholic Church on abortion. In a senate campaign, the slogan "Bill Brock Believes" may be a neat alliteration, but it is hardly informative as to what he believed. Criticized for being too vague, it really did not help much when the billboards were changed to read "Bill Brock Believes What We Believe." This was reducing to the absurd the tendency in many U.S. campaigns to be evasive on the issues and on ideology (Granberg, 1982). In regard to the average candidate in the United States, perceptual distortion is certainly a real possibility as a mode of dealing with cognitive imbalance.

The difficulty comes in providing a clear demonstration that assimilation and contrast have occurred and to separate these effects from other possibilities. When one observes subjective agreement between a person and that person's preferred party, this could result from perceptual distortion of the party's position, but it also could be the result of rational selection or persuasion.

Rational selection in this context refers to choosing the alternative that is closest to oneself. In Heider's model, the P-O sentiment is formed or altered on the basis of the degree of agreement between P-X and O-X. In other social psychological approaches, similarity leads to attraction (Byrne, 1971). Persuasion would refer to altering one's attitude on the issue, bringing about greater closeness between the P-X and O-X elements by changing the P-X element.

In fact, it is almost never the candidate's main goal to convince or persuade people to change their attitudes on some issue so that they conform more closely to the candidate's views. To be specific, we may not know how Walter Mondale really felt about a tax increase, but he had indicated, in his speech accepting the Democratic nomination in 1984, that he felt a tax increase would be necessary. He also went on to attribute duplicity to his opponent in claiming that President Reagan also would come to the view that a tax increase was necessary but only after the election. Most likely, Mondale cared little about whether the American people shared or would become persuaded to share his views about the necessity of a tax increase. As a pragmatic politician, what he really wanted was for 50.1 percent of the voters in the right states to vote for him. Persuasion of the public toward a candidate's views during a campaign could occur, but it would be regarded as incidental to the main question. Most campaign managers probably regard persuasion on issues as an irrelevant possibility. Panel analyses have indicated that it is hard (Markus, 1982), but not impossible (Abramowitz, 1978), to find evidence of a persuasion effect on substantive issues in the course of a political campaign.

Charles Judd, David Kenny, and Jon Krosnick (1983) looked at the sort of evidence in table 4.2 and figures 4.2 and 4.3 and were not convinced of claims regarding assimilation and contrast. What they questioned was not the occurrence of these two effects in political perception but rather their apparent asymmetry (proposition 5 above). Judd et al. also asserted that prior analyses were flawed by using an improperly specified model, by omitting a crucial variable (the candidate's real position), and by ignoring the problem of correlated measurement error. In their analysis, they sought to correct these flaws by using LISREL, and they purported to show that when all is said and done, assimilation and contrast occur and to roughly the same extent.

When Judd et al. (1983) approached the problem of political perception with LISREL, they viewed perception of Hubert Humphrey's position on the Vietnam War and perception of Humphrey's position on urban unrest as manifest indicators of a person's perception of Humphrey's position (on what remained unspecified). After their intensive analyses, Judd et al. (1983) still ended up with considerable assimilation and contrast. The only real question that they raise about prior research, aside from providing a more "elegant" demonstration, is whether there is asymmetry or not. Previous reports had observed assimilation to be stronger than contrast, and, indeed, it is even possible to read the results of Judd et al. (1983, p. 960, table 4) as containing asymmetry (Marks & Miller, 1987, pp. 80–81). Only by making the improbable assumptions that a persuasion effect was occurring on these issues, and that this persuasion effect was asymmetrical, were Judd et al. (1983) able to wipe out the apparent asymmetry in political perception.

The contribution of Judd et al. (1983) was to specify the models of political perception more precisely than had been done. Others had recognized the three processes of rational selection, persuasion, and perceptual distortion (e.g., Page & Brody, 1972; Shaffer, 1981), and the possibility of reciprocal causation (e.g., Granberg & King, 1980; Page & Jones, 1979), but Judd et al. laid out alternative models that were distinct from one another.

There remained the problem of how to separate the three effects when survey data were analyzed. A partial solution to this problem has been proposed (Granberg, 1987a; Granberg & Holmberg, 1986a, 1986b, 1988; Granberg, Kasmer, & Nanneman, 1988). It involves the creation of a new variable called placement of one's preferred candidate. Thus, for Bush supporters this would mean their perception of Bush, and for Dukakis supporters it would mean their perception of Dukakis. An eta coefficient is calculated to measure the association between where people place themselves and where they place the preferred candidate. The presumption is that this measure of association will reflect the joint operation of all three processes. That is, if people gravitate toward a candidate because of proximity (rational selection), if they alter their own self-placement to conform more closely with the position of a preferred candidate (persuasion), or if they distort the perception of their preferred candidate's position in the direction of their own position (misperception), any and all of these effects should be reflected in this "subjective agreement" eta. Then a second eta is based solely on where people place themselves as a function of candidate preference. The presumption is that this eta will reflect the effect of two processes (rational selection and persuasion).

Abramowitz (1978) correctly pointed out that this second eta does not enable one to distinguish between rational selection and persuasion. But suppose that is not one's purpose. If one wants an estimate of the combined effects of persuasion and rational selection, this second eta may be satisfactory. In this second eta, perception (other than self-perception) is not involved.

If this reasoning is sound, then the first eta (whose magnitude presumably results from all three processes) should always be as large or larger than the second eta (which taps only rational selection and persuasion). By implication, the difference between these two etas should reflect the strength of the third process, perceptual distortion. In the case of the perception of the preferred candidate, this would mean assimilation. Granberg, Kasmer, and Nanneman (1988) reported the first subjective agreement eta to be .50, averaging across eight scales from the 1984 U.S. election study, compared to .33 for the second eta. Elsewhere, it was shown that both eta values were much larger in Sweden than in the United States, but the difference between the two etas was about the same in both countries (Granberg, 1987a). This can be interpreted as indicating that the more democratic processes of persuasion and rational selection were occurring to a greater degree in Sweden, while perceptual distortion may have been occurring to about the same extent in both countries (Granberg & Holmberg, 1988).

Without question the two etas are legitimate calculations. Their interpretation is more tenuous. Even at best, this is a partial solution in that what you get are two coefficients, one which is the joint result of three effects, while the other is the joint result of two effects. A better solution would yield the joint effect of all three processes and would partition or apportion certain percentages of the overall effect to rational selection, persuasion, and perceptual distortion. Whoever devises such a solution and communicates it in a convincing manner certainly will have made an important advance.

In the meantime, if the two eta approach is essentially sound, though no more than a partial solution, it would argue against the notion that nothing important can be learned about political perception through the analysis of cross-sectional data. There are, of course, advantages of panel data in which the preferences, attitudes, and perceptions of the same individuals are traced across time, and such data have been extensively analyzed (e.g., Granberg & King, 1980; Granberg, Kasmer, & Nanneman, 1988; Markus, 1982; Shaffer, 1981). However, the timing of when things are measured is very crucial in panel analysis. For instance, an effect such as perceptual distortion may not be observable in panel data if the effect had already occurred before time 1 or if the interval between time 1 and time 2 is not appropriate (Krosnick, 1990a).

Political Cue Theory

The critiques offered by Shaffer (1981) and Judd et al. (1983) of previous analyses of political perception based on balance and social judgment theories, while intriguing, were essentially methodological and did not really change our understanding of political perception. More interesting, therefore, was the challenge offered by Pamela Conover and Stanley Feldman who in a series of articles proposed an alternative approach to the analysis of political perception—political cue theory (Conover, 1981; Conover & Feldman, 1982, 1986, 1989; Feldman & Conover, 1983). Displacement theory, emphasizing assimilation and contrast, is a relatively "hot," affectively charged theory, which proposes that perceptual distortion occurs because of ego involvement and one's affective orientation toward the candidates. Affect is thought to influence political perception. By comparison, political cue theory is relatively "cool," emphasizing cognition, information processing, and the drawing of inferences.

As a means of making sense of the complex political reality and as a cognitive shortcut, political cue theory depicts people as developing schemas. A schema in this context refers to a more or less integrated set of beliefs and implicit rules concerning a stimulus, including what goes with what, how things operate, and how cues can be used to infer features that go beyond information that is given. If the cues have validity, then the inferences drawn may be highly accurate. Inasmuch as it is not feasible for the average citizen to master the entire political agenda, schemas are used that streamline the process and make it more tractable. Obviously, great differences may exist between individuals in the levels of sophistication represented by these schemas (Brady & Sniderman, 1985; Converse, 1964; Luskin, 1987).

In experimental research, political perception is affected by providing cues or by making certain cues salient (Conover, 1981). Gender, class, education, accent, and ethnicity, all are cues that might be used to guess or estimate a person's attitude on questions pertaining to political perception. A central idea in political cue theory is that political parties act as abiding and reliable anchors, serving as strong cues in deriving political perceptions. In a strong party system, if you know someone to be an active member or leader of the Social Democratic party in Sweden or the Christian Democratic party in West Germany, this certainly would be used as a cue in impression formation. If the schema is reasonably well-developed in such a situation, a series of implications follow rather directly from the premise that a person is affiliated with a certain party.

For some observers, a single cue also can stigmatize a person. Knowing that a person is an ex-convict, a former mental patient, a homosexual, an immigrant from Haiti, these are cues that create an affective response in many people that may, in turn, influence their political perceptions. Traditionally in the United States, knowing that a person was Catholic, Jewish, black, or a woman was a strong enough cue for enough voters to make parties reluctant to nominate people with such characteristics for high office. Even though there has been a massive shift in U.S. public opinion in the direction of considering such cues to be irrelevant over the past fifty years, there is still a substantial minority (about 20 percent) who openly say that they would not vote for a woman or a black person for president, even if the individual was qualified and was nominated by the voter's preferred party. That is a considerable liability with which to begin a campaign.

In 1989 the mayor's contest in New York City pitted an Italian-American nominated by the Republican party, Rudolph Guiliani, against a black American, David Dinkins, nominated by the Democratic party. One young Jewish mother in Brooklyn was quoted as saying that it did not matter to her what Dinkins's relationship was to Jesse Jackson, the black presidential candidate in 1988 and leader of the Rainbow Coalition. The fact that Dinkins and Jackson had any relationship at all was enough to make her vote Republican for the first time (Reeves, 1989). In Heider's terms, Dinkins and Jackson have a unit relationship in that they are both black Americans. Beyond that, Jackson had offended many Jews by his reference to New York City as "Hymietown," and Jews may have doubted that Jackson shared their concern with the fate of Israel.

In any event, this serves to illustrate the use of cues in developing political perception, judgment, and behavior. Overall, there can be little doubt concerning the central premise of political cue theory. In 1988, for instance, perceptions of the parties' positions and the perceptions of the positions of the candidates nominated by those parties were not independent of one another. The correlation between where people placed the Democratic party and where they placed Michael Dukakis on the same scale was +.66, averaging across the nine scales in table 4.1. The comparable average correlation for the Republican party and George Bush in 1988 was +.67. The expectation was that this leader-party correlation would be even higher in a strong party system. This was confirmed when it was reported that in Sweden the correlation between perceptions of the ideological positions of a party and its leader was +.85, averaging across five parties (Granberg, 1987a).

The analyses of survey data based on political cue theory have emphasized, or one might say capitalized on, the relatively strong relationship between where people perceive a party to be in ideological space and where they perceive that party's nominee to be. When perception of a party's position and the person's self-placement are used to jointly predict perception of a preferred candidate's position, the party cue appears to exert the stronger effect. It is certainly reasonable to interpret that finding as supportive of political cue theory. The effect of the person's own attitude, the erstwhile assimilation effect, is reduced very substantially in such analyses, although it usually remains statistically significant (Conover & Feldman, 1982, 1986; Feldman & Conover, 1983; Granberg, 1987a; Jacoby, 1988). While Conover and Feldman raised doubts about the strength of assimilation and contrast effects, they did not question the asymmetry effect in which assimilation of a preferred candidate is a stronger tendency than contrast of a nonpreferred candidate.

In interpreting their regression analyses, it is appropriate to extend the argument by asking this question. What if individuals varied in self-placement, placement of a party, and placement of a party's nominee, but each individual placed the party and the party's nominee at exactly the same point? One can simulate such a situation by selecting, for instance, only those individuals who placed Bush and the Republican party at exactly the same point on the scale. These two variables would then be correlated at +1.0, and it would be impossible for any other variable to exert a statistically significant effect on perception of the candidate's position in such a hypothetical context. Nevertheless, would this necessarily mean that assimilation was not occurring? Suppose there was a moderate tendency, say +.45, for people to pull both their preferred candidate's position and the position of that candidate's party toward their own position. Such an effect could occur and yet be completely muffled in a regression analysis in the foregoing hypothetical case.

When one observes a strong correlation between perceptions of a party and the party's nominee, it is reasonable to ask whether the causal flow is predominantly in one direction. If the causal flow were predominantly from perception of a party's position to perception of a candidate's position, people should be less likely to say they "don't know" the party's position. Also, perceptions of the party's positions should be more stable. These hypotheses have been tested, but they were not supported (Granberg, Kasmer, & Nanneman, 1988; Wright & Niemi, 1983). Furthermore, panel analyses of people who gave their perceptions across time for Jimmy Carter, Gerald Ford, Ronald Reagan, and their two parties suggest that, if anything, people are probably more likely to derive their perceptions of the party's position from perception of the candidate's position than the reverse.

Since he was relatively unknown and a newcomer to the national political scene, perceptions of Jimmy Carter in 1976 are of special interest. As he was the Democratic party nominee, the situation seems like a natural context to apply political cue theory, especially on a traditional partisan question dealing with whether the government should play a role in guaranteeing everyone a job and an adequate standard of living. Yet, the fifty-five people who did not know where Carter was positioned on that dimension but did know the position of the Democratic party at time 1 did not appear to have derived their later perceptions of Carter's position from their earlier perceptions of the Democratic party's position ($r = +.17$, $p > .05$). On the other hand, the sixty-four people who knew Carter's position but not the Democratic position at time 1 may have derived their perception of the party's position from their earlier impression of Carter's position ($r = +.37$, $p < .01$). All in all, in a system such as that in the United States, it may not be tenable to hold that the primary flow is from perception of a party's position to perception of a candidate's position (Granberg, Kasmer, & Nanneman, 1988).

One study that provided evidence in support of political cue theory concerned "an anomaly in political perception." The anomaly concerned the perception of Senator Edward Kennedy's position on abortion. In 1984 the public tended to attribute an antiabortion position to Kennedy, despite his persistent pro-choice voting record. In fact, the public was even slightly more likely to attribute an extreme antiabortion position to Kennedy than they were to attribute that position to Ronald Reagan (Granberg, 1985). Why would that be considered anomalous? People who have analyzed political perceptions are struck by the fact that, while individuals distort and make errors, the public's perceptions in the aggregate of where parties and politicians stand on issues tend to be reasonably accurate (Page, 1978). There is also a certain irony in such perceptions in that Kennedy has come to be viewed with a special antipathy as a bête noire by activists in the antiabortion movement. Antiabortion activists seem to have had a special antagonism toward Catholic government officials (e.g., Supreme Court Justice William Brennan, Senator Kennedy, 1984 Democratic vice presidential candidate Geraldine Ferraro) who do not support making abortion illegal—people who ought to be "our natural allies," but who nonetheless oppose what "we" are trying to accomplish. Thus, ascribing an antiabortion position to Kennedy is a mistake that antiabortion activists would not make.

Insofar as this really is an anomaly, it would seem to be one that can be easily explained. People are probably making this aggregate error in political perception because they are using a misleading cue, namely the link between Kennedy and the Catholic Church. Some people may have reasoned, "You ask me what Kennedy's position is on abortion; well, perhaps I really don't know for sure, but I do know he's a Catholic. Catholics are known to oppose abortion, and therefore, I will guess that Kennedy is opposed to abortion." However, there is no way of proving that the underlying process involves use of the religious affiliation cue if we restrict the analysis to data from the national election study.

Therefore, an experiment was done in which the saliency of Kennedy's religious affiliation was manipulated. Half the people answered a series of questions designed to make Kennedy's religion salient, while the other half answered questions designed to make Kennedy's political affiliation salient. People who were led to think about Kennedy as a Catholic were much more likely to perceive him as taking an antiabortion position than people who were led to think about Kennedy as a liberal Democrat. This gave strong support to a cue interpretation of the erroneous perceptions of Kennedy's position on abortion (Granberg, 1985).

No one has yet identified or devised a definitive critical test between political cue theory and displacement theory. Perhaps the two theories are incommensurable in the philosophical sense. An alternative has been to try to derive hypotheses unique to one theory—a test where that theory has an implication but in which the other theory cannot be invoked as an alternative explanation. Thus, for instance, people have been singled out who say that they do not know the party's position on an issue but who express a candidate preference and place themselves and their preferred candidate on an issue scale. If these people show an apparent tendency to assimilate when placing their preferred candidate, they cannot be deriv-

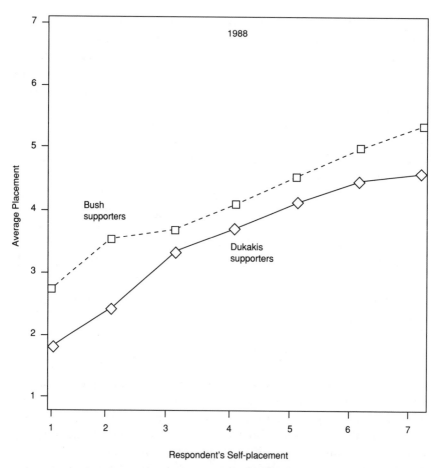

Figure 4.5. Average placement of the preferred candidate as a function of the person's own attitude among people who "don't know" the position of the preferred candidate's party. (Data are a composite of all scales in table 4.1.)

ing their estimate of the candidate's position from their perception of the party's position, since they have stated that they "don't know" that position.

Figure 4.5 shows relevant results from 1988. Among Dukakis supporters who did not know the position of the Democratic party (eta = .62 for 291 perceptions), as well as among Bush supporters who did not know the Republican party's position (eta = .57 for 323 perceptions), there was a substantial relationship between self-placement and perception of a preferred candidate's position. This result supports the assimilation hypothesis, and political cue theory does not offer an alternative explanation. Similar results have been reported for the four previous elections (Granberg, Kasmer, & Nanneman, 1988).

The Perception of Distance

A problem with the applications of cognitive balance theory and political cue theory to political perception is that they tend to focus on one perception at a time. If perceptions of political stimuli develop in relation to each other, then this relational quality is missed in many analyses (Krosnick, 1990b). An alternative that some have pursued involves the use of multidimensional scaling (e.g., Lund, 1974; Sherman & Ross, 1972). This may be useful if the goal is to give a descriptive account of how people differentiate a set of political stimuli in spatial dimensions. It is not easy to see how this form of analysis can be used to formulate or corroborate social-psychological theories.

If one limits the analysis to the distance between two parties and one dimension, the problem becomes analogous to estimating the distance between two trees. A direct question would be to ask people how far apart are the two trees. An indirect method would be to ask people to estimate the position of each tree and then to calculate the distance between the two estimates. The latter form of data is readily available in political surveys from many countries. If we are considering more than two trees but still only one dimension, we can sum and average all of the distances or take the standard deviation of the person's estimates as an indicator of the perceived distance.

A gestalt psychologist might suggest that one's own location relative to the position of the two trees would be crucial in determining one's perspective and, consequently, one's perception of distance. People halfway in between the two trees might perceive the greatest distance, and the perceived distance could decrease as one moved away from the midpoint in either direction. If so, we might expect an inverted U function between a person's own position on a scale and the perception of distance between two objects. Then there is the question of how great the distance would seem to the person who is well beyond either tree. St. Louis and Kansas City may seem very close to each other to someone in San Francisco or Washington, D.C., more so than to someone in St. Louis, Kansas City, or halfway in between the two in Columbia, Missouri.

When it comes to political stimuli, however, most people are not neutral. What if a person loves one tree and hates the other? Social-psychological theory implies that people situated halfway between two parties in ideological distance would have the least cause to prefer one party, and that the relative preference for one party over the other would increase as a person's position moves toward one party and away from the other. Such an affective orientation toward objects could influence the perception of these objects, including the distance between them. Social judgment theory, with its emphasis on the pull-push processes of assimilation and contrast, implies a U-shaped relationship between a person's own position and the perception of distance.

Specifically, suppose we have a 1–9 left-right scale, and the two objects are stationed at positions 3 and 7. If people at positions 1 and 9 pull the closer object toward themselves and push the farther object away from themselves psychologically, then people at the extremes of the scale ought to perceive a large distance. As people move toward the center of the scale, they might show similar tendencies, but the result would be for the perceived distance to gradually decrease as the person's own position moves toward the center.

What about the people whose own position is beyond the scale (not to say beyond the pale)? Recall the comment of third party candidate George Wallace in 1968 to the effect that "there's not a dime's worth of difference between the Democratic and Republican parties." If we take his words at face value, he is not saying where in ideological space the two parties are, but wherever they are, there is essentially no distance between them. This provided a hypothesis that the Wallace voters would perceive less distance between the Democratic and Republican nominees, Hubert Humphrey and Richard Nixon. Yet on the 1–7 Vietnam scale, Humphrey voters, Nixon voters, and Wallace voters each perceived, on average, 1.4 units of absolute distance between Humphrey and Nixon. On the 1–7 urban unrest scale, the three voting groups differed slightly in how much distance was perceived between Humphrey and Nixon. However, Humphrey voters perceived the most distance (2.0 units, on average), followed by Wallace voters (1.9), and then Nixon voters (1.8), and these averages were not significantly different. Thus, the hypothesis that supporters of an extremist candidate would perceive less distance between the mainstream candidates was not supported (Granberg & Brown, 1990).

On the question of the shape of the relationship between where people place themselves and the perception of distance, we have examined this matter in several different political contexts. Figure 4.6 shows the average perceived distance among more than 6,600 people who placed themselves and the two major party nominees somewhere on a 1–7 scale concerning whether the government ought to guarantee everyone a job

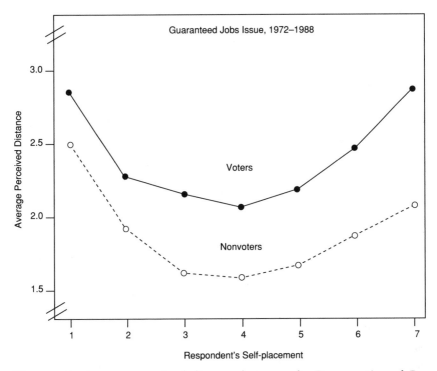

Figure 4.6. Average perceived distance between the Democratic and Republican candidates as a function of self-placement and voting, based on a combination of U.S. election studies, 1972–88.

and an adequate standard of living in one of the five most recent U.S. presidential election studies, 1972–88.[5] As might be expected, voters perceive more distance between the candidates than do nonvoters. However, for both voters and nonvoters, there is a U-shaped function between self-placement and the perception of distance. It is clear that people who placed themselves near one of the extremes perceived more distance between the two candidates than people who put themselves at or near the center of the scale.

The results in figure 4.6 are not peculiar to this issue, to a 1–7 scale, or to the United States. In England in 1983, people who placed themselves at or near the center of a twenty-one-point left-right scale perceived much less distance between the Labour and Conservative parties than did people who placed themselves toward either of the extremes. Similar results have been observed for the Netherlands and Sweden, countries with multiparty systems. So the finding in figure 4.6 has substantial generality (Granberg & Brown, 1990).

The question remaining is why this function exists between self-placement and the perception of distance. One possibility is a personal stylistic tendency. That is, people who use an extreme category to describe themselves may be inclined to use extreme categories when describing other people or political parties. In Sweden, people who spread the parties out more widely (i.e., perceived more distance) on an eleven-point left-right scale, also spread the parties and the party leaders out more widely on an eleven-point like-dislike scale. People who are strong partisans spread the parties out more widely on the left-right scale than people who lack an attachment to a party. Overall, the direct relationship between extremity of self-placement and the perception of distance holds consistent in regression analyses when the effects of other variables are controlled.

The pull of one's preferred party toward one's own position (assimilation) is implicated in the U-shaped function in figure 4.6. In Sweden in 1988 there was a relatively strong U-shaped function between where people placed themselves on a 0–10 left-right scale and the extent to which they spread out the seven parties on that same scale (eta $= .39$). However, when the perception of the person's most preferred party is removed, so that we are considering only how widely people spread out their six nonpreferred parties, the function is flattened and weakens considerably (eta $= .17$).

The perception of distance in politics is worthy of further attention in that it takes into account the relational nature of perceptions by considering more than one perception at a time. Moreover, it is relevant to normative democratic theory. If people perceive no distance or very little distance between the alternatives they confront in an election campaign, this certainly raises questions about whether the election is a meaningful exercise. If the perceived distance between alternatives increases across time, this could reflect an increasing political polarization in the society. It is possible to imagine a situation in which the distance is so great that a democratic situation becomes difficult, if not impossible, to sustain.

Perceived Distinctiveness and Political Polarization

Another approach that uses perceptions in relation to each other and seeks to relate the degree of distinctiveness of the alternatives to the degree of polarization between the voting groups is derived from V. O. Key's (1966) metaphor of the echo chamber.[6] Key's idea was that there ought to be an empirical relationship between how distinct the alternatives are from which voters choose and the extent to which voters are divided on that same dimension. The presumption is that voter groups echo back, in a slightly modulated form, the alternatives with which they are presented in elections. Thus, if the voter groups are not polarized on an issue or on ideology, this is often traceable to a lack of distinctiveness among the alternatives (Granberg & Holmberg, 1988, pp. 5–7). For this idea to be of interest, the concepts of distinctiveness and polarization must be based on independent measurements. Distinctiveness can be treated as a perceptual problem, while polarization involves an intergroup comparison.

There are probably many ways to assess these two concepts. However, it should be done in a manner that involves a similar method but different variables. One way is to superimpose the distribution of perceptions of party A on the perceptions of party B. Then the area of nonoverlap becomes the measure of *perceived distinctiveness*. Maximum distinctiveness (1.0) would be implied if the two distributions did not overlap at all. If they overlapped completely (i.e., coincided), this would imply minimum distinctiveness (.00). Voter group polarization can be assessed in a similar manner. That is, the distribution of self-placements by people who vote for party A can be superimposed on the self-placements of people voting for party B. In this case, the area of nonoverlap would measure *voter group polarization*. An example of how this works is shown in figure 4.7. In practice, distinctiveness and polarization are calculated as the area of nonoverlap divided by two. (If it were not divided by two, the area of nonoverlap could extend from .00 to 2.0.) As can be seen in the upper panel of figure 4.7, people's perceptions of Michael Dukakis and George Bush on the abstract liberal-conservative scale overlapped 46 percent, resulting in a distinctiveness score of .54. The lower portion of figure 4.7 shows that the self-placements by Dukakis and Bush supporters overlapped considerably, by 65 percent to be precise, resulting in a polarization score of .35. The distinctiveness and polarization scores for Walter Mondale and Ronald Reagan in 1984 were .46 and .37. These results are consistent with the idea that distinctiveness will exceed polarization on the same scale. However, the increase in distinctiveness from 1984 to 1988 was not accompanied by an increase in polarization.

Other comparisons can be made using different scales in a given election or even comparable scales in different countries (Inglehart & Klingemann, 1976; Sani & Sartori, 1983). The U.S. data from 1968 comfortably fit the echo chamber concept. That is, on both the Vietnam and urban unrest scales, candidate distinctiveness exceeded voter group polarization. More importantly, the candidates were more distinct and

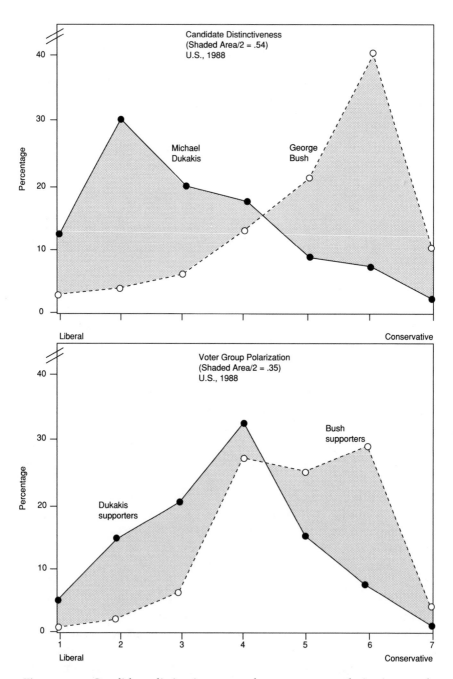

Figure 4.7. Candidate distinctiveness and voter group polarization on the liberal-conservative dimension in the 1988 U.S. presidential election.

the voter groups were more divided on urban unrest than on the Vietnam War issue. There was considerable division of opinion in the United States over the Vietnam War, but this division was almost completely independent of candidate preference in 1968.

Although it is somewhat difficult to compare a two-party system with a multiparty system, it appears that both distinctiveness and polarization are considerably higher in Sweden than in the United States (Granberg, 1987a). The Netherlands is in between the two other countries, although it is much more similar to Sweden. In all three countries, distinctiveness exceeds polarization; thus, the three data points comfortably fit on a theoretical curve.

One also can examine several issues in a given election, as shown in figure 4.8 for the U.S. presidential election of 1988. Eight issues (the scales from table 4.1 for aid to minority groups and aid to blacks are combined here) are analyzed in regard to the dual questions of how distinct the candidates are perceived to be and to what degree the voter groups are divided. The two candidates in 1988 were perceived as most distinct on the question of how large the military budget should be, and the two voting groups were most polarized on the abstract liberal-conservative scale. The candidates were perceived as least distinct on the question of how best to handle relations with the former Soviet Union, and the voter groups were least polarized on the scale pertaining to equality for women.

Overall, the results in figure 4.8 can be interpreted as supporting the echo chamber hypothesis. On each issue, perceived candidate distinctiveness exceeds voter group polarization, and at least some increase in polarization with increasing distinctiveness can be discerned. For each increase of .10 units on distinctiveness, there is an increase of about .06 units on polarization.

What conceivable results would be incompatible with Key's echo chamber concept? If we were to observe an instance in which voter group polarization exceeded party/candidate distinctiveness, or if we observed a flat or inverse function between distinctiveness and polarization, this would be incompatible with Key's hypothesis.

Political Perceptions and Behavior

Political perceptions can be treated as phenomena worthy of examination in their own right. People who prattle on about how great the American

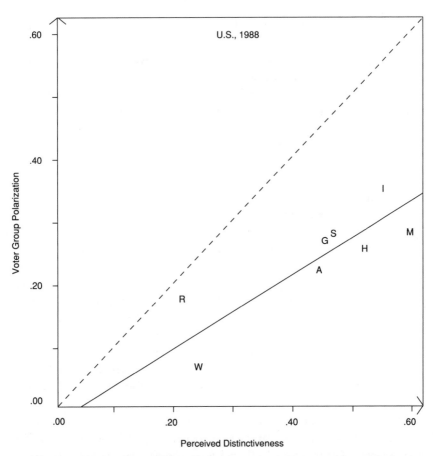

Figure 4.8. Perceived candidate distinctiveness and voter group polarization on eight scales in the 1988 U.S. presidential election. In this figure, I = liberal–conservative ideology, M = military spending, H = health insurance provided by government, S = social services, G = government guaranteed jobs and standard of living, A = aid to minority groups, R = relations with Russia, and W = women's rights to equality. See table 4.1 for the average placements on these scales.

political system is, or how well it is working, should look closely at the data on political perception. When citizens perceive the position of a party or candidate with a low level of consensus that exceeds a chance level by only a small margin, this ought to give pause (Granberg, 1987a). Of course, there are problems with measurement error, but a comparative perspective can be instructive. There is virtually no doubt that perceptual consensus as to where the parties or candidates stand is much lower in the United States than in many other countries. Insofar as distortions occur in perceptions, this is incompatible with a rational democratic model (Berelson, 1952).

For many people, perceptions take on interest (or they would assume a greater importance) if they can be shown to be related to behavior (Hurwitz, 1986). One test involved the link between similarity and attraction. The hypothesis that similarity causes attraction is well-established in social psychology (Byrne, 1971) and has a close counterpart in the political science literature on proximity voting. Given that people often assume similarity in the absence of strong evidence to the contrary, Rosenbaum (1986) suggested it might be more accurate to say that dissimilarity causes repulsion (Byrne, Clore, & Smeaton, 1986).

If we add perceptions as an intervening variable, then we can examine the relations among actual similarity, perceived similarity, and attraction. Once these variables have been identified, several analyses are implied. For instance, if the actual similarity between a person and a political party bore no relationship to the perceived similarity, it would imply a dreamworld type of autistic politics and certainly make us wonder about the ambiguity of the stimulus. If the perceived similarity predicted attraction and behavior, but was not itself grounded in actual similarity, this would hardly resemble a normative democratic model (Granberg & Holmberg, 1986a, 1988). If actual similarity influenced behavior without being mediated by perceptions, this would lessen the importance of understanding the process of political perception. Comparative research indicates that the correlation between perceived similarity and attraction is stronger than the correlation between actual similarity and attraction. Since attraction in the electoral context is strongly linked to behavior, this finding suggests that focusing on the perceptual process is not misguided.

It is possible in other ways to relate political perceptions, broadly conceived, to behavior. The classic bandwagon effect in elections implied an underlying perceptual process, along with a tacit assumption that people are motivated by a desire to be on the winning side or to avoid being socially isolated (Henshel & Johnston, 1987; Lazarsfeld, 1946; Lazarsfeld, Berelson, & Gaudet, 1948; Marsh, 1984; Uhlaner & Grofman, 1986). People perceive which side is leading or heading toward victory and form or alter their candidate preference to coincide with their perceptions. Does it really work that way? In 1988, whether people perceived Dukakis or Bush as more likely to win the election appeared to have a direct effect on voting for Dukakis or Bush, even after initial candidate preference was controlled. This result is consistent with the bandwagon hypothesis. However, in only one of nine previous U.S. elections (1900) was that regression coefficient significant (Granberg & Brent, 1983). An alternative is to examine the subsequent voting behavior of people who lack an intention at time 1 to see whether their behavior is consistent with the perceived or expected winner. In only one of ten tests (1976) was that relationship significant. Thus, considered together, a significant bandwagon effect was observed in only three of twenty tests using the 1952–88 Michigan election studies—hardly impressive evidence. Voting preferences are more volatile in primary elections than in general elections, and therefore it is reasonable that a bandwagon effect would be more likely in a primary election campaign (Bartels, 1985, 1987, 1988). However, it is doubtful that compelling evidence of a bandwagon effect can be adduced from cross-sectional data.

The other alternative, that perceptions are influenced by a person's affective orientation toward the candidates—the "wishful thinking" or "hedonic consistency" model (Babad & Yacobis, 1990; Granberg & Holmberg, 1986c; McGuire, 1981)—has received consistent support. Analysis of the 1980 U.S. election study found that perceptions of the public's inclination (expected winner) were influenced by the perception of recent poll results and by the perception of which candidate seems to be winning in the person's own state. These are effects of two cognitions on a third cognition and represent reasonable or quasirational information processing. On the other hand, the strongest effect seems to be exerted by a third variable, namely, which candidate the person prefers. This apparent effect of affect on cognition (or attitude on perception) can hardly be regarded as rational (Granberg & Brent, 1983).

This link between preference and perception can be analyzed within Heider's P-O-X model. P is still the person, O is now the entire electorate, and X is the issue of which candidate or party would be best for the country. If we assume that most people have a positive attitude toward the electorate (e.g., "the voters are not fools"), then perceiving disagreement between oneself and the electorate about which candidate should be elected would be a state of cognitive imbalance. Thus, expecting a preferred outcome—which is the case for about four out of five people in the United States (Granberg & Brent, 1983; Granberg & Holmberg, 1988)—can be interpreted as the result of the tendency toward cognitive balance. It also yields the intriguing, but as yet untested, prediction that people whose expected and preferred winner loses ought to change their attitude toward the electorate or toward the preferred candidate after the results of the election become known.

Related to this finding is the insight from Festinger's theory of cognitive dissonance (1957, 1964) that people should not necessarily change their attitudes toward a candidate solely because the candidate wins or loses. Rather it is when expectations are "violated," i.e., when a candidate wins or loses *unexpectedly,* that attitude change is anticipated (Granberg & Nanneman, 1986). Perceptions play a role here if we assume that a person's expectation regarding the likely winner is a perception (most broadly conceived) or based on perceptions.

Perceptions of the climate of opinion also are involved in the theory of the "spiral of silence," developed by Elisabeth Noelle-Neumann (1984), and these perceptions are expected to influence behavior. If people perceive their views as being in the minority, they will be less likely to express them. This differential inclination to express opinions will exert an effect, and the minority will gradually diminish. In this model, changes in perceptions precede changes in preferences. Minorities diminish sometimes, and some people may be motivated by the desire to avoid social isolation and ostracism, but it remains a difficult task to specify under what circumstances this model works. In a postmaterialist culture, with its emphasis on individualism and freedom of expression (Inglehart, 1985), the need for uniqueness may loom as large in human relations as the need to avoid social isolation.

Concluding Observations

Rather than issuing a general summons for more research on political perception, it may be more useful to indicate some specific lines of research that seem worthwhile. First, we do not really need more data, at least not more of the kind we already have. As indicated throughout this essay, a mountain of data exists on political perceptions that has been mined only sporadically. On the other hand, it is virtually inevitable that we shall get new data on political perception—at least with nearly every new election in every Western democracy. More valuable data on political perception will come from injecting experimental manipulations into surveys, unique situations, and the occasional natural experiment, the sort that happened in the conjunction between the Chernobyl nuclear disaster and the 1986 Dutch election.

As for specific problems, no one has adequately explained why on a series of issues a candidate is subject to perceptual distortion (i.e., assimilation and contrast) on some issues more so than on others. Some efforts to answer this question have been made, but it is not a simple matter to say why people appear to assimilate the position of a preferred candidate to varying degrees on different scales (Granberg, Harris, & King, 1981; Granberg & Jenks, 1977). Ambiguity and variance most likely play a role, but it has not been easy to nail down. If someone can solve that problem, or come close to a solution, it certainly ought to be worth a dissertation. One could say the same for the three-process (rational selection, persuasion, perceptual distortion) problem. Many people have looked into this matter, begun some analyses, and thrown up their hands in despair. It is not certain that it is solvable, but if a researcher knew that much, he or she probably would be able to come up with a viable and convincing solution.

Although some very interesting work has been done on perceptions of the personal characteristics of nominees (e.g., Esaiasson, 1990; Kinder, 1986a; Marcus, 1988), many additional possibilities are worth pursuing. It is often assumed that on issues and ideology, people draw their preferred party or candidate toward their own position, while on the matter of personal characteristics, people draw a preferred candidate toward their conception of an ideal leader (e.g., ideal president or prime minister) rather than toward themselves. For example, if I regard myself as relatively immature, and I think an ideal president is mature, it may be more likely that I will perceive my preferred candidate as similar to my conception of an ideal president than to my self-concept. That possibility, however, has not yet been demonstrated.

Moreover, people may not necessarily want an ideal candidate to have the exact position on issues as themselves. A pacifist may not necessarily want a pacifist president. Rather, a pacifist may prefer a candidate who would take conciliatory steps toward peace and cut the military budget by 25 percent. A person with extreme leftist views might regard as an ideal prime minister, under given circumstances, one who takes a position only slightly to the left of center. This is one of those cases where people assume that they know the answer, and therefore the relevant questions have not been posed to the public. On the questions of character and issues, there is an important distinction to be made between an ideal presidential candidate and an ideal president. We can assume that these concepts are not only analytically but empirically distinct.

In closing, the concepts used in this chapter (e.g., assimilation and contrast effects, political cues, consensus, distinctiveness and polarization) are useful building blocks in the analysis of political perception. At the same time, we should harbor no illusion that what has been presented in any way resembles an integrated theory. People doing research on political perception have been using theories of the middle range, and this chapter reflects that inclination. Clearly, there is an opportunity and a need for theoretical integration and advancement on this topic. It will be most interesting to see how future work on political perception builds on what is now thought to be true.

Notes

This chapter was written while I was Waernska Visiting Professor at the University of Göteborg. I wish to thank Thad Brown, Sören Holmberg, William Jacoby, Cees Van der Eijk, Ed Brent, Randy Kite, Mikael Gilljam, Ann Lawhorne, LeeAnn Debo, Teresa Hjellming, Patricia Shanks, and Billye Adams for their advice and assistance. I am solely responsible for the analyses and interpretation.

1. This is a very broad and arguably inappropriate use of the word perception. Historically, perception referred to the more or less immediate organization of the sensory stimulation impinging on an organism at a given time. When people were asked in an interview what they believed to be Hubert Humphrey's position on a 1–7 Dove-Hawk scale, neither Hubert Humphrey nor any of the public statements he may have made about the war in Vietnam was physically present at the time. Rather, the individual would have to rely on the cumulative set of impressions and memories built up about Humphrey. Technically, it would be more correct to refer to the answers as placement judgments, estimates, or attributions—but not perceptions (Granberg & Seidel, 1976). That battle for terminological purity has been fought, however, and lost. Thus, I opt here for the broad and now popular usage of the term, political perception.

2. Two of these scales, aid to minorities and aid to blacks, were used with a split sample design, with half of the sample randomly assigned to answer one or the other form. Table 4.1 shows the largest difference occurred on self-placement. People were slightly more liberal, and Dukakis was perceived to be slightly more liberal, when the wording was aid to minorities. Perceptions of Bush, and the Democratic and Republican parties, were not significantly affected by this variation in wording.

3. It should be noted that analyses of political perception have not exclusively used the terminology of social judgment theory. Some political scientists (e.g., Conover & Feldman, 1982; Krosnick, 1988a; Martinez, 1988; Page & Brody, 1972) have chosen to use terms from the psychoanalytic defense mechanisms to refer to essentially the same phenomena as what have been called here assimilation and contrast. Thus, displacement effects are referred to collectively as "rationalization," assimilation as "projection," and contrast as "negative projection." This choice may reflect one's theoretical predilection or it may be arbitrary,

but "negative projection" does seem a bit awkward. This terminological difference is the sort of implicit dispute about which only academicians could (but probably should not) get excited. Some people have felt that the concepts of assimilation and contrast are linked too closely to Sherif's social judgment theory. But it is now common for social scientists to use assimilation and contrast concepts with no reference whatever to Sherif's theory (e.g., Markovsky, 1988; Ottati et al., 1989). There is no question but that assimilation and contrast can be distinguished conceptually (as underestimating and overestimating distance, respectively) in a way that has no necessary linkage to the circumstances under which these displacement effects are predicted to occur under social judgment theory. Moreover, there may be just as close a linkage between projection as a psychological defense mechanism and psychoanalytic theory. (Negative projection appears to be an ad hoc label given to what occurs when people do the opposite of projection.)

Beyond that, it is well to reconsider that in psychoanalytic theory, projection referred to defending one's ego by attributing one's own *negative* qualities to other people. There seems to be little similarity between that concept of projection and how it has been used in the analysis of political perception. Unless one specifies otherwise, it is implied when using the term projection that people do it for the purpose of defending the ego. From what? From acknowledging that I have a certain disagreement with a candidate I happen to prefer? A more parsimonious approach may be that people engage in assimilation and contrast as forms of perceptual distortion, as a means of achieving, maintaining, or restoring cognitive balance. In any event, in practice it can be asserted that those who use the language of psychoanalytic defense mechanisms (rationalization, projection, negative projection) have been studying essentially the same phenomena associated with political perception.

4. Conover and Feldman (1982) reported more assimilation by those who made their decision early in the campaign. It seems likely that the time of decision is a reflection of involvement. However, this could be analyzed in a factorial design in which involvement and time of decision are independent variables. Martinez (1988) reported an analysis indicating that displacement effects increased as involvement increased, as if it were a new finding. This could be done only by failing to cite previous studies that were directly relevant (Granberg & Brent, 1974; Granberg & Seidel, 1976).

5. The sort of stacked analysis summarized in figure 4.6 was devised and executed by my colleague Thad A. Brown.

6. The analytical distinctions and modes of operationalizing concepts in this section emerged out of discussions with my former colleague William G. Jacoby.

David O. Sears

5. Symbolic Politics:
A Socio-Psychological Theory

Human beings are intensely concerned about remote and abstract political symbols, even though the emotional costs they pay and benefits they receive from such involvement are modest. These intense emotions have energized many of history's most devastating social, political, and religious conflicts. Why such intense emotions emerge from situations that often have so little tangible and personal at stake has long been a central puzzle for social scientists. This chapter proposes one psychological approach to the problem.

Political symbols often evoke and mobilize human emotions. Virtually every American war has been fought around such rallying symbols. The Boston Tea Party symbolized the colonials' rebellion against British authority. The Confederacy's attack on Fort Sumter and "Remember the Maine!" were the great rallying symbols for the Civil War and Spanish-American War. The sinking of the Lusitania served the same purpose before the United States entered World War I, as did "the sneak attack on Pearl Harbor" for World War II. Another effort to create the same kind of rallying symbol was the Gulf of Tonkin incident in 1964, which succeeded in mobilizing support in Congress but never in itself galvanized support among the general public. Nonetheless, the Vietnam War had its share of wonderfully symbolic phrases, such as the American army officer's statement that "we had to destroy it [a Vietnamese town] to save it," symbolizing for many the pointlessness of that conflict.

Pictures can serve as evocative symbols. One thinks of the marines raising the American flag on Mt. Suribachi on Iwo Jima, John F. Kennedy, Jr., saluting his father's coffin, Bull Connor's dogs attacking peaceful black demonstrators in Birmingham, Lyndon Johnson lifting his dog by its ears, a tearful young woman kneeling beside a fallen Kent State student, or a Vietnamese officer executing a suspected Viet Cong sympathizer by a bullet to the head.

People can serve as powerful symbols. Jesus, hanging on the cross, is perhaps the most widely known. People as revolutionary symbols are familiar to all of us: Washington, Bolívar, Garibaldi, Lenin, Castro, or Martin Luther King, Jr. People also can symbolize social evils. Marie-Antoinette's supposed "let them eat cake" comment or Nero's fiddling while Rome burned are examples. Adolf Hitler symbolized the Nazi horror. Richard Nixon, perhaps cursed forever by the Herblock cartoon character crawling out of a sewer, symbolized in the Watergate affair, deceptiveness and sleaze for many. Willie Horton, during the 1988 presidential campaign, came to symbolize a whole complex of problems in modern society: the mixture of sexuality and violence in whites' images of black males, and the excessive permissiveness of liberal Democratic crime policy. The villainy of Saddam Hussein stimulated widespread support for a remote war that appeared to many observers to have little direct connection to American interests.

Symbols are particularly useful for distinguishing the bad guys from the good guys. There is the spendthrift Congress ("tax and spend, tax and spend"), the communists, the KKK, Wall Street, drug kingpins, and welfare queens. Or, we have "good Americans," "honest working-class people," "the taxpayers," "senior citizens," or even "the people." We have "flower children," "brothers" and "homeboys" in urban ghettos, "war veterans," and "resistance fighters" (some more credible than others, perhaps, such as the distinction between France in 1943 and Nicaragua in 1983). "Woodstock" symbolized a Rousseauian ideal of peace and brotherhood.

When presented to us, all of these political symbols rivet our attention and evoke strong emotion. Usually, I will argue, it is emotion based on some enduring predisposition rather than on the tangible costs and benefits of the matters to which the symbol refers. This chapter offers a theory of individual psychology, described as a theory of symbolic politics, to explain this phenomenon. It also takes up the major alternatives to a symbolic politics theory in three contexts: the implicit theories of human nature undergirding political theories of democratic systems, the major classic general psychological theories, and contemporary sociopsychological research on information processing.

Democratic Theory and Human Nature

While most works of democratic theory do not self-consciously propose a psychological theory, they invariably rest on some implicit conception of human nature. And these conceptions have varied widely across time. For example, the gradual loosening of the dual holds of the medieval church and feudal society over ordinary people led during the Renaissance, as Albert Hirschman (1985) has noted, to a concern about control of the human passions. By the seventeenth century, European civilization seemed to be disintegrating in religious and factional wars. This led Thomas Hobbes, viewing man as narrowly self-interested, to baleful observations about the "war of all against all" and that human life was "nasty, brutish, and short." Three general solutions were later proposed for the societal problems raised, in the Hobbesian view, by the brutal selfishness of the individual human being in nature. Hobbes's notion was that only a "Leviathan," or omnipotent central authority, could hold society together. A second was the "deliberative government" model developed in England that involved the entire citizenry in a reasoning process of finding common interests as bases for adjudicating conflicts. This notion later emerged as the civic republican or civic virtue tradition in colonial New England in which the citizen's commitment to the community as a whole countered the selfishness of individual passions (Mansbridge, 1990; Reich, 1988). A third view asserted that such debates about the common interest only ignite the passions; they simply polarize people over their own self-serving interpretations of the community's interest. Rather, only calculated *self*-interest could restrain the passions, and indeed self-interest produced the greatest good for all through the invisible hand of the marketplace. The civic republican and rational self-interest traditions were blended by the Federalists and finally codified in the U.S. Constitution, as Mansbridge (1990) has noted.

These debates about homo politicus centered in a surprisingly consensual way on some simple dichotomies of human motivation. The most common dichotomy contrasts interest (selfish or self-interested action) with principle (high-minded action).[1] But interests come in more than one flavor, so pure self-interest is usually further distinguished from the individual's sense of group's interest, as in James Q. Wilson's distinction between material (self-interest), solidary (group interest), and purposive (principles) motives (Wilson & Clark, 1961). The economist Amartya Sen (1977) similarly distinguished egoistic motivation (the focal point of neoclassical economics) from "sympathy" (behavior that helps others with whom we identify) or "commitment" (which is particularly concerned with morals and plays an especially important role in creating public goods and work motivation). Amitai Etzioni (1988) also contrasted self-interest (the rational utility maximizer) and communal anchorage (embedding the individual in close interpersonal and group relationships) from a sense of morality. All of these typologies rest on the same general distinction, then, as Orren (1988, p. 24) has observed: "political research over the last thirty years suggests that personal self-interest, group identifications, and ideological goals all influence thought and action significantly. Most public opinion surveys probe for all three factors . . . with slight variations, these three general categories appear over and over in the social science literature."

The debate between neoclassical economics and civic republicanism yielded one further distinction, however, between self-interest and the public interest. Wilson and Banfield (1964), for example, explicitly contrast self-interested with public-regarding behavior. Public choice theorists passionately believe that self-interest dominates any possible public interest motives (e.g., Tullock, 1976). The description of congressmen's motives similarly center on reelection or on producing good public policy (Fenno, 1973; Mayhew, 1974). Citizens' voting behavior also has been viewed as motivated by self-interest (the voter's "pocketbook") or as being "sociotropic" (the interests of the nation as a whole) (Meehl, 1977; Kinder & Kiewiet, 1979).

Earlier Versions of Symbolic Politics

Others have approached mass politics by focusing on political symbols. In sociology there is the Durkheimian view that rituals and myths serve to unite groups within the society. For example, Gusfield (1963) suggests that in the early twentieth century temperance served as an "emblem of identity" in a diverse society. It has been even more common to contrast symbolic with literal readings of social behavior. The manifest, conventional understanding of social life is depicted as differing greatly from the "real" latent meanings underneath. For example, according to Gusfield (1963), the debate over prohibition was "really" a symbolic struggle between social groups (especially between Protestants and Catholic immigrants) for power and prestige, not an instrumental debate about how to handle substance abuse at an instrumental level (Gusfield & Michalowicz, 1984).

Murray Edelman's Symbolic Politics

The best-known use of the term "symbolic politics" comes from Murray Edelman's work (1964, 1971). His starting point is the assumption that the mass public consists largely of spectators acquiescent to the abstract and remote passing parade of political symbols but who are anxious about a threatening, complex world. Ordinary citizens, in his view, have only unstable and inconsistent political preferences, not firm ideological commitments that would resist the blandishments of elites. Political myth and ritual provide them with symbolic reassurance. Organized interest groups, on the other hand, do use politics instrumentally to directly and methodically maneuver for tangible benefits. Elites thus can easily manipulate mass publics by providing tension-reducing symbols (such as a political enemy, identification with a group, or attachment to a leader), which divert the public's energies into fruitless mass violence or political quiescence, such actions facilitating the interests of the elites. Though politics is apparently centered on tangible outcomes, then, it "really" only provides symbolic reassurance to the ordinary mass publics.

Edelman was more interested in developing a theory of politics than a psychological theory, but his ideas embody six key psychological propositions.

1. Crisis is ubiquitous, so people perceive threat and experience anxiety constantly. As with other mass society theories, most notably Erich Fromm's, it begins with a modern (post-Industrial Revolution) public that is alienated, anomic, socially isolated, and despairing. Its anxiety stems from continuous threats in a dangerous world, from the world's complexity, ambiguity, and novelty, and from a feeling that people cannot influence their own worlds. This endless anxiety produces a need for placation and reassurance to quiet resentments and doubts, and it leads to an "attachment to reassuring abstract symbols rather than to one's own efforts" (1964, p. 76).

2. The real world is so ambiguous and complex that people develop ambivalence toward political objects rather than real preferences (as in Converse's, 1970, notion of "non-attitudes"), and so are easily persuaded. This ambivalence makes them readily mobilizable by government and other elites.

3. Politics is a parade of abstract and remote symbols invested with passion. The human being is a symbolizing creature, one who especially creates and changes common meanings. Symbols are socially constructed, not inherent in political realities themselves, and are projections of ordinary people's wishes, hopes, fears, and fantasies.

4. Myth and ritual give meaning to the anxious person's life and the confusing events around him, thereby providing contentment and reassurance. Edelman's particular contribution has been to develop the realm of metaphors, myths, ritual, language, and other symbols as vehicles by which

elites manipulate the masses. Myths externalize inner tensions and impulses; metaphors simplify and give familiar meaning to the unknown, new, and remote; engagement in collective action reduces anxiety; and various forms of political language (such as hortatory, legal, administrative, or bargaining) give reassurance (see Edelman, 1978).

5. The complicated empirical world is therefore replaced by a few simple and archetypical myths, such as those that evoke enemies or an out-group, those that describe a benevolent leader who can save people from danger, those which assert that a nation/group can achieve victory if it will work and obey its leaders, those which contend that citizens' democratic participation (such as voting) controls government, those that public policy actually solves crises or public problems, and those which contend that incumbents actually are in control of events.

6. The distinction between self-interest and symbolic politics is central to Edelman's work. At a manifest level, politics centers on action to get specific, tangible benefits for groups, but the "real" nature of politics is symbolic. Nevertheless, in certain key respects people are depicted as acting with self-interest; most obviously, organized interest groups try to manipulate the government to serve their own interests.[2]

Empirical Research on Political Behavior

A competing set of ideas was developed contemporaneously by more empirically oriented survey researchers and psychologists. Several disparate lines of work have yielded findings that share the view that ordinary citizens' attitudes are organized by long-standing personal predispositions. The Columbia school focused on demographic predispositions (Lazarsfeld et al., 1948), primary group influence (Berelson, Lazarsfeld, & McPhee, 1954), and the reinforcement of predispositions by mass media communications messages (Klapper, 1960). The later "Michigan model" of voting behavior shared this emphasis on the role of predispositions: the individual acquired a standing party identification early in life, which influenced responses to election campaigns in adulthood (Campbell et al., 1960). Other work argued that such influential, long-standing attitudinal predispositions were acquired in preadult political socialization (Hyman, 1959; Easton & Dennis, 1969).

A subsequent line of research contrasted self-interest and symbolic politics as competing motives in mass politics. "Self-interest" was defined conceptually in terms of the impact of policy proposals or candidacies on the individual's personal life. Here, symbolic politics focused on the influence of long-standing symbolic predispositions (party identification, political ideology, racial prejudice). In a large number of studies, self-interest had much less influence on policy and candidate preferences than did long-standing predispositions (see Sears, Lau, Tyler, & Allen, 1980; Sears & Funk, 1991).[3]

The distinction between self-interest and symbolic politics resembles several other views that have driven empirical research. "Position issues," involving "self-interest of a relatively direct kind," have been distinguished from "style issues," involving "self-expression of a rather indirect, projective kind" (Berelson, Lazarsfeld, & McPhee, 1954, p. 184); "class politics," which revolves around simple economic issues of self-interest or group interest, from "status politics," which is based on the relative positions of individuals or groups (Bell, 1963); self-interest from ideology, e.g., "the pattern of responses to . . . domestic issues is best understood if we discard our notions of ideology and think rather in terms of primitive self-interest" (Campbell et al., 1960, p. 205; also see Bauer, Pool, & Dexter, 1963);[4] the "instrumental" functions of attitudes (based on the direct costs and benefits of the attitude object to the individual) from the symbolic (or "value-expressive") function (when the attitude becomes a means for expressing values and social identity; see Herek, 1986; Prentice, 1987).

The symbolic politics theory advanced by Edelman is similar in several respects to the theories of these political behavior researchers. In general, they view the ordinary person as relatively poorly informed about politics, as driven more by emotion than by cognition (so that neither requires a cognitive theory of information processing), and as often having inconsistent, concrete, unstable, or "morselized" political attitudes (Lane, 1962; Converse, 1964). However, the two views do diverge in one major respect. Edelman, like other mass society theorists, sees a rootless and normless mob that is vulnerable to the latest emotional pleas and is fundamentally unpredictable. But the central insight of some standing predispositions in research on political behavior points to the individual as responding in a more systematic and internally directed way to new information. In this view, party identification is stable, group loyalties or ethnic prejudices are strong, and voters are depicted as relatively resistant to change; media and election campaigns alike tend mainly to reinforce predispositions. So the voter is generally predictable (Campbell et al., 1960; Kelley & Mirer, 1974).

In short, the basic ideas described here as symbolic politics evolved out of two main sources: a radical critique of mass politics in democratic society, focusing on the role of symbols in manipulating the public; and empirically based analyses of public opinion and voting behavior that mirror survey data. The common elements form a distinctive theory of political psychology, though not usually explicitly recognized as such.

A Psychological Theory of Symbolic Politics

Let us begin with the "simple theory of symbolic politics" as first proposed (Sears, Huddy, & Schaffer, 1986) before adding more complex and recent elements.[5] This theory holds that people acquire stable affective responses to particular symbols through a process of classical conditioning, which occurs most crucially at a relatively early age. These learned dispositions may or may not persist through adult life, but the strongest—called "symbolic predispositions"—do. The most important of these predispositions in American politics include party identification, political ideology, and racial prejudice. Later in life, people respond to the daily flow of political attitude objects consistent with these standing predispositions. Any given attitude object is composed of one or more symbolic elements, and each conveys some meaning to the individual.[6] Attitudes toward the object as a whole reflect some combination of the affects previously conditioned to the specific symbols included in it. For example, attitudes toward "forced busing to integrate whites and blacks" would depend on affects toward such symbols as "force," "busing," "integration," "whites," and "blacks."

The adult individual, then, has numerous predispositions—learned affective responses that have been conditioned to specific symbols. When these symbols become salient later on, they should evoke consistent evaluations through a process of "transfer of affect," or cognitive consistency (see Lorge, 1936; Osgood & Tannenbaum, 1955).[7] It is assumed that people simply transfer affects from one symbol to another when they are linked to one another. As a result, the symbolic politics process is characterized by generally unthinking, reflexive, affective responses to remote attitude objects rather than by calculations of probable costs and benefits (whether personal or not). Also, since political attitudes reflect the affects previously conditioned to the specific symbols included in the attitude object, a simple symbolic politics theory suggests that affects are closely tied to the manifest symbolic content of a particular attitude object, without much generalization to manifestly dissimilar symbols or consideration of latent meanings (see Sears, Huddy, & Schaffer, 1986; Sears & Huddy, 1991).

A considerable volume of empirical research has been done using this framework, but a typical study should give its general flavor (Sears, Lau, Tyler, & Allen, 1980). A national survey of adults generated the data. The dependent variables were attitudes toward major policy issues (unemployment, national health insurance, busing, and law and order), while the predictors were the major symbolic predispositions (party identification, ideology, and racial attitudes) and indicators of personal self-interest. The symbolic predispositions had strong effects, while self-interest had virtually none.

While the data were consistent with the overall theory, they do not themselves reveal much about the symbolic politics process. Rather, the authors "simply appeal to the vast literatures on the preadult acquisition of partisanship, social values, and racial prejudice, on the one hand, and on cognitive consistency pressures on the other, for evidence of it" (p. 681). Subsequent work has looked more closely at the dynamics of long-term persistence of symbolic predispositions (Sears, 1983, 1989) and at those of symbolic processing (Sears & Huddy, 1991; Sears et al., 1986). This work will be discussed further at the appropriate time.

There are seven key propositions in the theory, then, which will be discussed in turn.

(1) Attitudinal predispositions can be identified that have a major impact on the adult's evaluation of political attitude objects. The strongest of these are described as "symbolic predispositions."

(2) Symbolic predispositions are strong attitudes normally acquired through classical conditioning in early life (though not necessarily in the preadult years). Their strength is dependent on a variety of factors, most prominently the frequency of exposure of pairing the political symbol with the evaluation in question and the consistency of the evaluations to which the individual is exposed later in life.

(3) These symbolic predispositions remain relatively stable through adult life.

(4) The symbolic meaning of an attitude object should influence evaluations of it.

(5) The particular symbols contained in an attitude object determine which predisposition it evokes. And if the symbolic meaning of the object changes, so may the specific predisposition that is evoked.

(6) The predisposition evoked by a particular attitude object depends on the semantic similarity between its symbolic meaning and specific predisposition.

(7) The process by which symbols evoke predispositions ("symbolic

processing") is automatic and affective. Among other things, cost-benefit calculations should play a relatively modest role.

Symbolic Predispositions

The core of the symbolic politics process is that standing learned predispositions are evoked by political symbols in the current informational environment. Most of the relevant research has concerned the origins, nature, and effects of these predispositions, with particular attention given to symbolic predispositions. These predispositions represent one end of a continuum of attitudes varying in affective strength; at the other end of this continuum, presumably, are "nonattitudes" that are highly unstable, unrelated to other attitudes, and unlikely to influence other preferences (Converse, 1970). They can be identified using three criteria: (1) of all the individual's attitudes, they are the most stable over time (stability); (2) they yield the most consistent responses over similar attitude objects (constraint); and (3) they are the most influential over attitudes toward other objects (power) (see Sears, 1969). Racial prejudice is a good example. It is relatively stable over time (Converse & Markus, 1979; Sears, 1983), relatively consistent over racially relevant areas such as schools, jobs, and housing (Sears, 1988), and is powerful in determining preferences toward racial policies and black candidates (Sears & Kosterman, 1991).

Much research has documented the influence of such predispositions over other political attitudes. For example, policy and candidate preferences often have been shown to be influenced by standing party identification (e.g., Campbell et al., 1960), social values (Feldman, 1988), racial attitudes (Sears, 1988), and antagonisms toward such groups as communists, Nazis, and the KKK (Sullivan, Piereson, & Marcus, 1982). Our own work has tested this impact of symbolic predispositions in a large number of studies: whites' racial attitudes influence opposition to busing (e.g., Kinder & Sears, 1981; Sears & Allen, 1984; Sears, Hensler, & Speer, 1979; Sears et al., 1980), affirmative action (Jessor, 1988; Sears & Kosterman, 1991), and black electoral candidates (Kinder & Sears, 1981; Sears, Citrin, & Kosterman, 1987); political ideology, opposition to communism, and support for the military influenced support for the Vietnam War (Lau, Brown, & Sears, 1978); party identification, ideology, and racial attitudes influenced support for the California tax revolt (Sears & Citrin, 1985); and basic values activated by symbols of injustice, inequity, or immorality produced mass protests (Sears & Citrin, 1985; Sears & McConahay, 1973).

The second proposition is that such symbolic predispositions are acquired relatively early in life. Extensive research on political socialization has investigated children's and adolescents' early affective responses to such symbols as the flag, the president, stigmatized racial groups, and the political parties (e.g., Easton & Dennis, 1969; Hyman, 1959; Katz, 1976). This early learning presumably yields such predispositions as party identification, racial prejudices, ethnic identities, basic values, nationalism, and attachment to various symbols of the nation and regime.

The third proposition is that these predispositions that are acquired early persist through life. Researchers on political socialization believed that childhood and early adolescent experiences were formative (Easton & Dennis, 1969; Hyman, 1959), whereas Mannheim (1952) pinpointed late adolescence as a critical period for the acquisition of lasting attitudes. Such theorizing led to the formulation of several alternative models of attitude change (and susceptibility to change) across a life span (Alwin, 1991; Sears, 1975, 1983). The question of attitudinal persistence during a lifetime has been extensively investigated, with research indicating support for both the "persistence" and the "impressionable years" viewpoints (see Sears, 1989, for a review; also Alwin & Krosnick, 1988; Converse & Markus, 1979; Sears, 1983). Especially interesting recent work has been done on the conditions for long-term attitude stability (Niemi & Jennings, 1991; Sears, Zucker, & Funk, 1992), on differences in persistence across attitude objects (Krosnick, 1991), and on socialization experiences later in life (Sigel, 1989).

At this point it would be useful to contrast the symbolic politics view with other extant theories about such predispositions. To reiterate, the symbolic politics view holds that most people in any mass public have some symbolic predispositions—attitudes that are stable, consistent, and powerful. It is likely that some of these attitudes are widespread among the public. But many other attitudes are much less crystallized, and at the extreme it is likely that a large number of attitude objects with which elites are preoccupied attract only "nonattitudes" in most members of the public.

This view is to be distinguished from the Converse (1970) "black and white model," which holds that most people respond to issue questions in a quasirandom fashion, with only a minority responding with a true and stable attitude.[8] At the other extreme, this view might be contrasted with "measurement error theory" (Zaller & Feldman, 1992), which holds that most people do have true attitudes that are relatively stable over time, though that stability is often empirically underestimated because of measurement error (Achen, 1975; Krosnick, 1991). From the perspective of a symbolic politics theory, the "black and white" theory both exaggerates the contrast between highly crystallized ("true") attitudes and poorly crystallized ones ("nonattitudes") and underestimates the role of the former, while the "measurement error" theory overestimates the stability and consistency of poorly crystallized attitudes.

A third, more recent approach might be called "construct sampling theory," as proposed separately in somewhat different forms by Zaller and Feldman (1992) and by Kinder and Nelson (1990). This approach proceeds from the assumption that people are often confused about the multiple considerations that are relevant to public policy. Because of this confusion, they do not have a fixed position or true attitude. Rather, they have a miscellaneous collection of often conflicting and always confusing separate ideas, called "considerations" by Zaller and Feldman and "raw ingredients" by Kinder and Nelson. When called on to express an opinion, people must construct a response out of these basic elements. The cognitive theory lying behind this view is that memory is a bin with many alternative constructs; long-term storage is huge, but short-term recall is small, so retrieval depends to some extent on chance and on recency of activation. As a consequence, when people are asked for an opinion, they respond off the "top of their head," to use the term applied by Taylor and Fiske (1978). The expressed opinion reflects which aspects come to mind at the moment, not a single "true attitude" or even a representative sampling of the full repertoire of the individual's relevant cognitive constructs. In this "construct sampling" theory, the constructs that are sampled are genuine beliefs, even though they may not be consistent with each other, and the same constructs are not likely to be evoked stably over time. But from the perspective of a symbolic politics theory, construct sampling underestimates the stability and consistency of highly crystallized attitudes. We will return to this question.

Symbolic Meaning

Only recently has attention begun to be devoted to the role of the evoking political symbols. Our fourth proposition suggests that symbolic meaning influences evaluations of the attitude object. And changes in symbolic meaning should do so as well. The symbols contained in the object can vary cross-sectionally among individuals at one point in time, or longitudinally within individuals over time. The effects of changes in symbolic meaning have been investigated in a number of contexts.

At the simplest level, naturalistic wording variations can show dramatic effects on evaluations of public policy, though they do not always do so. Support for intervention in the Korean War was considerably greater when it was described as intended "to stop the communist invasion of South Korea" than when it was simply described as "the war in Korea" (Mueller, 1973). Most people strongly oppose spending for "welfare" but support "helping the poor," "public assistance programs to the elderly and the disabled," and programs "for low-income families with dependent children," which together make up a major portion of welfare spending (see Sears & Citrin, 1985; Smith, 1987). Whites overwhelmingly oppose "busing" but support "racial integration of the schools" (Schuman, Steeh, & Bobo, 1985; Sears et al., 1979). In each case the differences may be caused by a variety of factors, but it seems likely that the presence of affectively loaded symbols such as "communists," "welfare," race, or minority cultures is critical.

Still, the symbolic politics view suggests some subtler effects of symbolic meaning, of which three might be mentioned here. First, most attitude objects contain multiple symbols. In the symbolic politics view, each such symbol should evoke the specific evaluation associated with it, with overall evaluation of the full attitude object being some simple function of those individual evaluations (such as a simple weighted average of them; see Anderson, 1971). For example, in one study, preadolescents' support for communists' civil liberties were predicted by evaluations of the general principle of free speech and of communism (Zellman & Sears, 1971). Whites' attitudes toward racial policies are a joint function of their racial attitudes and race-neutral predispositions (Sears & Kosterman, 1991; Sears et al., 1979; Sears et al., 1986). Similarly, whites' opposition to open housing for minorities is a joint function of evaluations of the minority group in question and evaluations of government-enforced fair housing in general (Schuman & Bobo, 1988).

A second point concerns the level of abstraction of political symbols. The conventional wisdom in political science and social psychology has been that abstract attitude objects are processed differently from concrete ones. Converse (1964) argued that relatively few voters possessed abstract ideological conceptualizations that would permit the deduction of specific policy attitudes; that is, few had "vertically constrained" belief systems in which abstract idea elements constrained concrete elements. On the other hand, deductive hierarchical structures play a more prominent role in contemporary social psychology as vehicles by which "cognitive misers" can minimize psychologically costly information-processing efforts. Such general-to-specific reasoning has been called "top-down" or "theory-driven" processing and is usually represented by a hierarchical structure in which abstract beliefs influence responses to more specific stimuli (Fiske & Taylor, 1991; Hurwitz & Peffley, 1987).

The simple symbolic politics view is considerably different from either of these viewpoints. It assumes that processing of political symbols depends on the evaluations associated with them, not the symbol's level of abstraction. Several findings indicate that political symbols presented at different levels of abstraction but referring to the same underlying reality do draw different responses, but this occurs because of differences in their manifest contents (and, presumably, the evaluations associated with them), not because of differences in abstraction. For example, most Americans prefer, in the abstract, "less government" to "more government." On the other hand, a large majority also consistently prefer that government services in specific areas (such as schools, police, public health, etc.) be maintained at least at current levels, not cut. But there is no evidence that these two sets of attitude objects are processed very differently, despite the difference in levels of abstraction. In one extensive study, both sets of attitude objects were explained by the same pre-dispositions (party identification, ideology, and racial attitudes), and both had similar effects on support for tax cuts (Sears & Citrin, 1985). A simple symbolic politics theory would explain the less favorable evaluation of the more abstract object as principally because of the different manifest symbolic content presented at each level of abstraction (and the different conditioned associations to those different symbols), not to the difference in level of abstraction per se (also see Sears et al., 1986).

A third case in point concerns social groups as attitude objects. Are they treated psychologically like any other political symbols? Much social science theory holds that they are not, that they have special meaning. For example, the conventional wisdom in social psychology has been that group identity is psychologically central to the individual, with self-esteem partially dependent on perceiving one's own group as superior to other groups (Tajfel, 1983). Similarly, a "sense of group position" is thought likely to generate racial prejudice when the dominant group feels threatened by other groups (Blumer, 1958). And groups are thought to be the most "central" of political attitude objects, so that political parties are perceived in terms of which groups they favor or oppose, voters adopting "ideologies by proxy" from the beliefs of their own groups, thus providing the psychological foundation for ego-involved attitudes (Bobo, 1983; Campbell et al., 1960; Converse, 1964; Sherif & Cantril, 1947). Similarly, group interest is said to be a powerful determinant of one's political preferences. But why it should be is perhaps a different matter. On the one hand, group interest may simply reflect the interdependence of the self's outcomes with the group's outcomes and behave like a variant of self-interest. The symbolic politics view, in contrast, is that a group represents an attitude object like any other and therefore evokes affective responses in the same manner. Groups may behave like other political symbols, mainly evoking symbolic predispositions (as in patriotism or nationalism or class solidarity), and they therefore may be best described in terms of symbolic politics (see Conover, 1988; Jessor, 1988; Sears, 1988). By this view, there is no fundamental difference in the processing of "Nazis," "Hitler," or "the Holocaust," or between "the middle class," "whites," "Ronald Reagan," or "tax cuts." A group symbol, then, would be just another attitude object with an evaluative loading.

What kinds of data are generated by the symbolic politics theory of group objects? Group evaluations should influence responses to specifically group-relevant policies and candidates. For example, people's willingness to extend civil liberties to a group depends on their evaluations of the group (Stouffer, 1955; Sullivan et al., 1982). But more than that, support for policies or candidacies associated with a particular group should be influenced specifically by evaluations of that group and not of other groups. So whites' attitudes toward racial policies and black candidates are influenced by their evaluations of blacks but not of whites (Sears & Kosterman, 1991), and non-Hispanics' attitudes toward bilingual education are influenced by evaluations of Hispanics (but not of other minorities or whites; Sears & Huddy, 1991). Similarly, racial equality values influence support for racial policies, and gender equality values influence support for gender policies but neither set of values is influenced by issues affecting the other group (Sears, Huddy, & Schaffer, 1986).

Classical analyses of group influence in mass politics add other variables but usually can be interpreted in a simple symbolic politics framework. For example, analyses of labor union or religious group influence on voting add roles for group identification and clarity of the group's political norms (Campbell et al., 1960; Converse et al., 1963). But group identification can be interpreted as mainly reflecting evaluation of the group (see Hovland, Janis, & Kelley, 1953).

The simple symbolic politics approach would prove insufficient, however, when motivational variables such as perceived outcome-interdependence of the self with the group play an important role beyond the effects of evaluations of the group symbol as a pure attitude object (Sears & Kinder, 1985; Jessor, 1988). For example, the symbolic politics approach would not explain white males' opposition to affirmative action policies if it were based in perceptions that white males themselves (or their group) were unfairly disadvantaged by them. Similarly, this approach would not explain social identity theory's "in-group bias" if it were based on the individual's feelings of self-esteem about social identity as a group member. Nor would it explain racial prejudice if based in the superiority feelings that Blumer (1958) and Sidanius and Pratto (1991) ascribe to socially dominant groups.

Changing Symbolic Meaning

An even less thoroughly investigated issue concerns the proposition that the symbolic meaning of an attitude object influences not only the evaluation of the object, but *which* predisposition is evoked.

Media framing. The symbolic meaning of a political attitude object may vary in how it is represented in the environment of communication. Gamson and Modigliani (1987) have described this meaning in terms of variations in the "framing" of an issue. Policy issues, they say, are always contested in a symbolic arena by groups of activists who try to give their own meaning to the issue. Each faction presents its case in terms of packages of ideas, within which is embedded a dominant frame—that is, a central organizing idea or story line, implying a particular policy alternative. The frame is displayed in "signature elements" that invoke the whole package through condensing symbols. Which frame dominates in the communications media may change over time as the political battle goes on. The persuasive success of any given frame depends on the "cultural resonances" or larger cultural themes it invokes. All this can be put in the language of symbolic politics: each frame presents a different symbolic meaning of the attitude object, including different symbolic elements, and its relative success depends on the symbolic predispositions it evokes.

Gamson and Modigliani (1987) empirical analysis traces changes over time in the dominant framing of the issue of affirmative action. "Remedial action" dominated in the 1960s and early 1970s, promoted by civil rights advocates who contended that blacks needed to be given extra help because past discrimination had handicapped them in economic competition. This approach appealed to antiracist, egalitarian themes. Over time, conservatives responded with a "no preferential treatment" frame, arguing that affirmative action gave minorities preferential treatment; this response appealed to the core American value of self-reliance. Finally, during the 1980s the "reverse discrimination" frame, in which non-minorities and males were depicted as discriminated against by affirmative action policies, became dominant. This development continued the self-reliance theme but added an appeal to egalitarianism.

Evoking new predispositions? Do changes in symbolic meaning in fact alter which predispositions are evoked? Certainly very different attitude objects do evoke different predispositions: "busing" evokes racial attitudes, while the "Korean War" evoked anticommunism. But the more critical implication is that changing the symbolic meaning of any *given* attitude object can evoke a new set of predispositions, as in Asch's observation that attitude change may result from "a change in the object of judgment, rather than in the judgment of the object" (1940, p. 458). For example, abortion can symbolize women's freedom of choice and evoke attitudes toward feminism and gender equality. Or it can symbolize murder of an unborn child and evoke attitudes toward that belief. This proposition could explain the effects of meaning variations on public opinion. A symbol like "choice" might evoke predispositions that boost support for abortion, while "murder" obviously would evoke much less helpful predispositions.

Evidence of various kinds that alters the symbolic meaning of an issue does indeed influence which predispositions it elicits. It has often been observed that at any given time the most salient political issues have the greatest weight in overall attitudes. For example, "important" issues have disproportionate weight in the voting decision (Krosnick, 1988; RePass, 1971). Making a single issue salient in a news broadcast has an "agenda-setting" effect, giving that issue greater weight over viewers' evaluations of presidential performance (Iyengar & Kinder, 1985). Analogously, changes over time in the salience of different issues influences their relative weights in voting decisions, as indicated by the importance of religion in the 1960 presidential election, civil rights in 1964, and foreign policy in 1980 and 1984 (Aldrich, Sullivan, & Borgida, 1989; Converse, Campbell, Miller, & Stokes, 1961; Converse, Clausen, & Miller, 1965). As the controversy about U.S. intervention in Central America mounted through the 1980s, that issue played an increasing role in the public's evaluations of President Reagan (Krosnick & Kinder, 1990).

Framing a particular issue in different ways also can activate different predispositions. Presenting bilingual education in terms of maintaining minority cultures (which, incidentally, generates more opposition to it among non-Hispanics; Sears & Huddy, 1991), as opposed to describing it as helping to promote English-language proficiency, enhances the influence of symbolic racism and nationalism over evaluations of bilingual education's effectiveness. Framing affirmative action as "reverse discrimination" evokes individualistic values, while framing it as "unfair advantage for minorities" evokes inegalitarian values (although in this case without influencing overall support for it; see Kinder & Sanders, 1990). Attitudes toward "helping the poor" are explained better by support for redistributive actions of government than are attitudes toward "welfare" (and the latter is much less popular; see Smith, 1987).

Yet variations in symbolic meaning do not always alter which predisposition is evoked. A political rose may sometimes be a rose by any other name, and the public may sniff it out accordingly. Various symbolic meanings of a particular attitude object simply may trigger the same underlying attitudinal dimension, consistent with the traditional definition of attitudes as *generalized* dispositions to respond to an object. A number of empirical examples can be cited for this point as well. Both "busing" and federal government action to enforce school integration so obviously focus on race that they evoke much the same racial attitudes, despite some other differences in symbolic meaning (Sears et al., 1979). Similarly, racial attitudes had much the same effect on evaluations of welfare and helping the poor (Smith, 1987) and on opposition to affirmative action whether framed as reverse discrimination or as unfair advantage (Kinder & Sanders, 1990). As already noted in our study of the California tax revolt, attitudes toward both "big government" and spending in specific service areas were explained by about the same mix of party identification, ideology, and racial attitudes (Sears & Citrin, 1985). In another series of comparisons, Kinder and Nelson (1990) found that framing variations did alter which predispositions best accounted for policy attitudes in some cases but not in many others. The authors concluded that frames matter "in locally sensible ways" but offered no general theory about it.

Matching predisposition to symbolic meaning. One can find, then, evidence consistent with the proposition that meaning variations affect which predisposition is evoked as well as evidence inconsistent with it. We need, therefore, to turn to the conditions that determine one or the other outcome. The proposition offered by a "simple symbolic politics theory" is that a particular predisposition will be evoked almost automatically in a template-matching fashion by an attitude object if the attitude objects are manifestly similar (Sears, Huddy, & Schaffer, 1986). For example, a black leader such as Jesse Jackson who forcefully advocates blacks' interests should readily evoke racial attitudes because they match the manifest content of the attitude object. At the other extreme, an attitude object should be unlikely to evoke a predisposition that is not at all similar to it; in other words, racial attitudes are not likely to be evoked by a proposal to ban offshore oil drilling.

However, this simple matching theory does not explain why political symbols sometimes evoke very dissimilar predispositions. For example, law-and-order issues such as judicial permissiveness or the death penalty frequently evoke racial attitudes, even though their manifest content is not explicitly racial (see Sears et al., 1980). To explain such findings requires the additional assumption that attitude objects can evoke dissimilar predispositions automatically when the individual has a belief system linking the two; i.e., when the similarity is only latent, not manifest (Sears, Huddy, & Schaffer, 1986).[9]

When these linking belief systems are broadly consensual, the symbol should elicit the predisposition just as universally as if the two were manifestly similar. Law-and-order issues presumably evoke whites' racial attitudes because so many people link them cognitively. In such cases almost everyone recognizes that the political rose is a political rose, and they respond appropriately. With manifest or consensual symbol predisposition similarity, then, the relevant predisposition should be evoked by the attitude object no matter what its particular symbolic meaning.

Widespread change of meaning effects should therefore be most likely to occur with latent similarity and no consensual linking belief systems. In such cases, symbolic meaning varies across members of the public, and consequently so does the predisposition normally evoked by the attitude object. But forcefully framing the issue in terms of a particular symbolic meaning could induce more uniformity on its meaning and on a belief system linking it to a particular predisposition. For example, the Japanese attack of Pearl Harbor presumably had the effect of coalescing Americans' diverse understandings of Japan around symbols associated with a "sneak attack," linking them consensually to hatred for national enemies.

By this reasoning, the cognitive match between symbolic meaning and predisposition is the key factor determining when symbolic meaning influences which predisposition is evoked. Variations in symbolic meaning should influence the evocation of predispositions with latent, nonconsensual similarity to the attitude object.[10]

We tested this conceptual analysis in our study of non-Hispanics' opinions about bilingual education (Sears & Huddy, 1991). As already noted, bilingual education has at least two common symbolic meanings: "cultural maintenance," which stresses English-language skills while also maintaining native-language skills, and "English as a second language" (ESL), which provides immersion in English with little use of the child's native language. Either way, bilingual education's manifest content concerns education and languages, so it should evoke attitudes toward foreign language instruction regardless of its symbolic meaning. The latent consensual content of bilingual education (as revealed in the perceptions of a majority of the public) is that it most often involves Spanish and that teaching foreign languages is an educational "frill." So the issue should evoke attitudes toward Hispanics and toward spending on educational frills regardless of symbolic meaning. The content of bilingual education's cultural maintenance variant emphasizes preservation of native languages over the "melting pot," so it should evoke attitudes toward minorities, immigrants, and the liberal Democratic social agenda more generally. The ESL variant, on the other hand, emphasizes simple educational practice, so it would seem more likely to evoke attitudes toward education.

To test these hypotheses, variations in symbolic meaning were manipulated experimentally by presenting each respondent in a national probability sample of non-Hispanics with one or the other version of bilingual education. As expected, the manifestly similar or latent/consensual predispositions were evoked at about the same level regardless of symbolic meanings. Anti-Hispanic affect and spending on foreign language instruction or other educational "frills" were correlated with attitudes toward bilingual education at the same level in both experimental conditions. In contrast, variations in symbolic meaning did affect the evocation of predispositions with only latent, nonconsensual similarity to bilingual education as a whole. Racial attitudes, partisan preferences, and traditional social values were correlated significantly with opposition to cultural maintenance but not with opposition to ESL. In short, symbol predisposition similarity was the key determinant of symbolic meaning effects: symbolic meaning affected the evocation of predispositions linked to the issue in latent but nonconsensual fashion, but not that of manifestly and/or consensually similar predispositions.[11]

Symbolic Processing

The theory of symbolic politics also describes a distinctive mode of information processing, which might be called "symbolic processing."

Its most notable characteristics are that it proceeds in terms of strong affective responses to political symbols. When we hear the word "democracy," we have a strong and immediate positive affect; when we encounter the symbol "Nazi," we have a strong and immediate negative response. Affect is central to this process, then, since political symbols are assumed to evoke strong emotions in the individual.[12]

It has long been recognized that evaluation is central to such core phenomena of social psychology as social perception, interpersonal attraction, attitudes, and prejudice. Early experiments on impression formation showed that the warm-cold dimension is an especially "central" dimension of person perception (Asch, 1946; Kelley, 1950). Later, Osgood, Suci, and Tannenbaum (1957) demonstrated that evaluation was the central dimension of meaning in a wide variety of areas of life; its importance was in no way limited to person perception. In the 1980s, Zajonc (1980, 1984) has proposed that affect may be a separate system altogether from cognition. For Zajonc, too, that is, evaluation is a universal component of all perception and meaning. But beyond that, affect is primary, basic, inescapable, irrevocable, difficult to verbalize, may well not depend on cognition, and may be distinctly separate from content or knowledge. Affective reactions are primary; they do not depend on prior cognitive appraisals, and indeed they may become completely separated from the content on which they were originally based, but then they may be cognitively justified. In this sense, affect does not depend on deliberate, rational, or conscious thought, and it may not even depend on unconscious mental activity.[13]

A contemporary illustration of affectively driven symbolic processing is "hot button" political advertising. Political campaigns devote much of their attention to trying to discover what issues or symbols evoke an emotional response; that is, what hits voters' hot buttons. The assumption is, as one specialist put it, "voting is a matter of the heart, what you *feel* about someone, rather than a matter of the mind. . . . [The mind] takes what the heart feels, and interprets it" (Diamond & Bates, 1984, p. 316). Certainly the hot button formula of many modern political ads, such as LBJ's "Daisy" television spot, Bush's "revolving-door justice" spot, or Reagan's "morning in America" ads, aim to evoke gut-level, affective responses (Kosterman, 1991).

A second aspect of symbolic processing is that it is cumulative and rapidly becomes detached from its informational origins. This parallels the notion of "on-line processing" (as opposed to "memory-based processing"; see Lodge, McGraw, & Stroh, 1989). As relevant information is encountered, the individual makes an evaluative judgment and then essentially keeps only a running tally, simply retrieving and updating that summary evaluation with later information but forgetting the actual pieces of evidence that contributed to it. Indeed, there is much evidence from experimental studies of impressions and attitudes that affective change is generally correlated only weakly with memory for the information that originally induced the change (see Anderson & Hubert, 1963; Fiske & Taylor, 1991).

Third, symbolic processing involves a relatively swift, reflexive, automatic triggering of an appropriate predisposition by a political symbol, guided by pressures toward affective consistency (Lorge, 1936; Osgood & Tannenbaum, 1955). In general, these consistency pressures are assumed to operate quickly and nondeliberatively. Consistent with this view, much of our research has shown that rational calculations of self-interest are weak forces in mass politics (Sears & Funk, 1991).

Finally, such consistency pressures tend to operate fairly narrowly and locally; indeed, one of the lessons of research on cognitive consistency was that people have a substantial tolerance for distant, indirect, general, or diffuse inconsistencies (see Abelson et al., 1968; Converse, 1964). As a result, any given symbol is not likely to evoke predispositions that are only distantly relevant to them. And the individual must be confronted with the association of the elements to induce pressure toward consistency; in the absence of such confrontation, pressures toward consistency tend to be weak.

Alternative Psychological Theories

The theory of symbolic politics deals with familiar phenomena, and many of the relevant data have been used to test other theories. Hopefully, one advantage of this theory lies in its scope; it purports to organize much evidence on mass attitudes with a limited set of assumptions. A second advantage is that it focuses attention on a particular process that is central to mass politics. The phenomena with which competing theories deal best are perhaps more peripheral or of more limited applicability. To illustrate, let me turn to other theories commonly used to explain mass political behavior. These theories are not mutually exclusive, or course. But they do differ at least in emphasis and in which theory best captures a particular phenomenon.

Motivational Theories

Motivational theories hold that attitudes are adopted because they fulfill the needs of the individual.[14] As noted, the most familiar motivational theory focuses on economic self-interest: political attitudes reflect individuals' efforts to maximize their own material well-being (see Citrin & Green, 1990; Mansbridge, 1990; Sears & Funk, 1991). This makes three separable assumptions: human behavior is selfishly motivated; it is focused on material goods in particular; and decision-making is rational within the constraints of available information.

A variant of this theory is that people try to maximize their own group interests, quite aside from their egoistic motives. For example, realistic group conflict theory suggests that ethnocentrism stems from intergroup competition over scarce resources (Bobo, 1988; LeVine & Campbell, 1972). Relative deprivation theory adds a second variant, expanding interests to include perceived personal deprivations relative to others, whether egoistic or fraternal (Runciman, 1966). A third variant focuses on the need for status rather than for material well-being. Some political movements may recruit people whose status has been threatened (e.g., Bell, 1963). Blumer (1958) held that people are motivated by protecting a "sense of group position," and Sidanius and Pratto (1991) contend that people are motivated by a need for "social dominance." Social identity theory (Tajfel, 1982b) has similarly suggested that intergroup competition arises partly from a need for a high-status group identity.

Attitudes also may serve the need for social adjustment, especially through conformity to the norms of primary groups (Berelson et al., 1954; Fetsinger, 1950). The social deprivations caused by the rootless and socially isolated quality of modern society were offered by the mass society theorists (e.g., Fromm, 1941; Kornhauser, 1959) as central motives for recruitment into mass movements. Contemporary sociologists, in similar fashion, speak of the need for solidarity, for a sense of common identity, shared fate, and commitment to defend the group (Coughlin, 1989; Fireman & Gamson, 1979).

A motivational assumption also is central to Edelman's version of symbolic politics theory; he assumes that the mass public's insecurities and needs for status are key motives that manipulative elites can play on. In contrast, our simple symbolic politics theory does not assume the involvement of any such motivational needs. Rather, positive or negative affects become associated with political symbols through a process of classical conditioning. People are emotionally invested in their values and attitudes, and challenges to them stimulate emotional responses. But there is no assumption that other needs are involved. This is a parsimonious view, but of course it requires empirical justification.[15]

Rational Choice

Rational choice models have become increasingly popular in analyses of political behavior. Beginning with the pivotal theorizing of Downs (1957), various scholars have argued that in fact voters make sensible judgments about the performance of public officials (Fiorina, 1981), that they choose candidates on the basis of issue proximity (Key, 1966), that economic issues are paramount in public choices (Kramer, 1971), and that public opinion itself is (at least in the aggregate) a rational response to real events (Page and Shapiro, 1992). In social psychology, rational choice theories also have some vogue. Early on, Ward Edwards put forward the expectancy-value theory of decision-making (1954), a tradition that continues in strength. For example, an influential theory of attitude-behavior linkages rests on an expectancy-value base and indeed is described as a "theory of reasoned action" (Ajzen & Fishbein, 1980; also see Feather, 1982).

The symbolic politics approach is considerably different. It views individuals as responding affectively on the basis of long-held and possibly anachronistic predispositions, rather than cognitively assessing current information in a realistic, sensible manner. It views people as somewhat resistant to change rather than as being open to good new information. Symbolic processing may ultimately serve rational ends for the individual or for the society, but if it does, it is not through a process of careful and rational deliberation or cost-benefit analysis.

Cognitive Miser

A final set of theories comes out of the social cognition tradition and depicts the individual as, in Shelley Taylor's (1981) deft words, a "cognitive miser," taking cognitive shortcuts, responding at a "top of the head" level to relatively subtle cognitive cues. Among the most prominent versions of this approach are Kahneman and Tversky's "cognitive heuristics" (1981), cognitive schema theory (Taylor & Crocker, 1981), and the cognitive categorization process (Fiske & Neuberg, 1990). All of these approaches begin with the observation that human information-processing capacity is limited. To save cognitive effort, people use cognitive shortcuts such as presumably diagnostic external cues or preexisting cognitive structures. Simon (1985) bases his notion of "bounded rationality" in economic decision-making on such observations.

This view also differs sharply from the symbolic politics perspective. To be sure, it also describes people as distorting current information, but doing so from an inability to process all available information and the resulting need to economize cognitively; since the individual cannot process all available information, shortcuts must be taken. The cognitive miser approach generally assigns a background role to affect or long-standing affective predispositions. To be sure, some versions do allow for "affective tags" on categories (see Fiske & Pavelchak, 1986), but affect is basically foreign to the key insights of the cognitive miser approach.

In short, the symbolic politics approach differs sharply in emphasis from, especially, the rational choice or cognitive miser perspectives. The rational choice view depicts a deliberate decision-maker objectively evaluating costs and benefits, while the cognitive miser approach sees a cerebral being desperately trying to husband his or her limited psychic energy in the midst of a torrent of information. The symbolic processor is reacting in a gut-level, automatic manner to emotionally evocative political and social objects. Of course, all three theories *can* be amended to explain phenomena central to the others. Their differences lie more in emphasis and in the core phenomena for which they are best fitted.

Attitude Accessibility

This symbolic politics theory has emerged from cross-sectional surveys of the general population. However, the phenomena it focuses on, and the underlying theory, are similar to those surveys developed in laboratory social psychology around the concept of "attitude accessibility" (Fazio, 1986), which extends basic memory models to the case of attitudes.

Symbolic theory begins with the assumption that long-term memory is an "associative network," a system of nodes connected by associational links (Anderson, 1983). For example, "Bush dislikes quotas" is stored as two nodes (Bush, quotas) and the link associating them (dislikes). Recall begins at one node, and activation spreads along the links between nodes (Collins & Loftus, 1975). These links are strengthened each time they are activated. To apply the model to attitudes requires thinking of "an attitude [as] essentially an association between a given object and a given evaluation" stored in long-term memory (Fazio, 1986, p. 214). The nodes of the network could be any kind of attitude object. When the attitude object is encountered, the attitude is activated and enters consciousness (i.e., is accessed). The process of activation is said to be automatic and spontaneous; it does not require reflection or attention (Fazio et al., 1986).

Priming

Some attitudes are chronically accessible, and so are likely to influence judgment and behavior whatever the context. That is, they are spontaneously accessible: "the mere presentation of an attitude object toward which the individual processes a strong evaluative association would automatically activate the evaluation" (Fazio, 1989, p. 157). For example, presenting positively evaluated words, even if only momentarily or subliminally, can speed response to other positively valenced stimuli (with symmetrical effects of priming negative affects; Fazio et al., 1986; Perdue et al., 1990; Devine, 1989).

Second, activating an accessible construct through priming should increase its impact over other attitudes, judgments, and behavior. For example, priming a particular trait construct gives it greater weight in impression formation. Bargh et al. (1988) presented subjects with a grouping of four words that contained the critical priming trait (e.g., "she, *outgoing,* is, was"), then with an ambiguous description of a person's behavior (e.g., "he monopolized the telephone where he lived"), and then asked for one word that best described this type of person. The primed adjective was more likely to be given.

Priming political attitudes has been shown experimentally to enhance their impact over candidate evaluations. Sherman and colleagues (1990) activated the categories of either foreign affairs (by presenting words such as "diplomat") or the economy (e.g., "fiscal"). Then they described a political candidate who was experienced in one area but inexperienced in the other. Evaluations of the candidate were most influenced by his level of experience in the area that had previously been primed. Similarly, "agenda-setting effects" show that emphasizing a particular issue in television news broadcasts increases that issue's weight in viewers' evaluations of presidential performance (Iyengar & Kinder, 1987). This can be thought of as another kind of priming effect: watching network coverage of a particular issue primes the individual's attitudes toward that issue, making them more accessible and more influential.

Chronic Accessibility

Some attitudes are more accessible than others on a long-term basis: "like any construct based on associative learning, the strength of the attitude can vary . . . this associative strength may determine the accessibility of the attitude from memory . . ." (Fazio, 1986, p. 214). Spontaneous activation, without prompting from situational cues or even extensive exposure to the attitude object itself, should occur primarily with highly accessible attitudes; that is, those with especially strong associative links between attitude object and evaluation. Even if not directly primed, highly accessible attitudes will dominate other attitudes. Other attitudes are not so strong and must be explicitly primed to have an effect, either through exposure to the attitude object or prompting from situational cues (Higgins & King, 1981).

This dimension of chronic accessibility, reflecting the strength of object-evaluation association, is analogous to a number of other concepts that bear on underlying attitude strength, such as "ego involvement" (Sherif & Cantril, 1947), "attitude centrality" (Converse, 1964), "attitude importance" (Krosnick, 1988), "conviction" about one's attitude (Abelson, 1988), or "public commitment" to an attitude (Hovland, Campbell, & Brock, 1957). In the language of symbolic politics, symbolic predispositions anchor one end of this dimension and nonattitudes anchor the other (Sears, 1983).[16]

The link between accessibility and attitude strength lies in the notion that attitudes are evaluations stored (along with relevant information) in long-term memory and varying in associative strength. Accessibility in memory does provide one potential explanation for the effects of attitude strength on resistance to change or influence over other attitudes. For example, Krosnick (1989) has suggested that the effects of attitude importance result from accessibility; more important attitudes are more accessible and therefore more easily evoked and more likely to influence other attitudes. Similarly, Fazio and his colleagues argue that more accessible attitudes produce higher attitude-behavior consistency, such as that between preelection candidate preference and actual vote (e.g., 1986a, 1986b).

Automatic Processing

This approach views chronically accessible social constructs as spontaneously and automatically activated in the presence of the attitude object.

Swift evaluative responses are the hallmark of the accessing of strong attitudes: people quickly classify objects into good and bad, particularly those objects that are associated with strong evaluations. This automatic processing can occur without conscious goals, control, attention, or awareness, and so it places minimal demands on processing capacity (Bargh, 1988, 1989). There are several versions of this automatic processing process, and they have a good bit in common.

One version distinguishes automatic from controlled processing (Shiffrin & Schneider, 1977). Automatic processing involves the spontaneous activation of a well-learned set of associations that have been developed through repeated activation in memory. An example offered by Devine (1989) is of conventional American racial stereotypes. They are learned early in life, before children develop the cognitive ability to critically evaluate them. Devine argues that these stereotypes represent a frequently activated, well-learned set of associations that are automatically activated in the presence of a group member (or symbolic equivalent of the target group) for virtually all Americans. In contrast, "controlled processing" is voluntary and requires conscious effort and active control by the individual. An example is the "theory of reasoned action" (Ajzen & Fishbein, 1980), which contends that behavior follows from behavioral intentions, which in turn are derived from attitudes toward the action and normative expectations in a conscious and deliberate way.

A second distinction, discussed earlier, is between "on-line" and "memory-based" processing (Hastie & Park, 1986). In on-line processing, the individual keeps a running tally of evaluations of the attitude object. Each new piece of information is simply absorbed as an incremental updating of that running tally, but the information itself is not necessarily stored. When the attitude is primed, the stored summary evaluation is retrieved, not the raw information on which it was based. As a result, evaluation is independent of remembered details. In contrast, in memory-based processing, attitudes are dependent on the retrieval of specific pieces of information from memory, and it is predictable from the mix of pro and con information retrieved from memory (McGraw et al., 1990). Experiments by Lodge et al. (1989) found on-line processing dominated in "impression-driven" conditions in which individuals were presented with various pieces of information about a political candidate and then were asked whether they liked or disliked the candidate. Memory-based processing appeared only in a "memory-driven" condition, in which the person was instructed simply to try to understand the information.

A third distinction is between "category-based" and "piecemeal" processing (Fiske & Pavelchak, 1986). In category-based processing, perceivers categorize other individuals immediately upon encountering them, and they categorize at a perceptual level rather than as a consequence of deliberate and conscious thought. The category carries an "affective tag" that transfers immediately to the evaluation of the target individual. Fiske and Neuberg (1990) argue that category-based processes typically have priority over more attribute-oriented, individuating processes, or "piecemeal processing," in which the stimulus person is processed in terms of his/her own individual attributes, with each individual piece of information being reviewed and integrated into the overall impression. A similar distinction between "category-based" and "person-based" processing has been developed by Brewer (1988) in her "dual-process model of impression formation."

One subtlety of the categorization process concerns the match of individual instance with general category. For Fiske and Neuberg (1990), categorization requires both the presence of the category label and the fit of the individual's attributes with the category. Sometimes a particularly apt single prototypical example is necessary to prime an underlying construct. Lord et al. (1984) showed that individuals' attitudes toward a particular stimulus person were consistent with their attitudes toward the overall group only when the individual was a prototypical exemplar of the group; this prototypicality presumably primed attitudes toward the group itself. Presumably, the process is one that involves feature-matching for similarity, as in our "schematic variant" of the theory of symbolic politics (Sears, Huddy, & Schaffer, 1986; also see Tversky, 1977; Brewer, 1988).

Several recently developed psychological concepts, then, parallel what we have described as symbolic processing: the "automatic activation of attitudes," "automatic processing," "on-line processing," and "category-based processing." All of these are highly affective rather than content-filled or cognitive; spontaneous rather than deliberate; cognitively effortless, making minimal demands on cognitive processes; automatic rather than intentional or voluntary; and oriented around symbolic representations.

A fourth distinction does not parallel these so neatly. This is the distinction between "peripheral" or "heuristic" processing and "central" or "systematic" processing (Chaiken, 1980; Petty & Cacioppo, 1986). Peripheral or heuristic processing describes attitude change resulting from cues, such as source expertness or attractiveness, other than the merits of the arguments. Central or systematic processing emphasizes deliberate and thoughtful processing of persuasive arguments, evaluating each argument for its validity. Peripheral/heuristic processing does parallel a piece of the symbolic or automatic processing picture in that the individual responds without thoughtful review of the detailed arguments. But this form of processing misses an equally central element: the swift and reflexive affective response based on strong object–evaluation associations (Kosterman, 1991). Central/systematic processing would seem to correspond more closely to controlled processing in that attitude change is dependent on piecemeal review of the individual arguments.

Applications to Mass Politics

In short, the core idea of a symbolic politics theory, as it has been developed in survey research on political behavior, is that strongly held affective predispositions are triggered automatically by attitude objects with relevant symbolic meaning. Quite independently, recent experimental work on attitudes has treated them in parallel fashion as elements in an associative network that vary in the strength of the object–evaluation association (i.e., in attitude strength). Those with the strongest associations are most accessible in memory and are evoked most automatically when primed with relevant stimuli. The notion of symbolic processing of political symbols relevant to symbolic predispositions would seem to have much in common with the notions of automatic processing of objects that activate chronically accessible attitudes, on-line processing, and category-based processing. All of them would seem to contrast with the concepts of controlled processing, memory-based processing, attribute-based processing, or central processing. But these latter literatures have been developed on the basis of experimental, laboratory research. Which of these modes of processing best fits the natural conditions of mass politics?

Presumably, controlled processing operates most commonly under conditions of greater information and attention. Yet it is clear that ordinary people usually do not have a great deal of political information (Sears, 1969; Kinder & Sears, 1985). Nor do they pay close attention to the political media; even though television is ubiquitous in our society, it usually receives diffused and distracted attention from the public, and that is particularly true of political messages (Kinder & Sears, 1985; Sears & Kosterman, 1991).

Automatic processing should be most common under conditions of strong object-evaluation associations. True, the mass public's attitudes toward the detailed issues of public life are frequently not very consistent or stable (Converse, 1964, 1970; Zaller & Feldman, 1992). On the other hand, they do have strong and stable attitudes toward the continuing political symbols of the era, and those are the attitudes that are evoked most often (Converse & Markus, 1979; Sears, 1983).

Whether affect or cognition plays a more important role in politics is an old debate (though usually framed by pitting passion against reason). But some suggestive preliminary data (Kuklinski et al., 1991) suggest that people's natural responses to civil liberties issues more closely resemble how they behave when affectively primed than when cognitively primed. Kuklinski et al. presented civil liberties dilemmas regarding a number of groups and asked an "affective" experimental group to approach them in terms of "your feelings, or the emotions you experience," while the "cognitive" group was asked to "think about the consequences of the action or event. . . ." The affective group behaved much like a no-instruction control group, suggesting to the authors that "individuals normally do little more than react viscerally to one or another group" (p. 17).

Most social psychologists seem to feel that automatic processing dominates in ordinary life. "It appears that most daily behaviors are not sufficiently consequential to induce people to undertake a controlled analysis" (Fazio, 1986, p. 238); "category-based processes seem to be the default option . . . under ordinary conditions, people simply do not pay enough attention to individuate each other" (Fiske and Neuberg, 1990, p. 21); "person-based encoding is the exception rather than the rule in . . . complex information settings" (Brewer, 1988, p. 3); and "on-line processing is . . . psychologically realistic in placing minimal information-processing demands on voters" (Lodge et al., 1989, p. 416) and is more common than memory-based processing (also see Hastie & Park, 1986; Fiske & Taylor, 1991).

But what are the conditions under which automatic as opposed to more controlled processing takes place? Are these most common in mass politics? For one thing, time pressure and limited attention, and indeed limited cognitive resources in general, promote category-based processing (Fiske & Neuberg, 1990). These, of course, are perennially at the heart of the problem with public participation in politics; the incentives are minimal, and there are many other demands on people's time, so politics is plainly one area of life in which decision-making shortcuts are likely to be found. Perhaps the cognitive miser is no less rational than Downs's (1957) rational nonparticipant.

Category-based processing requires the presence of appropriate categories, strongly established categories, and consistency of the target with the category (Fiske & Neuberg, 1990). To be sure, nonattitudes abound in politics. But both politicians and journalists try to frame issues and candidates in terms that can be readily linked to widespread, consensually understood predispositions. That is, the information environment in mass politics is heavily biased toward widely understood and shared categories. When that process is successful, the public is likely to be very effective in making its will known; if it is unsuccessful, the public will flounder and its voice is likely to be only dimly heard.

On-line processing is enhanced by an "impression set" in which the individual's goal is to develop an impression of another person, whereas memory-based processing is enhanced by the goal of remembering the informational details (Fiske & Taylor, 1991). And, in fact, an impression set is the ordinary person's orientation toward politics. The main practical decisions that voters must make are choices between candidates, which require impressions of those rivals. This is the focal point of much mass political conversation as well: "what do you think of X?"

A considerable body of experimental work argues that central processing, and consequent close attention to the merits of the arguments, is stimulated by personal involvement in the outcomes of issues (Petty & Cacioppo, 1986; Johnson & Eagly, 1989). In the political behavior literature this variable has been described as "self-interest" or the personal impact of political issues (Sears & Funk, 1991). Similarly, outcome interdependency with another person motivates closer attention to the details of that person's nature, especially short-term, task-oriented outcome dependency on the target (Fiske & Neuberg, 1990). However, such situations are relatively rare in politics. For the most part, the political choices faced by ordinary citizens do not have a major impact on their personal lives (Green, 1988; Sears & Funk, 1991).

Moreover, there is a good bit of evidence that people do not induce political preferences from the details of their own personal experiences. Rather, people appear to be slow to draw societal-level implications from *personal*-level information, and vice versa; political preferences and personal experiences seem to be cognitively compartmentalized. Extensive reviews of the literature on the political effects of self-interest have been published elsewhere and need not be reiterated. The best evidence is that self-interest has relatively little impact on political attitudes (Sears &

Funk, 1991). On the few occasions that self-interest does have great effects on public opinion, those effects tend to be cognitively narrow.

Some Implications

Let me close with two observations about the implications of this work for how we think about democratic governance. As Page and Shapiro (1992) have wisely noted in their recent book, a variety of perspectives on the general public is possible. Their perspective is of a fairly sensible and rational public, which does as well as can be expected given the limited and biased information it is given. The image of the public conveyed by the symbolic politics approach is greatly different; it sees a public emotional and reflexive in its responses to political symbols and relatively heedless of instrumentalities or realities. To be sure, practitioners of the symbolic politics approach see the public in the aggregate, and they concede that their view is not a good representation of the individual.

The symbolic politics model is most obviously geared to political conditions under which manipulation of the public is most likely to occur. By the reasoning laid out here, such efforts should be least fruitful on stimuli that have a clear, unambiguous, and consensual meaning. It has been difficult, for example, to change the meaning of busing because it is so widely viewed as a racial issue. On the other hand, manipulation should be easier on issues or candidates that lack consensual or manifest symbolism. When a new candidate, such as Michael Dukakis or Bill Clinton, comes onto the political scene, he is something of a black box, whose profile can be molded to elicit either positive or negative underlying predispositions—though presumably within some constraints based on reality.

Controlling the public agenda is required in order to control the symbolic meaning of an attitude object. Such control is politically consequential both in influencing overall public support for the object and in influencing which predisposition the object evokes. By manipulating the meaning of an issue such as crime, for example, as the Republican campaign did with the Willie Horton commercials in 1988, one can manipulate the role of a powerful and damaging predisposition such as racism. Similarly, regimes often manipulate national symbols to evoke loyalty and patriotism, which frequently has been done in recent times to mobilize secessionist sentiments in formerly communist nations.[17]

The normative impact of the symbolic politics process on democratic governance depends to a great extent on what symbols are salient in the public arena. If they evoke the uglier set of our predispositions—prejudice, ethnocentrism, nationalism, hostility toward the weak and disadvantaged—that is what we are likely to get. If they are symbols that appeal to our better sides—to our communitarian spirits, our selflessness, our idealism—that is what we are likely to get. To a considerable extent, political elites are prisoners of their times; events dictate what is placed on the public agenda. But let us not forget that no theory of good or bad times will explain variations in our leaders' appeals to the better or worse sides of human nature. In the United States the chaos of a new nation, Civil War, or a Great Depression have generated some of our most uplifting presidencies. As V. O. Key pointed out years ago (1961), political elites bear a considerable responsibility for the choices they offer the general public and therefore a considerable responsibility for the direction in which the public then turns.

Notes

1. For example, see Osgood (1953), *Ideals and Self-Interest in America's Foreign Policy.*

2. A later work by Elder and Cobb (1983) develops very similar ideas, though it is more systematic and considerably more linked to the political science mainstream. It too depicts the public as monitoring a passing parade of political symbols that are not greatly affected by personal experience. These symbols can mobilize people's anxieties (stemming from fraternal deprivation or status anxiety) or reassure (again through the trappings of power that convey the impression that a leader is in control, or by means of more public policies that "solve problems"). But here leaders must be careful not to offend the symbolic sensitivities of the public with such examples as big government, socialism, free enterprise, and bureaucracy. This departs from the "non-attituded" public of Edelman.

3. The empirical work began with an early study of the effects of race on voting behavior (Sears & Kinder, 1971, Kinder & Sears, 1981) and continued on racial policies (Sears et al., 1979; Sears et al., 1980; Sears & Allen, 1984), economic policies (Sears & Citrin, 1985; Sears et al., 1978; Sears et al., 1980), and war policies (Lau et al., 1978; Sears et al., 1983). Research by others than the original authors based on this paradigm has been conducted on taxes (e.g., Beck et al., 1990; Hadenius, 1986; Listhaug & Miller, 1985), racial policies (Kluegel & Smith, 1985; McClendon, 1985; McConahay, 1982), crime (Tyler & Lavrakas, 1983; Tyler & Weber, 1982), and attitudes toward welfare (Coughlin, 1989). For

reviews of this literature, see especially Citrin and Green (1990), Sears (1988), Sears and Funk (1991).

4. It should be said, though, that many other writers view ideology as stemming either from self-interest or group interest.

5. The most complete earlier descriptions of the psychology of "a simple theory of symbolic politics" have appeared in Sears (1983), Sears et al. (1980), and Sears et al. (1986).

6. The term "political symbol" refers to any affectively charged element in a political attitude object; it is not intended as a singular or special class of those elements. Whether the symbolic meaning of an object is fully apparent in its manifest content or is dependent on some cognitive structure it elicits in the individual is not prejudged by use of the term "symbolic meaning"; all that is intended is that the symbol convey some meaning to the individual.

7. The "transfer of affect" theory is better-described in terms of affective consistency than cognitive consistency, but congruity theory does not fundamentally differ from it (or indeed from the other cognitive consistency theories) in this respect; all deal primarily with reconciling inconsistent affects rather than with the cognitive processes that bound them together. For exceptions, see Abelson (1959, 1968b).

8. The characterization is perhaps overdrawn, since Converse selected an issue (public vs. private power) that he acknowledged to be highly obscure to the public, though intensely fought over in Congress. In later work (Converse & Markus, 1979) a great deal more stability was evident in a wider sample of issue attitudes.

9. In that earlier discussion, these belief systems were described as "cognitive schemas" (borrowing that concept from contemporary social psychology), and thus the extended version of the theory as a "schematic variant" of symbolic politics.

10. Note the contrast between this view and the "construct sampling theory" proposed by Kinder and Nelson (1990) and Zaller and Feldman (1992). Those researchers suggest that when asked for their opinion, people sample "considerations" or "raw ingredients" at random, or according to recency of activation. We are proposing a more systematic activation process based either in manifest semantic similarity or on underlying belief systems that link symbol to predisposition.

11. Additional evidence for the central role of cognitive similarity in determining the strength of symbolic meaning effects has emerged as an incidental by-product of other recent studies conducted for other purposes. Sears and Lau (1983) found that varying the salience of different dimensions of self-interest affected only the impact of cognitively relevant dimensions of self-interest, and only on cognitively relevant dependent variables. A study by Kinder and Sanders (1990) also found that symbolic meaning effects are limited to cognitively relevant predictors, and another by Krosnick and Kinder (1990) showed that these effects are limited to the most cognitively relevant dependent variable.

12. A recent example is the Perdue et al. (1990) demonstration that pairing nonsense syllables with in-group designators such as "we" or "ours" would lead to more favorable evaluations of the nonsense syllables than would pairing them with such out-group designators as "they" or "theirs," even when the latter were presented only briefly and subliminally prior to the nonsense syllable. While the difference between positive and negative affect is crucial to a symbolic politics theory, it does not concern itself with qualitatively different *kinds* of affecting each category. For example, fear is not differentiated from anger, or hope from pity, contrary to some current theories of emotion (see Marcus, 1990; Weiner, 1986; Roseman, Abelson, & Ewing, 1986). It may be that such distinctions will be valuable in the future.

13. There are objections to the Zajonc view. Lazarus (1984) has argued that prior to cognitive appraisal, especially of the personal significance of the stimulus, is necessary before the affective response occurs. Similarly, Weiner (1986) contends that cognitive attributions precede emotions; e.g., making an internal attribution for a positive outcome produces pride, whereas making an external, controllable attribution for a negative event produces anger.

14. The most comprehensive of these are the functional theories (Katz, 1960; Smith, Bruner, & White, 1956; Pratkanis, Breckler, & Greenwald, 1989) that proposed exhaustive taxonomies of the possible needs which an opinion might serve for an individual. As Herek (1986) and others have noted, in the scheme offered by Katz (1960) a symbolic politics process might be described as fulfilling a "value expressive" function; e.g., a strong egalitarian might oppose the KKK because she feels it contributes to inequalities in the society. But that conviction places a more specific interpretation on the symbolic politics process than we would choose to; the reaction might be a more reflexive revulsion to the KKK as an attitude object than a principled expression of a real value.

15. Our perspective also should be distinguished from an ego-defensive or more general personality approach, such as one concerned with authoritarian personality or Machiavellianism (Adorno et al., 1950; Christie & Geis, 1970). Symbolic predispositions may be linked to more general personality traits, but they need not be. Values, racial prejudices, and other such attitudes can be acquired through socialization in their own right, autonomous of other aspects of the individual's personality.

16. Not everyone would agree that all of these concepts can be reduced to a single dimension of attitude strength. Krosnick and Schuman (1988) and Raden (1985) raise such questions, and others (Johnson & Eagly, 1989) distinguish three different versions of ego involvement, of which "value-relevant" (aka "position involvement") most closely parallels attitude strength. It also should be noted that the psychological mainsprings of these various concepts vary somewhat. Sherif and Cantril (1947) and Converse (1964) suspected that the strongest ego involvements were anchored in some sense of group identity, while Abelson

(1988) describes "conviction" as deriving from emotional commitment, ego preoccupation, and cognitive elaboration.

17. This ignores the possibility that in some natural situations the direction of causality will be reversed: the predisposition itself may influence which symbolic meaning the attitude object takes on, rather than vice versa. For example, a particular set of political protests can "mean" an ugly resurgence of nationalism or an inspiring liberation from an imperial oppressor, depending on one's predisposition. We are not addressing this particular sequence here.

Roger D. Masters and Denis G. Sullivan

6. Nonverbal Behavior and Leadership:

Emotion and Cognition in Political

Information Processing

In the literature of political psychology, increased attention has been given to models of political information processing that stress the cost of information and cognitive analysis. For the citizen, time and effort are needed to learn about political issues and candidates. As a result, it is argued, voters use simple schemas or chronicities to simplify the way they process political information (Kraus & Perloff, 1985; Lau et al., 1988; Lodge et al., 1989). In one formulation, the voter is described as a "cognitive miser" who seeks to minimize these information costs in response to political life (Lau et al., 1988; Aldrich et al., 1988).

Interestingly enough, however, information-processing models often have ignored emotion, even though the attribution of a lasting emotional bias or valence to information is an effective device for simplifying the cognitive process. In this chapter we outline a theoretical explanation of the effects of leaders' nonverbal cues on the emotions and attitudes of citizens and then summarize a series of experiments that explore this process. Building on the increased use of experimental methods to assess how citizens process politically relevant information (Iyengar & Kinder, 1985, 1987; Iyengar, Peters, & Kinder, 1982; Kraus & Perloff, 1985; Lau & Sears, 1986; Lodge, McGraw, & Stroh, 1989), these studies presented viewers in both the United States and France with exemplars of leaders exhibiting different expressive behaviors, measuring episodic emotional responses and attitude changes caused by the viewing experience.

There are good reasons for assuming that the nonverbal behavior of leaders might be a relevant cue in the formation of public attitudes toward rivals for power. Western literature provides ample evidence that leaders attended to such behavior as a crucial element in establishing and maintaining dominant status (e.g., Shakespeare, III *Henry VI,* iii, 3, 168–

95; *Henry V,* iv, 1, 103–11; Milton, *Paradise Lost,* II.302–9); training in nonverbal behavior, and especially in facial display, was once an integral part of teaching rhetoric (Courtine & Harouche, 1988; for an example, see Scott, 1820). Such nonverbal cues play an important role in social interaction among nonhuman primates and human children (Hinde, 1982; Montagner, 1977; Kagan, 1988; Eibl-Eibesfeldt, 1989; Chance, 1989) and have increasingly been recognized as a basic element in theories of human social and political behavior (Frank, 1988; MacDonald, 1988; Masters, 1989a).[1]

Research in other fields has confirmed the importance of integrating the study of emotion and cognition as well as the role of nonverbal cues in social interaction. Social psychologists have shown that attitudes toward an observed person are shaped by emotional responses to the person's nonverbal behavior (Cacioppo & Petty, 1979; Lanzetta et al., 1985; Mc-Guire, 1985), and political scientists have begun to focus on the role of these variables in mediating attitude change (e.g., Marcus, 1988).

Although it should hardly be surprising that the sight of a face is an important cue in the social interactions of human beings (Darwin, 1965; Tranel & Damasio, 1985), research on the interactions between mothers and infants confirms that responses to facial cues are important predictors of the growing child's social behavior or personality (Izard, Hembree, & Huebner, 1987). Perhaps more surprising has been the discovery that the latency and habituation in processing the perception of faces by four-month-old infants is a significant predictor (along with mother-infant social interaction) of the child's verbal abilities at the age of one year and four years of age (Bornstein, 1988). In short, perception of the face seems to be implicated not only in social behavior and personality, but in some ways this system seems to be more generally linked to the capacity for associative learning.

Emotional Determinants of Political Judgment

How do political leaders evoke emotions and impressions that modify attitudes toward them? First, they are held accountable for the perceived consequences of their actions. In recent years, research has burgeoned on theories of "retrospective voting" in which voting choice is determined by cognitions about and emotional responses to the recent political past rather than prospectively to what candidates promise (Fiorina, 1981). Secondly, differences in candidate style in presenting the issues can lead voters to associate candidates more or less strongly with particular issues (Roseman et al., 1986). Thirdly, political leaders can elicit emotions and convey impressions by their nonverbal style, including voice quality and facial expressions (Lanzetta et al., 1985; Masters & Mouchon, 1986; Sullivan & Masters, 1988).

Evidence from the 1980s suggests that there has been a change in the basis for voter preference in the United States and Western Europe. Leadership style is now more important, while party loyalty has declined, in shaping levels of support or opposition to political leaders (Atkinson, 1984; Iyengar & Kinder, 1987). Television may be partly responsible for this development because viewers daily see close-up images of political leaders and newscasters exhibiting facial expressions that communicate emotion and suggest character (Mullen et al., 1986; Rosenberg et al., 1986). Moreover, such styles may affect the way in which citizens think about issues and political outcomes (Bower, 1981; Bower & Gilligan, 1982).

Before television, a leader's nonverbal cues were mainly seen by influential opinion leaders; when the general public learned of political discourse only through printed reports or by word of mouth, displays of emotion had their effect primarily by focusing the attention of opinion leaders who then disseminated some statements rather than others to the general public. As long as printing was the main source of political communication, therefore, leaders' messages often appeared as verbal statements when they reached the average citizen. Since television has increasingly exposed the citizens of all Western democracies to close-up images of their leaders, it is now of great practical as well as theoretical interest to study the effects of the way this medium evokes emotions and judgments in a modern society.

Television differs from print media in ways that can shape the political process, since in addition to combining visual and verbal stimuli, it provides frequent close-up images of known and powerful leaders.[2] As a result, the average citizen learns of events while watching a communicative medium that provides immediate impressions of leaders and events on a day-to-day basis. In this process it should hardly be surprising that the episodic emotions known to play a role in associative learning interact with cognitive cues in producing changes in the viewers' attitudes and opinions.

Over the past decade, research has shown that such emotions are important determinants of political attitudes toward presidential candidates (Abelson, Kinder, Peters, & Fiske, 1982). In the Abelson et al.

study, positive and negative emotional response scales were constructed from voter recall of specific emotion-evoking episodes for each candidate that involved the positive emotions of hope, happiness, pride, and sympathy and the negative emotions of anger, disgust, fear, and uneasiness. This study showed that responses toward the candidate on the two emotional scales and on trait attributions were roughly equal in weight, and that both played a stronger role in predicting attitude than did the traditional variables of party identification or issue position.[3]

In addition to the revival of interest in emotion as a determinant of attitudes toward leaders, research has again focused on voters' perceptions of the personal characteristics of political leaders. As early as 1966, Donald Stokes bemoaned the lack of an adequate theory of trait attributions. More recent research has shown that voters' impressions of a candidate's personality characteristics affect their political attitudes toward the candidate (Kinder 1986a; Popkin et al., 1976).

Kinder hypothesizes that voters consider the character of the candidate to be of central importance in their voting decision because they believe—rightly or wrongly—that character is fate, that candidate traits predict future performance. Thus, it is subjectively rational for voters to invest in the attribution of traits to candidates as long as the cost of such investment (Popkin et al., 1976) is relatively low. Although Popkin argues that "competence" is most important to voters because it is most predictive of performance, others (e.g., Page, 1978) include warmth, activity, strength, and honesty as traits of instrumental significance to voters. Kinder (1986a) has identified four traits—competence, integrity, leadership (strength or determination), and empathy—that voters attribute to candidates and which predict voters' overall evaluations of them.

In Popkin's investment theory of trait attribution, for example, voters combine free information (which is acquired as a by-product of other activities) with other relatively cheap information to make politically relevant trait attributions. Popkin argues that it is easier for voters to infer traits from such evidence than to calculate the effects of the candidate's party affiliation and issue position on his/her future behavior in office. Other analyses of political cognition reach similar conclusions by viewing the voter as a "cognitive miser" who seeks political information at a minimal cost (Aldrich et al., 1988; Lau et al., 1988).

While this explanation is reasonable, it leaves a critical question unanswered. Although emotional responses and trait attributions have been shown to be important determinants of voting decisions (Abelson, Kinder, Peters, & Fiske, 1982; Kagay & Caldiera, 1975; Kinder & Abelson,

1981), surprisingly little is known about how a political leader's verbal and nonverbal behavior evoke them (McGuire, 1985, esp. pp. 276–85). If voters seek easily interpretable cues when watching a leader on television, it is plausible to assume that they will pay attention to nonverbal behavior. Among these cues, it is likely that facial displays will be salient since they are frequently shown in television coverage of leaders (Masters et al., 1987) and since they transmit emotion and signal social status in all human cultures as well as among nonhuman primates (Ekman & Oster, 1979; Plutchik, 1980; Van Hooff, 1969). It is particularly important to focus on such cues because they provide an instance of the way episodic experience can be translated into lasting feelings and attitudes about politics.

This theoretical perspective integrates cognition and emotion in ways consistent with the results of research in cognitive neuroscience—a discipline that has rapidly developed in the past decade. Using techniques ranging from PET or NMR scanning of the entire human brain to the measurement of single cell responses during specific information-processing tasks, cognitive neuroscientists are rapidly transforming the understanding of how the central nervous system works (Gazzaniga, 1985).

These studies of the structure of the brain demonstrate the essential role of episodic and lasting emotion in cognition and confirm the importance of the face as a social stimulus among all primates. It has now been demonstrated, for example, that when the face of a conspecific is perceived and identified, a characteristic ensemble of neurons in the visual areas of the inferior temporal lobes ("inferotemporal cortex") is activated (Rolls, 1987, 1989a). This neuronal area, in turn, is closely linked with emotional responses mediated by the limbic system (especially the amygdala and hippocampus)—centers that are essential not only for emotion but for associative learning and memory (Mishkin & Appenzeller, 1987; Squire, 1987, esp. p. 336).

The temporal lobes are particularly important in social behavior. Among free-ranging nonhuman primates, damage to this structure seems to prevent bonding with others and results in the ostracism of the affected individual (Kling, 1986); human beings whose temporal lobes are damaged or destroyed not only exhibit the same behavioral traits but report an inability to establish emotional bonds or feelings when interacting with others (Kling, 1987). It is therefore of particular relevance that approximately 10 percent of the neurons in the visual pathway of the inferotemporal cortex of nonhuman primates are specialized in processing information of facial stimuli (Rolls, 1989a). The neuronal network for the perception of faces is thus an important component in the neuroanatomical structures underlying learning, memory, and social interaction in human beings as well as in nonhuman primates.

Ultimately, research in cognitive neuroscience and social psychology may suggest mechanisms that could explain many questions in political information processing. For example, often puzzling similarities and differences in cognition between men and women have been the subject of much discussion (e.g., Darcy, Welch, & Clark, 1987; Gilligan, 1982; Klein, 1987; MacDonald, 1988). Although reasons for observed gender differences remain highly controversial (Masters, 1989b; Masters & Carlotti, 1988), evidence like that presented here shows the need to go beyond conventional theories of political cognition. While the specific hypotheses of neuroscientists that relate to gender differences[4] lie outside the realm of political science, they suggest the importance of neurological processes if one is to understand the way in which facial displays and political attitudes relate to the experience of watching leaders on television.

Our theoretical approach to the role of impressions and emotions in shaping political attitudes thus combines the perspectives of ethology and social psychology in a way that is consistent with current work in cognitive neuroscience. Ethological theory emphasizes the importance of facial displays signaling attack, flight, or submission in regulating status and power relationships in primates (Chance, 1989; Hinde, 1982; van Hooff, 1969). Human facial displays corresponding to these functional categories—happiness/reassurance (H/R), anger/threat (A/T), and fear/evasion (F/E)—were chosen for research according to criteria summarized in table 6.1 (Masters et al., 1986). Because such displays play a role in social interaction among all human groups, it is hardly surprising that exemplars were plentiful in videotaped archives of American TV coverage of press conferences, party rallies, nominating conventions, and political speeches (Masters et al., 1987).

In the studies reported here, the naturally occurring images of leaders shown on TV have been used as experimental stimuli to assess what actually happens when citizens see leaders on a daily basis. The exemplars of facial displays, chosen on the basis of objective criteria derived from social psychology and ethology, are comparable to "visual quotes" of leaders that are typically shown on television news (Frey & Bente, 1989; Joslyn & Ross, 1986; Masters et al., 1987). The experimental results show that such facial displays can affect attitudes, emotions, and impressions in politically important ways. More recent research has replicated and reinforced many of the Abelson findings (Marcus, 1988).

Types of Nonverbal Display

In describing displays, ethologists have used Charles Darwin's insight that "antithetical" cues are likely to become salient through the process of natural selection (1965, pp. 50–65). Criteria for describing facial displays of happiness/reassurance, anger/threat, and fear/evasion are summarized in table 6.1. Hedonic (positive or pleasurable) behavior is contrasted from agonic (competitive or "negative") social interactions and emotions by such cues as smoothness of movement, tilting of the head, focusing then cutting off of eye contact, retracted or raised mouth corners and visible teeth in what we call the smile, visible crow's-feet at eye corners, etc. Agonic cues are further defined by the opposition between cues associated with threat or attack and those of fear, evasion, or submissiveness.

In human happy/reassuring displays, for example, eyebrows are likely to be raised (in contrast to the lowered brows in A/T), body movement to be smooth (in opposition to abrupt movements of flight or attack), and head tilted (as opposed to the rigid and forward motion of the head in signaling attack). Anger/threat is associated with lowered brows, widely opened eyelids, and staring gaze, forward or lowered mouth corners with no teeth or only lower teeth visible, absence of lateral head movement, and sometimes an abrupt upward vertical movement of the head. In contrast, fear/evasion is signaled by averted eye and head orientation, lowered head position, lowered and furrowed brows, and abrupt movement patterns.

These three gestures function as "unconditioned stimuli" in responses to others (e.g., Ekman & Oster, 1979; Lanzetta & Orr, 1980; Orr & Lanzetta, 1980) and are of special interest because ethological research shows their effects to depend on the power relationships and affective bonds between the emitter and the observer (de Waal, 1982; Lorenz & Leyhausen, 1973; van Hooff, 1969). Moreover, the observer's response, in addition to being dependent on the leadership status of the emitter, may feed back in a way that either enhances or weakens the leader's position (Chase, 1982; McGuire & Raleigh, 1986; Masters and Carlotti, 1988; Raleigh & McGuire, 1986).

We hypothesize that such facial displays are among the meaningful stimuli that can be determinants of viewers' trait attributions and emotional reactions to leaders. Both within cultures and across cultures, human beings accurately decode the emotion that a specific, expressive facial cue represents (Ekman & Oster, 1979). Because television frequently shows close-up, full face images of politicians who often rely

Table 6.1. Criteria for classifying facial displays.

	Anger/ Threat (A/T)	Fear/ Evasion (F/E)	Happiness/ Reassurance (H/R)
Eyelids	Opened wide	Upper raised/ Lower tightened	Wide, normal, or slightly closed
Eyebrows	Lowered	Lowered and furrowed	Raised
Eye orientation	Staring	Averted	Focused then cut
Mouth corners	Forward or lowered	Retracted, normal	Retracted and/or raised
Teeth showing	Lower or none	Variable	Upper or both
Head motion			
Lateral	None	Side-to-side	Side-to-side
Vertical	None	Down	Up-down
Head orientation			
To body	Forward from trunk	Turned from vertical	Normal to trunk
Angle to vertical	Down	Down	Up

Source: Masters, Sullivan, Lanzetta, McHugo, & Englis, 1986, table 2.

on simple, stereotyped emotional gestures for communicative purposes (Frey & Bente, 1989; Joslyn & Ross, 1986; Masters et al., 1987) and viewers interpret their meaning accurately (Masters et al., 1986; Sullivan & Masters, 1988), it seems reasonable to explore the extent to which this system provides the public with salient and relevant cues about leaders.

Our research, confirming work in psychology, shows that viewers distinguish such displays accurately and respond in emotionally different ways to them (Ekman & Oster, 1979; Masters et al., 1986). Real-time measures of psychophysiological reaction demonstrate that each of the three types of display (happiness/reassurance, anger/threat, and fear/ evasion) elicits different affective responses that are congruent with verbal reports of emotion (Englis, Vaughan, & Lanzetta, 1982; McHugo et al., 1985; Vaughan & Lanzetta, 1980). As a result, the viewer's self-reports of emotion seem to be "real" phenomena (and, indeed, probably not as likely to be influenced by the form and administration of questionnaires as are public opinion polls).

When seeing leaders, viewers react with more positive emotion to happiness/reassurance displays and with more negative emotion—anger and fear—to anger/threat or fear/evasion displays (Lanzetta et al., 1985; Masters et al., 1986; Sullivan & Masters, 1993a). Similar effects have been found when comparing emotional responses to neutral and H/R displays of all presidential candidates in both 1984 (Masters et al., 1985) and 1988 (Carlotti, 1988; Masters & Carlotti, 1988). Since such emotional responses to leaders' displays, like emotional responses to their policies and outcomes, sometimes shape attitudes toward them (Sullivan & Masters, 1988), exactly how does the process work?

A leader's expressive displays of emotion, if repeatedly seen, can modify viewers' attitudes directly by eliciting emotions (see Sullivan & Masters, 1988; Zajonc, 1982) or trait attributions (Abelson et al., 1982) that affect their attitude toward the leader. Although this chapter does not explore the issue, the causal path may be more complex. Rather than directly affecting attitudes, facial displays may elicit trait attributions that, in turn, arouse emotions that affect attitudes (Lazarus, 1984; Mandler, 1975). Or, conversely, an observer's emotional responses to a leader's displays may elicit attributions of traits that by a more cognitive process shape attitudes toward the leader.

Theories of political cognition thus need to include nonverbal cues that are capable of eliciting the affective responses known to be implicated in attitude formation and change.[5] The variables involved in the process by which facial displays can influence voters, however, are obviously complex. In addition to factors associated with the stimulus (the leader's identity, display behavior, and status as well as the context of the event), attributes of the viewer are known to modify the effects of any persuasive cue (Cacioppo & Petty, 1979; McGuire, 1985). In particular, it is to be expected that the extent to which the viewer has political information and the nature of these prior attitudes will be central determinants of affective and attitudinal responses.

Experimental Methods

While the studies summarized below were based on the same criteria for stimulus selection, experiments varied in design in order to elucidate different aspects of the system by which nonverbal cues elicit emotional and cognitive responses about leaders. These studies can be classed into four groups: (1) measures of display effects, using exemplars of a single leader such as Ronald Reagan exhibiting all three types of facial display (Masters et al., 1986; Sullivan & Masters, 1993b); (2) measures of psychophysiological responses using similar excerpts while measuring autonomic reactions and activation of facial muscles associated with emotional states (McHugo, Lanzetta, & Bush, 1987; McHugo et al., 1985); (3) measures of the effectiveness of displays in a more realistic setting, using different displays as silent cues embedded in the background of routine TV news stories (Sullivan & Masters, 1993a; Sullivan et al., 1984); and (4) measures of differences in the performance of similar display effects by competing leaders, using a neutral and a happy/reassuring display of competing candidates in an election (Sullivan & Masters, 1988). By showing the same excerpts of leaders to samples from the same subject population at different times or to samples from different subject populations at the same time, this last design also permitted study of the effects of the political context and status of the leader (Carlotti & Masters, in preparation; Sullivan & Masters, 1993b) as well as of the socioeconomic status of viewers. Additional research has included studies that (1) presented excerpts of Reagan to French viewers (Masters & Mouchon, 1986), (2) replicated features of the first and fourth type of study noted above, showing displays of three French leaders in France (Masters & Sullivan, 1989a, 1989b), (3) used a full presidential debate between Jimmy Carter and Gerald Ford in 1976 to measure the effect of the instant analysis or TV news commentary on the viewers' perceptions, emotions, and attitudes (Newton et al., 1987), and (4) assessed cognitive reactions to displays in real time.

In these studies, viewers were told that we were interested in the effects of the media on modern politics: virtually no subjects suspected that the purpose of our experiments was an assessment of facial display behavior.[6] After a standard pretest questionnaire in which viewers were asked to report information and attitudes concerning politics and rival leaders, videotaped excerpts of leaders were presented; after each segment, subjects were asked to describe the leader they had just seen, using 0–6 scales that have been validated at the psychophysiological level (McHugo et al., 1985) and elicit similar responses in both France and the United States (Masters & Mouchon, 1986; Masters & Sullivan, 1989a, 1989b). A posttest questionnaire was then used to assess changes of attitude that might be associated with the viewing experience (for typical questionnaire items, see Sullivan & Masters, 1988, appendix I).

Stimuli were selected to represent the three types of display according to the objective criteria outlined in table 6.1 and defined more completely elsewhere (Masters et al., 1986). For each leader being studied in an experiment, videotapes of routine television coverage were searched for the best available excerpt showing each type of display. After selection by one researcher, other observers recoded proposed excerpts using the same selection criteria; displays with discrepant ratings were dropped from the study.[7] While displays obviously varied not only in intensity but in homogeneity, viewer ratings of the type of display in both the United States and France confirm the accuracy of these selection procedures.

Although the experimental stimuli were sometimes shown to single viewers, notably in the studies of psychophysiological response, excerpts were usually presented to small groups of subjects who were instructed not to express their responses openly.[8] The channel of communication or "media condition" also was controlled. In studies of the first type described above, comparable groups saw identical displays with the sound-plus-image, image-only, sound-only—and, in one case, with filtered sound-plus-image and written text-only (Masters & Sullivan, 1989a, 1989b; Masters et al., 1986), while in the fourth or multicandidate type of experiment, the same excerpts were seen by half of each sample with image-only and the other half with sound-plus-image (Sullivan & Masters, 1988, 1989b). Political context was measured by repeating the same experimental paradigm using similar subjects at different moments in the election campaign (Carlotti & Masters, in preparation; Sullivan & Masters, 1988, 1993b); similarly, socioeconomic background was measured by simultaneously presenting the same stimuli to samples with different class and economic backgrounds.

Summary of Principal Results

Type of Display

Viewers accurately distinguish each type of nonverbal display—and each type elicits different patterns of psychophysiological and self-reported emotional response.

When viewers have seen the same leader exhibiting more than one type of display, descriptive scores of the leader's behavior in each excerpt (on 0–6 scales) show that the scale score congruent to the display as objectively defined ("happy" for H/R, "angry" for A/T, "fearful" for F/E) is always rated higher than other descriptive scales (Masters & Sullivan, 1989a; Masters et al., 1986). This was true for American viewers' descriptions of H/R, A/T, and F/E displays of President Reagan in five different media conditions (Masters et al., 1986) as well as of descriptions of H/R and N displays of candidates in the 1984 and 1988 elections (Carlotti & Masters, in preparation; Sullivan & Masters, 1988) and was confirmed for French viewers' responses to the same displays of Reagan (Masters & Mouchon, 1986, pp. 85–86) as well as for descriptions of H/R, A/T, and F/E displays of three French leaders.

Because a single verbal scale score may not be the best measure of decoding, descriptive ratings were factor-analyzed. Descriptive scores reflect two bipolar factors, one for reassurance (joyful and supportive vs. angry and threatening) and the other for dominance (strong vs. confused or evasive); here again, factor weights are highly similar in France and the United States (Masters & Sullivan, 1989b, table 1 and figures 1a–1b).[9] Each factor represents both the viewer's description of the emotion expressed and its communicative significance for the viewer. Whether measured by raw scale scores or by factor scores, the descriptive ratings of leaders' nonverbal display behavior shows similar patterns in two different cultures.[10]

Finally, a "centroid" cluster analysis of viewers' descriptions confirmed that verbal labels are used to decode nonverbal displays accurately (Masters et al., 1986, table 6), thereby indicating that viewers do indeed discriminate reliably between different behavioral episodes and use verbal labels consistently when perceiving different nonverbal displays (see Ekman & Oster, 1979).

While viewers' descriptions of a leader's behavior correspond to the type of display as objectively defined, experiments also show that viewers' attitudes toward the leader can influence their descriptions of his displays (Masters & Sullivan, 1989b, table 2). In general, such effects are more likely in a competitive context (Flohr, Tönnesman, & Pöhls, 1986; Kepplinger, 1990; Masters & Muzet, in preparation). Despite this qualification, however, descriptive scores are at least partially independent of verbal self-reports of emotion or of prior attitude toward the leader.

As will be shown, viewer perceptions of differences in display behavior affect their emotional responses; they respond with higher levels of emotion to displays judged to be more intense; this is true both for psychophysiological responses (McHugo, Lanzetta, & Bush, 1987) and for verbal self-reports. Moreover, emotional responses to the different displays (H/R, A/T, and F/E) affect viewers' attitudes toward the leader expressing the emotion (Carlotti & Masters, 1989; Sullivan & Masters, 1988, 1993a, 1993b). In the United States, emotional responses are more

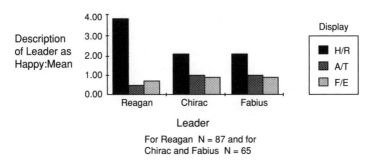

Figure 6.1. Viewers' impressions of leader as happy in the excerpt just seen: combined media conditions.

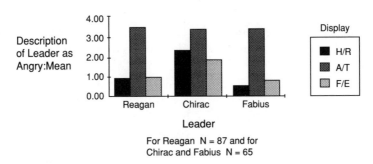

Figure 6.2. Viewers' impressions of leader as angry in the excerpt just seen: combined media conditions.

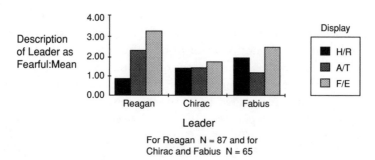

Figure 6.3. Viewers' impressions of leader as fearful in the excerpt just seen: combined media conditions.

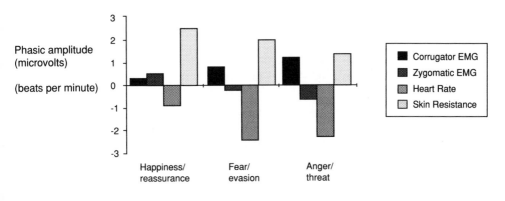

Facial Display

*The facial EMG and autonomic response measured as change from a pre-tape baseline. The skin response scale is in kilohms.

Figure 6.4. Autonomic changes during exposure to Reagan's facial displays: image-only. (McHugo et al. 1985)

positive after seeing H / R than after either A / T or F / E displays (Sullivan & Masters, 1993b, figs. 2a–2c), whereas in France there is little difference between the effects of H / R or A / T displays (Masters & Sullivan, 1989a, figs. 4a–4b).

Type of Emotional Response

Viewers' verbal self-reports of emotion during each excerpt correspond with psychophysiological responses known to be associated with emotional experience, reflecting similar hedonic and agonic dimensions of emotion in France and the United States.

While watching H / R, A / T, and F / E displays, viewers' facial muscle changes corresponded to the emotion expressed and were consistent with verbal self-reports of subjective feelings (fig. 6.4). Although viewers' psychophysiological responses to Reagan did not depend on their prior attitude toward him, attitude did have such an effect both on self-reported emotions in this study (McHugo et al., 1985, fig. 3) and on the same psychophysiological measures in a follow-up study with two competing politicians (Reagan and Gary Hart) as stimulus figures (McHugo, Lanzetta, & Bush, 1987). The latter study also confirmed that displays objectively defined as more intense elicited stronger psychophysiological responses.

Factor analysis of the verbal self-reports of emotional response showed that in both France and the United States viewers use verbal labels to map the same two dimensions of emotion, one hedonic or positive, and the other agonic or negative (Masters & Sullivan, 1989a; Masters et al., 1986). These dimensions (see table 6.2) correspond to those found in primate social behavior generally (Chance, 1976, 1989) as well as in social psychology and political science (Abelson et al., 1982; Marcus, 1988). In fact, the pattern of factor loadings found in our studies is almost identical to the results when public opinion poll data recording voters' feelings when they think about political leaders are analyzed (Masters et al., 1986, fig. 7). Episodic responses to nonverbal cues can therefore be reliably measured by verbal self-reports of emotion—and these reports track affective responses that are actually felt.

Posttest Attitude to Leader

Episodic emotions during the viewing experience contribute to potentially lasting attitude changes that result from the viewing experience; male viewers with neutral attitudes were most likely to change opinions because of silent nonverbal displays in T V newscasts.

The effects of episodic emotions felt during and immediately after the viewing experience can play an important role in attitude changes (McGuire, 1985). The mere experience of viewing rival candidates has short-term effects on viewers' attitudes; while seeing some leaders causes both critics and supporters to shift to more positive opinions, the sight of others may polarize previously neutral attitudes or actually reduce the strength of their support. In January 1984, before the New Hampshire primary, the experience of viewing Reagan's excerpts reduced the number of critics while attracting a higher proportion of supporters, whereas seeing Walter Mondale turned off his own supporters and increased the number of his critics (Lanzetta et al., 1985, table 4.4); at a comparable stage in the 1988 campaign, seeing excerpts of all of the candidates increased the number of those favorable to Jesse Jackson—and to a lesser extent to Hart and to Reagan—whereas both George Bush and Michael Dukakis had fewer supporters and more critics after the experience than before (Carlotti, 1988, table 9).[11]

Episodic emotional responses to displays, and especially to H/R excerpts, often contribute to these changes in attitude. For example, regression of posttest attitude toward each candidate on the independent variables—pretest attitude, self-reported net warmth (positive minus negative emotion) after seeing a H/R and after seeing a neutral display,

Table 6.2. Factor structure of emotional responses to Happy/Reassurance, Anger/Threat, and Fear/Evasion displays in France and the United States. (All media conditions combined) (United States N=145, France N=65)

Scale	Reagan		Chirac		Fabius	
	Positive	Negative	Positive	Negative	Positive	Negative
Joyful	.65	−.44	.79	−.08	.83	−.11
Interested	.81	−.07	.61	−.28	.64	−.16
Comforted	.82	−.31	.89	−.09	.88	−.10
Inspired	.83	−.22	.85	−.21	.84	−.24
Angry	−.07	.83	−.36	.68	−.30	.73
Fearful	−.12	.81	−.06	.84	.06	.77
Disgusted	−.25	.79	−.35	.76	−.21	.78
Confused	−.20	.59	−.03	.67	−.18	.63

*Cell entries are factor loadings from principal components factor analysis retaining and rotating by Varimax factors with eigen values > 1. The negative factor accounts for 33 percent of the total variance for Reagan, and 32 percent for Chirac and Fabius; the positive factor accounts for 32 percent for Reagan, 34 percent for Fabius, and 35 percent for Chirac. The American results are five media conditions: sound+image, sound-only, image-only, filtered sound, and transcript. In the French experiments, only the first three media conditions were used.
Source: Emotional Responses to Fabius and Chirac, Experiment at Université de Nanterre (Masters & Sullivan, 1986); emotional responses to Reagan, Experiment 2 at Dartmouth College (Masters et al., 1986). For the comparable factors for the French data when emotional responses to Le Pen are included along with Chirac and Fabius, see Masters and Sullivan (1986).

party identification, issue agreement, and assessed leadership ability— shows that the emotions elicited by H/R excerpts contributed significantly to posttest attitude toward each candidate for all Democrats in 1984 except Mondale, Ernest Hollings, and—in October 1984 but not January of that year—John Glenn (see table 6.3). Comparing responses of samples at the beginning and end of the 1984 campaign, moreover, the effect of emotional responses to Reagan's H/R display almost doubled from January to October, whereas the comparable responses to Mondale remained low in both studies (Sullivan & Masters, 1988, fig. 2).

Replication of this experimental design in the 1988 election produced mixed results. Before the 1988 New Hampshire primary, for example, emotional responses to H/R excerpts of Hart and Jackson had significant effects on posttest attitudes, whereas emotions felt during similar ex-

Table 6.3. Influence of viewers' pretest attitudes and emotional responses on their posttest attitudes at outset and conclusion of campaign.
(United States N=145, France N=65)

| Candidate | Attitude | Pretest Emotional Response to: | | | | | R² |
		Happy/ Reassuring display	Neutral display	Party identification	Issue agreement	Assessed leadership ability	
January 1984							
Reagan	.52	1.22	.90	−3.45	3.91	−2.00	.84
Mondale	.64	.48	.99	.73	1.73	−.92	.69
Hart	.45	1.21	1.22	−.64	.90	1.11	.43
Jackson	.39	1.50	.47	−.80	4.21	.44	.78
Glenn	.67	1.11	−.22	−.17	.26	.98	.57
McGovern	.91	1.38	.06	.02	.15	−1.66	.75
Cranston	.13	1.33	.41	−3.24	2.23	−.16	.41
Hollings	.59	1.14	.89	−1.53	1.29	3.15	.35
Askew	.22	1.90	.32	−3.12	5.18	−3.12	.32
October 1984							
Reagan	.22	2.01	.41	−.75	3.56	.41	.76
Mondale	.54	.55	1.00	−1.06	1.77	.60	.76
Hart	.61	1.43	−.45	−.05	2.96	.19	.69
Jackson	.32	1.83	−.08	.07	2.63	3.53	.83
Glenn	.56	.09	.74	−.12	2.75	.14	.37
McGovern	.53	.93	.10	−.15	3.83	.16	.59
Cranston	.36	1.59	−.05	−1.96	2.78	1.46	.47
Hollings	.60	.30	.52	−.57	−1.83	.53	.35
Askew	.45	1.57	.62	−2.07	.76	1.59	.47

Multiple regression analysis of posttest attitude to each candidate on a 0–100 "Thermometer" scale, combining responses to sound-plus-image and image-only presentation of displays. The relative weight of pretest attitudes and emotional responses has been measured by unstandardized partial regression coefficients. Statistically significant coefficients ($p<.05$) are underlined. Independent variables: pretest attitude (0–100 scale), "net warmth" of emotional response (joy plus comfort, minus anger plus fear) to each type of display, strength of self-reported party identification, issue agreement with leader, and assessment of candidate's leadership ability (on 0–6 scales). *Source*: Sullivan & Masters, 1988.

cerpts of either Bush or Dukakis did not have such effects (Sullivan & Masters, 1993b, table 6). In November 1988, just before the election, the same H / R excerpt of Hart did not have this effect, suggesting that loss of status or power reduces the impact of the emotions felt while seeing a leader; similarly, an excerpt of Reagan that had been highly evocative in 1984 failed to have similar results in both 1988 samples (Sullivan & Masters, 1993b, table 6 and appendix I). Although viewers' episodic emotional responses to the excerpts affected postexposure attitude for most candidates, moreover, the effect for some candidates stemmed from responses to the Neutral excerpt rather than the H / R excerpt.

Different types of viewers do not seem to respond to the viewing experience in the same way. Since the foregoing studies were done with comparable samples from the same Ivy League college, in November 1988 the same videotapes were shown to a sample of black students at Grambling State University as well as to students at Boston University. Not only did the non-Ivy League students often report emotional responses markedly different from the Ivy Leaguers after these excerpts, but effects of emotion on posttest attitude were not the same in each sample (Sullivan & Masters, 1993b). While the complicated interaction between cognition and emotion produces different effects on attitude depending on circumstances, however, episodic viewing experiences have modified attitudes to some leaders after all of our studies.

To assess whether the posttest attitude changes attributable to nonverbal displays could be more lasting, in another study attitudes toward President Reagan were measured twenty-four hours after the second day of the experiment in which silent excerpts of Reagan exhibiting H / R, A / T, or neutral facial displays were embedded in the background of routine newscast stories (Lanzetta et al., 1985; Sullivan & Masters, 1993a). For one category of viewers—males with neutral attitudes toward the president—displays had a significant effect on posttest thermometer scores (Lanzetta et al., 1985, fig. 4.5; Sullivan & Masters, 1993a, figs. 3a–3b).

Channel of Communication

In different media conditions, each type of display is discriminated from others, but the channel of communication influences the level of response elicited; in general, image-only presentations elicit stronger hedonic responses to H / R displays than do those accompanied by sound.

When the same displays of President Reagan were shown to viewers in

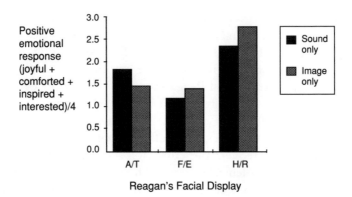

Figure 6.5. Positive emotional response to Reagan's display: image–only and sound–only media conditions. (Masters et al., 1986)

five different media conditions (sound-plus-image, image-only, sound-only, filtered-sound-plus-image, and text-only), we found the same patterns of descriptive scores and of emotional responses (Masters et al., 1986, fig. 1, tables 4 and 5) regardless of channel. While other studies confirm that similar display effects occur in different media conditions (e.g., Sullivan & Masters, 1988, table 3), responses do vary in ~~intensity~~ and significance when a leader is seen without being heard (image-only) or can be heard and seen at the same time.[12] Figure 6.5 shows the results for the image-only and sound-only media conditions.

When psychophysiological responses of emotion were measured, the display effects produced by H/R, A/T, and F/E excerpts of Reagan were stronger during image-only presentations than when the excerpts were shown with sound-plus-image; this difference was especially marked for the facial muscles of the mouth and eyebrows known to correlate with feelings of happiness and anger (Lanzetta et al., 1985, fig. 4.4; Masters et al., 1986, fig. 3). In particular, higher levels of positive affect were transmitted by H/R displays in the image-only condition, during which the zygomatic muscles associated with smiling were activated more strongly, and the corrugator muscles associated with both attentional focusing and anger were less activated, than during sound-plus-image presentations. The sound channel also seems to elicit stronger agonic responses than image-only presentations, perhaps because heart rate is increased by A/T and F/E excerpts when the sound is present but not when viewers see the image-only condition (Lanzetta et al., 1985, fig. 4.4).[13]

The effects of different kinds of displays on attitude, to be discussed further, may sometimes be influenced by media condition. When viewers watched all candidates during the 1984 American presidential campaign, the H/R excerpts of most leaders presented with sound-plus-image had a significant effect on posttest attitudes, whereas for two candidates—George McGovern and Hollings—this effect did not occur in image-only presentations of the same excerpts (Sullivan & Masters, 1988, table 3). Such effects of the channel of communication, however, also may be mediated by the gender of the viewer, since males seem more likely to be sensitive to independent effects of the media condition than do females.[14]

Performance Style of Leader

Nonverbal displays perceived as a mixture of distinct cues elicit weaker emotion, are less likely to activate prior opinions favorable to the leader, and produce less favorable attitude change.

In general, the homogeneity of a viewer's descriptive rating of a display, measured as the ratio of hedonic to agonic cues, predicts self-reported emotional response. In studies showing all candidates during the 1984 and 1988 American presidential elections, those leaders whose display behavior was described as more heterogeneous were less likely to elicit warm emotional responses and were less likely to be judged more favorably after the viewing experience (compare Masters et al., 1985, table 2, with Sullivan & Masters, 1988, table 3; Masters & Carlotti, 1988, pp. 18–22). In a French study in which viewers saw competing leaders, an individual whose display was described as more heterogeneous was less likely to elicit emotional responses that interacted with viewers' prior partisanship or attitude (Masters & Sullivan, 1989a, table 1).

Intensity of Display

Higher-intensity H/R displays elicit stronger psychophysiological responses, and the greater the difference between descriptions of the leader's neutral and his H/R display, the more that leader's H/R excerpt enhances viewers' emotional responses.

When viewers were shown a low-intensity and a high-intensity H/R excerpt of two leaders (Reagan and Hart), psychophysiological measures of affective response were significantly stronger during the more intense display (McHugo, Bush, & Lanzetta, 1987). In the 1984 presidential campaign, there was a strong correlation ($r^2 = .95$) between a sample's average descriptive rating of the intensity of a candidate's joy in the H/R excerpt and the average self-reported emotion of happiness (Sullivan & Masters, 1988, fig. 1). Similar—albeit slightly lower—correlations were found if each sample's average "net positive description" (ratings of "strong" plus "happy," minus ratings of "angry" plus "afraid") of each candidate's H/R excerpt was correlated with the average "net warmth" of emotional response (feelings of "happiness" plus "comfort," minus feelings of "anger" plus "fear") to the same excerpt (unpublished data).

These effects might result from positive emotions elicited by favorable attitudes toward the candidate and his party, or by a leader's facial conformation and performance style, rather than being produced by the display behavior itself. To control for the emotion aroused merely by seeing a candidate, the neutral display of each leader was used as a baseline to which descriptive ratings and emotional responses to the H/R excerpt of the same leader could be compared. Across several studies the intensity of the H/R excerpt was measured by the *difference* between average "net positive descriptions" of the neutral and the H/R excerpt of each leader; these intensity ratings were then correlated with the difference in net warmth of emotional response to the same two displays, thereby providing a measure of the enhanced emotion attributable to the H/R display while controlling for variables associated with the candidate and the subjects. Since individual descriptive scores do not always correlate with corresponding emotional response ratings (e.g., descriptions of candidate happiness and the viewer's self-reported emotions of happiness or joy), this measure provides a more accurate summary of effects ascribable solely to display intensity. Across thirty-five different leaders in five studies, there is again a high correlation ($r^2 = .81$) between described display intensity and felt emotional response.[15]

Pretest Attitude Toward Individual Leaders

Prior attitude generally influences emotional responses to excerpts of leaders, but these effects often depend on the type of display seen, the candidate's performance style, the political culture, and other variables implicated in leader-follower interactions.

Although it is hardly surprising that the attitudes or prejudices of viewers influence their emotional responses to leaders, the interactions between cognitive and affective factors are extremely complex. In some studies, even descriptions of the excerpts are influenced by prior attitude, with supporters describing given excerpts as exhibiting more strength

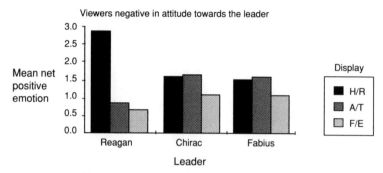

Figure 6.6. Viewers' net positive emotional responses to the expressive displays of Reagan in the United States and to those of Chirac and Fabius in France: combined media conditions. (Sullivan & Masters, 1993b)

and warmth, and critics seeing more anger and fear (Masters & Sullivan, 1989a, p. 6; Newton et al., 1987; Masters & Muzet, in preparation). Emotional response is even more sensitive to the viewer's prior attitude to a specific leader, but these effects of attitude on emotion interact with the kind of display seen, the performance style of the leader, the context of the viewing experience, and characteristics of the viewer such as socioeconomic status, political culture, or gender (Masters, 1991).

In general, of course, supporters respond to a leader with more positive emotion and less negative emotion—and hence greater affective "net warmth"—than do critics or neutral viewers. But supporters usually report stronger positive feelings and weaker negative ones after seeing a leader exhibiting H / R displays than after his F / E excerpts (Lanzetta et al., 1985, fig. 4.2; Masters & Sullivan, 1989b, figs. 2a, 2b, 3a, and 3b); A / T is intermediary, being more likely to resemble F / E displays for American viewers, whereas in France A / T does not generally differ from H / R in its effects on supporters and critics (figs. 6.6 and 6.7). As a result, there are often statistically significant interactions between prior attitude and display as determinants of episodic emotional responses to leaders (Sullivan & Masters, 1993a; Masters & Sullivan, 1989b, table 5).

In many contexts, critics seem less sensitive to differences in display behavior than do supporters (figs. 4a and 4b), but individual leaders may differ in the effects of their displays on supporters and critics (see Lanzetta et al., 1985, fig. 4.2; McHugo et al., 1985, fig. 3). In the French study just cited, for example, viewers' emotional responses to image-only excerpts

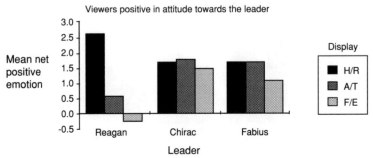

Figure 6.7. Viewers' net positive emotional responses to the expressive displays of Reagan in the United States and to those of Chirac and Fabius in France: combined media conditions. (Sullivan & Masters, 1993b)

of Jacques Chirac were influenced by prior attitudes, with his display behavior having little significant effect, especially on positive emotional responses, whereas prior attitude toward Fabius interacted with his displays in shaping viewers' emotions (Masters & Sullivan, 1989a, pp. 14–15; Masters & Sullivan, 1989b, table 5 and figs. 2 and 3). Finally, for some candidates who are not well known—like Alan Cranston and Reuben Askew in January of the 1984 American presidential campaign—prior attitude to the individual is not a significant predictor of emotional responses to the displays; three weeks before the election, however, pretest attitude also had become a significant predictor for these candidates (Sullivan & Masters, 1988, table 4).

The effects of prior attitude on emotion (and on posttest attitude) can, however, be mediated by a number of situational and personal factors. These include such diverse factors as: (1) mode of producing television newscasts, since silent displays in the background of newscasts can influence neutral viewers, whereas they are less likely to influence those with strong attitudes to a leader (Sullivan & Masters, 1993b; Lanzetta et al., 1985, fig. 4.5); (2) cueing by TV journalists, since neutral viewers are more likely than supporters to change their perceptions and responses on the basis of commentary accompanying a leader's appearance on television (Newton et al., 1987; see below); (3) status of a leader at the time of the experience, since the interaction of pretest attitude, display behavior, and emotional response can be strengthened by success during the course of a political campaign (Sullivan & Masters, 1988, fig. 2; see below). As will be further noted, socioeconomic attributes of the viewer and gender also can mediate the interactions between prior attitude, display behavior, and emotional response (Carlotti, 1988, pp. 82, 89, 91, 128, 131, 134).

Attitudes Toward Political Party, Ideology, or Issues

The viewer's partisanship and ideology are often less relevant as mediators of the effects of nonverbal cues than attitudes to the individual leader (especially in the United States).

Although it might seem self-evident that political information and commitment have an independent effect of viewers' reactions when they see leaders, the effects of partisanship and ideology are far from simple. By comparison with attitudes toward the leader being seen, partisanship and ideology are weaker as predictors either of emotional response (Masters, 1989b, figs. 3 and 4) or of posttest attitude (Sullivan & Masters, 1988, table 4; Sullivan & Masters, 1993b, appendix I). In general, however, strong political commitments reduce a viewer's tendency to be influenced by nonverbal cues or journalistic commentary during the viewing experience; hence, neutral and uninformed viewers are probably more likely to change opinions as a result of seeing leaders on TV than those with clearly defined attachments to the political right or left (Sullivan & Masters, 1993a, figs. 3a and 3c; Newton et al., 1987).

The mere fact of partisanship or ideological commitment is thus distinct from effects due to the congruence between the party or ideology of the viewer and of the leader being observed. Some leaders seem far more successful than others in eliciting responses that reflect the viewer's political attachments. During the 1984 campaign, for example, issue agreement—and, in January, partisanship—influenced posttest attitudes toward Reagan but not toward Mondale; for comparable samples in February and November 1988, posttest attitudes toward Bush and Jackson were significantly influenced by issue agreement but not by partisanship, whereas seeing Dukakis elicited posttest attitudes that were affected by both partisanship and issue agreement in February—and by neither in November (Sullivan & Masters, 1993a, appendix I).[16] Similarly, partisanship had a greater impact on the emotional responses of French viewers to excerpts of Chirac than of Fabius (Masters & Sullivan, 1989a, table 1).

Gender Differences

Although males and females often differ in the way that they respond to nonverbal cues, the pattern is far from simple; rather than having consistent differences in

*emotional response or attitude, it seems that gender effects are related to the way
that males and females process various cues.*

Despite the widespread presumption that females are more "sensitive"
to nonverbal behavior than males (Hall, 1978, 1987; Babchuck et al.,
1985), this conventional wisdom does not seem to apply when viewers
watch leaders on television. When silent excerpts of Reagan were edited
into the background of TV news stories, males rather than females were
more likely to accurately recall the type of silent displays they had
seen (Sullivan et al., 1991; Lanzetta et al., 1985, pp. 104–5) and neutral
males—but not females—expressed posttest attitudes that were significantly influenced by the embedded displays (Sullivan & Masters, 1993a,
fig. 3; Lanzetta et al., 1985, fig. 4.5). In other experiments it would seem
that the viewer's party identification is more likely to influence the male's
emotions and posttest attitudes, whereas interactions between prior attitude and the display that has been seen are more likely to be significant in
female responses (Masters, 1989b, tables 2 and 3, fig. 3; Masters &
Carlotti, 1988, figs. 1, 4a, and 4b).[17] In addition to these effects of the
display, however, are differences in the way males' and females' prior
attitudes or descriptions of the display relate to emotional responses and
attitude changes (Carlotti, 1988, pp. 89, 91, 128, 131, 134).

Several gender differences in processing specific nonverbal cues also
were found. Consistent with the general finding that females are more
likely to be risk-averse than males (Masters, 1989b, fig. 2), displays of
anger/threat seem generally to be more salient—and often more aver-
sive—to females. Gender sometimes has a significant influence on the
way a leader's display behavior is described (Plate, 1984), with males
being more likely to describe some excerpts as exhibiting high levels of
A/T (Carlotti, 1988, p. 116). After seeing newscasts with silent displays of
Reagan in the background, displays influenced immediate emotional
responses to the news story differently by gender (Sullivan & Masters,
1993a, fig. 5); in this study, females—but not males—were less likely to
attribute positive traits to the president if they had actually been exposed
to A/T than H/R displays (Sullivan & Masters, 1993b, table 3). Changes in
the status of a leader, as reflected in national opinion polls, also seem to influence the evocative effects of the same videotaped excerpts to a greater
degree for females than for males (Masters & Carlotti, 1988, fig. 5).

Other Individual Differences

*In addition to effects attributable to attitudes toward leaders, partisanship, or
ideology, differences in the viewer's overall knowledge about politics, sensitivity*

to nonverbal behavior, social background, or political culture can mediate the effects of facial display behavior.

(1) Information. Less-informed or naive viewers are more influenced by displays and cues than those with rich information or strong attitudes.

The best evidence of this effect concerned a study in which viewers watched the 1976 presidential debate between Ford and Carter either with or without network journalistic commentary, recorded responses to both leaders, and then saw a routine newscast story about the debate. While journalists' cues both in the commentary after the debate and in the newscast had an effect on all subjects, naive or relatively uninformed viewers were more affected by negative descriptions and judgments of both candidates (Newton et al., 1987).

(2) Culture. The description of facial displays and the structure of emotional responses is highly similar in France and the United States, but French viewers are more likely to respond with positive emotion to a/t displays, and prior attitude is more likely to interact with descriptions and emotional responses in France than in the United States.

Although these findings already have been indicated in passing, it is useful to summarize cross-cultural similarities and differences. The structure of words used to describe displays is essentially the same in France and the United States (Masters & Mouchon, 1986; Masters & Sullivan, 1989a, 1989b), as is the pattern of using verbal self-reports of emotional responses to the excerpts (see fig. 1 and table 2). American culture, however, does seem to have "ritualized" a/t in a different way from the French (see fig. 5). Whereas viewers in the United States respond more positively to h/r displays than to those of a/t, these two types of display behavior are less different in their effects on French viewers (see also Masters & Sullivan, 1989a, 1989b).

(3) Socioeconomic status of viewer, personality, and other viewer attributes. Recent work suggests that differences in social class or ethnicity as well as individual variations in sensitivity to nonverbal cues influence responses to the same stimuli of leaders (Sullivan & Masters, 1993b). Future research needs to focus more extensively on these factors that help to explain the complex ways in which emotion and cognition interact in large-scale populations (Masters, 1991).

Status of Leader

The more favorable the public opinion toward a powerful leader at the time of the experiment, the greater the evocative effect of the same display.[18]

For comparable samples drawn from the Dartmouth College student population, the enhanced net warmth of response attributable to President Reagan's H/R excerpt increased from January 1984 to November 1984, paralleling an increase in Reagan's net approval rating in the public opinion polls; a decline in support in public opinion between November 1984 and February 1988 was again paralleled by a decline in the effectiveness with which Reagan's H/R display elicited positive emotion. These changes attributable to Reagan's status were somewhat stronger for females than for males (Masters & Carlotti, 1988).

Viewing Context

In competitive contexts, prior attitude is more likely to be activated in response to display and viewing experience, and H/R displays are more likely to polarize supporters and critics.

In a study showing excerpts of President Reagan without any other leader, H/R, A/T, and F/E displays elicited EMG and autonomic responses that did not interact with the viewers' attitudes (McHugo et al., 1985); when Reagan and Hart were shown together in a subsequent study, the same psychophysiological measures interacted with the viewers' prior attitudes (McHugo, Bush, & Lanzetta, 1987).

Framing or Cueing

Not only were descriptions and emotional responses influenced by the news commentators' judgments, but instant analysis and subsequent news coverage had additive effects.

Interpretation of events by an authority figure or journalist influences viewers' emotional responses and attitudes toward leaders (see Iyengar & Kinder, 1987). Average descriptive ratings of the strength and happiness of both rivals in the presidential debate were lower—and descriptions of anger and fear higher—for viewers who saw an instant analysis critical of both candidates; similar differences occurred for emotional response and attitude. Later, after both groups of subjects saw a newscast story on the debate, ratings and attitudes declined further. The authoritative cues of journalists, moreover, had greater impact on naive viewers than on those with more sophisticated cognitive information (Newton et al., 1987).

Conclusions

The effects of facial displays, not to mention other nonverbal cues, seem to be of bewildering complexity. The simplistic dichotomies that long dominated discussions of human psychology—nature versus nurture, emotion versus cognition, or instinct versus learning—seem inadequate to account for the way that citizens respond when viewing powerful leaders on television. Instead, experimental evidence suggests how a wide range of factors are integrated when viewers process meaningful information about rival candidates or political leaders.

Although it seems paradoxical at first that facial displays should play such an important role in political information processing, recent research in neuroscience contradicts traditional approaches that isolate cognition and emotion. The "modular" or "parallel processing" models of the central nervous system (Gazzaniga, 1985; Mishkin & Appenzeller, 1987), now seemingly beyond question, have three essential implications for political psychology. First, it is only to be expected that a wide variety of verbal and nonverbal cues will interact when citizens engage in political behavior. Second, patterns of response should differ not only from one individual to another, but from one setting to another. Third, nonverbal cues like the facial displays studied here will sometimes—but not always—have significant effects in leader-follower relations.

That the face plays an unexpectedly important role in social behavior and cognitive information processing has become evident in a number of studies far removed from political psychology. Not only are the infant's responses to a mother's facial behavior a stable behavioral trait apparently associated with individual personality (Izard, Embree, & Heubner, 1987; Kagan, 1988; Kagan, Reznick, & Snidman, 1987), but latency and habituation in response to new faces at eight months of age predict verbal behavior at one year and four years of age (Bornstein, 1988). Reasons for these findings, moreover, can be found in the discovery of the neuroanatomical structures implicated in associative learning and memory, since the inferior temporal lobe and closely related sites specialized in processing facial cues are directly linked to components of the limbic system playing a central role in both social and cognitive behavior.

These results have practical implications, providing a more realistic approach to puzzles that have long confronted political psychology. From time to time, episodic events seem to change the political landscape. Often, however, the mechanisms that might account for these changes are puzzling. In the first polls after the Democratic nominating convention in July 1988, Dukakis led Bush; after the Republican convention, Bush received what journalists call a favorable "bounce" and took the lead in opinion polls. These changes, however, were sharply different for men and women. In July 1988, only 26 percent of females approved Bush, whereas 43 percent of males did so, while Dukakis was favored by

56 percent of females compared to 46 percent of males (*Wall Street Journal,* July 28, 1988, p. 52). In mid-August, after Bush's nomination, Dukakis trailed his rival 39 percent to 49 percent among males but only 42 percent to 44 percent among females. How might such short-term changes be explained?

Because presidential nominating conventions provide a focus of national attention, citizens are more likely to see rival leaders at these moments than in the routine periods of a campaign. It is surely plausible that emotional and cognitive responses during such focal events contribute to changes in public opinion (see Orren & Polsby, 1987). But episodic responses to rival leaders need to be studied in terms of the concrete cues presented to the viewer and the actual patterns of information processing capable of generating attitude change. On methodological grounds, experimental studies of responses to naturally occurring events in which citizens observe leaders seem necessary to account for opinion changes that are tracked by the polls; pragmatically, such experiments have the advantage of permitting an analysis of the way that nonverbal cues and verbal information might be integrated during the events that actually shape political life.

This analytic approach permits a more realistic assessment of the way that episodic memories are formed under the influence of perceptions and emotional responses at the moment of watching a leader, which thus might explain the enormous effects of campaign debates or focal events such as Edmund Muskie's "sobbing" in 1972 and Bush's acceptance speech in 1988. As we have shown, however, the interrelationship between the leader's nonverbal behavior, the viewer's emotions, and lasting attitudes is extraordinarily complex: at least sixteen different variables seem to be implicated in the system by which the citizen responds to the experience of watching a political leader.

This is not to say that the results are definitive or always easily explained. Consider again the differences in males' and females' episodic responses to Bush and Dukakis during the summer of 1988. Although gender differences in social and political behavior have frequently been demonstrated, theoretical explanations of these differences and plausible mechanisms to account for them have been highly controversial. By focusing on viewers' emotional and cognitive responses while they watch powerful leaders, it is at least possible to suggest that one way that gender might influence political life concerns modes of information processing (Masters, 1989b; Masters & Carlotti, 1988; see n. 3 of this chapter).

Ultimately, political psychology will need to build links between such everyday phenomena as the citizen's feelings and judgments about rival leaders and the discoveries of neuroscience. As a first step in this direction, more research is needed to explore episodic emotional and cognitive responses as they relate to long-term attitudes. While facial displays may be interesting in themselves as evidence of the way that presentational styles and expressive behavior relate to rhetoric and political effectiveness, at a deeper level the study of nonverbal cues in politics provides a valuable approach to the underlying process by which emotion and cognition are integrated in all political behavior.

Notes

1. On the importance of nonverbal communication in traditional political theory, see Bernard Mandeville, *Fable of the Bees* (Oxford: Clarendon Press, 1924), II, 286–87; Jean-Jacques Rousseau, *Second Discourse* (New York: St. Martin's Press, 1978), pp. 122–23.

2. In a recent study of nightly TV news, for example, leaders were visible on the screen during 14 percent of the duration of French newscasts, 17 percent of American newscasts, and 30 percent of German newscasts; a large proportion of these excerpts are brief "visual quotes" (less than six seconds) communicating an image without sound (Frey & Bente, 1989).

3. Of course, it can be assumed both that party identification is an influence prior to the episodic emotional responses and lasting attitudes toward each candidate that are formed during a campaign and that partisanship can shape attitudes toward the leader either directly or through indirect effects on such emotional responses. But without some understanding of the role of emotion in political information processing, it is hard to conceive of a theory linking short-term experiences with attitude change. On the importance of reintroducing emotion in areas of political analysis and theory that have been dominated by an exclusively "rationalistic" view of cognitive processing, see Baier (1987 and in press).

4. One hypothesis concerns patterns of cerebral lateralization that are entailed in cognition or emotion and which may vary by gender (Gazzaniga, 1985; Masland, 1981). For example, split brain studies show that both facial recognition and decoding of facial displays tend to be localized in the right hemisphere among monkeys and human beings, whereas discrimination tasks are left-hemispheric in monkeys—just as speech and abstract analysis are typically left-hemisphere functions in human beings. Because differences in the extent of lateralized information processing have repeatedly been found between men and women, especially with regard to social cues, males and females may differ in the pattern of cognitive processing even where they tend to agree—as they often

do—on the substantive matters (Masters, 1989b; Masters & Carlotti, 1988). Other neurological mechanisms, associated with the effects of sex hormones on the neonatal development of the hypothalamus, also might explain observed gender differences in the way that information is processed (Williams, 1989).

5. It need hardly be added that exploration of the way that leader's performance styles influence the public also will contribute to theories of leadership, particularly by filling the gap between scholarly theories (e.g., Barber, 1985; Burns, 1978) and journalistic accounts (e.g., Barnes, 1988; Kalb & Hertzberg, 1988; Suplee, 1988).

6. Since our experimental designs focus on within-subject differences in response to distinct displays (often by the same leader or leaders), or on between-group differences when comparable groups of viewers have an identical viewing experience with one or more experimental modifications, "demand-characteristics" are not likely to be associated with the significant effects reported below. Indeed, one could argue that the experience of watching television news provides a form of "priming," which is similar to the experimental setting insofar as the news commentator's introduction and statements "frame" the experience of watching a leader, much as did our experimental paradigm.

7. In some cases, as in the experiments using displays of all candidates during the 1984 and 1988 elections, it was extremely difficult to find good exemplars of happy/reassuring displays for some leaders. In the 1988 study, some candidates (Pete Dupont, Jack Kemp, Albert Gore, Paul Simon) were included in the design with a single, "mixed" excerpt in which no single type of display predominated (Carlotti, 1988, table 6). And, of course, differences in display intensity and homogeneity are one of the factors underlying differences in the political effectiveness of nonverbal behavior, since some leaders are more likely than others to show elements of tension or fear in their happy/reassuring facial displays (e.g., Suplee, 1988).

8. Since citizens normally watch television with others, this aspect of the experimental experience does not produce a situation totally unlike the one in which leaders are typically seen in contemporary societies.

9. Although two factors emerged from a factor analysis retaining factors with eigen-values greater than 1.0, an additional factor analysis retaining factors with eigen values greater than .80 resulted in three factors that were remarkably similar in composition across media conditions. In several of our early studies (Lanzetta et al., 1985, table 4.2; Masters et al., 1986, fig. 2) the three factors were labeled happiness/reassurance, anger/threat, and fear/evasion. When a comparable factor analysis was done for the descriptive scale scores of French subjects, three similar factors emerged (Masters & Sullivan, 1989a, fig. 2).

10. For the purposes of the analyses reported below, composite scales were formed, weighting each scale score by its factor loading, to measure both the subjects' impressions of the emotion expressed by the display and its communicative significance.

11. In contrast, when an adult sample saw the same excerpts of Dukakis and Bush after the Democratic convention in July, although viewers again responded with a shift away from Bush, females in this study shifted toward Dukakis after the viewing experience (Masters & Carlotti, 1988, figs. 3a and 3b).

12. This difference has considerable practical importance because television newscasts often show images of leaders without accompanying sound. In a cross-cultural study of nightly TV news in France, Germany, and the United States, a large proportion of these excerpts were found to be brief "visual quotes" (less than six seconds) communicating an image without sound (Frey & Bente, 1989).

13. The results of early exploratory studies show higher levels of self-reported hedonic responses to image-only excerpts as contrasted with higher levels of agonic response to sound-plus-image presentations (unpublished).

14. This possibility appeared in an exploratory, post hoc analysis, in which scale scores for each emotional response were regressed on attitude toward the leader or party identification, description of the display, and media condition (using dummy variables for presence or absence of either sound or image and sound-plus-image); controlling for the measures of attitude and for the viewer's descriptions of the display, media condition was less likely to influence females than males (Masters, 1989b, figs. 3 and 4). There is, however, further evidence of gender differences in responses to leaders in different media conditions (Carlotti, 1988, pp. 89, 91, 128, 131, 134) as well as experimental evidence from other contexts suggesting that this finding is plausible (Barchas & Mendoza, 1984).

15. That it is necessary to control for effects of cognitive or attitude variables when assessing intensity effects was confirmed by closer examination of excerpt-by-excerpt correlations between descriptive and emotional response measures. Although net description is usually strongly correlated with net emotional response to a single type of display, whether N or H/R, there are individual cases of counterempathy in response, in which greater "positive" description elicits more negative emotion (e.g., to Pat Robertson or Gary Hart in a February 1989 sample at Dartmouth College). Controlling for prior attitude by looking at difference scores, this effect of attitude on valence of emotion disappears (unpublished results).

16. Interestingly enough, for both samples at Dartmouth in 1988, partisanship ceased to affect posttest attitudes to Reagan, and issue agreement influenced attitudes only in November, even though the excerpts shown had been used in the 1984 study (Sullivan & Masters, 1989b, appendix I). For an explanation of this change in the effectiveness of the same stimulus material, see discussion of the role leader's status (below).

17. When gender is used as a factor in an analysis of variance, along with attitude toward the leader and the nature of display, interactive effects for gender by display and no main effect for gender can be interpreted as a confirmation that males and females are processing cues in a different way. Reanalysis of our studies

with this technique found a number of such interactions (Masters & Carlotti, 1988, tables 1 and 2).

18. In the 1988 study using displays of all presidential candidates, the intensity of the positive emotional response to Bush's H/R display did not rise significantly between February and November, nor did Dukakis's H/R display have significantly different effects over the course of the campaign. Because the experiment was designed to measure the change in emotional response over the campaign to the same display of each candidate, we chose the best available exemplar of a Bush and Dukakis H/R display from a very restricted set, and at the outset of the year Bush's display behavior was often perceived as blending fear with happiness (Suplee, 1988; Barnes, 1988). There is some evidence that changes in Bush's H/R display behavior over the course of the campaign (and particularly after the Republican convention) made him more evocative, whereas our study had to use an exemplar dating from the period before the first primaries.

James Sidanius

7. The Psychology of Group Conflict and the Dynamics of Oppression:
A Social Dominance Perspective

Why do people from one social group oppress and discriminate against the people from other groups? This is one of the most critical questions within the field of political psychology and one with which social scientists of all denominations are still struggling. This question is important because it covers such a broad array of human activities, including everything from mild forms of rivalry between youth gangs to the most virulent forms of international warfare and genocide. Most modern approaches to this question can be classified into five broad theoretical clusters. (a) Self-esteem enhancement models which view political attitudes and behavior as manifestations of basic character structure and intrapsychic dynamics (Adorno, 1950) or as mechanisms for the enhancement of the individual's self-esteem (e.g., Tajfel, 1978; Tajfel & Turner, 1986). (b) Rational actor models which assume that individuals adopt those political attitudes and behaviors which maximize or optimize their own personal or group-based material utilities (e.g., Downs, 1957; Mayhew, 1974; Niskanen, 1971). One of the most recent members of the rational actor cluster used to explain the dynamics of American race relations and racial policy is realistic group conflict theory, about which more will be said below (e.g., Bobo, 1983, 1988; Jackman & Muha, 1984; Sherif & Hovland, 1961). (c) Attitude consistency models which assume that group conflict is essentially driven by the individual's need to construct behaviors, values, attitudes and cognitions as internally consistent and meaningful wholes. One of the relatively early examples of theories within this cluster is Rokeach's belief similarity theory which essentially assumes that negative affect against minority groups is a function of the attitudinal and behavioral attributions made about that group (see Allen & Wilder, 1975; Byrne & Erwin, 1969; Hendricks, Bixenstine, & Hawkins, 1971; Hendricks & Hawkins, 1969; Insko & Robinson, 1967; Robinson & Insko, 1969; Rokeach, 1960; Serum & Myers, 1970; Tajfel, Sheikh, & Gardner, 1964). One of the most recent additions to this theoretical cluster is Symbolic Racism Theory which essentially views White opposition to redistribution social policies designed to help blacks as a function of "symbolic racism" rather than "old fashioned racism" (see Sears, 1988). We discuss this model in detail below.[1] (d) Biopolitical models are a relatively recent and closely related set of post-Darwinian theoretical perspectives which attempt to explain the dynamics of intergroup conflict either in terms of strategies designed to increase the inclusive fitness (i.e., reproductive success) of individual genes (the sociobiological variation) or in terms of the inclusive fitness of entire breeding population (i.e., the ethological variation; see e.g., Bailey, 1987; Mackenzie, 1978; Reynolds, Falger, & Vine, 1987; Somit, 1976; Thorson, 1970; Van den Berghe, 1978a, 1978b). (e) Finally, there exists a group of theories which are somewhat difficult to categorize because they are combinations of two or more of the above four categories. For lack of a better term, I will classify these as integrative models. The most recent arrival to this cluster, and a model which I shall be discussing in some detail in this chapter, is known as social dominance theory (see Sidanius & Pratto, 1991; Sidanius, Pratto, Martin & Stallworth, 1991).

From the theoretical clusters above, four theories have been or are becoming the focus of heated recent debate within political psychology. These include realistic group conflict theory, symbolic racism theory, social identity theory, and the biopolitical models of racism. In this chapter I shall attempt to sketch the major features, debates, advantages, and disadvantages of these four models and then present the fifth paradigm, which integrates a number of features of the previous four. This fifth model is social dominance theory.

Symbolic Racism Theory

In the early 1970s, social scientists began to argue that old-fashioned American racism characterized by public expressions of racial hatred, doctrines of (black) racial inferiority, and support for segregation was on the demise and was being replaced by racism of an entirely new breed, referred to as symbolic racism. This new, symbolic or modern racism consists of a combination of socialized anti-black affect and traditional American values such as the Protestant work ethic, belief in self-reliance and individual achievement. Among the more innovative positions that the symbolic racism school has taken, is the notion that political choice in general and whites' opposition to various racial policy positions regarding blacks in particular (e.g., busing, affirmative action), are driven neither by old-fashioned, "redneck" racism nor by individual self-interest, but rather by "symbolic attitudes" and "symbolic racism." For example, work by Kinder and Sears (1981) has shown that whites' preference for white vs. black political candidates has relatively little to do with perceived threats to the personal lives of whites (e.g., jobs, personal safety, children's schooling, etc.). Rather vote choice seemed to be largely determined by "symbolic" racial attitudes toward blacks (see also McConahay, 1982).

There are four major lines of criticism which have been leveled against symbolic racism theory (SRT). First, and most fundamentally, a number of critics have attacked the validity of the core concept itself. There is some empirical evidence indicating that what is being called "symbolic racism" is nothing more than simply old-fashioned racism in "drag"; this is to say old-fashioned racism expressed in less virulent and offensive ways (see Jacobson, 1985; Sniderman & Tetlock, 1986b; Weigel & Howes, 1985).

A second argument alleges that the symbolic racism literature contains a great deal of conceptual confusion over the meaning of central concepts, and the precise causal interconnections among these concepts. This confusion has been attributed to the fact that: (1) the three major symbolic racism theorists, Sears, McConahay, and Kinder, have all defined symbolic racism in slightly different ways; (2) some theorists have changed their definitions of symbolic racism over time; and (3) since all major symbolic racism theorists conceive of symbolic racism as being composed of "a blend of antiblack affect and traditional American moral values embodied in the Protestant ethic" (Kinder & Sears, 1981, p. 416), it is unclear whether or not a given person's opposition to a particular social policy (e.g., busing) is motivated by symbolic racism, anti-black affect, opposition to government intervention in general, or to some other factor(s).

A third attack against SRT comes from supporters of the "realistic group conflict" school (RGC; to be discussed below). In discussing the issue of whether or not self-interest really drives political choice, members of this school of thought have argued that symbolic racism theorists define self-interest in too narrow a fashion. The basic tension between symbolic racism and group conflict theories essentially involves two issues: (a) symbolic racism theory maintains that certain issues of public policy (e.g., busing, affirmative action, and voting for black candidates in elections), are NOT driven by rational self-interest. (b) Symbolic racial attitudes and political ideology do determine one's position on certain racially relevant issues of public policy, and voting for black candidates for public office. The "realistic" group conflict theorists maintain that not only are individuals interested in their personal welfare, but perhaps more importantly, they are also interested in the material interests of their reference social groups. Secondly, the realistic group conflict theorists maintain that political ideology primarily serves as a rationalization, masking concrete, group interests.

Supporters of the social dominance position (sD; to be discussed below) has voiced three objections to the sR paradigm. (a) Using structural equation analyses to test the causal assumptions of symbolic racism theory, Sidanius and his colleagues have argued that the symbolic racism model simply fails to give a statistically adequate explanation of their own empirical data (see Sidanius, Devereux, & Pratto, 1992). (b) Rather than a "new form of racism," the concept of symbolic racism is better thought of as a "legitimizing myth" (see discussion of this concept below). (c) The sD theorists have argued that symbolic racism theory suffers from theoretical parochialism. If symbolic racism theory is valid at all, this validity seems restricted to the domain of American, black vs. white racial conflict. The social dominance protagonists have argued that to be truly useful, a good theory of group conflict should be general and applicable across many different cultures and periods (see Sidanius & Pratto, 1990).

Realistic Group Conflict Theory

Realistic group conflict theory has a longer lifespan and appears to be more robust than the symbolic racism paradigm. The realistic group conflict paradigm basically assumes that ethnocentrism, intergroup discrimination and conflict are functions of real conflicts of interests over real things between real groups. Probably the most elegant experiment demonstrating this phenomena is Sherif and Hovland's now classic Robbers Cave Experiment (see Sherif & Hovland, 1961).

In this experiment, two groups of normally adjusted, white Protestant middle-class boys were sent to a three-week summer camp organized by a group of social psychologists in Robbers Cave, Oklahoma. Each group consisted of eleven boys and spent the first week of camp within their own groups and engaged in activities such as hiking, treasure hunting, etc. During this first week, sometimes referred to as Stage I, boys within each group got to know one another, establish their own group norms and routines and gave themselves group names, i.e., the "Rattlers" and the "Eagles." Neither group knew of the existence of the other. At the end of this first week the two groups were allowed to learn of the existence of one another. At stage II it was announced that there was to be a tournament between the two groups with the winning group to be awarded a rather expensive trophy and each member of the winning team to be given a medal and a four-bladed knife. In other words, the allocation situation was set up so as to constitute a zero–sum game. Very early on at the end of stage I, and as soon as the groups became aware of the other's existence, it was noticed that the two groups already began to form very negative stereotypes of one another. Of course, this situation only got much worse after the two groups began to compete actively. As a result of the competition structure among the two groups, one group finally winning the tournament and the continuing and escalating aggression between the two groups, the experimenters were finally forced to break off the experiment to avoid the possibility of the boys seriously injuring one another. Both quantitative and qualitative data revealed that this situation had created all of the expected characteristics of group ethnocentrism: (a) preference for in-group members as friend, (b) stereotyping of the out-group as "rotten cussers," "crybabies," "no-good cheats," and stereotyping of ingroup members as "brave," "friendly," "tough," etc., (c) overevaluation of ingroup products and underevaluation of outgroup products (see also replications by Blake & Mouton, 1962, 1979).

The results of the Robbers Cave experiment not only indicated that intergroup competition rather quickly leads to ethnocentrism and group conflict, but increased levels of intragroup morale, cohesiveness, and cooperation as well (see also Fiedler, 1967; Kalin & Marlowe, 1968; Vinacke, 1964). Therefore, the result of this experiment and others like it, seemed to give solid support for the notion that ethnocentrism and intergroup conflict are essentially a result of zero–sum conflicts over real and concrete assets. The implications for the attenuation of group conflict seemed equally clear; one must simply restructure situations in such a way as to eliminate their zero–sum character. However, as we shall see presently, the situation is not so simple.

Social Identity Theory

Among the major conclusions of the realistic group conflict approach was that (a) Groups form on the basis of developed internal interactions, interdependence and common norms among group members (referred to as "group formation"). (b) Group conflict and "ethnocentrism" are largely functions of "realistic" competition between groups over scarce resources. The work begun by Henri Tajfel at the University of Bristol was to challenge these two assumptions and as a result, have a major impact on the manner in which we conceptualize the dynamics of group conflict. Tajfel and his colleagues asked the fundamental question as to whether group formation and group competition were both sufficient and necessary conditions for the emergence of ethnocentrism and discrimination. The answer these researchers came on was that although group formation and concrete resource competition were certainly sufficient for the emergence of ethnocentrism and group conflict, they were by no means necessary (see Tajfel 1978, 1982a, 1982b; Tajfel, Flament, Billig, & Bundy, 1971; Tajfel & Turner, 1979).

The work of the Bristol school began by investigating the minimal conditions under which discrimination emerges. The somewhat surprising, counterintuitive, and disturbing answer that they stumbled upon was that the very cognition of "in-group" and "out-group" was a sufficient condition in and of itself to generate ethnocentric and discriminatory behaviors. In other words, neither group formation (i.e., in-group interactions, mutual dependence, common fate, common norms, etc.), nor "real" conflicts of interest were necessary for ethnocentrism and out-group discrimination to emerge. This conclusion was reached in the context of a now classical series of experiments known as the minimal groups paradigm.

The basic design of the minimal groups experiment consists of giving a sample of subjects some task, such as estimating the number of dots on a screen within a fraction of a second, and then informing the subjects that they are either "overestimators" or "underestimators." The subjects are also told that neither group is more accurate than any other group, just that these groups represent different perceptual styles. However, unknown to the subjects, the experimenter has assigned subjects to groups on a purely random basis, having nothing at all to do with perceptual style. Furthermore, the subjects do not actually meet other under- or overestimators or interact with them in any way (i.e., no group formation). Therefore, these groups are purely cognitive constructions, existing only in the subjects' minds. The second stage of the minimal groups paradigm consists of either allocating points to and/or making some kind of evaluative judgment about hypothetical individuals assumed to be either over- or underestimators. The subjects are not allowed to allocate points to themselves.

In the most simple and basic type of payoff matrix, subjects are instructed that they must choose one of fourteen payoff boxes such that a given number of points will be given to an anonymous member of group A when a given number of points is given to an anonymous member of group B (let's say the subject's in-group). The subjects are free to choose from among one of three basic strategies in allocating the rewards (note that each basic strategy also has intermediate positions): (a) maximum in-group favoritism, (b) maximum out-group favoritism, or (c) maximum fairness. The general result of this paradigm is the emergence of in-group favoritism. The subjects have a tendency to allocate more points to and make more positive evaluations of in-group than of out-group members and the results tend to be significantly more influenced by the in-group favoritism strategies than by group-fairness strategies. This in-group bias is interpreted as a form of ethnocentrism and emerges with groups whose "members" have no previous history of contact with one another or any history of existing as a group at all (see also Doise, 1988; Doise et al., 1972; Kahn & Ryen, 1972; Locksley, Ortiz, & Hepburn, 1980; Turner, 1978). Furthermore, this minimal in-group bias effect appears to be culturally transparent. Not only has it been observed using English samples, but also samples in Wales, Holland, the former West Germany, the United States, Switzerland, Hong Kong, and New Zealand (see Branthwaite & Jones, 1975; Dann & Doise, 1973; Doise & Sinclair, 1973; Howard & Rothbart, 1980; Locksley et al., 1980; Ng 1985; Vaughan, 1978). No culture has yet been discovered within which the minimal groups effects has not been found to operate.

Perhaps even more interesting are results which are found when people are given the choice between two other extreme strategies. In these matrices, besides opting for group fairness strategies, people also have the options of: (a) maximizing the joint return to both in-group and out-group or (b) maximizing ingroup-outgroup allocation at the cost of maximum in-group return. By choosing strategy (a), subjects can not only maximize the joint payoff, regardless of which group one belongs to, but can also maximize the absolute return to one's in-group. On the other hand, by choosing strategy (b), one maximizes the difference in return between in-group and out-group. However, by choosing this strategy, people are also maximizing group differences at the cost of maximization of ingroup profit. From a purely economic, rational actor perspective, alternative (b) is a most irrational strategy. Nonetheless, despite the patent economic irrationality of this option, the maximization of group differences at the cost of maximal in-group return is the option most often chosen.

Furthermore, pushing the minimalist aspect of this paradigm to its absolute limit, it was discovered that even when subjects are told that they are being divided into groups on a purely random basis by, for example, a toss of a coin or choice of a ticket in a lottery, and assigned to groups with meaningless names (e.g., "Kappas" and "Phis" or "A's" and "B's"), the in-group bias effect is still observed. This strategy seems to be consistent with a well-known Eastern European fable. One day God came upon Ivan, an impoverished farmer and said: "Ivan, I will grant you one wish; anything at all." Naturally, Ivan was very pleased at hearing this. God added: "However Ivan, anything I grant to you will be given to your neighbor twice over." After hearing this Ivan stood in silence for a few moments and finally said: "OK, God, take out one of my eyes."

These findings have some rather profound implications because they suggest that people are seemingly predisposed to discriminate against others even when such discrimination is not in their own material interest and the groups they are discriminating against do not even really exist.

Theoretical Explanations

How does the Bristol school explain these findings? Briefly, in order to simplify and manage the social universe, individuals establish cognitive categories of their social universe (e.g., "blacks," "whites," "homeless people"). The establishment of these categories are necessary for the individual to deal with the almost overwhelming complexity of the natural and social universes. Among the most important of these simplifications are the categories that represent social groups. Once these group categories are formed, the individual establishes group membership into one or several of them. Almost immediately upon the individual's psychological inclusion of self into one or several of these categories, each group then becomes associated with a set of behavioral expectations, dispositional attributions and positive or negative evaluations (e.g., "blacks are violent and stupid"; "Asians are industrious," etc.). These expectations, attributions, and evaluations are generally not idiosyncratic to the individual but compose a consensually accepted set; they are evaluations and expectations that almost everyone in a given social system accepts to one degree or another. One of the major motivational assumptions of social identity theory is that all people will strive to achieve a positive social identity. To the extent to which one's in-group is positively evaluated, the individual's need for positive social identity is satisfied. One of the ways that individuals can help manufacture positive social identity is via the process of discriminatory comparison of the in-group with some relevant out-group. These discriminatory comparisons can manifest themselves in actual discriminatory behavior toward members of the out-group and/or relative devaluation of out-group members and the out-group as a whole. On the other hand, if the comparison of the individual's in-group with some relevant out-group produces a negative self-evaluation, the individual is left with three major options. (1) Defection. The individual might choose to exit from her negatively evaluated social group and join another group which offers the opportunity of positive social identity. However, this option is only available if (a) the boundaries between social groups are permeable and the person can easily move from one group to the other or (b) the boundaries between groups are impermeable, but the individual is able to disguise herself and pass anyway. For example, in large sections of the United States, the boundaries between social classes are relatively permeable, and individuals have the option of moving up in the class system by a process of individual transformation (e.g., by changing income level, speech pattern, dress, social habits). On the other hand, unlike class groups, American ethnic groups are relatively impermeable and the individual is only able to defect if she can maintain a credible disguise (e.g., light-skinned blacks passing for white).

(2) Social Creativity. In order to achieve a positive comparative outcome, the individual might alter and/or redefine key elements of the comparison situation. There are three major ways to achieve this:

(a) *Dimensional Shift.* The individual might choose to compare the ingroup with some relevant outgroup with respect to a different dimension of comparison. For example, in comparing blacks to whites, a black child might choose to use the dimension of athletic prowess rather than family wealth as the appropriate dimension of group comparison.

(b) *Value Reassignment.* Members of disadvantaged groups might choose to reassign the value associated with their group membership by changing negative valences to positive valences. For example, instead of being ashamed of blackness and association with their African heritage, in the 1960s African Americans began to reassign the value attached to these characteristics by asserting that "black is beautiful!"

(c) *Relevant Group Selection.* Everything else being equal, it will be more advantageous for a low-status group to avoid comparing itself to a high-status group. Therefore, to achieve a positive outcome of the comparison process, a low status group will tend to choose a relevant comparison group of the same status as the ingroup or below.

(3) Social Competition. The ingroup may attempt to achieve positive distinctiveness by direct competition and confrontation with the high-status out-group. This confrontation will usually manifest itself in competition over material assets or value through collective political action (e.g., mass movements, rebellion, insurgency).

Difficulties of Social Identity Theory

Despite SIT's widespread and growing influence, Hinkle & Brown (1990), among others, have pointed out three major areas of inconsistency between the theoretical expectations of the model and empirical research findings. These difficulties involve: (1) rather consistent findings of out-group favoritism. (2) It is not clear along which dimensions in-groups will discriminate against out-groups and which dimensions they will not. (3) The evidence supporting the expectation of a strong, positive correlation between in-group identification and in-group favoritism is rather spotty and most inconsistent.

Of all the difficulties facing social identity theory, out-group favoritism is perhaps the most troublesome. The seriousness of this difficulty arises from the fact that out-group favoritism stands in direct contradiction to the model's theoretical assumptions. Although social identity theory does allow for situations in which out-group discrimination will not occur (i.e., individual mobility), there are no assumptions or mechanisms within the theory that will lead to the expectation of out-group favoritism. The existence of out-group favoritism is especially problematic with respect to low-status and subordinate groups. Because of their relatively disadvantaged social position, it is precisely members of low-status groups who should have the greatest motivation to engage in favorable and discriminatory out-group comparisons in order to bolster their sense of self-worth and self-esteem. For example, in a study by Yee and Brown (1989), children as young as three years were induced to participate in "egg/spoon" relay races. The children were given feedback that their teams were either fast or slow. Consistent with the general social identity perspective, the children within the "fast" group exhibited more positive evaluations of in-group members. However, contrary to what social identity theory would predict, the children within the "slow" group also tended to give the children in the "fast" group more positive evaluations as well. These results were found for three of four age groups. Furthermore, Brown (1978) reports similar results in a study of production, development, and toolroom workers at a British aircraft factory. The results showed no evidence of downrating or discrimination against the relatively high-status toolroom workers by the relatively low status production and development workers. However, although there was some evidence of development workers claiming superiority when comparing themselves to production workers, there was no evidence of reciprocal downrating of development workers by production workers. The production workers rated themselves as equal to the development workers. As mentioned by Hinkle and Brown (1990), these results can be explained by reasoning that (a) the production workers were comparing themselves with some other group outside of the work situation or (b) the work group did serve as a significant basis for social identity for the development group but not for the production group. Therefore, left within the constraints of social identity theory, it is difficult to determine a priori whether or not a given in-group will manifest in-group favoritism against a specific group within a specific context.

What is one to think when members of low-status groups display out-group favoritism and show no evidence of either individual upward mobility, social creativity, downrating of an alternative out-group or social competition? The general evidence seems to indicate that theoretically consistent in-group favoritism will only occur when the in-group occupies a social status as high or higher than the out-group. On the other hand, out-group favoritism seems to occur when the in-group occupies lower social status than the out-group, especially when the status continuum is perceived to be both legitimate and stable (see Brown, 1978; Sachdev & Bourhis, 1985; Skevington, 1981; Turner & Brown, 1978; van Knippenberg & van Oers, 1984).

I will refer to the phenomenon of out-group favoritism as a function of social status as a manifestation of asymmetrical in-group bias (to be discussed in detail). Although this behavior asymmetry phenomenon cannot be easily or seamlessly accommodated within the constraints of social identity theory, it is both accounted for and even derivable from social dominance theory (as we shall see).

The Biopolitical Approach

Like sociobiology, ethology and evolutionary psychology in general, the biopolitical approach to race and ethnicity is essentially a straightforward application of Darwinian principles to the domain of intergroup dynamics. Classical Darwinism basically asserts that the morphology and behavior of living organisms have evolved in response to the pressures and opportunities of their environments. Those morphological structures and behavioral repertoires that maximize the number of offspring an organism is able to produce will tend to survive and those morphological and behavioral characteristics and patterns which do not enable the organism to successfully reproduce will, over time, become extinct. Sociobiology and ethology have extended this basic reasoning to include also the social behaviors of animals and the highly complex social behaviors, mores and social institutions of homo sapiens. This implies that systems of complex social interactions among individual organisms of a particular species or group are subject to the same laws of natural selection as simpler morphological characteristics such as size, coloring, or diet, etc. Genes will survive through evolutionary time to the extent to which they are able to maximize inclusive fitness, or reproductive success within given environments. Besides the technique of reciprocal altruism, kin selection and nepotism are among the major mechanisms by which social organisms use to maximize inclusive fitness (see Ross, 1991; Shaw & Wong, 1989; Van den Berghe, 1987). In addition to its own reproductive activities, an organism can perpetuate its own genes by helping other organisms with which it is closely related. Everything else being equal, the greater the degree of genetic relationship, the greater this "altruism" is expected to be.

Keeping in mind that race and ethnicity are often based upon endogamous and thereby closely related groups (see especially Van den Berghe, 1978a), it is therefore easy to see how sociobiology and evolutionary psychology would explain ethnocentrism. Ethnocentrism can be viewed as essentially an expression of nepotism, which in turn, is a gene's way of maximizing its inclusive fitness. This principle is assumed to apply to all social organisms, to ants and human beings alike.

Human groups can be conceived as consisting of essentially two different categories: interest groups and primordial groups. Interest groups are based upon voluntary associations in which members share common concerns and in which there are reciprocal relations of support among members (e.g., social clubs, political parties, social classes). Primordial groups, on the other hand, are ascribed, endogamous entities in which members either have or perceive themselves to have common ancestry (e.g., families, clans, tribes). Ethnocentrism can, therefore, be regarded as nepotism with respect to one's primordial group. Within the biopolitical paradigm, not only are primordial groups universal across all human societies, highly salient, emotionally compelling, permanent, and capable of unleashing orgies of bloodshed and cruelty, but they are the first kinds of groups formed. Human beings are predisposed to form primordial groups.

There are a number of interesting points of intersection between social identity theory, realistic group theory, and the biopolitical paradigm of ethnocentrism. To begin, from social identity theory we will recall that the tendency to form ingroup-outgroup distinctions and to discriminate in favor of one's ingroup seems to be a universal and ubiquitous phenomenon. This fact is compatible with the observations of universal ethnocentrism made by ethologists and comparative anthropologists (see Eibl-Eibesfeldt, 1989; West, 1967). Thus the tendency to make ingroup-outgroup distinctions gives the appearance of being "hard-wired" and as such can be regarded as the psychological precondition for the development of primordial group loyalty. Seen in this light, one can then regard the "minimal group" within the framework of social identity theory as an "empty primordial group" or a "primordial proto-group." The minimal group functions as the psychological platform upon which highly salient and compelling primordial group identifications and loyalties are built. The biopolitical approach to ethnocentrism as nepotism is also consistent with empirical findings within the social identity tradition indicating that ethnocentrism is primarily expressed as discrimination in favor of the ingroup rather than discrimination against the out-group (see Brewer, 1979). Furthermore, like realistic group conflict theory, within the biopolitical paradigm of ethnocentrism, the entire perspective of ethnocentrism as nepotism must be seen within the larger context of scarce resource competition in which each gene pool is competing with other gene pools to maximize inclusive fitness.

Although the biopolitical paradigm of ethnocentrism and discrimination is in many ways elegant and parsimonious, its scientific value is limited by the fact that very few researchers have attempted to put it to empirical test in a manner which leads to nontrivial and clearly falsifiable predictions (e.g., see comments by Ross, 1991). Given this problem, and the fact that the model is regarded by contemporary social scientists as "politically incorrect," it should be no surprise that the biopolitical paradigm is among the least influential of the modern approaches to intergroup conflict.

Social Dominance Theory

Recently, Sidanius and his colleagues (see Sidanius, 1989; Sidanius & Pratto, 1991; Sidanius, Pratto, Martin, & Stallworth, 1991) have developed an alternative model of ethnocentrism and discrimination which incorporates many of the assumptions of social identity theory, neoclassical elitism theory (see Michels, 1962; Mosca, 1939; Pareto, 1979), evolutionary psychology, as well as literature within political attitude and public opinion research. Social dominance theory begins with the observation that all human societies are inherently group-based hierarchies and inherently oppressive. Following observations made by Van den Berghe (1978b), we assume that most modern social systems are composed of three related, yet distinctly different stratification systems: an age system, a sex system, and a group system. By group systems we are referring to the classification of individuals into clans, nations, races, caste, social classes, religious sects, etc. Traditional and technologically simpler societies are almost exclusively age and sex stratification systems, and as Karl Marx observed, group systems do not really emerge until societies become more technologically sophisticated and begin to amass economic surplus. Social dominance theory primarily concerns itself with sex and group systems of social hierarchy. We then go on to make four additional assumptions:

> (1) Human social systems are predisposed to form group-based social hierarchies. This social hierarchy consists of at least one Hegemonic group at its top and at least one Negative Reference Group at its bottom.

Human social systems consist of essentially two types of social hierarchies: (a) achieved hierarchies and (b) ascribed hierarchies. Achieved hierarchy comes closest to what one generally refers to as "meritocracy" and represents a social preference or status structure based on the socially useful and/or desirable characteristics possessed by a given individual. Ralph Johnson, a fourteen-year-old basketball star, might enjoy high social status among his peers, especially if his peers are basketball fanatics, for no other reason than the fact that he is a very good basketball player. Accordingly, in the schoolyard this group of boys is likely to develop a social hierarchy system, including a pecking order, based on the boys' relative abilities at basketball. With ascribed or group-based hierarchies, on the other hand, we have hierarchies based on one's membership in a particular primordial group. However, in complex human social systems, these two types of social hierarchies are not independent of one another. This is because access to the means of achieved social status mobility (e.g., education, specialized skills) are differentially accessible to different people depending upon their primordial group membership. This is to suggest that in complex, multigroup societies, this "achieved" component of social status and social mobility is, to a very significant degree, endogenous and dependent upon one's original primordial group membership.

Using Putnam's law of increasing disproportion (Putnam, 1976, pp. 33–37), in complex, multi-ethnic and multi-group societies, almost by definition, hegemonic groups are those whose proportional representation in decision making roles increase most sharply with the amount of power that these roles contain. The converse is true for negative reference groups.

(2) Males will tend to possess a disproportionate degree of political power. We refer to this as the Iron Law of Andrarchy.

This implies that all human social systems are andrarchical and that Putnam's law of increasing disproportion is assumed to apply to gender as well. The greater the power a given social role embraces, the greater the probability that role will be occupied by a male.

(3) Most common forms of group conflict and oppression (e.g., racism, sexism, nationalism, classism) can be regarded as different manifestations of the same predisposition toward group-based social hierarchy.

(4) The formation of social hierarchy and primordial groups are survival strategies adopted by humans.

Using evolutionary reasoning, the formation of primordial groups operating within the framework of group-based hierarchies can be seen as serving the goal of inclusive fitness by providing the socio-psychological reference point for the operation of kin selection and nepotism. There are two ways in which this might operate:

(a) Everything else being equal, social hierarchy might help to control internal conflict within social systems. Those with greater social status will serve as "conflict managers" to which those lower social status will tend to defer.

(b) In group competition for scarce resources, social groups which are hierarchically organized will have a competitive advantage over those social systems which are not hierarchically organized. This view is built on the assumption that proto- and early human troupes can be thought of as an ambulatory "attack and defense units," highly willing to exploit opportunities to attack weaker and/or less well-organized troupes and needing to be prepared against attack from rival troupes. Everything else being equal, military success will go to that troupe with the most efficient hierarchical organization. Therefore, those protohuman groups that could very quickly form hierarchical chains of command or were already hierarchically organized would have a

competitive advantage over those troupes that were horizontally or demo-
cratically organized.

Given these assumptions, social dominance theory primarily concerns
itself with the specific mechanisms by which social hierarchies are established and maintained and the consequences these mechanisms have for
the nature and distribution of social attitudes and the functioning of social
institutions within social systems. The processes by which all of this is
assumed to take place are sketched out in figure 7.1.

Starting from the extreme right-hand side of figure 7.1, the social
dominance model assumes that group-based social hierarchy is driven by
three basic processes, aggregated individual discrimination, aggregated
institutional discrimination and behavioral asymmetry. These processes
are driven, in part, by legitimizing myths, which in turn are effected by
group identity/social comparison processes and social dominance orientation. Finally, social dominance orientation will be significantly effected
by one's sex/gender; males should be significantly more social dominance oriented than females. For the remainder of this chapter I will
discuss each of these components and processes in detail.

Aggregated Individual Discrimination

These are the simple, daily, sometimes quite inconspicuous individual
acts of discrimination by individual$_A$ against individual$_B$. Examples of
such discrimination can be found in husband/wife family decision making, the decision of a given employer not to hire or promote a given
minority group member, or the decision of a given voter not to vote for a
given candidate due purely to that candidate's group membership (e.g.,
being Asian). When such acts of individual discrimination are aggregated
over many thousands of individuals each day and over many years, they
will tend to result in and/or maintain clear differences in social status
between groups.

Aggregated Institutional Discrimination

These are decisions made by public and private institutions such as
courts, corporations, schools, etc. which make differential allocations of
social resources to different social groups. These differential allocation
decisions have sometimes been referred to as institutional discrimination
(see Feagin & Feagin, 1978). Examples of this are discriminatory laws

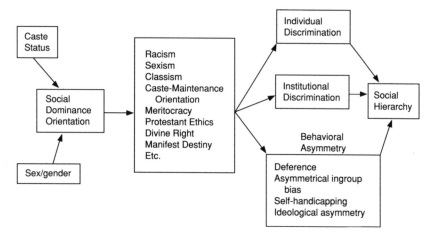

Figure 7.1. General Social Dominance model.

such as apartheid laws, institutionalized and sanctioned slavery, court decisions and salary scales rewarding different groups of workers different incomes. Besides the unequal distribution of social value, institutions also help maintain the integrity of the social hierarchy by the use of Systematic Terror. By systematic terror we are referring to use of violence or the threat of violence by high status individuals against lower-status individuals for the purpose of social hierarchy maintenance. There are three forms of systematic terror: (a) official terror, (b) semiofficial terror, and (c) unofficial terror. According to social dominance theory, all three forms of systematic terror are most likely to occur when members of negative reference groups are perceived to step out of place. This implies stepping out of their ascribed roles in the group-based social hierarchy. Systematic terror is likely to be most ferocious when this out-of-place behavior manifests itself in violence against members of the hegemonic group. This is especially so when negative-reference-group males sexually accost hegemonic females. We refer to this as the out-of-place principle. Therefore, systematic terror can be conceived of as a tool to encourage "deference" on the part of negative reference group members.

Official terror is manifested in legally sanctioned violence and the threat of violence perpetrated by organs of the state and that is disproportionately directed toward members of negative reference groups. The most salient example of such official violence is the disproportionate use of the death penalty against blacks and Hispanics in the United States. Not only are African Americans who commit homicide against European Americans more severely punished than European Americans who commit homicide against African Americans, but they are more severely punished than when they commit homicide against other African Americans, as well (see, e.g., Government Accounting Office, 1990; Sidanius, 1988). As a specific case in point, Paternoster (1983) showed that when blacks kill whites, prosecutors are *forty-four times more likely* to request the death penalty than when blacks kill other blacks.

Furthermore, at least within group- rather than sex-systems of social stratification, the validity of the out-of-place-principle does not appear to be restricted to the domain of race, but consistent with the expectations of social dominance theory, there is evidence indicating that it is applicable to group stratification systems in general rather than race systems in particular. For example, Farrell and Swigert (1978) divided crime victims and offenders into high and low socioeconomic status categories and then studied the factors which could reliably distinguish between four victim-status-offender-status groups. The sample included 444 defendants and 432 victims of criminal homicide between 1955 and 1973 from a large urban jurisdiction in the United States. Status was defined using Treiman's (1977) classification system. The researchers examined the ability of five variables to distinguish among the four offender-victim categories (a) use of private attorney, (b) trial (by jury), (c) bail, (d) offender's prior record and (e) final conviction severity. The results of the analysis disclosed that punishment severity made the largest contribution to the ability to distinguish among the offender-status—victim-status categories. Consistent with the out-of-place principle, low-status murderers of high-status victims received the most severe punishments. It is also interesting to note that in addition to receiving the most severe sanctions, violent crimes by negative-reference-group individuals against hegemonic-group individuals are also relatively rare (Karmen, 1984). Furthermore, there is reason to believe that official terror is quite widespread. For example, in a recent study of 138 countries, Amnesty International reported general, comprehensive and widespread state violence against ethnic and racial minorities. This terror consisted of mass arrests, trials without due process of law, extended detention without trial, beatings, torture of adults, and the torture of children in front of their parents, etc.

Semiofficial terror is violence or intimidation by internal security forces (e.g., police, secret police, paramilitary organizations) that is disproportionately directed against negative reference groups and that does not enjoy the legal and official sanction of the political and judicial systems. Examples of semiofficial terror are the death squads that have played such a prominent role in the politics of Central and South America. More recently, semiofficial terror was exemplified by the savage beating of Rodney King by police officers in Los Angeles on March 3, 1991. From a perspective of social dominance not only was the Rodney King affair not an aberration, as many police officials and politicians claim, but in contrast to many traditional group conflict models, the affair is also not a sign of "pathology," "lack of control," or "system failure." What one can witness in the videotape of the King beating was Los Angeles police operating, not only normally, but as it is supposed to operate. From the perspective of social dominance theory, the Rodney King beating was simply a routine exercise of deference enforcement.

Unofficial terror is that violence or threat of violence perpetrated by private individuals or small groups from the hegemonic strata against members of negative reference groups and that enjoys the tacit approval if not active participation of members of the security forces (e.g., lynchings by the Ku Klux Klan). Although this terror represents "private politics," it can be widespread in scope and comprehensive in its effects. For example, at least 3,400 African Americans were lynched in the United States between 1882 and 1927 (Pomper, 1970).

One implication of institutional discrimination and associated forms of terror is that the legal and criminal justice system will be one of the major instruments used in establishing and maintaining the hierarchical caste system. Clearly, the internal security and criminal justice systems are designed to maintain "law and order." However, from a social dominance perspective, the "law" is that which is determined by hegemonic groups, and the "order" is the defense and maintenance of the hierarchy of dominance. Therefore, contrary to the commonly held assumption that legal discrimination against members of subordinate groups are simply isolated examples of system "pathology" (e.g., the Rodney King case), social dominance theory suggests that the "law" will be used in a systematically discriminatory manner against members of negative reference groups.

However, at the same time that the legal and criminal justice systems must operate in a discriminatory manner for oppression to function smoothly, it is also extremely important that these mechanisms not appear to be openly discriminatory. In other words, it is crucial that the system be able to maintain plausible deniability (e.g., "We do not discriminate, and if there are instances of discrimination, these are the rare exceptions rather than the rule").

Many of these principles can be captured and summarized by social dominance theory's three Laws of Law. These state that when society's laws have been violated and everything else is equal: (a) The First Law of

Law: The expected level of negative sanction directed against members of negative reference groups will be greater than the expected level of negative sanctions directed against members of hegemonic groups. (b) The Second Law of Law: When violence is committed against members of Hegemonic groups by negative reference group members the level of negative sanctions directed against the perpetrator will be especially severe. (c) The Third Law of Law: The level of social dominance orientation (to be discussed below) of hegemonic members of the security forces (e.g., police, secret police) will be particularly great compared with other sectors of the population.

Behavioral Asymmetry

Besides the processes of individual and institutional discrimination, social hierarchy is also developed and maintained by behavioral asymmetry. By this term we mean that, on the average, the behavioral repertoires of individuals belonging to groups at different levels of the social hierarchy will show significant differences, differences that have been produced by the dynamics of and which, in turn, reinforce and perpetuate the group-based hierarchy system. This behavioral asymmetry is induced by socialization patterns, stereotypes, legitimizing myths (to be explained in more detail below), and the operation of systematic terror. There are at least four different varieties of behavioral asymmetry: (1) systematic out-group favoritism or deference, (2) asymmetrical in-group bias, (3) self-handicapping, (4) ideological asymmetry.

Deference or out-group favoritism can be said to occur when in-group members actually discriminate in favor of out-group members. Classical Uncle Tomming on the part of blacks toward whites is one of the clearest examples of deference behavior in recent American history. Also consistent with the expectations of social dominance theory and discussed above, a good deal of evidence shows that in reward allocation situations, out-group favoritism or deference is most often found in the behavior of low-status individuals toward higher-status individuals (see Brown, 1978; Sachdev & Bourhis, 1985; Skevington, 1981; Turner & Brown, 1978; Van Knippenberg & Van Oers, 1984). One of the best-known examples of out-group favoritism or deference of a low-status group toward a high-status group can be found in the Clark and Clark (1947) study in which black children preferred white over black dolls. (For more recent discussions of this "doll" approach to self-esteem, see Fine & Bowers, 1984; Powell & Hopson, 1988; Vaughan, 1986).

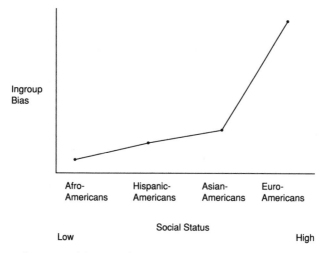

Figure 7.2. In-group bias as a function of primordial group social status.

Asymmetrical in-group bias could be viewed as a special case of out-group deference and occurs when, everything else being equal, the degree of in-group favoritism or nepotism (i.e., the default condition), is significantly lower among low-status than high-status people. One can make a strong case that opposition to interracial marriage and interracial dating reflects the degree preference for one's own group or in-group bias. If we can accept opposition to interracial marriage and interracial dating as one instantiation of in-group bias, then if in-group bias were perfectly symmetrical, one should expect all ethnic groups to be equally opposed to it (or in favor of it). However, social dominance theory predicts that not only will different ethnic groups show significantly different degrees of opposition to interracial marriage and interracial dating, but their opposition should be positively correlated with the social status of one's primordial group. The higher the social status, the weaker the support for this kind of "boundary crossing." Using a very large sample of University of Texas students, four major ethnic groups (i.e., European-Americans, Asian-Americans, Hispanic-Americans and African Americans) were ordered according to their empirically established relative social status (see Sidanius & Pratto, 1991) and their degree of in-group bias (i.e., attitudes toward interracial dating and marriage) were examined. The empirical results were found to be consistent with the expectations of social dominance theory (see fig. 7.2).

Not only were there highly significant differences in the level of in-group bias (i.e., opposition to interracial marriage and interracial dating, also known as caste-maintenance orientation); $(F3,4818)=64.69$, $p<10^{-11}$) as a function of ethnic group membership, but as social dominance theory would predict, this opposition shows a highly significant monotonic tendency to increase as a function of the social status of one's ethnic group (i.e., $F_{linear}[1,4818]=184.45$, $p<10^{-11}$).

Self-handicapping occurs when individuals from low-status primordial groups function significantly below their true abilities due to the lower expectations or stereotypes associated with their primordial group membership. These lower expectations and stereotypes exist both within their own minds and the minds of hegemonic group members. From a social dominance perspective, negative stereotypes of negative reference groups are important not only because of the discriminatory behavior they induce in members of hegemonic groups, but perhaps even more importantly because they serve as self-handicapping behavioral scripts for members of negative reference groups.

One example of the self-handicapping effect was first clearly and empirically demonstrated by Rosenthal and Jacobson (1968). These researchers informed elementary school teachers which children in their classes could be expected to show dramatic academic improvement in the coming school year, based on an assumably reliable "Harvard Test of Inflected Acquisition." In reality, this test did not actually exist and roughly one-third of the students were designated at random as "spurters." At the end of first and second grade school years, those students randomly designated as "spurters" showed significant and substantial improvement in their IQ scores in comparison to the control group. Furthermore, despite certain methodological problems with the original study, the effect has been replicated in more than one hundred studies and found to be stable (see Brophy, 1982). Furthermore, the research has also shown that just as higher teacher expectations can result in increased performance, low teacher expectations will also contribute to poor student performance. Follow-up research in this area has shown that the processes by which teachers communicate these lower expectations to low-expectation students include such things as (a) giving them less time to answer questions, (b) giving them more criticism for failure and (c) providing less eye contact (see Allington, 1980; Chaiken, Sigler, & Derlaga, 1974; Cooper & Baron, 1977; Taylor, 1979). Given the fact that social systems generally have lower expectations for members of negative reference groups, it is then easy to see how the net result of this will be self-handicapping, leading to differential access to the means of upward group mobility and thereby maintenance of the hierarchical status structure.

Ideological Asymmetry. Within the broad domain of politics, and intergroup behavior, one of the broadest and most predictively useful sociopolitical attitude domains is general liberalism-conservatism. This dimension will predict a wide number of political behaviors, including such things as voting behavior and support of various foreign and domestic policy initiatives. It can be thought of as a "generalized, political-behavior predisposition." Among other things, this predisposition will also predict racial and ethnic attitudes and behaviors. Furthermore, there is reason to suspect that the general left-right continuum will be related to the degree of in-group bias. However, the logic of behavioral asymmetry leads us to expect that, everything else being equal, the strength of this relationship will systematically vary as a function of the social status of a given caste. The higher the social status of the primordial group (or caste), the stronger this relationship is expected to be. For high-status and hegemonic groups we should expect a relatively strong relationship between in-group bias and generalized liberalism-conservatism; for negative reference groups we should expect a very weak relationship between in-group bias and generalized liberalism-conservatism. In other words, for hegemonic groups, the very important dimension of generalized political ideology is very much a function of the desire to maintain hegemonic social structure. For lower-status and negative reference groups, the general dimension of liberalism-conservatism will have relatively little to do with preference for one's own group or caste maintenance. Therefore, the degree to which the output of public policy is the result of the generalized political attitudes of hegemonic group members is the degree to which this public policy output is also likely to reflect the in-group bias of hegemonic groups and with relatively little counterbalancing from negative reference groups. The net result of all of this will be reinforced social hierarchy. We refer to this as the ideological asymmetry hypothesis.

To test this hypothesis, within each ethnic group of the large Texas sample previously discussed, Sidanius and Pratto tested a simple causal model in which (1) Gender helped determine both in-group bias (as before operationalized as opposition to interracial marriage or interracial dating) and political conservatism and (2) political conservatism was assumed to be determined by in-group bias. All of this implies three causal paths among the constructs.[2] Of these three paths (expressed as slopes), the researchers reasoned that the paths between sex and in-group

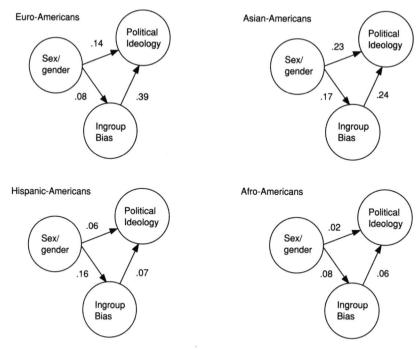

Figure 7.3. Political ideology as a function of in-group bias and sex/gender.

bias and political conservatism would show no significant differences over the four ethnic/social status groups. In other words, these relationships should be invariant over social status.[3] However, if the ideological asymmetry hypothesis is correct, the same should not hold for the path between in-group bias and political conservatism. Here it is expected that the higher social status of a primordial group, the stronger the path between in-group bias and political ideology should be. This is merely to imply that for hegemonic and high-status groups, political ideology will very much be a function of the desire to maintain caste distinctions between primordial groups, while for low-status and negative reference groups, political ideology will be largely independent of in-group bias. Multigroup, structural equation analyses disclosed that these expectations were confined. There were no statistically significant differences in the paths between sex/gender and in-group bias and political conservatism across the four ethnic groups. Consistent with the assumptions of social dominance theory, in each case, males were found to show slightly higher levels of in-group bias and be more politically conservative than females. Most importantly, however, and in direct support of the ideological asymmetry hypothesis, the higher the social status of the primordial group, the stronger the path between in-group bias and political conservatism. Using the unstandardized coefficients, the strongest path was found for the European-Americans (b=.39), and the weakest and essentially zero-path was found for the African Americans (b=.06; see fig. 7.3). In other words, for hegemonic European-Americans, political conservatism was quite substantially related to their desire to favor one's own group and maintain caste distinctions among ethnic groups, while for African Americans and Hispanic-Americans, political conservatism was largely irrelevant to these concerns.

These findings are also consistent with the empirical results from two other independent research teams not operating within the conceptual framework of social dominance theory. For example, Mercer and Cairns (1981) found that political conservatism was significantly correlated with anti-Catholic attitudes among Protestants in Northern Ireland but was not significantly correlated with anti-Protestant affect among Northern Irish Catholics. Likewise, Bahr and Chadwick (1974) uncovered that anti-Indian affect was significantly associated with general political conservatism among European Americans but was not associated with anti-white affect among Native Americans. The ideological asymmetry hypothesis is also consistent with Carmines and Stimson's (1982) findings that for European-Americans, political ideology is very much concerned with the issue of race.

The Subtheory of Legitimizing Myths

Public policy decisions, individual acts of discrimination, and behavioral asymmetry will tend to be affected by what we have termed legitimizing myths. Legitimizing myths are attitudes, values, beliefs, or ideologies that provide moral and intellectual support to and justification for the group-based hierarchical social structure and the unequal distribution of value in social systems. Legitimizing myths can be distinguished by three orthogonal characteristics: functional type, ideological flavor and robustness.

There are three broad functional types of legitimizing myths: paternalistic myths, reciprocal myths, and sacred myths. Paternalistic legitimizing myths justify social hierarchy and inequality by asserting that hegemonic groups are actually serving the interests of the entire society, including negative reference groups. This type of myth often asserts that the hegemonic group is functioning in a manner in which the negative reference group is quite incapable. A good example of a paternalistic legitimizing myth is the North American defense of chattel slavery, in which it was argued that slavery was actually benevolent and in the interests of blacks because they were simply incapable of attending to their own affairs. Using this argument, slavery was not only economically necessary but morally compelling (see Fitzhugh, 1854). Reciprocal myths justify social hierarchy by arguing that there is "equitable" exchange between hegemonic elites and other sectors of the population. Most representative democracies use arguments of this type. Sacred legitimizing myths support the hegemonic structure by arguing that the ruling elites have been given their positions by God, the "Ancestors," or as a result of virtuous deeds in previous lives. Two examples of this type of "myth" are the doctrines of the divine right of kings and papal infallibility.

Legitimizing myths come in at least three ideological flavors: left-wing, right-wing, and centrist/liberal. An example of a left-wing legitimizing myth includes Lenin's theory of the leading and central role of the communist party. This theory maintains that communists are the only individuals who truly understand the "real interests" of the working class and who are disciplined enough to serve those interests. As a result, in order to further the interests of the working class, the communist party should have absolute monopoly on state power.[4] Examples of right-wing legitimizing myths include beliefs such as the modern theories of European racial superiority and the white man's burden, the Monroe Doctrine, and Manifest Destiny. Finally, centrist/liberal legitimizing myths would include such things as the theory of meritocracy, the American Protestant work ethic and the myth of individual achievement.

Legitimizing myths are potent or robust to the extent to which they: (a) help to promote, maintain, or overthrow a given group-based hierarchy and (b) are well-anchored, attached to, and consistent with other centrally integrating conceptions of the "moral" and the "true" within social systems. Truly robust and potent legitimizing myths will be embraced by all major segments of the social systems and by members of negative reference groups as well as by members of the hegemonic group, even when these myths are clearly used to oppress the negative reference group. For example, belief in inherent white superiority (i.e., racism) was a very robust legitimizing myth in the antebellum South. This implies that blacks believed themselves to be inherently inferior almost to the same extent that whites believed themselves to be superior.[5] Therefore, in a very real sense, in the presence of very powerful and robust legitimizing myths, we can regard the exercise of oppression as a cooperative venture between oppressors and oppressed, and based upon shared ideologies and cosmologies. Another example of a very robust legitimizing myth from our own times is the Western thesis of meritocracy and individual achievement. This meritocracy myth is extremely powerful because it is so well-anchored and consistent with Westerner's and especially Americans' general notions of morality and fairness that the idea of advancement by merit takes on the appearance of self-evident truth.

Social Dominance Orientation

A key element of social dominance theory and the component that gives the theory its name, is social dominance orientation, or what we also sometimes refer to as the generalized imperial imperative. This construct concerns the degree to which individuals desire social dominance and superiority for themselves and their primordial groups over other groups. This "will to group dominance" will manifest itself not only in individual acts of discrimination but in adherence to numerous legitimizing myths and support for hierarchy-producing public policy.

It is at this point we shall refine our definition of legitimizing myths. Not only are legitimizing myths assumed to provide moral and intellectual justification for acts of individual and institutional discrimination, but they must be shown related to social dominance orientation. Consequently, a more comprehensive definition of a legitimizing myth would be any belief/attitude/value/ideology that can be demonstrated to be significantly related to social dominance orientation and acts of individual discrimination and/or support of hierarchy-producing public policy.

Group Identity and Social Comparison Processes

A number of assumptions from social identity theory are incorporated into the social dominance paradigm. First, social comparison processes are assumed to drive individual acts of in-group favoritism. Furthermore, like social identity theory, social dominance theory also assumes that these acts of individual, in-group favoritism will tend to enhance the self-esteem of the actor.

However, there are also some important differences between the two models. Unlike social identity theory, the sd perspective is firmly anchored to biopolitical, evolutionary, and system-functional explanations of discrimination and prejudice. Secondly, the social dominance para-

digm views in-group favoritism as simply one manifestation of a ubiquitous drive toward the establishment of group-based hierarchy systems,
the ultimate function of which is to aid the survival of breeding populations through evolutionary time. Third, and perhaps most importantly,
despite its cross-cultural robustness, the scope of social identity theory is
still rather limited. It is really designed to explain instances of in-group
favoritism rather than out-group hostility, aggression, and oppression.
For example, the social identity model would have great trouble explaining the brutal beating of Rodney King in 1991 by several members of the
Los Angeles police department in terms of in-group favoritism.

Social Dominance and Sex/Gender

Social dominance theory also posits that there will be a connection
between sex/gender and social dominance orientation indicating that
males will tend to have higher levels of social dominance orientation
(sdo) than females. For example, there is strong experimental evidence
to indicate that the levels of agonistic and dominance-oriented behavior
in males is affected by androgenization of the fetal brain and its subsequent sensitivity to testosterone and other androgens (see Kelly, 1985; see
also Scaramella & Brown, 1978). As a result, social dominance theory
views males as tending to function as hierarchy enforcers within social
systems. This is obviously not to imply that all males will be more
dominance-oriented than all females, any more than one can state that all
males will be taller than all females. The social dominance paradigm
merely implies that, everything else being equal,

$$E(SDO)_\delta > E(SDO)_\female.$$

The social dominance model views these sex differences as a complex
function of three factors: (a) the differential socialization of males and females, (b) inherent, genetic differences between males and females, and
(c) a complex and multilayered interaction between socialization and genetic factors. That males and females are exposed to different socialization environments is well recognized and relatively noncontroversial.
What is much less generally accepted is that there are also biological
factors that contribute to the differential political behavior and attitudes
of men and women.

One vector that appears to be involved in these biologically driven differences is the effects of androgens, particularly with regard to aggressive
and dominance-oriented behavior. There is mounting evidence that ag-

gressive and dominance-oriented behavior is positively correlated with androgen levels in human males.[6] For example, Christiansen and Knussmann (1987) examined the relationship between serum concentrations of testosterone ([T-sub(ser]), 5alpha-dihydrostestoterone (DHT), and the level of free testosterone in saliva (T-sub[sal]) and the behaviors exhibited on projective and standardized tests in 117 healthy men. These tests included measures of aggression including sexual aggressiveness and dominance. The results showed that all three androgens had reliable and positive correlations with the self-ratings of spontaneous aggression. Dominance had a positive and significant correlation to T-sub(ser) and DHT and DHT was negatively related to restraint of aggression. Furthermore, the ratio of DHT to T-sub(ser) was also found to be correlated with interest in sexual aggression. An additional example is a study by Mazur and Lamb (1980) that reported three experiments showing increasing testosterone levels with increasing social status. Males appear to experience heightened levels of androgen secretions when they defend or achieve a dominant social position and experience lowered levels of androgen secretion when they lose dominant social status. This implies, among other things, that different androgen levels might be both a cause and a result of different degrees of social status (see also Elias, 1981; Olweus et al., 1988; Salvador et al., 1987; Susman et al., 1987).

It also is interesting to note that although testosterone in males is associated with heightened levels of aggressive and dominance-oriented behavior, consistent with the subtheory of behavioral asymmetry, there is also some evidence that both the expression and effect of this aggression and dominance will systematically vary as a function of the individual's position in the social hierarchy. For example, in a recent study of 4,462 Vietnam veterans, Dabbs and Morse (1990) showed that for males in the lower half of the income distribution and education distribution, high testosterone was often associated with delinquent behavior of various kinds and ultimately with social sanctions and incarcerations. On the other hand, for men at higher levels of the social hierarchy, high levels of testosterone was not associated with social sanctions and incarcerations. There is some reason to suspect that high social status–high testosterone males are more likely to be found at the top of powerful social organizations. Using a little imagination, we can easily extrapolate these findings to the situation of slavery in the antebellum American South. Male slaves with high levels of testosterone were probably more likely to face severe sanction and have rather short life expectancies, while hegemonic white males with high levels of testosterone were probably more likely to either own or control large numbers of slaves. The general principle suggested here is that high testosterone males from negative reference groups are likely to face early death and social censorship while high testosterone males from hegemonic groups are likely to possess disproportionate amounts of social power. Although this recent testosterone research is both highly suggestive and provocative, what has yet to be established is a direct, causal relationship between male testosterone levels and other androgens on the one hand, and social dominance orientation and related attitudinal variables as defined within the context of social dominance theory. On the other hand, recent research by Sidanius and his colleagues has uncovered a fair amount of empirical support that is congruent with both the thesis of culturally invariant sex differences and the overall social dominance paradigm. Specifically, if the thesis of greater male social dominance orientation is correct, it should be relatively constant across ethnic group and culture. Within the logic of social dominance theory, one way in which this greater social dominance orientation will manifest itself is in higher levels of racism and ethnocentrism. To test the cultural/ ethnic generalizability of this hypothesis, Sidanius, Cling, and Pratto (1991) assessed antiblack racism among ten ethnic groups and/or nationalities who happened to be studying at the University of Texas. If SDT is correct, males should be significantly more racist than females across all cultures, and there should be no significant interaction between sex and ethnic group/culture. This is to say, that there should be no particular ethnic group and/or culture in which the racism difference between males and females is significantly larger or smaller than for any other ethnic/cultural group. The ethnic/cultural groups included (1) European-Americans, (2) African Americans, (3) Hispanic-Americans, (4) Native Americans, (5) Asian-Americans, (6) Hispanic nationals, (7) European nationals, (8) Asian nationals, (9) Middle Eastern and African nationals, as well as (10) "Others." Analysis of the data supported the hypothesis; The results showed a highly significant effect for greater male racism across ethnic group and/or culture. Further, despite the lack of difference in the sample of Asian nationals, there was no significant interaction between sex and ethnic group/culture. Even more telling, the sex/gender differences in racism were also invariant over different levels of gender role traditionalism.

These results are also consistent with empirical data on the cross-cultural consistency of sex stereotypes. For example, Williams and Best (1982) asked respondents in twenty-five countries which of three hundred adjectives best described males and females. The results showed very high cross-cultural agreement adjectives such as dominant, forceful, and strong were described as masculine, and submissive and sentimental were described as feminine.

Oppressive Equilibrium and Hierarchy Constraints

Although group-based social hierarchy and discrimination against negative reference groups are assumed to be found within all social systems, under "normal circumstances" this discrimination will tend to stabilize at a given level and not reach the point of genocide. We refer to this as the point of oppression equilibrium. This point will be established at the fulcrum between two competing sets of hierarchy regulators: (a) hierarchy enhancers and (b) hierarchy attenuators.

Hierarchy enhancers are those social institutions, traditions and ideologies which tend to favor and produce increasing degrees of group-based hierarchy within social systems (e.g., internal security forces, big business, and political conservatism).

Hierarchy attenuators are those social institutions, traditions, and ideologies that tend to promote greater degrees of social equality (e.g., public defenders, welfare organizations, charities, and political liberalism). Another factor contributing to hierarchy attenuation is the behavior of a hegemonic subgroup that we call patricians. Patricians are generally composed of elite members of the hegemonic group who have enjoyed a stable and high level of social status for a relatively long time. Because of this high and stable level of social status, patricians will also tend to enjoy higher levels of self-esteem and tend to feel quite personally secure in their hegemonic roles. This greater personal security and general well-being will allow them the opportunity of feeling and exhibiting greater sympathy for the plight of the negative reference groups and engage in acts of noblesse oblige. This heightened level of noblesse oblige or do-goodism will generally not be found among members of emerging elites, the nouveau riche, or other upwardly striving neohegemones. Because of the disproportionate amount of social influence enjoyed by patricians, their more "liberal" attitudes toward negative reference groups will have a disproportionate effect in the direction of hierarchy attenuation. The counterbalancing effects of these two hierarchy regulators helps to maintain a relatively stable level of group-based hierarchy over time.

If the subtheory of hierarchy regulators is correct, including the notion of hierarchy-enhancing and hierarchy-attenuating social institutions, then there is reason to suspect that each type of organization will attract personnel who are psychologically suited to the organization's function. Two recent studies by Sidanius and his colleagues seem to support this idea. Controlling for sex, race, and other factors, the studies show that students majoring in law and business administration (i.e., hierarchy-enhancing sectors) were significantly more dominance-oriented than students majoring in social work (i.e., hierarchy-attenuating sector). Furthermore, controlling for education, race, social class, age, and sex, data show that Los Angeles police officers had significantly higher social dominance scores than both college students and public defenders (see Sidanius, Pratto, Liu, & Shaw, 1991; Sidanius, Pratto, Martin, & Stallworth, 1991).

In sum, we posit that within relatively stable social systems, oppressive equilibrium or an oppression asymptote will be found at that point which simultaneously satisfies (a) the need to maintain as hierarchical a society as possible, but (b) does not allow the degree of social hierarchy to become either "morally" offensive or structurally destabilizing.

Short Summary of Social Dominance Theory

One could state: (1) All human societies are inherently group-based social hierarchies, hierarchies which have had functional utility for the survival of the human species over evolutionary time. (2) Most forms of oppression including racism, ethnocentrism (including the oppression of religious minorities such as Jews), sexism, nationalism, and classism and as well a number of other social attitudes, human drives, and social institutions function, in part, to help establish and maintain the integrity of this group-based, hierarchical structure.

As is now clear, social dominance theory takes a number of elements from earlier models of ethnic and racial conflict and combines them into a new synthesis. From symbolic racism theory it takes the idea that political attitudes and behavior are not necessarily or even primarily designed to maximize the individual's personal utility. From realistic group conflict theory comes the notion that the political choices and attitudes of individuals must often be seen within the context of group conflict over resource allocation. From social identity theory come the important notions that the conflict between groups is not necessarily or even primarily designed to maximize the absolute material return to the in-group but rather to maximize the relative return to the in-group, even at a substantial material cost. From evolutionary psychology come the notions that the ubiquitousness of ethnocentrism is most parsimoniously explained in terms of survival strategies of the human species. Finally, from classical and neoclassical elitism theories comes the notion of the functional value of ideology in the dynamics of social control. To these theoretical components, we have added a few new modules, including the concepts of (a) the functional utility of group-based social hierarchy, (b) social dominance orientation as a ubiquitous motive driving most group-relevant social attitudes, (c) behavioral asymmetry, and (d) hierarchy regulators, among other things. Clearly, then, social dominance theory has several intellectual parents, many and perhaps even most of whom would probably not approve of what we have done to their ideas. Nonetheless, we feel that this new synthesis combines some of the strongest components of these earlier models in ways that have the potential of producing both greater predictive validity and generalizability.

Broader Implications of Social Dominance Theory

If social dominance theory proves itself to be a robust and useful model of human political behavior across a wide domain of political systems, this would seem to have a number of implications for the formulation of social policy, not all of which seem particularly pleasant. To begin with, social dominance theory leads us to conclude that Martin Luther King's dream that all men be judged by the content of their character rather than by the color of their skin is not only a noble dream but an unattainable fantasy. Although African Americans might or might not always function as America's "negative reference group," the social dominance paradigm posits that there will always be some negative reference group and that, in the limit, this group will always be discriminated against.

Secondly, instead of regarding prejudice and discrimination as pathological or quasi-pathological conditions of the body politic, as has been predominantly the case within the social sciences since the end of World War II, social dominance theory regards prejudice, out-group discrimination, and the inequitable distribution of "value" as "normal" or default conditions huddled at the very heart and soul of politics as a process of human interaction. In many ways the difference between traditional models of prejudice and discrimination and the social dominance approach is similar to the conflict between contingency vs. inherency models of collective political violence (see Eckstein, 1980). Whereas contingency models consider political violence an unusual condition demanding an answer as to "Why?"; inherency models consider political violence a "normal" mode of human interaction, and when violence does not occur in conflict situations ask instead, "Why not?" Applied to the domain of ethnic and intergroup relations, rather than reacting with outrage and moral indignation to instances of racial, ethnic, and sex discrimination, the social dominance model will lead one to always expect discrimination against lower-status out-groups, in the limit.[7] It is, therefore, only in situations in which discrimination cannot be demonstrated that some kind of additional scientific "explanation" would be called for.

Thirdly, the social dominance model would lead us to suspect that any consciously manufactured, social policy effort directed toward the eradication of inequality and discrimination between hegemonic and negative-reference groups (e.g., blacks in the United States, untouch-ables in India, Turks in Germany, Gypsies in Hungary and Slovakia, Indians in the Amazon, Untouchables in India, Kurds in Iraq, Iran, and Turkey, etc.) such as affirmation action, equal housing, and antidiscrimi-nation laws will fail not only to achieve their publicly stated goals, but the efforts themselves will be ultimately unsustainable. According to the social dominance paradigm, the major reason for this is not that these public policies violate basic norms of fairness or the Protestant ethic, but because they tend to violate status boundaries between hegemonic and negative reference groups. Any efforts designed to alter status boundaries between hegemonic and negative reference groups are doomed to failure. What will be achieved, at best, is some alleviation in the *degree* of repres-sion so that this social hierarchy is no longer socially destabilizing or so "morally offensive."

Therefore, from the perspective of social dominance theory, the array of American Supreme Court decisions of the late 1980s: (a) striking down minority set-asides (*Richmond* v. *Croson*), (b) shifting the burden of proof from employers to employees in job discrimination cases (*Wards Cove* v. *Atonio*), (c) allowing claimants to attack consent decrees that purportedly support "reverse discrimination" (*Martin et al.* v. *Wilk et al.*), (d) restrict-ing the application of Title VII of the 1964 Civil Rights Act to apply to initial contracts rather than "post formation racial harassment in employ-ment" (*Patterson* v. *McLean Credit Union*), and (e) ruling that a lower court decision that striking black venirepersons from a black defendant's trial was not evidence of racial discrimination (*Tompkins* v. *Texas*) will not only have the affect reaffirming status differentials between hegemonic whites (particularly white males) and blacks but should also be seen as a return to a "normal" set of status relations. In other words, this end of "the Second Reconstruction" that we are now witnessing will lead to a result not terribly different from the end of the first, i.e., the clearly reestablished social domination of one group by another.

Fourthly, within the social dominance model it is expected that political and status equality between males and females will be extremely difficult, if not to say nearly impossible to achieve. This is not only because all complex societies are andrarchies, but because, in the limit, males are inherently more aggressive and dominance-oriented than females. If it is true that females are inherently oriented toward nurturance and the private sector, while males are oriented toward dominance and the public sector, it is difficult to see how females will ever achieve political parity with males without some extraordinary, ceaselessly applied effort on their part.

Finally, social dominance theory also contains implications for the attainability of democracy itself. Not only will status and political equity be extremely difficult if not impossible to achieve between social groups in general and between males and females in particular, but democracy itself would seem something of an unattainable goal. The fact that most social systems now in existence or which have ever existed, on careful inspection, have not even come close to being what most people would regard as democracies appears to support this grim expectation. Of course, the degree to which one should take this expectation seriously depends on exactly how one chooses to define the term democracy. For example, two popular dictionaries describe democracy as (a) "the absence of hereditary or arbitrary class distinctions or privileges," and (b) "a condition of equality and respect for the individual within the community." If political equality serves as an essential component in our definition of democracy, then it is, of course, clear that few if any governments are or ever have been democratic. However, if we choose not to make equality or the absence of privilege essential components of the concept and instead substitute the notion of the citizen's opportunity to choose among representatives of competing elites (i.e., polyarchy; see Dahl, 1971), competing hegemonic groups, or competing oligarchies, then a number of states would clearly have to be called democratic.

In sum, social dominance theory views society as inherently oppressive and group oppression to be the "normal," default condition of human relations. On the brighter side, although the social dominance model clearly implies that color-blind and truly democratic, multiethnic societies are probably not attainable, this does not imply that movement toward ethnic and gender equality and democracy is not possible at all. A comparison of nations around the world quickly reveals that some societies are a good deal more equitable and democratic than others. For example, using a number of different criteria, Sweden would probably have to be considered one of the most democratic nations in the modern world. It is the only country in the world that allows foreigner residents to vote in local elections and where women make up about 23 percent of the national legislature (Riskdagen). In most parliamentary states, women constitute only about 5 percent of the national legislature (Putnam, 1976). However, even in Sweden, if women enjoyed true political parity with men, 51 percent rather than 23 percent of the seats in parliament would be occupied by women. Given this fact, at least two clusters of questions immediately follow: (1) "How much equality is really possible? Does Sweden represent the most equitable and democratic society achievable or merely an anemic shadow of the possible?" (2) "What are the parameters of equality and democracy? That is to say, besides the obvious factors of history and tradition, what are the conditions and forces that will tend to make one social system more democratic and egalitarian than another?" These are, of course, huge questions that probably cannot be adequately attacked by political psychologists, given the technology presently available to us. Despite this limitation, however, it might still be profitable for us to pose the question, "What determines the level of discrimination in any given society?" It is to questions of this type that social dominance theory must direct its efforts in the future.

Notes

This research was partially supported by a grant from the Center for African-American Studies, UCLA. The author would also like to thank Tom Jessor and Marci Lobel for their valuable comments on earlier drafts of this essay.

1. For other members of this cluster, see Kleugel and Smith's "dominant ideology" theory (1986) and Katz and Hass's racial ambivalence model (1988). The most recent and perhaps most sophisticated member of this cluster is Turner's self-categorization theory, which has largely grown out of Tajfel's social identity theory but essentially views intergroup conflict, stereotyping and prejudice as the results of the individual's attempt to render to the social self more representative of the in-group social self than the out-group social self (see Turner, 1985; see also related "distinctiveness" model, i.e., McGuire, McGuire, Child, & Fujioka, 1978; McGuire & Padawer, 1976).

2. For an exact description as to how the constructs were measured, see Sidanius and Pratto (1993).

3. Note that the unstandardized coefficients based on the variance-covariance matrices were used to protect against the differences in path strength between the groups being unduly affected by differences in group variance.

4. Note that Leninist theory can also be regarded as a "paternalistic myth."

5. This type of shared racism has been referred to as consensual racism (see Sidanius, Pratto, Martin, & Stallworth, 1991).

6. See Christiansen and Knussman (1987), Dabbs and Morris (1990), Ehren-kranz, Bliss, and Sheard (1974), Elias (1981), Mazur and Lamb (1980), Olweus, Mattsson, Schalling, and Low (1988), Salvador, Simon, Suay, and Llorens (1987), Scaramella and Brown (1978), and Susman, Inoff, Nottelmann, Loriaux, et al. (1987).

7. By the term "in the limit," I am referring to long-range outcomes. For example, as with any statistical relationship, we cannot say that a specific white individual will discriminate against a specific black individual. However, given a statistical relationship that is greater than 0, we can predict that, in the long run, the average white will discriminate against the average black. In other words, we can be sure of discrimination "in the limit."

III

Information Processing and

Cognition

Research on all aspects of attitude formation, development and change was a principal focus of social psychologists in the period following World War II. In the late 1950s, psychological theories about attitudes, such as dissonance theory, began to be influenced by the insights of cognitive psychologists. In the early 1970s, attribution theory began to replace consistency theory as the dominant cognitive paradigm for attitude research.

This shift in approach began with Daryl Bem's reinterpretation (1967) of the classic "insufficient justification effect"—the finding that subjects who are given small incentives for engaging in counter-attitudinal behavior are more likely to undergo attitude change than subjects who are given large incentives. In the famous Festinger and Carlsmith (1959) study, for example, Stanford undergraduates who were paid one dollar for deceiving a fellow student by describing a particularly trivial and mindless task as intellectually challenging expressed more positive attitudes toward the task than other students who were paid twenty dollars to engage in the same deception. Dissonance theorists argued that the subjects who were paid the trivial sum perceived an uncomfortable inconsistency between their actions and attitudes which could only be resolved by altering their attitudes. Subjects who were paid the larger sum experienced no such tension because of the clear financial inducement. Bem's pathbreaking contribution was to suggest that subjects in the small reward condition did not experience any discomfort based on the inconsistency between attitude and behavior, but instead simply inferred their attitudes from their actions. These subjects reasoned that since they were provided but a token incentive to engage in the deception, their attitude must be consistent with their actions. Under this interpretation, cognition replaced motivation as the critical mediator of attitude change.

The rise of cognitive theories of attitudes in the 1970s and 1980s stimulated intense interest in the components and mechanisms of human cognition: attention, short-term and long-term memory, information storage and retrieval processes, recognition and generalization of stimuli, the logic of categorization, and related issues. The chapters included in this section, which are representative of the spread of the cognitive perspective to political psychology, explore particular cognitive processes applicable to the political domain, such as political information processing, the organization of political objects in memory, and the interplay between cognition and affect.

While political scientists have adopted the jargon of the cognitive approach enthusiastically, very few of them have actually employed the appropriate experimental methods and indicators of information processing (such as reaction time or response latency). For instance, the term "schema" abounds in the recent political psychology literature. A close look, however, reveals that more often than not, schemas are said to be either present or absent based on individuals' answers to public opinion survey questions. A voter is said to have a "candidate schema" if he or she mentions candidates' attributes in response to the question, "What do you like or dislike about the candidates?" Obviously, these researchers treat schemas as equivalent to strongly held attitudes or beliefs. In general, the cognitive aspirations of political psychologists have yet to be matched by the use of the appropriate experimental indicators of information processing.

The essays in Part 3 representing the cognitive perspective are faithful to the substance as well as the language of cognitive psychology. Based on their extensive program of research into the cognitive bases of political attitudes, Milton Lodge and Patrick Stroh demonstrate that when individuals acquire political information they proceed to immediately "update" their beliefs or impressions and then discard the information itself. In this manner, people economize on psychological effort. The authors thus draw a distinction between "information-based" (or memory-based) and "impression-based" models of political attitudes and preferences. Under their theory, since impressions are initially influenced by information, people may in fact be well "informed" despite their poor performance on tests of information.

Robert Wyer and Victor Otatti are also concerned with the sequence and structure of political cognition. Building upon models of social cognition and person perception developed by Wyer and Srull, they develop a general framework for tracking the progress of political information through the human mind from acquisition and encoding through categorization, storage, retrieval and, finally, inference. They then derive specific propositions for public opinion and voting studies. Wyer and Otatti are rigorously cognitive in their theorizing and in their experimental manipulations.

One of the paradoxes of the cognitive perspective is that it has served to rejuvenate research into the role of affect in political cognition. As Robert Zajonc (1980) has suggested, the presumption of cognitive primacy in human psychology may be ill-founded; the affective and cognitive components of information processing may function with relative autonomy. Zajonc's own research into the "mere exposure" effect is suggestive of such autonomy. In these studies (reviewed in Zajonc, 1980), repeated exposure to novel stimuli (such as Japanese ideographs) increases liking for the stimuli. The cognitive account of this effect is that people become familiar with objects through repeated exposure and that familiarity induces liking. Zajonc's evidence, however, demonstrates that repeated exposure to a stimulus enhances liking for it, and that this effect is independent of pure cognitive processing (for example, recognition). Zajonc concludes by urging researchers to abandon cognitive "imperialism": "affect should not be treated as . . . invariably postcognitive. The evolutionary origins of affective reactions that point to their survival value, their distinctive freedom from attentional control, their speed, the importance of affective discriminations for the individual, the extreme forms of action that affect can recruit—all of these suggest something special about affect. People do not get married or divorced, commit murder or suicide, or lay down their lives for freedom upon a detailed cognitive analysis of the pros and cons of their actions" (Zajonc, 1980, p. 172).

Zajonc's logic is particularly compelling in the area of politics. Political issues, movements, and candidates often represent "hot" stimuli in the sense that voters' emotional responses often take precedence over their beliefs and appraisals. The appeal of David Duke in the 1991 gubernatorial election in Louisiana and the impact of the Willie Horton advertisements in 1988 may have occurred more through affective arousal and less through a reasoned analysis of Duke's past background and ideology or Governor Dukakis's performance in the area of prison furloughs.

Taking Zajonc's argument seriously, Otatti and Wyer suggest in their next chapter that affect is an important ingredient of political information processing. Their essay itemizes a wide-ranging menu of research including alternative approaches to measuring affect and alternative theoretical accounts of the interplay between affective and cognitive variables.

In conclusion, there are signs that the information-processing perspective (which derives from experimental research) is gaining considerable favor among scholars who rely primarily upon survey research. Evidence is mounting, for instance, that cues made more accessible in the survey context play a more important role in generating opinion or attitude responses (see, for example, Zaller, 1992). Researchers have found that by focusing respondents' attention on particular considerations (at the expense of others) they can exert powerful effects on question answers (Lehman et al., 1991; Zaller and Feldman, 1988). Just as judgment and choice problems are resolved depending upon the manner in which the choice options are "framed," so are opinion responses contingent upon the wording and format of survey questions. In general, it seems safe to predict that the next decade will see considerable theorizing and research within this subfield of political psychology.

Milton Lodge and Patrick Stroh

8. Inside the Mental Voting Booth:
An Impression-Driven Process Model
of Candidate Evaluation

Contemporary political science models of candidate evaluation make robust information-processing assumptions about how citizens think about and choose among candidates, a common premise being that the direction and strength of one's preferences is a function of the mix of pro and con "evidence" in memory. In this sense, these are *memory-based* models, for whatever their premise—whether sociological, social-psychological, or rational—the information available in memory is said to directly inform how much one likes or dislikes a candidate. Yet, despite this reliance on memory, none of the major political science models provides an account of the mental processes involved in the formation, maintenance, or revision of the citizen's evaluation. In this sense, then, virtually all political science models of candidate evaluation are *black box models* in that they are silent about the processes that drive their explanations—information in, evaluation out—with no accounting of how voters actually go about converting campaign events into candidate evaluations (Berns, 1954; Herstein, 1981; and Rossi, 1956).

The reliance on black box explanations is rooted in the assumption that one's general assessment of the candidates is a direct function of what information voters can recollect about each candidate at the time they are called on to express their choice, whether in the voting booth or in reply to an interviewer's query. While the Columbia, Michigan, and Rochester approaches differ in what "considerations" they suppose the voter has available in memory (whether the candidate's partisan affiliation, personality, or policy positions), each starts from the premise that the voter's recollections provide a more or less accurate indicator of the factors actually contributing to the citizen's evaluation.

Kelley and Mirer (1974) state the classic case for these *memory-based* models: "The voter canvasses his likes and dislikes of the leading candidates and major parties involved in an election. Weighing each like and dislike equally, he votes for the candidate toward whom he has the greatest number of net favorable attitudes . . ." (p. 574). The basic assumption—shared by all the major contemporary political science models—is that the pro and con "evidence" recalled by respondents when asked for a candidate assessment directly mediates their evaluations. Were this generic account of the evaluation process a more or less faithful representation of how citizens actually form their preferences, it would surely simplify the modeling process, for if citizens can provide a more or less veridical account of the factors contributing to their impression, there would be no need to study the ongoing psychological processes that transform campaign stimuli into political preferences. All we would need do is have respondents recount their likes and dislikes. And this indeed is what we do routinely in electoral research—we ask respondents for their pros and cons, compute a tally, and predict the direction and strength of preference.

For the open-ended like-dislike and issue-proximity responses to stand as an explanation of voting choice, one must assume either (1) the information retrieved by the respondent represents a more or less accurate representation of the (salient) information they were exposed to and evaluated over the course of the campaign (Kelley & Mirer, 1974), or (2) that the mix of evidence retrieved from memory reflects the most relevant information encountered during the campaign, *plus* whatever information the respondent "reasonably" inferred about the candidate on the basis of some implicit theory of voting choice or stereotypes about, say, the candidate's party affiliation (Granberg, 1985; Conover & Feldman, 1986; Smith, 1989). Whichever, the information *currently available in memory,* whether accurately recollected or selectively filtered and inferred, provides the memory-based "datum" from which the sociological, social-psychological, and rational models derive their explanations.

Memory-based models construe recollections as the causal determinants of the direction and strength of one's candidate evaluation, hence the rationale for treating the voter as a black box. In fact, a positive correlation between voter memory and candidate evaluation is exactly what the various models report: respondents vote for the candidate amassing the most likes or fewest dislikes (Kelley & Mirer, 1974), or the candidate in closest proximity on the issue scales (Enelow & Hinich, 1984), or the candidate closest to the ideal personality profile (Kinder, 1986a). With each measure, predictions of voting choice reach upward of

95 percent accuracy. The problem, then, is not prediction but our *explanations of when and how* citizens go about forming their impression of candidates. At issue is the question: how much credibility can be placed on the citizen's memory of the reasons why he or she likes or dislikes a candidate?[1]

A major difficulty with memory-based models is that they are unable to distinguish between a host of psychological mechanisms underlying the judgmental process and consequently the causal ordering of relevant factors. Respondents may draw on stereotypes (e.g., partisan information) to justify their opinion or rationalize the evidence said to be informing their evaluation (e.g., Brody & Page, 1972; Converse, 1964; Hamill & Lodge, 1986; Hamilton, 1981; Johnson & Judd, 1983; Nisbett & Ross, 1980; Sebald, 1962). Stereotyping and rationalization effects, while pervasive, represent only two of many memorial biases that render memory-based models so problematical.

What we see as the most direct threat to the memory-causes-judgment assumptions of contemporary political science models is the demonstration in social and cognitive psychology of weak correlations between the actual mix of pro and con evidence in memory and the direction and strength of evaluations (Hastie & Park, 1986; Lichtenstein & Srull, 1987; Sherman, Zehner, Johnson, & Hirt, 1983; Srull & Wyer, 1988). Well-controlled laboratory experiments show that what people remember about other people, places, and things provides a relatively poor account of their evaluations (Lodge, McGraw, & Stroh, 1989). What citizens are likely to recollect about a candidate is their global assessment of him, not the specific considerations that actually entered into the evaluation (in an a priori sense), and to then rationalize their judgment with stereotypical inferences drawn from such group membership cues as the candidate's partisanship or race (Lingle & Ostrom, 1979). At best, one's recollections will represent a biased sampling of the actual causal determinants of the candidate evaluation (e.g., Anderson & Hubert, 1963; Dreben, Fiske, & Hastie, 1979; McGraw, Lodge, & Stroh, 1990; Reyes, Thompson, & Bower, 1980). At worst, the "evidence" in memory may reflect rationalizations thought up in support of the prior judgment (Pratkanis, 1989). In both cases the correlation between memory and judgment is spurious.

The failure to find empirical support for memory-causes-judgment assumptions across a broad range of judgmental tasks has spurred interest in a second type of model—what we call the *impression-driven model of candidate evaluation* (Lodge, McGraw, & Stroh, 1989; McGraw, Lodge & Stroh, 1990). This model abandons the strong memory-based assumptions characteristic of political science models of evaluation, focusing instead on the "on-line" formation of an "evaluation tally" (Hastie & Park, 1986; Wyer & Srull, 1986; see Bassili, 1989, for a review of this literature). Accordingly, when one's goal is to form an impression of some person, place, or thing, most people most of the time appear to simplify the judgmental process by spontaneously culling the affective value from the message *at the moment of exposure, and then immediately integrating this affective value into a summary counter that is stored in long-term memory.*

This "real-time" mode of information processing appears to operate whenever people see their information-processing task in terms of forming or updating an impression. This contrasts with those more demanding instances in which people set out consciously to learn and remember specifics about some person or event, as when perhaps expecting to have their opinions challenged, in which case memory-based processing would be prudent (Cohen, 1981; Hastie & Park, 1986; Lichtenstein & Srull, 1987; Ostrom, Lingle, Pryor, & Geva, 1980). When an impression is being formed on-line, citizens can act naturally as "cognitive misers" by simply storing this summary tally in memory and then in good conscience forgetting the specific considerations that went into their evaluation. Unless the information is particularly important or interesting, people appear to exert little effort to remember each bit once its affective value has been extracted.

The impression-driven mode of processing serves in part as an explanation for the fact that people can often tell you how much they like or dislike a book or movie but cannot recount the specific reasons for their reaction. When challenged to report the whys and wherefores for their evaluation, people are prone to tell you more than they know, most likely dredging up commonsensical rationalizations for their preferences (Nisbett & Ross, 1980; Wilson & Schooler, 1991). The implication of this literature is that the judgment process can be (and typically is) separate from and independent of the reporting process (Anderson & Hubert, 1963).

But what evidence outside the laboratory supports the impression-driven model of candidate evaluation? Something akin to our notion of impression-based processing is suggested by the Gant and Davis (1984) study of responses to the NES open-ended like–dislike questions where they find that "the most diffuse evaluations are reported first." From our perspective, voters, when asked for their evaluation of the candidates, simply retrieve and report their global impression. More telltale support comes from Graber's (1988) longitudinal study of the presidential campaign in which she compares what respondents read and heard during the campaign (as reported in a diary) to what they could later recollect about the candidates: "the fact that so little specific information can be recalled from a story does not mean that no learning has taken place. The information base from which conclusions are drawn may be forgotten, while the conclusions are still retained. This seems to happen routinely. Voting choices, for instance, often match approval of a candidate's positions even when voters cannot recall the candidate's positions or the specifics of the policy. In such cases, media facts apparently have been converted into politically significant feelings and attitudes and the facts themselves forgotten." The conversion of media events into feelings, followed by the forgetting of the instances, captures in broad sweep our on-line model of the candidate evaluation process. Impression-based processing implies that although citizens generally cannot accurately recount the specific bits and pieces of evidence that originally led to their preferences, the considerations that actually entered into their evaluation tally were factored in at the time of exposure and not held in abeyance until some future date when respondents would then be forced to construct an evaluation from whatever is available in memory.

We opt for the impression-driven model of candidate evaluation, in part because the empirical evidence points that way (Lodge, McGraw, & Stroh, 1989) and in part because an impression-driven model appears to better represent the citizen as a "bounded rationalist"—the individual need only retrieve the summary tally from long-term memory, not the bits and pieces of information that originally contributed to the evaluation. The choice between the impression-driven and memory-based models puts at stake how we model and explain the evaluation of political candidates and (we suspect) policy preferences. At issue are the questions: "What information will be integrated into an overall candidate evaluation? When? How?"

In this chapter we describe the rudiments of a process model of candidate evaluation, which—following the lead of Anderson (1983); Brewer (1988); Fiske and Pavelchak (1986); Hastie (1988), and Wyer and Srull (1986)—sets forth the basic components and mechanisms of a cognitively informed model of candidate evaluation. Our argument throughout is that researchers must understand how campaign events are processed inside the black box if we are to understand how citizens evaluate political events and make political choices. With this model, we hope to account for what we see as the most robust findings of prior research in individual voting behavior, these being (1) the perseverance of beliefs and prior evaluations in the face of new information, what are called "anchoring effects" on judgment and (2) its corollary, insufficient "adjustment" in the integration of new (short-term) information into a revised evaluation.

Part 1: Information Processing and Candidate Evaluation

We take as our starting point Walter Lippmann's (1922) view that reality ("the world outside") is far too complex to be comprehended as is, hence the need to build simplified "pictures in the head," which in turn guide the processing of new information. Accordingly, human beings do not respond to external reality, the world outside, but to a structured "representation of the environment which is in lesser or greater degree made up by man himself" (p. 10). To understand human behavior, one must know how the person comprehends the world.

The notion that information about the world is represented in memory in an organized way and that how this knowledge is structured affects the way we comprehend reality is not new (see Bartlett, 1932, who uses Aristotle as reference). What is new (this the hallmark of the "cognitive revolution") is the treatment of thinking as information processing, comprising distinct mechanisms and processes, that can be traced or reasonably inferred from how people perform specific mental tasks (Ericcson & Simon, 1984; Panchella, 1974). In contrast to the reliance on introspection that characterized earlier approaches to the study of thinking, the information-processing approach weds the experimental methods of psychology to age-old questions linking thought to action by means of the mind-as-computer metaphor (Gardner, 1985).

Two ideas can be seen as central to the cognitive approach to decision-making. First, thinking is information processing; and second, individuals can think about only so much information at once—the notion of bounded rationality (Newell & Simon, 1972; Simon, 1985). Given severe limitations on how much of what kinds of information people can process at any one time, decision-making is rarely optimal. If one's cognitive capacities were unlimited, decision-makers could simply compute their preferences and choose a course of action yielding the maximum expected utility. This "economic view" serves, perhaps, as a model of the mind of God, but certainly not as a working model of the mind of man. None but an idealized Downsian man could live up to this standard of rationality (Einhorn & Horgath, 1981). Facing complexity and lacking the machinery to optimize, human beings must be content to find solutions to their problems that are "good enough." Indeed, the information-processing approach challenges the claim of rational choice theorists that less-than-optimal decision-making behavior can be traced to an individual's consideration of marginal information costs or the implementation of well-considered habits (Wittman, 1991). From the cognitive perspective, suboptimal decision-making and "mistakes" are a direct consequence of how men and women are "hard-wired" by evolution (Losco, 1985). Human beings are constrained in the technical sense of being absolutely limited in their ability to process information (Fitts & Posner, 1967; Kantowitz, 1985; Simon, 1957; Slovic, 1972), hence, voters *do not* optimize because they *cannot* optimize.

Psychologically realistic models of the evaluation process must reflect the technical constraints inherent in human information processing. Within these limits, people reach "reasonable" conclusions in circumstances where they have no prospect of applying classical models of substantive rationality (Simon, 1978). Information processing requires effort, takes time, and is subject to systematic errors—all consequences of our limited resources and decision-making capabilities (Payne, 1976). What characterizes the contemporary information-processing approach from earlier attempts to psychologize political man is the attempt to take seriously the notion of man as a bounded rationalist.

Process Models: An Overview

The basic premise of the cognitive approach is that thinking is equivalent to information processing. The brain is seen as a system in which information is stored, retrieved, and operated upon (metaphorically) like a computer. The focus is on the chain of events that takes place throughout the judgment process. A psychologically informed model of evaluation should account for what information is attended to, how this information is stored in memory and retrieved, and how whatever information is available is integrated into a summary evaluation. Because mental activity cannot be directly observed, postulates describing basic processing mechanisms and functional components must be put forth to support a process model of the mind.

Human thinking and reasoning can be modeled in terms of "elementary information processes" (EIPS) operating in a small set of "functional components" (Sanford, 1987). Contemporary models of human information processing typically assume two functional components: (1) a very large permanent memory, called long-term memory, and (2) a small, temporary memory store, called working memory, where information is actively processed. A complete model of decision-making must describe how these two components interact across time—in our case how political stimuli are processed using "pictures in the head."

Basically speaking, information processed by the five senses triggers an encoding process that associates the stimulus (or some part of it) with existing patterns in long-term memory and then moves these familiar patterns into working memory. In this process, the existing patterns in permanent, long-term memory can be thought of metaphorically as a library of information whose main property is the storage of vast amounts of data. A basic finding of research on long-term memory—this evidence dating back more than a century—is that information is organized associatively, that is, meaningfully, in "packets" of conceptual knowledge and associations (Rumelhart & Norman, 1983; Rumelhart & Ortony, 1977; Schank, 1982). The fact that information in long-term memory is not stored in random fashion but is structured semantically accounts for much of the speed and coherence of human thought, as well as for many of the systematic biases that generate less-than-optimal information processing.

The semantically bundled units of associations in long-term memory are typically represented as nodes that are linked together into associational networks. A concept node is activated whenever a person sees, hears, reads, or thinks about that person, place, thing, or idea. Picture long-term memory as an enormous array of interrelated nodes or concepts. Nodes can be accessed directly by recognition (Washington's face on the dollar bill) or indirectly by the activation of attributes associatively linked to the nodes (the first president). In either case, what is retrieved and acted on is the information made available to working memory. Semantic networks provide a convenient and powerful formalism for representing knowledge in long-term memory. And, as we shall see, the depiction of political knowledge using node-link nomenclature provides a mechanism for depicting how people go about forming impressions and making decisions.

The second functional component of the information-processing system is working (or short-term) memory, the "place" where information is actively processed and integrated into impressions. Working memory corresponds to that set of things we are currently attending to at any given moment (Anderson & Hubert, 1963; Belmore, 1987; Fiske, 1980). Information in working memory is being actively considered, whereas information in long-term memory must first be activated (transferred to working memory) before it can be used.

Three characteristics of working memory make it the bottleneck of human information processing:

First, working memory has a *limited capacity*—limited, perhaps, to 7 ± 2 chunks of meaningful information (Miller, 1956). Thus, as new information is "moved" into working memory, information previously stored there must be pushed out. The limited capacity of working memory can be demonstrated when you try to copy a series of numbers from one sheet of paper to another; you will find it difficult to transfer more than five or six numbers at a time. To retain information in working memory requires constant, effortful rehearsal, as when you look up a number in the phone book and try to remember it over the time until you can start to dial it. The limited capacity of working memory renders only the most recently heeded information directly accessible to conscious thought.

The second characteristic of working memory and serious constraint on human information processing is the *serial nature of attention*. Because attention is a one-bit-at-a-time sequential process, a person can consciously attend to but a small number of facts and dimensions at a time, thereby limiting the depth and breadth of considerations that can be simultaneously taken into account when making judgments (Payne, 1982).

The third characteristic of working memory—this too a serious constraint on judgment and choice—is the *slow fixation rate* required to transfer information from working memory to long-term memory. To create or to revise a representation in long-term memory, associations must first be encoded ("written to memory") and associatively linked to other nodes in the knowledge structure. Processing times on the order of eight to ten seconds are required to assemble the bits and pieces of information in working memory and store them in long-term memory as a new "chunk" (Simon, 1978). Only upon being integrated into a network structure does information become knowledge, that is, usable information, not bits and pieces of fragmented data.

Taken together, the limited capacity and serial nature of working memory, as well as the relatively long fixation time required to transfer information from working memory to long-term memory, are the cornerstones of bounded rationality. They add up to what is called the

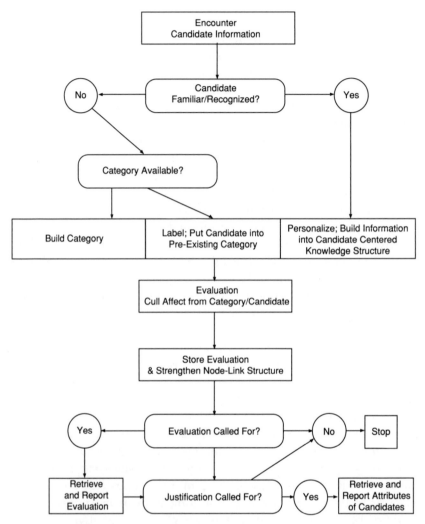

Figure 8.1. Flow diagram of Candidate evaluation.

"technical basis for bounded rationality," which is what we mean here when we speak of "cognitive limitations." Given that the judgment process cannot be directly observed, we need a clear specification of memory components and process-tracing procedures if we are to make reasonable inferences about what is going on inside their heads as people go about forming impressions (Ericsson & Simon, 1984). In figure 8.1 we display a flowchart model that depicts in broad sweep the steps in our impression-based model of the candidate evaluation process.

Taking our lead from Anderson (1983), Brewer (1988), Fiske and Pavelchak (1986), and Hastie (1988), this model posits four steps in the evaluation process: (1) a recognition phase in which the individual, on being exposed to a political message, searches for a match to an existing node structure in long-term memory; (2) the step when new information is linked to an existing knowledge structure; (3) an evaluation process in which the individual "computes" an overall impression from the information currently active in working memory and then "stores" this tally in long-term memory; and later (4), when called on to express a judgment, the stage when an individual retrieves this summary evaluation from long-term memory.

(1) Recognition

The first phase of our evaluation model is the identification stage of information processing. It represents a pattern-matching process in which a stimulus configuration (say, the headline, "Bush Wins New Hampshire Republican Primary") activates a search through long-term memory for categories whose features match those of the stimulus. The question being asked is "Does this instance or feature (here Bush) fit an existing category?" The individual is essentially asking "Who" or "what is that?" "Who is Bush?" "What is a Republican?" Or, more troublesome, "What is a primary?" Recognition occurs "automatically," that is, without conscious awareness of the search process involved (Neely, 1977). So, given a modicum of political savvy, the word "Bush" would not be ambiguous but would automatically activate the Bush-as-president memory structure rather than a Bush-as-plant category.

(2) Categorization

Categorization is the central act of information processing (Neisser, 1987; Rosch, 1978; Rosch & Mervis, 1975). At this point in the act of comprehension the process branches and the route taken depends on what category, if any, becomes activated in long-term memory. Leaving aside the arduous processes involved in creating new categories and piecing together new domain-specific knowledge structures, we posit two outcomes of a successful "fit-to-category" match, each dependent on the organization of one's existing memory structure for Bush: (a) labeling— if, for instance, George Bush is an ill-defined entity and is known only as an example of, say, the category "Republican," or (b) personalization—

if the citizen has developed a Bush-centered knowledge structure in memory.

Labeling. For those citizens disinterested in political affairs (except, of course, the scandalous kind), the news of Bush's victory in New Hampshire would conceivably activate the concept "Republican." If strongly enough motivated, the citizen might take the time to store "George Bush" as an instance of the superordinate category "Republican." In the labeling process the candidate automatically inherits the attributes of his category. So it may be that Bush, on being categorized as a Republican, acquires the most stereotypical attributes of the Republican label by default, perhaps enriching George Bush with such Republican attributes as his being "pro-rich," "pro-military," and "antiabortion." Some of these inferences may be a more or less accurate representation of the candidate's orientation, whereas other "default values" might misrepresent the candidate (Conover and Feldman, 1986, 1989).

Personalization. Our impression-driven model posits a developmental process in an individual's representation of political candidates. Over time, as political candidates become more familiar, many citizens will develop a candidate-centered knowledge structure in which the candidate becomes a distinct, relatively independent node in the network instead of being an instance of a superordinate category such as "Republican." At this stage the voter presumably has an image of the candidate—can recognize his picture and individuate him with distinct characteristics such as his being competent and opposed to tax increases. Assuming the citizen has developed a rich, personalized memory structure of George Bush, the fact that Bush won the New Hampshire primary can be stored as an attribute of the candidate node "Bush," along with such prototypical features of Bush as being Reagan's vice president, a "Republican," and being "antiabortion." The category header "George Bush" (think of the knowledge structure as now having the candidate's name as its label) as well as his key attributes can now be readily placed into working memory. Once deposited in working memory, the citizen is then consciously aware of George Bush and his attributes—being the vice president, a Republican candidate who opposes abortion, who scored a primary victory in New Hampshire.

(3) Evaluation

The third stage and most critical aspect of our impression-based model of candidate evaluation is (a) the computation of a summary evaluation of the candidate and (b) the storage of this tally in long-term memory with the candidate's name. Leaving aside for the moment how this evaluation is calculated and stored, the key aspect of this process is retrieval of the tally separately from the attributes that contributed to it. This process is thought to be characteristic of information processing when one's goal is to form a general impression of a person, place, or thing, rather than trying to remember facts. Once an evaluation is computed (at the time of exposure from all of the information in working memory), this summary tally is stored with the category header. This being the case, evaluative responses such as "I like him" are predicted to be very fast as one does not have to "go down" into the "mental library" to gain access to the affective values of the individual attributes stored with the category. More, when called on to express an evaluation, the individual can simply report the affective tally stored with the candidate's name (assuming the candidate is personalized) without having to compute a value from the stored category attributes. And—this a major plus of impression-based processing—given that one's evaluation is computed "on the fly," at the time of exposure, and not computed later from memory traces—we think it likely that one's summary evaluation will more accurately and more reliably reflect the citizen's evaluation of *all* of the information she was exposed to and considered than would be an evaluation based on what she can later remember (Lodge, McGraw, & Stroh, 1989).

(4) Reconstruction

The final step in the process deals with the expression of one's evaluations and, if demanded, the recounting of considerations said to be the evidence in support of one's overall impression. When called on to express an evaluation, we argue that an individual simply reports the affective tally stored with the candidate's name and does not compute an overall impression from the pro and con values available in memory. This being the case, people act as cognitive misers (Fiske & Taylor, 1991) by taking the simplest and most efficient course of action in evaluating the candidate (Fazio, Powell, & Herr, 1983). If, however, our citizen is asked to give the reasons for her evaluation, we think she will reconstruct the reasons *now thought to contribute to her impression*. This ratiocination process, relying as it does on whatever considerations are available in memory at the time the question is asked, is prone to serious and systematic errors (Hamill & Lodge, 1986; Nisbett & Wilson, 1977; Wilson & Schooler, 1991).

Our impression-based model holds that when respondents are asked for the "considerations" that contributed to their overall assessment, they do not accurately reproduce the actual factors that went into their evaluation. Why? First, because the affective tally is stored directly with the candidate's name in long-term memory, and secondly because the "facts" that originally contributed to the impression—having been "milked" of their affective value—were (in the name of cognition expediency) forgotten.

Having laid out the principal stages of our impression-driven model—recognition, categorization, evaluation, and reconstruction—we propose now to delve more deeply into the black box to specify the manner in which the candidate evaluation process might work. Our aim is to develop a working model of the candidate evaluation process that will incorporate the major findings of the political science literature on electoral behavior while not violating the constraints imposed by psychological realism.

Part 2: Specification of the Cognitive Processes

A cornerstone of any voting model is the citizen's political knowledge and predispositions. Each of the major political science models posits a starting point—typically, the preexistence of some group identification or ideal points at which the voter matches the political candidates. These long-term factors require (functionally speaking) that any general model of the candidate evaluation process must provide a "place" in memory for retaining one's beliefs and predispositions and a set of mechanisms for applying the knowledge available in memory to the processing of campaign information. Thus, all models—memory-based as well as impression-driven—rely on the content and structure of long-term memory; they differ in what information is in memory, when it got there, and how it is stored and accessed.

Although there are several ways to represent information in long-term memory, we opt to portray knowledge in graphic arrays known as knowledge structures or schemas (Alba & Hasher, 1983; Hastie, 1981; Taylor & Crocker, 1981). Knowledge structures in long-term memory are configurations of nodes linked to one another in a network of associations (Rumelhart & Norman, 1983). Nodes represent any of an entire range of concepts—from people (e.g., George Bush) to their discrete attributes (e.g., anti-taxes) and traits (e.g., tough) to abstractions (e.g.,

Republican) (see Chattopadhyay & Alba, 1988). Links, on the other hand, represent the association between one node and another.

On seeing a picture of former President Ronald Reagan, hearing his name, or simply thinking about him, the citizen represented in figure 8.2a is primed to associate [Reagan] with [Taxes] and [Republicans]. Each link between nodes represents a belief or "implicational relation" (Judd & Krosnick, 1988), what Collins and Quillian (1968) call a "referent" or "pointer" that describes the nature of the node-to-node relationship. Implicational relations can be positive (represented by a "+") or negative "−"). For example, figure 8.2b shows the concept [Reagan] to be negatively associated with [Taxes]; that is, our hypothetical citizen believes that Reagan opposes taxes. Likewise, [Reagan] is positively associated with [Republican]; thus, the citizen believes Reagan is an instance of the category Republican.

The strength of association between nodes is called "belief strength." The more strongly an individual believes that one concept is related to another, the greater the probability that activation of that node will activate its linked nodes in the network (Anderson, 1983; Collins & Loftus, 1975). Generally speaking, activation represents the "firing" or "energizing" of a particular node as a result of hearing, seeing, or thinking about that concept. In this process the activated node switches from being dormant to a state of readiness to be processed. An activated node has the potential to be moved into working memory and thereupon consciously thought about. On becoming activated, the node spreads "energy-like" activation along its links to other nodes. Hence, the activation of a node can result from either (1) direct exposure of a stimulus matching a node in long-term memory, or (2) indirectly by the spreading activation among related nodes. In our notation, belief strength is indicated in figures 2–7 by the size of the plus or minus sign depicting the implicative relation—the bigger the "+", the more strongly the nodes are positively associated. Alternatively, the larger the "−", the more strongly the nodes are negatively associated.

By way of example, the large plus sign in figure 8.2c implies that the concept [Reagan] is closely associated with the node [Republican]. This citizen believes that Reagan is a prototypical Republican. Conversely, the negative association of [Reagan] to [Taxes] is only moderate, as indicated by the relatively small minus sign, implying that our hypothetical citizen believes Reagan to be only moderately opposed to taxes. In short, the strength of the implicational relation indicates the strength of the belief that two nodes are associated.

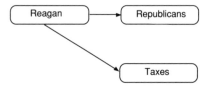

Figure 8.2a. Development of a simple node-link structure. (Note: the boxed concepts denote nodes, while the lines between the nodes denote associations.)

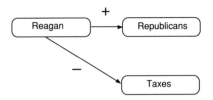

Figure 8.2b. Implicational relations between nodes. (Note: the "+" and "−" signs for each association denotes the implicational relation between each node, where "+" indicates the concepts are positively associated and "−" indicates the concepts are negatively associated.)

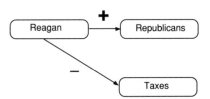

Figure 8.2c. Belief strength. (Note: the size of the implicational relation signs ("+" and "−") indicates the extent to which the citizen believes the concepts are related.)

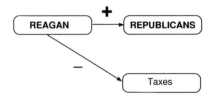

Figure 8.2d. Node strength. (Note: the size of the print within each circle indicates the strength and accessibility of the node.)

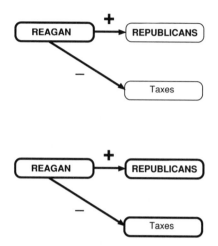

Figure 8.3. Spreading activation. (Note: thick lines between concepts indicate the presence of activation.)

Another characteristic of knowledge structures is "node strength." Node strength represents the accessibility of the node from long-term memory—the probability of a node being energized and moved into working memory. We treat node strength (one may think of it as long-term salience) as a function of the number of times that concept has been activated in the past, less some decay factor. In our notation, node labels printed in capital letters are stronger than node labels printed in lower-case letters. Figure 8.2d portrays the nodes [REAGAN] and [REPUBLICAN] as having great node strength, whereas the lower-cased node [Taxes] implies a relatively weaker node.

To depict the activation process we need a way to keep account of the amount of activation accumulating at each node and spreading from node to node throughout the network. In figure 8.3 the strength of node and link activation is portrayed by the thickness of the encircling lines that denote them. A thick-edged node indicates the activation of that node. Likewise, the activation spreading down a link is portrayed by the thickness of the line connecting the two nodes. Figure 8.3 depicts activation of the [Reagan] node and in the spreading of activation down the links energizing associated nodes. As a result of this spreading activation from [REAGAN], the [Republican] node fires first, given its greater node strength, the [Taxes] node next, thereupon depositing all three pieces of information into working memory. Our hypothetical citizen is now aware of Reagan's partisan affiliation and opposition to taxes. Taken together, belief strength and node strength interact to dictate what information makes its way into working memory and is thereby available as input into the candidate evaluation. What and how information gets deposited in working memory depends on the following activation rules.

First, the *exposure rule* states that when an external stimulus directly matches a node in long-term memory that node will fire and be automatically deposited in working memory. Much of human information processing is exposure-driven—the person is "in touch" with the environment whenever an "outside" stimulus configuration matches an existing pattern in long-term memory.

The second activation rule, a simplified version of Anderson's (1983) *fan rule,* states that all nodes directly linked to an activated node will themselves become activated (although not necessarily making their way into working memory), thereby potentially enriching the message by means of associations. From this perspective, inferences are made immediately, on line, from the "raw material" readily available in the message, not from memory traces (see Hastie & Pennington, 1989).

The final characteristics of node activation are *decay and strengthening rules,* these by and large derived from Anderson (1983). First, the activation level of nodes decays very quickly, eventually rendering them dormant. (This translates into the notion that almost all of long-term memory lies dormant at any moment in time; we are conscious of only those seven or so nodes currently energized in working memory.) If a node is not reactivated by either a direct stimulus match or by spreading activation, that node "turns off" (becomes inactive) within milliseconds. Second, unless they are activated, node strength and belief strength weaken as time passes; over time people tend to forget the associative links between people, objects, and events and are less apt to think about them. Third, the activation of a node increases its strength with repeated exposure, thereby making it more accessible to the evaluation process at some later date.

These decay and strengthening rules imply that abstract category labels (such as "Republican") and central personalities (such as "George Bush") should over time (given their repeated exposure) develop the greatest node strengths and also become more strongly linked to other nodes. For example, the concept [REPUBLICAN], implying as it does for many citizens a host of stereotypical expectations about leaders, groups, and issues (Hamill & Lodge, 1986), would likely be activated frequently, both directly and indirectly, in the course of conventional campaign coverage. Consequently, [REPUBLICAN] would become increasingly accessible (perhaps even "chronically" so) as a consideration in the evaluation of candidates (Bargh, 1984; Lau, 1986). In contrast, specific attributes—such as the detailed policy stands of the candidate—would probably have weaker node strengths because they are brought to our citizen's attention less frequently and are thereby rendered less accessible to her working memory. Finally, following from our discussion of spreading activation, strong nodes that are directly linked will have the strongest belief links between them, while directly linked weak nodes will have the weakest belief links between them (see Judd & Krosnick, 1988, for a closely related treatment).

Another aspect of human information processing that needs to be integrated into a dynamic model of evaluation relates to the decay of node strength and decay of link strength. Over time people forget. Note how much of human information processing is exposure-driven. Without repeated activation, nodes lose their strength (thereby making them less likely to work their way into working memory) and also lose their associational linkage to related concepts (thereby making them still less likely to be indirectly activated).

Whereas many models of information processing are strong in terms of their representation of the cognitive components of belief networks (e.g., nodes as concepts, links as beliefs), most are silent about the representation and role of affect in long-term memory. This is not terribly helpful for understanding the sociopolitical world that is characterized by affect-laden beliefs, or what Abelson (1968b) calls "hot cognitions." Given that our explicit goal is to develop a model of how the evaluations of candidates are formed, revised, and maintained, we must bring affect center-stage.

The simplest and perhaps most fruitful way of introducing affect into our model—following Fiske and Pavelchak (1986); Sears, Huddy, and Schaffer (1986); and Bower (1981)—is to posit that each node in addition to its cognitive content is affectively charged (represented by either a "+" sign depicting positive affect or "−" sign to indicate negative affect). These affective tags are portrayed in figure 8.4, which depicts the direction and strength of evaluations associated with each node in our hypothetical citizen's knowledge structure. For our purposes, affective strength varies from weak to strong as is notationally indicated by the size of plus and minus signs. To deal with a postulate in need of extensive testing, we further posit that affect-laden concepts decay much more slowly than do less affectively charged concepts. At this point it would be instructive to recap our model of long-term memory with an extended

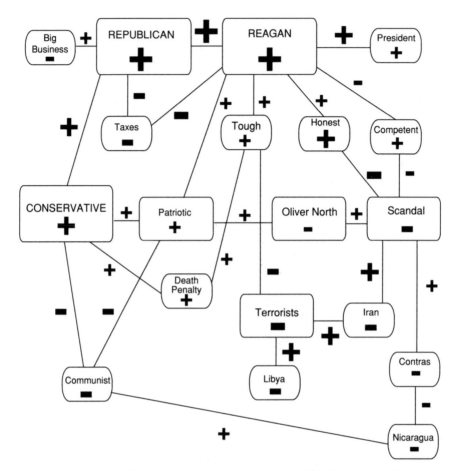

Figure 8.4. Complete knowledge structure and affective tags. (Note: the size of the "+" and "−" sign within each node indicates the direction and strength of citizen's evaluation for that concept.)

political example. Figure 8.4 illustrates each of the factors that have been discussed so far in our hypothetical knowledge structure.

Recall the nomenclature. First, the larger the printed label of the node, the greater that node's strength. Thus, [REAGAN] has greater node strength than does the node labeled [Oliver North], implying that [REAGAN] can be more easily activated than [Oliver North]. Second, the more intense one's affect, the larger the respective (+) or (−) tag attached to that node. [REAGAN] is evaluated more positively than the node [Tough], while [Scandal] is evaluated more negatively than [Oliver

North]. Third, implicational relations among connected nodes are indicated by either a plus (+) or minus (−) sign attached to the link. A plus indicates a positive implicational belief (here, Reagan is thought to be honest), a minus indicates a negative implicational belief (Reagan opposes Taxes). Fourth, the larger the size of each plus or minus sign appended to the link relating two nodes, the stronger that belief is held. For example, this citizen strongly believes that [REAGAN] and [REPUBLICAN] are related, but also acknowledges, albeit weakly, that [REAGAN] is not [competent].

Let us now describe in general terms how activation might spread through this hypothetical knowledge structure to produce such statements of belief as "Reagan favors big business" and such sentiments as "I like Reagan." We start from the premise that activation is triggered whenever a person sees, hears, or thinks about any particular node. So, seeing Reagan's picture in the evening newspaper would fire the Reagan node and instantaneously spread activation to those beliefs thought to characterize the [President]. Nodes receiving activation are [REAGAN] "is − a" [REPUBLICAN] and he opposes [Taxes]. He also is [Patriotic], [Tough], [honest], and not too [competent]. If our good citizen continues to think about Reagan, activation would cascade through the network, bringing other associations to mind. The firing of [REPUBLICAN] would spread activation to [CONSERVATIVE] and [big business]. Assuming now that [CONSERVATIVE] fires, its activation spreads back to the [Patriotic] node as well as to the anti-[communist] node. (Imagine this activation process occurring simultaneously along other node-link paths as well.)

If at this point our hypothetical citizen were to describe her beliefs and feelings about Reagan, she would report liking him. If then asked the reasons why, she would cite the items in working memory, first mentioning his Republican affiliation, then noting his opposition to taxes, his conservatism, and his patriotism. The process of spreading activation ceases when the individual directs attention elsewhere or when new environmental stimuli impinge on the senses and thereby force their way into consciousness. (More on this later.)

As with all contemporary process models of judgment, our model depends on the exchange of information between long-term and working memory. Working memory holds the limited amount of information that the person is attending to at any moment in time (Ericsson & Simon, 1984). It can be represented as a "buffer" that holds only the most highly activated nodes in long-term memory. The crucial aspect of this "work area" relates to its limited capacity, as the amount of free "work space" determines how much information can enter into a candidate evaluation. Given that working memory can hold only a small number of node-link-node associations at any one time, its limited capacity constitutes the principal constraint within which evaluations occur. Psychologically realistic models of candidate evaluation must operate within these constraints on working memory.

Generally speaking, the exchange of information between long-term and short-term memory can be described in the following working memory cycle. First, environmental stimuli that successfully match corresponding nodes in long-term memory are automatically deposited in working memory. So, a headline reading "Reagan Praises Bush" places both names in working memory. Next, activation spreads from these "stimulus-activated" nodes to adjacent nodes. Whether these indirect associations make their way into working memory depends on a set of enter-exit rules, the most important being that only the strongest of these "secondary" nodes (along with their affective tags and implicational relations) will be deposited in the working memory buffer, up to capacity.

The third step in the working memory cycle (the focus of this chapter's next section) is the process whereby the affective weight of each node that successfully works its way into working memory gets added to the summary tally appended to the candidate's name. Fourth, once the summary tally is bonded to the candidate's name, each of the nodes passing through working memory is strengthened, as are the implicational relations between these nodes. Therefore, the repeated pairing of concepts (e.g., Reagan: Republican) strengthens their association by strengthening the nodes themselves, as well as their linkage, thereby increasing the likelihood that one concept will activate the other. Clearly, the greater the number of nodes and links that are used, the greater their activation potential. With repeated exposure or indirect activation, what were once tenuous associations can become tenaciously held beliefs.

The final step in the judgmental cycle relates to forgetting: nodes in working memory decay quickly unless they are rekindled either by being reactivated directly by repeated exposure or indirectly by associated nodes in the network. In either case, memory retains the candidate's name along with the strongest resident nodes from the previous step. But now, to keep abreast of the flow of information, the next string of incoming stimuli automatically pushes out the weakest nodes in working memory and the cycle begins again, with the new stimulus nodes becoming integrated into the summary evaluation. This working memory cycle, which gives precedence first to whatever information the individual is exposed to and then to the strongest associations in one's belief system, can account for the direction and strength of one's overall evaluation of political candidates (see Hastie, 1988, for a similar treatment).

An Example of Information Exchange

Figure 8.4 also illustrates how political information wends its way in and out of working memory. To make this illustration both realistic and manageable, we limit to five the number of nodes that can reside simultaneously in working memory. Assume that our hypothetical citizen sees Reagan's picture in the newspaper. This exposure activates [REAGAN] and soon after lights up [Tough], [honest], in-[competent], [President], opposition to [Taxes], and [Patriotic]. Of these energized associations, only the [REAGAN] node plus the strongest associations with him (here, Republican, Conservative, Patriotic, and anti-Tax) possess enough strength to make their way into working memory. And, critical to our impression-based model of evaluation, along with these concepts come their affective tags and implicative relations to the stimulus object [REAGAN].

Working memory is now full; the five-node capacity has been reached. At this juncture, the only way another concept and belief could enter working memory (and thereby contribute to our citizen's evaluation) would be if its node strength exceeded that of any node already residing in working memory. According to our model, this could happen in one of two ways: either the associates in working memory decay, thereby freeing up space, or another stimulus is encountered that exceeds the strength of those nodes already in working memory. For example, the mere mention of "Terrorists" in the caption of Reagan's picture could activate that node which exceeds the strength of the [Patriotic] node and thereupon pushes the [Patriotic] node from working memory. The stimulus [TERRORIST] would also activate its associated concepts, but these would be too weak to push out any other node currently residing in working memory.

Before turning to a description of how information from long-term memory is integrated into an evaluation tally in working memory, let us summarize the key concepts characterizing the exchange of cognitive and affective information. The basic characteristics of long-term memory are (1) node strength, the inherent strength or accessibility of a node that determines the ease with which it is brought to mind; (2) belief strength, the strength of association between connected nodes; (3) affective tags, the evaluative weight of each node; and (4) the implicational relation believed to exist between connected nodes. These factors are brought into consciousness through the mechanism of spreading activation whereby energy passes from node to node. Working memory, on the other hand, has one chief characteristic: it is limited to only a small amount of information that can be processed at any given time. To compensate for this limitation, which is especially serious given that information is constantly streaming by, working memory operates according to rules that serve to constantly shuffle information in and out of memory. Finally, the actual process of forming an evaluation occurs in working memory by integrating the affective weights of nodes into a running attitude tally toward the candidate. Taken together, we believe these considerations represent the rudiments for a cognitively realistic process model of candidate evaluation. Let us now try a pencil-and-paper simulation of the candidate evaluation process.

Part 3: A Process Model of Candidate Evaluation

All process models of candidate evaluation rely from start to finish on the exchange of information between long-term and working memory. Having spelled out the basic components and elementary mechanisms of the impression-driven model, let us describe how citizens might go about evaluating candidates over the course of a campaign. Our portrayal of how long-term and working memory interact to produce candidate evaluations follows the process depicted in figure 8.1.

Working memory holds the key to what information gets integrated into a candidate evaluation. In our earlier research (Lodge, McGraw, & Stroh, 1989; McGraw, Lodge, & Stroh, 1990), only the information to which a person was exposed made its way into working memory and was thus integrated into the summary evaluation. Our current thinking makes the more realistic assumption that inferences as well as the stimuli one directly encounters enter into the evaluation. Candidate evaluations are updated on the fly as associations move in and out of working memory (Hastie, 1988).

We propose that when a node is "moved" into working memory, its affective tag is immediately integrated into an on-line tally or summary attitude that is attached to the candidate. If that node is subsequently "bumped" from working memory, either because its strength has decayed or a stronger node bumps it out, its affective weight has nonetheless contributed to the summary evaluation of the candidate. The integration rule is simple: *all information that makes its way into working memory is immediately integrated into the candidate evaluation.* Therefore, the citizen's evaluation is a function of all of the information she was exposed to and inferred, not the bits and pieces of information she can later remember.

Once this information in working memory is summed up, the tally is simply added onto the candidate's preexisting affective tag. This can be stated more formally as

$$\text{Evaluation (t)} = (1 - d) * \text{Prior Evaluation (t} - 1) + \text{Input (t) [Affect\_Tag}_1 + \text{Affect\_Tag}_2 + \dots \text{Affect\_Tag}_n]$$

where the summary evaluation of the candidate equals the preexisting evaluation, with a decay coefficient (d) that varies between 0 and 1, plus the affective tags of the new inputs present in working memory. Assuming a random input of new affective tags, the overall evaluation stabilizes most rapidly for small values of (d). Contrariwise, large values of (d) result in the summary evaluation largely reflecting the input of new affective tags. For the time being, let us assume (d) increases monotonically over time; that is, the new overall evaluation largely reflects the initial evaluation over short periods, and new inputs over long periods. (See Dreben, Fiske, & Hastie, 1979, for a similar treatment.) Keep in mind that the evaluation tally is updated continually as each new association enters working memory, and the capacity of working memory is five nodes (including the candidate's name, which comes with its evaluative tally attached). The summary tally reflects the simple summation of all affective tags passing through working memory.[3]

The cognitive literature suggests that our integration rule captures the robust finding in psychology of primacy effects on impression formation—the heavy weight given to information encountered early in a communication—as well as the often-noted impact of strong beliefs on an evaluation. Furthermore, since exposure to stimuli automatically moves nodes into working memory, our integration rule is sensitive to historical as well as short-term events (Campbell, Converse, Miller, & Stokes, 1960; Fiorina, 1981). This on-line integration of information is the hallmark of the impression-driven model of evaluation and reflects, we believe, a reasonable heuristic for bounded rationalists to form and update their evaluations.

The incorporation of primacy effects, belief strength, and short-term stimulus effects is straightforward. First, this model of information exchange and affective integration captures the impression-driven dynamics spelled out by Norman Anderson (1982) whereby the impact of a piece of information on an impression is weighted by its order in the flow of the message—the very first pieces of information integrated into the impression count more than do later pieces. First impressions count most heavily in an overall evaluation because they (1) generate the initial set of strong inferences, which then (2) occupy a place in working memory to the exclusion of weaker inferences drawn from subsequent stimuli. Thus, a noticeable "primacy effect" should be observed when the impact of information upon evaluation is assessed (see Asch, 1946; Hamilton, Fallot, & Hautaluoma, 1978; in political science, see McGraw, Lodge, & Stroh, 1990; Sostek & Sostek, 1981).

Second, our model takes into account the impact of strong beliefs on evaluations (Fishbein & Ajzen, 1975). Since information with the greatest node strength is most likely to be moved into working memory and stands the least chance of being bumped, the model insures that strong beliefs and their most accessible concepts will contribute most to the overall evaluation. Since category labels (such as "Republican") and the nodes directly connected to them (for example, pro "defense spending") are most likely to have great node strength (by dint of their frequent exposure in conventional campaign coverage), they are most likely to be integrated into the evaluation counter.

Insofar as exposure to campaign stimuli automatically deposits that information into working memory, the development of one's candidate evaluation is sensitive to the short-term forces of the campaign, as the repetition of facts, arguments, and images strengthens nodes and their linkages and thereby increases the likelihood of their becoming central features of the candidate's image. The impact of these processes, of course, is mediated by the strength of the affective tags brought into working memory. Accordingly, items that carry the strongest affective weight will have the greatest proportional impact on candidate evaluations.

A final characteristic of working memory controls what information about candidates people store in long-term memory. Our model states that if a node resides in working memory, the node will be linked to and stored with the candidate name in long-term memory, given the following provisos. If such a node-link-node connection already exists, then it will be strengthened; if such a link does not exist, it will (given sufficient motivation) be created (although with minimal strength, thereby leaving it vulnerable to decay and forgetting).

It follows from these conditions that working memory determines what information people will remember about candidates and what factors contribute to the overall evaluation, because if some piece of information does not possess enough strength to push its way into working memory, it goes unheeded and thereby has no effect on the evaluation of the candidate. Again, note the strong effect of exposure on working memory and consequently on the strength of nodes and associations in long-term memory. Taken together, we have the rudiments for a rather efficient information-processing system, as it is the strong nodes with firmly established links to other associates in the knowledge structure that are most likely to contribute to the candidate evaluation, not the flotsam of the campaign (see Hendrick, 1972; Reeder & Coovert, 1986).

The Formation of Candidate Evaluations

Knowledge—what people know and how they use what they know to form their impressions—is central to the modeling of candidate evaluations. As noted earlier in our flowchart depiction of impression formation (fig. 8.1), we propose a four-stage model of this evaluation process: (1) a recognition phase in which the individual, on being exposed to a political message, tries to match the stimulus to an existing node structure in long-term memory; next (2) a categorization process in which the new information is linked to an existing memory structure—most probably to a leader, group, or issue category; (3) an evaluation process in which the individual computes a summary impression from the information currently active in working memory; then stores this tally in long-term memory (and updates the node and link strength of all the information that made its way into working memory); and later (4) when called on to express a judgment, the individual retrieves a facsimile of this evaluation tally from long-term memory.

To trace this process, let us run a paper-and-pencil simulation of George Bush during the 1988 primary season through the eyes of a citizen who starts out knowing little about Bush other than that he is Reagan's vice president and a Republican. From our perspective, categorization is the central act of information processing as individuals begin the evaluation process by searching for a pattern in long-term memory that matches the stimulus configuration. Information processing, at least initially, is expectation-driven as people attempt to fit incoming information into their preformed knowledge structures about politics.

Let us now trace the activation process in figure 8.4 as our citizen reads the newspaper headline "George Bush Wins Republican Nomination." First [BUSH], then the [REPUBLICAN] node fires, thereupon energizing those nodes associated with it: [REAGAN], [CONSERVATIVE], anti-[Tax] and pro-[big business]. The first five of these nodes, being the strongest, pop into working memory, thereupon filling its five-byte capacity and thereby precluding the [big business] node from making its way into working memory. Under everyday circumstances, people are confronted with a steady stream of messages that demand attention and stimulate trains of thought. Thus, if our voter were now to read about George Bush's "antiterrorist program," within milliseconds the anti-[Tax] node would be bumped from working memory as the anti-[Terrorist] node became activated. If our voter were not exposed to any more information, the knowledge structure portrayed in figure 8.5 would result. At this point, the voter's evaluation of Bush reflects the integration of the affective tags of all the nodes that passed through working memory, including the affective weight of those items that had been bumped, here the anti-[Tax] node. The process is expressed in this regression equation:

Evaluation (t) = (1 − d) o + Input (t) (REPUBLICAN + REAGAN + CONSERVATIVE + Anti-Tax) + (anti-TERRORIST)

Our citizen's evaluation of Bush is highly positive, given the positive values of [REAGAN], [REPUBLICANS], [CONSERVATIVE], anti-[Tax], and anti-[TERRORIST]. If our voter did not encounter any more information about Bush, she would simply store this summary attitude with the candidate's name (at the "George Bush" header) and update the strengths of the nodes and links in long-term memory. Implicit here, albeit not specified, is the notion that the forgetting curve is steeper than the learning curve.

Of course, for some people the categorization of George Bush as a Republican is not a firmly established connection in long-term memory, and consequently the headline information does not match a preexisting category in long-term memory. This being the case—but given a modicum of political interest and the natural inclination of people to simplify the world by categorization—we expect this individual would infer one or another category label from the message, perhaps from the Bush-Reagan association. In this instance, the activation of the Bush-Reagan association could well be strong enough to push its way into working memory and carry with it some of the network's stronger inferences.

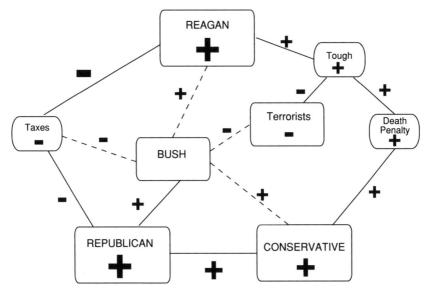

Figure 8.5. Knowledge network of George Bush. *Note:* Solid lines connecting a concept to Bush indicate that item being associated with Bush directly (by exposure), while dashed lines indicate concepts associated with Bush by inference (spreading activation).

At this point, the evaluation of the candidate would be moderately negative, as the implication that George Bush is anti-Communist (a plus) cannot overcome our citizen's initial (and relatively heavily weighted) negative reaction to [Contras] and [Scandal]. But, the news report continues: "Along with other conservatives, George Bush advocates the death penalty for cop killers." This phrase activates [CONSERVATIVE] and [death penalty] nodes (in fig. 8.4), and it now dawns on our voter that George Bush is [Tough], a [REPUBLICAN], and [Patriotic], as activation flows from the message concepts. At this juncture [Contras], [Nicaragua], [Scandal], and anti-[communist] get bumped from working memory, first by [death penalty] and then by [Tough], [CONSERVATIVE], and [REPUBLICAN].

Over this short time our hypothetical voter's evaluation of George Bush has grown moderately positive, the actual integration looking like this:

Evaluation (t) = (1 − d) Evaluation (t−1) + Input (t) ([Contra + Nicaragua] + [scandal + anti-Communist]) and then

Evaluation (t) = (1 − d) Evaluation (t−1) + Input (t) [death penalty + Tough + CONSERVATIVE + REPUBLICAN]

As noted, we expect the initial decay term (d) to be relatively small in the last integration since virtually no time passed between the working memory cycles. Additionally, it is noteworthy here that the initial stimuli, although weak, nonetheless had an impact on the evaluation. The [Contra] and [Nicaragua] tags initially entered the overall evaluation as they entered working memory first. Once our voter classified Bush as a [CONSERVATIVE] [REPUBLICAN], however, nodes of lesser strength had little chance of contributing to the evaluation. Therefore, as activation spreads through the network, it becomes increasingly difficult for other associations to push their way into working memory and contribute to the candidate evaluation, unless of course they are stimulated directly by exposure. Critically, all of the information that works its way into working memory gets counted; the summary attitude or tally reflects everything people attended to, not just what they can later remember. Also, the strongest nodes (and their implicational links) exert an especially strong effect on the attitudinal tally since they dominate a person's thoughts as information cycles through working memory.

By the end of the message, the eight pieces of information that entered working memory would be restored to the George Bush network in long-term memory with each node and link strengthened, as portrayed in figure 8.6. If now asked "Why do you like George Bush?" our citizen would draw on this memory structure. Since each node and link possesses a different strength, and thus varies in its likelihood of being placed in working memory, it follows that our voter would probably tell us how she likes the "fact" that Bush is a conservative Republican who is tough—the strongest nodes attached to the candidate. Then, if pressed for more reasons, she could go on to describe the candidate as being anti-Communist and in favor of the death penalty. All well and good, but we must remember that while these relatively weak associations did indeed contribute to the candidate evaluation, they are not likely to be available later, as their strength, if not repeatedly summoned into working memory by direct exposure, would decay over time.

As depicted in our flowchart model, people can form their candidate evaluation in either of three ways. First, they can simply rely on the category information in which the candidate was initially placed. In this

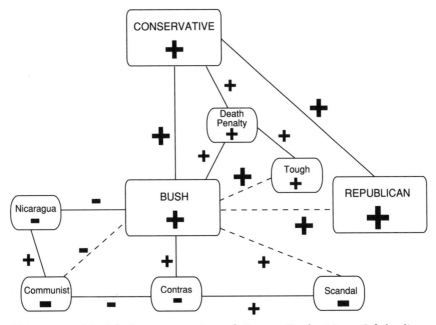

Figure 8.6. Modified representation of George Bush. *Note:* Of the lines emanating from the Bush node, solid lines indicate the item being associated directly with Bush (upon exposure), while dashed lines indicate items associated with Bush by means of inference from another item.

case, called "top-down processing," the initial evaluation of Bush comes exclusively from the voter's evaluation of a small set of considerations cued by a powerful diagnostic stimulus cue such as the category label "Republican." We expect that information encountered after this categorization will have relatively little impact on the evaluation because such strong category labels and their closely linked attributes would dominate working memory. The second manner in which people may form evaluations is in a more "piecemeal," "bottom-up" fashion in which the citizen tries to build a category from bits and pieces of fragmented information that do not as yet match a readily available node-link structure in long-term memory (Fiske & Pavelchak, 1986; Fiske & Ruscher, 1989). Unless and until an available category can be found or created, such evaluations, based as they are on an impoverished knowledge structure, will be unstable. The third and, we think, most common evaluative framework is by means of a candidate-centered network, to which we now turn.

Personalization

Over the course of a presidential campaign, most voters are thought to develop what we call an "individuated" or "personalized" knowledge structure in which each of the major candidates becomes a candidate-centered knowledge structure in our citizen's long-term memory. Once this individuated node–link network develops, it easily can be enriched with such candidate-specific attributes as his personal traits and idiosyncrasies (Hastie & Kumar, 1979), as well as be instantiated by his stands on specific issues. Once this type of memory structure forms, the citizen possesses the conceptual wherewithal to quickly and efficiently integrate into her evaluative tally the candidate-focused information so characteristic of contemporary media coverage of presidential campaigns.

The development of a candidate-centered knowledge structure is based on exposure to information that individuates the candidate from being a mere instance of a more abstract category such as "Republican." If this information merely reinforces prior expectations (as when a Republican candidate espouses what are generally viewed as Republican-type policies), the original pattern of associations simply strengthens. Here, each repetition makes it increasingly difficult for other news to displace these initial impressions from working memory. On the other hand, if the flow of information exposes one to new candidate-specific facts and images, then slowly, with repeated exposure, this new information leaves its mark in long-term memory, perhaps with individuating images of George, Barbara, and Millie, which could eventually grow strong enough to influence one's evaluative tally.

This personalization process is most likely to develop over the course of a campaign as candidates try to create a fresh view of their party and themselves by emphasizing distinctive policy positions, images, and associations, or by some salient short-term factor entering the public mind. The extent to which these campaign events become meaningful (that is, get linked to existing nodes in the voter's knowledge structure) depends primarily on the number of repetitions to which the individual is exposed. For instance, in the early days of the 1988 campaign Bush appeared repeatedly before a prominently displayed American flag (critics saying "he wrapped himself in the flag"), his aim apparently to link himself to a symbol of patriotism. In our hypothetical citizen's mind, this [patriotism] node was not very accessible, at least initially, given the strong weights attached to Bush's partisan identification. However, with repeated pairings of flag and candidate, an association builds, with each repetition increasing the strength of [flag].

Forgetting and Reconstruction

From our perspective, translating one's evaluative tally into a voting choice is simple and direct (even simpler and more direct than Kelley & Mirer's [1974] "simple act of voting" rule)—the attitude tagged to each candidate's name pops into working memory, the affective weights are compared, and the candidate with the highest positive value is preferred. This mode of processing is set in motion when individuals see their primary task as assessing how much they like a person, place, or thing, and is especially effective when—as is normally the circumstance—the flash images and soundbites of modern news coverage compete for time and space in working memory. To satisfy information-processing goals under these environmental constraints, people simply integrate the surface components of the message (the stimuli themselves) along with any directly linked associations that quickly and automatically come to mind.

In contrast, the job of dredging up reasons for one's preferences is a memory-based task and as such is difficult and especially prone to error (Nisbett & Wilson, 1977; Sentis & Burnstein, 1979; Woll & Graesser, 1982). When acting as a survey respondent, for example, individuals are typically freed from the time constraints that characterize, say, watching the evening news and are encouraged to search long-term memory more extensively and report as many likes and dislikes as possible. This distinction between tasks—evaluating candidates in "real time" versus answering survey questions—proves to be crucial in our modeling of voting behavior. When called on to answer questions, people are encouraged to go beyond the "surface components" and immediate inferences that characterize impression formation and seek out plausible reasons for their beliefs. We see the process working this way. First, the voter retrieves the candidate header and affective tag from long-term memory as well as those concepts most closely associated with him. These nodes (as discussed earlier) are likely to be abstractions and general impressions, as these have the strongest and most numerous links in the network, and therefore will be reported first (see Johnson & Judd, 1983, for evidence supporting this contention). Thus, we often sense how strongly we feel about something but are unable to recount the specific reasons why.

Next, as the voter continues to scan memory in search of supporting evidence for her evaluation, she brings other pieces of information to mind: "What do I like about Bush?" She is actively searching her memory for information. Any concepts associated with Bush, even those remotely connected by inference, stand a chance of coming to mind and being cited as considerations in her evaluation. But only when people make a concerted effort to keep account of the evidence are they likely to dredge up the facts. For most citizens in the normal course of events, the formation of a general impression appears to be the most natural goal of political information processing. When operating in an impression-driven mode, voters are not expecting to be quizzed, hence the likelihood that some of the likes and dislikes elicited by question-answering will not be the considerations that entered into her on-line evaluation.

What arguments can be mustered in support of our claim that what voters remember about a candidate does not reflect the actual information on which their liking or disliking of the candidate is based? Phrased differently, what is the evidence for the notion of two distinct memory processes, one for the formation and updating of impressions, the other, memory-based, for the recollection and reconstruction of pros and cons?

The idea that voter recollections often do not reflect the actual considerations and processes that produced their evaluation stems from two related processes in our model. The first—this a cornerstone of Zajonc's (1980) argument on the "primacy of affect in human judgment"—is that affect decays slowly (if at all), whereas cognitive linkages (i.e., node and belief strengths) fade quickly from long-term memory unless repeatedly reactivated; thus it is that people can often tell us what they like without being able to cite the reasons why. As time passes and particular associations with the candidate go unreinforced, these cognitive components of the knowledge structure decay, perhaps at an exponential rate as did the nonsense syllables studied by Ebbinghaus (1964). As they fade in strength relative to other memory traces, the likelihood of their being retrieved decreases further as other, competing nodes gain in node strength. Consequently, we expect certain kinds of nodes, such as partisan labels and personality traits, to remain relatively active and strong, as they are constantly reactivated or easily inferred and popped into working memory, and thereby repeatedly contribute to the evaluation. However, other factors once relevant to the initial evaluation are forgotten over the course of the campaign. Thus, *forgetting-as-decay* alters the information available to working memory simply as a function of time and infrequent exposure, whereas one's affective reactions to a candidate persevere because the candidate's name header repeatedly enters working memory along with its affective tag and different sets of affect-laden associations.

A second reason for challenging the often-made assumption that recollections are a valid basis for evaluating candidates is the idea of *forgetting-as-inference*. After forgetting a number of considerations relevant to her candidate evaluation (as per the forgetting-as-decay process), our good citizen must now recount the reasons for her impression—i.e., she must come up with a reasonable accounting for her evaluation or else appear uninformed and shallow. Memory search is not random; typically, inferences drawn from the available impressions and labels in working memory are cognitively and evaluatively consistent with any overall impressions (Judd, Drake, Downing, & Krosnick, 1991; Lui & Brewer, 1988; Pratkanis, 1989; Wilson & Schooler, 1991; Woll & Graesser, 1982). In-depth searches through memory are prone to produce a logical set of rationalizations which, while showing a strong, positive correlation with evaluation, is not the set of considerations that went into the evaluation. Indeed, the voter is probably unaware that she strayed so far from the factors that actually entered into her evaluation of the candidates. As such, rationalizations interfere with the recollection of (decayed) actual considerations. In short, we discount the notion that voters actually "sort through" their knowledge structure and accurately exact the "causally significant" pieces of information. An example of the effect of interference on recall is portrayed in figure 8.7.

As depicted here, six items contributed to our voter's evaluation of Bush: REPUBLICAN, REAGAN, anti-TAXES, CONSERVATIVE, death penalty, and TOUGH. When asked for reasons why she likes Bush, our voter would probably mention his being a tough, conservative Republican who is associated with Ronald Reagan. All well and good, but if pressured by the inevitable probe "Anything else?" she might now mention the "fact" that Bush is "tough on" terrorists. Why? Given sufficient time, activation spreading through the knowledge structure will eventually light up TERRORISTS, which then displaces the weakest concept occupying working memory. This serves as an example of how someone might draw a stereotypical inference from an actual attribute of the candidate, although that stereotypical inference (from TOUGH to TERRORISTS in this case) did not contribute to the original evaluation of the candidate. Indeed, in this case, saying that "Bush is tough on terrorists" is a rationalization, a reason given for liking a candidate that did not contribute much to the actual evaluation but is merely consistent with the evaluation. Another example can be drawn from this scenario in which the voter is asked for her dislikes of the candidate. She would search through her knowledge structure representing Bush until she happens on the "fact" that Bush favors big business (by virtue of his being a Republican). Again, attributing "favors big business" to Bush is a stereotype-induced inference from Republican that had nothing to do with the voter's evaluative tally regarding the candidate.

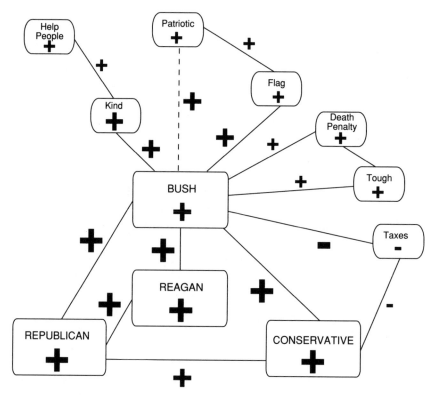

Figure 8.7. Illustration of interference process.

Thus, long-term memory decay and systematic biases in memory search can produce spurious evidence of memory-causes-judgment effects *when in fact the causal arrow points from judgment to evidence*. The moral here is that when a voter operates in a processing mode different from that in which the evaluation was formed (memory-based with effortful search versus impression-driven with rapid interpretation), interference from stereotypes and rationalizations can render the mix of pros and cons in memory spurious to the evaluation. Thus, from our perspective, the single most reliable element of the knowledge structure is the summary evaluation—the affective tag linked to the candidate's header—whereas the least reliable component of the citizen's recollections are the memory-based pros and cons purported to have caused the evaluation.

Indeed, our model entirely transforms the interpretation of memory-based measures, both the open-ended like/dislike responses and the responses to the closed-ended issue questions. From the perspective of on-line processing, the level of conceptualization expressed in the open-ended responses does not necessarily indicate the quality of the voter's information or decision-making calculus. Rather, these post hoc recollections represent the product of memory-based processes and, as such, do not necessarily represent the voter's political sophistication or reflect the actual considerations that informed an evaluation. Similarly, the notion of issue constraint is likely to reflect a straightforward "judgment-causes-memory" effect.

Part 4: Conclusion

Although most models of the candidate evaluation process prove to be powerful predictors of preferences and voting choice, these models operate under the assumption that voters provide interviewers with a more or less veridical account of how and what attitudes and beliefs actually contributed to their assessment of candidates and issues. This assumption underlies most contemporary efforts to model the evaluation of political candidates. Why else ask respondents to recount their likes and dislikes or recollect the attributes of candidates? Unfortunately, this basic assumption strikes us as psychologically implausible and proves to be empirically untenable. Thus, it becomes incumbent on us to look inside the black box and develop a psychologically realistic model of the candidate evaluation process.

Our impression-driven model, taking its lead from Norman Anderson's (1982, 1988) "dual process model," holds that memory-based processing is distinct from and independent of impression-based processing. Memory-based processing comes to the fore when the individual has foreknowledge of the need to recollect the evidence, is motivated to keep account of this evidence, and has the time to contemplate its ramifications, whereas the impression-driven mode of processing is engaged when time is short, there is no expectation of need to later reproduce the considerations entering a judgment, or the citizen sees her task as forming or upgrading an impression. From this perspective, answering questions is memory-based, while the evaluation process is impression-driven.

When applied to the study of political behavior, a cognitively informed, impression-driven model operates within well-known constraints on human information processing. First and foremost, people have a limited attention span; they cannot integrate very many pieces of information at once. Also, people are constrained by the "pictures in their heads," by the knowledge networks they use to structure the environment and interpret events. Finally, whereas people are inherently limited in their ability to remember facts and report on their thought processes, they are whizzes when it comes to generating plausible justifications for their opinions and actions. While these post facto reasons will of course correlate with the evaluation, they are not likely to be an accurate representation of the actual causal factors.

We see the impression-based model of the evaluation process as a viable alternative to memory-based models, not only because it does not rely on an individual's ability to accurately recollect the reasons for their preferences, but because impression-driven processing strikes us as an "ecologically efficient" manner for developing preferences. The impression-driven model, in emphasizing the spontaneous culling of affect from relevant information at the time of exposure, appears to circumvent the most serious constraints on human information processing. When citizens see their goal in terms of forming an impression (as is normally the case, we think), they can simply extract the affective weight from whatever facts that make their way into conscious memory and store this overall attitude with the candidate's name in long-term memory. We see this process as a reasonable and, in Simon's (1985) terms, a "procedurally rational" way for the citizen to go about choosing among candidates.

Finally, whereas most psychological models of evaluation set themselves in direct opposition to rational-choice, utility-maximization models (Herstein, 1981), we do not. Rather, we see impression-driven processing as a reasonable and generally effective method for informing one's judgments because the summary tally is based on all of the information that the individual attends to and infers from prior experience, not the information one can recollect at some later point. The evaluation process is one of continually updating a tally, not reconstructing an argument. This is not to say we think human information processors are "optimizers," but simply that when it comes to making affective judgments, people appear to have developed a sound and efficient set of procedures for extracting the feeling component from whatever information they are exposed to. By operating on-line, they are able to make judgments "in the context of the message" (i.e., as the information is before their eyes), rather than later under the different and largely irrelevant conditions of being quizzed. From our perspective, then, the voter's often-noted inability to cite many reasons for preferring one candidate over another is not necessarily because "voters are fools," but more likely because they see their task in terms of forming a general impression of the candidates and proceed as rather efficient processors of campaign information.

Notes

Much of the original research carried out at Stony Brook on impression-based processing was supported by a grant from the National Science Foundation [SES 8819974].

1. To avoid the cumbersome "he/she" and "her/him," let us refer to the gender of citizens as female, since there are more of them, and when referring to candidates use the masculine pronouns, since there are more of them, all the while implying no support whatsoever for present inequities.

2. This "integration rule" is similar to the Fishbein and Ajzen (1975) expectancy-value model of attitude formation: $A_o = \Sigma\, b_i e_i$ where A_o represents the person's attitude toward object o; b_i represents the belief linking the object to attribute i; and e_i represents an evaluation of attribute i. Here, the person's attitude simply represents the integration of all attributes linked to the candidate at the time of the attitude expression, whereas in our model, attributes fade over time and the dynamic integration of attributes is made up of the attributes in working memory at the time of exposure.

Robert S. Wyer, Jr., and Victor C. Ottati

9. Political Information Processing

In this chapter we provide a general theoretical framework for conceptualizing the cognitive processes that underlie the use of information to make political judgments. This is a difficult task for two reasons. First, very little research on political judgment per se bears directly on these matters. Second, research in other areas of social judgment has typically been performed under conditions that differ in many important respects from those that exist in political judgment situations outside the laboratory. The purpose for which people expect to use the information they receive is a critical determinant of the mental operations they perform on this information, the cognitive representations they form from it, and therefore the judgments and decisions they ultimately make (Srull & Wyer, 1986). For this reason alone, it is hazardous to generalize empirical findings in one domain to others in which the type of information presented, the way it is conveyed, and the purpose for which it is used are likely to differ. Our analysis of political information processing is therefore speculative. Our aim, however, is not to propose a definitive theory of political judgment. Rather, we provide a conceptual framework for conducting research on political judgment that can be used as a springboard for a more refined and elaborated formulation in the future.

An information-processing approach to social judgment (Wyer & Srull, 1986, 1989) focuses on several component stages of cognitive functioning that mediate the use of information to make a judgment or behavioral decision: (a) the interpretation of individual pieces of information in terms of previously formed trait and evaluative concepts that are accessible at the time the information is received, (b) the organization of this encoded information into a mental representation of its referent,

(c) the storage of the representation in memory, (d) the later retrieval of the information, along with other knowledge about its referent, (e) an assessment of the implications of this information and knowledge for the judgment or decision to be made, and (f) the transformation of the results of this assessment into an overt response. These stages of processing will be discussed more fully. To focus our discussion, we concentrate on the voter's use of information to evaluate a political candidate or to make a voting decision. However, similar considerations arise for voters in making other types of judgments.

In discussing each stage, we first review theory and research in other areas of social judgment that bear on these issues. Then, we evaluate the implications of this work of political decision-making. Finally, we propose a preliminary conceptualization of political information processing that takes into account many of the phenomena we have identified.

Encoding Processes

Information can often be interpreted in terms of more than one concept. A person's statement that the Ku Klux Klan should be allowed to hold public meetings, for example, could be interpreted as either "racist" or as "civil libertarian." Under such conditions, which of several alternative concepts is most likely to be applied?

People typically do not conduct a detailed evaluation of the alternative concepts that might potentially be applied to a piece of information. Rather, they tend to apply the concept that comes to mind most easily at the time (Bargh, 1984; Higgins & King, 1981; Wyer & Srull, 1986, 1989). This concept, however, is unlikely to capture every implication of the original information. This observation's importance derives from the fact that once information is encoded into memory in terms of a set of concepts, these encodings, rather than the original information, are later retrieved and used as bases for judgments (Carlston, 1980; Higgins, Rholes, & Jones, 1977; Srull & Wyer, 1979). Consequently, implications of the original information that are not captured by the abstract encodings are not considered. In this regard, it is important to note that once information has been encoded into memory in terms of one set of concepts, it is unlikely to be retrieved and interpreted later in terms of other concepts that are accessible at the time that a judgment or a decision is made (Srull & Wyer, 1979). Consequently, factors that affect the concepts that come to mind when new information is first acquired have an important and enduring effect on the interpretation of this information and, therefore, the nature of its influence on later judgments and decisions.

Determinants of Concept Accessibility

1. Frequency and recency of prior use. The accessibility of a concept in memory is determined in part by the frequency and recency with which the concept has been used in the past (Higgins, Bargh, & Lombardi, 1985; Srull & Wyer, 1979). Life goals, values, and past experiences can influence the frequency with which certain concepts have been used and thus can produce differences in the "chronic" accessibility of these concepts. As a consequence, there are often systematic individual differences in the interpretation of information that can be generalized over situations (Anderson, Reynolds, Schallert, & Goetz, 1976; Bargh, Bond, Lombardi, & Tota, 1986; Bruner, 1951; Klinger, 1977).

On the other hand, fortuitous events that one experiences a short time before information is received also can activate concepts that are used to interpret this information and, as a result, can influence judgments of the object to which the information refers (Higgins & King, 1981; Wyer & Srull, 1989). These effects often can occur without someone being aware of the conditions that activated the concepts that are applied (Bargh & Pietromonaco, 1982).

2. Information-processing objectives. Concepts also can be activated by one's goals at the time the information is received, or by the purpose for which one expects to use the information. People who simply wish to comprehend the information they receive may not interpret it in terms of any more abstract concepts than are necessary to understand it at a basic, descriptive level (Wyer & Srull, 1986, 1989). Thus, a person's behavior, or a statement the person makes, is not spontaneously encoded in terms of more abstract trait concepts unless an interpretation in terms of these concepts is necessary to attain a higher-order processing objective (e.g, to form an impression of the person). (For indirect evidence of this contingency, see Wyer & Gordon, 1982). Moreover, when subjects do have a specific judgmental objective at the time they receive information, they are likely to activate and apply concepts that are particularly useful in attaining this objective. These concepts may affect the interpretation of the information. For example, a man with the objective of deciding whether someone will be a good legislator might activate a prototype of a "good legislator" and attempt to interpret information about the person in terms of attributes that compose this prototype. In doing so, he may ignore other interpretations that, in principle, are equally appropriate.

3. Effects of prior knowledge and expectations. A third general determinant of the concepts that someone is likely to bring to bear on information is the already acquired knowledge about the person or object to which the information pertains or, alternatively, about a group or category to which the target belongs. For example, knowledge that the referent of a message is a congressman from Mississippi might activate a stereotype of someone with racist attitudes, whereas information that the referent is a member of the American Civil Liberties Union (ACLU) might activate a stereotype of a civil libertarian. Concepts activated by these stereotypes could influence the interpretation of information that the referent approves of the Ku Klux Klan's right to hold public meetings.

For the initial information about a target to affect the interpretation of later information, it may need to be presented a sufficient time before the second set of material for a concept of the target to be formed on the basis of it alone. This contingency was identified by Hong and Wyer (1990). Subjects initially received information that a commercial product was manufactured in either a country that was known for high-quality products or a country that was known for inferior products. Then, either immediately or the next day, the subjects received additional information about specific attributes of the product. When only a short time separated the two sets of information, the product's country of origin was simply treated as a favorable or unfavorable attribute that influenced evaluations of the product in much the same way as other attributes. When a long delay separated the two sets of information, however, subjects formed an initial impression of the product as favorable or unfavorable, based on the country of origin information alone. Concepts associated with this impression were then used to interpret the later attribute information, thus affecting the impact of this information on product judgments. The implications of these findings for political information processing will be noted presently.

Other Effects of Concept Accessibility

The above discussion has focused on the effect of an activated concept on the interpretation of individual pieces of information. This effect is typically reflected by perceptions that the information's implications are more similar to those of the concept than would otherwise be the case (an "assimilation" effect). However, two additional effects of concept accessibility on the encoding of information are important.

Contrast effects. Although most of the research on the influence of concept accessibility indicates that these concepts produce assimilation effects on the interpretation of information, there are two conditions in which they can have the opposite effect.

(1) People are sometimes aware that the concepts which come to mind when they receive information were activated for reasons that have nothing to do with this information. In such conditions, they consciously suppress the use of these concepts in an attempt to avoid being biased (Lombardi, Higgins, & Bargh, 1987; Martin, 1986). This sometimes can lead to *contrast* effects of the activated concept on judgments. Imagine that subjects are told that someone has advocated giving the Ku Klux Klan the right to hold public meetings. Suppose they believe that the reason "racist" came to mind when receiving the information resulted from a recent experience that had nothing to do with the person to whom this information referred. They might then suppress the use of this concept, thereby increasing the likelihood of interpreting it as "civil libertarian." Consequently, they might interpret the implications of the statement as more favorable than they would if "racist" had not been activated by the earlier experience.

(2) Contrast effects also can occur when the features of information about a referent are diametrically opposite to features of the activated concept. For example, suppose the information conveys dishonesty, whereas the activated concept is "honest." In such conditions the concept (or objects that exemplify it) might be used as a standard of comparison in evaluating the implications of the information. This means, for example, that a moderately dishonest behavior might be judged as even more dishonest if a concept that exemplifies an extreme degree of honesty has been activated than if it has not. These effects can occur regardless of whether the events that activate the concept are relevant to the judgment task (Manis, Nelson, & Shedler, 1988) or not (Herr, 1986).

Selective encoding. The concepts activated at the time that information is received may affect not only *how* individual pieces of information are interpreted but *which* pieces are actually encoded into memory. That is, information is more likely to be encoded if the concepts necessary to interpret it come to mind easily than if they do not. Consequently, information that can be interpreted in terms of easily accessible concepts is relatively more likely to become part of the representation formed of the referent, and, therefore, is more likely to be retained in memory (Wyer & Srull, 1989). As a result, this information is more likely to be recalled and used later as a basis for judgments.

The effects of selective encoding are most apparent when concepts involved are activated in the course of pursuing a particular goal to which they are relevant. Lingle, Geva, Ostrom, Leippe, and Baumgardner (1979) found that subjects recalled information about a job candidate better if it was relevant to the job for which the person was applying than if it was irrelevant. Apparently, concepts activated by the job specification were used to encode and organize the former information but not the latter. (For other evidence of processing objectives on selective encoding, see Wyer, Srull, Gordon, & Hartwick, 1982.) Lingle et al.'s findings are of particular relevance to political judgment. People with the objective of evaluating a person for public office, for example, may spontaneously activate a prototype of someone whom they believe to be suitable for the job. As a consequence, information about the candidate that can be interpreted in terms of the attributes composing the prototype may be encoded into memory, whereas other information (although potentially relevant to other processing objectives) may not be. Consequently, the latter information will not be recalled if a situation later arises to which it is relevant.

Selective encoding also can result from the accessibility of concepts that have been activated for other, goal-irrelevant reasons. Bower, Gilligan, and Monteiro (1981), for example, showed that the concepts activated by the subjects' mood at the time that information was presented led them to selectively encode those aspects of the information to which the concepts were applicable. Consequently, these aspects of the information were better remembered than other aspects.

Implications for Political Judgment

Although the research cited above has generally been performed outside the domain of political judgment, its implications for political information processing are fairly obvious. An example helps to convey these implications. Suppose the first information one acquires about a political candidate includes the candidate's party affiliation. This information is later followed by descriptions of the candidate's stands on several issues. Knowledge of the candidate's party membership might activate concepts associated with his or her political ideology (e.g., liberal or conservative). To this extent, research and theory summarized above suggest the following hypotheses:

(1) If features of the candidate's issue stands are similar to those of concepts activated by the candidate's party membership, they are likely to be interpreted as more consistent with the ideology implied by this membership than they otherwise would be.

(2) If features of the candidate's issue stands are dissimilar to those of

concepts activated by the candidate's party membership, these stands may be contrasted. That is, they may be interpreted as even more inconsistent with the ideology implied by the candidate's party membership than they otherwise would be.

(3) If a candidate's stands on issues can be interpreted in terms of concepts activated by his or her party membership, they are more likely to be encoded into memory than those that cannot be so interpreted. Therefore, the former issues should be relatively better recalled. (Some additional considerations arise in making this prediction, as will be noted in the next section.)

(4) For the above effects to occur, however, two conditions are necessary: (a) Subjects must have the goal of forming an impression of the candidate, or of deciding his or her suitability for office, when the information is received. (b) The candidate's party and appearance must be conveyed a sufficient time before the candidate's issue stands are learned for a separate stereotype-related concept of the candidate to be formed on the basis of these characteristics. Otherwise, they may simply be treated as attributes of the candidate that affect judgments in much the same way as other attributes.

Although these predictions follow from the research and theory we have cited, several other factors must be taken into account in evaluating their plausibility and generalizability. In particular, we have described the encoding of information into memory as a relatively passive process. That is, people simply try to understand the information they receive by comparing its features with those of concepts to which the information is potentially relevant. This assumption overlooks the fact that the candidates' stands on many issues not only provide information about the candidate but function as persuasive communications that have implications for people's *own* beliefs about the issues. To this extent, information about these stands is likely to elicit other cognitive responses than those that underlie the effects we thus far have considered (Petty & Cacioppo, 1986). For example, people are likely to tend to counterargue positions with which they disagree, but to elaborate on and marshal support for positions with which they agree. The effects of this cognitive activity on recall of these positions could override the selective encoding effects implied by hypothesis 3 above. Research described in the next section provides an instance.

Further considerations arise when people have already developed an evaluative concept of a candidate at the time they receive information about the candidate's stands on issues. If their concept of the candidate is favorable, they might actively attempt to interpret the candidate's issue positions as consistent with their own. Alternatively, they might change their own opinions to make them more congenial to the candidate's. In contrast, subjects who have formed a negative concept of a candidate at the time they learn about his position on an issue might counterargue the candidate's positions and actively attempt to interpret them as inconsistent with their own views. In any event, it is important to bear in mind that the cognitive activities that affect the interpretation of a candidate's positions on issues are often more extensive than those we have considered in this section. These possibilities should be explored empirically.

Organizational Processes

Once the individual pieces of information about a person have been encoded in terms of previously formed concepts, a mental representation of the person is theoretically formed on the basis of these encodings. This representation is then stored in memory at a location that pertains to its referent. The representation may later be retrieved for use in making judgments and decisions for which it has implications.

Three questions are embodied in this brief description. In this section we consider the content and structure of the representations that are formed from any given body of information. In the next section we discuss the processes that govern the storage of these representations and their later retrieval for use in making judgments.

The Representation of Persons

A detailed conceptualization of the mental representations that are formed from information about a person has been proposed by Srull and Wyer (1989) (see also Wyer & Srull, 1989). This formulation has typically been applied under conditions in which subjects are given a list of behaviors with instructions to form an impression of the person who performed them. In some cases, the behaviors are accompanied by favorable or unfavorable trait adjective descriptions of the person. (Alternatively, subjects are told that the person belongs to a group with whom certain traits are stereotypically associated.) These conditions theoretically stimulate subjects to engage in several cognitive activities. (The first is akin to selective encoding as discussed in the previous section.)

(1) Subjects interpret the person's behaviors in terms of trait concepts

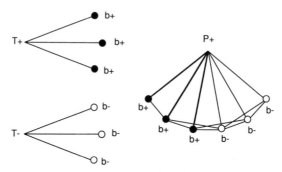

Figure 9.1. Hypothetical (a) trait behavior clusters and (b) evaluative person representation formed from descriptions of a person's behavior under instructions to form an impression of the person. *T* and *b* and *P* denote trait concepts, behaviors, and the evaluative person concept, respectively. Subscripts denote favorableness. Wider pathways denote stronger associations.

that they exemplify. The concepts they use are often ones that have been activated by initial trait adjective descriptions of the person, or by a group to which the person belongs, as well as factors of the sort discussed in the preceding section. This activity produces associations between the behaviors and the activated trait concepts. The representations that result can be conveyed metaphorically as shown on the left side of figure 9.1, where trait and behavior concepts are represented by nodes and the associations between them by pathways.

(2) Subjects extract an evaluative concept of the person as favorable or unfavorable. This concept is generally based on the initial information presented. Once the concept is formed, subjects think about the person's behaviors with reference to this concept as well. This leads the behaviors to become associated with the concept.

(3) When subjects encounter a behavior that is inconsistent with their evaluative concept of the person, they engage in two activities: (a) *Inconsistency resolution*. Subjects think about the behaviors in relation to others that the person has performed in an attempt to understand why it occurred. This activity leads associations to be formed among the behaviors. (b) *Bolstering*. Subjects review other behaviors of the person that are consistent with their central concept of him or her in an attempt to confirm the concept's validity. This activity strengthens the association of the behaviors with the concept. Thus, if the central person concept is favorable (P+), the representation that emerges resembles that shown on the right side of figure 9.1, where b+ and b− are favorable and unfavorable behaviors, and wider pathways denote stronger associations.

(4) The representations (both the trait behavior clusters and the evaluative person representation) are stored independently of one another at a memory location pertaining to the person. Note that a given behavior is often represented twice: once in a trait behavior cluster and once in the evaluative person representation.

Theoretically, the cognitive activity that underlies bolstering leads behaviors that are consistent with the central person concept to be more strongly associated with it than are behaviors that are inconsistent with it (see fig. 9.1). However, the activity involved in inconsistency resolution leads to the formation of more associative pathways to inconsistent behaviors than to consistent ones. Both of these factors (the strength of a behavior's association with the central person concept and the number of ways it can be accessed) potentially affect the ease of recalling a behavior. Inconsistency resolution appears to occur spontaneously, as information is presented, whereas bolstering occurs only if subjects have sufficient time available once inconsistency resolution has been attempted. Consequently, inconsistent behaviors are often recalled better than consistent ones.[1] When sufficient time is available to think about the behaviors, however (either as they are represented or subsequently), subjects engage in bolstering. This activity increases the ease of recalling consistent behaviors to a level that can exceed that of inconsistent ones (Wyer, Budesheim, Lambert, & Martin, 1987; Srull & Wyer, 1989).

In many cases, the representations that are formed of a person are domain-specific. That is, subjects form different concepts that pertain to each situation or role and organize the person's behaviors around the particular concept to which they are relevant (see Trafimow & Srull, 1986; Wyer & Martin, 1986). Thus, for example, people who have a concept of a man as friendly at work but a tyrant at home might be most likely to recall unfavorable behaviors that the man performs at the office, but favorable behaviors he performs in the home environment.

Implications for Political Information Processing

In principle, a person's opinion statements constitute behaviors that vary in their consistency with the trait and evaluative concepts that have been formed of this person. To this extent, the person memory model described above is potentially applicable in conceptualizing the representations that are formed from information about a political candidate's stands on issues as well as other behaviors the candidate might perform. However, two factors come into play in political information processing that are not directly taken into account by the model in its present form.

(1) In the conditions in which the person memory model has usually been applied, the source of the information presented is unfamiliar, and there is no reason to question the source's motives in conveying it. In the political arena, however, information is often conveyed for purposes other than simply to be informative. In particular, it is intended to persuade the recipient of a particular point of view and therefore is likely to be biased, if not simply inaccurate. In these cases, recipients are often likely to think about the pragmatic implications of information (i.e., why the information is being conveyed) as well as its semantic implications for the persons or objects to which it refers.

(2) The information presented in most tests of the person memory model has concerned people and events with which subjects were unfamiliar. In contrast, information acquired outside the laboratory usually concerns actual people and events about which recipients have prior knowledge. This is particularly true in the case of opinion statements. In these conditions, recipients are likely to think about the consistency of the information they receive with their general knowledge about the issues to which it refers as well as its consistency with expectancies for its source.

Some evidence of the importance of these considerations has been obtained. In a study by Wyer, Budesheim, and Lambert (1990), for example, subjects listened to a conversation that two persons had about a mutual acquaintance. They were told to form an impression of the target person being discussed. Instead, however, they spontaneously formed impressions of the speakers, based on the speaker's descriptions of the target. (That is, they formed favorable concepts of speakers who described the target favorably, but unfavorable concepts of speakers who described him unfavorably.) Then they used these concepts as standards of comparison when they were asked to evaluate the target later. As a result, the representations that were formed from the information were different from those shown in figure 9.1, despite the fact that the actual information presented about the person being discussed was the same.

In a study more directly relevant to political judgment (Wyer, Lambert, Gruenfeld, & Budesheim, 1991), subjects first received information about a political candidate consisting of (a) favorable or unfavorable trait descriptions, and (b) a characterization of him as either a conservative Republican or a liberal Democrat. This initial information was followed by descriptions of both overt behaviors that the person had performed and opinion statements that conveyed either a liberal or conservative point of view. Subjects had better recall of overt behaviors that were evaluatively inconsistent with an initial concept they formed of the target based on his combined traits and ideology. Thus, these results replicated those of previous person memory research. However, subjects had better recall of opinion statements with which they personally disagreed, regardless of the statements' consistency with the candidate's ideology or the favorableness of the concept that subjects formed of him on the basis of this ideology. These findings were not attributable to either subjects' lack of memory for the candidate's ideology or their failure to perceive the ideological implications of his stands on issues. Rather, they indicate that subjects thought about the candidate's statements of opinion, unlike his overt behaviors, with reference to their prior knowledge of the issues at hand, thinking more extensively about statements that were inconsistent with this knowledge regardless of the statements' consistency with expectations that subjects had formed of their source.

The difference between subjects' cognitive responses to opinion statements and their responses to overt behaviors requires further investigation. Pending this research, however, it seems likely that the representations that are formed of political candidates from the set of information that is often acquired about them differs in important ways from those implied by the person memory model. Consequently, applications of the model in this domain should be made with some caution.

Storage and Retrieval

The Organization of Information in Long-Term Memory

The conceptualization outlined above implies that several different representations can be formed of a person. Separate representations are particularly likely to be constructed when information about the person is received at different times. How are these representations stored in memory, and what factors underlie their later retrieval?

A theoretical formulation of social information processing by Wyer and Srull (1986, 1989) provides a possible answer. The model, which is metaphorical, assumes that the information one receives for a particular purpose is stored in long-term memory in a content-addressable storage bin that refers to the person, object, or event to which the processing objective is relevant. Each bin is identified by a header, which consists of a set of features that are strongly associated with the referent and that, separately or in combination, permit the bin to be identified. For example, the features of the header might include the candidate's name, political party, and personal appearance (i.e., a visual image). To the extent that some features of the candidate elicit affective reactions, the header also could include concepts of these reactions.

Each cognitive representation formed from information about a referent constitutes a different unit of knowledge, and each of these units is stored in a bin on top of previously deposited units. The number and complexity of these knowledge units might vary. That is, one unit might consist of a single attribute, or a previous judgment of the referent; another might be a configuration of attributes and behaviors (e.g., fig. 9.1); while a third might be a visual image, or an episodic representation of a sequence of behavioral events. Whatever the nature of a given knowledge unit, it is stored in the bin and consequently can be retrieved independently of other units.

A unit of knowledge is not stored in all of the bins to which it is relevant. Rather, it is deposited in only those bins whose referents are the focus of processing objectives that exist when it is formed or thought about. Thus, for example, one's representation of a politician's speech on disarmament might be stored in a "politician" bin if the listener has the goal of forming an impression of the politician, but in a "disarmament" bin if the listener's goal is to learn something about disarmament. In the latter case, the representation would not be retrieved if the recipient is later asked to evaluate the politician and searches for judgment-relevant information in the "politician" bin.

Retrieval Processes

People who are required to make a judgment do not retrieve and use all of the knowledge they have accumulated that potentially bears on this judgment (Kahneman, Slovic, & Tversky, 1982; Nisbett & Ross, 1980; Taylor & Fiske, 1978; Wyer & Hartwick, 1980). Rather, they sample only a subset of information that they consider to be representative of the pool of knowledge they have acquired and, therefore, to be a sufficient basis for the judgment they are required to make. Wyer and Srull postulate a priority system to govern the knowledge that people are likely to consider.

Specifically, assume that someone has formed several representations of a person on the basis of information acquired at several different times and has stored these representations in a referent bin pertaining to the person. If the recipient of this information is later asked to make a judgment or decision regarding the person, the following steps are theoretically performed.

(1) The recipient first scans working memory for judgment-relevant information. This means that any information that has been very recently acquired, or old information that has been very recently thought about, may be retrieved and used independently of the knowledge that exists in long-term memory.

(2) If no judgment-relevant information is found in working memory, the recipient compiles a set of probe cues consisting of features that specify the referent of the information being sought and identifies a bin in long-term memory whose header contains these features. When such a bin is identified, the recipient scans the remainder of the header for features that are relevant to the judgmental objective at hand. If such features are found, the recipient uses them as a basis for judgment without consulting the contents of the bin itself.

(3) If the header features do not have clear implications for the judgment, the recipient performs a top-down search of the bin for a knowledge unit whose central concept is directly relevant to the judgment to be made. If the concepts defining two or more knowledge units have implications for the judgment, the unit that is nearest to the top of the bin (i.e., the one that has been deposited most recently) is the most likely to be identified and used.

(4) If a knowledge unit whose central concept has direct implications for the judgment or decision cannot be identified, the recipient searches for a representation whose central concept is primarily evaluative (see fig. 9.1) and bases the judgment on both (a) the evaluative implications of this central concept and (b) the descriptive implications of the features associated with it, identified through a partial review of these features.

(5) If a representation whose central concept is evaluative cannot be found, the recipient retrieves a sample of feature-specific knowledge units that are contained in the bin, assesses the implications of these individual features, and computes a judgment on the basis of these implications.

(6) When a judgment-relevant knowledge unit is identified, its position in the bin remains intact. However, a *copy* of the unit is retrieved and operated on, and once the processing is completed, this copy is returned to the top of the bin from which it was drawn. This increases the likelihood that this knowledge unit (or a copy of it) will be retrieved and used again.

In combination, these principles have many implications, a few of which are worth noting.

(1) Judgment-relevant information is retrieved from a bin that is directly relevant to the person or object being judged. As we pointed out,

much of the knowledge we acquire about a particular referent may not be stored in a bin pertaining to this referent. Consequently, this knowledge is normally not considered when judgments of the referent are made.

(2) Although people are able to recall specific information they have received about a person or object if they are required to do so, they often do not use this information as a basis for their judgments. Such specific information is used only if (a) a judgment cannot be made on the basis of features that are contained in the referent bin header and (b) a knowledge unit whose central concept has direct implications for the judgment cannot be identified. For these reasons, there often is little relation between the judgments that are made of a person or object and the implications of the information that people can recall about the referent when they are explicitly asked to do so (Hastie & Park, 1986; Lichtenstein & Srull, 1987; Lodge, McGraw, & Stroh, 1989).

(3) Different concepts and knowledge may be used to make different types of judgments, and the implications of these sources of information may conflict.

(4) Judgments of a referent that can be based on the features of a bin header are likely to be fairly invariant over time. In contrast, judgments that require the use of knowledge that is contained in the bin itself may be rather unstable, varying with how recently the knowledge has been acquired or previously thought about.

Implications for Political Judgment

Several features of this model make it potentially useful for conceptualizing the cognitive representation of information about political candidates. For example, the model allows for the possibility that several different subsets of knowledge about a candidate are acquired at different times and stored in memory independently. It also specifies the conditions in which these subsets of knowledge are likely to be retrieved and used. Finally, it implies that many judgments of a candidate are based on general, categorical, or affective criteria without considering the implications of the specific pieces of knowledge that one has acquired about the candidate (e.g., the candidate's voting record or positions on issues).

A rigorous application of the formulation to political judgment, however, requires several assumptions about the conditions in which features become part of a referent bin header. For example:

(1) A candidate's personal appearance and party membership are often among the first things one learns about a candidate. An initial evaluative

concept of the candidate is therefore likely to be formed on the basis of this initial information. Whether this concept and its associated features continue to be used as a basis for judging the candidate, however, theoretically depends on whether they have been repeated often enough to become strongly associated with the candidate's name and, therefore, to become part of the header of the bin that pertains to the candidate.

(2) In general, the candidate's stands on particular issues are treated as behaviors of the candidate that compose the situation-specific representations contained in the bin. In some cases, however, a candidate's stand on a particular issue can become a header feature. This is particularly likely when the candidate's campaign is focused on a particular issue, or if the candidate for other reasons has become strongly identified with an issue. It also could occur when an issue is considered to be of considerable importance and the candidate's stand on it elicits strong affective reactions. These conditions ultimately must be specified more clearly.

Despite these ambiguities, the formulation developed by Wyer and Srull to account for the way in which information about people is organized and stored in memory, and how these representations are used to make judgments, provides an initial framework for conceptualizing the organization, storage, and retrieval of information about political candidates. At the same time, several unique aspects of political judgment situations must be taken into account in applying the theory in these situations. The conceptualization of political judgment that we propose later in this chapter addresses certain of these questions.

Inference Processes: Judgments of Single Individuals

Most research on person memory and judgment has been conducted under conditions in which one's objective is to form an impression of and evaluate a single individual. In many political judgment situations, however, one must make a comparative judgment of two or more persons. The processes that underlie comparative judgments, and the influence of different types of information on these judgments, may differ from those involved in single-person judgments.

Both types of judgment are important. In this section, we concentrate on single-person inferences. In doing so, we note some additional factors that theoretically and empirically influence the extent to which people rely upon general concepts of the target (e.g., those activated by the target's group membership or the social category to which the person belongs) as a basis for judgments rather than performing a detailed computation on the basis of the target's individual features. These factors include (a) the anticipated difficulty of the judgment to be made, (b) the interval between the receipt of different types of information and between the information and judgments, and (c) the role of affect in inference processes. Then, in the next section, we turn to a discussion of comparative judgment processes.

Determinants of the Use of Category-Based Criteria for Judgment

1. Judgment task difficulty. People are likely to base their judgments on detailed information about a person if the information has clear implications for the judgment and the judgment is easy to compute. When a judgment is difficult to make on the basis of this information, however, people are likely to default to the use of more general, category-based criteria as heuristics. For example, they may activate a stereotype on the basis of the target's group membership and may use features of this stereotype as criteria for judging the target without bothering to perform a piecemeal analysis of the target's individual attributes (see Bodenhausen & Lichtenstein, 1987; Bodenhausen & Wyer, 1985). Bodenhausen and Lichtenstein (1987), for example, gave subjects information about a court case that included an indication of the defendant's ethnicity and also specific details that bore on his guilt or innocence. The specific case information was typically used as a basis for judgment when subjects anticipated making a trait judgment that required little cognitive effort. However, when subjects expected to judge the defendant's guilt (an assessment that required an analysis and integration of several different facts with conflicting implications), they defaulted to the use of categorical, stereotype-based criteria instead.

This does not necessarily mean that subjects who make category-based judgments entirely ignore the individuating information. Bodenhausen and Wyer (1985) found that subjects' recall of different types of judgment-relevant information was affected by the stereotypes they had activated earlier. One explanation of this is that subjects, having made an initial judgment on the basis of categorical criteria, selectively processed the information they received later in an attempt to corroborate this judgment. However, this cognitive activity did not lead them to alter the judgment they ultimately reported.

2. Time delay between category activation and individuating information. Providing information that a person belongs to a group or category does not in itself guarantee that a concept of the person will be formed on the basis of the information. When the category is included along with other information about the target, and subjects have a specific judgmental objective in mind, it might simply be treated as an attribute of the target that is used as a basis for judgment (in much the same way as other attributes) without being used to form a more general concept of the target in its own right.

Two studies suggest that this is true. Futoran and Wyer (1986) found that when the gender of a candidate for a job was presented along with a series of personality attributes, it was used as an attribute of the target that influenced job suitability judgments independently of and in addition to other attributes. (The effect of gender could not be attributed to the influence of judgments on subjects' beliefs that the candidate had other job-relevant attributes.) That is, subjects treated gender as an attribute that was relevant to job effectiveness in its own right, independently of other attributes that were stereotypically associated with it.

Similarly, the aforementioned study by Hong and Wyer (1990) showed that when a product's country of origin was presented along with information about specific attributes of the product in the same experimental session, each type of information had an independent influence on subjects' judgments of the product's quality. When subjects learned the product's country of origin twenty-four hours before they read about the product's judgment-relevant attributes, however, the effect of country of origin on judgments was increased.

In combination, these studies suggest that when people receive information with a particular judgmental objective in mind and the target's group membership is presented along with more specific information, this membership is treated as one of several attributes of the target and does not activate a more general stereotype. When it is conveyed some time before the more specific information, a separate stereotype-based concept of the target may be formed from it, and, as a result, its impact on judgments is greater.

3. Time delay between information presentation and judgment. We noted earlier that once information has been encoded in terms of more general concepts, the effects of these encodings on judgments increase over time. This suggests that if a person is identified as an exemplar of a general group or category on the basis of initial information presented, the effects of this categorization on judgments will increase over time in relation to the effects of the more specific, individuating information that was conveyed (Srull & Wyer, 1979). Therefore, for example, suppose subjects have formed an initial concept of a political candidate as liberal or conservative, or as an effective leader, on the basis of a subset of the initial information about him. The impact of these concepts on later evaluations of the candidate may increase over time in relation to the influence of the candidate's specific behavior and stands on issues.

4. *The role of category-triggered affect.* People often use their internal affective reactions to a stimulus as information about how well they like it (Schwarz & Clore, 1983; Strack, Martin, & Stepper, 1988; for a review, see Schwarz & Clore, 1987). Moreover, this judgmental criterion may be given priority over the descriptive implications of judgment-relevant information (Strack, Schwarz, & Gschneidinger, 1985). In the present context, this suggests that the influence of general concepts of a person on judgments of the person will be particularly great when these concepts elicit strong emotional reactions. If people have previously conditioned positive or negative affective responses to a group or social category, information that someone belongs to this group or category may elicit these reactions. The reactions may then be used to infer one's "feelings" about the person, and the effect of these inferences on judgments can override the influence of more descriptive judgment-relevant criteria.

5. *Typicality.* Two recent theoretical formulations of the conditions in which categorical and piecemeal information is used as a basis for judgment point out still other factors to consider. Fiske and Pavelchak (1986; see also Fiske & Neuberg, 1990) suggest that the use of a person's category membership (or the affect elicited by it) as a basis for judgment depends on the extent to which the person's individual attributes match those that are typical of category members. That is, people first determine whether the target is a good or bad exemplar of the category, based on descriptions of the target's specific attributes. If they conclude that the target is typical, they base their judgments on the affective reactions to the *category* independently of the evaluative implications of the target's individual features. If they conclude that the target is atypical, however, they base their judgments on a piecemeal analysis of the evaluative implications of the target's features themselves. Alternatively, they attempt to identify a subcategory of the more general one with which the target's features are consistent (e.g., "liberal Republican") and base their judgment on their evaluation of this subcategory (Fiske & Neuberg, 1990).

A qualification of these predictions has been suggested by Brewer (1988). She postulates that a critical determinant of category-based vs. piecemeal-based judgments is the extent to which judges are personally involved in the judgment to be made. That is, personally involved judges are likely to engage in analytic, piecemeal processing regardless of the target's typicality. In contrast, uninvolved subjects typically base their judgments on categorical criteria, attempting to subcategorize the target when he or she is a poor exemplar of the more general category to which he belongs.

Implications for Political Judgment

To summarize, category-based criteria for judging a person are more likely to have an influence when (a) judgments are made a relatively long time after judgment-relevant information is presented (Wyer & Srull, 1989); (b) the judgment is expected to be difficult (Bodenhausen & Lichtenstein, 1987); (c) there is a substantial interval between (i) learning the person's membership in a stereotyped category and (ii) learning the individuating information about the person's attributes (Hong & Wyer, 1990); (d) the stereotyped group or category to which the person belongs elicits strong affective reactions (Strack et al., 1985); (e) the person's individuating features suggest that he or she is a typical member of the category (Fiske & Pavelchak, 1986); (f) judges are not personally involved in the judgment task (Brewer, 1988). Any or all of these factors might come into play in political judgment situations.

A study by Wyer, Budesheim, Shavitt, Riggle, Melton, and Kuklinski (1991) raises still further considerations concerning the effects of time delay. In this study, subjects (nonacademic employees) listened to a videotaped nonpolitical speech of a political candidate that was delivered in a style that conveyed either a favorable or unfavorable impression. The speech was followed either immediately or one day later by a radio interview in which the candidate's issue positions were conveyed. The issue stands conveyed either a liberal or a conservative ideology. The interval between the latter information and subjects' evaluations of the candidate was also varied. The direct effect of the candidate's speech on evaluations of him was substantial, but decreased over the time between the speech and judgments. Although this decrease is not surprising, it disconfirmed speculations that visual information is retained in memory longer than verbal information and therefore has a relatively greater impact on judgments as time goes on (see Reyes, Thompson, & Bower, 1980).

More provocative is the evidence that the candidate's speech affected the way subjects thought about his issue stands and therefore the nature of their influence on judgments. Specifically, when the subjects saw the speech twenty-four hours before hearing about his positions on issues, they based their judgments of the candidate on their personal agreement with these stands, and the ideological implications of the stands had no influence. When they listened to the speech immediately before the information on issue stands, however, subjects based the judgments on the ideology conveyed by the candidate's issue positions (and its similarity to the subjects' own ideologies), and their agreement with the individual positions had no influence. These data suggest that the salience of categorical (image-related) information at the time that subjects encountered the candidate's stands on issues stimulated them to think more categorically about the issue information that supported those stands as well, and so they based their judgments on the more general implications of the candidate's positions on issues regardless of whether they personally agreed or disagreed with them.

Comparative Judgment Processes

Although the findings of Wyer et al. (1991) are provocative, their generalizability is constrained by the nature of the judgment task. That is, only one candidate was considered. In many political judgment situations, people are required to make a *comparative* judgment of two or more candidates. Comparative judgments often appear to involve different inference processes than do judgments of single candidates, and these processes are more likely to involve the use of stereotype-related criteria.

The difference between processes of absolute and comparative judgment is not self-evident. People who are confronted with a comparative judgment of two or more individuals could in principle form an impression of each person separately in much the same way they would evaluate the person if considered in isolation. Then, having done so, they could simply compare the overall evaluations of each person to determine their relative preference. This strategy is particularly likely when no common bases for comparison exist. In political judgment situations, however, specific bases for comparison often do exist. That is, candidates belong to different parties; they differ in speech style, attractiveness, and general personality; they endorse differing positions on a common set of issues. Under these conditions, people may not separately form independent impressions of each candidate. Rather, they may conduct a dimension-by-dimension comparison of the candidates, and they may base their relative preferences on the number of judgment-relevant criteria on which one candidate is superior to the other (for a survey of several specific comparative judgment strategies, see Montgomery, 1983).

The difference between comparative and single-candidate judgments was made salient in a series of studies by Riggle, Ottati, Kuklinski, Wyer, and Schwarz (1989). In one study, subjects received information about a member of the U.S. House of Representatives consisting of (a) an attractive or unattractive photograph, (b) an indication of the candidate's party affiliation, and (c) the candidate's votes on a series of bills. In this condition, judgments of the candidate were based almost exclusively on the candidate's voting record, and the effects of his party affiliation and physical attractiveness had little effect.[2] In a second study, however, subjects were asked to make comparative judgments of two candidates who differed from one another with respect to each of the three characteristics and then to separately evaluate each candidate. The pattern of these judgments was different from the pattern that emerged when only one candidate was judged. Specifically, subjects appeared to give a candidate a favorable evaluation if he rated favorably on two of the three criteria, and the candidate received an unfavorable evaluation if he rated unfavorably on two of the three criteria. This was true regardless of which two criteria were involved. Moreover, when two of the three criteria had similar implications, the third factor had no effect at all. Therefore, in contrast to absolute judgments, comparative judgments were influenced by all three criteria.

Additional Considerations

If the differences we observed between single-candidate and comparative judgments are generalized to situations outside the laboratory, their implications are provocative. Single-person judgments are most likely to be made in off-election years when politicians are not involved in campaigning. In contrast, comparative judgments are most likely to occur during an election when the opposing candidates have been identified. Taken at face value, the results obtained in Riggle et al.'s (1989) studies would suggest that a candidate's stands on issues are more likely to influence judgments of an incumbent during the period in which he or she is not actively seeking office, whereas stereotype-activated, image-related criteria are more likely to come into play during an election campaign. If this is the case, it raises an interesting question. Does one's evaluation of an incumbent during his or her term in office (which may be based on positions on issues) affect the comparative judgment that is made later, when the person is running for reelection? Or, is one's evaluation of the incumbent recomputed using comparative strategies similar to those described above? The effects of incumbency on voting decisions might be worth considering in this context.

In evaluating the generalizability of these results to political judgment situations outside the laboratory, two other considerations arise.

(1) Unlike the conditions constructed by Riggle et al. (1989), people in actual political judgment situations normally receive information about candidates at different times, and the information does not always pertain to the same issues. (Consequently, one candidate's stand on a given issue may be known, whereas the other candidate's stand on this issue may not be.) These conditions mitigate against a direct issue-by-issue comparison of the candidates and, therefore, increase the likelihood that people evaluate each candidate separately, much as they would under single candidate judgment conditions. Moreover, to the extent that direct comparisons are attempted, they must be made between the implications of new information presented about one candidate and one's *memory* for comparable information acquired about the other candidate in the past. The complexity of this comparison decreases the likelihood of its being performed, at least at the time of judgment.

(2) Our interpretation of Riggle et al.'s (1989) study assumes that the candidate is preferred who has the greatest number of desirable characteristics. However, many voting decisions are undoubtedly based on *negative* criteria. In other words, we do not vote for candidate A because of any features of A that we consider particularly desirable. Rather, we vote for A because we cannot tolerate B, and A is the lesser of the two evils.

To the extent that this is the case, the decision strategy could be distinctly different from those we have considered so far. For example, a person who finds that one of two candidates is abominable may not bother to compare this candidate feature-by-feature with the other. Rather, the person may simply scan the opponent's known attributes to see that they are above the critical *threshold of acceptability*. If they are, the person may vote for the opponent even if some of the opponent's attributes (although above the threshold) are less desirable than those of the first candidate. This "satisficing" strategy might be adopted without any direct comparison of the candidates in respect to other issues.

A Conceptual Integration

We have identified many factors that can potentially affect the processing of political information. These factors come into play at several different stages of processing. In this section we propose a conceptualization of political judgment that incorporates many of the empirical phenomena we have identified and the conclusions we have drawn concerning their implications for political judgment. In doing so, we attempt to capture many of the conditions in which political information is acquired and used in nonlaboratory situations.

The model has three distinct parts. The first pertains to the formation of a concept of a candidate on the basis of the first information received about him or her. The second concerns the processing of information that is acquired sometime after the initial concept of the candidate has been formed. The third part focuses on the process of making a judgment or a voting decision. In each case, consideration is given to the role of information that has been received about alternative candidates as well as about the candidate in question.

In describing the model, we restrict our consideration to three types of information about a candidate: physical appearance, party affiliation, and stands on specific issues.[3] In addition, we assume that people acquire the information about a candidate with the implicit objective of evaluating the candidate and deciding whether to vote for this candidate or an alternative. This latter restriction on the model's applicability is particularly important. When people acquire information about a candidate for other purposes, or with no particular objective in mind, other considerations may arise that are not taken into account by the formulation.

The model is summarized in figure 9.2. This figure conveys the sequence of cognitive activities and decisions that theoretically occur in the course of receiving information about a particular candidate and the priorities that are given to different criteria at the time a judgment or voting decision is made. The model can be conveyed more formally in the terms of twelve postulates. For convenience, three postulates are stated in terms of the concepts and terminology used by Wyer and Srull (1986, 1989) in the model of social information-processing described earlier.

Initial Concept Formation (Postulates 1–4)

Postulate 1. If subjects receive information about a previously unknown political candidate in the absence of information about the candidate's stands on specific issues, they form a general concept of the candidate on the basis of (a) party affiliation, (b) physical appearance and personal mannerisms, or both. (Features of this concept can include both a visual

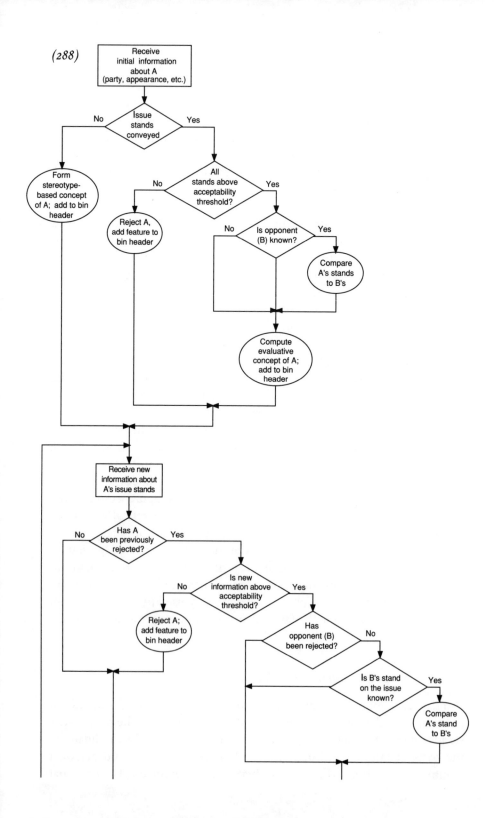

(288)

(Figure 9.2. continued)

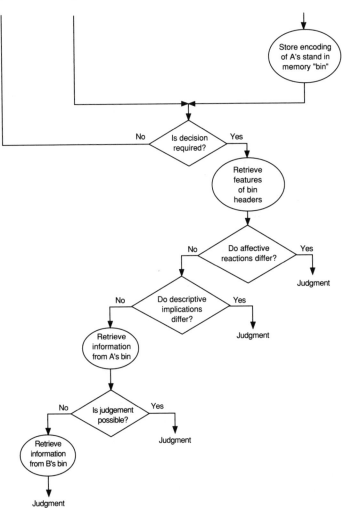

Figure 9.2. Flow diagram of the steps postulated to intervene between the receipt of initial information about a political candidate, A, and judgments of whether to vote for this candidate or an alternative, B. Rectangles denote external events, circles denote cognitive activities, and diamonds denote decision points.

representation of the candidate and affective reactions to him or her that are elicited by the information.)

Postulate 2. When a candidate's stands on particular issues are conveyed in the initial information about him, subjects compute the candidate's similarity to themselves in political orientation on the basis of these stands and form a concept of the candidate as a result of this computation. In this case, the candidate's physical appearance and party membership (if available) function as additional attributes that may or may not be of sufficient importance to influence the concept that is formed.

Note that these postulates take into account the evidence that physical appearance and party membership both appear to influence the evaluative concept that is formed of a candidate when these factors are presented in isolation (Asher, 1983; Riggle et al., 1989, experiment 1), but have little influence on this concept when they are accompanied by information concerning the candidate's stands on specific issues (Riggle et al., 1989, experiment 2). In addition, they are consistent with evidence that category-based criteria are not the primary basis for forming an initial concept of the target when more specific attribute (e.g., issue) information is available (Hong & Wyer, 1990; Riggle et al., 1989, experiment 2).

Postulate 3. If a candidate's attribute, or stand on a political issue, is below a recipient's threshold of acceptability, the recipient will form a concept of the candidate as "unacceptable" on the basis of this information about political stand alone, regardless of the candidate's other qualities.

This postulate recognizes that certain issue positions, or other personal characteristics, can often be a sufficient basis for rejecting a candidate. When this is the case, the remaining information about the candidate is not taken into account in the evaluative concept that is formed.

Postulate 4. Once an evaluative concept of the candidate has been formed, this concept, along with the candidate's name, party affiliation, political orientation (if known), and physical appearance, become features of the header of a referent bin that pertains to the candidate.[4] In contrast, the specific information on which the concept was based is not contained in the header but is stored in the bin itself.

Encoding of New Information (Postulates 5–9)

After an initial concept of a candidate has been formed, additional information about the candidate's issue stands may be received. The next five postulates specify the way in which this new information is processed.

Postulate 5. New information about a candidate will activate the features of a header of a referent bin that pertains to this candidate. If one of these features is "unacceptable," or if the evaluative implications of another header feature are below the threshold of acceptability, the new information will receive no further processing.

Postulate 6. If the concepts that compose a candidate's referent bin header do not indicate that the candidate is unacceptable, and if these concepts have implications for the interpretation of new information about the candidate, this interpretation is made.

Postulate 6 therefore recognizes that new information about a candidate's stands on issues is often interpreted in terms of previously formed general concepts of the candidate. It does not specify, however, which specific concepts are employed. The interpretation of issue stands as liberal or conservative might be influenced by the candidate's party affiliation. Its interpretation as favorable or unfavorable, however, might be influenced by header features that are evaluative in nature (e.g., concepts based on the basis of the candidate's physical attractiveness or other concepts that are descriptively irrelevant to the candidate's position on issues). In some instances, however, a candidate's stands on issues are interpreted with reference to those of the candidate's opponent.

Postulate 7. If no information is available about a candidate's opponent at the time the candidate's stand on an issue is learned, or if the opponent has been declared unacceptable on the basis of previous information, the candidate's position on the issue is encoded as favorable or unfavorable in *absolute* terms. If, however, the opponent is potentially acceptable and his or her position on the issue is known, the candidate's stand on this issue is compared to the opponent's and is encoded in *relative* terms.

Thus, a candidate's stand might be encoded as "in favor of increased defense spending" if the opponent's stand on this matter is unknown. However, if the opponent is a strong proponent of the Strategic Defense Initiative (Star Wars), the same stand might be encoded as only "somewhat in favor of increased defense spending." Note that such an encoding does not reflect the particular standard that gave rise to it. This means that if the encoding is retrieved later, its implications might be evaluated in relation to a *different* standard. Therefore, the stand might be interpreted as less favorable toward defense spending than the original information had actually implied. (For evidence of this phenomenon in other domains, see Higgins & Lurie, 1983; Sherman, Ahlm, Berman, & Lynn, 1978).

One implication of postulate 7 is that the encoding of issue stands is not symmetric. That is, suppose the opponent's position is already known at the time that the candidate's stand is learned. Then, the candidate's stand is encoded in relation to the opponent's, but the opponent's stand is *not* recoded in relation to the candidate's. Rather, it retains its initial, context-free value.

Postulate 8. Representations that are formed of the candidate on the basis of new information are deposited in the candidate's referent bin independently of other, previously formed representations.

Postulate 9. If the evaluative implications of the new information about a candidate have been encoded and the evaluative implications of these encodings are below the threshold of acceptability, a feature reflecting this conclusion (e.g., "unacceptable") is added to the header of the candidate's bin. (The information on which this conclusion is based is stored in the bin itself.)

Considered in combination, these postulates have several interesting implications. For example, new information about a candidate, A, should only affect one's overall concept of A if its implications fall below the threshold of acceptability (postulate 9). Moreover, the encoding of this information into memory depends on whether both A and the opponent are considered viable candidates. If A already has been rejected, the new information is not processed extensively (postulate 5), and so it is unlikely to be remembered. If A's opponent (B) has been rejected, the information about A will be encoded in absolute terms and, therefore, its interpretation will not depend on B's stand on the issue (postulate 7). Only if A and B are *both* acceptable candidates will A's stand be encoded in relative terms and, therefore, be influenced by B's position.

Decision-Making (Postulates 10–12)

The information-acquisition processes implied by postulates 1–9 continue until the recipient is asked to report a preference for the candidates (or, alternatively, is called upon to vote). Three postulates govern the criteria on which this judgment is based and the relative priority that is given to these criteria.

Postulate 10. To decide between two candidates, a person first consults the headers of the bins that pertain to the candidates and compares the affective reactions that are elicited by the concepts contained in these headers. If these reactions do not differ, the person assesses the descriptive implications of the header concepts for the likelihood that each candidate supports the person's own views. Only if a decision cannot be made on the basis of these criteria are the specific contents of the bins themselves considered.

Postulate 11. Information about a candidate is sought only until the amount obtained is deemed sufficient to justify a decision.

Postulate 12. One bin is searched at a time. The search for information is top-down, and so the information nearest the top of the bin is the most likely to be retrieved and used. If an absolute judgment is required, the judgment is based on features in the bin that have been encoded in absolute terms. If a comparative judgment is required, the judgment is based on features that have been encoded in relative terms.

Postulates 10–12 reflect the implications of Strack et al.'s (1985) evidence that the primary criterion for evaluative judgments is *affective*. That is, if the general concepts associated with a candidate elicit strong affective reactions that differ from those associated with the opponent, these reactions will be used as a basis for the decision regardless of the descriptive implications of the concepts for the candidate's political ideology and its similarity to the subjects' own orientation. Only if these affective reactions do not adequately discriminate the candidates will subjects consider the descriptive implications of the information they have available.

Postulate 12, that only one bin at a time is searched for judgment-relevant information, has interesting implications. In an election campaign, people are likely to learn a candidate's stands on some issues before learning the opponent's positions on these issues, but they do not learn the candidate's stands on other issues until after the opponent's views become known. According to postulate 6, they should encode the former stands in absolute terms, but should encode the latter stands in relative terms. To the extent that a voting decision is based on a comparison of the two candidates' issue stands, conditions can arise in which the decision will depend on which candidate is thought about first and, therefore, which candidate's bin happens to be consulted. (To take an extreme example, this would arise if candidate A is preferred to candidate B on all issues in which B's stand was learned before A's, whereas B is preferred to A in all cases in which A's stand was learned before B's.)

Still other implications can be derived from postulate 12. Specifically, the search for information in a bin is from the top down. In general, this means that the most recently acquired knowledge is nearest the top of the bin, and, therefore, is most likely to be retrieved and used. Space does not permit us to evaluate these implications in detail (for a fuller discussion of these effects, see Wyer & Srull, 1986, 1989).

Final Remarks

We have attempted to apply theory and research in the area of social information processing to political judgment and decision-making. We have undoubtedly raised more questions than we have answered. In many instances, major ambiguities exist, and the generalizability of conclusions that are drawn is unclear.

Our recognition of these ambiguities should not be interpreted as pessimism. With the use of innovative research designs that are sensitive to the types of political judgment situations that exist outside the laboratory, the problems can be overcome. In the area of political judgment, as in other areas of scientific inquiry, it is often more difficult to ask the right questions than to come up with the right answers. Although social information-processing formulations have not yet come up with answers, they at least provide a framework within which fundamental questions about political judgment and decision-making can be asked. Our objective in this chapter has been to raise certain of these questions within the context of such a framework. Although we are just beginning to conduct systematic research on these questions, meaningful answers may not be too far off.

Notes

This paper was prepared with funds provided in part by National Institute of Mental Health Grant MH 3-8585. The research on political judgment reported therein was conducted with funds provided by the University of Illinois Survey Research Laboratory in collaboration with Ellen Riggle, James Kuklinski, and Norbert Schwarz. Appreciation is extended to these collaborators, and also to other members of the Political Judgment Research Group—Sharon Shavitt, Lee Budesheim, and Jeff Melton—for stimulating many of the ideas presented in this chapter, and to the University of Illinois Social Cognitive Group for valuable feedback concerning much of the theory and research on which the ideas are based.

1. When subjects have very little time to think about the behaviors in relation to one another, of course, neither inconsistency resolution nor bolstering can occur. In these cases, inconsistent behaviors and consistent behaviors are both recalled poorly, and neither has a recall advantage over the other (Srull, 1981; Wyer, Budesheim, Lambert, & Martin, 1988).

2. That the candidate's attractiveness fails to have an influence in this study conflicts with evidence obtained by Wyer et al. (1991). The photographs used in

this study created a less vivid impression of the candidate than the speech information presented by Wyer et al. (1991) and for this reason it might have had less effect. However, the candidate's attractiveness did affect subjects' evaluations when comparative judgments were made, as will be noted.

3. The restriction of our consideration to these three attributes does not deny the importance of other candidate attributes such as ethnicity or gender. These attributes, like the ones we consider, are likely to have their impact through their mediating influence on beliefs that the candidate will support one's interests and will be effective in public office. To this extent, the conceptual framework we propose would be applicable in understanding the effects of these characteristics as well.

4. For simplicity in presenting the conceptualization, this postulate ignores the assumption noted earlier that these features do not become part of the bin header until they have reoccurred with sufficient frequency to become strongly associated with the candidate. A refinement of the conceptualization would presumably need to take this contingency into account.

Victor C. Ottati and Robert S. Wyer, Jr.

10. Affect and Political Judgment

Recent years have witnessed an increasing concern with the cognitive mechanisms that underlie political judgment and behavior (Ferejohn & Kuklinski, 1990; Lau & Sears, 1986). Much of this work has focused on the cognitive processes that underlie the use of information to make voting decisions. This emphasis contrasts with earlier work that was devoted to the prediction of political behavior without regard to its cognitive mediators.

Although there have been many advances in our understanding of the cognitive aspects of political judgment, certain important considerations have been neglected. In particular, social judgments and decisions are often greatly influenced by affective reactions that are elicited by the people or objects being judged or by the information presented about them. The importance of taking these reactions into account is supported by evidence indicating that cognitive and affective process mechanisms are interrelated, with one often influencing the other (Clarke & Fiske, 1982; Isen, 1984; Wyer & Srull, 1989). However, the role of these affective mechanisms in political decision-making has rarely been investigated (for exceptions, see Fiske, 1986; Roseman, Abelson, & Ewing, 1986). This chapter attempts to set an agenda for a comprehensive examination of the role of affect in cognitive functioning by considering both the antecedents and consequences of affective responses.

Before doing so, however, it is necessary to state more precisely the meaning of "affect" and to distinguish among several different theoretical constructs to which it is relevant. Then, we will consider theory and research that employ these constructs and consider its relevance to the political judgment process.

What Is Affect?

In this chapter we conceptualize affect as a physiological state that is experienced as either pleasant (positive affect) or unpleasant (negative affect). This is surely not the only way to conceptualize an affective state. For example, one could consider physiological or bodily reactions that occur without phenomenological awareness. We assume, however, that it is the *experience* of an affective state that is most directly related to the interplay between affect and cognitive processing. For our purposes, therefore, we do not distinguish between affect per se and the experience of affect. Furthermore, we acknowledge that pleasant and unpleasant affective states can be experienced in ways that are more differentiated than simply positive or negative. For example, individuals may distinguish "sad" from "fearful" unpleasant states. We also assume that affective states can be produced by external stimuli, internally generated thoughts, or physiological changes (e.g., an upset stomach). As we will elaborate, however, the specific determinants of an affective state are not always clearly identifiable by the person who experiences it.

Although affective reactions are not always directly observable, they can provide the basis for a variety of overt judgments and behavioral decisions. The link between affective reactions and overt judgments is more firmly established in some instances than in others. In this chapter we discuss four constructs that are relevant to a consideration of affect: (a) evaluations of an object or a particular feature of an object, (b) emotional reactions to an object, (c) mood, and (d) affective arousal. These constructs vary in the extent to which they assume that affective reactions are enduring or transitory, diffuse or object-specific, and are consciously labeled or unlabeled by the person who experiences them.

Evaluation. Social psychologists typically construe evaluations of a stimulus as estimates of the individual's liking or disliking for it. When an evaluation pertains to an object as a whole, it is typically referred to as an "attitude" (e.g., an attitude toward George Bush). An evaluative judgment may be based in part on a conditioned affective response to the object that is relatively enduring and permanent. Evaluative judgments may also be influenced by transitory sources of affect (e.g., one's mood at the time of judgment) that are incorrectly attributed to the object being judged.

Objects possess features, qualities, or attributes. For example, a political candidate may possess the features "liberal," "in favor of decreased defense spending," and "charismatic." These individual features may elicit affective reactions that contribute to someone's overall evaluation of the candidate. It is not necessarily the case, however, that the affect elicited by the object as a whole is predictable from the affect elicited by its individual characteristics. We also will consider this matter.

It is important to note that in many instances evaluations of an object might not be based on affective reactions at all. Political psychologists often measure attitudes toward a political candidate using a "feeling thermometer." The link between such judgments and affective reactions is not always clearly established. These judgments could, in principle, reflect "cold" evaluative inferences that are associated with little if any physiological activity.

Emotional responses to an object. Emotional reactions to an object are typically more transitory than attitudes toward an object. That is, they are episodic "feeling events" that occur during a circumscribed period and are attributed to a specific object or event toward which one's attention is directed. For example, a person may indicate that "Reagan made me feel angry when he made that joke about bombing the Soviets." As this example suggests, the label given to emotional responses is often more highly differentiated than simply "positive" or "negative." Thus, "happy" is distinguished from "hopeful," and "angry" is distinguished from "fearful."

Mood. "Mood states," like emotional responses to an object, are transitory or episodic affective reactions that occur for circumscribed periods. Unlike emotional responses, however, they are not cognitively associated with any particular eliciting stimulus. Thus, a person can be in a happy mood without being able to designate a cause or reason for being in such a state (Schwarz & Clore, 1983).

The distinction between emotional reactions and mood states is clearer in principle than in practice. Similar terms are often used to denote both conditions. A person who reports that a particular event made him feel sad would be said to have an emotional reaction to the event, whereas a person who reports feeling sad for no particular reason would be inferred to be in a sad mood. Put another way, emotional responses to a specific stimulus may be transformed into a mood state if these responses persist in the absence of thought about the objects or events that originally elicited them. Alternatively, a mood could give rise to an emotional reaction if a person who experiences the mood attributes the affect being experienced to a particular source that is not, in fact, the one that actually elicited it.

Affective arousal. Affective arousal states, like mood states, are epi-

Table 10.1. Characteristics of four theoretical constructs to which affect is relevant.

	Duration of affective reactions	Specificity of affective reactions	Labeling of affective reactions
Evaluations	enduring	object-specific	labeled
Emotional responses	transitory	object-specific	labeled
Mood	transitory	diffuse	labeled
Affective arousal	transitory	diffuse	unlabeled

sodic and are not necessarily directed at any particular object. However, they differ from mood states in that they are not cognitively labeled. That is, depending on the circumstances, a person may come to label the same arousal state as "euphoria" or "anger" (Schachter, 1964). According to this view, all affective states are characterized by some level of physiological arousal that is not specific to their quality or valence.

The four constructs described above are summarized in table 10.1 as a function of whether the affective reactions associated with them are relatively enduring or transitory, object–specific or diffuse, and whether the reactions are labeled or unlabeled. Note that with the exception of affective arousal, the reactions implied by each construct include a cognitive component. Thus, an "evaluation" reflects the favorableness of an individual's reaction to a cognitively represented object or some particular feature of that object. A "mood" is an affective reaction that has been cognitively labeled as belonging to some conceptual category ("sad," etc.). And, an "emotional response" to an object is a feeling state that is assigned both a cognitive label (e.g., "I feel angry") and cognitively attributed to a particular eliciting stimulus (e.g., "Reagan is making me feel angry"). As such, an examination of the role of affect necessarily entails an analysis of the affect–cognition relationship.

The literature on the role of affect in judgment often fails to distinguish between the various constructs noted above. The theoretical and empirical issues that surround the role of each construct are nevertheless very different. In the remainder of this chapter we will first consider theory and research that bear either directly or indirectly on the antecedents of affective reactions of the sorts that these constructs imply. After this discussion, we will turn to each construct and consider its role in social and political judgment.

Determinants of Affective Reactions

Recent theory and research on the determinants of affect has focused on two different issues. The first concerns the extent to which affective reactions to a stimulus are cognitively mediated. The second issue concerns the extent to which the affective reactions that underlie judgments of a stimulus result from a piecemeal analysis of the evaluative implications of its unique individuating attributes or, alternatively, are elicited by more global criteria (e.g., the stimulus object's membership in a social category).

The Role of Cognition in Determining Affective Reactions

Affective reactions to a stimulus person or object are often elicited by attributes of the stimulus of which the perceiver is well-aware. More-over, thinking about a person or object that is not physically present can elicit an emotional or affective response. Many theorists (e.g., Arnold, 1960; Lazarus, 1984) assume that emotional responses follow from an initial cognitive appraisal of the stimulus. This appraisal may often reflect the relevance of the stimulus to future goal attainment (Roseman, 1979; see also Foa & Kozak, 1985). A stimulus that is perceived to increase the probability of attaining a desirable outcome (or to decrease the probability of attaining an undesirable outcome) elicits a positive affective reaction. A stimulus that is believed to decrease the probability of attaining a desirable outcome (or to increase the probability of attaining an undesirable outcome) elicits a negative affective reaction. The question is whether such cognitive appraisals are *necessary* for the elicitation of affect. The answer to this question is controversial.

Unattributed cognitive appraisal models. According to some cognitive appraisal theorists (e.g., Ittelson, 1973; Lazarus, 1984), emotions are sometimes elicited by cognitive responses to a stimulus configuration as a whole, independently of the individual features that compose it. For example, a situation may be perceived as threatening and, therefore, may elicit fear, without identifying any particular aspect of the situation. Such undifferentiated appraisals are, nonetheless, cognitions. That is, they constitute holistic cognitive responses to a stimulus configuration that do not require an analysis of its individual features and, therefore, can occur without a conscious identification of these features. (In a sense, this sort of response is no different from one's recognition of a letter string as a word without a detailed analysis of the individual letters.) Such undifferentiated cognitive responses could stimulate an affective reaction at the time one is exposed to the configuration without awareness of which specific aspects of the configuration are primarily responsible for it. One consequence is that the affective reaction might later be attributed to factors other than those that actually gave rise to it. In the political domain, for example, an undifferentiated cognitive appraisal of a politician's nonverbal behavior during a speech could elicit fear. This fear, however, might later be misattributed to the content of the candidate's message.

Inference-free models. Still other theorists (see Zajonc, 1984) have argued that emotional responses can occur without any prior cognitive appraisal whatsoever. According to classical conditioning theory, an object can become associated with a stimulus that elicits an affective response. Once the association is formed, the object might later elicit the affective reaction even when the original stimulus is not present. These associations conceivably occur without conscious awareness. Zajonc (1984) has argued that emotion can be triggered by untransformed "pure sensation." In support of this claim, he cites evidence indicating that preferences for a stimulus can be affected by repeated exposures to it even when the exposure times are below the recognition threshold (Kunst-Wilson & Zajonc, 1980; Wilson, 1979). Although Zajonc's (1984) interpretation of these findings has been strongly challenged (Birnbaum, 1981; Lazarus, 1984), its implications are worth noting. In the present context, for example, a perceiver could experience emotional reactions to a situation in which a political candidate is present without knowing what elicited these reactions. Later, these reactions might be evoked by the candidate, even when other features of the stimulus situation were originally responsible for them.

Facial feedback models. A special case of an inference-free model focuses on the role of facial feedback on the subjective experience of emotion. Proprioceptive feedback from different facial expressions may be associated with certain affective or emotional states and, therefore, may elicit these states (Buck, 1980; Cupchik & Leventhal, 1974; Izard, 1971, 1977, 1981; Kraut, 1982; Laird, 1981; Strack, Martin, & Stepper, 1988; Tomkins, 1962, 1979, 1981; Winton, 1986). Thus, a perceiver's emotional responses to someone may be determined in part by the perceiver's own facial expressions when the person is thought about or when information about the person is presented. This has further implications in light of the fact that perceivers tend to mimic the facial expressions of the people they are observing (Bartolucci, 1984; Bavelas, 1986; Dimburg, 1982; Meltzoff & Moore, 1977). Suppose, therefore, that a person who observes a political candidate unconsciously mimics the candidate's facial expressions. As a result, the observer might experience affective reactions that are elicited by the observer's own expressions. Of course, if these reactions result from an unconscious tendency to mimic the candidate's facial expression, they may be consciously misattributed to some other feature of the candidate (e.g., the candidate's verbal message).

The exact nature of this process, however, is subject to debate. According to the cognitivist position (e.g., Buck, 1985), facial feedback is a matter of self-perception. For example, the person feels his/her jaw become tense and infers "I must be angry." According to the inference-free model of facial feedback (Zajonc, Murphy, & Inglehart, in press), however, this mediating cognitive step is unnecessary. That is, proprioceptive feedback from a person's facial expression triggers a series of physiological responses that directly influence the person's emotional state. The implications of these alternative interpretations for political judgment are considered in more detail later.

Categorical vs. Piecemeal Bases for Affective Reactions

Here we focus on cognitively determined affective reactions and consider the nature of the cognitive appraisals that determine these reactions. Global affective reactions to a person, when cognitively mediated, are elicited by one or more characteristics of the person. These characteristics could include specific attributes and behaviors that are unique to the individual. However, they also could include a general category (black, Republican, etc.) in which the person can be placed. In this case, the question arises as to which type of information is most likely to be the source of the affective reactions that are used to evaluate the person.

Piecemeal processing models. An object can be viewed as a bundle of attributes. Associated with each attribute may be an evaluative "tag" that reflects one's subjective evaluation of it (or, theoretically, the affect that is elicited by it). A person who is required to evaluate the object may combine the implications of these tags to arrive at an overall summary evaluation. This computational process has been described algebraically in a number of ways, including summation (Fishbein & Ajzen, 1975) and averaging (Anderson, 1965, 1971).

These piecemeal integration models have their political counterparts in the voting behavior literature. For example, Kelly and Mirer (1974) assume that the voter subjectively computes the number of advantages and disadvantages of voting for each alternative political candidate and votes for the candidate for whom the difference between these numbers is greatest. A similar assumption is made by Campbell et al. (1960) when computing indices of the attitudes they assume to determine voting behavior.

Rational choice theorists (e.g., Downs, 1957) focus more specifically on a candidate's stands on various policy issues. They depict the voter as computing the "expected utility" of voting for a candidate on the basis of the desirability (or undesirability) of the candidate's position along each of a number of policy dimensions. Spatial models (Enelow & Hinich, 1985) conceptualize this utility in terms of the distance between the candidate's actual position along a dimension and the voter's ideal point along the dimension. In any case, the integration rule implicit in these models is also piecemeal. That is, the voter accumulates pieces of information about the candidate's stands on a number of policy issues and computes an overall evaluation of the candidate by combining the utilities associated with these stands.

Category-based judgments. The question is whether people do, in fact, always perform the computations described above in forming an attitude toward a person. Fiske and Pavelchak (1986) postulate that when people believe that someone is a typical member of a social category (e.g., liberal, Democrat, Catholic, etc.), they base their evaluation of the person on their reactions to this category and ignore the affect associated with the person's individual features. Only if the person appears to be an atypical member of a category do people resort to a piecemeal assessment of the affective implications of the person's individual attributes.

It should be noted that when judgments are category-based, the social category does *not* simply function as an attribute of the person that is "added" to other, individuating attributes to arrive at an overall judgment. To the contrary, affective reactions to the social category (and perhaps attributes associated with it) *supplant* the affective reactions to the person's individuating attributes. By relying on the social category, the individual obviates the cognitive costs associated with considering the idiosyncratic attributes of the particular instance and simply bases the judgment on information previously associated with the social category taken as a whole.

Psychological research bearing on this postulate has focused on the impact of gender and ethnic stereotypes on judgments (Bodenhausen & Lichtenstein, 1987; Deaux & Lewis, 1984; Futoran & Wyer, 1986; Locksley, Borgida, Brekke, & Hepburn, 1980). In combination, this research suggests that complexity of the judgment task influences the relative extent to which a respondent relies on piecemeal or category-based information when forming a judgment. For instance, Bodenhausen and Lichtenstein (1987) found that subjects used individuating attribute information about a person when they anticipated making a simple judgment but relied on category-based information (i.e., ethnicity) when they anticipated making a complex judgment. In evaluating the generalizability of these findings, however, it is important to note that in none of the studies cited were subjects asked to evaluate persons when two or more category-based criteria were available. When two such criteria are salient, combining their implications to arrive at a judgment may require processes similar to those performed during a piecemeal analysis of the individuating information. Because political candidates are often simultaneously members of more than one social category (e.g., black, Democrat, etc.), a consideration of this multiple-category situation is of some importance (see Wyer & Ottati chapter in this volume for a more detailed treatment of this question).

In addition, it is important to reiterate an ambiguity noted earlier. That is, we have framed our discussion in this section in terms of the extent to which the affective reactions elicited by piecemeal or categorical information about a person are used as a basis for evaluations of the person. However, there is no direct evidence that the results we have cited have anything at all to do with subjects' internal affective reactions. One could simply assume that evaluative judgments are based purely on the semantic implications of the information available, independently of any affective reactions that are elicited by this information. To validate the assumption that affective reactions are elicited by either categorical or individuating information, and that judgments are based on these reactions rather than on semantic aspects of the information, more innovative research strategies are needed. We shall discuss certain viable strategies presently.

Consequences of Affective Responses

In this section we turn specifically to the judgmental consequences of affective reactions. The theoretical and empirical issues that have been examined in this area depend on the particular affect-related construct that researchers have chosen to consider. We will discuss each construct in turn, in each case limiting our consideration to issues that are of relevance to political judgment and decision-making.

Effects of Attitudes on Political Judgment

Our discussion of piecemeal and categorical processing in the previous section was, in effect, concerned with attitude formation. Implicit was the assumption that attitudes toward a person are determined by beliefs that the person has certain attributes or belongs to certain social categories. However, not only can beliefs affect attitudes, but attitudes, once formed, can influence beliefs. In the political arena, for example, perceptions of candidates' stands on issues could in part be rationalized consequences of attitudes toward the candidates that were developed for other reasons (e.g., Brent & Granberg, 1982; Brody & Page, 1972; Kinder, 1978; Page & Brody, 1972). Specifically, a voter might simply assume that a liked candidate holds an agreeable position and a disliked candidate holds a disagreeable one.

This sort of inferential strategy, which may reflect the use of an affective balance heuristic (Heider, 1958), should lead voters to assimilate a liked candidate's position toward their own position and to contrast a disliked candidate's position away from their own (Brent & Granberg, 1982; Granberg & Brent, 1974, 1980; Kinder, 1978). Evidence that people's perceptions of a liked candidate's positions on issues are positively correlated with the voter's own positions is consistent with this possibility.[1]

The status of a belief as a determinant or a consequence of an attitude is inherently rooted in the prior question of whether the belief is based on objective criteria or on the balance heuristic.[2] Although the above research provides evidence that a balance heuristic is applied in inferring candidates' positions on issues, it does not indicate the extent to which this influence overrides the effect of objective information that one has acquired concerning the candidate's positions.

A study by Ottati, Fishbein, and Middlestadt (1988) bears on this question. At the time of the Reagan-Mondale presidential election campaign in 1984, respondents were given belief statements describing the two candidates' stands on a number of issues and were asked to indicate the likelihood that each statement was true along a scale from -3 (unlikely) to $+3$ (likely). Some of these belief statements were generally true; that is, they accurately reflected the candidates' publicly expressed positions (e.g., Reagan favors an increase in defense spending; Mondale favors a decrease in defense spending). Others were generally false (e.g., Reagan favors a decrease in defense spending; Mondale favors an increase in defense spending). Measures of the respondents' attitudes toward each candidate and the respondents' own positions on each issue also were obtained.

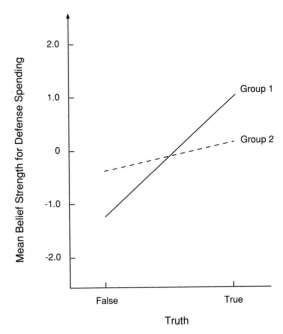

Figure 10.1. Mean belief strength for the defense spending issue as a function of truth. Means are plotted for Group 1 and Group 2 separately.

Based on these measures, the belief statements were coded as balanced if they implied that a liked candidate agreed with the respondent on the issue of concern or, alternatively, that a disliked candidate disagreed with the respondent. Correspondingly, the statements were coded as imbalanced if they implied that a liked candidate disagreed with the respondent or that a disliked candidate agreed with the respondent. For each issue under consideration, subjects were divided into two groups. In group 1, the true statements were balanced, and the false statements were imbalanced. In group 2, the true statements were imbalanced, and the false statements were balanced. In other words, the truth value of the belief statements was positively confounded with balance in group 1 and negatively confounded with truth in group 2.

If balance is irrelevant to a subject's reported beliefs, the statements' truth value should have similar effects on the beliefs reported by both groups of subjects. Yet if balance, in addition to truth value, contributes to these judgments, the apparent effect of the statements' truth on belief judgments should be greater when the confound between truth value and balance is positive (group 1) than when it is negative (group 2).

In fact, the latter is the case. Figure 10.1 shows subjects' beliefs in statements describing candidates' views on defense spending as a function of the truth value of these statements. (Data pertaining to other statements were comparable.) The results are very clear. Belief strength was jointly determined by *both* the truth of the statements and the balance heuristic. Respondents rated objectively true sentences as more likely to be true than objectively false ones. The influence of the balance heuristic is also apparent, however. That is, the effect of statements' truth value on subjects' beliefs in them was greater when their truth value was positively confounded with balance (group 1) than when it was negatively confounded with balance (group 2). That is, balance contributed to subjects' reported beliefs over and above the truth value of the statements.

One additional aspect of the results is noteworthy. Truth value had a positive influence on subjects' beliefs even when balance was negatively confounded with it (group 2). In other words, the balance effects did not outweigh the influence of objective information that subjects had acquired concerning these statements. Taken together, these findings indicate that beliefs about a political candidate operate as *both* determinants (reasons) *and* consequences (rationalizations) of attitudes toward the candidate.

Effects of Emotional Responses on Political Judgment

Abelson, Kinder, Peters, and Fiske (1982) have shown that emotions and beliefs (cognitions) can operate as partially unique predictors of attitudes toward a candidate. Conover and Feldman (1986) have made a similar claim when predicting evaluations of the government's handling of the economy. In both cases, these findings have been explained in terms of Zajonc's (1984) inference-free model of affect described earlier in this chapter. That is, insofar as emotional responses arise independently of any prior cognitive appraisal, these emotions should influence global evaluations of a candidate independently of cognition. However, Markus (1988) has shown that beliefs about the candidates' stands on the issues operate as important determinants of emotional responses to them. This raises the question of whether emotional responses do indeed contribute to evaluations independently of the beliefs that give rise to them.

Some evidence bearing on this conclusion has been reported by Ottati (1988). For one thing, he showed that respondents are easily capable of generating explanations for their emotional responses to a candidate. Two different emotional reactions could have the same explanation, of course. (For example, a person may indicate that Reagan's joke about bombing the Soviets instigated both anger and nervousness.) However, if one takes this fact into account, the evaluative implications of subjects' explanations for their emotions completely accounts for the influence of these emotions on candidate evaluations.

To demonstrate this possibility, Ottati (1988) performed a stepwise regression analysis of subjects' thermometer ratings of President Reagan as a function of their reported positive and negative emotional reactions to him and their explanations for these reactions. The proportion of belief explanations that were positive, the proportion of explanations that were negative, and the proportions of emotions that were positive and negative were used as predictor variables. When positive and negative belief indices were entered at step 1 of the analysis, the additional contribution of emotion indices to ratings was nonsignificant.

If beliefs or cognitive appraisals determine emotional responses, it is not surprising that they account for the influence of these responses on reported attitudes. As such, Ottati's (1988) results seriously challenge the popular notion that emotional responses operate independently of beliefs in determining political attitude judgments (a notion that has achieved the status of "fact" among many political scientists). Note, however, that the correlational nature of these data does not permit an inference-free model to be ruled out completely. The beliefs reported by subjects in Ottati's (1988) and Markus's (1988) studies could conceivably be post hoc rationalizations that were generated by subjects at the time of judgment and were not determinants of these emotions. Thus, the unattributed cognitive appraisal and inference-free models are not unequivocally disconfirmed by these results.

The above ambiguity reflects a more general problem with using correlational data as evidence of the process mechanisms that underlie relations between emotional reactions, beliefs, and judgments. For example, suppose that indices of emotional reactions *had* contributed to unique variance in judgments as has been the case in other studies (Abelson et al., 1982; Conover & Feldman, 1986). This would not necessarily indicate that the reactions were not mediated by cognitive appraisals. One could simply argue that subjects did not remember all of the appraisals that originally elicited their emotional reactions to the candidate being judged, and so the belief index did not capture all of the variance in emotional responses that resulted from these appraisals. If this were the case, the emotions would contribute to the prediction of attitude over and above subjects' *reported* beliefs despite the fact that these emotions were completely determined by cognitive appraisals at the time the emotions first occurred. In short, correlational findings do not allow one to disentangle the process mechanisms that underlie the observed effects. Experimental strategies for attaining this objective are discussed in the final section of this chapter.

The Effects of Mood on Political Judgment

To reiterate, subjects' explanations for their affective responses may not always reflect the actual determinants of these responses. That is, respondents are not always fully aware of the actual source of their affective reactions. To address the questions raised above, therefore, it is useful to consider the role of preattributed affective responses. As such, this section focuses on the effects of mood on political judgments. In the following section the influence of affective arousal will be considered.

The affect or emotion that is elicited by a stimulus does not dissipate immediately once the stimulus is no longer thought about. Consequently, the affective reactions that a person experiences at any moment can be the net result of several different external or mental events that have recently occurred (e.g., a recent stimulus event, memory, or internal physiological change). When people are asked to make a judgment to which their affective or emotional reactions are relevant, they often are unable to distinguish clearly between their reactions to the particular stimulus they are asked to judge and the residual affect they are experiencing for other reasons. Consequently, this extraneous affect can influence the judgment they make.

This phenomenon is well-documented (Schwarz & Clore, 1987). In a study by Schwarz and Clore (1983, experiment 2), for example, subjects were asked in a telephone interview how satisfied they were with their lives as a whole. They reported greater life satisfaction on sunny days (which presumably put them in a good mood) than on rainy days (which put them in a bad mood). Interestingly, this effect was diminished when the experimenter incidentally mentioned the weather, thus reminding subjects of the true source of their affective state. Other, more direct manipulations of subjects' mood states have similar effects (Schwarz & Clore, 1983, experiment 1). These effects also are diminished when subjects are induced to attribute their feelings to factors that are irrelevant to the judgment they are asked to make.

Other possible influences of the effect of mood on judgment should be noted in this context. For example, Isen, Clark, Shalker, and Karp (1978) postulate that the effect of mood on judgment is mediated by an increase in the cognitive accessibility of information that is evaluatively consistent with the mood state. Thus, positive features of an object are more accessible when a person is in a good mood, whereas negative features are more accessible when a person is in a bad mood. To the extent that evaluative judgments are based on accessible material, this view suggests that the effect of mood on judgments of an object is mediated by its effect on the accessibility of information relevant to these judgments. Isen et al. report results that are consistent with this hypothesis. That is, subjects who were put into a positive mood by giving them a free gift evaluated the performance of their TV service more favorably than did control, neutral-mood subjects.

Note, however, that these results would be equally compatible with the "mood-as-information" hypothesis introduced by Schwarz and Clore (1983). To the extent that receiving a gift elicited positive affective reactions, and these reactions had not dissipated by the time that subjects were asked to make judgments, subjects may have attributed these reactions in part to the stimulus they were asked to rate, and, therefore, used them as a basis for reporting their feelings about the stimulus. Be that as it may, the effects of mood on information accessibility cannot account for the contingency of Schwarz and Clore's findings on the salience of alternative explanations for the mood they were in. (That is, the increased accessibility of mood-consistent information in memory, or the use of this information to make judgments, should not depend on the availability of such explanations.) Consequently, it seems justifiable to assume that although the influence of mood on the accessibility of judgment-relevant knowledge can conceivably contribute to the effects of mood on judgment, the informational properties of subjects' affective reactions clearly play a role as well.

The influence of mood on judgments of political candidates has not been extensively investigated. Preliminary research by Ottati, Riggle, Wyer, Schwarz, and Kuklinski (1989), however, suggests that this influence exists. Subjects in their study were placed in a positive, neutral, or negative mood state by having them recall a pleasant, neutral, or unpleasant past experience. Then, as part of an ostensibly unrelated experiment, subjects were given a description of a political candidate's voting record and were asked to evaluate the candidate. The information consisted of votes on ten issues that conveyed a political orientation (liberal or conservative) that was either similar or dissimilar to the subject's own. Mean thermometer ratings of the candidate are presented in table 10.2 as a function of the candidate's voting record and the subjects' mood. Not

Table 10.2. Mean favorableness ratings of a candidate as a function of issue similarity and affective state.

	Affective state		
	Positive	Neutral	Negative
Dissimilar issue profile	33.6	29.3	25.0
Similar issue profile	83.6	78.0	75.9

surprisingly, evaluations of the candidate were more favorable when his voting record was consistent with their own political orientation. However, the subjects' mood appeared to influence their evaluations independently of the candidate's voting record. These preliminary findings do not specify the exact process underlying the effect of mood. They do suggest, however, that transitory moods can influence evaluations of political candidates in much the same manner that they affect other types of judgments (Schwarz & Clore, 1983; Strack, Schwarz, & Gschneidinger, 1985).

Experimental evidence of this kind may shed light on the current success of "feel good" political campaigning. By surrounding the candidate with upbeat visual and auditory montages (e.g., music, balloons, beautiful scenery), political strategists could be eliciting positive affective responses that viewers mistakenly attribute to the candidate. This evidence also bears on a question raised earlier. That is, if affective responses to an extraneous stimulus are experienced as emotional responses to the candidate, these emotional responses can later influence evaluations *independently* of beliefs about the candidate's attributes. Of course, it is not necessary for the factors that elicit emotions to be entirely unrelated to the person being judged. For example, episodic affective responses to a candidate that were originally stimulated by cognitive appraisals of the candidate might become dissociated from these appraisals. Later, these affective responses could be recalled and could influence judgments of the candidate independently of the cognitions that originally gave rise to them.

A conceptualization of political judgment by Lodge, McGraw, and Stroh (1989) is worth noting in this context. They suggest that citizens continually update their evaluations of candidates as they receive more information about them. At any given time these updated evaluations determine judgments of the candidate independently of the specific information on which earlier judgments were based. This updating process may conceivably describe how affective reactions that underlie judgments of a candidate are augmented by the accumulation of affect-laden information. That is, not only judgment-relevant information about a candidate, but extraneous factors that lead affective reactions to be attributed to the candidate could enter into the updating. These factors could therefore have an enduring rather than transitory influence on judgments. Furthermore, this effect would not be explainable in terms of the voter's beliefs about the candidate's characteristics.

Effects of Affective Arousal on Political Judgment

The experience of affect is typically accompanied by physiological arousal. However, a given level of arousal may be associated with several different emotional states. Thus, people who experience arousal may not always be clear about the affective state it implies unless situational cues exist that permit them to interpret it. A classic study by Schachter and Singer (1962) provides evidence of this contingency. That is, epinephrine-injected subjects labeled their arousal as "euphoria" when situational cues suggested that they should be happy. However, they labeled their arousal as "anger" when situational cues suggested that they should be angry. These effects were most pronounced when subjects were unaware of the actual source of the arousal they were experiencing. Similar effects may occur when there are multiple possible sources of arousal and the contribution of each source is difficult to isolate. Cantor, Zillman, and Bryant (1974), for example, found that when subjects have engaged in rigorous physical activity, they attribute a portion of the arousal produced by this activity to other factors, and, therefore, their judgments of their affective reactions to persons and objects are influenced.

This possibility has implications for political judgment. Suppose subjects are exposed to political information at the time they experience an arousing personal event. Part of the arousal elicited by this event may be incorrectly attributed to the information and therefore may influence the subjects' interpretations of their emotional responses to it. For similar reasons, the arousal elicited by one political event may influence perceptions of the intensity of one's emotional responses to some other event. For example, if a president's speech conveys a danger of military conflict, the arousal elicited by these remarks may be misattributed to the president himself. Moreover, the label that is assigned to this arousal may depend on predispositions to view the president favorably or unfavor-

ably. That is, people who are predisposed to view the president negatively may label their reaction as anger or fear, whereas those who are
disposed to view the president positively may label their reaction as
pride. These interpretations, once made, could mediate other judgments
about the president.

Effects of this kind could be deliberately produced. For example, it
might be useful to avoid the elicitation of extraneous arousal when an
incumbent must report on unpleasant political developments (e.g., the
federal deficit). When reporting on pleasant developments, however, the
elicitation of arousal could work to the candidate's advantage. These
strategies could be used to minimize the intensity of negative reactions to
the incumbent's handling of unpleasant developments and to increase the
intensity of positive affective reactions to the incumbent's handling of
pleasant developments.

Future Directions

In attempting to take a closer look at the role of affective reactions in
political judgments, this chapter has raised many questions. A given
empirical finding may reflect a number of different processes. Not only
must the conceptualization of these processes be made more precise, but
a methodology must be developed for evaluating the alternative processes and circumscribing the conditions in which they are likely to
apply.

In this regard, correlational analyses based on survey data have stimulated considerable interest in the role of episodic affect as a determinant of
political judgment (e.g., Abelson, Kinder, Peters, & Fiske, 1982; Conover & Feldman, 1986). These studies have alerted the political science
community to the importance of studying affect. To gain a fuller understanding of the causal properties of affective process mechanisms, however, innovative experimental approaches may be necessary.

Many of the ambiguities surrounding the interpretation of existing
research concern the causal priority of affective and cognitive factors in
the judgment process. That is, it is unclear exactly when cognitions
determine affective responses and when they are simply the rationalized
consequence of these responses. Another ambiguity concerns the nature
of the so-called "independent" influence of affect on political judgments.
Does this independent effect indicate that respondents were not cog-
nizant of the course of their affective reactions at the time they originally

occurred? Or were the emotional responses originally elicited by cognitive appraisals of the candidate that were later forgotten at the time the judgments were made? Either of these possibilities could produce an influence on candidate evaluation that is not explained by accessible beliefs about the candidate.

Experimental manipulations of mood can begin to address some of these issues. Misattribution methodology similar to that employed by Schwarz and Clore (1983) could be useful in evaluating when people base their judgments on their affective reactions to candidates.

In this regard, it is important to distinguish between the influence of affect experienced at the time of stimulus exposure from the influence of affect experienced at the time of judgment. This distinction is particularly relevant in understanding voting decisions, which typically occur after information about a candidate has been received. Experimental variations of the time at which affect is experienced or attributed may help to evaluate these different effects.

These and other experimental strategies could serve to further our understanding of affective process mechanisms and the manner in which they influence political judgments.

Notes

This chapter was prepared with funds provided in part by National Institute of Mental Health grant MH 3-8585. The research on political judgment reported herein was conducted with funds provided by the University of Illinois Survey Research Laboratory in collaboration with Ellen Riggle, James Kuklinski, and Norbert Schwarz. Appreciation is extended to these collaborators, and also to other current members of the Political Judgment Research Group—Sharon Shavitt, Lee Budesheim, and Jeff Melton—for stimulating many of the ideas presented, and to the University of Illinois Social Cognition Group for valuable feedback concerning much of the theory and research on which the ideas are based.

1. In fact, advocates of the asymmetry hypothesis have argued that balance effects influence perceptions of positively evaluated candidates more than they do for negatively evaluated candidates (Brent & Granberg, 1982; Granberg & Brent, 1974, 1980; Kinder, 1978). However, this claim also has been challenged (Judd, Kenney, & Krosnick, 1983; Ottati, Fishbein, & Middlestadt, 1988). In any case, because the asymmetry hypothesis is not directly related to the central concerns of this chapter, it is not elaborated here.

2. An objectively rooted belief also may instigate persuasion effects. That is,

voters may adjust their own position to make it similar to that endorsed by a liked candidate (Brody & Page, 1972; Page & Brody, 1972). In this case, beliefs about the candidate's stand on an issue serve to determine the voter's own position without necessarily determining the voter's attitude toward the candidate. In other words, the status of a belief as being rooted in objective criteria is not a sufficient basis for arguing that it determines attitude. However, it is a necessary condition for making this argument.

IV

Decision Making and

Choice

Making decisions is like speaking prose, as Herbert Simon once observed. Somehow, people manage to decide all kinds of questions instinctively and effortlessly. It is no wonder that understanding decision-making is central to a number of disciplines, from economists who wonder about utility maximization, to philosophers who wonder about free will.

Political psychology provides a particularly interesting laboratory for decision-making research because it represents two of the principal competing perspectives on the subject. According to the theory of rational choice, decision-makers are determined to optimize outcomes; they seek decisions that maximize their gain and minimize their cost. Rational choice theorists typically assume that individuals have well-defined and stable preferences that conform to several normative criteria. According to the norm of transitivity, for example, if a person prefers outcome A over outcome B, and B over C, she must pick A over C.

In addition to requirements of preference structure, rational choice theorists expect that decision-makers are systematic in assessing the relevant evidence. In the classical game-theoretic approach, for instance, players must update their beliefs about their opponents probablistically in light of evidence about their actions. In effect, rational decision-makers are sensitive to base rates and the logic of conditional probability (see, for example, the discussion in Tsebelis, 1990).

As these two assumptions illustrate, the rational choice theorist's vision of decision-making is one that calls for considerable sophistication or motivation. The decision-maker must know what the relevant set of outcomes looks like, have a preference that is well-behaved, and be vigilant to relevant evidence.

The image of the decision-maker propagated by social-psychological research could not be more different. Decision-makers are seen as casual and lazy. Rather than attempting to maximize gain, they seek to "satisfice" and do only what is necessary to reach acceptable outcomes. Moreover, the manner in which decision-makers treat evidence is fraught with a variety of logical and statistical errors. Far from being Bayesian in their approach to probability, people habitually ignore base-rate information and are willing to generalize from very few instances. This belief in the "law of small numbers" extends so far that people often make strong generalizations from single and atypical instances. Finally, there is considerable evidence that preferences are not invariant over differences in context and presentation. Kahneman and Tversky have demonstrated in a number of ingenious experiments that when outcomes are depicted as gains (relative to some baseline), people choose the outcome that is more certain, yet when the identical outcomes are depicted as relative losses, people choose the outcome with greater risk (see Kahneman & Tversky, 1982).

The divergence between the economic and psychological perspectives suggests a continuum of decision-making behavior with possible end points of "vigilant" and "casual" decision-making (for a related discussion of "central" versus "peripheral" decision paths, see Petty & Cacioppo, 1986). The important questions, then, concern the circumstances under which particular strategies are adopted and the particular characteristics of individuals that foster movement toward one or other of these extremes. For example, one might expect that decisions with grave consequences are reached more systematically than decisions that are trivial in their impact. In fact, one of the more telling criticisms directed at the psychological work on decision-making is that it typically poses issues or choices for which the "decision-maker" (usually a college sophomore) has little incentive to be vigilant. It is one thing to find that base-rate information is ignored when people are asked to decide whether "Joe, who goes to the movies twice a week, is an extrovert"; it is quite another to find that people ignore base-rate information when purchasing home insurance. Alternatively, decision-making may be a learned skill, and some people are more adept than others at maximizing gain. This fundamental question about the antecedents of decision-making style is the subject of Tetlock's contribution. Tetlock seeks to identify both contextual and individual-level determinants of "integrative complexity." The integratively complex decision-maker is able to incorporate multiple perspectives (e.g., the senator who considers the economic, social, and political consequences of reduced social welfare programs when deciding how to vote on budget cuts) and sees the connections between these perspectives (e.g., the trade-off between short-term economic benefits and long-term social costs). Tetlock's research program has identified both dispositional and contextual factors that make decision-makers more or less integratively complex. Contrary to intuition, Tetlock demonstrates that integratively complex decision-making does not always produce the best outcome and that the expert decision-maker is one who knows when the costs of integrative complexity outweigh the benefits.

The chapters by Jervis and Popkin both epitomize the psychological perspective on decision-making, i.e., reasoning by heuristics and shortcuts. In Jervis's analysis, the decision-makers are foreign policy and diplomatic officials; for Popkin, the decision-making arena is presidential election campaigns in which ordinary citizens choose between candidates about whom they have little information. Political decision-makers, Jervis and Popkin both suggest, cope with complexity by oversimplifying. Policy-makers tend to discount the importance of circumstantial and chance influences on the actions of their opponents, whom they view instead as behaving according to stable motives. Ordinary citizens are led to think about political candidates according to considerations made more available to them through patterns of news media coverage. More importantly, Popkin shows that voters make sense of political campaigns by employing simple scripts and scenarios for assessing the character of political candidates and their suitability for public office.

It is not clear when and how the rational choice and psychological perspectives on decision-making will intermarry. One area in which the two perspectives are susceptible to comparative scrutiny concerns attitudes toward risk. Rational choice theorists typically assume that individuals' preferences and their underlying attitudes toward risk are invariant across contexts. As noted earlier, however, psychological research (well illustrated by Kahneman & Tversky, 1982, 1984) indicates that attitudes toward risk are subject to considerable flux depending on the manner in which choice or decision outcomes are presented. The chapter by Ansolabehere and Iyengar investigates the impact of economic information on evaluations of the president in order to shed light on voters' attitudes toward risk. Are Americans more prone to punish the president for a falling economy than they are to reward him for good times? The authors show that questions of "negativity" in political evaluation can be traced to attitudes toward risk. Their results indicate that citizens tend to be strictly risk-averse when evaluating the president according to past economic conditions, and that their evaluations based on past economic conditions are unaffected by the manner in which these conditions are depicted in television news reports. However, when individuals evaluate the president according to their expectations of future economic conditions, they are susceptible to significant presentation effects. In short, Ansolabehere and Iyengar suggest that elements of the rational choice and psychological perspectives on decision making are both present in "economic voting."

Stephen Ansolabehere and Shanto Iyengar

11. Information and Electoral Attitudes:
A Case of Judgment Under
Uncertainty

The ability of citizens to control the actions of their elected representatives is generally regarded as the definition of democratic government. A vigilant public presumably is knowledgeable about public affairs. Three decades of public opinion research, however, have shown American voters to be largely inattentive to politics and government. For example, slightly less than half of those surveyed by the National Election Study in the 1980s could name their congressman, and fewer still could recall the name of the challenger who was running against the incumbent in their district (Jacobson, 1987). A study of the 1978 congressional elections found that only 20 percent of the people who had a position on an issue were capable of indicating where both candidates in their district stood on that issue (Hinckley, 1981).

Such modest levels of political information among the electorate have important consequences for the democratic process. Typically, it is taken for granted that uncertainty is a barrier to effective representation. Presumably, when voters are uninformed, they are less able to express their wants, and politicians are less able to interpret public opinion polls and election outcomes (see Ferejohn, 1990). Recently, scholars have begun to investigate the relationship between voter uncertainty and electoral outcomes focusing on two particular questions. First, how do voters choose between candidates or policies when they are uncertain about the prospects associated with the different alternatives? A considerable body of research by psychologists, economists, and others addresses this issue, but only a handful of these studies pertain to political choices. Second, how does the level of information among the electorate affect the responsiveness of elected leaders? While it is generally assumed that uncertainty among voters gives politicians greater latitude in office, some recent theoretical work suggests that in some circumstances uncertainty may force politicians to work harder to remain in office.

In this chapter we are primarily concerned with the first of these questions. We contrast economic and psychological perspectives on how voters cope with uncertainty. Both perspectives assume that citizens have preferences (utilities) about candidates or policies and that people are uncertain about the consequences of their electoral choices. However, economic and psychological models diverge in their treatment of individuals' responses to uncertainty. While economists assume that people are able to assess probabilities accurately, psychologists argue that individuals' beliefs about probabilities are subject to various biases and errors. After examining the ramifications of this distinction for political choice, we review the evidence on economic voting under uncertainty. While voters are generally found to be risk-averse, there is evidence that they do err in computing probabilities in particular contexts. Finally, we discuss the implications of economic and psychological models of judgment for the electoral responsiveness of public officials.

Two Views of Political Choice Under Uncertainty

Homo Economicus

Under economic theory, voters are rational actors. They have well-formed preferences and choose between alternatives so as to maximize personal utility. Personal utilities depend, among other things, on the consequences of governmental activities such as entitlement payments, economic performance, taxes, and the quality of public education. Economic man, then, chooses the candidate or party that represents the combination of governmental activities that will bring him the highest utility.

In the real world, the assessment of governmental performance is complicated considerably by uncertainty. Uncertainty shapes the campaign strategies of candidates (Alesina & Cukierman, 1987) and also influences the judgments of voters. Most voters are poorly informed and lack familiarity with abstract concepts such as the gross national product or the consumer price index; they are therefore unable to assess with much confidence the meaning of a great deal of significant data on the economy's performance. Voters also are unaware of particular government actions such as a change in the Federal Reserve's money fund discount rate. Moreover, the outcomes of governmental policies are not perfectly tied to the policies themselves. The economy, for example, is volatile and susceptible to unpredictable events and fluctuations. Voters must project past and current governmental performance into at least the near future. Unexpected local, national, or international events make those forecasts unreliable.

The uncertainty surrounding voters' assessments of current and future economic conditions has important implications for models of voting. First, voters' attitudes toward uncertainty will enter into determinations of personal utility and, hence, their evaluations of candidates. If, for instance, people are averse to less-certain (riskier) alternatives, they will prefer candidates about whom they know more. Second, voters may make errors in assessing the expected value of alternatives. To the extent that these errors are systematic, we expect patterns will exist in the ways that people use information in evaluating candidates.

Attitudes toward risk and the formation of expectations are both most clearly understood in terms of gambling. Suppose that an individual is offered a choice between $1 as a sure thing and a gamble that offers payoffs of $2 and $0 half of the time. Even though the expected value of the gamble and the sure thing are equivalent, the alternatives may not be perceived as equivalent. Some people may prefer to avoid uncertainty and choose the certain $1, while others may prefer to take chances and choose the gamble. The former group is risk-averse, while the latter is risk-seeking. Persons who are indifferent to equivalent certain and uncertain outcomes are considered risk-neutral.

What has gambling to do with voting and other political decisions? According to economic theory, all decisions are fundamentally the same. People first calculate the expected value (generally, the average value) of the alternatives at hand. They then assign utilities to each of the alternatives according to the expected value of each alternative weighted by their attitudes toward risk. Finally, people choose the alternative that maximizes utility.

As with gambling, a person's taste (or distaste) for uncertainty influences the assignment of utilities to specific candidates. To the extent that a voter dislikes uncertainty, she will avoid lesser-known candidates. Similarly, voters who seek risk may prefer a lesser-known challenger to a better-known incumbent, all other things being equal. In short, attitudes toward risk are important characteristics of voters' comparisons of candidates. (For empirical evidence and further elaboration, see Brady & Ansolabehere, 1989; Radcliff, 1990.)

Measuring the effect of voters' attitudes toward risk on electoral decisions is complicated, even in the more manageable setting of the economic model. How voters weigh the risks associated with different candidates depends on how uncertainty enters their choices, which in turn depends on what voters take as the standard by which they judge the performance of the government. The basic idea behind the measurement of risk is to compare the expected (or average) utility of the outcome to the utility of the "certainty equivalent." The expected utility (EU) of the outcome is the utility that the individual expects to receive as an empirical matter. When calculating their EU, individuals first assign utilities to alternative outcomes and then average these utilities by weighting each alternative by its probability of occurrence. The utility of the "certainty equivalent" is the utility that the individual would ascribe to his best prediction of social and economic conditions if it were certain that those conditions would in fact materialize.

For example, consider how an individual votes on the basis of his income. He supports the government if the utility of the income received when the incumbent party is in office exceeds the utility of the income received when the opposition governs. There is a certain amount of ambiguity about which policies the incumbent party intends to pursue if it wins another term. Specifically, suppose that the incumbents will pursue policy A with probability 0.8 and policy B with probability 0.2 and that the individual will experience an increase in income of $1,000 with policy B and an increase in income of $5,000 with policy A. Under the usual statistical analysis, his best prediction of future economic conditions is that he will experience an increase in income of $1,800 (i.e., $0.8 \times$ $1,000 + 0.2 \times $5,000$). The utility of the certainty equivalent takes $1,800 as the basis of his judgment. That is, if he were certain that he would experience an $1,800 increase in income, his utility for that amount would be U$_{1800}$. By contrast, the individual's expected utility will be the weighted average of the utility associated with a $1,000 increase in income and of the utility associated with a $5,000 increase in income. Thus, EU equals $0.8 \times$ U$_{1,000} + 0.2 \times$ U$_{5,000}$.

Attitudes toward risk can now be expressed in terms of comparisons between the expected utility and the utility of the certainty equivalent. A voter is risk-seeking if the former exceeds the latter, risk-averse if the latter exceeds the former, and risk-neutral if the two utilities are equal. In terms of our example, an individual is risk-averse if U$_{1,800} > 0.8 \times$ U$_{1,000} + 0.2 \times$ U$_{5,000}$ and risk-seeking if U$_{1,800} < 0.8 \times$ U$_{1,000} + 0.2 \times$ U$_{5,000}$. The magnitude of the distance between the two is a rough

Figure 11.1. Economic models: utility functions when people are risk neutral, risk seeking, and risk averse.

measure of attitude toward risk. A mathematically equivalent but somewhat simpler way of expressing the same concept is to classify attitudes toward risk according to the shape of the utility function. The utility function of the risk-averse voter is concave (i.e., it has a negative second derivative), of the risk-seeking voter it is convex (i.e., it has a positive second derivative), and of the risk-neutral voter it is linear (i.e., it has a zero second derivative). These three cases are presented in the three panels of figure 11.1.

The identity of the graphs in figure 11.1 with the earlier definitions of attitudes toward risk is easily appreciated when one considers the behavior of the risk-averse voter. The point $1 on the horizontal axis represents the sure outcome in our example of the gamble (or certainty equivalent for the economic voter). The expected utility of the gamble can be seen by plotting the utilities of the two payoffs—$2 and $0—and drawing a cord between these two points. The expected utility of the gamble that gives an even chance of $2 or $0 is the point on the cord above $1. Notice that this point on the cord lies below the value corresponding to the utility of the sure outcome. Put simply, the individual would prefer the sure thing to the gamble, even though on average they yield the same amount of cash. Geometrically, this demonstrates that the utility assigned to the sure outcome exceeds the expected utility of the gamble. In fact, for any gamble, the risk-averse voter will always assign greater utility to a sure outcome than to a risky alternative. All functions that have this property are shaped like the one depicted in panel C of figure 11.1.

Further reflection on figure 11.1 reveals that a number of controversies in the psychology of voting behavior can be understood in simple economic terms. For example, several researchers find that voters have a negativity bias in their evaluations of the president. That is, a downturn in the economy brings dramatic decreases in presidential popularity, but an improvement in the economy boosts presidential popularity only modestly (Campbell et al., 1960; Fiorina & Shepsle, 1989; Key, 1966; Lau, 1982). This asymmetry can be explained in terms of attitudes toward risk. Specifically, figure 11.1 shows that for risk-averse voters the increase in utility brought about by a one-unit increase in income is subject to diminishing marginal returns. This is precisely what is meant by a negativity bias: risk-averse voters are less sensitive to increases than to decreases in income. Risk aversion then means that incumbents will suffer more from a downturn in the economy than they will benefit from an upswing. The converse is true for risk-seeking voters: they are more sensitive to increases than to decreases in economic performance and will, therefore, tend to reward incumbents if the economy shows even slight gains.

Negativity biases are one example of a phenomenon discovered by psychologists that can be subsumed within the economic model. Work in recent years by cognitive psychologists, however, presents a more direct challenge to homo economicus.

Homo Psychologicus

A crucial assumption behind the economic analysis of judgment under uncertainty is that attitudes toward risk depend only on individuals' utilities and are not affected by the particular ways in which problems are presented. In the area of voting, this principle is questionable, for most Americans have a limited store of political information, and, since that information is of dubious value outside the act of voting, they are unlikely to put much effort into predicting political events. Moreover, the mass media are the major source of information, and television and newspaper stories may report insufficient, irrelevant, or inaccurate information. It is likely, therefore, that voters will resort to rules of thumb to compute statistical expectations and that their calculations will be susceptible to a variety of biases, depending on the manner in which information is presented.

Cognitive psychologists have identified a variety of information-processing biases, the most relevant of which is framing. The concept of framing is based on experiments in which subjects exhibit either risk-averse or risk-seeking behavior depending on whether outcomes are presented as probable losses or probable gains. The classic example of framing is that when offered the choice between a certain gain and a gamble, people prefer the former, but when the identical choice is expressed as a choice between a certain loss and a gamble, they prefer the latter (Kahneman & Tversky, 1984). Researchers typically treat this reversal as indicative of framing, but in fact it is one of several possible framing effects. For example, one might imagine the opposite reversal in choices. Individuals might exhibit risk-accepting behavior in the domain of gains, but risk-averse behavior in the domain of losses. For the sake of this discussion, we refer to the classic type as Type A framing and the alternative as Type B framing.

Thinking about how people gamble makes the distinction between Type A and Type B framing more concrete. Suppose there are two different casinos. In one, people pay an admission fee; in the other, they are paid to come to the casino. Which casino induces more gambling once people are inside? Classical (Type A) framing predicts that people are more likely to gamble in the first casino. Type B framing, however, implies that people are more willing to gamble in the second case than in the first. That is, people are more prone to gamble when given an inducement, but less prone when they pay a fee.[1]

This reversal in choices caused by framing (known as the "preference-reversal" phenomenon) clearly violates the invariance principle of economics—the assumption that preference orders for outcomes are unaffected by the manner in which the outcomes are described. There is a large literature concerning the degree to which the invariance assumption is met in a variety of circumstances. (See, for example, Grether & Plott, 1979; Kahneman & Tversky, 1984.) Here, we are concerned with the reason for the reversal and the evidence for the different types of framing.

In the appendix to this chapter we show that framing results when risk-averse individuals hold excessively optimistic beliefs in one domain (losses or gains) and realistic or pessimistic beliefs in the other. Specifically, Type A framing implies that in the domain of losses individuals place too much weight on their belief that beneficial events will occur and tend to downplay the likelihood of harmful events. Type B framing implies the opposite pattern of beliefs. In the two-casino example, Type A framing would occur when people exaggerate their chances of winning back their losses, but accurately predict or downplay their chances of winning when they are ahead. Type B framing would arise because individuals would harbor excessively optimistic beliefs when gambling in the casino that paid them to come, but that the optimism would vanish if they were to play in the casino that charged admission.

As with economic models, we can measure attitudes toward risk in psychological models by examining the shape of the utility functions.

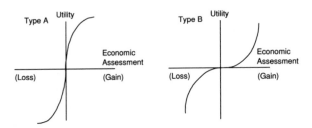

Figure 11.2. Psychological models: utility functions when people exhibit Type A and Type B framing effects.

The contrast between these two types of framing is depicted in figure 11.2. The top panel exhibits classical framing. In the domain of gains, individuals are averse to uncertainty, and, as a result, their utility functions are concave. However, in the domain of losses, individuals are willing to accept riskier alternatives, and their utility functions are convex. The bottom panel shows Type B framing. Here, individuals are risk-seeking in the domain of gains and risk-averse in the domain of losses.

Overall, the critical difference between the economic and psychological models of voting under uncertainty concerns the processing of information. In all three of the economic models, voters' attitudes toward risk (and their resulting utility functions) are independent of the manner in which economic information is presented. Both psychological models predict that attitudes toward risk and the resulting behavior depend on the presentation of information. Most economic models of voting lead us to expect either negativity or symmetry in political evaluations, corresponding to risk-aversion and risk-neutrality, respectively. If the electorate deviates from this norm, however, we can expect either positivity biases (risk-seeking) or a mix of positivity and negativity biases, caused by different sorts of framing.

Evidence

Empirical research on perceptions of risk has flourished in economics and psychology and even in applied disciplines like management and behavioral medicine. Only a modest amount of empirical work in voting behavior and public opinion, however, explores individuals' reactions to electoral uncertainties. Most research on voting behavior implicitly treats voters as risk-neutral by using statistical models in which specific independent variables have linear effects on turnout and voting choice. Micro-level studies of economic voting, for example, regress vote intention on assessments of the economy (Fiorina, 1981; Kiewiet, 1983), a procedure which implies that utilities are linear in the economic variables. Several studies have incorporated nonlinear terms to capture curvature in the utility functions of voters (e.g., Bartels, 1986), and only two experimental studies have tested the claims of cognitive psychologists using voting decisions (Ansolabehere, Iyengar, & Simon, 1990; Quattrone & Tversky, 1988).

Beginning with Kernell's (1977) study of negative voting, researchers have grappled with asymmetries and nonlinearities in voting decisions. The thrust of the literature has been to see if deteriorations in the health of the economy affect incumbents' approval ratings more than improvements. There is considerable evidence that negative voting is generated by risk-aversion (Ansolabehere, 1988; Lau, 1985).

Apart from the literature on negative voting, economic research on voting behavior has used a standard econometric technique to measure voters' attitudes toward risk. Citizens are assumed to form preferences about candidates on the basis of some indicator, say, income or ideology. The indicator is related to the preferences through a utility function, and the statistical problem is to approximate the shape of that function. Tobin (1958) showed that the indicator and the square of the indicator can be used as independent variables in a regression to approximate the shape of the utilities. What is more, the sign of the coefficient on the square of the indicator measures attitudes toward risk. If that coefficient is positive, then the individual is risk-seeking; if the coefficient is negative, the individual is risk-averse; and if the coefficient is zero, the individual is risk-neutral. Tobin's technique has been applied in studies of both issue voting and economic voting. Hinich and Enelow (1984), Bartels (1986), and Brady and Ansolabehere (1989) all find that voters are consistently risk-averse in primary and general elections.

In all of these studies, attitudes toward risk are assumed to be constant. Questions of presentation are, thus, irrelevant. Two experimental studies have tested for possible presentation effects in voting. Quattrone and Tversky (1988) administered a series of experiments in which people were given information about the economy or a public policy and then asked to choose a candidate or party. Political choices in these experiments were couched as lotteries and gambles. In one study, for example, subjects were told that party A will produce inflation of 12 percent, while party B will produce inflation of 0 percent with a probability of .5, and inflation of 24 percent with a probability of .5. In all cases, Quattrone and Tversky found strong evidence of Type A framing. These experiments, though not particularly realistic, serve as a useful demonstration that voting decisions are subject to framing.

Ansolabehere, Iyengar, and Simon (1990) examined the voting choices of (nonstudent) subjects in a more realistic but less well-controlled experiment. In this experiment, subjects were shown a fifteen-minute clip of a news program into which one or another two-minute treatment story had been inserted. The treatments consisted of reports that described the economy as either bad or good (in the present) and then as about to get better or worse. The objective was to locate people in the domain of losses or of gains and then measure the shape of their utilities for equivalently good and bad news. The results of the study indicated that when people used retrospective evaluations of the economy to judge the incumbent president, they were risk-averse. However, when they used prospective evaluations, they exhibited Type A framing effects.

In sum, research on voter uncertainty has centered on measuring attitudes toward risk. The basic conclusion is that voters tend to be risk-averse. Citizens also are prone to make cognitive errors, and those errors seem to be prevalent when voters think about the future rather than the past. Importantly, no one has examined what beliefs voters actually hold, or how malleable these beliefs are. At this point, speculation about the consequences of uncertainty, then, is principally informed by the notion that voters are risk-averse. Clearly, more work needs to be done on the changeability of beliefs if theorists are to understand the role of uncertainty in electoral processes.

Implications

At the beginning of this essay we noted a recent shift in the focus of research on information in democratic processes. Scholars working with the tools of economics have developed a deeper theoretical understanding of the ways in which voters and politicians behave in elections and of the way that elected officials respond to changes in public opinion. In this section we examine the nature of representation when voters fit either homo economicus or homo psychologicus.

V. O. Key (1966) was perhaps the first to point out that a poorly informed electorate could still exert considerable control over elected officials. He noted that the responsible electorate cares chiefly about economic and social conditions and, accordingly, punishes incumbents for bad times and rewards them for good times.

The implication of risk-aversion in this setting is simple. Voters will punish politicians more strongly for bad times than they will reward them for good times. Concavity of voters' utilities means that a decrease in personal income will lead to a large decrease in utility, while the corresponding increase in income will produce only a modest increase in utility. Consequently, the presence of uncertainty and risk aversion among voters means that economic downturns will hurt politicians' approval ratings more than economic upswings will help them. As a result, incumbents must work harder simply to stay in office when there is uncertainty, and the worse that economic conditions become, the harder the incumbent must run.

Key also noted that judgments about the performance of the government are not made in isolation but in response to information, giving rise to his famous description of the electorate as "an echo chamber." In the area of economic performance, voters may judge the government on the basis of personal (egocentric) circumstances or national (sociotropic) conditions (Kinder & Kiewiet, 1979). While egocentric considerations are learned primarily through personal experience, information about national conditions is learned primarily from the media and campaigns. This raises the prospect that politicians may be able to turn voters' uncertainty into an electoral advantage by being purposefully vague or by emphasizing only good or only bad economic news.

Alesina and Cukierman (1987) present an interesting case in which the incumbent administration can use electoral ambiguity to its advantage. Shepsle (1972) had shown that in a single election with risk-averse voters the best strategy a candidate can pursue is to be unambiguous. Shepsle looked at a race with two candidates in which each promised a policy position and chose a level of ambiguity associated with that promise. Mathematically, the promise was represented as a mean and the ambiguity as a variance. Shepsle showed that competition between the two candidates in a single election reduced the variance to zero—i.e., no ambiguity associated with policy positions. Building on this model, Alesina and Cukierman (1987) constructed a model of elections in which risk-averse citizens vote on the basis of economic performance, and the incumbent party is interested in winning election to more than just one term. The incumbent administration in this example manipulates fiscal policy to stimulate the economy. The authors show that under some conditions the incumbent administration will have to increase the immediate variability in economic performance to maximize its chances of reelection over future terms. Hence, there is some electoral incentive to increase the uncertainty that voters face.

In sum, lack of knowledge among voters creates an interesting tension in representative politics. On the one hand, risk aversion among voters forces politicians to work harder simply to stay in office. On the other hand, the ability of politicians to manipulate information occasionally produces an electoral advantage to uncertainty. The conditions under which one of these two forces—negativity among voters and manipulation by candidates—dominates have not been spelled out in any systematic manner.

Despite the compelling evidence of cognitive errors in reasoning under uncertainty, there is very little work that demonstrates the importance of framing to political reasoning. Most applications seem to be in the theory of international relations where "misperception" has long been thought to be a cause of war (e.g., Jervis, 1976). Some recent game-theoretic work on misperception demonstrates that the key problem is optimism. Highly optimistic beliefs are often destabilizing in two-player games, but it is hard to tease more general lessons out of these examples (Kreps, 1990; Stein, 1982).

In addition to their work in international relations, communications scholars have investigated the impact of differing news "frames" on political beliefs (see Gamson & Modigliani, 1986; Iyengar, 1991). These studies show that the manner in which the news media present political issues affects how the public reasons about these issues. When television news frames poverty in episodic terms by dwelling on the plight of a particular poor person, viewers are likely to attribute responsibility for poverty to the characteristics of poor people. However, when the news frames poverty in thematic terms by focusing on collective outcomes and general concepts, individuals attribute responsibility for poverty to society and government (see Iyengar, 1991). The upshot of this work is that when the news media concretize and personalize national issues, the effect is to absolve public officials from responsibility. In this sense, framing impedes electoral responsiveness in that elected officials are less likely to be held accountable for national problems.

Conclusion

Economic models of electoral behavior reveal that political uncertainty among voters does not necessarily impede their ability to control elected representatives. Because of risk aversion, incumbent politicians are penalized disproportionately for economic downturns and must strive to avoid them. For an administration this may mean manipulating economic policy instruments to keep the economy healthy (Bloom & Price, 1975). For individual congressmen this may mean that they must provide services for constituents, thereby unhitching themselves from national conditions (Cain, Ferejohn, & Fiorina, 1988). Politicians retain some advantage, however, since the government and political candidates can powerfully influence the flow of information. When candidates and parties look beyond the immediate election, there are sometimes strategic advantages to political ambiguity, and in such situations politicians may be less constrained by public preferences.

The challenge that cognitive psychology presents to economic models of voting is profound. The invariance principle—one of the basic assumptions of these models—may be violated by the realities of voting behavior. The presence of cognitive errors in voters' judgments means that many of the implications of rational choice models must be reconsidered. As yet, very little has been done along those lines.

Authors such as Fiorina (1990) and Grether and Plott (1979) defend the rational choice paradigm as a theory of politics, but not necessarily as a theory of reasoning, since there are few if any predictions about politics generated by the psychological paradigms. Furthermore, as the argument goes, experimental psychologists may be able to induce cognitive errors, but it is not clear that these errors manifest themselves as anything more than just noise. We agree, and we believe that more theorizing is needed to develop the political and electoral consequences of cognitive errors. Along these lines, we propose the following research agenda.

First, there needs to be an explicit, positive theory of cognitive errors. Kahneman and Tversky's "prospect theory" (1979) is a step in the right direction. These authors suggest that the crux of the matter is not the existence or nonexistence of utility functions, but the nature of subjective probability, or judgment. Their experiments reveal that people's subjective probabilities do not always add to one, that people are overconfident about infrequent events, and that they place too much weight on familiar events. In the language of probability theory, subjective probabilities are subadditive and asymmetric, when the true probabilities are additive and symmetric. Beyond this first pass, there is little theoretical work on the characteristics of subjective probabilities.

Second, rational choice theorists need to incorporate these errors into their models. Specifically, how do subadditive and asymmetric subjective probabilities affect people's attitudes toward risk and the measurement of risk in areas such as insurance, investment, and competition under uncertainty?

Turning to the convergence of economic and psychological models, there are three areas of political science research where prospect theory may yield insights: spatial competition, public goods, and bargaining. Electoral models of spatial competition are widely used in political science. They generate the robust prediction that candidates and parties will converge to or purport to represent the ideal point of the median voter. Spatial competition under uncertainty produces a similar result. In political campaigns, however, candidates do not merely announce their political positions. They attack and criticize the positions of their opponents. William Riker has analyzed the partisan pamphlets and announcements distributed during the campaign to ratify the U.S. Constitution. He found that the Anti-Federalists chiefly attacked the proposal, hoping to exploit the sorts of errors induced by framing. Studies of political campaigns suggest that a similar motivation may account for candidates' extensive use of attack advertising. As yet, however, there is no theory of spatial competition that predicts when candidates will attack each other rather than merely promote themselves.

Models of public goods have been applied chiefly to political participation. Here, the predictions of rational choice theory diverge wildly from empirical reality. If it is irrational for people to vote or to join groups, why do people donate millions of dollars each year to public interest groups and political action committees, and why does slightly more than half of the public vote in U.S. presidential elections? The economist's standard response to these facts is to invoke "psychic utility"—people participate because of their sense of duty as citizens. Psychological studies suggest an alternative explanation: citizens' overconfidence that their votes, protests, or contributions will result in influence.

Finally, models of bargaining have been widely used to describe legislative behavior. The basic prediction of these models is that minimal winning coalitions form in legislatures. Empirically, however, few bills are passed by majorities of size 50 percent + 1, and many important bills (such as rivers and harbors legislation in Congress) are approved unanimously. The problem here is that models of bargaining are highly sensitive to assumptions and often predict too many equilibrium outcomes. One possible solution is Thomas Schelling's notion of "focal points." According to Schelling, people focus on outcomes that are particularly desirable, familiar, or traditional, and bargaining is oriented toward those outcomes. For example, negotiations over the federal budget begin with last year's allocations and appropriations, and attempts at zero-based budgeting are rare and difficult to implement. In essence, last year's budget acts as an anchor for current negotiations.[2] Here, prospect theory is likely to make fundamental contributions. The notion of anchoring in prospect theory justifies a particular equilibrium selection rule (focal points) and may produce specific predictions about the outcomes of legislative bargains.

To conclude, theories of rational choice and cognitive psychology have yet to address each other. The research agenda we recommend is one way of bridging this divide. The theory of rational choice has produced a fairly integrated set of propositions about the political world. Empirically, however, these propositions have met with mixed success. Cognitive psychologists, by contrast, have uncovered several empirical regularities in human choice but have made little progress toward a general theory. We believe that economic and psychological models can converge at some middle ground. Psychologists need to specify the systematic consequences of cognitive errors on individuals' subjective beliefs, while rational choice theorists need to incorporate the effects of these errors in their models of political competition and bargaining.

Appendix

To demonstrate the implications of framing, consider an individual who is risk-averse when using the true probabilities of events, but who exhibits Type A framing when left to use her own subjective beliefs. Let a and b be two alternatives; p is the true probability of winning a; $1 - p$ is the true probability of winning b; and $c = pa + (1 - p)b$ is the certainty equivalent. When p is unknown, the individual substitutes her subjective beliefs π for p and $1 - \pi$ for $1 - p$. In addition, when c is a positive number (i.e., when we are in the domain of gains), she uses π_+, and when the certainty equivalent is $-c$, a negative number, she uses π_-.

Risk-aversion with the correct beliefs means that the following inequalities must hold in the positive and negative domains:

(1) $$U(c) > pU(a) + (1-p)U(b)$$
(2) $$U(-c) > pU(-a) + (1-p)U(-b).$$

The preference reversal generated by subjective beliefs means that the first inequality continues to hold when the individual uses her subjective probabilities, but the second is violated with her subjective beliefs. This is

(3) $$U(c) > \pi_+ U(a) + (1-\pi_+)U(b)$$
(4) $$U(-c) < \pi_- U(-a) + (1-\pi_-)U(-b).$$

The preference reversal phenomenon is described by all four inequalities. In the absence of cognitive errors, the individual has consistently risk-averse preferences. Systematic mistakes in calculating probabilities lead to changes in the inequalities in the *negative* domain.

What do these inequalities imply about the relationship between p and π? Adding inequalities (2) and (4) reveals that

$$\pi_- U(-a) + (1-\pi_-)U(-b) > pU(-a) + (1-p)U(-b),$$

which reduces to

(5) $$\pi_- > p.$$

Simply put, the preference reversal occurs in the domain of losses because people hold optimistic subjective beliefs.

Adding inequalities (1) and (3) yields

$$2U(c) > (p + \pi_+)U(a) + (1 - p + 1 - \pi_+)U(b),$$

which reduces to

(6) $$\pi_+ > 2[(U(b)-U(c))/(U(b)-U(a))] - p.$$

This inequality is somewhat less obvious than (5), but we can describe its implications by taking first and second derivatives with respect to p. The first derivative is

$$\frac{\partial \pi_+}{\partial p} > \frac{2(b - a)}{u(b) - u(a)} u'(c)$$

which is always positive, since $b > a$ and utility is increasing. The second derivative is

$$\frac{\partial^2 \pi_+}{\partial p^2} > \frac{2(b - a)^2}{u(b) - u(a)} u''(c)$$

The number on the righthand side of the inequality is negative, so the inequality implies that π_+ cannot be too concave.

Figure 11.3 depicts the range of beliefs that are implied by the preference reversal phenomenon. The first panel is the domain of losses. Here inequality (5) must hold. The second panel is the domain of gains. Here inequality (6) must hold. The first derivative implies that π_+ is increasing in p. The second derivative implies that π_+ may be concave, i.e., π_+ may lie above p, but not too concave, otherwise preferences in the positive domain will reverse as well, leaving us with behavior that looks risk-accepting. Any belief below the concave boundary in the second panel is consistent with the observed concavity of the utilities.

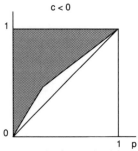 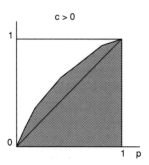

Figure 11.3. Beliefs implied by framing.

Similar derivations show that the converse sort of beliefs are implied by Type B framing.

Notes

1. The economic models hold that individuals' preferences about risks and proclivities to gamble are independent of any fees or inducements.

2. This is distinct from the idea that the status quo is an alternative to any other proposal, because the default in budgeting is not last year's budget but no budget at all.

12. The Drunkard's Search

Just like the drunk who looked for his keys not where he dropped them, but under the lamppost where the light was better, people often seek inadequate information that is readily available, use misleading measures because they are simple, and employ methods of calculation whose main virtue is ease (for previous uses of this metaphor, see Kaplan, 1964, and Betts, 1983). For example, in 1949 when Senator Joseph O'Mahoney tried to convince his colleagues not to cut the air force budget, he argued: "We do not need details here. All we need to know is that this . . . is a reduction from a 58-group air force to a 48-group air force. In my judgment, a 58-group air force would be too little" (Schilling, 1962, p. 129). This argument is straightforward and makes minimal demands on one's ability to find and process information. But it is not satisfactory. Even a person who believed that the air force should be larger than fifty-eight groups still should want to know the costs and effectiveness of smaller forces. If a much larger force was beyond reach, one could prefer a force of forty-eight groups to one that was ten groups larger if the gap in effectiveness was relatively slight and the cost difference very great. Furthermore, the most important consideration might not be the size of the air force, but its composition, training, state of readiness, and supplies. It is also possible that expansion might profitably be delayed a few years if changes in technology were in the offing.

Of course, information and decision costs must be considered when judging the availability of a decision-making procedure, and methods that seem irrational when these factors are ignored can become rational once they are weighed (for example, see Downs, 1957; Jervis, 1989a; Riker & Ordeshook, 1973; Stigler, 1961). But there is more to it than this. In many cases, searching further or looking at less obvious criteria could significantly increase the chance of a better decision at a manageable cost. Without being able to specify exactly how much effort would be optimal, it seems likely that people seize on easier ways of processing and calculating information than they would if they were fully aware of what they were doing.[1]

Ways of Decreasing the Burden of Cognition

Simple Models and Decision Rules

The propensity to conserve cognitive resources in seeking and processing information manifests itself in several forms. First, people prefer simple decision rules and unitary causal accounts to ones that posit a multiplicity of factors and causal paths. In areas in which they are expert, people may reject an explanation as too simple, but even here there may be more lip service than actual avoiding of simplicity. In some contexts, simplicity is valued for well-thought-out reasons: parsimony is a criteria for a good scientific theory not only because it increases the theory's power (i.e., the ability to explain a lot with relatively few independent variables), but because at least some scientists believe that the phenomena they are trying to capture are themselves parsimonious. But finding parsimony at the end of data collection and analysis is one thing; assuming it from the start is another.

Two linked manifestations of the preference for seeing a minimum of causal factors are the propensity of people to believe conspiracy theories and the hesitancy of even sophisticated observers to give full credit to the role of chance and confusion. Conspiracies are complicated in one sense—they involve a large number of activities that may seem bewildering. But the underlying causation is simple: everything is knit together into a coherent plan. The drive to see conspiracies varies across personalities and cultures, but a general cognitive bias also is important. Even those who reject one or another of these theories often sense the attractiveness of an explanation that ties so many odd bits of behavior together. It sometimes takes a great deal of training and experience to produce a reaction against this kind of explanation as being "too neat to be true."

If the belief in conspiracies is common, the resistance to accepting a large role for chance is almost universal. People see order even in random data. They seek parsimony even when it is not present. Thus, they are slow to explain the policies of states in terms of a multiplicity of bureaucratic factors or a multiplicity of changing motives; other states are seen as coordinated and Machiavellian when in fact they may be blundering and incoherent (Jervis, 1976).

A similar pattern is displayed when people are asked to report how many kinds of evidence they used to arrive at a decision (e.g., on which stocks to buy, on what disease a patient has, on whether to admit an applicant to graduate school). People claim to use a large number of cues, but statistical analysis of the pattern of their choices indicates that they rely on only very few. People also report that they look for complex interactive patterns (i.e., they would buy a stock if indicator A were high and B were low or if B were low and A were high, but not if both were either high or low) when in fact they treat the same variables in a simple additive manner (see Dawes & Corrigan, 1981). In the same way, when people search for the solution to puzzles in experimental settings, they focus on rules with only one element. They are slow to explore the possibility that the required answer is conjunctive (i.e., the presence of two or more elements) and even slower to think of possibilities that are disjunctive (i.e., one element present but another absent). This was a clear result of Bruner, Goodnow, and Austin's *A Study of Thinking* in which subjects were asked to reconstruct the rule by which an item was determined to belong to a category established by the experimenter. The task was relatively easy if having an attribute was both a necessary and sufficient cause for inclusion in the category; it was more difficult if having such an attribute was necessary but not sufficient; it was beyond most people's reach when there were several sufficient conditions.[2]

In much the same way, people avoid value trade-offs (Jervis, 1976). That is, they often reach a decision based on how the alternative policies are likely to affect one value although several are at stake. Furthermore, people generally fail to realize that this is what they are doing; instead, they think they have looked at several value dimensions and conveniently found that the preferred course of action is best on all counts. This would imply that the world is simply and benignly arranged, a belief that most people would reject if it were explicitly posed. But people act as though the world were so arranged in part because making trade-offs, especially when values of very different kinds are involved, places strain on cognitive abilities. To take the example of buying a house, how would one go about balancing cost, size, proximity to public transportation, noise, estimated future value, and other considerations? How would these different values be measured by a common yardstick? Although people hesitate to acknowledge that they do not go through the sort of trade-offs that full rationality would call for, they must concentrate on one or two values.

Certainty

The preference for simple calculations also is revealed by people's tendency to think in terms of certainties and, when they must employ probabilities, to use round numbers, especially 50 percent. Cognitive resources are conserved by declaring that many alternatives are simply impossible. Sometimes a more sophisticated formulation is called up: "The chance that X will occur is so unlikely that it is not worth thinking about." But conditions can change that increase the likelihood of X without triggering further consideration for it. The preference for absolutes also is found in experiments: people who are shown statements of the form "Some X are Y" and "All (or No) X are Y" are more likely to remember the former as being the latter than vice versa (Dawes, 1966).

A related device is for the person to refuse to consider complicating factors. Thus, during the Cold War it seems that the American intelligence community paid little attention to the possibility of extensive deception and that analysts who raised this problem were not taken seriously.[3] Because this stance was not limited to those with a benign view of the USSR, the best explanation is the need to keep one's task manageable. It was hard enough to try to estimate Soviet capabilities and intentions; to constantly have had to doubt much of the information that one was using would have made the problem intolerably complex. All of one's time and intellectual energy would have been taken up by trying to tell what information was deceptive, and very little time would have been left for the main job. So it is not surprising that analysts often ignored a great deal of evidence that in retrospect clearly indicated deception. The Germans in World War II similarly failed to grasp any of the innumerable clues that their spy network in England had been "turned" and taken over by the British. Although the British blatantly used the network to deceive the Germans on the location of the invasion of the Continent, even after D-Day the Germans continued to take the reports from their "agents" at face value, much to the amazement of the British.

Benchmarks and Analogies

The burdens of calculation are further reduced by the use of benchmarks to guide decisions. Round numbers often serve this function. Thus,

Herbert York (1970) explained that the Atlas missile was designed to be able to carry a one-megaton warhead in large part because, having ten fingers, we build our number system on the base of ten. Similarly, although considerations of both strategy and domestic politics were important in determining the rough number of Minuteman missiles President Kennedy decided to procure in the early 1960s, the advantage of the figure 1,000 as compared with, say, 875 or 1,163 was that it was a round number. The other side of this coin is that when a person wants others to believe that a figure she has selected was the result of complex and detailed calculations, she will pick a number that is *not* round.

Benchmarks also can be provided by other people's behavior. States often compare their performance with other states, even when this comparison is not fully appropriate. Or an actor will copy another actor believing (or acting as though he believes) that the two of them are in such similar positions and have such similar interests that they can save themselves a lot of cognitive work simply by following the other's lead. It would be hard to otherwise explain the call for an American Fractional Orbiting Bombardment System after the Soviets had tested one, or NATO's drive to match the Soviet's SS-20. (Even if many people had other motives for urging the deployment of intermediate range missiles and only used the SS-20s as an excuse, the fact that they believed that other audiences would find this excuse persuasive needs to be explained.)

When people try to determine whether a policy has succeeded, they often use two related measuring rods. First, if the situation is competitive, they ask who won and who lost. This is appropriate if the situation is zero-sum, but it will be misleading if both sides could be better off (or worse off) than they would have been had alternative courses of action been followed. Even when misleading, the question often is asked because it is easier to answer than a more complex one would be. Under some circumstances, actors ask whether they are gaining (or losing) more than another, and doing so is sensible when the nature of the interaction makes relative position or standing crucial, as is often the case when power or status are involved. But use of this measure does not seem to be restricted to situations where it fits.

The second benchmark is to compare the result of the interaction to the result of previous ones. Doing better than before is equated with winning, which in turn is equated with success. A good example is provided by the way that observers—at least American observers—judged American policy in 1986 after the Soviets arrested Nicholas Daniloff and the United States gained the reporter's freedom by complex trade. Politicians and reporters alike compared this exchange to similar cases in the past, often arguing that the United States "lost" because Soviet spies previously had been kept in jail longer and more dissidents had been released in similar trades. Setting aside the difficulties in deciding whether the circumstances of earlier cases really were the same, what is crucial here is that many people jumped from the judgment that the Soviets did better this time to the conclusion that they "won"—that is, "set a precedent that would make Western governments think twice about arresting Soviet spy suspects."[4] But even if this trade was more palatable to the Soviets than earlier ones, it may not have been so attractive as to tempt them to repeat the adventure. By the same token, the terms of the trade could have been worse than in previous cases without being excessively costly. But the baseline of the past establishes our expectations, and so we concentrate on deviations from it, even if logically they do not carry much meaning.

Other benchmarks are more ad hoc, rising out of the prominent features of the environment. For example, when President Johnson "began to search for the elusive point at which the costs of Vietnam would become unacceptable to the American people, he always settled upon mobilization, the point at which reserves would have to be called up to support a war that was becoming increasingly distasteful to the American public" (Schandler, 1977, p. 56). Although Johnson's view may have been correct, he neither sought a way around the ceiling nor considered whether a shorter war with mobilization might have been more acceptable than a longer and inconclusive one fought with fewer men. Instead, the ceiling was taken as an absolute prohibition. In the same way, when a person is considering a major purchase, he may well set an upper limit on what he is willing to spend and not consider going higher even for something of greater value. As these examples show, benchmarks can be used by the actor to restrain himself. In moments of calm, he can construct barriers that are difficult for him to break through under circumstances of temptation. Furthermore, as Thomas Schelling (1960) has shown, benchmarks can be particularly useful when several people are involved; they can provide a way for people to coordinate their behavior and can guide bargaining. But these functions also depend in part on the fact that benchmarks are artificially attractive.

Using Common Dimensions

People also can ease their burden of calculation by comparing alternatives only on the dimension that they have in common. This is fully rational if that dimension is the most important one; but the method will be employed whether or not this is the case, as is brought out by an experiment in which subjects are asked to compare pairs of students. For each student there were scores on two dimensions; one was common to both of them and was different for each. For example, one student might have scores for English skills and need for achievement, while the other would have scores on English skills and aptitude for quantitative analysis. In their evaluations, subjects weighed the common dimensions more heavily: the student with the higher English skill was likely to be rated as superior overall, even if the gap on this dimension was slight, and the student who lagged here did extremely well on the unique dimension. Furthermore, neither cautioning subjects about the effect nor giving them feedback as to the "correct" answers changed their method. Interestingly, when the subjects were questioned after the experiment, they denied that they had given extra weight to the common dimension (Slovic, 1975; Slovic & MacPhillmay, 1974). This discredits one obvious explanation that would undermine my argument: people could give extra weight to any dimension that was held in common on the not unreasonable grounds that the very fact that it was common indicates that it was important.

Few foreign policy cases are as clear as this experiment, although the way in which states compare each others' military strength (discussed below) fits this pattern. In other cases as well, it seems at least plausible that a policy which is believed to be superior to the alternatives on the one dimension that is shared by all will have a major advantage. Although the noncognitive explanation of the importance of the common dimension cannot be dismissed—any policy proposal will have to speak to the concern that is most deeply felt—ease of comparison is still likely to play a role.

In a related manifestation of the same impulse, one reason why the American armed services after World War II were a bit slower to see the Soviet Union as a threat than were the other parts of government was that each branch of the services tended to examine the single dimension that concerned it the most. When they looked into the future, each military service saw its potential enemies as those states that had, or could develop, extensive capabilities that resembled theirs or that could be countered by their service. "Air Force planners eyed a renascent Germany or Japan as the most probable enemies because both possessed the technology to develop strategic air power. Certain that only nations with a strategic bombing capability would dare wage war in the future, they dismissed the Soviet Union as a foe because it failed to develop a strategic force during the war and appeared to lack both technology and doctrine to do so for at least twenty or thirty years. The navy also minimized the Russian threat, since the Soviets demonstrated no more flare for battleships than for bombers" (Sherry, 1977, p. 168; also see Davis, 1966; Smith, 1970). Of course, the Soviet Union had a large army, but because it could not be used to attack the United States, it did not alarm the army's planners. Bureaucratic politics cannot explain this way of thinking because each service had an interest in detecting the Soviet menace; judging the Soviet Union on the most salient military dimension was such a powerful cognitive shortcut that it was employed even though doing so would not maximize the military's role or budget.

Using Only the Most Readily Available Information

To ease calculations, people concentrate on questions about which they have a good deal of information, pay most attention to the factors on which they are best-informed, and attribute the causes to variables with which they are familiar. Of course, outside the laboratory it is hard to tell which way causality runs (and it may be reciprocal); people seek information about factors that they believe are important. But this is not the entire story, as Tversky and Kahneman's research on availability shows. Tversky and Kahneman have found that ease of recall strongly influences judgments in ways that cannot be explained by the rational seeking and using of information. For example, if a person is asked whether the number of words beginning with a particular letter is greater than the number of words in which the letter appears third, he is likely to answer in the affirmative because it is easier to recall the first letters of words. But this ease of recall is not a good measure of frequency. The fact that it is hard for us to call to mind words with a given third letter does not mean that such words are uncommon (Tversky & Kahneman, 1973).

As with the other effects we have discussed, the impact of readily available information often is not conscious. Thus, experiments have shown that if the salience of a factor is increased, people will treat that factor as of greater importance, even though they do not understand the manipulation and probably would deny that the manipulation had any effect on them (Fiske & Taylor, 1991). For example, while actors usually attribute their own behavior to the stimuli they confront, and observers attribute the behavior to the actor's internal characteristics, if videotapes are used to change the actors' and the observers' perspectives, the attributions change correspondingly (see Arkin & Duval, 1975; Regan & Toten, 1975; Storms, 1973). Similarly, differences in interpretation of events often can be traced to differences in the information that is salient, with each person attributing greater importance to the factors with which he is most familiar.

For many of the same reasons, "individuals tend to accept more responsibility for a joint project than other contributors attribute to them" (Ross & Sicoly, 1979, p. 322). This is true for couples' beliefs about how much each of them contributes to routine household chores and major decisions; it also is the case for subjects in problem-solving experiments. That the effect is present, although attenuated, when the group product is criticized shows that ego gratification cannot entirely explain the bias. Further evidence that what is at work is the propensity for people to attribute primary responsibility to factors about which they are most aware—which is usually things they have said or done—is supplied by an experimental manipulation. If the experimenter heightens the subject's recollection of the other person's actions, the subject will accord the other person a greater share of the responsibility for the outcome.[5]

In foreign policy as well, the degree to which a factor is seen as influential depends in part on the amount of information that the decision-maker has about it. What the decision-maker is most likely to know about are his own worries and plans, thus contributing to the egocentric nature of inference. This bias is not necessarily a self-serving one—the actor does not always see himself in a favorable light. Rather, people place themselves at the center of others' attention, believing that others are reacting to them or trying to affect them. Since the decision-maker knows about his state's policy in great detail, it will be relatively easy for him to find some element in it that could have been the cause or the object of the other state's actions. By contrast, many of the other possible causes of the other state's behavior are seen only in dim outline.

It was to correct this propensity and to better understand Soviet behavior in the Strategic Arms Limitation Treaty (SALT) negotiations that Marshall Shulman, as Secretary of State, Cyrus Vance's assistant, kept a chart of what he called "correlated activities" (Talbott, 1979, pp. 80, 120, 146), which showed all the events that were likely to be affecting the Russians, not only those which were of primary interest to the United States. Of course, people can draw inferences only when they have some information to work with. But rarely are they aware of the degree to which hidden factors could be more powerful than those about which they are informed. They implicitly assume that factors not in their purview are unimportant.[6]

It also is easier to see how a new technology fits into one's own plans than it is to see how an adversary might use it. The difficult task of discerning the implications of new developments can be made easier by using a framework that the person already understands well—most often his nation's capacities and intentions. He will have much less information on how the other side might employ the new device and so will pay less attention to this problem or, when he studies it, will implicitly assume that the other side will see it as he does. This was the pattern in many of the Royal Navy's attempts to grasp the implications of new technologies before World War I. When trying to understand how the torpedo boat would change warfare, both those who urged its adoption and those who denied its importance paid most attention to how it could be used in the close blockade that the Royal Navy planned to institute in the event of war. Little thought was given to how England's enemies might use torpedo boats to thwart the blockade, a mission that they could in fact perform well (Cowpe, 1977). Similarly, most of the discussion of submarines was in terms of their utility to the British, which was slight. Only a few people shared Lord Balfour's insight: "The question that really troubles me is not whether *our* submarines could render the enemy's position intolerable, but whether *their* submarines could render our position untenable" (Kennedy, 1977).[7] Some of this effect may be explained by the tendency of military commanders to think in terms of taking the initiative rather than having to react to what the adversary is doing. But probably at least as important is the fact that they can make the problem of judging new weapons less intractable by concentrating on how they could use them rather than trying to guess how the other side might do so, a question about which there is less information and whose answer requires the use of a less familiar mental framework.

In a variant of this pattern, states assume that other states will use their weapons in the same way that the state is planning. This makes some sense because a great deal of thought presumably went into developing the state's own plans and, if the problems and outlook of other states are similar, they are likely to come up with similar answers. But even if these conditions do not hold, the simplifications that are permitted by assuming that they do hold exert such a strong attraction that decision-makers are not likely to abandon them. Thus, in the 1930s the British believed that the Germans planned to use air power in the same way that the British did—that is, in strategic attacks on the adversary's homeland. There was little in German military doctrine to lead to this conclusion and German airplanes were not suited to this mission, but those factors were not sufficient to destroy the illusion of symmetry (see Jervis, 1982).

Until shortly before the outbreak of World War II, the British Air Ministry made the same kind of assumption the basis for its estimates of the size of the German air force. It thought that "the best criteria for judging Germany's rate of expansion were those which governed the rate at which the RAF could itself form efficient units" (Hinsley et al., 1979, p. 299). Up to the mid 1970s, the United States thought that Soviet nuclear doctrine resembled American views even though Soviet history, context, and civilian-military relations were very different. Beliefs about how the Soviets would use specific weapons similarly proceeded on the assumption that they would adopt the American pattern, and it took several years before U.S. analysts realized the Soviets' large missiles were not targeted as we would have used them, but instead were aimed at the U.S. command and control structure (Steinbruner, 1981).

Consequences

Inertia

The first consequence of the need to simplify calculations is that incrementalism is encouraged. Decision-making is made much easier if the person searches only for alternatives when the current policy is failing badly, limits the search to policies that are only marginally different from the current one, concentrates on the particular value dimension that is causing trouble, evaluates only a few alternatives, and adopts the first alternative that puts the person above an acceptable level of satisfaction. Furthermore, some of these processes operate at the perceptual level as well as at later and more conscious levels of decision-making. Thus, people engage in "perceptual satisficing"—i.e., rather than waiting, collecting more information, and comparing several accounts, each of which is at least minimally satisfactory, they accept the first image or belief that makes minimal sense out of data. Once an initial belief is formed, even if the person means it to be tentative, it will tend to become solidified because all but the most discrepant evidence will be assimilated to it; people will not search for new beliefs or images as long as the ones that they hold are not clearly inadequate (for further discussion, see Jervis, 1976).

Linked to this characteristic is the tendency for a policy to continue even as the rationales for it shift. In the case of nations, many explanations for inertia stem from bureaucratic, domestic, and international politics; vested internal interests often support continuity, and their policies constitute commitments that are hard to break. But in many cases this phenomenon has a cognitive component as well. Once a person has worked through the arguments that led him to a conclusion, he is likely to conserve his resources by not reexamining it unless he has to. As the reasons that originally led to the policy erode, they often are gradually replaced by new and sometimes incompatible ones. Thus, an experiential-induced belief can persevere even when the person is told that the evidence which established it is false (see Jervis, 1976; Ross, Lepper, & Hubbard, 1975). A similar process may be at work in cases—such as the call for foreign aid and the preference for Pakistan over India—that have seen a relatively constant policy supported by changing rationales.

Ignoring Interaction Effects

A second consequence of the need to keep calculation manageably simple is that problems which involve many interrelated elements often are analyzed as though each element were separate (Dawes, 1971; Dawes & Corrigan, 1981; Einhorn, 1972; Jervis, 1991). While people think they are using interactive models and complex methods of calculation, in fact they implicitly assume additivity. People are better at seeing what variables are important than they are at combining them. This is consistent with Cyert and March's (1963) finding that organizations deal with complexity by dividing up problems into smaller ones and seeking separate solutions for each part of them ("factored problems—factored solutions").

The same patterns appear in political decision-making. Interactive models place enormous strain on our cognitive abilities and, even when we know they are appropriate, we shy away from using them. Thus, the flaw in the Royal Navy's analysis of the threat posed by air power to battleships in the interwar period: "Although specific problems . . . such as the effect of underwater explosives were occasionally analyzed in depth, there was little continuing research into the . . . problem as a whole" (Till, 1977, p. 119). Taken one at a time, the problems might be manageable, but when combined the threat could be overwhelming. The German analysis in late 1916 and early 1917 employed the same shortcut and similarly produced erroneous results. In deciding whether to adopt unrestricted submarine warfare, the Germans estimated the amount of goods that Britain needed to maintain her position and the numbers of ships that the Germans thought they could sink. The conclusion was that they could quickly reduce the flow of material coming into Britain to below the minimum level; thus, Britain would sue for peace before the impact of U.S. entry into the war could be felt. While the specific calculations were accurate, the influence of one of the factors on the others was neglected. That is, once the United States entered the war, the British were willing to suffer what earlier would have been an intolerable loss of shipping because they realized that if they held on a bit longer the tide would turn (Ikle, 1971).[8]

The pattern of dividing up problems and examining each solution in isolation contributes to the propensity for states to follow policies that embody conflicting elements. To say that the right hand does not know what the left hand is doing is not quite accurate: rather the right hand does not pay any attention to the implications of the left hand's activities. Thus, in the interwar period Japan acted as though its policies toward China would not influence the prospects for relations with the West (Iriye, 1969). Similarly, in 1918 the French ministry of war supported Japanese intervention in Siberia but "tended to ignore the obvious consequences of this policy on [French] relations with the Bolsheviks, or preferred to treat European Russia and Siberia as two separate theaters of action" (Carley, 1976, p. 432).

Net Assessment

The drunkard's search is illustrated by the way that the British judged German air power in the 1930s and American analysts compared Soviet and American nuclear strength throughout the cold war. In both cases, the basic question asked was "Who is ahead?" not "Do we have sufficient military force to support our foreign policy?" A glance at almost any article on what is called nuclear or strategic balance shows a preoccupation with the question of whether or not the United States trails the Soviet Union. Carrying this approach to its absurd end, Secretary of Defense Caspar Weinberger argued that the United States had to spend as much as the Soviets did. But this general error was not committed only by hawks. While doves used different indicators and argued that the situation was one of parity or U.S. superiority, they framed the question in the same way. Similarly, in the interwar period both Neville Chamberlain and Winston Churchill focused on the question of whether the United Kingdom had what they called "air parity" with Germany.

But this approach, while simple, is highly misleading. Most obviously, the United States and the USSR could have had equal numbers of strategic forces, but the weapons could have been configured in such ways that both sides had first-strike capability, thus creating tremendous instability. While everyone knew of this danger, it sometimes was lost sight of in comparing the size of the two sides' forces. Even less frequently recognized was the fact that depending on the task and context, a state could have more military power than its adversary and still not have enough, or that it could be inferior and still have more than it needed. In the interwar period, air parity might have been sufficient to deter a direct attack on England, but not enough for "extended deterrence" against German expansion to the east. Similarly, the analysis of many hawks during the cold war implied that a significant margin of superiority—perhaps what Herman Kahn called a "not-incredible first strike capability"—was needed if the American commitment to NATO was to be credible (Kahn, 1960). The implication of the arguments of many doves was that significantly less than parity was needed, certainly to protect the United States, and probably to protect vital European interests as well. But the logic of both positions was abandoned when much of the debate focused on the question of who was ahead, which is a much more manageable question than estimating how much was enough to deter the Soviets and how various configurations of forces could have contributed to terminating a war in the least possible unfavorable way.[9]

In general, it is very difficult to estimate what would happen in the event of a war—the "outputs" of the weapons. The interaction of what each side will do is terribly complex. It is much easier to measure the "inputs"—what weapons each side has—even though the relationship between these and the outputs is tenuous. So, just as the drunk looks under the lamppost, so it is that analysts use inputs to judge military balance.

Little attention was paid to the composition of the forces on both sides, and numbers of planes often were compared without separating fighters from bombers. On some occasions, the British fighter force was compared to the German one and the bombers were compared to those of the adversary. But while fighters would sometimes meet in an air battle, bombers never would. What was really needed was some way of judging how many German bombers could penetrate British defenses on a sustained basis and how much damage they could do.[10] Similarly, one wanted to know how much the British bombers could damage German targets. So comparing each side's bombers with the other's fighters and antiaircraft guns would have made some sense. Even this would have omitted many crucial factors, such as the ability of defenders to disperse or hide and the ability of the attackers to navigate across hostile terrain in good weather and in bad—in the first year of the war, few British bombers could find their way to their targets. But at least such a measure would have been closer to what would affect the outcome of a war than the simple comparison that was used.

Furthermore, in looking at inputs people have a preference for absolutes, for examining what is most easily quantified, and for stressing what they have most information on. Thus, in the 1930s the British judged comparative air strength by counting the number of planes each side had. Sometimes they distinguished the total number from what they called "first-line" aircraft—planes of the most modern design—but even this degree of complexity was often dropped (Gilbert, 1967). This was not because the British treated the whole question of the comparison casually. There were long debates over how to calculate first-line strength (Gilbert, 1967), but the attempts to push beyond this measure were few and desultory.

Quality of the aircraft was omitted from most calculations. For example, the British official history notes that in looking at the effectiveness of a planned expansion of their bombers, the British took "no account of the fact that paper plans were . . . actively being made within the Air Ministry to incorporate the new heavy four-engined machines into the bomber force" (Gibbs, 1976, p. 569). (While those who favored a stronger bomber component had an interest in underestimating British strength, strategic misrepresentation cannot explain why those who opposed the air ministry's plans ignored the question of quality.) Government critics like Churchill who called for a rapid expansion of the RAF also generally ignored the linked questions of what aircraft were ready for production and whether it would have been better to postpone increased procurement until a new generation of planes was available.

Quality of personnel likewise was given short shrift. Although the Germans suffered from the "teething problems" associated with a young and expanding force, questions of training, morale, and maintenance were generally ignored. Similarly, emphasis on numbers of planes usually excluded consideration of each side's production capacity, which was vital for sustaining and increasing its force in wartime. A country might be stronger with a somewhat smaller standing air force supported by large and flexible production facilities than it would be with a larger force that would not be maintained in the face of wartime losses. But production facilities remained marginal to the British estimates of the military balance (for exceptions, see Gilbert, 1967, pp. 631–35, 650, 671–72; also see Slessor, 1956).

This pattern of assessment was not limited to air power. In judging their naval strength before World War I, the British also relied exclusively on numerical comparisons without consideration of quality. As the battles showed, seamanship, strength of armor, accuracy of fire, ship design, and the effectiveness of shells were extremely important, and the German superiority in the latter two categories cost the British dearly. The impact of factors such as these also shows up in ground combat. In 1940, French tanks were superior to German tanks in numbers and roughly equal in quality. Tactics, training, morale, coordination, and political will made all the difference. But even had planners been aware of their importance, it is doubtful whether they could have developed sufficient understanding of them to have usefully employed them in their analysis.

In summary, British decision-makers concentrated on what was relatively easy to measure at the expense of trying to develop more complex, but more revealing, measures of relative strength. By implicitly assuming that both sides were planning to use their airplanes in the same way, which they could have learned was not correct, they were able to concentrate on only one dimension, just as the experimental subjects did. The yardstick they employed was distinguished only by the extent to which it facilitated comparisons and decisions. It gave them manageable simplicity, summary numbers they could hold in their minds and easily use.

The same pattern was apparent during the cold war. Heavy reliance was placed on "static indicators"—numbers of missiles and warheads, the amount of throw-weight, and the extent of the damage that each side could do to the other. (The indicators of latter capability were themselves derived from highly oversimplified calculations.)[11] Although there was some discussion of "counter-balancing asymmetries," arguments often were couched in terms of which side was ahead on any of these dimensions. For example, in the fall of 1981 many officials in the United States were disturbed by reports that Soviet missiles had become more accurate than American missiles, just as in other periods there was fear that the Soviets were developing better bombers than the United States possessed. Calculations are facilitated by such comparison, but this conservation of cognitive resources is purchased at the price of answering questions that make no sense. The accuracy of each side's missiles or the quality of its bombers were significant, but the direct comparison of these factors was not. Each weapons system should have been evaluated in terms of its ability to carry out its mission; an increase in, say, the quality of Soviet bombers may have had important implications for U.S. air defense, but it said nothing about the utility of American bombers. There may have been reasons to be disturbed if Soviet missiles were extremely accurate, but comparison with the accuracy of American missiles says nothing about the ability of either side's forces to carry out useful missions.

At first glance, numbers of bombers and missiles (or their destructive capabilities) would seem to make more sense. But they do not. As noted earlier, whether the state is ahead or behind its adversary in strategic weaponry says little about the question of whether the state's military force is adequate for its foreign policy. Furthermore, in a counterforce war in which strategic forces are to be attacked, what is crucial is the match between the numbers and characteristics of the weapons (particularly accuracy) on the one hand and the numbers and characteristics of the targets (particularly their hardness) on the other.[12] This complex matter is not illuminated by comparing the two sides' weapon systems themselves. One side could have more weapons, warheads, throw-weight, or even hard-target kill capability than the other yet be less able to wage a counterforce war than the adversary because the latter's forces are more protected than the former's. To come closer to what we want to know, we need to consider the state's ability to locate the adversary's forces and communicate with its own, but here again knowing—or estimating— which side is "ahead" in this regard does not tell us which side's forces, if either, could complete their required missions.

Arms control negotiations show the same concern with equality of static indicators, especially numbers of missiles and warheads. Indeed, the Jackson amendment passed in the wake of SALT I agreements required that future treaties should "not limit the United States to levels of intercontinental strategic forces inferior to the limits provided for the Soviet Union" (Wolfe, 1979, p. 301). In the months that followed its passage, this somewhat vague prescription hardened into a mandate for a force of the same size as that of the USSR, and Henry Kissinger's attempts to gain agreement within the United States on proposals embodying "offsetting asymmetries" failed because opponents were able to rally forces in and outside of government to the misleading standard of equality. Furthermore, even more sophisticated analysts, who saw that there was no magic in equality, generally argued that lower numbers of weapons would make the world safer and paid surprisingly little attention to the goal of stability that arms control was initially designed to

reach and whose relationship to reduced numbers was only problematical (Schelling, 1985).[13]

Similar intellectual shortcuts are revealed by the tendency to compare
how well American forces would have done in a first strike with how well
the USSR would have done if struck first. In fact, while both of these
estimates were significant, it does not matter who was "ahead" in this
regard. Both sides cannot simultaneously strike first, and these capabilities can never be matched against each other. The degree of first-strike
capability that the United States needed was not a function of the damage
that the Soviets could have done if they had struck first.

When output is measured in terms of civilian rather than military
damage, a parallel flaw often appears. One of Nixon's criteria for "essential equivalence" was that the Soviet Union not be able to do more
damage to the United States than the United States could do to it.[14]
Winston Churchill made the same point in 1934: "I believe that if we
maintain at all times in the future an air power sufficient to enable us to
inflict as much damage upon the most probable assailant, upon the most
likely potential aggressor, as he can inflict upon us, we may shield our
people effectually in our times from all those horrors that I have ventured
to describe" (Gilbert, 1967, p. 574). But in neither case was such a simple
yardstick appropriate. States do not decide to go to war on the basis of
comparisons between how much they will suffer and much harm will
come to their adversaries. If decision-makers are even minimally rational, they compare their estimates of the probable gains and losses of
going to war with what the state expects the situation to be if it does not
attack. Thus an aggressor could be deterred even if a state thought it
could inflict more damage than it would receive or, in other circumstances, could attack even if it thought this balance was reversed. Such
assessments of damage also fit the drunkard's search metaphor in their
omission of many factors whose importance is matched only by the
difficulty of measuring them, such as long-term casualties and environmental effects of nuclear war.

There is little dispute on these points: all analysts agree that it is better
to use "dynamic indicators" that attempt to capture the likely courses of
wars fought under various conditions. But such measures are much more
expensive in terms of time and cognitive resources and do not yield
simple and straightforward summary numbers. Because they involve a
large number of variables of widely different kinds and are highly sensitive to conditions and context—e.g., how the war starts, what each side's
targeting strategy is, how well the weapons work, etc.—they do not lend

themselves to easy comparison over time or between two adversaries. Thus, it is not surprising that static indicators remained popular; for all their inadequacies, they are relatively easy to develop and use.

Even dynamic indicators pay little attention to factors that, while crucial, are particularly difficult to capture, such as command, control, and communications. The survival and efficiency of these systems would have an enormous impact on the way that any war could be fought and terminated—indeed a significant advantage on this dimension would more than outweigh a major disadvantage in numbers of missiles. But we know so little about how these systems would function in wartime that they do not figure in our assessments.

In the same way, political factors that would have influenced the outcome of a limited war were left out of most analyses of the strategic balance. We hardly need to be reminded that the victor in Vietnam was incomparably weaker than its adversary on all standard military indicators. The outcome of any war that ends through negotiations will be strongly influenced by the stakes each side has in the conflict, each side's willingness to bear pain, each side's fear that the war will continue and grow even more destructive, and each side's perception of how the other side stands on these dimensions (for further discussion, see Jervis, 1984). But since these factors—which may be highly situation-specific—are so hard to estimate and complicate analysis enormously, they too are neglected.

Most attempts to assess the strategic balance also conformed to our model in that they pretended to greater certainty than the information actually permitted. They did not deal adequately with the large number of unknowns that characterize the complex weapons systems that have never been used. Would missiles have been as accurate when fired over the North Pole as they were on test ranges? Could a large number of missiles have been fired simultaneously? How vulnerable were various targets? (We could not have been certain about the hardness of our own missile silos, let alone those of the Soviets.) How would nuclear explosions have affected communications systems? What would be the environmental effects of a war? This list could be readily expanded even if we ignored questions about human behavior. Indeed, there may be crucial questions that we do not even know enough to ask—only in the past decade did people think about the effects of explosions on world climate.

These uncertainties are so enormous that they present insurmountable obstacles to a complete and thorough analysis. But what is striking from the standpoint of common sense, but expected by the model of the drunkard's search, is that few discussions contained any sensitivity analysis. That is, they did not explain how the results would have differed if the assumptions on which they were based were altered. Instead, most analyses of the effects of various strikes presented misleadingly firm conclusions about the expected consequences of nuclear war. One used to read, for example, that a Soviet first strike would probably destroy all but fifty U.S. ICBMs. But while this claim might have been based on the best estimate, what was generally ignored was that the number of ICBMs might have been much higher or lower. In other words, this number represented some sort of average of the uncertainties and concealed the extent to which the result could have been wildly different if any of the assumptions were incorrect. It matters a great deal how likely it is that an outcome will be radically different from the best estimate—e.g., whether all missiles in a first strike might miss their targets. Only occasionally did one get some of this information in the form of a range of 50 percent, 75 percent, or 90 percent within which the analysts were certain that the outcome would fall. In the overwhelming majority of cases, the prediction came in the form of a misleadingly precise estimate of the likely outcome rather than in a presentation of the range of outcomes within which the actual result was likely to occur. It often will turn out that if one wants 90 percent certainty, the range will be so wide that the analysis is extremely difficult to use.[15] At bottom is the problem that to dwell on the unknowns could render the calculations unmanageable, as perhaps the problems themselves are.

In both the 1930s and the cold war, one can argue that it made sense for the actors to use illogical but simple measures because others whom the actors wanted to influence considered them accurate measures of strategic power. A self-fulfilling prophecy was then at work. For example, the British were under pressure to build a "shop window" force (one that had no reserves) because the Germans would count only these planes, and so deterrence would be maximized. As the minutes of a British cabinet meeting paraphrased the secretary of state for air's explanation

> of his proposed bomber expansion program, he pointed to the crux of the matter, that military considerations as such really had little to do with the issue; . . . arguing that "the policy now being considered was designed largely as a gesture to check Herr Hitler's continual demands. . . ." The program that resulted [from these deliberations] had no function other than to produce the same size front line as Germany was expected to have in April 1937. No notion of wartime use of such a force [or of the fact that Britain was more

vulnerable than Germany and had more alliance commitments] . . . entered into the considerations. (Smith, 1986, pp. 156–57)

Similarly, during the cold war the United States had to be concerned with the throw-weight balance or the warhead balance because the Soviets, NATO allies, and neutrals believed that the side that was ahead on these dimensions was more likely to stand firm and prevail in disputes. A full discussion of this question would take us off the track (for further discussion, see Jervis, 1989b), but it should be noted that this consideration cannot be the entire explanation for the phenomenon. Not only is there no direct evidence to support the claim that others see the strategic military balance in this way—the Germans did not in the 1930s and the Soviets probably did not during the cold war—but purely military analyses that are not concerned with second-order political implications display the same pattern of using only easily available information. What is in control, I think, is the pressure to simplify in order to conserve our time, energy, and cognitive resources.

Summary

We find the story of the Drunkard's Search humorous because we recognize that it is not entirely fictitious: people do look where the light is brightest. Nor is it entirely foolish: the costs of gathering and processing information need to be taken into account by any intelligent decision-maker. But the pattern cannot be entirely explained by the rational search for and use of information. The data that analysts and decision-makers use are often more distinguished by their ready availability than by their relation to the questions being asked. Like people in their everyday lives, statesmen tend to see a minimum of causal factors at work, minimize uncertainty, use simple benchmarks and analogies, and make comparisons that are manageable but inappropriate. Intellectual resources are conserved, but at a high price.

Notes

1. People, then, are "cognitive misers," but the results may be a greater degradation in the quality of the decision-making than is often realized. (The phrase "cognitive misers" comes from Fiske & Taylor, 1991; this concept, as they

acknowledge, comes from Simon, 1957.) Also see Braybrooke and Lindblom, 1963; Lindblom, 1959, pp. 74–88.

2. Similarly, when people are asked to determine the rule that generates a string of numbers or letters, they almost always stop after having found a way of producing positive cases; they do not see if cases that the rule says should be negative in fact are so.

3. Unfortunately, at least some of those within the U.S. government who have worried about deception have developed such exaggerated claims and fears that the whole enterprise had been somewhat discredited. Examples are James Angleton, who was in charge of counterintelligence for the CIA, and David Sullivan, a former CIA analyst who has published his arguments in "Evaluating U.S. Intelligence Estimates," in Roy Goodson, ed., *Intelligence Requirements for the 1980s: Analysis and Estimates,* pp. 49–73.

4. Serge Schemann, "A Limited Success for Gorbachev," *New York Times,* October 1, 1986.

5. Ross and Sicoly also discuss the extent to which information disparities, selective coding of data, or selective retrieval are the mechanisms through which this bias acts. They stress the latter, but the point is not crucial here. For a further discussion of the existence of "self-serving biases," see the literature cited in Ross and Sicoly (1979) and in Tetlock and Levi, 1982.

6. Thus, telling someone about a possible factor is likely to increase the weight he will give to it. See Fischhoff, Slovic, and Lichtenstein, 1978.

7. An exception was the British analysis of airships. By 1911 they had come to see this weapon as Germany's and had concentrated on how to defeat them, not on how to use them for their own purposes. See Higham, 1977.

8. The German error may well have been a motivated one growing out of the intractable dilemma she faced.

9. Indeed, the whole question of how the military balance would affect the termination of war is terribly complex and filled with uncertainties. The assumptions made by current American deterrence theory, though, are both simple and very plausible. For further discussion, see Jervis, 1984.

10. The British estimates of how much damage would be done by each ton of bombs that landed was also highly inaccurate. For a good discussion, see Bracken, 1977. But this error was not entirely cognitive.

11. For good discussions of the technique of net assessment, see Baugh, 1984; Seiler, 1983; and Pry, 1990. Pry purports to link the present dynamic analyses that could shed light on how a nuclear war might end but in fact commits many of the errors described here.

12. This assumes that the targets are protected by being difficult to destroy, not by being difficult to find.

13. Elsewhere I have argued that the emphasis on numbers makes sense in terms of the symbolic nature of arms control, *The Meaning of the Nuclear Revolution* (1989c, pp. 221–25).

14. See, for example, Secretary of Defense Melvin Laird's testimony in House of Representatives, Subcommittee on the Department of Defense, Appropriations for the FY 1973 Defense Budget and FY 1973–77 Program, 92nd Congress, 2nd Session, February 22, 1972. For further discussion, see Jervis, *Meaning of the Nuclear Revolution,* pp. 16–19.

15. Furthermore, even this approach assumes that it is legitimate to apply statistical analysis to estimating an event that has never occurred and that can occur only once. This is not to claim that any other kind of method could be used, but only to remind us of the inherent difficulty of dealing with this question.

Samuel L. Popkin

---

13. Decision Making in Presidential Primaries

Presidential primaries are one of the more intriguing anachronisms of American elections, fascinating and bedeviling participants and bystanders with their volatility. Virtually unknown candidates, like Jimmy Carter in 1976, can in a matter of weeks become the presidential preference of a plurality of their party; other candidates, like Senator Edward Kennedy in 1980, can lose commanding three-to-one leads to become decided underdogs even before the first vote. Candidates strapped for cash can scrape together money for a few commercials and immediately rise in the polls, as Gary Hart did in Iowa in 1980; others, like John Connally in 1980, can spend over $14 million and win only one delegate to his party's convention.

Surges and declines of support for a candidate are related to the ways that voters think about the kind of person they want to be president, and about the policies they want their party to pursue. They reflect the ways in which people use and acquire information, the way in which elections are framed, the ways people read the array of candidates, and the fact that people vote strategically. In this chapter I use research in the cognitive psychology of choice and judgment to analyze this process.

Voters' lack of factual civics book information is well-established (Delli Carpini and Keeter, 1989). Grappling with this deficiency among voters, scholars who work in the economic tradition begun by Anthony Downs's classic *An Economic Theory of Democracy* have shown that voters use information shortcuts to compensate for the information they lack and to keep track of the information they do have (Downs, 1957). Information shortcuts, such as party identification, allow voters to make political choices with incomplete information—that is, to reach a decision without data to support it.

However, in primary elections, people also go beyond the information they already have by using cues that enable them to call on beliefs about people and institutions. They absorb cues and then flesh out a scenario, or narrative, with their "default values"—the information they assume to be associated with the cue in the absence of contradictory information about the specific situation (Lau & Sears, 1986).

Assembling, assessing, and incorporating information into a coherent narrative takes time and is a selective—hence creative—process. We assemble when we think; and the more we are stimulated, the more we think, computing on the fly, adjusting our categories and the data we use dynamically (Kahneman & Miller, 1986; Lakoff, 1987; Lodge, McGraw, & Stroh, 1989). The cognitive research that explains how narratives are assembled includes studies that focus on the representativeness, availability, and framing of information. We incorporate information that forms a narrative, which we assess by judgment by representativeness, the clinical equivalent of goodness-of-fit testing. When we assemble information, we do not use all that we know at one time. We incorporate information that fits our point of view, or frame, and we incorporate information that we have used recently—that is, available information.

From this research, we can draw several principles that help explain how voters make evaluations and choices. The findings about how people assemble information into narratives lead to a kind of Gresham's law of information. Just as the original Gresham's law was that bad money drives good money out of circulation, small amounts of new personal information in campaigns can dominate large amounts of old impersonal information, permitting hitherto unknown candidates to surge ahead of better-known candidates.

The cognitive psychology literature also leads researchers to the calculation shortcuts that people use when choosing one favorite from an array of candidates. When potential voters make choices among candidates, particularly in primaries, they "know" many things about the candidates from the information they obtain and the meaning they ascribe to it based on their default values. However, they do not have in mind the same characteristics for each candidate. This disparity means that the way in which voters evaluate candidates is affected by the ways in which they formulate comparisons of them. When people compare candidates on the basis of the candidates' most obvious differences, rather than the most important ones, they are conducting the equivalent of a Drunkard's Search, looking for their lost car keys under the streetlight because it is easier to search there (Kaplan, 1964). This search strategy reflects the ways in which voters formulate their choices.

Taken together, the Drunkard's Search, Gresham's law of information, and pseudo-certainty effects provide a theoretical explanation consistent with the pattern of rise and fall among new candidates in presidential primaries. Further, the same cognitive principles suggest explanations for the declines of older, established candidates before the first results are known.

Representativeness

When millions of voters cast ballots for candidates about whom they knew nothing a few weeks prior to a primary, and when people judge a candidate's past record on the basis of campaign appearances, they are assessing past or future political performance on the basis of assessments of how well a candidate fits their scenarios or scripts. Such goodness-of-fit assessments involve the use of a representativeness heuristic (Kahneman & Tversky, 1972; for a summary of recent efforts by economists to deal with the "unsettling" experimental confirmations of representativeness, see Grether, 1990). Representativeness is a heuristic, a rule of thumb, for judging the likelihood that a person will be of a particular kind by how similar he is to the stereotype of that kind of person. In other words, if we judge how likely it is that a candidate will do the right things by how well he fits our ideas about what kind of person does the right thing, rather than by considering how likely it is that a person with a particular record would do the right thing, we are using the representativeness heuristic in our judging. In the case of voting behavior, the most critical use of this heuristic involves projecting from a personal assessment of a candidate to an assessment of what kind of a leader he was in previous positions or to an assessment of what kind of president he will be in the future.

When voters see a new candidate on television and assess what kind of a president he would be from his media character and demographic characteristics, they are extrapolating from observed personal data to unobserved personal data, and from personal data to future presidential policies and performance. When voters judge how a candidate will run the government from how he manages his campaign, or whether he will have an honest administration from perceptions of his personal honesty, they are making large extrapolations with little or no discomfort, or even an awareness, that they are extrapolating.

When voters make these jumps—assessing character from interviews or from observing the candidate with his family and then predicting future presidential performance from these personal traits—they are making intuitive predictions by representativeness (Kahneman & Tversky, 1972). When making such judgments by representativeness, people compare their evidence about a candidate with their mental model of a president. They judge the likelihood of a candidate's being a good president by how well the evidence about him fits the essential features of their model of a good president (Kahneman & Tversky, 1972). Representativeness, then, is a form of clinical goodness-of-fit testing.

Demographics and résumés are important because of our talent for developed narratives about others. From fragments of information and random observations of behavior, we can develop full-blown causal narratives about kinds of people, and these narratives are so suggestive that we are not aware of the limited data from which we are generating them. In other words, the representativeness research is psychology's way of testing whether a picture really is worth a thousand words.

The tendency to imagine whole people from specific traits and isolated observations of character is strengthened by our willingness to assume that we are learning about character whenever we observe behavior. We explain our own behavior in terms of situational constraints and incentives, but when we judge the behavior of others, we assume that it reveals character. Your behavior tells me what kind of a person you are; mine reflects my environment. Obviously, this critical difference increases the amount of information about character that we acquire and subsequently use in assembling our views of others.

The original research by Kahneman and Tversky on representativeness suggested that no background information about a person would be integrated into the impression drawn from personal behavior. Subsequent research, however, has shown that historical information—what the psychological researchers call base-rate information—will be integrated when it is comprehended as causally related to character formation and when it is not pallid, remote, or abstract (Zukier & Pepitone, 1984).

Past votes by a political candidate frequently are not easily assimilated into a picture, but a host of tags do become integrated, such as environmentalist, union member, fundamentalist, right-to-lifer, militant, feminist, military veteran, draft dodger, Rhodes scholar, Eagle Scout, or astronaut. When candidates who were previously unknown to voters stump through living rooms, supermarkets and barbershops of Iowa and New Hampshire, voters use lists of background data. Voters learn that Jimmy Carter was a governor, Gary Hart a senator, and George Bush an ambassador, congressman, and CIA director. They also integrate this information into their images of candidates. However—and this is the critical point—they will decide what kind of a governor Jimmy Carter was and what kind of a president he will be not on the basis of knowledge about his performance as governor of Georgia but on their assessment of how likely it is that Jimmy Carter, as a person, was a good governor.

If people knew enough about politics, they could generate a picture of a politician in the same way they generate pictures of other people from knowing their demographics and personality traits. Tell a political junkie how a politician has voted, and what kind of district or state he is from, and the junkie, after considering the interplay of personal preferences and political necessities, can tell you something about the politician's character and beliefs. But few people have enough knowledge about the organization of government and the dynamics of legislation to do this; most find it far easier to develop a personal narrative and then assess political character from personal character.

Gresham's Law of Political Information

Because we generate narratives about kinds of people, it is easier to take personal data and fill in the political facts and policies than to do the reverse. This has an important political implication in decision-making, and evaluation, campaign behavior, or personal behavior can dominate political history.

Judgment by representativeness means that people can quickly shift the data base from which they judge candidates. A voter may have information about the past accomplishments of a candidate, but when the voter is exposed to the candidate on television, the voter may judge future performance solely by how presidential the candidate appears, ignoring evidence about past performance. Furthermore, personal evidence is so compelling that candidates who have become known personally and recently come to appear more attractive than candidates with less recent images.[1]

Presidential appearance, particularly in the short run, can seem to voters to be an adequate basis for predicting presidential success in the future. This can occur because in comparing personal information and political behavior, one is comparing facts with stories. Personal data gathered from observing the candidate generates a story about the candidate—what he is like and is likely to do if elected. The information about votes, offices held, and policy positions taken does not generate a full story and may not even be joined with the personal data. Narratives are more easily compiled and they are retained longer than facts about persons. Further, narratives require more negative information before they change (Bruner, 1986). When judgments of likelihood are made by representativeness, people do not integrate personal data with background data easily or at all. Personal data can dominate or even obliterate background data; "when worthless specific evidence is given, prior probabilities are ignored."[2]

This is a point where the cognitive literature seems to me more optimistic than warranted about the use of information. Daniel Kahneman has written that "distant labels or incidents will be ignored when evidence that is closer to the target . . . is available" (Kahneman & Miller, 1986). But his own work shows that this contention does not always hold true. Recent data of one form dominate distant data of the same form, but when some data are personal narratives and some are political facts, distant personal data can dominate more recent impersonal material.

In elections, our Gresham's law of political information means that personal information can drive more relevant political information out of consideration. Thus, there can be a perverse relationship between the amount of information voters are given about a candidate and the amount of information they actually use: a small amount of personal information can dominate a large amount of historical information about a past record.

In one context—campaign information versus past voting records—this Gresham's law is both strong and discouraging. Personally uninspiring politicians with a career of solid accomplishments get bypassed in primaries for fresh new faces with lots of one-liners but no record of accomplishment. In the context of low-information rationality and information shortcuts, however, the law is somewhat less bleak; there are many low-information cues that are proxies for political records which voters may pick up and incorporate into their assessments of future performance.

New Candidates

The ability to judge by representativeness explains why it is possible for new candidates to do well against established heavyweights in the early primaries. If people could not assemble full and coherent images from personal observations, well-established candidates with records would dominate primaries—except when voters were so unhappy with them that they were willing to gamble on new faces.

From a psychological point of view, voters do not necessarily gamble when they select new candidates over better-known candidates because the comparisons they make are clinical. In comparing candidates, the process of projection—judging future likelihoods by representativeness—does not automatically take account of different levels of information about the candidates. If voters were statisticians, they would integrate personal data with historical data and then adjust their predictions to account for the quantities of information on which the predictions were based. In statistical terms, voters would regress for limited information so that the extent to which they predicted that performances would deviate from the norm would depend on the quantity of data that are the basis for the prediction.

If a small number of data about one candidate suggest that he would be a good president, and a large number of data suggest the same thing about another candidate, statisticians would say that it is more likely that the second candidate will do well; they would discount the prediction based on fewer data. But voters are not statisticians, and they do not automatically discount, or regress, for limited data. They are, at best, clinicians, and they will be as confident in predictions made from flimsy and remote data as they will be in predictions made from substantial and recent data (Kahneman & Miller, 1986).

Jimmy Carter provides a clear example of how fast people believe they know "something" about a candidate and feel able to rate him. Carter was the governor of Georgia and had no national television exposure prior to the 1976 primary. He won the Iowa primary in January, received some national publicity, and then received a lot of national publicity after winning the New Hampshire Democratic primary the next month, but few Americans outside Georgia or Florida would have heard of him a month before he won in New Hampshire. Gerald Ford had been president nearly nineteen months by February 1976 and had accumulated far more media coverage than Carter. Despite the disparity in amounts of exposure and duration of time over which people had a chance to observe the two men, however, people who knew of Carter were able to place him on issues almost as readily as those who knew Ford (Conover & Feldman, 1989).

Walter Mondale's famous campaign query about Gary Hart, "Where's the beef?" was an attempt to make voters aware of how little they knew about Hart. President Ford's campaign against Jimmy Carter in 1976 also largely focused on pointing out how little voters knew about him. The very fact that better-known candidates need to work so hard to remind voters how little they know about some of the new candidates emphasizes just how far a small amount of personal data can go for new candidates, particularly when the data are consistent and clear.

Framing and Availability

While the representativeness literature emphasizes that information gets used when it can be incorporated into a coherent picture, the framing literature emphasizes formulation effects: people can generate many different narratives, and what we incorporate into a picture or narrative depends on the point of view or frame that we use. The decision frame has been defined as "decision-maker's conception of the acts, outcomes, and contingencies associated with a particular choice. The frame that the decision-maker adopts is controlled partly by the formulation of the problem and partly by the norms, habits, and personal characteristics of the decision-maker" (Tversky & Kahneman, 1981, p. 453). The frame "determines how a task is conceived, what kind of evidence is considered, and the cognitive strategy employed" (Zukier & Pepitone, 1984). The frame matters because different reference points, or points of view, bring forth different information and attitudes.[3] As Aristotle noted, it adds to an orator's influence if "his hearers should be in just the right frame of mind."[4]

Framing is to psychology as role theory is to sociology. Role theory tells us that we can present many different personas to others. At different times of the day, we can be a spouse, a parent, a child, a worker, a partisan, a customer, or a patient. By showing us these possibilities, role theory also says that we do not use all of ourselves at any one time. Framing tells us that since we cannot look at a person or a situation from all perspectives at the same time, we cannot use all of ourselves when we view others. Both framing and role theory, then, are about the ways that we divide ourselves and about which parts of ourselves we use in presenting ourselves or in viewing the ways in which other people present themselves.

When Framing Matters

Framing effects occur whenever altering the formulation of a problem, or shifting an observer's point of view, changes the information and ideas that the observer will use when making decisions. Framing effects, in other words, occur only when there is differentiation in the ways that we can think about a subject. If the same information and metaphors always come to the fore no matter how many questions about a subject are formulated, there is no differentiation and hence no possibility of framing effects. There also is no framing if there is a single dominant attitude about a subject. If people integrated all of their atttitudes about candidates and parties into a single measure, there would be no framing effects; the single measure would have the same explanatory power in all situations. Or if people had different attitudes about a candidate or a party but had one attitude that dominated all others, again framing would not matter.

Framing effects are not an artifact of causal responses to low-salience subjects. People who care about a subject, who think about their responses, and who are certain of their beliefs are equally susceptible to framing effects (Krosnick & Schuman, 1988). Whenever there is more than one way to think about a subject, there can be framing effects.

There are limits to framing. Certainly some information is always brought to the fore, regardless of perspective. Similar to people with rose-colored glasses, some subjects, no matter how they are viewed, and no matter how choices or problems are formulated, evoke the same dominant attitudes and ideas in some people. In general, you can frame all of the people some of the time and some of the people all of the time, but you cannot frame all of the people all of the time.[5]

It is, of course, always an empirical issue whether framing matters: that is, whether there is so little information that differentiation is impossible, or whether there are such strong dominant evocations or such specific lenses that perspectives do not matter. The evidence is strong that framing matters in presidential politics. Shanto Iyengar and Donald Kinder have experimentally confirmed three points: there is enough differentiation in peoples' images of presidents for formulation effects to matter; changing people's ideas about the problems facing the president changes the way that people think about presidents; changing the way that people think about presidents affects their assessments of presidents—and, by extension, candidates—as well as their votes (Iyengar & Kinder, 1987).[6]

Calculation Shortcuts

The cognitive literature also has considered how people in their decision-making use calculation aids as they search among candidates. Making complex calculations to "maximize expected value" is difficult for all of us, and we are frequently unsure of our choices or projections. We are more confident and comfortable in making some estimates and choices than in others, for example, when we are able to use calculation short-cuts.

One problem in making choices is resolving contradictions and incon-sistencies. When all of the evidence points the same way because the data are consistent, we do not have to resolve contradictions or decide how to weigh the evidence for one conclusion against the evidence for another. Internal consistency—when all evidence points in the same direction—also raises confidence (Kahneman & Tversky, 1973).

Another problem is assessing probabilities. People are confused, even repelled, by vague probabilities (Bewley, 1986).[7] When people find them-selves in situations where they must implicitly compare the likelihood of different outcomes, they become less confident. When they are dealing with easy calculations of likelihood, however, they are more confident in their choices. When they can think of "always" or "never," the proba-bilities of one or zero, they overrate the accuracy of their predictions (Kahneman & Tversky, 1973). People also find it difficult to calculate when choices require separate assessments of gains and losses. Lotteries with only gains are more attractive than bets with gains and losses, even if the mixed bet has a higher expected return (Kahneman & Miller, 1986). Finally, people are more confident in making predictions from the more reliable to the less reliable measure, even though actual accuracy is the same in either direction (Kahneman & Tversky, 1973).

Some types of data and probabilities make it easier for people to calculate and choose. People always overvalue consistent information and find it easier to use than inconsistent information; they find informa-tion that is all good or bad more valuable than mixed information; and they prefer positive bets to mixed bets. When people use these shortcuts, they are more confident in their decisions. The most confident projec-tions are made when there are what can be termed pseudocertainty effects, the types of data and probabilities that give people strong as-surance in their predictions by offering them easy and clear calculations.

As I have said, people with consistent data are more confident than people with inconsistent data about their predictions. At the beginning of a primary campaign, the data offered to voters often are all positive or all negative; therefore, people often are most confident in political predic-tions that are most likely to be inaccurate and subject to later revision.

When people can use "always or never," for example, they are making predictions near the tail of the distribution; when they are more confident in a little consistent data than in a large amount of inconsistent data, they are not correcting for the amount of data but for the ease of assessing the data. Because of pseudocertainty effects, overvaluing of the "always or never," finding information that is all good or all bad more valuable than mixed information, and preferring positive to mixed bets, people are most confident about their least accurate projections (Kahneman & Miller, 1986).

The Drunkard's Search

The calculation shortcuts that people use in making choices of all kinds, and the pseudocertainty principles underlying their calculations, demonstrate that people have difficulty making choices when they must integrate data about several factors. When there are several factors, or when some indicators point to one choice and others to a different one, people are, in effect, being pushed to weigh the pluses and minuses, to assign weights to the different features they care about. People have a general aversion to making trade-offs and instead search for a way to make their choices one-dimensional, to make a choice between apples and oranges a choice among fruits.[8] As Robyn Dawes (1979) has noted: "People are good at picking out the right predictor variables and coding them. . . . People are bad at integrating information from diverse and incomparable sources" (p. 574).

People particularly need search aids in situations such as primaries when they possess different kinds and qualities of information about each candidate. The way they make use of shortcuts in searching among complex choices results in a Drunkard's Search among obvious differences.

The Drunkard's Search is a widely recognized information shortcut, but it also is a calculation shortcut. By telling us where to look, it also tells us how to choose, how to use easily obtained information in making comparisons and choices. People are particularly likely to use one-dimensional searches—focusing on a single issue or attribute—when there is no dominant alternative. Such a procedure "avoids mental strain and provides a compelling argument" (Tversky, Sattah, & Slovic, 1988, p. 372).

When faced with an array of candidates where some are known well and some are known poorly, and all of them are known in different and noncomparable ways, voters will seek a clear and accessible criterion for comparing them. This usually means looking for the sharpest differences among the candidates that can be related to government performance.

When complicated choices involving many different issues are simplified to a single dimension, which dimension is chosen is important. Focusing on an attribute tends to increase the mutability of that attribute, and increased mutability increases the weight of an attribute. Since increased awareness of alternatives tends to increase the perceived importance of a feature, the search process, by focusing on a particular feature among many, gives disproportionate weight to that feature, even if it originally was of lesser importance (Kahneman & Miller, 1986).

Front-runners can be a reference point for voters and for other candidates. At the beginning of a primary season, voters will not know anything about many of the candidates and will consider information about only a few of them from the whole field. If there is a front-runner, the voter is likely to consider that candidate when evaluating other candidates, both because the front-runner is likely to be known and because the front-runner is considered viable.

A Drunkard's Search among candidates depends on the characteristics of the front-runner and can lead to peculiar dynamics. Do front-runners affect the agenda in primaries? Candidates and their strategists believe they do (Drew, 1985). Research about decision-making, in fact, supports the idea that it matters whether there is a front-runner and that it matters who the front-runner is.[9] The way in which front-runners set the stage affects the dynamics and relative fortunes of the other candidates. Whether it is always bad to be the front-runner, however, is a more complicated question.

When there is a front-runner, the other candidates frequently describe themselves with reference to how they differ from this candidate, and these features of the front-runner become focal points of candidate comparison. The increased attention placed on these features leads to increased awareness of alternatives, which in turn increases the importance that voters place on these features in evaluating candidates. This process places relatively less importance on the features of the front-runner that are not discussed but are taken for granted. For example, in 1984 as the other candidates made numerous references to Walter Mondale's endorsement by the AFL-CIO, the salience of attitudes toward political endorsements by labor increased.

When the front-runner is well enough known so that voters are aware of his warts and blemishes, these faults can be magnified in the primaries. Just as people are more comfortable with sins of commission than sins of omission, and more confident making predictions from the more reliable to the less reliable measure, they will be more confident with searches made comparing from the better-known to the less well-known candidates, or from the incumbent to the challenger. Therefore, it can be a disadvantage to be the front-runner. When the front-runner is well-known, his warts and blemishes can be magnified in the primaries. If voters had the same types of information about each candidate, they could compare the candidates on the feature they considered most important, or even on many criteria, not just those features that are advantageous to the challengers.

The Rise of New Candidates

The Drunkard's Search makes it easier for new candidates to define themselves. In primaries, voters have vastly different kinds and amounts of information about the candidates, which leads them to use the Drunkard's Search to compare the candidates, sorting them out by a few prominent criteria.

When there is a well-known trait on which the other candidates distinguish themselves from the front-runner, the communications of the less-known candidates become easier. They communicate by means of negatives, telling voters what they are not, and letting voters fill in the rest with default values and representativeness. It was easy for voters to decide that George Bush was not a voodoo economist or a bomb thrower, that Jimmy Carter was not a "typical" politician, that Jerry Brown was not a Southern fundamentalist, and that Gary Hart was not a tool of unions or blacks.

Negative Framing and Surges

Poorly known candidates can communicate through negatives, framing themselves as "not" whatever people do not like about the front-runner. Since people fill in missing information with "default values," they can "know enough" about the new candidate to support him for president because they have combined what they know about the candidate's attributes with what they know about the front-runner. No candidate has ever acknowledged this point more trenchantly than Gary Hart. In 1984, after he won two primaries in the middle of the campaign, Senator Hart told an interviewer: "Mondale's had to face cruelly twice, twice, the fact that a majority of this party wants someone else. . . . He think's I'm his problem. I'm not his problem. He's his problem."[10]

The first stage in the creation of constituencies is likely to be the "not" stage, where disparate constituent elements rally around a candidate on the basis of the ways in which he differs from a well-known candidate—on the basis of what he is not. A new candidate is most likely to emerge, therefore, in situations where this type of communication is easiest; and a surge of support for that candidate is most likely when he appears to be the obvious solution to a coordination game. The situation most favorable to this phenomenon will occur when the field of candidates is like Snow White and the Seven Dwarfs, a prominent and well-known candidate and a host of poorly known challengers.[11]

Patterns of support for the front-runner determine where support for fresh faces comes from, and the image of the front-runner determines which issues and personal characteristics that other candidates emphasize. Further, the issues that other candidates use to distinguish themselves from the front-runner become more salient as the campaign progresses.

The sudden emergence of new candidates in the context of a coordination game occurs only when there is dynamic framing—when the categories people use to examine the candidates are constructed out of the array of candidates. People do not assess the candidates separately and vote for the one with the highest expected value; they use a Drunkard's Search over the whole field. The coordination game also presupposes a critical inferential rule: "My enemy's enemy is my friend." People can switch to a new candidate when their initial favorite fares poorly because their negative framing of the candidate—as "not Reagan" or "not Mondale," for example—precludes the possibility that the voter is closer to Reagan or Mondale than to the new candidate (Brady & Sniderman, 1985; Brody, Sniderman, & Kuklinski, 1984).

New candidates excite interest because they tap hopes created by voters thinking about the better-known candidates. When there is an explicit or implicit discontent with our existing choices, victories by newcomers trigger surges of hope. As different as politics and love may be, the initial euphoria of new love and the utopian enthusiasm for a newly emergent candidate are both examples of low-information infatuation. The bubbles that lift new candidates reflect Stendahl's observation about amour that "realities model themselves enthusiastically on one's desires." In other words, the way we see little-known objects of desire depends on what we are looking for. Our hopes frame our realities.

Crystallization

The surge for new candidates depends in part on the particular framing of the candidate against the front-runner. When the framing changes, support for the newcomer can break down because voters use more information about the challenger and make more complete comparisons of the two candidates. New candidates are likely to be known mainly from campaign behavior and personal attributes, and the publicity given to the early winners often is all personal data and all positive. These candidates can get large lifts from the negative framing of better-known candidates. In 1980 George Bush was the "un-Reagan" candidate; in 1984 Reagan was the "un-Mondale."

The use of the representativeness heuristic makes it easy for people to assess future political performance by projecting from personal data about the candidate. Further, when the data are consistent and positive, the ease of using them leads to pseudocertainty effects—overly optimistic projections from limited information. The collapse of the bubble for the fresh new candidate is most likely when pseudocertainty effects no longer operate in projections of future performance. Regardless of how much new information about a candidate becomes known, pseudocertainty effects do not operate when data are inconsistent, and when the "always" and "never" in a voter's projections are replaced by "sometimes." This explains why negative campaign behavior can have so much impact at a particular point in a campaign.

Henry Brady and Richard Johnston in an important analysis (1987) of voter evaluations of candidates show that as candidates become known, their images become more differentiated, or "crystallized"; that is, people evaluate and rate candidates differently in different situations. As people develop a more differentiated picture, they become less dependent on personal attributes for projecting future behavior and more concerned with the candidates' political position. As voters learn more about a candidate, or as they discover that they know less than they thought, they sometimes discover that they prefer a different candidate. The rapid decline of candidates who surge favorably early in campaigns occurs because of new information about their stands or competence, not because of changes in voter expectations about the candidates' chances of electoral success. When pseudocertainty effects are eliminated, projections of future performance become less extreme, and the choice becomes one between two candidates who have both positive and negative traits and positions. Thus, the sudden collapses that occur in primaries and general elections depend on quirks in the ways people process data and frame their information about candidates. When we understand these quirks, we can predict how and when the overconfident projections of voters will collapse. This also emphasizes the increasing knowledge about candidates that takes place during a campaign. When voters see a candidate in new situations, they learn to view the candidate differently (Brady, 1989).

Old Information in New Contexts: *The Cases of Edward Kennedy, John Glenn, John Connally, and Gary Hart*

When the presidential primaries begin, there can be rapid changes in evaluation and preferences. In particular, there are always relatively well-known political figures who are unable to convert preferences based on their record into votes at the polls. These declines reflect political reasoning about what kind of persona a president should have. They also reflect how the reasoning that voters do in primaries is affected by the new information they receive—in effect, from a politician's pre-primary résumé to an electronic "interview" with him during the campaign.

Henry Jackson, John Connally, John Glenn, Howard Baker, and Gary Hart, to name five prominent examples in 1988, were preferred by 10 to 30 percent of their parties before the primaries began, but they had little or no success in converting these early preferences into actual votes. In 1980 Senator Edward Kennedy led President Carter by nearly three to one, but he fell in the national polls almost as soon as he announced his candidacy for president—a bandwagon effect in reverse. In 1983 Senator Glenn was within three points of Walter Mondale for months; he had as much support in 1983, in fact, as Ronald Reagan had in 1979 or 1975, yet his ratings fell and support faded rapidly.

In 1986 and 1987 Gary Hart was the leading contender for the Democratic nomination for president until he was involved in a personal scandal aboard the yacht *Monkey Business* with Donna Rice. When the scandal occurred, Senator Hart's ratings dropped, but he still led the field, and not because of a lack of known alternatives; most of his support came from knowledgeable and interested voters. Nevertheless, he received fewer than 1 percent of the votes in Iowa and fewer than 4 percent in New Hampshire. As voters were contacted by the campaigns and stimulated to watch debates and think about the candidates, Hart's support began to sink.[12]

The research on representativeness, framing, and availability shows that people do not incorporate all of their information about political figures into one overall assessment. If we had ready-made categories in which all of our information was stored, changing the perspective would not affect what information is used. But that is not the case, and since we are not using and integrating all of our information all of the time, any change of frame or any stimulation that increases the amount of time we spend thinking about a person or a choice can affect our evaluations and preferences.

The declines in support for Kennedy, Glenn, Connally, and Hart are consistent with the argument that when voters evaluate candidates as potential presidents, they try to imagine what they will do in office. This increases the weight they give to personal factors, which means that personal information matters more as voters begin to think about their choice. Thinking about the future involves evaluating scenarios. If people find it easier to project from personal data than from political data, then representativeness, coupled with a limited knowledge of politics, increases the importance of personal data. Thus, declines in ratings are consistent with the notion that most voters have vague and ill-defined notions of all of the jobs that presidents do, and they therefore evaluate presidential aspirants on personal grounds, projecting from personal characteristics and competence to future performance. It is possible that these changes in support are the result of more thinking, and not of framing, but it is the new context that prompts more thinking. Either way, these declines are consistent with Gresham's law of information.

Conclusion

Anthony Downs never explicitly considered just how voters combined new and old information, or how recent events affect their ongoing assessment of parties, but his work generally leads to what can be called neo-Bayesian assumptions. In Bayesian statistical analysis, decisions are not based solely on old information or solely on new information, but on a weighted combination of the two, with the weights assigned to reflect the information content of each type. But this idea takes no account of how content is weighed. The cognitive research suggests that a small amount of new information is usually given more weight than a large amount of old information whenever the new information is personal and the old information is abstract and hard to fit into a narrative. It also suggests that a small amount of old information may receive more weight than a large amount of new information in at least three situations: when the old information becomes more important in a new context, when the old information is easier to incorporate, or when the old information is easier to use in comparing candidates.

Campaign analysis must begin to explain what kinds of data are compelling to voters and how voters combine old and new data.[13] This means, in particular, learning why some forms of information are more easily used than others and why all information is not necessarily informative: "Some kinds of information that the scientist regards as highly pertinent and logically compelling are habitually ignored by people. Other kinds of information, logically much weaker, trigger strong inferences and action tendencies. We can think of no more useful activity for psychologists who study information processing than to discover what information their subjects regard as information worthy of processing" (Nisbett, Borgida, Crandall, & Reed, 1982, p. 116).

There is another reason that people do not act like crude statisticians: they cannot easily integrate all of their information; their choices are context-sensitive. "Preferences are not simply read off from some master list; they are actually constructed in the elicitation process. Furthermore, choice is contingent or context sensitive. . . . An adequate account of choice, therefore, requires a psychological analysis of the elicitation process and its effect on the observed response" (Tversky, Sattah, & Slovic, 1988, p. 371).

The cognitive literature shows ways that voters process and absorb information and infer meaning. Taken together, the Drunkard's Search, Gresham's law of information, and pseudocertainty effects provide a theoretical explanation consistent with the patterns of the rises and declines of new candidates in presidential primaries. When we understand these quirks, we can predict how and when overconfident projections of voter behavior will collapse.

Notes

1. Ronald Reagan fell 26 points in one month in the 1980 Iowa pre-primary polls when he chose not to campaign in the state and skipped a debate with other candidates. I believe, and I believe the surveys support me, that this decline resulted from a dominance of recent personal evidence for the active campaigners over past evidence about Reagan, not from any concern that he skipped the

campaign because he was getting old, or from local resentment that he was downplaying Iowa.

2. I substitute the phrase "background data" for Kahneman and Tversky's "knowledge of base rates."

3. Evaluations and choices are susceptible to formulation effects, as Daniel Kahneman and Amos Tversky (1984) note, "because of the nonlinearity of the value function and the tendency of people to evaluate options in relation to the reference point that is suggested or implied" (p. 346).

4. *The Rhetoric and Poetics of Aristotle,* pp. 90–91.

5. The limits to framing are in part a consequence of ways that people consciously guard against framing effects by organizing their lives to counter them (Simon, 1985).

6. Iyengar and Kinder do not discuss framing explicitly. Nevertheless, their experiments and their parallel statistical analyses of public opinion polls and network news offer strong evidence of formulation effects—framing—in politics.

7. Bewley notes that this is one of the implications of the Ellsberg Paradox.

8. I am particularly indebted to Robert Abelson for help with this section.

9. Candidates do not think that it is actually bad to be ahead, just that it is bad to be labeled as ahead, or as the probable winner.

10. *Newsweek,* June 4, 1984, p. 21.

11. For another typology, see Bartels (1988, chap. 7).

12. CBS News/*New York Times* polls from Iowa and New Hampshire in January 1988.

13. I am not suggesting, however, that more sophisticated Bayesian models cannot be developed that are consistent with the findings of cognitive psychology. Indeed, I hope, and assume, that by pointing out the discrepancies between elemental Bayesian ideas and the cognitive findings, I contribute to stimulating the next round of developments in decision theory and formal modeling of voting.

Philip E. Tetlock

14. Cognitive Structural Analysis of Political Rhetoric: *Methodological and Theoretical Issues*

Political pundits lavish attention on the opinions that high-level policy-makers express on issues of the day. All of this attention is not altogether surprising. The opinions that policy-makers express are often useful clues to future decisions with major national and international consequences (Graber, 1976). It is surprising, however, that observers devote so little attention to *how* policy-makers appear to think—to the styles of reasoning they use in explaining and justifying their views to others. For instance, do policy-makers see solutions to problems as essentially simple (all considerations pointing to one conclusion) or complex (competing values must be weighed against each other)? Are policy-makers tolerant or intolerant of alternative ways of looking at issues? Do policy-makers deduce positions from general principles or reason inductively from specific experiences and cases?

We can learn much about both policy-makers and the world in which they operate by carefully examining their styles of political reasoning. Much also can be revealed from careful examination of variables in the real world that covary with styles of political reasoning. There are substantial individual differences in styles of reasoning (Putnam, 1971; Tetlock, 1984). There are, moreover, significant relationships between these individual differences and political attitudes and policy stands. Styles of reasoning also vary as a function of situational variables, including political role (Tetlock, 1981a; Tetlock et al., 1984), the issues under discussion (Tetlock, 1984, 1986; Tetlock & Boettger, 1989b; Tetlock et al., 1985), and levels of stress and threat created by the environment (Staw et al., 1981; Suedfeld and Tetlock, 1977).

This chapter describes a series of studies that explore both individual differences and situational correlates of styles of political reasoning in a variety of subject populations, ranging from college undergraduates to U.S. senators to British parliamentarians to members of the former Soviet Politburo. The chapter is divided into two sections. The first describes the stylistic dimension of reasoning on which my own work has focused: conceptual or integrative complexity. I also provide a brief review of integrative complexity theory. The second section describes laboratory and archival studies that probe relationships of integrative complexity and a variety of attitudinal, personality, and situational variables. I argue that a comprehensive explanation of the findings must draw on a number of theoretical traditions, including personality theories, role theories, and theories of cognitive processing under uncertainty and value conflict. I conclude by sketching an integrative functionalist framework that helps to organize existing findings, to stimulate the generating of new hypotheses, and to point to profitable directions for future research.

Theoretical Background

Integrative complexity theory was originally developed to explain individual differences in the complexity of the cognitive rules that people use to analyze incoming information and to make decisions (Harvey et al., 1961; Schroder et al., 1967). The theory focused on two cognitive stylistic variables: differentiation and integration. Differentiation refers to the number of evaluatively distinct dimensions of a problem that are taken into account in interpreting events. For instance, a politician might analyze policy options in an undifferentiated way by placing options into one or two value-laden categories: the "good socialist policies" that promote redistribution of wealth and the "bad capitalistic policies" that preserve or exacerbate inequality. A highly differentiated approach would recognize that different policies can have many, often contradictory, effects that cannot be readily classified on a single evaluative dimension of judgment—for example, effects on the gross national product, the government deficit, interest rates, inflation, unemployment, the balance of trade, and a host of other economic and political variables. Integration refers to the development of complex connections among differentiated characteristics. (Differentiation is thus a prerequisite for integration.) The complexity of integration depends on whether the decision-maker perceives the differentiated characteristics as operating in isolation (low integration), in first-order or simple interactions (the effects of A on B depend on levels of C—moderate integration), or in multiple contingent patterns (high integration). Common examples of integration include references to value trade-offs (e.g., how much unemployment are we willing to endure as a society in order to bring inflation under control?), attempts to explain why "reasonable people" view the same problem in different ways (e.g., which position you take on the abortion debate depends on the stands you take on a mixture of constitutional, religious, and medical issues), and recognition of the need to take into account the joint—not just the separate—impact of causal variables on an outcome (e.g., the Federal Reserve Board will risk recession and raise interest rates only if several unlikely contingencies simultaneously arise: continuing growth in the federal deficit combined with new signs of weakness in the dollar and the reemergence of inflation in the domestic economy. And even then, the board may not act if it is an election year).

Advocates of the early trait view of integrative complexity (or conceptual complexity as it was then known) relied heavily on the semi-projective Paragraph Completion Test for assessing individual differences in cognitive functioning. Subjects were presented with sentence stems (e.g., Rules . . . , When I am criticized . . .) and asked to complete each stem and write at least one additional sentence. Trained coders rated subjects' responses on a seven-point scale designed to measure the integrative complexity of subjects' thinking in the topic area. Scores of 1 reflected low differentiation; scores of 3 reflected moderate to high differentiation, but low integration; scores of 5 reflected moderate to high differentiation and moderate integration; and scores of 7 reflected high differentiation and high integration (development of complex comparison rules to integrate differentiated perspectives). Scores of 2, 4, and 6 represented transition points between adjacent levels.

Two points concerning the integrative complexity coding system deserve mention. First, with adequate training (two to three weeks), coders can rate verbal responses for integrative complexity with high levels of reliability (Pearson product-moment correlations between .85 and .95).[1] Second, the complexity coding system focuses on the cognitive *structure*, not the *content*, of expressed beliefs and is not biased for or against any particular philosophy. One can be simple or complex in the advocacy of a wide range of political positions.

Early laboratory research using the Paragraph Completion Test showed that systematic individual differences do, indeed, exist in integrative complexity. The test demonstrated predictive power in a variety of experimental contexts, including Inter-Nation Simulations of crisis decision-making (Driver, 1965; Schroder et al., 1967; Streufert & Streufert, 1978), studies of bargaining and negotiation behavior (Pruitt & Lewis, 1975; Streufert & Streufert, 1978), and studies of attitude change (Crano & Schroder, 1967; Streufert & Fromkin, 1972). Relative to subjects who were integratively simple, those subjects who were classified as integratively complex used a broader range of information in forming impressions of others and in making decisions, were more tolerant of dissonant or incongruent information, and were more likely to be successful in achieving mutually beneficial compromise agreements in bargaining games.

Such empirical successes notwithstanding, it became clear by the late 1960s that a static trait model of integrative complexity was inadequate. Integrative complexity of cognitive functioning at a given time was not just a function of stable dispositional variables; several experiments indicated that situational factors also influenced integrative complexity (Driver, 1965; Schroder et al., 1967). Some environments were much more conducive to complex information processing than were others. Schroder et al. (1967) and Streufert and Streufert (1978) explicitly recognized this point in their "interactionist theories" of integrative complexity—theories stipulating that (1) moderate levels of threat, time pressure, and information load are most likely to promote integratively complex styles of thinking; and (2) individual differences in integrative complexity determine how people react to changing levels of these environmental variables.

Another critical development in the evolution of integrative complexity theory and research occurred in the mid-1970s. Prior to that time, research on the integrative complexity construct was primarily limited to experimental studies that examined the interactive effects of dispositional integrative complexity (assessed by the Paragraph Completion Test) and situational variables (environmental stressors) on subjects' selection of "low-involvement" response options (endorsing attitudes or making decisions with no important consequences for the subjects' own futures or those of others). The external validity limitations of such studies are well-known (see Janis & Mann, 1977; Tetlock, 1983d). In an innovative study of revolutionary leaders, Suedfeld and Rank (1976) showed that, unlike other measures of cognitive style that are linked to specific paper-and-pencil tests (e.g., the Dogmatism or Tolerance of Ambiguity scales, the Embedded Figures Test), the integrative complexity coding system is not tied to the coding of only Paragraph Completion Test responses. They also found that integrative complexity was a powerful predictor of which revolutionary leaders were and were not successful in retaining power after the success of their revolutionary movements.

Since then, a large number of studies have used the integrative complexity coding system to analyze a broad range of archival documents and to test an even broader range of hypotheses (Levi & Tetlock, 1980; Raphael, 1982; Suedfeld et al., 1977; Suedfeld & Tetlock, 1977; Tetlock, 1979, 1981a, 1981b, 1983a, 1983b, 1984; Tetlock et al., 1984, 1985).[2] These novel methodological applications of the coding system have enormously expanded the data base of integrative complexity theory. The coding system has been used to analyze diplomatic communications during major international crises, transcripts of Japanese cabinet meetings prior to the decision to attack the United States in 1941, pre- and postelection speeches of American presidents, confidential interviews with members of the British House of Commons, policy statements of U.S. senators, judicial opinions of Supreme Court justices, American and Soviet foreign policy rhetoric, and policy pronouncements of members of the former Soviet Politburo and Central Committee Secretariat. The "nomological network" (Cronbach & Meehl, 1955) surrounding the integrative complexity construct has expanded to include not only individual difference predictions, but a wide array of hypotheses concerning situational determinants of complex information processing that even the later "interactionist" theories of integrative complexity had not anticipated (e.g., hypotheses concerning the effects of role demands, accountability, groupthink, and value conflict on integrative complexity of functioning). Indeed, as we shall see, the very identity of integrative complexity as a purely cognitive construct has been challenged.

In brief, data generation has in this case outpaced theory generation (a situation similar in some respects to the state of cognitive dissonance literature in the late 1960s). In the next section I will examine some of the major findings that have emerged from the new wave of political psychology research on integrative complexity and will propose explanatory principles for organizing and interpreting these findings.

Some Major Recent Findings

Lewin's classic formula, Behavior = f(Person, Environment), summarizes a good deal of what has been learned about determinants of integrative complexity during the past twenty years. Today, we know that integrative complexity possesses some attributes of a relatively stable individual difference variable (moderate consistency across time, situations, and issues) and some attributes of a relatively context-specific variable (predictable variation as a function of situational and issue variables). Although much remains to be learned, we also have made some progress in delineating boundary conditions for when it is more or less useful to think of integrative complexity as an individual-difference versus context-specific variable. In short, our understanding of integrative complexity has itself become much more integratively complex.

The research on individual differences in integrative complexity among political leaders has largely focused on the relationships between political ideology and integrative complexity. The key question has been whether individuals who differ in ideological orientation (e.g., isolationists versus internationalists, liberals versus conservatives) also differ in the complexity of their styles of reasoning about policy issues. Two theoretical viewpoints (both of which treat integrative complexity as a stable dispositional property of the perceiver) have dominated speculation on this topic: the "rigidity-of-the-right" and "ideologue" hypotheses. The rigidity-of-the-right hypothesis derives from well-known work on the authoritarian personality. Authoritarian personality theory traces a cluster of beliefs—including political-economic conservatism, ethnocentrism, and cynicism and pessimism about human nature—to deeply rooted psychodynamic conflicts that, in turn, can be traced to the early parent-child relationship. Ambivalence toward authority figures motivates people to project their unacceptable hostile impulses onto outgroups toward whom they then adopt punitive stances. Conservative and nationalistic attitudes in this view frequently serve ego-defensive functions. Individuals who identify with the sociopolitical right are more likely than their centrist and left-wing counterparts to feel threatened by ambiguous or counterattitudinal information that challenges their political worldviews (information that, by implication, also challenges the elaborate network of defense mechanisms they have evolved to cope with unconscious needs and conflicts).

Critics, however, were quick to note the insensitivity of the above argument to "authoritarianism of the left" (Rokeach, 1956; Shils, 1958). An alternative view—the ideologue hypothesis—asserts that, although advocates of left-wing and right-wing political causes take dramatically different positions on many policy issues, they display very similar styles of reasoning about these issues. Differences in the content of left-wing and right-wing belief systems should not be allowed to obscure fundamental similarities in how ideologues organize and process political information. True believers (regardless of their cause) are held to be more dogmatic, intolerant of ambiguity, and integratively simple than their moderate counterparts who have resisted the absolutist doctrines of the left and right. In part, this relationship emerges because people with simple, dogmatic cognitive styles are naturally drawn to belief systems that offer clear-cut causal analyses of what is wrong with society and clear-cut solutions to those problems. There is a special affinity between the individual's cognitive structure and the cognitive structure of extremist ideologies. And, in part, this relationship emerges because extremist groups—in order to maintain in-group cohesion and identity in a hostile world—need to draw sharp ideological and group boundaries. In short, extremist groups "need" enemies.

Early Support for the Rigidity-of-the-Right Hypothesis

Tetlock (1981b) carried out the first of a series of studies of individual differences among U.S. senators in the integrative complexity of their policy statements. The study's primary goal was to test hypotheses derived from McClosky's (1967) classic study of personality correlates of isolationist foreign policy sentiment in the American public. On the basis of three national surveys in the 1950s in which a large battery of personality and attitude scales were administered, McClosky concluded that isolationists differed from nonisolationists on a variety of dimensions. Isolationists—particularly "jingoistic" or nationalistic ones who sought to insulate the United States from the rest of the world by overwhelming superiority of force—were more tolerant of ambiguity, closed to new experiences, prone to dichotomous (good-bad) forms of thinking, and likely to express strong positive affect toward in-groups (patriotic Americans) and strong negative affect toward out-groups (foreigners, communists). McClosky argued that psychodynamic processes similar to those hypothesized to underlie the authoritarian personality (Adorno et al., 1950) influenced the content and structure of isolationist belief systems. For instance, he proposed that the rigidly chauvinistic overtones in isolationism represented means of coping with severe inner conflicts and feelings of inferiority.

Tetlock (1981b) tested the generalizability of McClosky's psychological portrait of the isolationist to senators who held office in the 82nd Congress (1951–52). Speeches of senators were subjected to both integrative complexity coding and a complementary coding technique—

evaluative assertion analysis—for measuring the intensity of speakers' attitudes toward in-group and out-group symbols (see Osgood et al., 1956). Tetlock used the coding techniques to analyze randomly selected passages from foreign policy speeches of senators who had been classified, on the basis of Guttman scaling of their foreign policy voting patterns, as isolationist, ambivalent isolationist, and internationalist. The results strongly supported McClosky's analysis. Isolationists were much less integratively complex than nonisolationists. Relative to nonisolationists, isolationists also evaluated out-groups more negatively and in-groups more positively. Ambivalent isolationists fell between these two groups. Discriminant analysis indicated that the content-analytic indicators were powerful joint predictors of isolationist orientation. One highly significant discriminant function emerged that accounted for 41 percent of the total variation and permitted correct classification of 66 percent of the senators into the isolationist, ambivalent, and nonisolationist categories, against a chance accuracy rate of 37 percent.

McClosky, in short, appears to have been correct. Isolationist sentiment in the early post–World War II period—among both elites and followers—seems to have been a posture of belligerency in international affairs, one that had "more to do with hostility against foreign nations and disavowal for the well-being of others than with the considered assessment of the risks arising from foreign entanglements" (McClosky, 1967, p. 104). The isolationist relies heavily on "dichotomous thought processes, that lack breadth or perspective and that seek to exclude whatever is different, distant, or unfamiliar" (p. 107).

Tetlock (1983b) conducted a follow-up study of individual differences in integrative complexity among senators in the 94th Congress (1975–76)—a study that explored the relationships between complexity of (public) styles of reasoning and overall liberalism-conservatism of voting records.

Like the McClosky work on personality correlates of foreign policy preferences, research on cognitive stylistic correlates of liberalism-conservatism had been limited—until 1983—to self-report personality and attitude scales administered to survey respondents and college students. Stone (1980) concluded in his review of this literature that the preponderance of evidence is consistent with the rigidity-of-the-right hypothesis and inconsistent with the ideologue hypothesis. He noted that across a variety of measurement instruments and subject populations, right-wing respondents appear more dogmatic, intolerant of ambiguity, and conceptually undifferentiated than their left-wing and moderate counterparts (e.g., Barker, 1963; McClosky, 1967; Neumann, 1981; Wilson, 1973). These findings do not, of course indicate that there is no authoritarianism of the left (Eysenck, 1981). They indicate only that in twentieth-century Western democracies (e.g., Britain, the United States, Sweden) certain cognitive stylistic traits occur more frequently among members of the public conventionally classified as being on the sociopolitical right.

Many of these studies suffered from serious methodological problems. One recurring problem is potential ideological or content bias in self-report measures of cognitive style. A strong case could be made that "conservative" answers to scales designed to measure dogmatism, moral development, and tolerance of ambiguity lead to lower scores than do liberal answers (e.g., Johnson & Hogan, 1981). From this standpoint, the relation between cognitive style and political ideology may be a tautology. A second important objection concerns the seriousness of the respondents' commitment to the political views that they endorse. Are the respondents expressing more than vague sympathies or antipathies toward groups and causes? Disconcerting doubts on this score are raised by the substantial impact of question-wording manipulations (Schuman & Presser, 1981) and of response sets (acquiescence and social desirability) on the political positions that people stake out for themselves.

Although content-analytic archival studies suffer from serious inferential limitations of their own (see the qualifications that need to be attached to the results reported by Tetlock, 1983b), such studies allow us to avoid many of the methodological objections raised to the personality-and-politics literature. The data analysis techniques employed—integrative complexity coding (Schroder, Driver, & Streufert, 1967) and evaluative assertion analysis (Osgood, Saporta, & Nunnally, 1956)—allow one to derive cognitive structural indices that are, by definition, independent of the content of the arguments analyzed. It is possible to advance conceptually differentiated or undifferentiated claims in support of polar opposite positions on the political spectrum (Suedfeld & Rank, 1976; Tetlock, 1983a, 1984). And it is relatively easy for archival investigators to obtain access to articulate and influential advocates of a broad range of political positions. Moreover, the individuals under study are clearly not just expressing questionnaire opinions off the tops of their heads; they have made major personal commitments to particular ideological stands.

Tetlock (1983b) tested the rigidity-of-the-right and ideologue hypotheses by coding the integrative complexity of randomly selected passages drawn from speeches of senators whose voting records had been classified by political action groups (with almost perfect consensus) as extremely liberal, moderate, or extremely conservative. He found that senators with conservative voting records in the 94th Congress made less integratively complex policy statements (M = 1.79) than their moderate (M = 2.51) or liberal (M = 2.38) colleagues. This finding remained significant after controlling for a number of potential confounding variables, including political party affiliation, education, age, years of service in the Senate, and types of issues discussed.

These results converge impressively with previous work on nonelite samples, work which indicates that right-wing respondents score more highly than moderate and left-wing respondents on self-report measures of dogmatism, intolerance of ambiguity, and cognitive simplicity (for reviews, see Stone, 1980; Wilson, 1973). Nonetheless, two problems complicate interpretation of the results. The first problem stems from relying on public statements for inferring the cognitive styles of senators. Public policy statements may shed more light on how senators seek to influence other political actors (colleagues, the executive branch of government, the press) than on how senators actually think about policy issues. In short, conservatives may differ from moderates and liberals in *rhetorical* style, not *cognitive* style. The second problem stems from the limited ideological range of positions represented in the U.S. Senate. A defender of the ideologue hypothesis could argue that there were not enough representatives of the ideological left to provide a fair test of the hypothesis (i.e., there is no influential socialist or communist party in the United States). To clarify these issues, Tetlock (1984) and Tetlock et al. (1984, 1985) carried out a set of additional studies of the complexity-ideology relationship.

Later Support for the Ideologue Hypothesis

Tetlock (1984) reported a study that provided a stronger test of the complexity-ideology relationship than the earlier Tetlock (1983b) study of senators. The raw data consisted of confidential in-depth interviews that the political scientist Robert Putnam (1971) conducted with ninety-three members (MPs) of the British House of Commons. There is good reason to believe that impression management motives exerted much less influence on what the politicians said in this setting than in more public settings such as press conferences or in Parliament (see Putnam, 1971, for relevant evidence). The politicians interviewed were willing on several occasions to criticize their own party and even themselves in the course of the discussions. In addition, the politicians who were examined represented a wider variety of ideological positions than exists in the U.S. Senate. The MPs included extreme socialists (who favored the nationalization of all major industries), moderate socialists (who favored a mixed economy or balance of private and public enterprises), moderate conservatives (who favored limited denationalization of industry), and extreme conservatives (who opposed any government intervention in the economy).

Coders rated the integrative complexity of statements randomly drawn from the interviews with the MPs (Tetlock, 1984). The results revealed highly significant differences among the four ideological groups. Moderate socialists (M = 3.07) discussed issues in more integratively complex terms than extreme socialists (M = 2.17), moderate conservatives (M = 2.65), and extreme conservatives (M = 1.97). Moderate conservatives were more complex than extreme conservatives and extreme socialists. Extreme conservatives and socialists, the two groups most dissimilar in the content of their political beliefs, had the most similar levels of integrative complexity. After controlling for a variety of background variables as well as belief and attitudinal variables assessed in the Putnam research, these relationships between political ideology and integrative complexity remained highly significant.

In addition to its relationship to political ideology, integrative complexity was correlated with a host of relevant cognitive stylistic variables assessed in the original Putnam (1971) research. From these correlations emerges a more detailed portrait. The more integratively complex the politician, the more likely he or she was to (a) deemphasize the differences between the major political parties; (b) be tolerant of opposing viewpoints; (c) think about issues in relatively nonideological terms; and (d) be unconcerned with assigning blame for societal problems. In short, integrative complexity was associated with a pragmatic, open-minded, and nonpartisan worldview.

What interpretation should one attach to the links between political ideology and integrative complexity? At first glance, the data appear to vindicate advocates of the ideologue hypothesis. When the confidential statements of politicians who represented a wide spectrum of ideological positions were analyzed, extremists of the left and right were found to be similar to each other in styles of reasoning, but different from individuals closer to the center of the political spectrum. The ideologue hypothesis, however, leaves important questions unanswered. Why does the point of maximum integrative complexity consistently appear to be displaced to the political left of center? Why, for instance, were both liberals and moderates more integratively complex than conservatives in the U.S. Senate? Why were moderate socialists more integratively complex than moderate conservatives in the British House of Commons? The ideologue hypothesis is not explanatory, but rather descriptive. It simply asserts that as one departs from an ill-defined political center or midpoint, one is increasingly prone to view issues in simple, dichotomous terms. What determines where this mysterious midpoint lies? Why are liberals and moderate socialists apparently closer to it than conservatives? Why was it necessary to go as "far out to the political left" as "radical socialists" to find a marked decline in the integrative complexity of thought? Advocates of the ideologue hypothesis need to offer defensible and explicit criteria for specifying the conditions that must be satisfied to test the hypothesis.

A Value Pluralism Model of Ideological Reasoning

Both the rigidity-of-the-right and ideologue hypotheses assume that it is possible to map multidimensional political belief systems onto a unidimensional left–right measurement scale. Such mapping exercises can be done, of course, but the price in loss of knowledge is substantial. People try to achieve a wide range of objectives through political action—objectives that often do not correlate nearly as highly as one would expect if one assumed that people structure their thought along conventional ideological lines (Converse, 1964; Lane, 1973). It is not hard, for example, to identify people (including policy elites) who are liberal on social welfare policy but conservative on defense, conservative on social welfare policy but liberal on defense, or liberal or conservative across the board except, say, on environmental protection and civil liberties issues. Researchers ignore this multidimensional variation at their peril. As we shall see in the next section (ideology-by-issue interactions), the relationships between integrative complexity and political ideology take different forms in different issue domains.

Equally problematic, it is often unclear how to define the left–right continuum in non-Western political systems. For instance, Tetlock and Boettger (1989b) note the enormous problems that arise in applying the rigidity-of-the-right and ideologue hypotheses to the former Soviet Union. They found that reformist Soviet politicians (advocates of at least limited political liberalization and economic decentralization) tended to be more integratively complex than traditionalists (opponents of these measures). This finding could be construed as support for the ideologue hypothesis. Traditionalists arguably represent the extreme left, which resists the introduction of market mechanisms and individual incentives into the centrally planned Soviet economy; reformers arguably represent the right, which is willing to compromise Marxist-Leninist principles in order to stimulate efficiency and individual initiative and creativity (an effort to achieve some form of mixed economy). As one moves in from the far (rigid state control) left, one discovers greater integrative complexity. Alternatively, this same finding could be construed as support for the rigidity-of-the-right hypothesis. Soviet traditionalists, like American conservatives, are arguably more likely to be authoritarian personalities who are deeply committed to traditional in-group symbols and to resent attempts to tamper with system fundamentals (e.g., the Protestant or socialist work ethic, law and order, free enterprise or central planning, support for "free world" or "progressive" regimes abroad). As one moves toward the right (more ethnocentric, nationalistic forms of ideology), one discovers less integrative complexity.

To avoid conceptual dilemmas of this sort, we need a theoretical model that satisfies three key requirements. The model should not force political belief systems into a simple one-dimensional classification scheme. The model should allow for the possibility that advocates of different viewpoints reason in more or less complex patterns in different issue domains. The model also should not be limited to descriptive correlational hypotheses (e.g., as one moves in this or that direction on an attitude continuum, integrative complexity of reasoning rises or falls). The model should focus on the underlying social-cognitive processes that shape the complexity of political thought. And, finally, the model should yield reasonably specific predictions concerning the forms that complexity-ideology relationships will take in different issue domains and political systems. The model, in brief, should be simultaneously subtle and falsifiable.

The value pluralism model of ideological reasoning is an attempt to fill this theoretical void. The value pluralism model can be summarized in the following two general sets of propositions. (1) Underlying all political ideologies are core or "terminal" values (Lane, 1973; Rokeach, 1973, 1979) that specify what the ultimate goals of public policy should be (e.g., economic efficiency, social equality, individual freedom, crime control, national security). Ideologies vary not only in the types of values to which they assign high priority (Rokeach, 1973), but in the degree to which high-priority values are acknowledged to be in tension or conflict with each other. In monistic ideologies, high priority is attached to only one value or set of values that, it is claimed, are highly consistent with each other. In pluralistic ideologies, high priority is attached to values that are recognized to be in frequent, even intense, conflict with each other. Important values often point to contradictory policies (e.g., "I value social equality, but dislike paying for it through taxes," "I want to protect the environment, but don't want to slow economic growth"). (2) Advocates of the "most pluralistic" ideologies should exhibit the most integratively complex styles of reasoning. This prediction is based on Abelson's (1959, 1968b) influential work on the strategies people use for resolving cognitive inconsistency in belief systems. Abelson maintained that, *whenever feasible,* people prefer modes of resolving cognitive inconsistency that are simple and require minimal mental effort. (People, in this view, are "lazy organisms" or "cognitive misers"; (Fiske & Taylor 1991; McGuire, 1969). Simple modes of resolving inconsistency are feasible when the conflicting values activated by a policy choice are of very unequal strength. It is then easy to deny the less important value and to bolster the more important one, a process that consistency theorists described as a "spreading of alternatives."

By contrast, simple modes of inconsistency reduction are much less practical for advocates of pluralistic ideologies. When conflicting values are of approximately equal strength, denial of one value and bolstering of the other are much less plausible coping strategies (Abelson, 1959, 1968b). People must turn to strategies that demand more effort, such as differentiation (e.g., distinguishing the impact of policies on conflicting values) and integration (developing rules or schemata for coping with trade-offs between important values). For instance, in domestic policy debates, liberals and social democrats are most committed to the often conflicting values of social equality and economic freedom (see Rokeach, 1973, 1979). They are therefore under the greatest psychological pressure to take into account the effects of policy proposals on both values as well as to develop guidelines or criteria for finding appropriate compromises between the two values (compromises that may, of course, have to take different forms in different economic and political circumstances).

To summarize, the value pluralism of an ideology determines both the frequency with which people experience cognitive inconsistency and the complexity of the strategies they rely on to cope with inconsistency. A value pluralism analysis of the complexity-ideology relationship has several noteworthy advantages. It not only helps to explain existing data, but it leads to a variety of novel and testable theoretical predictions—a number of which have subsequently been supported.

With respect to existing data, the value pluralism model is well-positioned to explain why several studies have found that advocates of centrist and moderate left-wing causes tend to interpret issues in more integratively complex ways than do advocates of conservative causes. Evidence from survey studies of the general public and from content analyses of political writings suggests that advocates of centrist and moderate left-wing causes are more likely to hold at least partly contradictory values. They are likely to value both social equality and economic freedom, economic growth and environmental protection, civil liberties and crime control, and deterring aggressors and avoiding spirals of conflict. From this standpoint, the point of maximum integrative complexity is often displaced to the left of center because that is the point of maximum value pluralism, at least on many issues (Sniderman & Tetlock, 1986c).

The value pluralism model also clarifies how far to the sociopolitical left or right one must go for integrative complexity to decline, i.e., to the point where conflict between core values begins to diminish sharply. For instance, in domestic policy debates, one would expect to—and actually does—find a sharp reduction in integrative complexity as one moves from moderate socialists (who, according to Rokeach, 1973, place nearly equal importance on freedom and equality) to extreme socialists (for whom concern for equality seems to dominate concern for individual economic rights). Similarly, one would expect to find—and does—a reduction in integrative complexity as one moves from moderate socialists to moderate conservatives (for whom economic freedom is a dominant value) to extreme conservatives (for whom economic freedom is the overwhelmingly dominant value.)

Although the value pluralism model can account for existing data on ideological "main effects" in integrative complexity, the model strongly implies that traditional trait analyses of the complexity-ideology relationship are useful only within limits. We should not assume that certain ideological groups will always be more integratively complex than other groups; rather, we should expect ideology-by-issue and ideology-by-role interactions in the integrative complexity of styles of reasoning.

Ideology-by-Issue Interactions in Integrative Complexity

One key determinant of the feasibility of simple modes of resolving value conflict is the degree to which the policy domain under discussion activates conflicting values of approximately equal strength. And value conflict may well be most intense in different issue domains for different ideological groups. For instance, American conservatives in the 1980s experienced their most intense value conflicts over such issues as defense spending (e.g., national security versus fiscal restraint or economic recovery) or compulsory military service (e.g., national security versus individual liberty). Liberals experienced their most intense value conflicts over such issues as redistributive income policies (e.g., equality versus economic efficiency or individual economic rights).

Two studies have revealed support for ideology-by-issue interaction predictions of the value pluralism model. In one study, Tetlock et al. (1985) examined the relations between integrative complexity and political ideology among U.S. Supreme Court justices who served on the Court between 1946 and 1978. The study assessed the integrative complexity of opinions that each of twenty-five justices authored (or at least signed) as well as the overall liberalism-conservatism of each justice's voting record (Tate, 1981). Consistent with past work on senators, justices with liberal and moderate voting records exhibited more integratively complex styles of reasoning than did justices with conservative voting records. However, these relationships between integrative complexity and political ideology were more powerful on cases involving economic conflicts of interest (e.g., labor versus management, business versus government) than on cases involving civil liberties issues (e.g., First Amendment due process and questions). Tetlock et al. argued that civil liberties issues were more likely to activate shared elite values— common to both liberals and conservatives—such as constitutional protections for freedom of speech and press and due process of law (see McClosky & Brill, 1983). The competing ideological groups were less likely, therefore, to experience differential value conflict on these issues. By contrast, much less value consensus probably existed on the economic conflict of interest cases (see Chong et al., 1983). Good reasons exist, moreover, for suspecting value conflict in this policy domain to be more intense for liberals than for conservatives (a policy domain that frequently activates conflicts between private economic interests and public ones).

In a second study, Tetlock (1986) obtained direct experimental evidence for the hypothesized role of value conflict in promoting integratively complex thought. Two types of information were collected from a nonelite (college student) sample: (1) subjects' rank-order evaluations of the importance of each of eighteen terminal values from the Rokeach Value Survey (values included national security, natural beauty, economic prosperity, equality, and freedom); (2) subjects' support for six public policy positions and their thoughts on each issue (e.g., redistributive income policies, domestic CIA activities, defense spending). Each of the public policy issues had been selected on the basis of pretest scaling data which indicated that the issue brought at least two values from the Rokeach Value Study into conflict (e.g., the defense spending question was phrased in such a way as to activate tension between the values of national security and economic prosperity). On five of six issues a significant trend was found for people to report more integratively complex thoughts to the degree that the issue domain activated conflicting values that people held to be (a) important in their value hierarchy and (b) close to equally important. This study provides strong evidence that the intensity of value conflict between basic political values does indeed influence the complexity of thought in that domain.

These data have important implications for existing theories of cognitive style and decision-making. The data suggest that the sharp distinction that some cognitive-style theorists have drawn between the content and structure of thought processes is an artificial one (Schroder et al., 1967; Streufert & Streufert, 1978; Suedfeld, 1983). What people think (the basic values they hold and the types of problems they are trying to solve) often constrains how they think (the complexity of their reasoning). Content and structure are closely intertwined, and efforts to analyze structure in isolation from content can produce highly misleading conclusions. Debates over the cross-issue or cross-situation generality of individual differences in complexity of thought also need to be reformulated. It should be possible to find evidence for either specificity or generality depending on whether the issues sampled in a study activate similar conflicting values and depending on the correlations that exist among respondents' values (see Bowers, 1973, on the futility of the trait versus situation debate in general).

Political Roles and Integrative Complexity

Intensity of value conflict is a major, but not the only possible, determinant of the integrative complexity of people's reasoning about a policy domain. For instance, political roles appear to exert an important influence. Some roles seem to encourage integrative complexity; others, integrative simplicity.

A particularly powerful variable in this regard is the distinction between being "in power" (the policy-making role) and "out of power" (the opposition role). Governing a country—developing policies one actually expects to implement—is generally a more integratively complex task than opposing the government. In a world of scarce resources, the policy-making role inevitably requires making unpopular trade-off decisions (Katz & Kahn, 1978; Thurow, 1980) that, at least in democracies, must be justified to skeptical constituencies motivated to argue against positions one has taken (e.g., explaining to various interest groups why it was not possible to satisfy all of their conflicting demands). Integrative complexity is needed both at the level of private thought (to work out viable compromise policies that at least partly satisfy major constituencies) and of public rhetoric (to develop cogent two-sided appeals that sensitize antagonized constituencies to the complexity of the policy-making role) (see McGuire, 1985; Tetlock, 1983a).

There are far fewer pressures on opposition politicians to think or speak in integratively complex terms. The mass electorate possesses little knowledge of major policy issues and little motivation to think carefully about political messages or to defend the government (see Kinder & Sears, 1985; Sniderman & Tetlock, 1986b). The essence of the opposition role is to rally antigovernment sentiment—a goal that is most effectively achieved not by evenhanded "on the one hand" and "on the other" rhetoric, but by constructing easily understood (integratively simple) and memorable attacks on the government. In the opposition role, one is free to find fault, to focus selectively on the shortcomings of proposals advanced by those in power and on the advantages of one's own proposals.

Several studies support the claim that the policy-making role encourages integrative complexity. Suedfeld and Rank (1976), for instance, observed that revolutionary leaders (from several nations) made more integratively complex statements after coming to power than before coming to power. Perhaps even more telling, Suedfeld and Rank (1976) also found that revolutionary leaders who retained power in the postrevolutionary period were much more likely to display such upward shifts in integrative complexity than were leaders who failed to retain power. Tetlock (1981a) observed a similar upward shift in the integrative complexity of policy statements that American presidents issued during election campaigns and immediately after coming to power (postinauguration). Most twentieth-century presidents apparently have believed that, although integratively simple rhetoric is useful for rallying popular support during elections, it is politically prudent once they have assumed office to present issues in more integratively complex terms. Tetlock et al. (1985) have even found evidence for the "in-power"/"out-of-power" complexity shift among (life-tenured) Supreme Court justices. Judicial opinions for the majority (which thus have the force of law) tended to be more integratively complex than dissenting or minority opinions. And Tetlock and Boettger (1989) have reported that "reformist" Soviet politicians became more integratively complex after Gorbachev and his political allies gained working control of the Politburo and Central Committee Secretariat.

Transitions in political roles do not, however, affect all ideological groups equally. Tetlock et al. (1984) examined the integrative complexity of liberal, moderate, and conservative senators in five congresses, three dominated by liberals and moderates (the 82d, 94th, and 96th) and two dominated by conservatives (the 83rd and 97th). Tetlock et al. found that liberals and moderates were more integratively complex than conservatives in the Democratic-controlled 82nd, 94th, and 96th congresses, replicating the earlier Tetlock (1983b) findings. However, when the political balance of power shifted in favor of conservatives (e.g., in 1953 and 1981 when the Republicans gained control of both the Senate and the presidency), the complexity-ideology relationship disappeared. No significant differences existed in integrative complexity as a function of political ideology. Interestingly, this pattern resulted from *sharp declines* in the integrative complexity of liberals and moderates in the Republican-dominated congresses, not to an increase in the integrative complexity of conservatives. Conservatives displayed much more traitlike stability in integrative complexity both within and across congresses.

In a similar vein, Tetlock and Boettger found that whereas reformist politicians in the former Soviet Union increased the integrative complexity of their policy statements on coming to power, traditionalist Soviet politicians were relatively unaffected by the power transition. Soviet traditionalists, like American conservatives, displayed more trait-like stability in their levels of integrative complexity across time.

These findings point to an important qualification to the value pluralism model's prediction of greater integrative complexity among liberals and moderates than among conservatives. Liberals and moderates may present issues in more integratively complex terms only when they are forced, so to speak, by their political role to confront the tensions between basic values inherent in their ideological outlooks. Conservatives, with their presumably more internally consistent value systems, are relatively unaffected by shifts in political role. There is less potential value conflict that they can be forced to confront.

It also should be noted that the archival evidence on links between political roles and integrative complexity is highly consistent with recent experimental evidence on the effects of accountability on complexity of reasoning. The policy-making role is, in a sense, one of high accountability. One can be called on by a variety of constituencies to justify what one has done. Moreover, one is potentially accountable not only for the short-term consequences of one's policies, but for the (more unpredictable) long-term consequences. The opposition role, in a sense, is of low accountability. One has the rhetorical freedom to focus single-mindedly on the flaws in the other side's position. Experimental data suggest that the types of accountability created in policy-making roles are indeed likely to promote integratively complex reasoning by subjects on policy issues (see Tetlock, 1983a, 1983e, 1985b; Tetlock & Kim, 1987). Accountability, especially to unknown or multiple constituencies, appears to encourage subjects to engage in "preemptive self-criticism"—to attempt to anticipate a variety of potential critics' objections to the policy stands subjects have taken.[3]

The Normative Issue: *When Is It Better to Be More Complex?*

The answer to the question When is it better to be more complex? is complex itself. To begin, it is critical to distinguish the adaptive value of integrative complexity at two very different levels of analysis: public rhetoric and private thought. With respect to public rhetoric, it is not hard to imagine political situations in which it is to one's advantage to feign simplicity—to present issues in stark, evaluatively polarized terms in order to rally popular support for a cause (e.g., by convincing the electorate of the incompetence or venality of one's opposition, by convincing hard-liners within a revolutionary movement of one's ideological purity) or to demonstrate one's resolve to an adversary (e.g., by striking a tough initial bargaining posture). Although it may be a little more difficult to imagine, there also undoubtedly are political situations in which it is to one's advantage to feign complexity—to pretend to respect alternative points of view that one, in fact, holds in contempt (e.g., to appease an influential constituency or to pull together a coalition government). In brief, different political situations call for rhetorical responses of widely varying levels of integrative complexity.

   The above argument points to a paradoxically simple answer to the original question of whether it is better to be integratively simple or complex. The shrewd politician uses an integratively complex set of *private* decision rules in determining whether it is prudent to be integratively simple or complex in *public* statements in particular situations. From this point of view, simplicity in many situations may be a sign of complexity.

Is it always better, however, to be integratively complex at the level of private thought? Careful analysis suggests two persuasive reasons for a negative answer. First, and perhaps most obvious, one needs to take into account the cognitive and motivational costs of complexity—the time required for integratively complex thought (time in many business and political situations translates into money and even lives) and the effort required by integratively complex thought (it is not easy or pleasant to acknowledge trade-offs among important values or the possibility that one has already made major mistakes). As contingency decision theorists have long been aware (e.g., Einhorn & Hogarth, 1981; Payne, 1982; Simon, 1957), people must decide how to decide. Implicitly or explicitly, they must judge whether the likely benefits of complex information processing outweigh the likely costs. Second, there is no guarantee that the benefits will indeed outweigh the costs. Integratively complex thought is neither a necessary nor a sufficient condition for making wise political decisions. It is possible to be complex and wrong. A leader may see trade-offs when none exist, see intricate interactive relationships among causal variables when only one or two "main effects" are present, and be willing to "see the point of view" of expansionist states that claim to be motivated by purely defensive concerns. And it is possible to be simple and right. A leader may correctly conclude that the long-term well-being of his or her people is best served by persistently pursuing a particular policy line and not allowing events to deflect policy off that course. Simple heuristics can serve decision-makers well even in highly complex, probabilistic environments (e.g., Kleinmuntz & Kleinmuntz, 1981).

There is no simple normative rule that, once the relevant situational parameters have been specified, points to an optimal level of integrative complexity in political reasoning. Here, the experimental literature is a useful guide. We know there are situations in which experimental manipulations that encourage integratively complex thought lead to improved judgmental performance. Integratively complex information processors are less likely to make confident judgments about the personalities of others in response to fragmentary and unrepresentative behavioral evidence (Tetlock, 1985b), are more likely to change their first impressions of others in response to new evidence (Tetlock, 1983b), and are less likely to be excessively confident in the correctness of their factual beliefs and predictions (Tetlock & Kim, 1987). And we know that there are some situations in which experimental manipulations that encourage integrative complexity interfere with judgmental performance. Tetlock and

Boettger (1989b), for instance, report that integratively complex thinkers are more susceptible to the "dilution effect" (Nisbett, Zukier, & Lemley, 1981) than are integratively simple thinkers. Complex thinkers attempt to integrate a variety of information in sizing up situations and in making predictions—a tendency that is often adaptive, but quite maladaptive in environments in which there is only *one* predictively valid cue surrounded by a host of irrelevant, distractor cues. The result is that, relative to simple thinkers, complex thinkers inappropriately "dilute" (make less extreme) predictions. A recent experiment may have identified another setting in which integrative complexity can be maladaptive. A simulation of the cost-benefit decision-making of the Food and Drug Administration found that complex thinkers were more likely than simple thinkers to procrastinate and buckpass to avoid making decisions that would impose costs on others, even if a much larger group stood to gain and there was little prospect of further evidence changing that estimate.

In other words, empirical research and logical analysis converge on a common conclusion. One's assessments of the soundness of political judgments and decisions should hinge on much more than the structural complexity of the reasoning that underlies the judgments and decisions; such assessments also should hinge on the *content* of the reasoning and on one's assumptions about the nature of the political environment confronting the decision-makers. From a normative standpoint, the integrative complexity construct can be usefully broken down into a 2 x 2 Peabody (1967) plot in which the denotative and connotative meanings of the construct are disentangled. Integrative simplicity may signify simple-minded inability or stubborn unwillingness to recognize the true complexity of the world, or it may signify keen appreciation for the underlying simple processes at work in an only superficially complex world. Integrative complexity may signify cognitively sophisticated appreciation for the true complexity of the world or it may signify muddled or indecisive patterns of thinking that are insensitive to the simple processes that actually drive events.[4] Judgments of procedural rationality ultimately hinge as much on ontology as on psychology.

Concluding Remarks: *The Need for a Flexible Functionalist Framework*

The data discussed in this chapter can be viewed from a wide range of theoretical perspectives. There is something for almost everybody. Advocates of authoritarian personality theory can point to the frequently replicated and powerful relationship between integrative simplicity and political conservatism. They also can point to the greater trait-like consistency of conservative thought. Advocates of the ideologue hypothesis can note the cognitive stylistic similarities between extreme conservatives and socialists in the British House of Commons. Role theorists and symbolic interactionists can note that how people think about political issues depends on the institutional role they occupy and the political balance of power. Advocates of the value pluralism model can note that how people think about political issues depends on the degree to which issues bring important values into clear conflict with each other.

Given the range of findings reported here, it is tempting to agree with McGuire's (1983) radically contextualist perspective on theory-testing in social psychology. All hypotheses, he argues, are under some conditions true. Research is a "discovery process to make clear the meaning of the hypothesis, disclosing its hidden assumptions and thus clarifying the circumstances under which it is false" (McGuire, 1983, p. 7). From this standpoint, work on the links between cognitive style and political ideology has been successful in illuminating boundary conditions for the applicability of the rigidity-of-the-right and ideologue hypotheses. Both hypotheses highlight certain interesting empirical regularities but blind us to others—in particular, to the impact of value conflict, political role, and accountability demands on political thought. Many people (although not all) display styles of political reasoning that are much more responsive to situational demands than the personality-trait perspectives led us to expect.

What kind of theory can explain all of the data? My current nomination would be for an updated version of the classic functionalist theories of Smith, Bruner, and White (1956) and Katz (1960). From a functionalist perspective, the key theoretical question is: Of what use to a person is a particular pattern or style of political reasoning? It is possible to organize existing research findings by invoking a fairly small number of functionalist postulates:

(1) All other things being equal, people generally prefer integratively simple styles of political reasoning. Integratively simple reasoning requires relatively little mental effort (people are assumed to be "cognitive misers") and makes few emotional demands (it does not require acknowledging painful value trade-offs). These straightforward assumptions help to explain why integrative complexity scores tend to be so positively skewed (it is not unusual for 50 percent or more of the assigned scores to be at the lowest scale value).

(2) People can be motivated to think in integratively complex ways.

Integratively complex reasoning is especially useful in coping with both intrapsychic and political conflict. The value pluralism model, for example, suggests that complex reasoning is a common coping response to intrapsychic conflict—to policy problems that clearly bring important values in conflict (e.g., lives vs. economic growth, liberty vs. crime control). Work on political roles and accountability suggests that complex reasoning is more common when people expect to be held personally responsible for the consequences of their actions or when people need to justify their actions to constituencies with unknown or conflicting policy preferences.

(3) Individual differences exist in thresholds for the activation of coping responses to integrative complexity. Some individuals—in both archival and experimental settings—show remarkably little variability in the integrative complexity of their political reasoning. These highly consistent individuals also tend to have low average scores on the complexity scale and to be politically conservative. From the perspective of authoritarian personality theory, this finding is not surprising (individuals with fragile psychic systems should feel particularly threatened by ambiguity and rely on integratively simple coping responses). The psychodynamic interpretation is not, however, the only possible functionalist explanation. These individuals may, for example, find the cognitive strain of integratively complex reasoning to be especially unpleasant (Tetlock, 1986). Or they may have concluded, in a rational metacognitive way, that the net benefits of integrative simplicity outweigh those of complexity in the decision-making environments they typically confront.

The list of functionalist themes invoked here is by no means exhaustive. Other motives—for example, concern for cognitive mastery or for protecting one's self-image or social image—undoubtedly play important roles in shaping how people think (Tetlock, 1985b). The various functional goals also come into conflict with each other. Minimilization of mental effort quickly collides with the goal of finding integratively complex solutions to policy problems that satisfy opposing values or constituencies. Maintaining psychological equilibrium in authoritarian personalities often may make it difficult to accept the accommodations and trade-offs necessary to achieve other personal or social goals. It is certainly reasonable to expect a functionalist theory of political thought to be both more comprehensive in specifying motives and more precise in specifying interrelations among motives than I have been here. I have simply sketched the general form that a functionalist explanation of the data will probably have to take.

Finally, it is appropriate to close with a warning. McGuire's contextualist perspective reminds us not to grow too attached to our theories. The first-order interactions of today can easily become the second- or higher-order interactions of tomorrow. Research to date has revealed that the complexity-ideology relationship depends on the intensity of value conflict activated within an issue domain and on one's social-political role. Future research may well show that increased integrative complexity of thought is by no means the only possible coping response to intense intrapsychic or political cross-pressures. Some people may respond by rigid, defensive bolstering, denial, or procrastination (Janis & Mann, 1977; Tetlock, 1985a; Tetlock, Boettger, & Skitka, 1989). Future research may reveal that in some political contexts, extremism is associated with greater cognitive flexibility and multidimensionality than centrism. And future research may reveal that in some political contexts, opposition factions display more integratively complex patterns of reasoning than do ruling factions. The functionalist perspective per se is not testable (it is possible to generate post hoc functionalist explanations for any finding). The functionalist perspective is, however, heuristically provocative; it leads to new ways of thinking about the content, structure, and adaptability of political thought. And, perhaps most important, the functionalist perspective is sufficiently flexible to accommodate the complex, context-dependent relationships that so frequently emerge in this line of inquiry.

Notes

Preparation of this chapter was assisted by the Institute on Global Conflict and Cooperation and by the Institute of Personality and Social Research at the University of California, Berkeley. Correspondence concerning this chapter should be sent to Philip E. Tetlock, Department of Psychology, 3210 Tolman Hall, University of California, Berkeley, CA 94720.

1. Although training coders to reliably assess the integrative complexity of texts is a fairly time-consuming process, integrative complexity coding is considerably less time-consuming than such content analysis systems as cognitive mapping (Axelrod, 1976) and evaluative assertion analysis (Osgood et al., 1956). And integrative complexity scores are highly correlated with relevant cognitive structural indices derived from these other techniques (e.g., Levi & Tetlock, 1980; Tetlock, 1979, 1981b).

2. A number of methodological precautions need to be taken in this type of archival research—precautions taken in all of the major studies discussed in this chapter. Perhaps the most obvious and elementary safeguard is the employment

of double-blind coding procedures. Coders should be unaware of the hypotheses being tested and, to the extent possible, the sources of the materials coded. In scoring controversial material, it also is helpful to include coders on the research team from diverse political viewpoints and to check on potential ideological contamination of coding judgments by planting "test paragraphs" (simple and complex paragraphs that cover a broad range of political positions). It is useful to remind coders repeatedly that there is no necessary relationship between the structural complexity of an argument and their judgments of its moral or political appropriateness (a key theme of the complexity coding manual). It is not hard to find integratively complex advocacies of positions that, given contemporary political norms, are widely viewed as immoral (e.g., the complex arguments of antiabolitionists in pre-Civil War America or complex arguments of classical economic theorists in the early nineteenth century in opposition to aid to starving children). Nor is it hard to find examples of integratively simple statements that now provoke wide moral approval (e.g., simple arguments of those who opposed the appeasement of Nazi Germany in the 1930s or de jure segregation in the American South).

3. Integratively complex thought is by no means the only possible coping response to accountability demands. Tetlock, Boettger, and Skitka (1989) report experimental support for the hypotheses that (a) people who are accountable to an audience with known views cope by moving their views toward those of the prospective audience (strategic attitude shifting), but do not become more or less integratively complex; (b) people who are accountable to an audience with unknown views cope by thinking in more integratively complex ways (preemptive self-criticism); (c) people who are accountable for positions they have already taken (and are difficult to reverse) cope by thinking in less integratively complex ways (defensive bolstering). These coping strategies need not always be mutually exclusive. Politicians may rely on shifting combinations of coping strategies: moving toward a complex, middle-ground position when accountable to conflicting or unknown constituencies, and downplaying differences with the audience except when those differences are undeniable—in which case, they may bolster or engage in overjustification.

4. The argument here is strikingly reminiscent of Brunswik's (1956) ecological functionalism. Integratively simple information processors (who rely on only one or two nonredundant "proximal" cues in making inferences about true states of the world) are likely to perform well in environments characterized by simple ecological function forms but to run into serious difficulty in more complex environments (environments in which proximal cues are related to true states of the world in subtle interactive or nonlinear patterns). There is no guarantee that integratively complex information processors will successfully master complex ecological function forms, but they certainly have a better chance of doing so than integratively simple thinkers.

References

Abelson R. 1959. Modes of resolution of belief dilemmas. *Journal of Conflict Resolution*, 3, 343–352.

―――. 1968a. Simulation of social behavior. In G. Lindzey and E. Aronson (eds.), *The Handbook of Social Psychology*, vol. 2. 2nd ed. Reading, MA: Addison-Wesley.

―――. 1968b. Psychological implication. In R. Abelson et al. (eds.), *Theories of Cognitive Consistency: A Sourcebook*. Chicago: Rand McNally.

―――. 1988. Conviction. *American Psychologist*, 43, 267–275.

Abelson, R., Aronson, E., McGuire, W., Newcomb, T., Rosenberg, M., and Tannenbaum, P. (eds.). 1968. *Theories of Cognitive Consistency: A Sourcebook*. Chicago: Rand McNally.

Abelson, R., Kinder, D., Peters, M., and Fiske, S. 1982. Affective and semantic components in political person perception. *Journal of Personality and Social Psychology*, 42, 619–630.

Abramowitz, A. 1978. The impact of a presidential debate on voter rationality. *American Journal of Political Science*, 22, 680–690.

Achen, C. 1975. Mass political attitudes and the survey response. *American Political Science Review*, 69, 1218–1231.

Acton, J. 1907. *Historical Essays and Studies*. London: Macmillan.

Adorno, T., Frenkel-Brunswik, E., Levinson, D., and Sanford, N. 1950. *The Authoritarian Personality*. New York: Harper.

Ajzen, I., and Fishbein, M. 1980. *Understanding Attitudes and Predicting Social Behavior*. Englewood Cliffs, NJ: Prentice-Hall.

Alba, J., and Hasher, L. 1983. Is memory schematic? *Psychological Bulletin*, 93, 203–231.

Aldrich, J., Borgida, E., Rahn, W., and Klein, S. 1988. Is voter decision-making candidate centered? Presented at annual meeting of American Political Science Association, Washington, DC, September 2.

Aldrich, J., Sullivan, J., and Borgida, E. 1989. Foreign affairs and issue voting:

do presidential candidates "waltz before a blind audience?" *American Political Science Review*, 83, 123–141.

Alesina, A., and Cukierman, A. 1987. Asymmetric information and policy consequences in a two-party system. NBER Working Paper No. 2468.

Allen, V., and Wilder, D. 1975. Categorization, belief similarity and intergroup discrimination. *Journal of Personality and Social Psychology*, 32, 971–977.

Allington, R. 1980. Teacher interruption behaviors during primary grade oral reading. *Journal of Educational Psychology*, 72, 371–377.

Almond, G. 1954. *The Appeals of Communism*. Princeton, NJ: Princeton University Press.

Almond, G., and Verba, S. 1963. *The Civic Culture*. Boston: Little, Brown.

Alwin, D. 1991. Aging, personality and social change. In D. Featherman, R. Lerner, and M. Perlmutter (eds.), *Life-span Development and Behavior,* vol. 12. Hillsdale, NJ: Lawrence Erlbaum Associates.

Alwin, D., and Krosnick, J. 1988. Aging, cohorts, and change in political orientation: exploring the aging-attitude stability relationship. Presented at annual meeting of International Society of Political Psychology, Secaucus, NJ.

Anderson, J. 1983. *The Architecture of Cognition*. Cambridge, MA: Harvard University Press.

Anderson, N. 1971. Integration theory and attitude change. *Psychological Review*, 78, 171–206.

———. 1982. *Methods of Information Integration Theory*. New York: Academic Press.

———. 1988. A functional approach to person cognition. In T. Srull and R. Wyer (eds.), *Advances in Social Cognition: A Dual Process Model of Impression Formation*. Hillsdale, NJ: Lawrence Erlbaum Associates.

Anderson, N., and Hubert, S. 1963. Effects of concomitant verbal recall on order effects in personality impression formation. *Journal of Verbal Learning and Verbal Behavior*, 2, 379–391.

Anderson, N. H. 1965. Averaging versus adding as a stimulus-combination rule in impression formation. *Journal of Experimental Psychology*, 70, 394–400.

Anderson, R., Reynolds, R., Schallert, D., and Goetz, E. 1976. Frameworks for comprehending discourse. Technical Report No. 12. Urbana: Laboratory of Cognitive Studies in Education, University of Illinois.

Anderson, T. 1978. Becoming sane with psychohistory. *The Historian,* 41, 1–20.

Ansolabehere, S. 1988. Rational choice and the puzzle of negative voting: a random utilities model of the vote. Presented at annual meeting of Midwest Political Science Association.

Ansolabehere, S., Iyengar, S., and Simon, A. 1990. Good news, bad news, and economic voting. Presented at annual meeting of American Political Science Association.

Arad, Y. 1987. *Belzec, Sobibor, Treblinka: The Operation Reinhard Death Camps*. Bloomington: Indiana University Press.

Archer, D., and Gartner, R. 1984. *Violence and Crime in Cross-National Perspective.* New Haven, CT: Yale University Press.

Ariès, P. 1960. *L'enfant et la vie familiale sous l'ancien régime.* Paris: Plon. ([1962]. R. Baldick, trans., *Centuries of Childhood: A Social History of Family Life.* New York: Knopf.)

———. 1977. L'homme devant la mort. Paris: Éditions du Seuil. ([1981]. H. Weaver, trans., *The Hour of Our Death.* New York: Knopf.)

Arkin, R., and Duval, S. 1975. Focus of attention and causal attribution of actors and observers. *Journal of Experimental Social Psychology,* 11, 427–438.

Arnold, A. 1960. *Emotion and Personality.* New York: Columbia University Press.

Aronson, E., Turner, J., and Carlsmith, J. 1963. Communicator credibility and communication discrepancy as determinants of opinion change. *Journal of Abnormal and Social Psychology,* 67, 31–36.

Asch, S. 1940. Studies in the principles of judgments and attitudes: II. determination of judgments by group and by ego standards. *Journal of Society Psychology,* 12, 433–465.

———. 1946. Forming impressions of personality. *Journal of Abnormal and Social Psychology,* 41, 258–290.

Asher, H. 1983. Voting behavior research in the 1980s: an examination of some old and new problem areas. In A. Finifter (ed.), *Political Science: The State of the Discipline.* Washington, DC: American Political Science Association.

Atkinson, M. 1984. *Our Master's Voices: The Language and Body Language of Politics.* London: Methuen.

Axelrod, R. 1973. Schema theory: an information processing model of perception and cognition. *American Political Science Review,* 67, 1248–1273.

———. 1976. *Structure of Decision.* Princeton, NJ: Princeton University Press.

———. 1983. *The Evolution of Cooperation.* Cambridge, MA: Harvard University Press.

Babad, E., and Yacobis, E. 1990. Wish and reality in voters' predictions of election outcomes. Unpublished manuscript, Hebrew University of Jerusalem.

Babchuck, W., Hames, R., and Thomason, R. 1985. Sex differences in recognition of infant facial expressions of emotion: the primary caretaker hypothesis. *Ethology and Sociobiology,* 6, 89–102.

Bahr, H., and Chadwick, B. 1974. Conservatism, racial intolerance and attitudes toward racial assimilation among whites and American Indians. *Journal of Social Psychology,* 94, 45–56.

Baier, A. 1987. Getting in touch with our feelings. *Topoi,* 6, 89–97.

———. In press. What emotions are about. In J. Tomberlin (ed.), *Philosophical Perspectives.*

Bailey, K. 1987. *Human Palepsychology: Applications to Aggression and Pathological Processes.* Hillsdale, NJ: Lawrence Erlbaum Associates.

Bailyn, B., and Fleming, D. (eds.). 1969. *The Intellectual Migration.* Cambridge, MA: Harvard University Press.

Barber, J. 1985. *The Presidential Character: Predicting Performance in the White House*. Englewood Cliffs, NJ: Prentice-Hall.

Barbu, Z. 1960. *Problems of Historical Psychology*. Westport, CT: Greenwood Press.

Barchas, P., and Mendoza, S. (eds.). 1984. *Social Cohesion: Essays Toward a Sociophysiological Perspective*. Westport, CT: Greenwood Press.

Bargh, J. 1984. Automatic and conscious processing of social information. In R. Wyer and T. Srull (eds.), *Handbook of Social Cognition*, vol. 3. Hillsdale, NJ: Lawrence Erlbaum Associates.

Bargh, J. A. 1988. Automatic information processing: implications for communication and affect. In L. Donohew, H. E. Sypher, and E. T. Higgins (eds.), *Communication, social cognition, and affect* (pp. 9–32). Hillsdale, NJ: Erlbaum.

———. 1989. Conditional automaticity: varieties of automatic influence in social perception and cognition. In J. Uleman and J. Bargh (eds.), *Unintended Thought*. New York: Guilford Press.

Bargh, J., Bond, R., Lombardi, W., and Tota, M. 1986. The additive nature of chronic and temporary sources of construct accessibility. *Journal of Personality and Social Psychology*, 50, 869–878.

Bargh, J., Lombardi, W., and Higgins, E. 1988. Automaticity of chronically accessible constructs in person × situation effects on person perception: it's just a matter of time. *Journal of Personality and Social Psychology*, 55, 599–605.

Bargh, J., and Pietromonaco, P. 1982. Automatic information processing and social perception: the influence of trait information presented outside of conscious awareness on impression formation. *Journal of Personality and Social Psychology*, 43, 437–449.

Barker, E. 1963. Authoritarianism of the political right, center, and left. *Journal of Social Issues*, 19, 63–74.

Barnes, F. 1988. Campaign '88: a fine romance. *New Republic*, July 11, 1988, pp. 10–12.

Barnes, H. 1925. *Psychology and History*. New York: Century.

Barnouw, V. 1985. *Culture and Personality*. 4th ed. Homewood, IL: Dorsey Press.

Baron, S., and Pletsch, C. (eds.). 1985. *Introspection in Biography: The Biographer's Quest for Self-Awareness*. Hillsdale, NJ: Analytic Press.

Barraclough, G. 1978. *Main Trends in History*. New York: Holmes and Meier.

Bartels, L. 1985. Expectations and preferences in presidential nominating campaigns. *American Political Science Review*, 79, 804–815.

———. 1986. Issue voting under uncertainty. *American Journal of Political Science*, 30, 709–728.

———. 1987. Candidate choice and the dynamics of the presidential nominating process. *American Journal of Political Science*, 31, 1–30.

———. 1988. *Presidential Primaries and the Dynamics of Public Choice*. Princeton, NJ: Princeton University Press.

Bartlett, F. 1932. *Remembering*. Cambridge: Cambridge University Press.

Bartolucci, G. 1984. Nonverbal disturbances attributed to schizophrenic psychoses. *Comprehensive Psychiatry*, 25, 491–502.

Barzun, J. 1974. *Clio and the Doctors: History, Psycho-History, Quanto-History*. Chicago: University of Chicago Press.

Bassili, J. 1989. *On-line Cognition in Person Perception*. Hillsdale, NJ: Lawrence Erlbaum Associates.

Bauer, R., de Sola Pool, I., and Dexter, L. 1963. *American Business and Public Policy*. New York: Atherton Press.

Baugh, W. 1984. *The Politics of Nuclear Balance*. New York: Longman.

Baumeister, R. 1986. *Identity: Cultural Change and the Struggle for Self*. New York: Oxford University Press.

Bavelas, J. B., Black, A., Lemery, C. R., and Mullett, J. 1986. "I show how you feel": motor mimicry as a communication act. *Journal of Personality and Social Psychology*, 50, 322–329.

Beck, P., Rainey, H., and Traut, C. 1990. Disadvantage, disaffection, and race as divergent bases for citizen fiscal policy preferences. *Journal of Politics*, 52, 71–93.

Beer, F., Healy, A., Sinclair, G., and Bourne, L. 1987. War cues and foreign policy acts. *American Political Science Review*, 81, 701–715.

Bell, D. 1960. *The End of Ideology*. Glencoe, IL: Free Press.

———. (ed.). 1963. *The Radical Right: The New American Right*. New York: Doubleday.

Bellah, R., Madsen, R., Sullivan, W., Swidler, A., and Tipton, S. 1985. *Habits of the Heart: Individualism and Commitment in American Life*. Berkeley: University of California Press.

Belmore, S. 1987. Determinants of attention during impression formation. *Journal of Experimental Psychology: Learning, Memory and Cognition*, 13, 480–489.

Bem, D. 1967. Self-perception: an alternative interpretation of cognitive dissonance phenomena. *Psychological Review*, 74, 183–200.

Bendersky, J. 1988. Psychohistory before Hitler: early military analyses of German national psychology. *Journal of the History of the Behavioral Sciences*, 24, 166–182.

Bendix, R. 1952. Complaint behavior and individual personality. *American Journal of Sociology*, 58, 292–303.

Benedict, R. 1946. *The Chrysanthemum and the Sword*. Boston: Houghton Mifflin.

Berelson, B. 1942. The effects of print upon public opinion. In D. Waples (ed.), *Print, Radio, and Film in a Democracy*. Chicago: University of Chicago Press.

———. 1952. Democratic theory and public opinion. *Public Opinion Quarterly*, 16, 313–330.

Berelson, B., Lazarsfeld, P., and McPhee, W. 1954. *Voting: A Study of Opinion Formation in a Presidential Campaign*. Chicago: University of Chicago Press.

Berns, W. 1954. Voting studies. In Herbert Storing (ed.), *Essays on the Scientific Study of Politics*. New York: Holt, Rinehart and Wilson.

Betts, R. 1983. Conventional strategy: new critics, old choices. *International Security*, 7, 141–143.

Beyerchen, A. 1977. *Scientists Under Hitler*. New Haven, CT: Yale University Press.

Binion, R. 1976. *Hitler Among the Germans*. New York: Elsevier.

Birke, L. 1986. *Women, Feminism, and Biology: the Feminist Challenge*. New York: Methuen.

Birnbaum, M. H. 1981. Thinking and feeling: a skeptical review. *American Psychologist*, 36, 99–101.

Blackburn, G. 1984. *Education in the Third Reich*. Albany: State University of New York Press.

Blake, R., and Mouton, J. 1962. The intergroup dynamics of win-lose conflict and problem-solving collaboration in union-management relations. In M. Sherif (ed.), *Intergroup Relations and Leadership*. New York: Wiley.

———. 1979. Intergroup problem solving in organizations: from theory to practice. In W. G. Austin and S. Worchel (eds.), *The Social Psychology of Intergroup Relations*. Monterey, CA: Brooks/Cole.

Blatt, S., with Blatt, E. 1984. *Continuity and Change in Art: The Development of Modes of Representation*. Hillsdale, NJ: Lawrence Erlbaum Associates.

Bloom, H., and Price, D. 1975. Voter response to short-run economic conditions. *American Political Science Review*, 69, 1240–1253.

Blumler, H. 1958. Race prejudice as a sense of group position. *Pacific Sociological Review*, 1, 3–7.

Bobo, L. 1983. Whites' opposition to busing: symbolic racism or realistic group conflict? *Journal of Personality and Social Psychology*, 45, 1196–1210.

———. 1988. Group conflict, prejudice, and the paradox of contemporary racial attitudes. In P. Katz and D. Taylor (eds.), *Eliminating Racism: Profiles in Controversy*. New York: Plenum.

Bock, P. 1988. *Rethinking Psychological Anthropology*. San Francisco: Freeman.

Bodenhausen, G., and Lichtenstein, M. 1986. Social stereotypes and information-processing strategies: the impact of task complexity. *Journal of Personality and Social Psychology*, 52, 871–880.

———. 1987. Social stereotypes and information processing strategies: the impact of task complexity. *Journal of Personality and Social Psychology*, 52, 871–880.

Bodenhausen, G., and Wyer, R. 1985. Effects of stereotypes on decision-making and information-processing strategies. *Journal of Personality and Social Psychology*, 48, 267–282.

Bogue, A. 1983. *Clio and the Bitch Goddess: Quantification in American Political History*. Beverly Hills, CA: Sage.

Bornstein, M. 1988. Mothers, infants, and the development of cognitive competence. In H. Fitzgerald, B. Lester, and M. Yogman (eds.), *Theory and Research in Behavioral Pediatrics,* vol. 4. New York: Plenum.

Bower, G. 1981. Emotion, mood and memory. *American Psychologist,* 36, 129–148.

Bower, G., and Gilligan, S. 1982. Emotional influences in memory and thinking: data and theory. In S. Fiske and M. Clark (eds.), *Affect and Social Cognition.* Hillsdale, NJ: Lawrence Erlbaum Associates.

Bower, G., Gilligan, S., and Monteiro, K. 1981. Selectivity of learning caused by affective states. *Journal of Experimental Psychology: General,* 110, 451–483.

Bowers, K. 1973. Situationism in psychology: analysis and a critique. *Psychological Bulletin,* 80, 307–336.

Bracken, P. 1977. The unintended consequences of strategic gaming. *Simulation and Games,* 8, 300–315.

Brady, H. 1989. Is Iowa news? In P. Squire (ed.), *The Iowa Caucuses and the Presidential Nominating Process.* Boulder, CO: Westview Press.

Brady, H., and Ansolabehere, S. 1989. The nature of utility functions in mass publics. *American Political Science Review,* 83, 143–163.

Brady, H., and Johnston, R. 1987. What's the primary message? In G. Orren and N. Polsby (eds.), *Media and Momentum.* Chatham, NJ: Chatham House.

Brady, H., and Sniderman, P. 1985. Attitude attribution: a group basis for political reasoning. *American Political Science Review,* 79, 1061–1078.

Branthwaite, A., and Jones, J. 1975. Fairness and discrimination: English vs. Welch. *European Journal of Social Psychology,* 5, 323–328.

Braudel, F. 1949. *La Méditerranée et le monde méditerranéen à l'époque de Philippe II.* Paris: Colin. ([1972]. S. Reynolds, trans., *The Mediterranean and the Mediterranean World in the Age of Philip II.* New York: Harper and Row.)

Braybrooke, D., and Lindblom, C. 1963. *A Strategy of Decision.* New York: Free Press.

Brent, E., and Granberg, D. 1982. Subjective agreement with the presidential candidates of 1976 and 1980. *Journal of Personality and Social Psychology,* 42, 393–403.

Brewer, M. 1979. In-group bias in the minimal intergroup situation: a cognitive-motivational analysis. *Psychological Bulletin,* 86, 307–324.

———. 1988. A dual process model of impression formation. In T. Srull and R. Wyer (eds.), *Advances in Social Cognition,* vol. 1. Hillsdale, NJ: Lawrence Erlbaum Associates.

Brodie, F. 1981. *Richard Nixon: The Shaping of His Character.* New York: Norton.

Brody, R., and Page, B. 1972. Comment: the assessment of policy voting. *American Political Science Review,* 66, 450–458.

Brody, R., Sniderman, P., and Kuklinski, J. 1984. Policy reasoning in political issues: the problem of racial inequality. *American Journal of Political Science,* 28, 75–94.

Bronfenbrenner, U. 1979. *The Ecology of Human Development*. Cambridge, MA: Harvard University Press.

Brophy, J. 1982. Research on the self-fulfilling prophesy and teacher expectations. Presented at annual meeting of American Educational Research Association, New York City.

Brown, J. 1936. *Psychology and the Social Order*. New York: McGraw-Hill.

Brown, R. 1978. Divided we fall: An analysis of relations between sections of a factory work-force. In H. Tajfel (ed.), *Differentiation Between Social Groups: Studies in the Social Psychology of Intergroup Relations*. London: Academic Press.

Brown, R., Tajfel, H., and Turner, J. 1980. Minimal group situations and intergroup discrimination: comments on the paper by Aschenbrenner and Schaefer. *European Journal of Social Psychology*, 10, 399–414.

Brugger, R. (ed.). 1981. *Our Selves/Our Past: Psychological Approaches to American History*. Baltimore: Johns Hopkins University Press.

Bruner, J. 1951. Personality dynamics and the process of perceiving. In R. Blake and G. Ramsey (eds.), *Perception: An Approach to Personality*. New York: Ronald.

——. 1986. *Actual Minds, Possible Worlds*. Cambridge, MA: Harvard University Press.

Brunswik, E. 1956. *Perception and the Representative Design of Experiments*. Berkeley: University of California Press.

Buck, R. 1980. Nonverbal behavior and the theory of emotion: the facial feedback hypothesis. *Journal of Personality and Social Psychology*, 38, 811–824.

——. 1985. Prime theory: an integrated view of motivation and emotion. *Psychological Review*, 92, 389–413.

Burns, J. 1978. *Leadership*. New York: Harper and Row.

Byrne, D. 1971. *The Attraction Paradigm*. New York: Academic Press.

Byrne, D., Clore, G., and Smeaton, G. 1986. The attraction hypothesis: do similar attitudes affect anything? *Journal of Personality and Social Psychology*, 51, 1167–1170.

Byrne, D., and Erwin, C. 1969. Attraction toward a Negro stranger as a function of prejudice, attitude similarity and the stranger's evaluation. *Human Relations*, 22, 397–404.

Cacioppo, J., and Petty, R. 1979. Attitudes and cognitive response: an electrophysiological approach. *Journal of Personality and Social Psychology*, 37, 2181–2199.

Cain, B., Ferejohn, J., and Fiorina, M. 1988. *The Personal Vote*. Cambridge, MA: Harvard University Press.

Calhoun, D. 1973. *The Intelligence of a People*. Princeton, NJ: Princeton University Press.

Campbell, A., Converse, P., Miller, W., and Stokes, D. 1960. *The American Voter*. New York: Wiley.

Campbell, A., Gurin, G., and Miller, W. 1954. *The Voter Decides*. Evanston, IL: Row, Peterson.

Campbell, D., 1969. Ethnocentrism of disciplines and the fish-scale model of omniscience. In M. Sherif and C. Sherif (eds.), *Interdisciplinary Relationships in the Social Sciences*. Chicago: Aldine.

Cantor, J., Zillmann, D., and Bryant, J. 1974. Enhancement of experienced sexual arousal in response to erotic stimuli through misattribution of unrelated residual excitation. *Journal of Personality and Social Psychology*, 32, 69–75.

Cantril, H. 1965. *The Pattern of Human Concerns*. New Brunswick, NJ: Rutgers University Press.

Cargas, H. 1985. *The Holocaust: An Annotated Bibliography*. 2nd ed. Chicago: American Library Association.

Carley, M. 1976. French intervention in Russia. *Journal of Modern History*, 48, 420–443.

Carlotti, S., Jr. 1988. The faces of the presidency: individual differences in responses to non-verbal behavior of American leaders. Senior fellow's thesis, Dartmouth College.

Carlotti, S., Jr., and Masters, R. 1993. How television influences voters: emotion, nonverbal cues, and momentum. In preparation.

Carlson, J. 1990. Subjective ideological similarity between candidates and supporters. *Political Psychology*, 11, 485–492.

Carlston, D. 1980. Events, inferences and impression formation. In R. Hastie, T. Ostrom, E. Ebbesen, R. Wyer, D. Hamilton, and D. Carlston (eds.), *Person Memory: The Cognitive Basis of Social Perception*. Hillsdale, NJ: Lawrence Erlbaum Associates.

Carmines, E., and Stimson, J. 1982. Racial issues and the structure of mass belief systems. *Journal of Politics*, 44, 2–20.

Cash, W. 1941. *The Mind of the South*. New York: Knopf.

Chaiken, S. 1980. Heuristic versus systematic information processing and the use of source versus message cues in persuasion. *Journal of Personality and Social Psychology*, 39, 752–766.

Chaiken, A., Sigler, E., and Derlaga, V. 1974. Nonverbal mediators of teacher expectation effects. *Journal of Personality and Social Psychology*, 30, 144–149.

Chance, M. 1976. The organization of attention in groups. In M. von Cranach (ed.), *Methods of Inference from Animal to Human Behavior*. The Hague: Mouton.

———. 1989. *Social Fabrics of the Mind*. Hillsdale, NJ: Lawrence Erlbaum Associates.

Chase, I. 1982. Behavioral sequences during dominance hierarchy formation in chickens. *Science*, 216, 439–440.

Chattopadhyay, A., and Alba, J. 1988. The situational importance of recall and inference in consumer decision-making. *Journal of Consumer Research*, 15, 1–12.

Childers, T. 1984. *The Nazi Voter*. Chapel Hill: University of North Carolina Press.

Chong, D., McClosky, H., and Zaller, J. 1983. Patterns of support for democratic and capitalistic values in the United States. *British Journal of Political Science,* 13, 401–440.

Christiansen, K., and Knussmann, R. 1987. Androgen levels and components of aggressive behavior in men. *Hormones and Behavior,* 21, 170–180.

Christie, R., and Geis, F. 1970. *Studies in Machiavellianism.* New York: Academic Press.

Citrin, J., and Green, D. 1990. The self-interest motive in American public opinion. In S. Long (ed.), *Research in Micropolitics,* vol. 3. Greenwich, CT: JAI Press.

Clark, K., and Clark, M. 1947. Racial identification and preference in Negro children. In T. Newcomb and E. Hartley (eds.), *Readings in Social Psychology.* New York: Holt, Rinehart and Winston.

Clark, M. S., and Fiske, S. T. 1982. *Affect and Cognition.* Hillsdale, NJ: Lawrence Erlbaum Associates.

Cloninger, R. 1987. A systematic method for clinical description and classification of personality variants. *Archives of General Psychiatry,* 44, 573–588.

Cocks, G. 1979. The Hitler controversy. *Political Psychology,* 1, 67–81.

———. 1985. *Psychotherapy in the Third Reich: The Göring Institute.* New York: Oxford University Press.

———. 1986. Contributions of psychohistory to understanding politics. In M. Hermann (ed.), *Political Psychology.* San Francisco: Jossey-Bass.

Cocks, G., and Crosby, T. 1987. *Psychohistory: Readings in the Methods of Psychology, Psychoanalysis, and Medicine.* New Haven, CT: Yale University Press.

Cohen, C. 1981. Goals and schemata in person perception. In N. Cantor and J. Kihlstrom (eds.), *Personality, Cognition and Social Interaction.* Hillsdale, NJ: Lawrence Erlbaum Associates.

Coles, R. 1986. *The Political Life of Children.* Boston: Atlantic Monthly Press.

Collins, A., and Quillian, M. 1968. Retrieval time from semantic memory. *Journal of Verbal Learning and Verbal Behavior,* 8, 240–247.

Collins, A., and Loftus, E. 1975. A spreading-activation theory of semantic processing. *Psychological Review,* 82, 407–428.

Conover, P. 1981. Political cues and perception of candidates. *American Politics Quarterly,* 9, 427–448.

———. 1988. The role of social groups in political thinking. *British Journal of Political Science,* 18, 51–76.

Conover, P., and Feldman, S. 1982. Projection and the perception of candidates' issue positions. *Western Political Quarterly,* 35, 228–244.

———. 1986. The role of inference in the perception of political candidates. In R. Lau and D. Sears (eds.), *Political Cognition.* Hillsdale, NJ: Lawrence Erlbaum Associates.

———. 1989. Candidate perception in an ambiguous world: campaigns, cues, and inference processes. *American Journal of Political Science,* 33, 912–940.

Converse, P. 1964. The nature of belief systems in mass publics. In D. Apter (ed.), *Ideology and Discontent.* New York: Free Press of Glencoe.

——. 1970. Attitudes and non-attitudes: continuation of a dialogue. In E. Tufte (ed.), *The Quantitative Analysis of Social Problems.* Reading, MA: Addison-Wesley.

Converse, P., Campbell, A., Miller, W., and Stokes, D. 1961. Stability and change in 1960: a reinstating election. *American Political Science Review, 55,* 269–280.

Converse, P., Clausen, A., and Miller, W. 1965. Electoral myth and reality: the 1964 election. *American Political Science Review, 59,* 321–336.

Converse, P., and Markus, G. 1979. Plus ça change . . .: the new CPS election study panel. *American Political Science Review, 73,* 32–49.

Conway, J. 1969. *The Nazi Persecution of the Churches, 1933–1945.* New York: Basic Books.

Cooper, H., and Baron, R. 1977. Academic expectations and attributed responsibility as predictors of professional teacher's reinforcement behavior. *Journal of Educational Psychology, 69,* 409–418.

Coser, L. 1984. *Refugee Scholars in America.* New Haven, CT: Yale University Press.

Coughlin, R. (ed.). 1989. *Reforming Welfare: Lessons, Limits, and Choices.* Albuquerque: University of New Mexico Press.

Courtine, J., and Claudine, H. 1988. *Histoire du Visage: Exprimer et Taire ses Émotions, XVIe—Début XIXe Siècle.* Paris: Rivages.

Cowpe, A. 1977. The Royal Navy and the Whitehead torpedo. In B. Ranft (ed.), *Technical Change and British Naval Policy: 1960–1939.* New York: Holmes and Meier.

Craik, K. 1988. Assessing the personalities of historical figures. In W. Runyan (ed.), *Psychology and Historical Interpretation.* New York: Oxford University Press.

Crano, W., and Schroder, H. 1967. Complexity of attitude structure and processes of conflict resolution. *Journal of Personality and Social Psychology, 5,* 110–114.

Crockett, W. 1974. Balance, agreement and subjective evaluations of the P-O-X triads. *Journal of Personality and Social Psychology, 29,* 102–110.

Cronbach, L. 1975. Beyond the two disciplines of scientific psychology. *American Psychologist, 30,* 116–127.

——. 1986. Social inquiry by and for earthlings. In D. Fiske and R. Shweder (eds.), *Metatheory in Social Science.* Chicago: University of Chicago Press.

Cronbach, L., and Meehl, P. 1955. Construct validity in psychological tests. *Psychological Bulletin, 52,* 281–302.

Cupchik, G., and Leventhal, H. 1974. Consistency between expressive behavior and the evaluation of stimuli: the role of sex and self-observation. *Journal of Personality and Social Psychology, 30,* 429–442.

Cyert, R., and March, J. 1963. *A Behavioral Theory of the Firm.* Englewood Cliffs, NJ: Prentice-Hall.

Dabbs, J., and Morris, R. 1990. Testosterone, social class, and antisocial behavior in a sample of 4,462 men. *Psychological Science,* 1, 209–211.

Dahl, R. 1956. *A Preface to Democratic Theory.* Chicago: University of Chicago Press.

Dahl, R. A. 1961. *Who Governs? Democracy and Power in an American City.* New Haven, CT: Yale University Press.

———. 1971. *Polyarchy: Participation and Opposition.* New Haven, CT: Yale University Press.

Dahl, R., and Lindblom, C. 1953. *Politics, Economics and Welfare.* New York: Harper and Row.

Dann, H., and Doise, W. 1974. Ein neuer methodologischer ansats sur experimentellen erforschung von intergroupen-beziehungen. *Zeitschrift für Sozialpsychologie,* 5, 2–15.

Darcy, R., Welch, S., and Clark, J. 1987. *Women, Elections, and Representation.* New York: Longman.

Darwin, C. 1965 [1872]. *The Expression of the Emotions in Man and Animals.* Chicago: University of Chicago Press.

Davies, A. 1980. *Skills, Outlooks and Passions: A Psychoanalytic Contribution to the Study of Politics.* Cambridge: Cambridge University Press.

Davies, J. 1962. Toward a theory of revolution. *American Sociological Review,* 27, 5–19.

Davis, V. 1966. *Post-War Defense Policy and the U.S. Navy.* Chapel Hill: University of North Carolina Press.

Dawes, R. 1966. Memory and distortion of meaningful written material. *British Journal of Psychology.* 57, 77–86.

———. 1971. A case of graduate admissions: application of three principles of human decision making. *American Psychologist,* 26, 180–188.

———. 1979. The robust beauty of improper linear models in decision making. *American Psychologist,* 34, 571–582.

Dawes, R., and Corrigan, B. 1981. Linear models in decision making. *Psychological Bulletin,* 81, 95–106.

Dawidowicz, L. 1975. *The War Against the Jews, 1933–1945.* New York: Bantam Books.

Deaux, K., and Lewis, L. L. 1984. Structure of gender stereotypes: interrelationships among component and gender label. *Journal of Personality and Social Psychology,* 42, 991–1004.

Delli Carpini, M., and Keeter, S. 1989. Political knowledge of the U.S. public: results from a national survey. Presented at annual meeting of American Association for Public Opinion Research.

Devine, P. 1989. Stereotypes and prejudice: their automatic and controlled components. *Journal of Personality and Social Psychology,* 56, 5–18.

de Waal, F. 1982. *Chimpanzee Politics*. London: Jonathan Cape.

———. 1984. Sex differences in the formation of coalitions among chimpanzees. *Ethology and Sociobiology*, 5, 239–268.

Diamond, E., and Bates, S. 1984. *The Spot: The Rise of Political Advertising on Television*. Cambridge, MA: MIT Press.

Dimburg, U. 1982. Facial reactions to facial expressions. *Psychophysiology*, 19, 643–647.

Dimsdale, J. (ed.). 1980. *Survivors, Victims, and Perpetration: Essays on the Nazi Holocaust*. Washington, DC: Hemisphere.

Direnzo, G. (ed.). 1977. *We, the People: American Character and Social Change*. Westport, CT: Greenwood Press.

Doise, W. 1986. Mass psychology, social psychology, and the politics of Mussolini. In C. F. Graumann and S. Moscovici (eds.), *Changing Conceptions of Crowd Mind and Behavior* (pp. 69–82). New York: Springer-Verlag.

———. 1988. Individual and social identities in intergroup relations. *European Journal of Social Psychology*, 18, 99–111.

Doise, W., Csepeli, G., Dann, H., Gouge, C., Larsen, K., and Ostell, A. 1972. An experimental investigation into the formation of intergroup representations. *European Journal of Social Psychology*, 2, 202–204.

Doise, W., and Sinclair, A. 1973. The categorization process in intergroup relations. *European Journal of Social Psychology*, 3, 145–157.

Dollard, J. 1937. *Caste and Class in a Southern Town*. New Haven, CT: Yale University Press.

Dollard, J., and Miller, N. 1950. *Personality and Psychotherapy*. New York: McGraw-Hill.

Dollard, J., Miller, N., Doob, L., Mowrer, O., and Sears, R. 1939. *Frustration and Aggression*. New Haven, CT: Yale University Press.

Downs, A. 1957. *An Economic Theory of Democracy*. New York: Harper and Row.

Dreben, E., Fiske, S., and Hastie, R. 1979. The dependence of item and evaluative information: impression and recall order effects in behavior-based impression formation. *Journal of Personality and Social Psychology*, 37, 1758–1768.

Drew, E. 1985. *Campaign Journal: The Political Events of 1983–1984*. New York: Macmillan.

Driver, M. 1965. A structural analysis of aggression, stress and personality in inter-nation simulation. Institute Paper 97, Lafayette, IN: Institute for Research in the Behavioral, Economic, and Management Sciences, Purdue University.

Easterlin, R. 1980. *Birth and Fortune: The Impact of Numbers on Personal Welfare*. New York: Basic Books.

Easton, D., and Dennis, J. 1969. *Children in the Political System: Origins of Political Legitimacy*. New York: McGraw-Hill.

Ebbinghaus, H. 1964 [1885]. *Memory: A Contribution to Experimental Psychology*. New York: Dover.

Eckstein, H. 1980. Theoretical approaches to explaining collective political violence. In T. R. Gurr (ed.), *Handbook of Political Violence*. New York: Free Press.

Edelman, M. 1964. *The Symbolic Uses of Politics*. Urbana: University of Illinois Press.

———. 1971. *Politics as Symbolic Action: Mass Arousal and Quiescence*. Chicago: Markham.

———. 1978. *Political Language*. New York: Academic Press.

Edwards, A. L. 1957. *Techniques of Attitude Scale Construction*. New York: Appleton-Century-Crofts.

Edwards, W. 1954. The theory of decision-making. *Psychological Bulletin*, 51, 380–417.

Ehrenkranz, J., Bliss, E., and Sheard, M. 1974. Plasma testosterone: correlation with aggressive behavior and social dominance in man. *Psychosomatic Medicine*, 36, 469–475.

Eibl-Eibesfeldt, I. 1989. *Human Ethology*. New York: Aldine De Gruyter.

Einhorn, H. 1972. Expert measurement and mechanical combination. *Organizational Behavior and Human Performance*, 7, 86–106.

Einhorn, H., and Hogarth, R. 1981. Behavioral decision theory: processes of judgment and choice. *Annual Review of Psychology*, 32, 153–188.

Eiser, J. 1971. Enhancement of contrast in the absolute judgment of attitude statements. *Journal of Personality and Social Psychology*, 17 (January), 1–10.

Eiser, J., and Stroebe, W. 1972. *Categorization and Social Judgment*. London: Academic Press.

Ekman, P., and Oster, H. 1979. Facial expressions of emotion. In *Annual Review of Psychology*, vol. 30. Palo Alto, CA: Annual Reviews Press.

Elder, C., and Cobb, R. 1983. *The Political Uses of Symbols*. New York: Longman.

Elias, M. 1981. Serum cortisol, testosterone, and testosterone-binding globulin responses to competitive fighting in human males. *Aggressive Behavior*, 7, 215–224.

Elms, A. 1976. *Personality in Politics*. New York: Harcourt Brace Jovanovich.

Elster, J. (ed.). 1986. *Rational Choice*. New York: New York University Press.

Enelow, J., and Hinich, M. 1985. *The Spatial Theory of Voting: An Introduction*. New York: Cambridge University Press.

Englis, B., Vaughan, K., and Lanzetta, J. 1982. Conditioning of counterempathetic emotional responses. *Journal of Experimental and Social Psychology*, 18, 375–391.

Ericsson, K., and Simon, H. 1984. *Protocol Analysis: Verbal Reports as Data*. Cambridge, MA: MIT Press.

Erikson, E. 1942. Hitler's imagery and German youth. *Psychiatry*, 5, 475–493.

———. 1958. *Young Man Luther: A Study in Psychoanalysis and History*. New York: Norton.

———. 1969. *Gandhi's Truth*. New York: Norton.

———. 1975. *Life History and the Historical Moment*. New York: Norton.

Erikson, E., and Hofstadter, R. 1967. The strange case of Freud, Bullitt, and Wilson. *New York Review of Books,* February 9, pp. 3–8.

Erikson, E. H. 1963. *Childhood and society.* New York: Norton.

Esaiasson, P. 1990. Folker tycker om partiledarna. In M. Gilljam and S. Holmberg (eds.), *Rött Blått Grönt: En bok om 1988 års val.* Stockholm: Bonniers.

Etzioni, A. 1988. *The Moral Dimension: Toward a New Economics.* New York: Free Press.

Eysenck, H. 1981. Left-wing authoritarianism: myth or reality? *Political Psychology,* 3, 234–239.

Farley, J. 1938. *Behind the Ballots.* New York: Harcourt, Brace.

Farrell, R., and Swigert, V. 1978. Legal disposition of inter-group and intra-group homicides. *Sociological Quarterly,* 19, 565–576.

Fazio, R. 1986. How do attitudes guide behavior? In R. Sorrentino and E. Higgins (eds.), *Handbook of Motivation and Cognition: Foundations of Social Behavior.* New York: Guilford Press.

———. 1989. On the power and functionality of attitudes: the role of attitude accessibility. In A. Pratkanis, S. Breckler, and A. Greenwald (eds.), *Attitude Structure and Function.* Hillsdale, NJ: Lawrence Erlbaum Associates.

Fazio, R., Powell, M., and Herr, P. 1983. Toward a process model of the attitude-behavior relation: accessing one's attitude upon mere observation of the attitude object. *Journal of Personality and Social Psychology,* 44, 723–735.

Fazio, R., Sanbanmatsu, D., Powell, M., and Kardes, F. 1986. On the automatic activation of attitudes. *Journal of Personality and Social Psychology,* 50, 229–238.

Fazio, R., and Williams, C. 1986. Attitude accessibility as a moderator of the attitude-perception and attitude-behavior relations: an investigation of the 1984 presidential election. *Journal of Personality and Social Psychology,* 51, 505–514.

Feagin, J., and Feagin, C. 1978. *Discrimination American Style: Institutional Racism and Sexism.* Englewood Cliffs, NJ: Prentice-Hall.

Feather, N. (ed.). 1982. *Expectations and Actions: Expectancy-Value Models in Psychology.* Hillsdale, NJ: Lawrence Erlbaum Associates.

Feierabend, I., and Feierabend, R. 1966. Aggressive behaviors within politics, 1948–1962: a cross-national study. *Journal of Conflict Resolution,* 10, 249–271.

Feldman, S. 1988. Structure and consistency in public opinion: the role of core beliefs and values. *American Journal of Political Science,* 32, 416–440.

Feldman, S., and Conover, P. 1983. Candidates, issues and voters: the role of inference in political perception. *Journal of Politics,* 45, 812–839.

Fenno, R. 1973. *Congressmen in Committees.* Boston: Little, Brown.

Ferejohn, J. 1990. Information and the electoral process. In J. Ferejohn and J. Kuklinski (eds.), *Information and Democratic Processes.* Urbana: University of Illinois Press.

Ferejohn, J. A., and Kuklinski, J. H. 1990. *Information and the Democratic Process.* Urbana, IL: University of Illinois Press.

Festinger, L. 1950. Informal social communication. *Psychological Review*, 57, 271–282.

———. 1957. *A Theory of Cognitive Dissonance*. Evanston, IL: Row, Peterson.

———. 1964. *Conflict, Decision, and Dissonance*. Stanford, CA: Stanford University Press.

Festinger, L., and Carlsmith, J. 1959. Cognitive consequences of forced compliance. *Journal of Abnormal and Social Psychology*, 58, 203–210.

Fiedler, F. 1967. The effect of inter-group competition on group member adjustment. *Personnel Psychology*, 20, 33–44.

Fine, M., and Bowers, C. 1984. Racial self-identification: the effects of social history and gender. *Journal of Applied Social Psychology*, 14, 136–146.

Fiorina, M. 1981. *Retrospective Voting in American National Elections*. New Haven, CT: Yale University Press.

———. 1990. Information and rationality in elections. In J. Ferejohn and J. Kuklinski (eds.), *Information and Democratic Processes*. Urbana: University of Illinois Press.

Fiorina, M., and Plott, C. 1978. Committee decisions under majority rule. *American Political Science Review*, 72, 575–598.

Fiorina, M., and Shepsle, K. 1989. Is negative voting an artifact? *American Journal of Political Science*, 33, 423–439.

Fireman, B., and Gamson, W. 1979. Utilitarian logic in the resource mobilization perspective. In M. Zald and J. McCarthy (eds.), *The Dynamics of Social Movements*. Cambridge, MA: Winthrop.

Fischhoff, B., Slovic, P., and Lichtenstein, S. 1978. Fault trees: sensitivity of estimated failure probabilities to problem representation. *Journal of Experimental Psychology: Human Perception and Performance*, 4, 330–344.

Fishbein, M., and Ajzen, I. 1974. Basis for decision: an attitudinal analysis of voting behavior. *Journal of Applied Social Psychology*, 4, 95–124.

Fishbein, M., and Ajzen, I. 1975. *Belief, Attitude, Intention and Behavior: An Introduction to Theory and Research*. Reading, MA: Addison-Wesley.

Fiske, S. 1980. Attention and weight in person perception: the impact of negative and extreme behavior. *Journal of Personality and Social Psychology*, 38, 889–906.

———. 1986. Schema-based versus piecemeal politics: a patchwork quilt, but not a blanket, of evidence. In R. R. Lau and D. O. Sears (eds.), *Political Cognition: The Nineteenth Annual Carnegie Symposium on Cognition*. Hillsdale, NJ: Lawrence Erlbaum Associates.

Fiske, S., and Neuberg, S. 1990. A continuum of model impression formation, from category-based to individuating processes: influences of information and motivation on attention and interpretation. In L. Berkowitz (ed.), *Advances in Experimental Social Psychology*, vol. 23. New York: Academic Press.

Fiske, S., and Pavelchak, M. 1986. Category-based vs. piecemeal-based affective responses: developments in schema-triggered affect. In R. Sorrentino and E. Higgins (eds.), *Handbook of Motivation and Cognition* (pp. 167–203). New York: Guilford Press.

Fiske, S., and Ruscher, J. 1989. On-line processes in category-based and individuating impressions: some basic principles and methodological reflections. In J. Bassili (ed.), *On-Line Cognition in Person Perception*. Hillsdale, NJ: Lawrence Erlbaum Associates.

Fiske, S., and Taylor, S. 1991. *Social Cognition*, 2nd ed. New York: McGraw-Hill.

Fitts, P., and Posner, M. 1967. *Human Performance*. Belmont, CA: Brooks/Cole.

Fitzhugh, G. 1854. *Sociology for the South*. Richmond, VA.

Flohr, H., Tönnesmann, W., and Pöhls, U. 1986. Studying leader-follower relationships from an ethological perspective. Presented at fifth international conference on human ethology, Tutzing, West Germany, July 27–31.

Foa, E. B., and Kozak, M. J. 1985. Emotional processing of fear: exposure to corrective information. *Psychological Bulletin*, in press.

Foucault, M. 1961. *Folie et déraison: Histoire de le folie à l'âge classique*. Paris: Plon. ([1965]. R. Howard, trans., *Madness and Civilization: A History of Insanity in the Age of Reason*. New York: Pantheon Books.)

———. 1984. *Histoire de la sexualité*, vol. 3: *La souci de sois*. Paris: Gallimard. ([1986]. R. Hurley, trans., *The History of Sexuality*, vol. 3: *The Care of the Self*. New York: Pantheon Books.)

Frank, R. 1988. *Passions Within Reason*. New York: Norton.

Frei, D. 1986. *Perceived Images: U.S. and Soviet Assumptions and Perceptions in Disarmament*. Totowa, NJ: Rowman and Allanheld.

Freud, S. 1953 [1913]. *Totem and Taboo*. Standard ed., vol. 13. London: Hogarth Press.

———. 1955 [1921]. *Group Psychology and the Analysis of the Ego*. Standard ed., vol. 18. London: Hogarth Press.

———. 1957 [1910]. *Leonardo da Vinci and a Memory of His Childhood*. In Standard ed., vol. 2. London: Hogarth Press.

———. 1957 [1930]. *Civilization and Its Discontents*. Standard ed., vol. 17. London: Hogarth Press.

———. 1961 [1927]. *The Future of an Illusion*. Standard ed., vol. 21. London: Hogarth Press.

———. 1964 [1939]. *Moses and Monotheism*. Standard ed., vol. 23. London: Hogarth Press.

Freud, S., and Bullitt, W. C. 1967. *Thomas Woodrow Wilson, 28th President of the U.S.: A Psychological Study*. Boston: Houghton Mifflin.

Frey, S., and Bente, G. 1989. Mikroanalyse Medienvermittelter Informationsprozesse zur Anwendung zeitreihen-basierter Notationsprinzipien auf die Untersuchung von Fernsehnachrichten. Kölner zeitschrift für soziologie und sozialpsychologie, sonderheft 30–1989, *Massenkommunikation*, 515–533.

Frey, S., Hirshrunner, H., Florin, A., Daw, A., and Crawford, R. 1983. A unified approach to the investigation of nonverbal and verbal behavior in communication research. In W. Doise and S. Moscovici (eds.), *Current Issues in European Social Psychology*. Cambridge: Cambridge University Press.

Fridlund, A., and Izard, C. 1983. Electromyographic studies of facial expressions of emotions and patterns of emotion. In J. Cacioppo and R. Petty (eds.), *Social Psychophysiology: A Sourcebook.* New York: Guilford Press.

Friedländer, S. 1971. *L'Antisémitisme Nazi: Histoire d'une psychose collective.* Paris: Editions du Seuil.

———. 1978. *History and Psychoanalysis.* New York: Holmes and Meier.

———. 1984. *Reflections of Nazism.* New York: Harper and Row.

Fromm, E. 1941. *Escape from Freedom.* New York: Holt.

———. 1973. *The Anatomy of Human Destructiveness.* New York: Holt, Rinehart and Winston.

Funk, C., and Sears, D. 1990. Are we reaching undergraduates? a survey of course offerings in political psychology. Presented at meeting of International Society of Political Psychology, Washington, DC.

Futoran, G., and Wyer, R. 1986. Effects of traits and gender stereotypes on occupational suitability judgments and the recall of judgment-relevant information. *Journal of Experimental Social Psychology,* 22, 475–503.

Gamson, W., and Modigliani, A. 1986. Media discourse and public opinion on nuclear power. Unpublished paper, Boston College.

———. 1987. The changing culture of affirmative action. *Research in Political Sociology,* 3, 137–177.

Gant, M., and Davia, D. 1984. Mental economy and voter rationality: the informed citizen problem in voting research. *Journal of Politics,* 46, 132–153.

Gardner, H. 1985. *The Mind's New Science: A History of the Cognitive Revolution.* New York: Basic Books.

Gaxie, P. (ed.). 1985. *Explication du vote.* Paris: Presses de la Fondation Nationale des Sciences Politiques.

Gay, P. 1985. *Freud for Historians.* New York: Oxford University Press.

Gazzaniga, M. 1985. *The Social Brain.* New York: Basic Books.

Geertz, C. 1973. *The Interpretation of Cultures.* New York: Basic Books.

———. 1983. *Local Knowledge: Further Essays in Interpretive Anthropology.* New York: Basic Books.

Genovese, E. 1960. The medical and insurance costs of slaveholding in the cotton belt. *Journal of Negro History,* 65, 141–155.

George, A. 1980. *Presidential Decision-making in Foreign Policy: On the Effective Use of Information and Advice.* Boulder, CO: Westview Press.

George, A., and George, J. 1964 [1956]. *Woodrow Wilson and Colonel House: A Personality Study.* New York: Dover.

Gergen, K. 1973. Social psychology as history. *Journal of Personality and Social Psychology,* 26, 309–320.

———. 1982. *Toward Transformation in Social Knowledge.* New York: Springer-Verlag.

Gergen, K., and Gergen, M. (eds.). 1984. *Historical Social Psychology.* Hillsdale, NJ: Lawrence Erlbaum Associates.

Gibbs, N. 1976. *Grand Strategy: Rearmament Policy.* London: Her Majesty's Stationer's Office.

Gilbert, M. 1967. *Churchill.* Englewood Cliffs, NJ: Prentice-Hall.

Gilligan, C. 1982. *In a Different Voice.* Cambridge, MA: Harvard University Press.

Gilmore, W. 1979. Paths recently crossed: alternatives to psychoanalytic psychohistory continued. *Psychohistory Review*, 7, 26–42.

———. 1984. *Psychohistorical Inquiry: A Comprehensive Research Bibliography.* New York: Garland.

Glad, B. 1973. Contributions of psychobiography. In J. Knutson, *Handbook of Political Psychology.* San Francisco: Jossey-Bass.

———. 1980. *Jimmy Carter: In Search of the Great White House.* New York: Norton.

Goffman, E. 1959. *The Presentation of Self in Everyday Life.* New York: Doubleday.

———. 1961. *Asylums: Essays on the Social Situation of Mental Patients and Other Inmates.* New York: Doubleday.

Goodall, J. 1986. *The Chimpanzees of Gombe.* Cambridge, MA: Harvard University Press.

Googin, M. 1984. The ideological content of presidential communications: the message-tailoring hypothesis revisited. *American Politics Quarterly*, 12, 361–384.

Gordon, S. 1984. *Hitler, Germans and the "Jewish Question."* Princeton, NJ: Princeton University Press.

Gordon, S., and Wyer, R. 1987. Person memory: category-set-size effects on the recall of a person's behaviors. *Journal of Personality and Social Psychology*, 53, 648–662.

Gorer, G. 1948. *The American People.* New York: Norton.

Government Accounting Office. 1990. *Death Penalty Sentencing: Research Indicates Patterns of Racial Disparities.* Washington, DC: GAO Report to Senate and House Committee on the Judiciary. GAO/GGD-90-57.

Graber, D. 1976. *Verbal Behavior and Politics.* Urbana: University of Illinois Press.

———. 1988. *Processing the News: How People Tame the Information Tide.* New York: Longman.

Granberg, D. 1982. Social judgment theory. In M. Burgoon (ed.), *Communications Yearbook*, 6, 304–329.

———. 1985. An assimilation effect in perceptions of Sweden's political parties on the left-right dimension. *Scandinavian Journal of Psychology*, 26, 88–91.

———. 1987a. Candidate preference, membership group, and estimates of voting behavior. *Social Cognition*, 5, 323–335.

———. 1987b. A contextual effect in political perception and self-placement on an ideology scale: comparative analyses of Sweden and the U.S. *Scandinavian Political Studies*, 10, 39–60.

Granberg, D., and Brent, E. 1974. Dove-hawk placements in the 1968 election: application of social judgment and balance theories. *Journal of Personality and Social Psychology,* 29, 687–695.

———. 1980. Perceptions of issue positions of presidential candidates. *American Scientist,* 68, 617–625.

———. 1983. When prophecy bends: the preference-expectation link in the U.S. presidential elections, 1952–1980. *Journal of Personality and Social Psychology,* 40, 833–842.

Granberg, D., and Brown, T. 1990. The perception of ideological distance. Paper presented at meetings of the Midwest Political Science Association, Chicago.

Granberg, D., and Campbell, K. 1977. Effect of communication discrepancy and ambiguity on placement and opinion change. *European Journal of Social Psychology,* 7, 137–150.

Granberg, D., Harris, W., and King, M. 1981. Assimilation but little contrast in the 1976 U.S. presidential election. *Journal of Psychology,* 108, 241–247.

Granberg, D., and Holmberg, S. 1986a. Preference, expectations, and voting behavior in Sweden's referendum on nuclear power. *Social Science Quarterly,* 66, 379–392.

———. 1986b. Political perception in Sweden and the U.S.: analyses of issues with explicit alternatives. *Western Political Quarterly,* 39, 7–28.

———. 1986c. Subjective ideology in Sweden and the United States. In R. Braungart and M. Braungart (eds.), *Research in Political Sociology,* 3, 107–143. Greenwich, CT: JAI Press.

———. 1988. *The Political System Matters: Social Psychology and Voting Behavior in Sweden and the United States.* Cambridge: Cambridge University Press.

———. 1990. The person positivity and principal actor hypotheses. *Journal of Applied Social Psychology,* 20, 1879–1901.

Granberg, D., Jefferson, N., Brent, E., and King, M. 1981. Membership group, reference group, and the attribution of attitudes to groups. *Journal of Personality and Social Psychology,* 40, 833–842.

Granberg, D., and Jenks, R. 1977. Assimilation and contrast in the 1972 election. *Human Relations,* 30, 623–640.

Granberg, D., Kasmer, J., and Nanneman, T. 1988. An empirical examination of two theories of political perception. *Western Political Quarterly,* 41, 29–46.

Granberg, D., and King, M. 1980. Cross-lagged panel analysis of the relation between attraction and perceived similarity. *Journal of Experimental Social Psychology,* 16, 573–581.

Granberg, D., and Nanneman, T. 1986. Attitude change in an electoral context as a function of expectations not being fulfilled. *Political Psychology,* 7, 753–765.

Granberg, D., and Robertson, C. 1982. Contrast effects in estimating the policies of the federal government. *Public Opinion Quarterly,* 46, 43–53.

Granberg, D., and Seidel, J. 1976. Social judgments of the urban and Vietnam issues in 1968 and 1972. *Social Forces, 55,* 1–15.

Gray, J. 1982. *The Neuropsychology of Anxiety.* New York: Oxford University Press.

Green, D. 1988. Self-interest, public opinion, and mass political behavior. Unpublished doctoral dissertation, University of California, Berkeley.

Greenstein, F. 1975. *Personality and Politics: Problems of Evidence, Inference, and Conceptualization.* New York: Norton.

Grether, D. 1990. Testing Bayes rule and the representativeness heuristic: some experimental evidence. Social Science Working Paper No. 724, California Institute of Technology.

Grether, D., and Plott, C. 1979. Economic theory of choice and the preference reversal phenomenon. *American Economic Review, 69,* 623–638.

Greven, P. 1977. *The Protestant Temperament: Patterns of Child-rearing, Religious Experience, and the Self in Early America.* New York: Meridian.

Gurr, T. R. 1970. *Why Men Rebel.* Princeton, NJ: Princeton University Press.

Gusfield, J. 1963. *Symbolic Crusade.* Urbana: University of Illinois Press.

Hadenius, A. 1986. *A Crisis of the Welfare State?: Opinions About Taxes and Public Expenditure in Sweden.* Stockholm: Almqvist and Wiksell.

Hall, J. 1978. Gender effects in decoding nonverbal cues. *Psychological Bulletin, 85,* 845–857.

———. 1987. On explaining gender differences: the case of nonverbal communication. In P. Shaver and C. Hendrick (eds.), *Sex and Gender.* Beverly Hills, CA: Sage.

Hamill, R., and Lodge, M. 1986. Cognitive consequences of political sophistication. In R. Lau and D. Sears (eds.), *Political Cognition.* Hillsdale, NJ: Lawrence Erlbaum Associates.

Hamilton, D. 1981. *Cognitive Processes in Stereotyping and Intergroup Behavior.* Hillsdale, NJ: Lawrence Erlbaum Associates.

Hamilton, D., Fallot, R., and Hautaluoma, J. 1978. Information salience and order effects in impression formation. *Personality and Social Psychology Bulletin, 4,* 44–47.

Hamilton, D., Katz, L., and Leirer, V. 1980. Cognitive representation of personality impressions: organizational processes in first impression formation. *Journal of Personality and Social Psychology, 39,* 1050–1063.

Hamilton, R. 1981. *Who Voted for Hitler?* Princeton, NJ: Princeton University Press.

Hamilton, R., and Wright, J. 1986. *The State of the Masses.* New York: Aldine.

Harvey, O., Hunt, D., and Schroder, H. 1961. *Conceptual Systems and Personality Organization.* New York: Wiley.

Hastie, R. 1981. Schematic principles in human memory. In E. Higgins, C. Herman, and M. Zanna (eds.), *Social Cognition: The Ontario Symposium,* vol. 1. Hillsdale, NJ: Lawrence Erlbaum Associates.

———. 1986. A primer of information-processing theory for the political scientist. In R. Lau and D. Sears (eds.), *Political Cognition: The Nineteenth Annual Carnegie-Mellon Symposium on Cognition*. Hillsdale, NJ: Lawrence Erlbaum Associates.

———. 1988. A computer simulation of person memory. *Journal of Experimental Social Psychology*, 24, 423–447.

Hastie, R., and Kumar, P. 1979. Person memory: personality traits as organizing principles in memory for behaviors. *Journal of Personality and Social Psychology*, 37, 25–38.

Hastie, R., and Park, B. 1986. The relationship between memory and judgment depends on whether the judgment task is memory-based or on-line. *Psychological Review*, 93, 258–268.

Hastie, R., and Penningon, N. 1989. Notes on the distinction between memory-based and on-line judgments. In J. Bassili (ed.), *On-Line Cognition in Person Perception*. Hillsdale, NJ: Lawrence Erlbaum Associates.

Hastie, R., Penrod, S., and Pennington, N. 1983. *Inside the Jury*. Cambridge, MA: Harvard University Press.

Hausner, G. 1966. *Justice in Jerusalem*. New York: Holocaust Library.

Heider, F. 1946. Attitudes and cognitive organization. *Journal of Psychology*, 21, 107–112.

———. 1958. *The Psychology of Interpersonal Relations*. New York: Wiley.

Hendricks, C. 1972. Effects of salience of stimulus consistency on impression formation. *Journal of Personality and Social Psychology*, 22, 219–222.

Hendricks, C., Bixenstine, E., and Hawkins, G. 1971. Race versus belief similarity as determinants of attraction. *Journal of Personality and Social Psychology*, 17, 250–258.

Hendricks, C., and Hawkins, G. 1969. Race and belief similarity as determinants of attraction. *Perceptual And Motor Skills*, 29, 710.

Henshel, R., and Johnston, W. 1987. The emergence of bandwagon effects: a theory. *Sociological Quarterly*, 28, 493–511.

Herek, G. 1986. The instrumentality of attitudes: toward a neofunctional theory. *Journal of Social Issues*, 42, 99–114.

Hermann, M. (ed.). 1986. *Political Psychology*. San Francisco: Jossey-Bass.

Herr, P. 1986. Consequences of priming: judgment and behavior. *Journal of Personality and Social Psychology*, 51, 1106–1115.

Herstein, J. 1981. Keeping the voters limits in mind: a cognitive process analysis of decision making and voting. *Journal of Personality and Social Psychology*, 40, 843–861.

Higgins, E., Bargh, J., and Lombardi, W. 1985. The nature of priming effects on categorization. *Journal of Experimental Psychology: Learning, Memory and Cognition*, 11, 59–69.

Higgins, E., and King, G. 1981. Accessibility of social constructs: information processing consequences of individual and contextual variability. In N. Cantor and J. Kihlstrom (eds.), *Personality, Cognition and Social Interaction*. Hillsdale, NJ: Lawrence Erlbaum Associates.

Higgins, E., and Lurie, L. 1983. Context, categorization and recall: the "change-of-standard" effect. *Cognitive Psychology, 15*, 525–547.

Higgins, E., Rholes, W., and Jones, C. 1977. Category accessibility and impression formation. *Journal of Experimental Social Psychology, 13*, 141–154.

Higham, C. 1983. *Trading with the Enemy*. New York: Delacorte.

Higham, R. 1977. The peripheral weapon in wartime. In G. Jordan (ed.), *Naval Warfare in the 20th Century*. London: Croom Helm.

Himmelweit, H., Humphries, P., and Jaeger, M. 1985. *How Voters Decide*. Milton Keynes, Eng.: Open University Press.

Hinckley, B. 1981. *Congressional Elections*. Washington, DC: Congressional Quarterly Press.

Hinde, Robert. 1982. *Ethology*. Glasgow: Collins.

Hinich, M., and Enelow, J. 1984. *Spatial Models of Voting*. New York: Cambridge University Press.

Hinkle, S., and Brown, R. 1990. Intergroup comparisons and social identity: Some links and lacunae. In D. Abrams and M. Hogg (eds.), *Advances in Social Identity Theory*. New York: Harvester Wheat Sheaf.

Hinsley, F. (with E. Thomas, C. Ransome, and R. Knight). 1979. *British Intelligence in the Second World War*. New York: Cambridge University Press.

Hirschleifer, J. 1987. *Economic Behavior in Adversity*. Chicago: University of Chicago Press.

Hirschman, A. 1985. Against parsimony. *Economics and Philosophy, 1*, 7–21.

Hoess, R. 1959. *Commandant of Auschwitz*. London: Pan Books.

Hoffman, L. 1982. Psychoanalytic interpretations of Adolf Hitler and Nazism, 1933–1945: a prelude to psychohistory. *Psychohistory Review, 11*, 68–87.

Hoffman, P. 1977. *The History of the German Resistance, 1933–1945*. Cambridge, MA: MIT Press.

Hofstadter, R. 1944. *Social Darwinism in American Thought, 1860–1915*. Philadelphia: University of Pennsylvania Press.

Höhne, H. 1969. *The Order of the Death's Head: The Story of Hitler's SS*. New York: Coward-McCann.

Holmberg, S., and Esaiasson, P. 1988. *De folkvalda: En bok om Riksdagsledamöterna och den Representiva Demokratin i Syerige*. Stockholm: Bonniers.

Hong, S., and Wyer, R. 1990. Determinants of product evaluation: effects of the time interval between knowledge of a product's country of origin and information about its specific attributes. *Journal of Consumer Research, 17*, 277–288.

Horney, K. 1937. *The Neurotic Personality of Our Time*. New York: Norton.

Hovland, C. 1959. Reconciling conflicting results derived from experimental and survey studies of attitude change, *American Psychologist, 14*, 8–17.

Hovland, C., Campbell, E., and Brock, T. 1957. The effects of "commitment" on opinion change following communication. In C. Hovland et al., *Order of Presentation in Persuasion*. New Haven, CT: Yale University Press.

Hovland, C., Janis, I., and Kelley, H. 1953. *Communication and Persuasion*. New Haven, CT: Yale University Press.

Howard, J., and Rothbart, M. 1980. Social categorization and memory for in-group and out-group behavior. *Journal of Personality and Social Psychology*, 38, 301–310.

Hughes, J. 1983. *Emotion and High Politics: Personal Relations at the Summit in Late Nineteenth-Century Britain and Germany*. Berkeley: University of California Press.

Hunter, F. 1953. *Community Power Structure: A Study of Decision Makers*. Chapel Hill: University of North Carolina Press.

Hurwitz, J. 1986. Issue perception and legislative decision making. *American Politics Quarterly*, 14, 150–185.

Hurwitz, J., and Peffley, M. 1987. How are foreign policy attitudes structured? a hierarchical model. *American Political Science Review*, 81, 1099–1120.

Hyman, J. 1959. *Political Socialization*. Glencoe, IL: Free Press.

Ikle, F. 1971. *Every War Must End*. New York: Columbia University Press.

Imai, M. 1986. *Kaizen: The Key to Japan's Competitive Success*. New York: Random House.

Inglehart, R. 1985. Aggregate stability and individual-level flux in mass beliefs systems: the level of analysis paradox. *American Political Science Review*, 79, 97–116.

Inglehart, R., and Klingemann, H. 1976. Party identification, ideological preference and the left-right dimension among western mass publics. In I. Budge, I. Crewe, and D. Farlie (eds.), *Party Identification and Beyond: Representations of Voting and Party Competition*. New York: Wiley.

Inkeles, A. 1983. *Exploring Individual Modernity*. New York: Columbia University Press.

Inkeles, A., and Smith, D. 1974. *Becoming Modern: Individual Change in Six Developing Countries*. Cambridge, MA: Harvard University Press.

Insko, C., and Robinson, J. 1967. Belief similarity versus race as determinants of reactions to Negroes by southern white adolescents: a further test. *Journal of Personality and Social Psychology*, 7, 216–221.

Insko, C., Songer, E., and McGarvey, W. 1974. Balance, positivity, and agreement in the Jordan paradigm: a defense of balance theory. *Journal of Experimental Social Psychology*, 10, 53–83.

Inter-University Consortium for Political and Social Research. 1988. *Guide to Resources and Services, 1987–1988*. Ann Arbor: University of Michigan, Institute for Social Research.

Iriye, A. 1969. *After Imperialism*. New York: Atheneum.

Isen, A. M. 1984. Toward understanding the role of affect in cognition. In R. S. Wyer and T. K. Srull (eds.), *Handbook of Social Cognition*. Hillsdale, NJ: Lawrence Erlbaum Associates.

Isen, A. M., Clark, M., Shalker, T. E., and Karp, L. 1978. Affect, accessibility of material in memory, and behavior: a cognitive loop? *Journal of Personality and Social Psychology,* 36, 1–12.

Ittelson, W. H. 1973. Environment perception and contemporary perceptual theory. In W. H. Ittelson (ed.), *Environment and Cognition.* New York: Seminar Press.

Iyengar, S. 1991. *Is Anyone Responsible?: How Television Frames Political Issues.* Chicago: University of Chicago Press.

Iyengar, S., and Kinder, D. 1985. Psychological accounts of agenda-setting. In S. Kraus and R. Perloff (eds.), *Mass Media and Political Thought: An Information-Processing Approach.* Beverly Hills, CA: Sage.

———. 1987. *News That Matters: Television and American Opinion.* Chicago: University of Chicago Press.

Iyengar, S., Peters, M., and Kinder, D. 1982. Experimental demonstrations of the "not-so-minimal" consequences of television news programs. *American Political Science Review,* 81, 848–858.

Izard, C. E. 1971. *The Face of Emotion.* New York: Appleton-Century-Crofts.

———. 1979. *The Maximally Discriminative Facial Movement Coding System.* Newark, DE: University of Delaware.

———. 1981. Differential emotions theory and the facial feedback hypothesis of emotion activation: comments on Tourangeau and Ellsworth's "The role of facial response in the experience of emotion." *Journal of Personality and Social Psychology,* 40, 350–354.

Izard, C., Hembree, E., and Heubner, R. 1987. Infants' emotion expressions to acute pain: developmental change and stability of individual differences. *Developmental Psychology,* 23, 105–113.

Jackman, M., and Muha, M. 1984. Education and intergroup attitudes: moral enlightenment, superficial democratic commitment, or ideological refinement? *American Sociological Review,* 49, 751–769.

Jackman, M., and Senter, M. 1983. Different, therefore unequal: beliefs about trait differences between groups of unequal status. In D. Treiman and R. Robinson (eds.), *Research in Social Stratification,* Greenwich, CT: JAI Press.

Jacobson, C. 1985. Resistance to affirmative action: self-interest or racism? *Journal of Conflict Resolution,* 29, 306–329.

Jacobson, G. 1987. *The Politics of Congressional Elections.* New Haven, CT: Yale University Press.

Jacoby, W. 1988. The impact of party identification on issue attitudes. *American Journal of Political Science,* 32, 643–661.

Janis, I. 1982. *Victims of Groupthink.* 2nd ed. Boston: Houghton Mifflin.

———. 1989. *Crucial Decisions: Leadership in Policymaking and Crisis Management.* New York: Free Press.

Janis, I., and Mann, L. 1977. *Decision Making.* New York: Free Press.

Jaynes, J. 1976. *The Origin of Consciousness in the Breakdown of the Bicameral Mind.* Boston: Houghton Mifflin.

Jennings, M. 1987. Residues of a movement: the aging of the American protest generation. *American Political Science Review,* 81, 367–382.

Jennings, M., and Niemi, R. 1981. *Generations and Politics.* Princeton, NJ: Princeton University Press.

Jervis, R. 1976. *Perception and Misperception in International Politics.* Princeton, NJ: Princeton University Press.

———. 1982. Deterrence and perception. *International Security,* 7, 14–19.

———. 1984. *The Illogic of American Nuclear Strategy.* Ithaca, NY: Cornell University Press.

———. 1986. Representativeness in foreign policy judgments. *Political Psychology,* 7, 483–505.

———. 1989a. Political psychology—some challenges and opportunities. *Political Psychology,* 10, 481–493.

———. 1989b. Rational deterrence: theory and practice. *World Politics,* 41, 199–201.

———. 1989c. *The Meaning of the Nuclear Revolution.* Ithaca, NY: Cornell University Press.

———. 1991. Systems effects. In R. Zeckhauser (ed.), *Strategic Reflections on Human Behavior.* Cambridge, MA: MIT Press.

Jervis, R., Lebow, R., and Stein, J. 1985. *Psychology and Deterrence.* Baltimore: Johns Hopkins University Press.

Jessor, T. 1988. Personal interest, group conflict, and symbolic group affect: explanations for whites' opposition to racial equality. Unpublished doctoral dissertation, University of California, Los Angeles.

Johnson, B., and Eagly, A. 1989. Effects of involvement on persuasion: a meta-analysis. *Psychological Bulletin,* 106, 290–314.

Johnson, J., and Hogan, R. 1981. Moral judgments as self-presentations. *Journal of Research in Personality,* 15, 57–83.

Johnson, J., and Judd, C. 1983. Overlooking the congruent: categorization biases in the identification of political statements. *Journal of Personality and Social Psychology,* 45, 978–996.

Jöreskog, K., and Sörbom, D. 1984. *LISREL VI: Analysis of Linear Structural Relationships by the Method of Maximum Likelihood.* Mooresville, IN: Scientific Software.

Joslyn, R., and Ross, M. 1986. Television news coverage and public opinion in the 1984 primaries. Presented at annual meeting of American Political Science Association, Washington, DC.

Judd, C., Drake, R., Downing, J., and Krosnick, J. 1991. Some dynamic properties of attitude structures: context-induced response facilitation and polarization. *Journal of Personality and Social Psychology,* 60, 193–202.

Judd, C., Kenny, D., and Krosnick, J. 1983. Judging the positions of political candidates: models of assimilation and contrast. *Journal of Personality and Social Psychology,* 44, 952–963.

Judd, C., and Krosnick, J. 1988. The structural bases of consistency among political attitudes: effects of political expertise and attitude importance. In A. Pratkanis, S. Beckler, and A. Greenwald (eds.), *Attitude Structure and Function*. Hillsdale, NJ: Lawrence Erlbaum Associates.

Judd, C., and Lusk, C. 1984. Knowledge structures and evaluative judgments: effects of structural variables on judgment extremity. *Journal of Personality and Social Psychology*, 46, 1193–1207.

Kagan, J. 1988. Biological bases of childhood shyness. *Science*, 240, 167–171.

Kagan, J., Reznick, J., and Snidman, N. 1987. The physiology and psychology of behavioral inhibition in children. *Child Development*, 58, 1459–1473.

Kagay, M., and Caldeira, G. 1975. "I like the looks of his face": elements of electoral choice, 1952–1972. Presented at annual meeting of American Political Science Association.

Kahn, A., and Ryen, A. 1972. Factors influencing the bias toward one's own group. *International Journal of Group Tensions*, 2, 33–50.

Kahn, H. 1960. *On Thermonuclear War*. Princeton, NJ: Princeton University Press.

Kahneman, D., and Miller, D. 1986. Norm theory: comparing reality to its alternatives. *Psychological Review*, 93, 124–139.

Kahneman, D., Slovic, P., and Tversky, A. (eds.). 1982. *Judgment Under Uncertainty: Heuristics and Biases*. New York: Cambridge University Press.

Kahneman, D., and Tversky, A. 1972. Subjective probability: a judgment of representativeness. *Cognitive Psychology*, 3, 445–452.

———. 1973. On the psychology of prediction. *Psychological Review*, 80, 237–251.

———. 1982. The psychology of preferences. *Science*, 246, 136–142.

———. 1984. Choices, values, and frames. *American Psychologist*, 39, 341–350.

Kalb, M., and Hertzberg, H. 1988. *Candidates '88*. Dover, MA: Auburn House.

Kalin, R., and Marlowe, D. 1968. The effects of intergroup competition, personal drinking habits and frustration in intra-group cooperation. Proceedings of 76th annual convention of the American Psychological Association.

Kantowitz, B. 1985. Channels and stages in human information processing: a limited analysis of theory and methodology. *Journal of Mathematical Psychology*, 29, 135–174.

Kaplan, A. 1964. *The Conduct of Inquiry*. San Francisco: Chandler.

Karmen, A. 1984. *Crime Victims: An introduction to Victimology*. Monterey, CA: Brooks/Cole.

Katona, G. 1975. *Psychological Economics*. New York: Elsevier.

Katz, D. 1960. The functional approach to the study of attitudes. *Public Opinion Quarterly*, 24, 163–204.

Katz, D., and Kahn, R. 1978. *The Social Psychology of Organizations*. 2nd ed. New York: Wiley.

Katz, I., and Hass, R. 1988. Racial ambivalence and American value conflict:

correlational and priming studies of dual cognitive structures. *Journal of Personality and Social Psychology, 55,* 893–905.

Katz, P. 1976. The acquisition of racial attitudes in children. In P. Katz (ed.), *Towards the Elimination of Racism.* Elmsford, NY: Pergamon Press.

Kelley, H. 1950. The warm-cold variable in first impressions of persons. *Journal of Personality,* 18, 431–439.

Kelley, S., Jr., and Mirer, T. 1974. The simple act of voting. *American Political Science Review,* 68, 572–591.

Kelly, D. 1985. Sexual differentiation of the nervous system. In E. Kandel and J. Schwartz (eds.), *Principles of Neural Science.* New York: Elsevier.

Keniston, K. 1971. Psychological development and historical change. *Journal of Interdisciplinary History,* 2, 329–345.

Kennedy, P. 1977. Fisher and Tirpitz compared. In G. Jordan (ed.), *Naval Warfare in the 20th Century.* London: Croom Helm.

Kepplinger, H. 1990. The impact of presentation techniques: theoretical aspects and empirical findings. In F. Biocca (ed.), *The Psychological and Semantic Processing of Televised Political Advertising.* Hillsdale, NJ: Lawrence Erlbaum Associates.

Kernell, S. 1977. Presidential popularity and negative voting: an alternative explanation of the midterm congressional decline of the President's party. *American Political Science Review,* 71, 44–66.

Key, V. O., Jr. 1949. *Southern Politics in State and Nation.* New York: Knopf.

———. 1961. *Public Opinion and American Democracy.* New York: Knopf.

———. 1966. *The Responsible Electorate.* Cambridge, MA: Harvard University Press.

Kiewiet, R. 1983. *Macroeconomic and Micropolitics.* Chicago: University of Chicago Press.

Kinder, D. 1978. Political person perception: the asymmetrical influence of sentiment and choice on perceptions of presidential candidates. *Journal of Personality and Social Psychology,* 36, 859–871.

———. 1986a. Presidential character revisited. In R. Lau and D. Sears (eds.), *Political Cognition.* Hillsdale, NJ: Lawrence Erlbaum Associates.

———. 1986b. The continuing American dilemma: white resistance to racial change 40 years after Myrdal. *Journal of Social Issues,* 42, 151–171.

Kinder, D., and Abelson, R. 1981. Appraising presidential candidates: personality and affect in the 1980 campaign. Presented at annual meeting of American Political Science Association.

Kinder, D., and Kiewiet, R. 1979. Economic discontent and political behavior: the role of personal grievances and collective economic judgments in congressional voting. *American Journal of Political Science,* 23, 495–527.

Kinder, D., and Nelson, T. 1990. Experimental investigations of opinion frames and survey responses. Report to the National Election Studies Board.

Kinder, D., and Sanders, L. 1990. Mimicking political debate with survey questions: the case of white opinion on affirmative action for blacks. *Social Cognition,* 8, 73–103.

Kinder, D., and Sears, D. 1981. Prejudice and politics: symbolic racism versus racial threats to the good life. *Journal of Personality and Social Psychology,* 40, 414–431.

———. 1985. Public opinion and political action. In G. Lindzey and E. Aronson (eds.), *Handbook of Social Psychology,* vol. 2. 3rd ed. New York: Random House.

King, M. 1978. Assimilation and contrast of presidential candidates' issue positions. *Public Opinion Quarterly,* 41, 515–522.

Klapper, J. 1960. *The Effects of Mass Communications.* Glencoe, IL: Free Press.

Klein, E. 1987. *Gender Politics.* Cambridge, MA: Harvard University Press.

Kleinmuntz, D., and Kleinmuntz, B. 1981. Systems simulation decision strategies in simulated environments. *Behavioral Science,* 26, 294–305.

Kleugel, J., and Smith, E. 1986. *Beliefs About Equality.* Hawthorne, NY: Aldine de Gruyter.

Kling, A. 1986. Neurological correlates of social behavior. In M. Gruter and R. Masters (eds.), *Ostracism: A Social and Biological Phenomenon.* New York: Elsevier.

———. 1987. Brain mechanisms and social/affective behavior. *Social Science Information,* 26, 375–384.

Klinger, E. 1977. *Meaning and Void: Inner Experience and the Incentives in People's Lives.* Minneapolis: University of Minnesota Press.

Kluckhohn, C., and Murray, H. 1948. Personality formation: the determinants. In C. Kluckhohn, H. Murray, and D. Schneider (eds.), *Personality in Nature, Society, and Culture.* Rev. ed. New York: Knopf.

Kluegel, J., and Smith, E. 1983. Affirmative action attitudes: effects of self-interest, racial affect, and stratification beliefs on whites' views. *Social Forces,* 61, 797–824.

Knutson, J. (ed.). 1973. *Handbook of Political Psychology.* San Francisco: Jossey-Bass.

Kornhauser, W. 1959. *The Politics of Mass Society.* Glencoe, IL: Free Press.

Kosslyn, S. 1988. Aspects of cognitive neuroscience of mental imagery. *Science,* 240, 1621–1626.

Kosterman, R. 1991. Political spot advertising and routes to persuasion: the role of symbolic content. Unpublished doctoral dissertation, University of California, Los Angeles.

Kramer, G. 1971. Short-term fluctuations in U.S. voting behavior, 1896–1964. *American Political Science Review,* 65, 131–143.

Kraus, S., and Perloff, R. (eds.). 1985. *Mass Media and Political Thought.* Beverly Hills, CA: Sage.

Kraut, R. E. 1982. Social presence, facial feedback, and emotion. *Journal of Personality and Social Psychology,* 42, 853–863.

Krech, D., and Crutchfield, R. 1948. *Theory and Problems of Social Psychology.* New York: McGraw-Hill.

Kren, G., and Rappoport, L. 1980. *The Holocaust and the Crisis of Human Behavior.* New York: Holmes and Meier.

Kreps, D. 1990. *An Introduction to Microeconomic Theory.* Princeton, NJ: Princeton University Press.

Krosnick, J. 1988a. Psychological perspectives on political candidate perception: a review of research on the projection hypothesis. Presented at annual meeting of Midwest Political Science Association, Chicago.

———. 1988b. The role of attitude importance in social evaluation: a study of policy preferences, presidential candidate evaluations, and voting behavior. *Journal of Personality and Social Psychology,* 55, 196–210.

———. 1988c. Attitude importance and attitude change. *Journal of Experimental Social Psychology,* 24, 240–255.

———. 1989. Attitude importance and attitude accessibility. *Personality and Social Psychology Bulletin,* 15, 297–308.

———. 1990a. Americans' perceptions of presidential candidates: a test of the projection hypothesis. *Journal of Social Issues,* 46, 159–182.

———. 1990b. Government policy and citizen passion: a study of issue publics in contemporary America. *Political Behavior,* 12, 59–92.

———. 1991. The stability of political preferences: comparisons of symbolic and nonsymbolic attitudes. *American Journal of Political Science,* 35, 547–576.

Krosnick, J., and Kinder, D. 1990. Altering the foundations of support for the president through priming. *American Political Science Review,* 84, 497–512.

Krosnick, J., and Schuman, H. 1988. Attitude intensity, importance, and certainty and susceptibility to response effects. *Journal of Personality and Social Psychology,* 54, 940–952.

Kuklinski, J., Riggle, D., Ottati, V., Schwarz, N., and Wyer, R. 1991. The cognitive and affective bases of political tolerance judgments. *American Journal of Political Science,* 35, 1–27.

Kunst-Wilson, W. R., and Zajonc, R. B. 1980. Affective discrimination of stimuli that cannot be recognized. *Science,* 207, 557–558.

LaBarre, W. 1945. Oriental character structure. *Psychiatry,* 8, 319–342.

Ladurie, E. 1978. *Le territoire de l'historien,* vol. 2. Paris: Gallimard. ([1981]. S. Reynolds and B. Reynolds, trans., *The Mind and Method of the Historian.* Chicago: University of Chicago Press.)

Laird, J. D. 1974. Self-attribution of emotion: the effects of expressive behavior on the quality of emotional experience. *Journal of Personality and Social Psychology,* 29, 475–486.

Lakoff, G. 1987. *Women, Fire and Dangerous Things.* Chicago: University of Chicago Press.

Lambert, A., and Wyer, R. 1990. Stereotypes and social judgment: the effect of typicality and group heterogeneity. *Journal of Personality and Social Psychology,* 59, 676–691.

Lane, R. 1959. *Political Life: Why and How People Get Involved in Politics.* Glencoe, IL: Free Press.

———. 1962. *Political Ideology: Why the American Common Man Believes What He Does.* Glencoe, IL: Free Press.

———. 1973. Patterns of political belief. In J. Knutson (ed.), *Handbook of Political Psychology.* San Francisco: Jossey-Bass.

Langer, W. 1972. *The Mind of Adolf Hitler: The Secret Wartime Report.* New York: Basic Books.

Lanzetta, J., and Orr, S. 1980. Influence of facial expressions on the classical conditioning of fear. *Journal of Personality and Social Psychology,* 39, 1081–1087.

Lanzetta, J., Sullivan, D., Masters, R., and McHugo, G. 1985. Emotional and cognitive responses to televised images of political leaders. In S. Kraus and R. Perloff (eds.), *Mass Media and Political Thought.* Beverly Hills, CA: Sage.

Larson, D. 1985. *Origins of Containment: A Psychological Explanation.* Princeton, NJ: Princeton University Press.

Lasch, C. 1979. *The Culture of Narcissism: American Life in an Age of Diminishing Expectations.* New York: Norton.

Lasswell, H. 1930. *Psychopathology and Politics.* Chicago: University of Chicago Press.

———. 1935. *World Politics and Personal Insecurity.* New York: McGraw-Hill.

———. 1948. *Power and Personality.* New York: Norton.

Lau, R. 1982. Negativity in political perceptions. *Political Behavior,* 4, 353–378.

———. 1985. Two explanations for negativity effects in political behavior. *American Journal of Political Science,* 29, 119–138.

———. 1986. Political schemata, candidate evaluations and voting behavior. In R. Lau and D. Sears (eds.), *Political Cognition.* Hillsdale, NJ: Lawrence Erlbaum Associates.

Lau, R., Brown, T., and Sears, D. 1978. Self-interest and civilians' attitudes toward the Vietnam war. *Public Opinion Quarterly,* 42, 464–483.

Lau, R., and Sears, D. (eds.). 1986. *Political Cognition.* Hillsdale, NJ: Lawrence Erlbaum Associates.

Lau, R., Smith, R., and Fiske, S. 1988. Framing effects, political schemata, and political persuasion. Presented at annual meeting of American Political Science Association, Washington, DC, September 2.

Lazarsfeld, P. 1946. Mutual effects of statistical variables. In P. Lazarsfeld, A. Pasanella, and M. Rosenberg (eds.), *Continuities in the Language of Social Research.* New York: Free Press.

Lazarsfeld, P., Berelson, B., and Gaudet, H. 1948. *The People's Choice.* 2nd ed. New York: Columbia University Press.

Lazarus, R. S. 1982. Thoughts on the relations between emotion and cognition. *American Psychologist,* 37, 1019–1024.

———. 1984. On the primacy of cognition. *American Psychologist,* 39, 124–129.

Lebow, R. 1981. *Between Peace and War: The Nature of International Crises.* Baltimore: Johns Hopkins University Press.

Lehman, D., Krosnick, J., West, R., and Fan, L. 1991. The focus of judgment effect: a question wording effect due to hypothesis confirmation bias. Presented at annual meeting of American Association for Public Opinion Research, Phoenix.

Leighton, A. 1945. *The Governing of Men*. Princeton, NJ: Princeton University Press.

Levi, A., and Tetlock, P. 1980. A cognitive analysis of the Japanese decision to go to war. *Journal of Conflict Resolution*, 24, 195–212.

LeVine, R., and Campbell, D. 1972. *Ethnocentrism: Theories of Conflict, Ethnic Attitudes, and Group Behavior*. New York: Wiley.

LeVine, R., and Shweder, R. (eds.). 1984. *Culture Theory: Essays on Mind, Self, and Emotion*. Cambridge: Cambridge University Press.

LeVine, R., and White, M. 1986. *Human Conditions: The Cultural Basis of Educational Developments*. New York: Routledge and Kegan Paul.

Lewis, O. 1961. *Children of Sánchez*. New York: Random House.

Lichtenstein, M., and Srull, T. 1987. Processing objectives as a determinant of the relationship between recall and judgment. *Journal of Experimental Social Psychology*, 23, 93–118.

Lifton, R. 1986. *The Nazi Doctors*. New York: Basic Books.

Lindblom, C. 1959. The science of muddling through. *Public Administration Review*, 19, 74–88.

Lingle, J., and Ostrom, T. 1981. Retrieval selectivity in memory-based impression judgments. *Journal of Personality and Social Psychology*, 37, 180–194.

Lingle, J., Geva, H., Ostrom, T., Leippe, M., and Baumgardner, M. 1979. Thematic effects of person judgments on impression organization. *Journal of Personality and Social Psychology*, 37, 674–687.

Lippmann, W. 1922. *Public Opinion*. New York: Macmillan.

Lipset, S. 1960. *Political Man: The Social Bases of Politics*. Garden City, NY: Doubleday.

Listhaug, D., and Miller, A. 1985. Public support for tax evasion: self-interest or symbolic politics? *European Journal of Political Research*, 13, 265–282.

Locksley, A., Borgida, E., Brekke, N., and Hepburn, C. 1980. Sex stereotypes and social judgment. *Journal of Personality and Social Psychology*, 39, 821–831.

Locksley, A., Ortiz, V., and Hepburn, C. 1980. Social categorization and discrimination behavior: extinguishing the minimal intergroup discrimination effect. *Journal of Personality and Social Psychology*, 39, 773–783.

Lodge, M., McGraw, K., and Stroh, P. 1989. An impression-driven model of candidate evaluation. *American Political Science Review*, 83, 99–119.

Lodge, M., Stroh, P., and Wahlke, J. 1990. Black-box models of candidate evaluation. *Political Behavior*, 12, 5–18.

Loewenberg, P. 1971. The psychohistorical origins of the Nazi youth cohort. *American Historical Review*, 76, 1457–1502.

———. 1975. Psychohistorical perspectives on modern German history. *Journal of Modern History*, 47, 229–279.

———. 1983. *Decoding the Past: The Psychohistorical Approach*. New York: Knopf.

———. 1988. Psychoanalytic models of history: Freud and after. In W. Runyan (ed.), *Psychology and Historical Interpretation*. New York: Oxford University Press.

Lombardi, W., Higgins, E., and Bargh, J. 1987. The role of consciousness in priming effects on categorization. *Personality and Social Psychology Bulletin*, 13, 411–429.

Long, S. (ed.). 1981. *The Handbook of Political Behavior*. 5 vols. New York: Plenum.

Lord, C., Lepper, M., and Mackie, D. 1984. Attitude prototypes as determinants of attitude-behavior consistency. *Journal of Personality and Social Psychology*, 46, 1254–1266.

Lorenz, K., and Leyhausen, P. 1973. *Motivation of Human and Animal Behavior*. New York: Van Nostrand Reinhold.

Lorge, I. 1936. Prestige, suggestion, and attitudes. *Journal of Social Psychology*, 7, 386–402.

Losco, J. 1985. Evolution, consciousness and political thinking. *Political Behavior*, 7, 223–247.

Lui, L., and Brewer, M. 1988. Recognition accuracy as evidence of category-consistency effects in person memory. *Social Cognition*, 2, 89–107.

Luker, K. 1984. *Abortion and the Politics of Motherhood*. Berkeley: University of California Press.

Lund, T. 1974. Multidimensional scaling of political parties: a methodological study. *Scandinavian Journal of Psychology*, 15, 108–118.

Luria, A. 1971. Towards the problem of the historical nature of psychological processes. *International Journal of Psychology*, 6, 259–272.

———. 1976. *Cognitive Development: Its Cultural and Social Foundations*. Cambridge, MA: Harvard University Press.

Luskin, R. 1987. Measuring political sophistication. *American Journal of Political Science*, 31, 856–899.

Luttbeg, N. 1981. Balance theory as a source of where political parties stand on the issues. In N. Luttbeg (ed.), *Public Opinion and Public Policy*. Itaska, IL: F. E. Peacock.

Lynd, R., and Lynd, H. 1937. *Middletown in Transition: A Study in Cultural Conflicts*. New York: Harcourt Brace.

McAdams, D., and Ochberg, R. (eds.). 1988. *Psychobiography and Life Narratives*. Durham, NC: Duke University Press.

McClelland, D. 1961. *The Achieving Society*. Princeton, NJ: Van Nostrand.

———. 1975. *Power: The Inner Experience*. New York: Irvington Publishers.

McClendon, M. 1985. Racism, rational choice, and white opposition to racial change: a case study of busing. *Public Opinion Quarterly*, 49, 214–233.

McClosky, H. 1958. Conservatism and personality. *American Political Science Review*, 52, 27–45.

———. 1967. Personality and attitude correlates of foreign policy orientation. In J. Rosenau (ed.), *Domestic Sources of Foreign Policy*. New York: Free Press.

McClosky, H., and Brill, A. 1983. *Dimensions of Tolerance: What Americans Believe About Civil Liberties*. New York: Russell Sage.

McCluskey, K., and Reese, H. (eds.). 1984. *Life-Span Developmental Psychology: Historical and Generational Effects*. New York: Academic Press.

McCombs, M. 1981. The agenda-setting approach. In D. Nimmo and K. Sanders (eds.), *Handbook of Political Communication*. Beverly Hills, CA: Sage.

McConahay, J. 1982. Self-interest versus racial attitudes as correlates of anti-busing attitudes in Louisville: is it the buses or the blacks? *Journal of Politics*, 44, 692–720.

———. 1983. Modern racism and modern discrimination: the effects of race, racial attitudes and context on simulated hiring decisions. *Personality and Social Psychology Bulletin*, 9, 551–558.

McConahay, J., and Hough, J. 1976. Symbolic racism. *Journal of Social Issues*, 32, 23–45.

MacDonald, K. 1988. *Social and Personality Development: An Evolutionary Synthesis*. New York: Plenum.

McGrath, J., and McGrath, M. 1962. Effects of partisanship on perception of public figures. *Public Opinion Quarterly*, 26, 236–248.

McGraw, K., Lodge, M., and Stroh, P. 1990. On-line processing in candidate evaluation: the effects of issue order, issue importance, and sophistication. *Political Behavior*, 12, 41–58.

McGuire, M., and Raleigh, M. 1986. Behavioral and physiological correlates of ostracism. In M. Gruter and R. Masters (eds.), *Ostracism: A Social and Biological Phenomenon*. New York: Elsevier.

McGuire, W. 1968. The structure of human thought. In R. Abelson, E. Aronson, W. McGuire, T. Newcomb, M. Rosenberg, and P. Tannenbaum (eds.), *Theories of Cognitive Consistency: A Sourcebook*. Chicago: Rand McNally.

———. 1969. Theory-oriented research in natural settings: the best of both worlds for social psychology. In M. Sherif and C. Sherif (eds.), *Interdisciplinary Relationships in the Social Sciences*. Chicago: Aldine.

———. 1976. Historical comparisons: testing psychological hypotheses with cross-era data. *International Journal of Psychology*, 11, 161–183.

———. 1981. The probabilogical model of cognitive structure and attitude change. In R. Petty, T. Ostrom, and T. Brock (eds.), *Cognitive Responses in Persuasion*. Hillsdale, NJ: Lawrence Erlbaum Associates.

———. 1983. A contextualist theory of knowledge: its implications for innovation and reform in psychological research. In L. Berkowitz (ed.), *Advances in Experimental Social Psychology*, vol. 16. New York: Academic Press.

———. 1985. Attitudes and attitude change. In G. Lindzey and E. Aronson (eds.), *Handbook of Social Psychology,* vol. 2. 3rd ed. New York: Random House.

———. 1986a. A perspectivist looks at contextualism and the future of behavioral science. In R. Rosnow and M. Georgoudi (eds.), *Contextualism and Understanding in Behavioral Science: Implications for Research and Theory.* New York: Praeger.

———. 1986b. The vicissitudes of attitudes and similar representational constructs in twentieth century psychology. *European Journal of Social Psychology,* 16, 89–130.

———. 1988. The structure of individual attitudes and of attitude systems. In A. R. Pratkanis, S. J. Breckler, and A. G. Greenwald (eds.), *Attitude Structure and Function.* Hillsdale, NJ: Lawrence Erlbaum Associates.

McGuire, W. J., and McGuire, C. V. 1991. The content, structure, and operation of thought systems. In R. S. Wyer, Jr. and T. K. Srull (eds.), *Advances in social cognition,* vol. 4. Hillsdale, NJ: Lawrence Erlbaum Associates.

McGuire, W., McGuire, C., Child, P., and Fujioka, T. 1978. Salience of ethnicity in the spontaneous self-concept as a function of one's ethnic distinctiveness in the social environment. *Journal of Personality and Social Psychology,* 36, 511–520.

McGuire, W., and Padawer, S. 1976. Trait salience in the spontaneous self-concept. *Journal of Personality and Social Psychology,* 33, 743–754.

McHugo, G., Lanzetta, J., and Bush, L. 1987. The effect of attitudes on emotional reactions to expressive displays of a political leader. Unpublished manuscript, Dartmouth College.

McHugo, G., Lanzetta, J., Sullivan, D., Masters, R., and Englis, B. 1985. Emotional reactions to expressive displays of a political leader. *Journal of Personality and Social Psychology,* 49, 1513–1529.

Mack, J. 1971. Psychoanalysis and historical biography. *Journal of the American Psychoanalytic Association,* 19, 143–179.

Mackenzie, W. 1978. *Biological Ideas in Politics.* New York: Viking, 1978.

Maital, S. 1982. *Minds, Markets and Money: Psychological Foundations of Economic Behavior.* New York: Basic Books.

Mandeville, B. 1924. *The Fable of the Bees.* Oxford: Clarendon Press.

Mandler, G. 1975. *Mind and Emotion.* New York: Wiley.

Manis, M. 1961. The interpretation of opinion statements as a function of recipient attitude and source prestige. *Journal of Abnormal and Social Psychology,* 63, 82–86.

Manis, M., Nelson, T., and Shedler, J. 1988. Stereotypes and social judgment: extremity, assimilation and contrast. *Journal of Personality and Social Psychology,* 51, 493–504.

Manis, M., et al. 1976. Social psychology and history: a symposium. *Personality and Social Psychology Bulletin,* 2, 371–444.

Mannheim, K. 1952. The problem of generations. In P. Kecskemeti (ed.), *Essays on the Sociology of Knowledge.* London: Routledge and Kegan Paul.

Mansbridge, J. (ed.). 1990. *Beyond Self-Interest.* Chicago: University of Chicago Press.

Manuel, F. 1972. The use and abuse of psychology in history. In F. Gilbert and S. Graubard (eds.), *Historical Studies Today.* New York: Norton.

Marcus, G. 1988. The structure of emotional response: 1984 presidential candidates. *American Political Science Review,* 82, 737–761.

————. 1990. Emotions and politics: hot cognitions and the rediscovery of passion. Presented at annual meeting of International Society of Political Psychology, Washington, DC.

Marcus, S. 1984. *Freud and the Culture of Psychoanalysis.* Boston: Allen and Unwin.

Markovsky, B. 1988. Anchoring justice. *Social Psychology Quarterly,* 51, 213–224.

Marks, G., and Miller, N. 1987. Ten years of research on the false-consensus effect: an empirical and theoretical review. *Psychological Bulletin,* 102, 72–90.

Markus, G. 1982. Political attitudes during an election year: a report on the 1980 NES panel study. *American Political Science Review,* 76, 538–560.

Marsh, C. 1984. Back on the bandwagon: the effect of opinion polls on public opinion. *British Journal of Political Science,* 15, 51–74.

Martin, L. 1986. Set/reset: the use and disuse of concepts in impression formation. *Journal of Personality and Social Psychology,* 51, 493–504.

Martindale, C. 1981. *Cognition and Consciousness.* Homewood, IL: Dorsey.

————. 1984. The evolution of aesthetic taste. In K. Gergen and M. Gergen (eds.), *Historical Social Psychology.* Hillsdale, NJ: Lawrence Erlbaum Associates.

Martinez, M. 1988. Political involvement and the projection process. *Political Behavior,* 10, 151–167.

Marwick, A. 1981. *The Nature of History.* 2nd ed. London: Macmillan.

Masters, R. 1989a. *The Nature of Politics.* New Haven, CT: Yale University Press.

————. 1989b. Gender and political cognition. *Politics and the Life Sciences,* 8, 3–39.

————. 1991. Linking ethology and political science. In M. Watts (ed.), *Biopolitics: Ethological and Physiological Approaches.* San Francisco: Jossey-Bass.

Masters, R., and Carlotti, S., Jr. 1988. The gender gap revisited. Presented at annual meeting of International Political Science Association, Washington, DC.

Masters, R., and Mouchon, J. 1986. Les gestes et la vie politique, Le Français dans le Monde, no. 203. Paris: Hachette.

Masters, R., and Sullivan, D. 1989a. Nonverbal displays and political leadership in France and the United States. *Political Behavior,* 11, 121–153.

————. 1989b. Facial displays and political leadership in France. *Behavioural Processes,* 19, 1–30.

Masters, R., Sullivan, D., Feola, A., and McHugo, G. 1987. Television coverage of candidates' display behavior during the 1984 Democratic primaries in the United States. *International Political Science Review,* 8, 121–130.

Masters, R., Sullivan, D., Lanzetta, J., and McHugo, G. 1985. Leaders' facial displays as a political variable. Presented at annual meeting of International Political Science Association, Paris.

Masters, R., Sullivan, D., Lanzetta, J., McHugo, G., and Englis, B. 1986. The facial displays of leaders: toward an ethology of human politics, *Journal of Social and Biological Structures,* 9, 319–343.

Mayhew, D. 1974. *Congress: The Electoral Connection.* New Haven, CT: Yale University Press.

Mayhew, H. 1986 [1861]. *London Labour and the London Poor.* New York: Penguin.

Mazlish, B. 1972. *In Search of Nixon: A Psychohistorical Inquiry.* New York: Basic Books.

———. 1977. Reflections on the state of psychohistory. *Psychohistory Review,* 5 (4), 3–11.

Mazur, A., and Lamb, T. 1980. Testosterone, status, and mood in human males. *Hormones and Behavior,* 14, 236–246.

Mead, M. 1942. *And Keep Your Powder Dry.* New York: Morrow.

Meehl, P. 1977. The selfish voter paradox and the thrown-away vote argument. *American Political Science Review,* 71, 11–30.

Mensch, T. 1979. Psychohistory of the Third Reich: a library pathfinder and topical bibliography of English-language publications. *Journal of Psychohistory,* 7, 331–354.

Mercer, G., and Cairns, E. 1981. Conservatism and its relationship to general and specific ethnocentrism in Northern Ireland. *British Journal of Social Psychology,* 20, 13–16.

Michels, R. 1962 [1911]. *Political Parties: A Sociological Study of the Oligarchical Tendencies of Modern Democracy.* New York: Free Press.

Milgram, S. 1974. *Obedience to Authority.* New York: Harper and Row.

Miller, A. 1986. *The Obedience Experiments: A Case Study of Controversy in Social Science.* New York: Praeger.

Miller, G. 1956. The magical number seven, plus or minus two: some limits on our capacity for processing information. *Psychological Review,* 63, 81–97.

Miller, J. 1978. *Living Systems.* New York: McGraw-Hill.

Miller, L., and Sigelman, L. 1978. Is the audience the message? a note on LBJ's Viet Nam statements. *Public Opinion Quarterly,* 42, 71–80.

Miller, N., and Dollard, J. 1941. *Social Learning and Imitation.* New Haven, CT: Yale University Press.

Miller, W., and Godwin, K. 1977. *Psyche and Demos: Individual Psychology and the Issues of Population.* New York: Oxford University Press.

Mills, C. 1959. *The Sociological Imagination.* New York: Oxford University Press.

Mishkin, M., and Appenzeller, T. 1987. *The Anatomy of Memory.*

Montagner, H. 1977. Silent speech. *Horizon—BBC2,* Videotape.

Montgomery, H. 1983. Decision rules and the search for a structure: towards a process model of decision making. In P. Humphreys, O. Svenson, and A. Vari (eds.), *Analyzing and Aiding Decision Processes*. Amsterdam: Elsevier.

Morita, A., Reingold, E., and Shimomura, M. 1986. *Made in Japan: Akio Morita and the Sony Corporation*. New York: Dutton.

Mosca, G. 1939 [1896]. *The Ruling Class: Elements of Political Science*. New York: McGraw-Hill.

Mueller, J. 1973. *War, Presidents, and Public Opinion*. New York: Wiley.

Mullen, B., et al. 1986. Newscasters' facial expressions and voting behavior of viewers: can a smile elect a president? *Journal of Personality and Social Psychology*, 51, 291–295.

Myrdal, G. 1944. *An American Dilemma*. New York: Harper.

Namier, L. B. 1955. *Personalities and Powers*. London: Hamish Hamilton.

Naroll, R., Bullough, V., and Naroll, F. 1974. *Military Deterrence in History: A Pilot Cross-Historical Survey*. Albany: State University of New York Press.

Neely, J. 1977. Semantic priming and retrieval from lexical memory: roles of inhibitionless spreading activation and limited capacity attention. *Journal of Experimental Psychology: General*, 106, 226–254.

Neisser, U. (ed.). 1987. *Concepts and Conceptual Development: Ecological and Intellectual Factors in Categorization*. Cambridge: Cambridge University Press.

Nesselroade, J., and Baltes, P. 1974. Adolescent personality development and historical change: 1970–1972. *Monographs of the Society for Research in Child Development*, 39, serial no. 154.

Neumann, R. 1981. Differentiation and integration in political thinking. *American Journal of Sociology*, 86, 1236–1268.

Neustadt, R. E., and May, E. 1986. *Thinking in Time: The Uses of History for Decision Makers*. New York: Free Press.

Newcomb, T. 1943. *Personality and Social Change*. New York: Dryden.

Newell, A., and Simon, H. 1972. *Human Problem Solving*. Englewood Cliffs, NJ: Prentice-Hall.

Newton, J., Masters, R., McHugo, G., and Sullivan, D. 1987. Making up our minds: effects of network coverage on viewer impressions of leaders, *Polity*, 20, 236–246.

Ng, S. 1985. Biases in reward allocation resulting from personal status, group status and allocation procedure. *Australian Journal of Psychology*, 37, 297–307.

Nie, N., Verba, S., and Petrocik, J. 1976. *The Changing American Voter*. Cambridge, MA: Harvard University Press.

Niemi, R., and Jennings, M. 1991. Issues and inheritance in the formation of party identification. *American Journal of Political Science*, 35, 970–988.

Nimmo, D., and Savage, R. 1976. *Candidates and Their Images: Concepts, Methods, and Findings*. Pacific Palisades, CA: Goodyear.

Nisbett, R., Borgida, E., Crandall, R., and Reed, H. 1982. Popular induction: information is not necessarily informative. In D. Kahneman, P. Slovic and

A. Tversky (eds.), *Judgment Under Uncertainty: Heuristics and Biases.* New York: Cambridge University Press.

Nisbett, R., and Ross, L. 1980. *Human Inference: Strategies and Shortcomings of Social Judgment.* Englewood Cliffs, NJ: Prentice-Hall.

Nisbett, R., and Wilson, T. 1977. Telling more than we know: verbal reports on mental processes. *Psychological Review,* 84, 231–259.

Nisbett, R., Zukier, H., and Lemley, R. 1981. The dilution effect: nondiagnostic information weakens the implications of diagnostic information. *Cognitive Psychology,* 13, 248–277.

Niskanen, W., Jr. 1971. *Bureaucracy and Representative Government.* Chicago: Atherton Press.

Noelle-Neumann, E. 1984. The spiral of silence: a theory of public opinion. *Journal of Communication,* 24, 43–51.

Nunn, C., Crockett, J., Jr., and Williams, J., Jr. 1978. *Tolerance for Nonconformity: A National Survey of Americans' Changing Commitment to Civil Liberties.* San Francisco: Jossey-Bass.

Olson, M., Jr. 1965. *The Logic of Collective Action.* Cambridge, MA: Harvard University Press.

Olweus, D., Mattsson, Å., Schalling, D., and Low, H. 1988. Circulating testosterone levels and aggression in adolescent males: a causal analysis. *Psychosomatic Medicine,* 50, 261–272.

Orr, S., and Lanzetta, J. 1980. Facial expressions of emotion as conditioned stimuli for human autonomic responses. *Journal of Personality and Social Psychology,* 38, 278–282.

Orren, G. 1988. Beyond self-interest. In R. Reich (ed.), *The Power of Public Ideas.* Cambridge, MA: Ballinger.

Orren, G., and Polsby, N. (eds.). 1987. *Media and Momentum.* Chatham, NJ: Chatham House.

Osgood, C. 1953. Ideals and self-interest in America's foreign policy.

Osgood, C., Saporta, S., and Nunnally, J. 1956. Evaluative assertion analysis. *Litera,* 3, 47–102.

Osgood, C., Suci, G., and Tannenbaum, P. 1955. *The Measurement of Meaning.* Urbana: University of Illinois Press.

Osgood, C., and Tannenbaum, P. 1955. The principle of congruity and the prediction of attitude change. *Psychological Review,* 62, 42–55.

Ostrom, T. 1966. Perspective as an intervening construct in the judgment of attitude statements. *Journal of Personality and Social Psychology,* 3, 135–144.

———. 1988. Computer simulation: the third symbol system. *Journal of Experimental Social Psychology,* 24, 381–392.

Ostrom, T., Lingle, J., Pryor, J., and Geva, N. 1980. Cognitive organization of person impressions. In R. Hastie, et al. (eds.), *Person Memory: The Cognitive Basis of Social Perception.* Hillsdale, NJ: Lawrence Erlbaum Associates.

Ottati, V. 1988. The cognitive and affective determinants of political judgments.

Presented at annual meeting of American Political Science Association, Washington, DC, September.

———. 1990. Determinants of political judgments: the joint influence of normative and heuristic rules. *Political Behavior*, 12, 159–179.

Ottati, V., Fishbein, M., and Middlestadt, S. 1988. Determinants of voters' beliefs about the candidates' stands on the issues: the role of evaluative bias heuristics and the candidates' expressed message. *Journal of Personality and Social Psychology*, 55, 517–529.

Ottati, V., Riggle, E., Wyer, R., Schwarz, N., and Kuklinski, J. 1989. Cognitive and affective bases of opinion survey responses. *Journal of Personality and Social Psychology*, 57, 404–415.

Ottati, V., and Terkildsen, N. 1989. Perceptions of the candidates' stands on the issues: the role of projection and the candidates' expressed message. Presented at annual meeting of Midwest Political Science Association, Chicago.

Ottati, V., and Wyer, R. 1991. The cognitive mediators of political information processing. In J. Ferejohn and J. Kuklinski (eds.), *Information and the Democratic Process*. Urbana: University of Illinois Press.

Page, B. 1976. The theory of ambiguity. *American Political Science Review*, 70, 742–752.

———. 1978. *Choices and Echoes in Presidential Elections*. Chicago: University of Chicago Press.

Page, B., and Brody, R. 1972. Policy voting and the electoral process: the Vietnam War issue. *American Political Science Review*, 73, 1071–1089.

Page, B., and Jones, C. 1979. Reciprocal effects of policy preferences, party loyalties and the vote. *American Political Science Review*, 66, 979–985.

Page, B., and Shapiro, R. 1992. *The Rational Public: Fifty Years of Trends in Americans' Policy Preferences*. Chicago: University of Chicago Press.

Panchella, R. 1974. The interpretation of Reaction Time in information Processing Research. In B. Kantowitz (ed.), *Human Information Processing: Tutorials in Performance and Cognition*. Hillsdale, NJ: Lawrence Erlbaum Associates.

Pareto, V. 1979 [1901]. *The Rise and Fall of the Elites*. New York: Arno.

Park, B., and Rothbart, M. 1982. Perception of out-group homogeneity and levels of social categorization: memory for the subordinate attributes of in-group and out-group members. *Journal of Personality and Social Psychology*, 42, 1051–1068.

Patai, R. 1973. *The Arab Mind*. New York: Scribners.

———. 1977. *The Jewish Mind*. New York: Scribners.

Paternoster, R. 1983. Race of victim and location of crime: the decision to seek the death penalty in South Carolina. *Journal of Criminal Law and Criminology*, 74, 754–785.

Patterson, T. 1980. *The Mass Media Election: How Americans Choose Their President*. New York: Praeger.

Pavelchak, M. 1986. Category-based versus piecemeal-based affective responses:

developments in schema triggered affect. In R. Sorrentino and E. Higgins (eds.), *The Handbook of Motivation and Cognition: Foundations of Social Behavior.* New York: Guilford Press.

Payne, J. 1976. Task complexity and contingent processing in decision making: an information search and protocol analysis. *Organizational Behavior and Human Performance,* 16, 366–387.

————. 1982. Contingent decision behavior. *Psychological Bulletin,* 92, 382–402.

Peabody, D. 1985. *National Characteristics.* New York: Cambridge University Press.

Perdue, C., Dovidio, J., Gurtman, M., and Tyler, R. 1990. Us and them: social categorization and the process of intergroup bias. *Journal of Personality and Social Psychology,* 59, 475–486.

Petty, R., and Cacioppo, J. 1981. *Attitudes and Persuasion: Classic and Contemporary Approaches.* Dubuque, IA: Brown.

Petty, R., and Cacioppo, J. 1986. *Communication and Persuasion: Central and Peripheral Routes to Attitude Change.* New York: Springer-Verlag.

Plate, E. 1984. The double-bind phenomenon in politics: the influence of non-verbal expressive behavior of male and female candidates on impression formation. Senior honor's thesis, Dartmouth College.

Plato. (Bloom, ed.). 1968. *The Republic.* New York: Basic Books.

Plutchik, R. 1980. *Emotion: A Psychoevolutionary Synthesis.* New York: Harper and Row.

Pomper, G. N. 1970. *Elections in America.* New York: Dodd, Mead.

Poole, K., and Zeigler, H. 1985. *Women, Public Opinion, and Politics: The Changing Political Attitudes of American Women.* New York: Longman.

Popkin, S., Gorman, J., Phillips, C., and Smith, J. 1976. Comment: what have you done for me lately?: toward an investment theory of voting. *American Political Science Review,* 70, 779–805.

Popper, K. R. 1945. *The Open Society and Its Enemies.* London: Routledge. (Rev. ed. [1966]. Princeton, NJ: Princeton University Press.)

Powell, H., and Hopson, D. 1988. Implications of doll color preferences among black preschool children and white preschool children. *Journal of Black Psychology,* 14, 57–63.

Pratkanis, A. 1989. The cognitive representation of attitudes. In A. Pratkanis, S. Breckler, and A. Greenwald (eds.), *Attitude Structure and Function.* Hillsdale, NJ: Lawrence Erlbaum Associates.

Pratkanis, A., Breckler, S., and Greenwald, A. (eds.). 1989. *Attitude Structure and Function.* Hillsdale, NJ: Lawrence Erlbaum Associates.

Prentice, D. 1987. Psychological correspondence of possessions, attitudes, and values. *Journal of Personality and Social Psychology,* 87, 993–1003.

Protess, D., and McCombs, M. (eds.). 1991. *Agenda Setting: Readings on Media, Public Opinion, and Policymaking.* Hillsdale, NJ: Lawrence Erlbaum Associates.

Pruitt, D., and Lewis, S. 1975. Development of integrative solutions in bilateral negotiation. *Journal of Personality and Social Psychology*, 31, 621–633.

Pry, P. 1990. *The Strategic Nuclear Balance*. New York: Crane Russak.

Purkitt, H. E., and Dyson, J. W. 1986. The role of cognition in U.S. foreign policy toward southern Africa. *Political Psychology*, 7, 507–532.

Putnam, R. 1971. Studying elite culture: the case of ideology. *American Political Science Review*, 65, 651–681.

———. 1976. *The Comparative Study of Political Elites*. Englewood Cliffs, NJ: Prentice-Hall.

Quattrone, G., and Tversky, A. 1988. Contrasting rational and psychological analyses of political choice. *American Political Science Review*, 82, 719–736.

Rabinowitz, G., and MacDonald, S. 1989. A directional theory of issue voting. *American Political Science Review*, 83, 93–121.

Radcliff, B. 1990. Cyclical majorities and voter rationality in American presidential elections. Presented at annual meeting of Midwest Political Science Association.

Radding, C. 1985. *A World Made By Men: Cognition and Society*. Chapel Hill: University of North Carolina Press.

Raden, D. 1985. Strength-related attitude dimensions. *Social Psychology Quarterly*, 48, 312–330.

Raleigh, M., and McGuire, M. 1986. Animal analogues of ostracism: biological mechanisms and social consequences. In M. Gruter and R. Masters (eds.), *Ostracism: A Social and Biological Phenomenon*. New York: Basic Books.

Raphael, T. 1982. Integrative complexity theory and forecasting international crises. *Journal of Conflict Resolution*, 26, 423–450.

Rawls, J. 1971. *A Theory of Justice*. Cambridge, MA: Harvard University Press.

Reeder, G., and Coovert, M. 1986. Revising an impression of morality. *Social Cognition*, 4, 1–17.

Reeves, R. 1989. New York election, may the least-offensive man win. *International Herald Tribune*, November 6, p. 1.

Regan, D., and J. Toten. 1975. Empathy and attribution: turning observers into actors. *Journal of Personality and Social Psychology*, 32, 850–856.

Reich, R. (ed.). 1988. *The Power of Public Ideas*. Cambridge, MA: Ballinger.

Reinarman, C. 1987. *American States of Mind: Political Beliefs and Behavior Among Public and Private Workers*. New Haven, CT: Yale University Press.

Reiss, I. 1986. *Journey into Sexuality: An Exploratory Voyage*. Englewood Cliffs, NJ: Prentice-Hall.

RePass, D. 1971. Issue salience and party choice. *American Political Science Review*, 65, 389–400.

Reychler, L. 1979. *Patterns of Diplomatic Thinking: A Cross-National Study of Structural and Social-Psychological Determinants*. New York: Praeger.

Reyes, R., Thompson, W., and Bower, G. 1980. Judgmental biases from differing availabilities of arguments. *Journal of Personality and Social Psychology*, 39, 2–12.

Reynolds, V., Falger, V., and Vine, I. 1987. *The Sociobiology of Ethnocentrism: Evolutionary Dimensions of Xenophobia, Discrimination, Racism and Nationalism.* Beckenham, Kent: Croom Helm.

Richardson, L. 1960. *Statistics of Deadly Quarrels.* Pittsburgh: Boxwood Press.

Ricoeur, P. 1967. *The Symbolism of Evil.* (E. Buchanan, trans.) New York: Harper and Row.

Riesman, D. 1961 [1950]. *The Lonely Crowd: A Study of the Changing American Character.* New Haven, CT: Yale University Press.

Riggle, E., Ottati, V., Kuklinski, J., Wyer, R., and Schwarz, N. 1989. Bases of political judgment: the role of a candidate's physical attractiveness, party membership and voting record. Unpublished manuscript, University of Illinois.

Riker, W., and P. Ordeshook. 1973. *An Introduction to Positive Political Theory.* New York: Harper and Row.

Robinson, J., and Insko, C. 1969. Attributed belief similarity-dissimilarity versus race as determinants of prejudice: a further test of Rokeach's theory. *Journal of Experimental in Research Personality,* 4, 72–77.

Rokeach, M. 1956. Political and religious dogmatism: alternative to the authoritarian personality. *Psychological Monographs,* 70, no. 18, whole no. 425.

———. 1960. *The Open and Closed Mind: Investigations into the Nature of Belief Systems and Personality Systems.* New York: Basic Books.

———. 1973. *The Nature of Human Values.* New York: Free Press.

———. 1979. *Understanding Human Values: Individual and Social.* New York: Free Press.

Rokkan, S. 1962. The comparative study of political participation: notes toward a perspective on current research. In A. Ranney (ed.), *Essays on the Behavioral Study of Politics.* Urbana: University of Illinois Press.

Rolls, E. 1987. Information representation, processing, and storage in the brain: analysis at the single neuron level. In J. Changeux and M. Konishi (eds.), *The Neural and Molecular Bases of Learning.* New York: Wiley.

———. 1989a. The processing of face information in the primate temporal lobe. In V. Bruce and M. Burton (eds.), *Processing Images of Faces.* London: Ablex.

———. 1989b. The representation and storage of information on neuronal networks in the primate cerebral cortex and hippocampus. In R. Durbin, C. Miall, and G. Mitchison (eds.), *The Computing Neuron.* Reading, MA: Addison-Wesley.

Rosch, E. 1978. Principles of Categorization. In E. Rosch and B. Lloyd (eds.), *Cognition and Categorization.* Hillsdale, NJ: Lawrence Erlbaum Associates.

Rosch, E., and Mervis, C. 1975. Family resemblances: studies in the internal structure of categories. *Cognitive Psychology,* 7, 573–605.

Roseman, I. 1979. Cognitive aspects of emotion and emotional behavior. Presented at meeting of American Psychological Association, New York, September.

Roseman, I., Abelson, R., and Ewing, M. 1986. Emotion and political cognition: emotional appeals in political communication. In R. Lau and D. Sears (eds.), *Political Cognition*. Hillsdale, NJ: Lawrence Erlbaum Associates.

Rosenbaum, M. 1986. The repulsion hypothesis: on the nondevelopment of relationships. *Journal of Personality and Social Psychology*, 51, 1156–1166.

Rosenbaum, R. 1989. Too young to die. *New York Times Magazine*. March 12, pp. 32–35, 58, 60–61.

Rosenberg, S., Bohan, L., McCafferty, P., and Harris, K. 1986. The image and the vote: the effect of candidate presentation on voter preference. *American Journal of Political Science*, 30, 108–127.

Rosenthal, R., and Jacobson, L. 1968. *Pygmalion in the Classroom: Teacher Expectations and Pupils' Intellectual Development*. New York: Holt, Rinehart and Winston.

Ross, L., and Anderson, C. 1982. Shortcomings in the attribution process. In B. Kahneman, P. Slovic, and A. Tversky (eds.), *Judgment Under Uncertainty: Heuristics and Biases*. New York: Cambridge University Press.

Ross, L., and Lepper, M., and Hubbard, M. 1975. Perseverance in self perception and social perception: biased attributional processes in the debriefing paradigm. *Journal of Personality and Social Psychology*, 32, 880–892.

Ross, M. 1991. The role of evolution in ethnocentric conflict and its management. *Journal of Social Issues*, 47, 167–185.

Ross, M., and Sicoly, F. 1979. Egocentric biases in availability and attribution. *Journal of Personality and Social Psychology*, 37, 322–337.

Rossi, P. 1956. Four landmarks in voting research. In E. Burdick and A. Brodbeck (eds.), *American Voting Behavior*. New York: Free Press.

Rotter, J. 1966. Generalized expectancies for internal versus external control of reinforcement. *Psychological Monographs*, 80 (1), whole no. 609.

Rousseau, J.-J. 1964. *The First and Second Discourses* (R. Masters, ed.). New York: St. Martin's Press.

———. 1978. *The Social Contract, with Geneva Manuscript and Political Economy*. (R. Masters, ed.). New York: St. Martin's Press.

Rumelhart, D., McClelland, J., and the PDP Research Group. 1986. *Parallel Distributed Processing*, vols. 1–3. Cambridge, MA: MIT Press.

Rumelhart, D., and Norman, D. 1983. Representation in memory. In R. Atkinson, R. Herrnstein, G. Lindzey, and R. Luce (eds.), *Handbook of Experimental Psychology*. New York: Wiley.

Rumelhart, D., and Ortony, A. 1977. The representation of knowledge in memory. In B. Anderson, R. Spiro, and J. Montague (eds.), *Schooling and the Acquisition of Knowledge*. Hillsdale, NJ: Lawrence Erlbaum Associates.

Rummel, R. 1972. *The Dimensions of Nations*. Beverly Hills, CA: Sage.

Runciman, W. 1966. *Relative Deprivation and Social Justice*. London: Routledge and Kegan Paul.

Runyan, W. 1981. Why did Van Gogh cut off his ear?: the problem of alternative explanations in psychobiography. *Journal of Personality and Social Psychology,* 40, 1070–1077.

———. 1982. *Life Histories and Psychobiography: Explorations in Theory and Method.* New York: Oxford University Press.

———. 1983. Idiographic goals and methods in the study of lives. *Journal of Personality,* 51, 413–437.

———. 1984. Diverging life paths: their probabilistic and causal structure. In K. Gergen and M. Gergen (eds.), *Historical Social Psychology.* Hillsdale, NJ: Lawrence Erlbaum Associates.

———. 1986. Life histories in anthropology: another view. *American Anthropologist,* 881, 181–183.

———. 1988a. Progress in psychobiography. *Journal of Personality,* 56, 293–324.

———. 1988b. Reconceptualizing the relationships between history and psychology. In W. Runyan (ed.), *Psychology and Historical Interpretation.* New York: Oxford University Press.

———. 1988c. A historical and conceptual background to psychohistory. In W. Runyan (ed.), *Psychology and Historical Interpretation.* New York: Oxford University Press.

———. 1990. Individual lives and the structure of personality psychology. In A. Rabin et al. (eds.), *Studying Persons and Lives.* New York: Springer.

Russett, B., Alker, H., Deutsch, K., and Lasswell, H. 1964. *World Handbook of Political and Social Indicators.* New Haven, CT: Yale University Press.

Sachdev, I., and Bourhis, R. 1985. Social categorization and power differentials in group relations. *European Journal of Social Psychology,* 15, 415–434.

Salvador, A., Simon, V., Suay, F., and Llorens, L. 1987. Testosterone and cortisol responses to competitive fighting in human males: a pilot study. *Aggressive Behavior,* 13, 9–13.

Sani, G., and Sartori, G. 1983. Polarization, fragmentation and competition in western democracies. In H. Daalder and P. Maier (eds.), *Western European Party Systems: Continuity and Change.* Beverly Hills, CA: Sage.

Sapiro, V. 1986. *Women in American Politics.* Palo Alto, CA: Mayfield.

Scaramella, T., and Brown, W. 1978. Serum testosterone and aggressiveness in hockey players. *Psychosomatic Medicine,* 40, 262–265.

Schachter, S. 1964. The interaction of cognitive and physiological determinants of emotional state. In L. Berkowitz (ed.), *Advances in Experimental Social Psychology,* vol. 1. New York: Academic Press.

Schachter, S., and Singer, J. 1962. Cognitive, social, and physiological determinants of emotional state. *Psychological Review,* 69, 379–399.

Schandler, H. 1977. *The Unmaking of a President.* Princeton, NJ: Princeton University Press.

Schank, R. 1982. *Dynamic Memory: A Theory of Reminding and Learning in Computers and People.* New York: Cambridge University Press.

Schelling, T. 1960. *The Strategy of Conflict*. Cambridge, MA: Harvard University Press.

———. 1985. What went wrong with arms control? *Foreign Affairs*, 64, 219–233.

Scheman, S. 1986. A limited success for Gorbachev. *New York Times*, October 1.

Schilling, W. 1962. The politics of national defense: fiscal 1950. In W. Schilling, P. Hammond, and G. Snyder (eds.), *Strategy, Politics and Defense Budgets*. New York: Columbia University Press.

Schlenker, B. 1974. Social psychology and science. *Journal of Personality and Social Psychology*, 29, 1–15.

Schoenwald, R. 1973. Using psychology in history: a review essay. *Historical Methods Newsletter*, 71, 9–24.

Scholl, I. 1983. *The White Rose: Munich 1942–43*. Middletown, CT: Wesleyan University Press.

Schroder, H., Driver, M., and Streufert, S. 1967. *Human Information Processing*. New York: Holt, Rinehart and Winston.

Schubert, G. 1985. Sexual differences in political behavior, *Political Science Reviewer*, 15, 1–66.

———. 1987. Sexual politics: some biosociopsychological problems. *Political Psychology*, 8, 61–94.

Schuman, H., and Bobo, L. 1988. Survey-based experiments on white racial attitudes toward residential integration. *American Journal of Sociology*, 94, 273–299.

Schuman, H., and Presser, S. 1981. *Questions and Answers in Attitude Surveys: Experiments on Question Form, Wording and Context*. New York: Academic Press.

Schuman, H., Steeh, C., and Bobo, L. 1985. *Racial Trends in America: Trends and Interpretations*. Cambridge, MA: Harvard University Press.

Schwartz, G., Fair, P., Salt, P., Mandel, M., and Klerman, G. 1976. Facial muscle patterning to affective imagery in depressed and nondepressed subjects. *Science*, 192, 489–491.

Schwartz, T. 1990. Social sciences, disciplinary divisions, and the consequences of coherence. Presented at annual meeting of International Congress of Sociology, Madrid.

Schwarz, N., and Clore, G. 1983. Mood, misattribution, and judgments of well-being: informative and directive functions of affective states. *Journal of Personality and Social Psychology*, 45, 513–523.

———. 1987. How do I feel about it? the informative function of affective states. In K. Fiedler and J. Forgas (eds.), *Affect, Cognition and Social Behavior*. Toronto: Hogrefe International.

Scott, W. 1820. *Lessons in Elocution; or, a Selection of Pieces in Prose and Verse for the Improvement of Youth in Reading and Speaking*. Leicester: Hori Brown.

Scribner, S., and Cole, M. 1981. *The Psychology of Literacy*. Cambridge, MA: Harvard University Press.

Sears, D. 1969. Political behavior. In G. Lindzey and E. Aronson (eds.), *Handbook of Social Psychology*, vol. 2. Rev. ed. Reading, MA: Addison-Wesley.

————. 1975. Political socialization. In F. Greenstein, and N. Polsby (eds.), *Handbook of Political Science,* vol. 2. Reading, MA: Addison-Wesley.

————. 1983. The persistence of early political predispositions: the roles of attitude object and life stage. In L. Wheeler and P. Shaver (eds.), *Review of Personality and Social Psychology,* vol. 4. Beverly Hills, CA: Sage.

————. 1986. College sophomores in the laboratory: influences of a narrow database on social psychology's view of human nature. *Journal of Personality and Social Psychology,* 51, 515–530.

————. 1987. Political psychology. *Annual Review of Psychology.* Palo Alto, CA: Annual Reviews.

————. 1988. Symbolic racism. In P. A. Katz and D. A. Taylor (eds.), *Eliminating Racism: Profiles in Controversy.* New York: Plenum Press.

————. 1989. Whither political socialization research? the question of persistence. In O. Ichilov (ed.), *Political Socialization, Citizenship Education, and Democracy.* New York: Teachers College Press.

Sears, D., and Allen, H. 1984. The trajectory of local desegregation controversies and whites' opposition to busing. In N. Miller and M. Brewer (eds.), *Groups in Contact: The Psychology of Desegregation.* New York: Academic Press.

Sears, D., and Citrin, J. 1985. *Tax Revolt: Something for Nothing in California.* Cambridge, MA: Harvard University Press.

Sears, D., Citrin, J., and Kosterman, R. 1987. Jesse Jackson and the southern white electorate in 1984. In L. Moreland, R. Steed, and T. Baker (eds.), *Blacks in Southern Politics.* New York: Praeger.

Sears, D., and Funk, C. 1990. Graduate education in political psychology in the United States. Presented at meeting of International Society of Political Psychology, Washington, DC.

————. 1991. The role of self-interest in social and political attitudes. In M. Zanna (ed.), *Advances in Experimental Social Psychology,* vol. 24. Orlando, FL: Academic Press.

Sears, D., Hensler, C., and Speer, L. 1979. Whites' opposition to "busing": self-interest or symbolic politics? *American Political Science Review,* 73, 369–384.

Sears, D., and Huddy, L. 1991. The symbolic politics of opposition to bilingual education. In J. Simpson, and S. Worchel (eds.), *Conflict Between People and Peoples.* Chicago: Nelson-Hall.

Sears, D., Huddy, L., and Schaffer, L. 1986. A schematic variant of symbolic politics theory, as applied to racial and gender equality. In R. Lau and D. Sears (eds.), *Political Cognition.* Hillsdale, NJ: Lawrence Erlbaum Associates.

Sears, D., and Kinder, D. 1971. Racial tensions and voting in Los Angeles. In W. Z. Hirsch (ed.), *Los Angeles: Viability and Prospects for Metropolitan Leadership.* New York: Praeger.

————. 1985. Whites' opposition to busing: on conceptualizing and operationalizing group conflict. *Journal of Personality and Social Psychology,* 48, 1141–1147.

Sears, D., and Kosterman, R. 1991. Is it really racism? the origins and dynamics of symbolic racism. Presented at annual meeting of Midwest Political Science Association, Chicago.

Sears, D., and Lau, R. 1983. Inducing apparently self-interested political preferences. *American Journal of Political Science*, 27, 223–252.

Sears, D., Lau, R., Tyler, T., and Allen, H. M., Jr. 1980. Self-interest vs. symbolic politics in policy attitudes and presidential voting. *American Political Science Review*, 74, 670–684.

Sears, D., and McConahay, J. 1973. *The Politics of Violence: The New Urban Blacks and the Watts Riot.* Boston: Houghton Mifflin.

Sears, D., Steck, L., Lau, R., and Gahart, M. 1983. Attitudes of the post-Vietnam generation toward the draft and American military policy. Presented at annual meeting of International Society of Political Psychology, Oxford.

Sears, D., Tyler, T., Citrin, J., and Kinder, D. 1978. Political system support and public response to the 1974 energy crisis. *American Journal of Political Science*, 22, 56–82.

Sears, D., Zucker, G., and Funk, C. 1992. Gender and ideological change in the 1960s and 1970s: a longitudinal study. Presented at annual meeting of *American Political Science Review*, Chicago.

Seiler, G. 1983. *Strategic Nuclear Force Requirements and Issues.* Maxwell Air Force Base, AL: Air University Press.

Sen, A. 1977. Rationality and morality: a reply. *Erkenntnis*, 11, 225–232.

Sentis, K., and Burnstein, E. 1979. Remembering schema consistent information: effects of a balance schema on recognition memory. *Journal of Personality and Social Psychology*, 37, 2200–2211.

Serum, C., and Myers, D. 1970. Prejudice and perceived belief dissimilarity. *Perceptual and Motor Skills*, 30, 947–950.

Shaffer, S. 1981. Balance theory and political cognitions. *American Politics Quarterly*, 9, 291–320.

Shaw, R., and Wong, Y. 1989. *The Genetic Seeds of Warfare: Evolution, Nationalism and Patriotism.* Boston: Unwin and Hyman.

Shepsle, K. 1972. The strategy of ambiguity: uncertainty and electoral competition. *American Political Science Review*, 66, 555–568.

Sherif, M., and Cantril, H. 1947. *The Psychology of Ego-Involvements.* New York: Wiley.

Sherif, M., and Hovland, C. 1961. *Social Judgment: Assimilation and Contrast Effects in Communication and Attitude Change.* New Haven, CT: Yale University Press.

Sherif, M., and Sherif, C. 1969. Interdisciplinary coordination as a validity check: retrospect and prospects. In M. Sherif and C. Sherif (eds.), *Interdisciplinary Relationships in the Social Sciences.* Chicago: Aldine.

Sherif, C., Sherif, M., and Nebergall, R. 1965. *Attitude and Attitude Change: The Social Judgment-Involvement Approach.* Philadelphia: Saunders.

Sherman, S., Ahlm, K., Berman, L., and Lynn, S. 1978. Contrast effects and their relationship to subsequent behavior. *Journal of Experimental Social Psychology*, 14, 340–350.

Sherman, S., Mackie, D., and Driscoll, D. 1990. Priming and the differential use of dimensions in evaluation. *Personality and Social Psychology Bulletin*, 16, 405–418.

Sherman, R., and Ross, L. 1972. Liberalism-conservatism and dimensional salience in the perception of political figures. *Journal of Personality and Social Psychology*, 23, 120–127.

Sherrod, D. 1972. Selective perception of political candidates. *Public Opinion Quarterly*, 28, 483–496.

Sherry, M. 1977. *Preparing for the Next War: American Plans for Post-War Defense, 1941–45*. New Haven, CT: Yale University Press.

Shiffrin, R., and Schneider, W. 1977. Controlled and automatic human information processing: II. Perceptual learning, automatic attending, and a general theory. *Psychological Review*, 84, 127–190.

Shils, E. 1958. Ideology and civility: on the politics of the intellectual. *Sewanee Review*, 66, 950–980.

Shorter, E. 1975. *The Making of the Modern Family*. New York: Basic Books.

———. 1986. Paralysis: the rise and fall of an "hysterical" symptom. *Journal of Social History*, 19, 549–582.

Sidanius, J. 1988. Race and sentence severity: the case of American justice. *Journal of Black Studies*, 18, 273–281.

———. 1989. The psychology of political conflict: a social dominance perspective. Presented at annual meeting of Society of Experimental Social Psychology, Los Angeles.

Sidanius, J., Cling, B., and Pratto, F. 1991. Ranking and linking as a function of sex and gender role attitudes. *Journal of Social Issues*, 47, 131–149.

Sidanius, J., Devereux, E., and Pratto, F. 1991. A comparison of symbolic racism theory and social dominance theory: explanations for racial policy attitudes. *Journal of Social Issues*.

Sidanius, J., and Pratto, F. 1991. The inevitability of oppression and the dynamics of social dominance. In P. Sniderman and P. Tetlock (eds.), *Prejudice and Politics in American Society*. Stanford, CA: Stanford University Press.

Sidanius, J., Pratto, F., Liu, J., and Shaw, J. 1991. Police attitudes and the dynamics of social power: some implications of social dominance theory. Unpublished manuscript.

Sidanius, J., Pratto, F., Martin, M., and Stallworth, L. 1991. Consensual racism and career track: some implications of social dominance theory. *Political Psychology*, 12, 691–721.

Sigel, R. 1964. Effect of partisanship on the perception of political candidates. *Public Opinion Quarterly*, 35, 554–562.

———. (ed.). 1989. *Political Learning in Adulthood*. Chicago: University of Chicago Press.

Silberpfennig, J. 1945. Psychological aspects of current Japanese and German paradoxa. *Psychoanalytical Review,* 32, 73–85.

Simon, H. 1957. *Models of Man.* New York: Wiley.

———. 1978. Rationality as a Process and Product of Thought. *American Economic Review: Proceedings,* 68, 1–16.

———. 1981. *The Sciences of the Artificial.* 2nd ed. Cambridge, MA: MIT Press.

———. 1985. Human nature in politics: the dialogue of psychology with political science. *American Political Science Review,* 79, 293–304.

Simonton, D. 1984. *Genius, Creativity, and Leadership.* Cambridge, MA: Harvard University Press.

Singer, J., and Small, M. 1972. *The Wages of War, 1816–1965: A Statistical Handbook.* New York: Wiley.

Skevington, S. 1981. Intergroup relations and nursing. *European Journal of Social Psychology,* 11, 43–59.

Skinner, Q. 1985. *The Return of Grand Theory in the Human Sciences.* Cambridge: Cambridge University Press.

Slessor, J. 1956. *The Central Blue.* London: Cassell.

Slovic, P. 1972. From Shakespeare to Simon: speculations—and some evidence—about man's ability to process information. *Oregon Research Institute Monograph,* 12.

———. 1975. Choice between equally valued alternatives. *Journal of Experimental Psychology: Human Perception,* 1, 280–287.

Slovic, P., and D. MacPhillmay. 1974. Dimensional commensurability and cue utilization in comparative judgment. *Organizational Behavior and Human Performance,* 11, 172–194.

Smelser, N., and Smelser, W. (eds.). 1970. *Personality and Social Systems.* 2nd ed. New York: Wiley.

Smelser, W., and Smelser, N. 1981. Group movements, sociocultural change, and personality. In M. Rosenberg and R. Turner (eds.), *Social Psychology: Sociological Perspectives.* New York: Basic Books.

Smith, M. 1986. *British Air Strategy Between the Wars.* Oxford: Clarendon Press.

Smith, M., Bruner, J., and White, R. 1956. *Opinions and Personality.* New York: Wiley.

Smith, P., 1970. *The Air Force Plan for Peace.* Baltimore: Johns Hopkins University Press.

Smith, T. 1987. That which we call welfare by any other name would smell sweeter: an analysis of the impact of question wording on response patterns. *Public Opinion Quarterly,* 51, 75–83.

Sniderman, P., and Tetlock, P. 1986a. Reflections on American racism. *Journal of Social Issues,* 42, 173–187.

———. 1986b. Symbolic racism: problems of motive attribution in political analysis. *Journal of Social Issues,* 42, 129–150.

———. 1986c. Interrelations between political ideology and public opinion. In

M. Hermann (ed.), *Handbook of Political Psychology*, vol. 2. San Francisco: Jossey-Bass.

——. 1986d. Public opinion and political ideology. In M. Hermann (ed.), *Handbook of Political Psychology*, vol. 2. San Francisco: Jossey-Bass.

Somit, A. 1976. *Biology and Politics*. Paris: Mouton.

Sorokin, P. 1962 [1937–41]. *Social and Cultural Dynamics*, vols. 1–4. New York: Bedminster Press.

Sostek, A., and Sostek, A. 1981. Impressions of presidents: effects of information, time and discrepancy. *Bulletin of the Psychonomic Society*, 17, 187–189.

Spindler, G. (ed.). 1978. *The Making of Psychological Anthropology*. Berkeley: University of California Press.

Spitzer, H. M. 1947. Psychoanalytic approaches to the Japanese character. In G. Róheim (ed.), *Psychoanalysis and the Social Sciences*. New York: International Universities Press.

Squire, L. 1987. Memory: neuronal organization and behavior. In V. Mountcastle, F. Plum, and S. Geiger (eds.), *Handbook of Physiology—the Nervous System*, vol. 5. Bethesda, MD: American Physiological Society.

Srole, L. 1956. Social integration and certain corollaries: an exploratory study. *American Sociological Review*, 21, 709–716.

Srull, T. 1981. Person memory: some tests of associative storage and retrieval models. *Journal of Experimental Psychology: Human Learning and Memory*, 7, 440–463.

Srull, T., and Wyer, R. 1979. The role of category accessibility in the interpretation of information about persons: some determinants and implications. *Journal of Personality and Social Psychology*, 37, 1660–1672.

——. 1986. The role of chronic and temporary goals in social information processing. In R. Sorrentino and E. Higgins (eds.), *Handbook of Motivation and Cognition*. New York: Guilford Press.

Srull, T., and Wyer, R. 1989. Person memory and judgment. *Psychological Review*, 96, 58–83.

Stannard, D. 1980. *Shrinking History: On Freud and the Failure of Psychohistory*. New York: Oxford University Press.

Staw, B., Sandelands, L., and Dutton, J. 1981. Threat-rigidity effects in organizational behavior: a traditional analysis. *Administrative Science Quarterly*, 26, 501–524.

Stearns, C., and Stearns, P. 1986. *Anger: The Struggle for Emotional Control in America's History*. Chicago: University of Chicago Press.

Stein, A. 1982. When misperception matters. *World Politics*, 34, 505–526.

Stein, G. 1988. Biological science and the roots of Nazism. *American Scientist*, 76, 50–58.

Steinbruner, J. 1981. Nuclear decapitation. *International Security*, 6, 17–22.

Steiner, J. 1980. The ss yesterday and today: a sociopsychological view. In

J. Dimsdale (ed.), *Survivors, Victims and Perpetrators: Essays on the Nazi Holocaust*. Washington, DC: Hemisphere.

Stepansky, P. 1977. *A History of Aggression in Freud*. New York: International Universities Press.

Stierlin, H. 1976. *Adolf Hitler, A Family Perspective*. New York: Psychohistory Press.

Stigler, G. 1969. The economics of information. *Journal of Political Economy*, 69, 213–225.

Stocking, G. (ed.). 1987. *Malinowski, Rivers, Benedict and Others: Essays on Culture and Personality*. Madison: University of Wisconsin Press.

Stokes, D. 1966. Some dynamic elements in contests for the presidency. *American Political Science Review*, 60, 19–28.

Stone, L. 1977. *The Family, Sex and Marriage in England, 1500–1800*. New York: Harper and Row.

———. 1981. *The Past and the Present*. Boston: Routledge and Kegan Paul.

Stone, W. 1980. The myth of left-wing authoritarianism. *Political Psychology*, 2, 3–20.

Storms, M. 1973. Videotape and the attribution process. *Journal of Personality and Social Psychology*, 27, 165–175.

Stouffer, S. 1955. *Communism, Conformity, and Civil Liberties*. New York: Doubleday.

Strack, F., Martin, L., and Stepper, S. 1988. Inhibiting and facilitating conditions of the human smile: a non-obtrusive test of the facial-feedback hypothesis. *Journal of Personality and Social Psychology*, 54, 768–777.

Strack, F., Schwarz, N., and Gschneidinger, E. 1985. Happiness and reminiscing: the role of time perspective, affect, and mode of thinking. *Journal of Personality and Social Psychology*, 49, 1460–1469.

Streufert, S., and Fromkin, W. 1972. Complexity and social influence. In J. Tedeschi (ed.), *Social Influence Processes*. Chicago: Aldine.

Streufert, S., and Streufert, S. 1978. *Behavior in a Complex Environment*. Washington, DC: Winston.

Suedfeld, P. 1983. Authoritarian leadership: a cognitive-interactionist view. In J. Held (ed.), *The Cult of Power: Dictators in the Twentieth Century*. New York: Columbia University Press.

Suedfeld, P., and Rank, A. 1976. Revolutionary leaders: long-term success as a function of changes in conceptual complexity. *Journal of Personality and Social Psychology*, 34, 169–178.

Suedfeld, P., and Tetlock, P. 1977. Integrative complexity of communications in international crises. *Journal of Conflict Resolution*, 21, 169–184.

Suedfeld, P., Tetlock, P., and Ramirez, C. 1977. War, peace, and integrative complexity: United Nations speeches on the Middle East problem. *Journal of Conflict Resolution*, 21, 427–442.

Sullivan, D. 1980. Evaluating U.S. intelligence estimates. In R. Godson (ed.),

Intelligence Requirements for the 1980s: Analysis and Estimates. New Brunswick, NJ: Transaction Books.

Sullivan, D., and Masters, R. 1988. "Happy warriors": leaders' facial displays, viewers emotions, and political support." *American Journal of Political Science,* 32, 345–368.

———. 1993a. In A. Somit, and S. Peterson (eds.), *Research in Biopolitics.* Greenwich, CT: JAI Press.

———. 1993b. Nonverbal behavior, emotions, and democratic leadership. In G. Marcus and R. Hanson (eds.) *Reconsidering the Democratic Public.* University Park: Pennsylvania State University Press.

Sullivan, D., Masters, R., Lanzetta, J., Englis, B., and McHugo, G. 1991. "Facial displays and political Leadership: some experimental findings." In G. Schubert and R. Masters (eds.) *Primate Politics.* Carbondale: Southern Illinois University Press.

Sullivan, J., Piereson, J., and Marcus, G. 1982. *Political Tolerance and American Democracy.* Chicago: University of Chicago Press.

Sullivan, D., Pressman, J., Page, B., and Lyons, J. 1974. *The Politics of Representation.* New York: St. Martin's Press.

Suplee, C. 1988. Sorry, George, but the image needs work. *Washington Post,* July 10, 1988, pp. C1, C4.

Susman, E., Inoff, G., Nottelmann, E., and Loriaux, D. 1987. Hormones, emotional dispositions, and aggressive attributes in young adolescents. *Child Development,* 58, 1114–1134.

Swados, F. 1941. Negro health on ante-bellum plantations. *Bulletin of the History of Medicine,* October, 460–461.

Sydnor, C. 1977. *Soldiers of Destruction.* Princeton, NJ: Princeton University Press.

Szalai, A., and Andrews, F. 1980. *The Quality of Life: Comparative Studies.* Beverly Hills, CA: Sage.

Szonyi, D. 1985. *The Holocaust: An Annotated Bibliography and Resource Guide.* New York: Ktav.

Tajfel, H. 1978. *Differentiation Between Social Groups: Studies in Intergroup Relations.* London: Academic Press.

———. 1982a. The social psychology of intergroup relations. *Annual Review of Psychology,* 1, 149–178.

———. 1982b. *Social Identity and Intergroup Relations.* Cambridge: Cambridge University Press.

Tajfel, H., Flament, C., Billig, M., and Bundy, R. 1971. Social categorization and intergroup behavior. *European Journal of Social Psychology,* 1, 149–178.

Tajfel, H., Sheikh, A., and Gardner, R. 1964. Content of stereotypes and the inference of similarity between members of stereotyped groups. *Acta Psychologica,* 22, 191–201.

Tajfel, H., and Turner, J. 1979. An integrative theory of intergroup conflict. In

W. Austin and S. Worchel (eds.), *The Social Psychology of Intergroup Relations.* Monterey, CA: Brooks/Cole.

———. 1986. The social identity theory of intergroup behavior. In S. Worchel and W. Austin (eds.), *Psychology of Intergroup Relations.* Chicago: Nelson-Hall.

Talbott, S. 1979. *Endgame.* New York: Harper and Row.

Tate, P. 1981. Personal attribute models of the voting behavior of U.S. Supreme Court justices: liberalism in civil liberties and economics decisions, 1946–1978. *American Political Science Review,* 75, 355–367.

Taylor, J. 1962. *Negro Slavery in Louisiana.* Baton Rouge: Louisiana State University Press.

Taylor, M. 1979. Race, sex and the expression of self-fulfilling prophesies in a laboratory teaching situation. *Journal of Personality and Social Psychology,* 37, 897–912.

Taylor, S. 1981. The interface of cognitive and social psychology. In J. Harvey (ed.), *Cognition, Social Behavior, and the Environment.* Hillsdale, NJ: Lawrence Erlbaum Associates.

Taylor, S., and Crocker, J. 1981. Schematic bases of social information processing. In E. Higgins, C. Herman, and M. Zanna (eds.), *Social Cognition: The Ontario Symposium,* vol. 1. Hillsdale, NJ: Lawrence Erlbaum Associates.

Taylor, S., and Fiske, S. 1978. Salience, attention, and attribution: top of the head phenomena. In L. Berkowitz (ed.), *Advances in Experimental Social Psychology,* vol. 11. New York: Academic Press.

Terkel, S. 1967. *Division Street: America.* New York: Pantheon Books.

Terkel, S. 1970. *Hard Times.* New York: Pantheon Books.

Tetlock, P. 1979. Identifying victims of groupthink from public statements of decision makers. *Journal of Personality and Social Psychology,* 37, 1314–1324.

———. 1981a. Personality and isolationism: content analysis of senatorial speeches. *Journal of Personality and Social Psychology,* 41, 737–743.

———. 1981b. Pre- to post-election shifts in presidential rhetoric: impression management or cognitive adjustment? *Journal of Personality and Social Psychology,* 41, 207–212.

———. 1983a. Accountability and complexity of thought. *Journal of Personality and Social Psychology,* 45, 74–83.

———. 1983b. Policy-makers' images of international conflict. *Journal of Social Issues,* 39, 67–86.

———. 1983c. Accountability and perseverance of first impressions. *Social Psychology Quarterly,* 46, 285–292.

———. 1983d. Cognitive style and political ideology. *Journal of Personality and Social Psychology,* 45, 118–126.

———. 1983e. Psychological research on foreign policy: a methodological overview. In L. Wheeler (ed.), *Review of Personality and Social Psychology,* vol. 4. Beverly Hills, CA: Sage.

———. 1984. Cognitive style and political belief systems in the British House of Commons. *Journal of Personality and Social Psychology*, 46, 365–375.

———. 1985a. Integrative complexity of American and Soviet foreign policy rhetoric: a time-series analysis. *Journal of Personality and Social Psychology*, 49, 1565–1585.

———. 1985b. Integrative complexity of policy reasoning. In S. Kraus and R. Perloff (eds.), *Mass Media and Political Thought*. Beverly Hills, CA: Sage.

———. 1985c. Accountability: a social check on the fundamental attribution error. *Social Psychology Quarterly*, 48, 227–236.

———. 1985d. Accountability: the neglected social context of judgment and choice. In B. M. Staw and L. Cummings (eds.), *Research in Organizational Behavior*, vol. 7. Greenwich, CT: JAI Press.

———. 1986. A value pluralism model of ideological reasoning. *Journal of Personality and Social Psychology*, 50, 819–827.

Tetlock, P., Bernzweig, J., and Gallant, J. 1985. Supreme Court decision making: cognitive style as a predictor of ideological consistency of voting. *Journal of Personality and Social Psychology*, 48, 1227–1239.

Tetlock, P., and Boettger, R. 1989a. Accountability: a social magnifier of the dilution effect. *Journal of Personality and Social Psychology*, 57, 388–398.

———. 1989b. Cognitive style and political ideology in the Soviet Union. *Political Psychology*, 10, 209–231.

Tetlock, P., Boettger, R., and Skitka, L. 1989. Social and cognitive strategies of coping with accountability: conformity, complexity, and bolstering. *Journal of Personality and Social Psychology*, 57, 632–641.

Tetlock, P., Hannum, K., and Micheletti, P. 1984. Stability and change in senatorial debate: testing the cognitive versus rhetorical style hypothesis. *Journal of Personality and Social Psychology*, 46, 621–631.

Tetlock, P., and Kim, J. 1987. Accountability and judgment processes in a personality prediction task. *Journal of Personality and Social Psychology*, 52, 700–709.

Tetlock, P., and Levi, A. 1982. Attribution bias: on the inconclusiveness of the cognition-motivation debate. *Journal of Experimental Social Psychology*, 18, 68–88.

Tetlock, P., and McGuire, C. 1986. Cognitive perspectives on foreign policy. In S. Long (ed.), *Political Behavior Annual*, Boulder, CO: Westview Press.

Tetlock, P., and Manstead, A. 1985. Impression management versus intrapsychic explanations in social psychology: a useful dichotomy? *Psychological Review*, 92, 67–82.

Thorson, T. 1970. *Biopolitics*. New York: Holt, Rinehart and Winston.

Thurow, L. 1980. *The Zero-Sum Society: Distribution and the Possibilities for Economic Change*. New York: Basic Books.

Till, G. 1977. Airpower and the battleship in the 1920's. In B. Ranft (ed.), *Technical Change and British Naval Policy, 1860–1939*. London: Hodder.

Tobin, J. 1958. Liquidity preference as behavior toward risk. *Review of Economic Studies*, 25, 65–86.

Tomkins, S. S. 1962. *Affect, Imagery, Consciousness I: The Positive Affects*. New York: Springer Verlag.

———. 1979. Script theory: differential magnification of affects. In H. E. Howe, Jr., and R. A. Dienstbier (eds.), *Nebraska Symposium on Motivation*, vol. 26 (pp. 201–236). Lincoln: University of Nebraska Press.

———. 1981. The role of facial response in the experience of emotion: a reply to Tournageau and Ellsworth. *Journal of Personality and Social Psychology*, 40, 355–357.

Trafimow, D., and Srull, T. 1986. The situation specificity of mental representations of another. Unpublished manuscript, University of Illinois.

Tranel, D., and Damasio, A. 1985. Learning without awareness: an autonomic index of facial recognition by prosopagnosics, *Science*, 1218, 1453–1454.

Treiman, D. 1977. *Occupational Prestige in Comparative Perspective*. New York: Academic Press.

Trunk, I. 1979. *Jewish Responses to Nazi Persecution*. New York: Stein and Day.

Tsebelis, G. 1990. *Nested Games: Rational Choice in Comparative Politics*. Los Angeles: University of California Press.

Tucker, R. 1973. *Stalin as Revolutionary, 1879–1929: A Study in History and Personality*. New York: Norton.

———. 1988. A Stalin biographer's memoir. In W. Runyan (ed.), *Psychology and Historical Interpretation*. New York: Oxford University Press.

Tullock, G. 1976. *The Vote Motive*. London: Institute for Economic Affairs.

Turner, H., Jr. 1985. *German Big Business and the Rise of Hitler*. New York: Oxford University Press.

Turner, J. 1978. Social categorization and social discrimination in the minimal group paradigm. In H. Tajfel (ed.), *Differentiation Between Social Groups: Studies in the Social Psychology of Intergroup Relations*. London: Academic Press.

———. 1982. Towards a cognitive redefinition of the social group. In H. Tajfel (ed.), *Social Identity and Intergroup Relations*. Cambridge: Cambridge University Press.

———. 1985. Social categorization and the self-concept: a social-cognitive theory of group behavior. In E. J. Lawler (ed.), *Advances in Group Processes*, vol. 2. Greenwich, CT: JAI Press.

Turner, J., and Brown, R. 1978. Social status, cognitive alternatives and intergroup relations. In H. Tajfel (ed.), *Differentiation Between Social Groups: Studies in the Social Psychology of Intergroup Relations*. European Monographs in Social Psychology, no. 14. London: Academic Press.

Turner, J., and Singleton, R. 1978. A theory of ethnic oppression: toward a reintegration of cultural and structural concepts in ethnic relations theory. *Social Forces*, 56, 1001–1018.

Turner, J., Singleton, R., and Musick, D. 1984. *Oppression: A Socio-History of Black-White Relations in America*. Chicago: Nelson-Hall.

Tversky, A. 1977. Features of similarity. *Psychological Review,* 84, 327–352.

Tversky, A., and Kahneman, D. 1981. Availability: a heuristic for judging frequency and probability. *Cognitive Psychology,* 5, 207–232.

———. 1983. Extensional versus intuitive reasoning: the conjunction fallacy in probability judgments. *Psychological Review,* 90, 293–315.

Tversky, A., Sattah, S., and Slovic, P. 1988. Contingent weighting in judgment and choice. *Psychological Review,* 95, 364–374.

Tyler, T., and Lavrakas, P. 1983. Support for gun control: the influence of personal, sociotropic, and ideological concerns. *Journal of Applied Social Psychology,* 13, 392–405.

Tyler, T., and Weber, R. 1982. Support for the death penalty: instrumental response to crime, or symbolic attitude? *Law and Society Review,* 17, 21–45.

Uhlaner, C., and Grofman, B. 1986. The race may be close but my horse is going to win: wish fulfillment in the 1980 presidential election. *Political Behavior,* 8, 101–129.

Upshaw, H. 1969. The personal reference scale: an approach to social judgment. In L. Berkowitz (ed.), *Advances in Experimental Social Psychology,* vol. 4. New York: Academic Press.

Upshaw, H., and Ostrom, T. 1984. Psychological perspective in attitude research. In J. Eiser (ed.), *Attitudinal Judgment.* New York: Springer-Verlag.

Van den Berghe, P. 1978a. Race and ethnicity: a sociobiological perspective. *Ethnic and Racial Studies,* 1, 401–411.

———. 1978b. *Man in Society: A Biosocial View.* New York: Elsevier North Holland.

Van der Eijk, C., Irwin, G., and Niemöller, K. 1986. The Dutch parliamentary election of May, 1986. *Electoral Studies,* 5, 289–296.

Van Hooff, J. 1969. The facial displays of catyrrhine monkeys and apes. In D. Morris (ed.), *Primate Ethology.* New York: Doubleday Anchor.

———. 1973. A structural analysis of the social behavior of a semi-captive group of chimpanzees. In M. Cranach and I. Vine (eds.), *Social Communication and Movement.* New York: Academic Press.

Van Knippenberg, A., and van Oers, H. 1984. Social identity and equity concerns in intergroup perceptions. *British Journal of Social Psychology,* 23, 351–361.

Vaughan, G. 1978. Social categorization and intergroup behavior in children. In H. Tajfel (ed.), *Differentiation Between Social Groups.* London: Academic Press.

———. 1986. Social change and racial identity: issues in the use of picture and doll measures. *Australian Journal of Psychology,* 38, 359–370.

Vaughan, K., and Lanzetta, J. 1980. Vicarious instigation and conditioning of facial expressive and autonomic responses to a model's expressive display of pain. *Journal of Personality and Social Psychology,* 38, 909–923.

Veroff, J., Douvan, E., and Kulka, R. 1981. *The Inner American: A Self-Portrait from 1957 to 1976.* New York: Basic Books.

Vinacke, W. 1964. Intra-group power differences, strategy, and decisions in inter-triad competition. *Sociometry,* 27, 25–50.

Vine, I. 1987. Human nature and sociocultural processes in intergroup discrimination. In V. Reynolds, V. Falger, and I. Vine (eds.), *The Sociobiology of Ethnocentrism: Evolutionary Dimensions of Xenophobia, Discrimination, Racism and Nationalism*. Beckenham, Kent: Croom Helm, 1987.

Volkan, V., and Itzkowitz, N. 1984. *The Immortal Attatürk: A Psychobiography.* Chicago: University of Chicago Press.

Waite, R. 1977. *The Psychopathic God: Adolf Hitler.* New York: Basic Books.

Walker, N. 1988. What we know about women voters in Britain, France, and West Germany, *Public Opinion*, May/June, pp. 49–55.

Warner, W., and Lunt, P. 1941. *The Social Life of a Modern Community.* New Haven, CT: Yale University Press.

Warr, P., Barter, J., and Brownbridge, G. 1983. On the independence of positive and negative affect. *Journal of Personality and Social Psychology*, 44, 644–651.

Weigel, R., and Howes, P. 1985. Conceptions of racial prejudice: symbolic racism reconsidered. *Journal of Social Issues*, 41, 117–138.

Weiner, B. 1986. *An Attributional Theory of Motivation and Emotion.* New York: Springer-Verlag.

Weinstein, F. 1980. *The Dynamics of Nazism: Leadership, Ideology, and the Holocaust.* New York: Academic Press.

Weinstein, F., and Platt, G. 1973. *Psychoanalytic Sociology.* Baltimore: Johns Hopkins University Press.

Wertsch, J. 1985. *Vygotsky and the Social Formation of Mind.* Cambridge, MA: Harvard University Press.

West, L. 1967. The Psychobiology of Racial Violence. *Archives of General Psychiatry*, 16, 645–651.

White, R. (ed.). 1986. *Psychology and the Prevention of Nuclear War.* New York: New York University Press.

Whiting, J., and Child, I. 1953. *Child Training and Personality.* New Haven, CT: Yale University Press.

Whyte, W. 1943. *Street Corner Society.* Chicago: University of Chicago Press.

Whyte, W. 1949. The social structure of the restaurant. *American Journal of Sociology*, 54, 302–310.

Williams, J., and Best, D. 1982. *Measuring Sex Stereotypes: A Thirty-Nation Study.* Beverly Hills, CA: Sage.

Wilson, G. 1973. *The Psychology of Conservatism.* New York: Academic Press.

Wilson, J., and Banfield, E. 1964. Public-regardingness as a value premise in voting behavior. *American Political Science Review*, 53, 876–887.

Wilson, J., and Clark, P. 1961. Incentive systems: a theory of organization. *Administrative Science Quarterly*, 6, 129–166.

Wilson, T., and Schooler, G. 1991. Thinking too much: introspection can reduce the quality of preferences and decisions. *Journal of Personality and Social Psychology*, 60, 181–192.

Wilson, W. R. 1979. Feeling more than we know: exposure effects without learning. *Journal of Personality and Social Psychology*, 37, 811–821.

Winter, D. 1973. *The Power Motive.* New York: Free Press.

Winton, W. M. 1986. The role of facial response in self-reports of emotion: a critique of Laird. *Journal of Personality and Social Psychology,* 59, 808–812.

Wittman, D. 1991. Contrasting rational and psychological analyses of political choice. In K. Monroe (ed.), *The Economic Approach to Politics: A Critical Assessment of the Theory of Rational Action.* New York: Harper/Collins.

Wolfe, T. 1979. *The SALT Experience.* Cambridge, MA: Ballinger.

Woll, S., and Graesser, A. 1982. Memory discrimination for information typical or atypical of person schemata. *Social Cognition,* 1, 287–310.

Wright, J., and Niemi, R. 1983. Perceptions of candidates' issue positions. *Political Behavior,* 5, 209–223.

Wyer, R., Bodenhausen, G., and Srull, T. 1984. The cognitive representation of persons and groups and its effect on recall and recognition memory. *Journal of Experimental Social Psychology,* 20, 445–469.

Wyer, R., and Budesheim, T. 1987. Person memory and judgments: the impact of information that one is told to disregard. *Journal of Personality and Social Psychology,* 53, 14–29.

Wyer, R., Budesheim, T., and Lambert, A. 1990. Cognitive representation of conversations about persons. *Journal of Personality and Social Psychology,* 58, 218–238.

Wyer, R., Budesheim, T., Lambert, A., and Martin, L. 1987. Person memory: the priorities that govern the cognitive activities involved in person impression formation. Unpublished manuscript, University of Illinois.

Wyer, R., Budesheim, T., Shavitt, S., Riggle, E., Melton, R., and Kuklinski, J. 1991. Image, issues and ideology: the processing of information about political candidates. *Journal of Personality and Social Psychology,* 61, 533–545.

Wyer, R., and Gordon, S. 1982. The recall of information about persons and groups. *Journal of Experimental Social Psychology,* 18, 128–164.

Wyer, R., and Hartwick, J. 1980. The role of information retrieval and conditional inference processes in belief formation and change. In L. Berkowitz (ed.), *Advances in Experimental Social Psychology,* vol. 13. New York: Academic Press.

Wyer, R., Lambert, A., Gruenfeld, D., and Budesheim, T. 1991. Political memory and judgment: the effects of ideology, opinions, traits and behaviors on the evaluation of politicians. Unpublished manuscript, University of Illinois.

Wyer, R., and Martin, L. 1986. Person memory: the role of traits, group stereotypes and specific behaviors in the cognitive representation of persons. *Journal of Personality and Social Psychology,* 50, 661–675.

Wyer, R., and Srull, T. 1986. Human cognition in its social context. *Psychological Review,* 93, 322–359.

———. 1989. *Memory and Cognition in Its Social Context.* Hillsdale, NJ: Lawrence Erlbaum Associates.

Wyer, R., Srull, T., Gordon, S., and Hartwick, J. 1982. The effects of taking a perspective on the recall of prose material. *Journal of Personality and Social Psychology,* 43, 674–688.

Wyer, R., and Unverzagt, W. 1985. The effects of instructions to disregard information on its subsequent recall and use in making judgments. *Journal of Personality and Social Psychology,* 48, 533–549.

Wyman, D. 1984. *The Abandonment of the Jews: America and the Holocaust, 1941–45.* New York: Pantheon Books.

Yinger, J. 1965. *Toward a Field Theory of Behavior.* New York: McGraw-Hill.

York, H. 1970. *Race to Oblivion.* New York: Simon and Schuster.

Zajonc, R. 1980. Feeling and thinking: preferences need no inferences. *American Psychologist,* 35, 151–175.

———. 1982. On the primacy of affect. *American Psychologist,* 39, 117–123.

Zajonc, R., Murphy, S., and Inglehart, M. 1989. Feeling and facial efference: implications of the vascular theory of emotion. *Psychological Review,* 96, 395–416.

Zaller, J. 1992. *The Nature and Origin of Mass Opinion.* New York: Cambridge University Press.

Zaller, J., and Feldman, S. 1992. Answering questions versus revealing preferences: a simple model of the survey response. *American Journal of Political Science,* 96, 579–616.

Zeckhauser, R. (ed.). 1991. *Strategic Reflections on Human Behavior.* Cambridge, MA: MIT Press.

Zellman, G., and Sears, D. 1971. Childhood origins of tolerance for dissent. *Journal of Social Issues,* 27, 109–136.

Zukier, H., and Pepitone, A. 1984. Social roles and strategies in prediction: some determinants of the use of base-rate information. *Journal of Personality and Social Psychology,* 47, 351–359.

Zullow, H., and Seligman, M. 1989. Pessimistic rumination predicts defeat of presidential candidates, 1900–1984. *Psychological Inquiry.*

Index

Abelson, R., 152–53, 155, 307, 393
Abnormal psychology, 55
Abortion, 76–77, 89, 96–97, 129, 382
Abstract ideas, 125–26
Academe, 5, 60, 62
Acceptability threshold, 286, 290, 291, 292
Accountability, 399, 405 n.3
Achieved hierarchies, 196–97
Adolescents: attitude formation in, 66; executions of, 77; in Nazi Germany, 47; personality studies of, 19; political thought in, 28; symbolic predispositions and, 123
Adorno, T., 14, 20
Advertisements, 85, 133
Affect: in candidate evaluation, 237–38, 248–50; category-based processing and, 141, 282; classical conditioning and, 135–36; cognitive attributions and, 148 n.13; cognitive linkages and, 258; cognitive miserliness and, 137; cognitive priming and, 143; displacement theory on, 93; distance perception and, 100; group evaluation and, 148 n.12; in impression formation, 262; intentions and, 80–81; judgment and, 223, 293, 296–320; knowledge structure and, 243–44, 248; memory and, 134; Nazism studies and, 50; nonverbal behavior and, 150–82; perception and, 108; peripheral/heuristic processing and, 142; psychobiography and, 57; rational self-interest and, 115; selective encoding and, 269; symbols and, 113, 114, 117, 120, 133. *See also* Moods

Affirmative action policies, 128–29, 130
African Americans. *See* Blacks
Agenda setting, 28, 145–46
Aggregated discrimination, 198–202
Aggression: "attitudes and voting behavior" era research on, 29; authoritarian personality and, 20; cross-national differences in, 32; frustration and, 19–20; inevitability of, 215–16; male, 211; "personality" era research on, 16. *See also* Terror
Agonic emotion, 163–64, 168, 169
Agonic social interaction, 156, 210
Agreement effect, 76, 79
Aircraft workers, 192–93
Air power: pre–World War I, 359 n.7; World War I, 349–50; interwar, 347–48, 351–52, 355, 357–58
Ajzen, I., 136, 140, 263 n.2
Alesina, A., 331–32
Ambiguity: advantages of, 333; cognitive consistency and, 134; in election campaigns, 89, 331; integrative simplicity and, 403; in racist/civil libertarian propositions, 268; social judgment theory of, 83–84, 86. *See also* Uncertainty
Analogies, 342–43
Anchoring effects, 230
Anderson, Norman, 250, 261
Andrarchy, 197
Androgens, 210–11
Anger, 299, 308
Annaliste school, 27
ANOVA, 70–71
Anthropology, 25, 34, 37, 53, 61

Contributors

Shanto Iyengar is Professor of Political Science and Communications Studies at the University of California, Los Angeles. He is the author of *Is Anyone Responsible?: How Television Frames Political Issues*, *News That Matters: Television and American Opinion* (with Donald R. Kinder), and *American Politics in the Age of Television* (with Stephen Ansolabehere and Roy Behr).

William J. McGuire is Professor of Psychology at Yale University and is the leading authority in the area of attitude change. His most recent publication is *The Content, Structure, and Operation of Thought Systems*.

Stephen Ansolabehere, Department of Political Science, University of California, Los Angeles

Donald Granberg, Department of Sociology, University of Missouri

Robert Jervis, Department of Political Science, Columbia University

Milton Lodge, Department of Political Science, SUNY at Stony Brook

Roger D. Masters, Department of Government, Dartmouth College

Victor C. Ottati, Department of Political Science, SUNY at Stony Brook

Samuel L. Popkin, Department of Political Science, University of California, San Diego

William McKinley Runyan, School of Social Welfare, University of California, Berkeley

David O. Sears, Department of Psychology, University of California, Los Angeles

James Sidanius, Department of Psychology, University of California, Los Angeles

Patrick Stroh, Department of Political Science, Carnegie-Mellon University

Denis G. Sullivan, Department of Government, Dartmouth College

Philip E. Tetlock, Department of Psychology, University of California, Berkeley

Robert S. Wyer, Jr., Department of Psychology, University of Illinois, Urbana-Champaign